War and Popular Culture

War and Popular Culture

Resistance in Modern China, 1937–1945

CHANG-TAI HUNG

University of California Press

BERKELEY   LOS ANGELES   LONDON

Chapters 2, 3, and 4 incorporate material previously printed in the following publications and revised for this book:

"Female Symbols of Resistance in Chinese Wartime Spoken Drama," *Modern China* 15.2 (April 1989): 149–177. Reprinted by permission of Sage Publications, Inc.

"War and Peace in Feng Zikai's Wartime Cartoons," *Modern China* 16.1 (January 1990): 39–83. Reprinted by permission of Sage Publications, Inc.

"Paper Bullets: Fan Changjiang and New Journalism in Wartime China," *Modern China* 17.4 (October 1991): 427–468. Reprinted by permission of Sage Publications, Inc.

"The Fuming Image: Cartoons and Public Opinion in Late Republican China, 1945 to 1949," *Comparative Studies in Society and History*, forthcoming. Reprinted by permission of the Society for the Comparative Study of Society and History.

University of California Press
Berkeley and Los Angeles, California
University of California Press, Ltd.
London, England

Library of Congress Cataloging-in-Publication Data
Hung, Chang-tai.
    War and popular culture : resistance in modern China, 1937–1945 / Chang-tai Hung.
        p.   cm.
    Includes bibliographical references and index.
    ISBN 0-520-08236-2 (alk. paper)
    1. Arts, Chinese—20th century.   2. Sino-Japanese Conflict, 1937–1945—Art and the war.   3. China—Civilization—1912–1949.   I. Title.
NX583.A1H86   1994
700—dc20   93-4738

Printed in the United States of America
9   8   7   6   5   4   3   2   1

For Wai-han

Contents

Illustrations

Abbreviations

DGB	*Dagong bao* (Impartial daily; original title *L'Impartial*). Tianjin, Hankou, Chongqing, Hong Kong, 1931–1945.
GM	*Guangming* (Light). Shanghai, June 1936–October 1937.
JFRB	*Jiefang ribao* (Liberation daily). Yan'an, 1941–1947.
JWMH	*Jiuwang manhua* (National salvation cartoons). Shanghai, September–November 1937.
JWRB	*Jiuwang ribao* (National salvation daily). Shanghai, Guangzhou, Guilin, 1937–1941.
KDD	*Kang dao di* (Resisting till the end). Hankou, Chongqing, January 1938–November 1939.
KRZZY	*Kang-Ri zhanzheng shiqi Yan'an ji ge kang-Ri minzhu genjudi wenxue yundong zhiliao* (Materials on the literary movement in Yan'an and other anti-Japanese democratic base areas during the War of Resistance). 3 vols. Edited by Liu Zengjie et al. Taiyuan: Shanxi renmin chubanshe, 1983.
KZWY	*Kangzhan wenyi* (Resistance literature and art). Hankou, Chongqing, May 1938–May 1946.
KZWYYJ	*Kangzhan wenyi yanjiu* (Studies on resistance literature and art). Chengdu, 1982–.
LY	*Lunyu* (The analects). Shanghai, September 1932–August 1937.
QGXJ	*Quanguo manhua zuojia kangzhan jiezuo xuanji*

(Selected works of Chinese cartoonists on the War of Resistance). Edited by Huang Miaozi. N.p.: Zhanwang shuwu, 1938.

SDMH   *Shidai manhua* (Modern cartoons). Shanghai, January 1934–June 1937.

XJCQ   *Xiju chunqiu* (Drama annals). Guilin, November 1940–October 1942.

XJSD   *Xiju shidai* (Drama times). Shanghai, May 1937–August 1937.

XWJZ   *Xinwen jizhe* (The reporter). Hankou, April 1938–March 1941.

XWXSL   *Xinwenxue shiliao* (Historical materials on the new literature). Beijing, 1978–.

XWYJZL   *Xinwen yanjiu ziliao* (Research materials on journalism). Beijing, 1979–.

YZF   *Yuzhou feng* (Universal wind). Shanghai, Guangzhou, Guilin, September 1935–1947.

ZGHJYD   *Zhongguo huaju yundong wushinian shiliao ji* (Historical materials on the Chinese drama movement of the last fifty years). Edited by Tian Han et al. 3 vols. Beijing: Zhongguo xiju chubanshe, 1985.

Acknowledgments

In writing this book I have benefited from the support, advice, and encouragement of many individuals. My profound gratitude goes first to three historians. Joseph W. Esherick read the original manuscript with great care and offered numerous invaluable suggestions for improvement. R. David Arkush encouraged me to refine and refocus my arguments. And Arif Dirlik challenged me to reexamine the theoretical underpinnings of this study. Their advice has saved me from many errors and helped to make this a better book.

Two friends deserve special thanks. Mark A. Greene of the Minnesota Historical Society had the patience to review countless pages and to offer counsel and assistance when they were most needed. The text has benefited greatly from his constant probing and his remarkable sense of style. Paul Clark of the University of Auckland, New Zealand, also gave generously of his time and read the original draft with critical shrewdness.

Other constructive criticisms and good cheer came from Lyman P. Van Slyke, Charles W. Hayford, and Jeffrey C. Kinkley. They read the manuscript in whole or in part, and their trenchant comments provided the basis for some rewriting. My colleagues in the History Department at Carleton College, especially Robert E. Bonner, Diethelm Prowe, and Carl D. Weiner, generously shared with me their extensive knowledge of the resistance movements in Europe during the Second World War.

I owe a special debt of gratitude to the late Haldore Hanson, who provided valuable information about wartime Yan'an and other Communist border regions. I am also indebted to Zhu Jiefan, Pao-liang Chu, Shuen-shuen Hung, Perry Yu, Yuan Yimu, Robert E. Entenmann, Mariko Kaga, and Qiguang Zhao for bringing relevant materials to my attention.

A good many institutions helped keep this endeavor afloat. In particular, I would like to thank the National Endowment for the Humanities for a summer stipend in 1988 and a research fellowship in 1990. A grant from the Committee on Scholarly Communication with the People's Republic of China enabled me to conduct crucial interviews and collect much-needed materials in China in the fall of 1989. Carleton College assisted my research by granting me, through the Faculty Development Endowment Program, several awards in the past few years to finance two trips to Taiwan and facilitate the gathering of materials relevant to this project.

This study would not have been possible without generous assistance from many libraries and their staffs. In particular, I am grateful to the Hoover Institution's East Asian Collection at Stanford (where I began the research for this book in 1986), the Harvard-Yenching Library, the East Asian Library at the University of California at Berkeley, the East Asian Library at Columbia University, the National Library in Beijing, Beijing Normal University Library, Beijing University Library, Shanghai Library, Fudan University Library, and the Institute of Modern History Library at Academia Sinica in Taibei.

The staff of the University of California Press made work on this book a pleasure with their gentle guidance and meticulous attention to detail. I am especially grateful to Sheila Levine for her encouragement and enthusiasm for this project. Laura Driussi, Amy Klatzkin, and Monica McCormick provided editorial advice. Anne Canright copyedited the manuscript with a keen eye to both style and presentation.

A note on format and sources is in order here. The *pinyin* romanization system has been used throughout (with the exception of Sun Yat-sen, whose Cantonese approximation is long familiar in the West). As for sources, this book makes use of an assortment of published and unpublished materials: wartime newspapers and magazines, official and unofficial pamphlets, plays, cartoons, diaries, memoirs, biographies, letters, and personal interviews. Many participants in China's War of Resistance (whose names appear in the appendix) gave me much help, information, and advice. One of the most rewarding experiences in writing contemporary history is the opportunity to engage in face-to-face dialogue with the subjects of one's study. As is evident throughout the book, talking to them shed new light on questions that texts alone cannot answer. Needless to say, all interpretations and conclusions in this book are entirely my own, and I alone am responsible for any shortcomings that remain.

Finally, gratitude of a more personal kind must be recorded as well. My daughter, Ming-mei, and my son, Ming-yang, have the wonderful patience to tolerate an oftentimes preoccupied father, and I wish to thank them for bringing their joy and energy into my life. And, as always, I am immeasurably grateful to my wife, Wai-han Mak, for sharing together the good times and the hard, and for the countless ways she has given love and support to this project. It is to her that this book is dedicated.

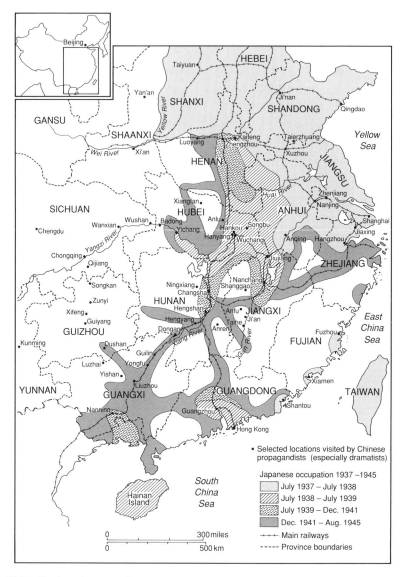

- • Selected locations visited by Chinese propagandists (especially dramatists)

Japanese occupation 1937–1945
- July 1937 – July 1938
- July 1938 – July 1939
- July 1939 – Dec. 1941
- Dec. 1941 – Aug. 1945
- ╼╾╾ Main railways
- ----- Province boundaries

China During the War of Resistance, 1937–1945

Based on *The Cambridge History of China*, vol. 13: *Republican China, 1912–1949*, pt. 2, ed. John K. Fairbank and Albert Feuerwerker (Cambridge: Cambridge University Press, 1986), p. 549; Hong Shen, *Kangzhan shinian lai Zhongguo de xiju yundong yu jiaoyu* (Shanghai: Zhonghua shuju, 1948), pp. 5–6; and *Baqian li lu yun he yue—Yanju jiudui huiyilu*, ed. Yanju jiudui duishi bianji weiyuanhui (Shanghai: n.p., n.d.), pp. 367–473.

Introduction

The Japanese attack at the Marco Polo Bridge (Lugouqiao) about ten miles west of Beijing on 7 July 1937, which set off full-scale war between China and Japan (the Sino-Japanese War of 1937–1945; known in China as "The War of Resistance Against Japan" [Kang-Ri zhanzheng]), probably did not surprise many Chinese. After all, the Japanese had been intensifying their aggression in northern China since the Twenty-one Demands of 1915, and in 1931 had seized Manchuria. It was only a matter of time, many believed, before this intermittent, undeclared war between the two countries would erupt into open combat. Yet the idea that China and Japan were *actually* at war was unsettling and frightening. To the Chinese, war meant that China's sovereignty was being openly and unjustly trampled; it meant that the nation had to confront an enemy whose ambitions knew no bounds and whose superior war machine could bring ruin and suffering to the Chinese people. When the battle shifted to Shanghai in August 1937, it became clear that the conflict would not be easily or quickly resolved. A mixture of shock and anger gripped the entire nation.

The eruption of full-scale war with Japan dealt a devastating blow to the Nationalist (Guomindang; GMD) government's efforts to recentralize its authority and revive the economy.[1] It also ended Jiang Jieshi's (Chiang Kai-shek, 1887–1975) chance of crushing the Communist forces, who were isolated in the barren and sparsely populated Shaanxi province with Yan'an as their capital. The war uprooted the Nationalists from their traditional power base in the urban and industrial centers of east China, especially along the lower Yangzi River, and forced them to move to the interior. At the same time, it afforded an

1

ideal opportunity for the Communists to expand their influence in north China and so become a true contender for national power by the end of the war.

For many Chinese resisters, the clash with Japan turned out to be a unifying force and an ennobling experience. The Marco Polo Bridge Incident released a passionate outpouring of patriotic enthusiasm, temporarily uniting dissenting voices and disparate interest groups. The deafening call for "national salvation" was heard everywhere. The idea of resistance against Japanese aggression, a much-talked-about notion before the war, now crystallized into something tangible and emotional. Like the Great Wall, the Marco Polo Bridge became a compelling symbol of China's unity and rapidly took its place in resistance lore. Immediately after the incident, for example, a stream of spoken dramas appeared bearing the name of the famous bridge, including the popular three-act play *Defend the Marco Polo Bridge* (*Baowei Lugouqiao*), a joint product of sixteen dramatists speaking out in solidarity against the invaders.[2]

Ironically, for some frustrated intellectuals the war could not have come at a better time. While granting that armed conflict was brutal and inhuman, they argued that it nevertheless raised hopes of solving China's myriad problems. They looked at war as an antidote to malaise and chaos, and as an opportunity to break the shackles of tradition and offer new vistas for China. To them, the past two decades had been a time of despair and uncertainty. The euphoria kindled in the early Republican years had long since evaporated. After years of continued Japanese threat and dreams of political reform repeatedly dashed, a mixture of cynicism and pessimism overwhelmed the youth of the post–May Fourth generation.[3] Despite some progress made toward economic growth and political integration by the Nationalist government on the eve of the war,[4] the country was still largely fragmented. Regional militarists remained a serious threat to the government, and the armed conflict between the Nationalists and the Communists continued unabated. Political instability bred fear and fueled great discontent in society.

"Perhaps a nation long plagued by deeply divided regional interests will finally come together?" were the hopeful words of the editors of the literary journal *Light* (*Guangming*) in July 1937.[5] With the Japanese attack on the Marco Polo Bridge, all kinds of differences, both political and intellectual, seemed to disappear overnight. China suddenly found itself united. War, like it or not, commanded everyone's attention and emotions. It pulled the nation together, forcing people to endure the traumatic experience collectively. Could the war be the beginning of national regeneration? If nothing else, some thought that war could furnish a much-needed sense of direction and purpose to a country so long divided and discouraged. "Is war so dreadful? Not at all! Our four hundred million people are eagerly looking forward to its arrival. We welcome it because this is the time that we can liberate ourselves [from oppression]," proclaimed the poet Zang Kejia (1905–).[6]

But what was to be done? The poet Mu Mutian (1900–1971) sounded a battle cry: "We must use war to answer war."[7] It was clear from the beginning that the determination and resources required to resist and ultimately defeat the invader lay no longer simply in the soldier's courage at the front, but in the will of the people to rally behind the government. A fragmented country could make the enemy's task of occupation and exploitation of China a relatively simple matter. To Chinese resisters, the people's consciousness about the war and the home front morale became as important as the outcome of campaigns on the battlefield in determining the future. "To save China we must develop the mass movement," stated one writer, summing up this attitude succinctly.[8]

To rally people together and convey the exigencies of the hard times successfully, Chinese resisters knew they had to plan carefully, establish a nationwide network of communication, and create new channels for the dissemination of information. In brief, their aim was to activate an unprecedented, ambitious propaganda campaign aimed at mobilizing every citizen and utilizing every resource in the country. But given China's vast size, the enormous regional differences, and the lack of modern means of transportation, deciding even where to begin did not prove easy. Resistance intellectuals turned increasingly toward a few urban popular culture forms—spoken dramas, cartoons, and newspapers—for help, transforming them into popularizing media.

This book addresses the important but often ignored issue of the rise and spread of urban popular culture during the War of Resistance, particularly how this culture was politicized and popularized by Chinese resisters to wage a concerted battle against the invading Japanese. The war was a critical period in the spread of popular culture from urban enclaves, especially cities like Shanghai, to the vast rural hinterland, a move that turned the nation's attention increasingly toward the countryside. The resisters' use of highly politicized spoken drama symbols, patriotic cartoon images, and combative newspaper languages in communication with the populace changed the fundamental nature and discourse of wartime popular culture. During the war, while the Nationalists used popular culture largely as a patriotic tool, the Communists refashioned it into a new "people's culture." Capitalizing on the shift of awareness to the countryside, the Communists imbued popular culture with a rural, socialist content and portrayed the border regions under their control as the future of China. In the end it was the Communists, not the Nationalists, who succeeded in utilizing the developments in the popular culture of the GMD areas for their own political ends, a fact that contributed to their victory in the civil war (1945–1949).

The twists and turns in the course of the popular culture campaign in wartime China, especially its development in the Communist-held border regions, must be examined within the larger historical context of the war with Japan. The campaign can be divided into two stages. An early period of high morale and intense activity from 1937 to 1939 saw patriotic Chinese intellectuals and artists roaming the villages and towns of the interior provinces to spread the gospel of resistance, each group using a different tool to reach the rural masses. In the case of dramatists, for example, street plays became the staple in their propaganda arsenal. But as the fighting settled into a stalemate in 1939 and the early enthusiasm waned, Chinese dramatists, now physically exhausted and mentally drained, gravitated back to the cities. The trend now was toward more historical plays and traditional dramas, aimed once again at urban audiences. This was a period of digging in and waiting, but also a time of growing discontent among intellectuals with the GMD government's ineptitude, corruption, and increasing censorship.

The Japanese invasion in July 1937 divided China essentially into three zones: the Japanese-occupied territories, the Guomindang-controlled areas, and the Communist-held regions. The first and the most bitter phase of the war lasted sixteen months, until the fall of Wuhan (the triple cities of Wuchang, Hankou, and Hanyang) and Guangzhou in October 1938. By late 1938 the Japanese, with superior air power and armored troops, controlled the main coastal cities and major railway lines. The Japanese advance, however, was met with stiff resistance from the Chinese. During the ninety-day defense of Shanghai (August–November 1937), Jiang Jieshi threw his best, German-trained divisions into service, battling the Japanese to a standstill. Even so, the superior military might of Japan finally prevailed. The battle of Shanghai, moreover, proved to be extremely costly for the Nationalists: as many as 250,000 Chinese troops—the nucleus of

Jiang Jieshi's finest forces—were killed or wounded, and the road to the capital, Nanjing, was left wide open. When the city fell in late December 1937, the invaders unleashed the notorious "Rape of Nanjing" —wanton destruction, rape, robbery, and random killing, leaving over 200,000 dead and the city in ruins.[9]

The carnage in Nanjing only strengthened the Chinese will to resist. Despite being outgunned and ill trained, some Chinese troops, with great determination and under capable leadership, occasionally managed to mount a successful fight. In April 1938, for example, at the town of Taierzhuang in southern Shandong, the forces of Nationalist General Li Zongren (1891–1969) trapped and inflicted heavy casualties on Japanese troops who were attempting to link with other divisions in north and central China for the forthcoming campaign against Wuhan. For the Chinese, the Battle of Taierzhuang had great symbolic meaning, in that it shattered the myth of Japanese invincibility. This first major Chinese victory provided a glimmer of hope in difficult times and soon figured prominently in the resistance culture: it quickly established itself as one of the most popular topics in wartime spoken dramas and political cartoons. But the Taierzhuang triumph was short-lived; in May, the Japanese took the town and the nearby key railway junction of Xuzhou. Wuhan fell in October.

Following a new scorched earth strategy—in essence "trading space for time" in the hope of frustrating Japanese offensive operations in the vast interior—the GMD government retreated to Hankou and then to Chongqing, a city a thousand miles upriver in Sichuan that was to remain China's wartime capital until the end of the war in 1945.[10] The government's withdrawal to the interior also quickened the vast migration of urban Chinese (especially intellectuals), industrial enterprises, and universities from Japanese-occupied territories to the hinterland.

The fall of Wuhan and Guangzhou in October 1938 ended the first phase of the war. The fighting presently settled into a long and costly stalemate. Unable to secure final victory and fearful of being seriously overextended, the Japanese turned to consolidate their hold over eastern and northern China through various puppet regimes, among them Wang Jingwei's (1883–1944) new "National Government" in Nanjing. They also cut off the GMD's supply lines in southern China and waged a relentless air war against the interior cities, including Kunming and Guilin. Chongqing, though safe from land attack, was flattened by Japanese bombers.

China fought very much alone until December 1941, when the

United States entered the war after the Pearl Harbor attack. Still, the Japanese offensive did not cripple the nation's will to resist. On the contrary, it created an unprecedented wave of patriotism and an uncommon spirit of national unity in the early war years. Nowhere was this more evident than in the dedicated commitment of Chinese intellectuals and artists to the resistance cause and in the second united front between the Nationalists and the Communists.

Initiated by the literati, a campaign for the resistance was quickly taking shape based on popular culture. Traveling drama and cartoon propaganda troupes were formed and dispatched to interior China. The campaign reached a crescendo in March 1938 when the All-China Resistance Association of Writers and Artists (Zhonghua quanguo wenyijie kangdi xiehui; ACRAWA) was established in Hankou to map out a resistance plan. The association's slogan, "Literature must go to the countryside! Literature must join the army!" became a call to arms. What emerged was a nationwide popular culture crusade to raise public consciousness about the conflict.

On the political front, shortly after the war broke out, in September 1937, the Nationalists and the Communists entered into their second alliance, temporarily submerging their enmity in the face of an invasion. The Red Army was reorganized as the Eighth Route Army, and the Communist forces south of the Yangzi River were turned into a second fighting force named the New Fourth Army. Mao Zedong (1893–1976) and other Communist leaders were elected to serve on the newly created People's Political Council. Leading Communist intellectuals such as Guo Moruo (1892–1978) were recruited into the Political Department in the Military Affairs Commission (responsible for coordinating the war effort), in charge of crucial propaganda work.

This united front, however, like the first one of 1923–1927, was marked by mutual suspicion and friction. Mao insisted that the Communists should remain independent and autonomous, in sharp contrast to his chief rival, Moscow-influenced Wang Ming (Chen Shaoyu, 1904–1974), whose position was "Everything through the united front." In 1939 armed clashes erupted as the Nationalists attempted to restrict the activities of the Communists. After the New Fourth Army Incident of January 1941, in which the Nationalist forces almost wiped out the Communist troops in southern Anhui, the second united front ceased to exist except as a scrap of paper.

The Sino-Japanese conflict exhausted the Nationalists. The later war years saw the magnification of some of the major weaknesses in the government: massive corruption, harsh censorship, and political repression, the inability to control a vicious inflationary spiral, and Jiang Jieshi's increasingly centralized, authoritarian rule together with his distrust of the mass movement all combined to undermine the government's mandate to rule. As the earlier exhilaration and high morale continued to erode, intellectuals and artists became ever more critical of the government. All the while, by contrast, the Communists were aggressively expanding their territorial control, both behind Japanese lines and in GMD areas throughout north and east-central China. By the end of the war they had become a formidable military and political force. Their ingenious use of popular culture to foster an image of a new China would soon contribute to their ultimate seizure of power.

In this study the term *popular culture* refers to a series of modern urban culture forms—spoken dramas, cartoons, and newspapers—that gained prominence and popularity in China in the early decades of this century and had a great impact during the war. That is, the term does not mean the customs, beliefs, and rituals of a particular group of people such as peasants or artisans; rather, it designates certain kinds of literature or art that are widely diffused and generally accepted by the people in a particular social setting at a particular period of time.[11] While the former type of study focuses on a community, the latter begins with a cultural artifact. The two, however, are complementary and to a certain extent overlap; in the words of Natalie Davis, they "have the same ultimate goals: the careful explication of values, beliefs, and customs and their relation to social milieu," and they are both needed for "the study of *mentalités*."[12] This "literary-cultural" approach allows us to examine how a specific cultural artifact—such as a cartoon—can cross cultural lines and transcend group affiliations. It presents us with a sharper societal dynamic by asking how the artifact in question was created. Who created it? For what purpose? How was it communicated? Who was the intended audience? In brief, the literary-cultural approach establishes the cultural artifact within a certain context and tells us how it moves and interacts in different milieus.

Urban popular culture forms were ideal as media of communication. Popular because they were "favorite, acceptable, pleasing," and "intended for or suited to ordinary people,"[13] they became the most potent tools in shaping the minds and sentiments of the common people during the War of Resistance. Yet the increased use of urban popular culture forms in the early decades of this century, like the growing interest in folk culture, such as folk songs and legends, among young

Chinese folklorists in the same period, was not without controversy. Many conservative intellectuals, in fact, viewed it with alarm as a sign of the cultural deterioration. Although the distinction between "high" culture—such as poetry, Confucian classics, philosophical treatises—and "low" culture—such as regional dramas and popular religions—remained nebulous in Chinese tradition,[14] the traditional elites' attitude toward folk and popular culture tended to be condescending. The elites viewed folk culture genres as unsophisticated and unworthy of study because of their predominantly rural basis, vulgar content, and oral mode of transmission.[15] In their eyes, moreover, urban popular culture forms produced standardized and inferior products—the results of commercialization and industrialization; to them, "popular" implied faceless anonymity and the loss of a distinct identity. Culture, once the embodiment of noble ideals and great artistic traditions, had degenerated into a shoddy commodity. Traditional painters, for instance, saw the cartoon as a mediocre art form catering merely to mass consumption (see chapter 3). This negative view resonated with that of such Western conservatives as Matthew Arnold and José Ortega y Gasset, who viewed with alarm the rapid material changes in modern society, including the increasing popularization of art.[16]

The eruption of the war with Japan, however, suddenly made these urban culture forms important. They were, after all, convenient tools for espousing and conveying patriotic messages to the general public. Poignant in imagery (such as cartoons), easy to produce and disseminate to a large and varied audience (such as newspapers and tabloids), and charged with emotion (such as patriotic plays), they came to be used primarily for their political, not literary, character. Indeed, the war changed the very nature of Chinese popular culture. No longer a strictly urban product with a heavy dose of commercialism, popular culture was quickly refashioned into a propaganda medium aimed primarily at the rural audience. The politicization of popular culture, to be sure, did not begin with the war. When Japanese militarists intensified their aggression in China after the Manchurian (Mukden) Incident of September 1931, a number of artistic devices were remolded by intellectuals into tools of defense against outside intrusion. The street play *Lay Down Your Whip* (*Fangxia nide bianzi*) was a case in point (see chapter 2). Still, the organized, nationwide resistance movement did not commence until after the war broke out in the summer of 1937; and *Lay Down Your Whip* did not become one of the most influential anti-imperialist, anti-Japanese propaganda plays until the early years of the war.

For wartime Chinese intellectuals, propaganda was undoubtedly an important weapon in the resistance arsenal. Because of its pejorative connotations, however, the importance of propaganda has often been ignored. Propaganda is in fact not an aberration but a basic ingredient of the political process; contrary to the public perception, moreover, it does not consist only of lies and falsehood. As David Welch puts it, "It operates with many different kinds of truth—from the outright lie, the half truth, to the truth out of context."[17] Even the most mendacious propaganda effort must entertain some truths to be effective. It must appeal to human reasoning, not just to emotional instincts. Thus Chinese wartime propaganda was an act of persuasion, combining feelings and facts. Moreover, the Chinese word *xuanchuan* (propaganda), meaning to inform and to propagate, carries a more positive connotation than its English counterpart. Granted that it is still a form of advocacy and conveys a particular point of view, *xuanchuan* lacks the negative implication of manipulation. It is in this more positive sense that the term *propaganda* is used throughout the book.

Spoken dramas were one of the first urban culture forms to which the resisters turned for patriotic cause. The formation of traveling dramatic troupes immediately after the war broke out demonstrated both the urgent need to spread information to the rural interior and the desire to create a new channel for communicating with the people. Wartime spoken dramas, especially street plays, attempted to engage a mass audience in a novel face-to-face dialogue. In their ambitious, and sometimes frustrating, attempt to galvanize public support for the war cause and to spur national consciousness, Chinese dramatists also systematically cultivated patriotic symbols. Like Joan of Arc, who stands for French patriotism, such female symbols as Hua Mulan were revived in Chinese spoken dramas to inspire unity and devotion to the nation at a critical time. Combative and appealing, these symbols provided spiritual strength and a political rallying point. To nourish a feeling of solidarity, Chinese dramatists also frequently invoked the past, recalling the glory of China's resistance against outsiders. Tradition brought familiarity and, more important, a sense of identity and cohesiveness.

The message of unity was simultaneously delivered through the visual arts, notably political cartoons. As the resisters found out, the cartoon was a uniquely efficient means for presenting ideas in spontaneous and often biting images. Unlike symbols, which convey ideas and judgments through suggestion or association and often carry multiple meanings,[18] images in general are imitations or representations of objects or people; they delineate outer reality more faithfully, in a graphic form, portraying phenomena as they can be directly perceived.[19] Because cartoons are easily reproducible, they proved a convenient and powerful propaganda tool. Relying on directness, common imagery, and sometimes deliberate vulgarity to make a point, as well as being readily comprehended and frequently entertaining, cartoons could cut to the heart of things with a power and immediacy unparalleled among other media. Good cartoons, as the resisters found out, must tell their story simply, at a glance. Wartime cartoonists thus juxtaposed unambiguous images of the heroism of Chinese soldiers and the brutality of Japanese troops to convey a battle between right and wrong, good and evil. The grisly images of war were designed to arouse public anger against the Japanese and to draw sympathy for the suffering innocents at home.

Among the print media, newspapers occupied a central place in wartime popular culture. With them, too, a transformation took place. As coastal urban centers fell into the hands of the advancing Japanese, newspapers were forced to relocate to interior cities and towns, and journalists took refuge with them. This decentralization of the press was accompanied by a change of style in reporting and writing. Not only did newspapers appear in different forms, such as tabloids, and in many locations in the hinterland to meet the growing public demand for basic war information, but their language also became more direct and accessible. Writing with emotion and an unabashed commitment to the national cause, Chinese journalists were as much interested in *what* they reported as in *how* they reported. They registered personal observations, used down-to-earth language, and became more responsive to the reader. Nevertheless, the personal style of wartime newspaper writing ran into conflict with the much talked about prewar goal of objectivity in reporting. In the end, patriotism—the appeal to emotions—prevailed over a professional ideal.

Newspaper reportage was but one of many forms of wartime political rhetoric. Indeed, despite the call for unity, political rhetoric was not used in a uniform manner during the war. It changed in function over time and was used by different people for different purposes. While nonpartisan intellectuals such as Lao She filled political language with emotion, Chinese Communists turned it into an instrument of political suasion and class struggle. Lao She, for example, used slogans like "Resisting until the end" (*kang dao di*) to signal a kind of Sisyphean determination to defend the nation at whatever cost; the Communists, for their part, invented terms such as "turning over" (*fanshen*) or "liberation" (*jiefang*) to announce the arrival of a new social order and to create a feeling of camaraderie among people of the lower orders. But descriptions such as *fanshen* and *jiefang* were no mere rhetorical exercise; they constituted powerful political calls for change in the social system and, ultimately, an attack on the Nationalists.

This book, however, does not focus solely on urban culture forms. It also explores a variety of predominantly rural folk art genres, largely oral in transmission and anonymous in composition—folk songs, drum singing, storytelling, and so on—that were not replaced by urban popular culture forms as the latter were introduced in earnest by the resisters to the villages. Instead, the two groups were used collectively and often interchangeably by the resisters for propaganda purposes. The distinction between the two thus became ambiguous, in practice if not in theory. And the Communists turned out to be the great promoters and ingenious practitioners of this new trend.

In studying Chinese wartime popular culture, especially patriotic symbols, I found Clifford Geertz's idea of culture as a collectively held system of symbols and meanings helpful. Geertz sees culture as a discourse, an "ensemble of texts," rather than a superorganic entity.[20] For him, every form of human behavior involves symbolic actions that can be subjected to semiotic analysis and decoded. Similarly, patriotic symbols of resistance and the emotionally charged political language created by Chinese intellectuals during the war were meant to nourish a "symbolic universe of patriotism" among the populace, to foster a dialogue with the audience and convince them that victory would prevail in the end.

The Geertzian conception of culture as symbolic behavior allows historians to study the past through nonliterary sources and to examine power relations as mirrored by informal mechanisms. Cultural practices can be politicized without elaborate, systematic governmental intervention; indeed, rituals and village operas can wield as much, if not more, influence on the community as governmental declarations or laws.[21] Working through mostly nongovernmental channels and nonverbal means, Chinese resisters brought the ideas of unity, courage, and sacrifice directly to the grass roots through peripatetic village propaganda teams, street plays, posters, and drum singing rather than by means of formal, institutional arrangements. Wartime culture was an accumulation of images and symbols through which intellectuals communicated among themselves and with the public. Such symbols constituted a collective form of experience that can be "decoded" only within the "world of significance" created by the conflict with the Japanese. It is in this broad sense that "culture" in the Geertzian definition is used in this study.[22]

The transformation and politicization of wartime popular culture centers on resistance politics. Here, "politics" is not meant in the narrow sense of the structure of government or parties; rather, it is interpreted as "political culture"—that is, ideas, attitudes, and feelings about the unfolding political and military crisis. It is about, in Victor Turner's words, "idealism, altruism, patriotism."[23] Political culture focuses on the dynamics of politics, its forms, its development, its public dimensions, and its impact on society. It links politics to the full range of human activities.[24] It suggests ways to study the influence of cultural artifacts and the symbolic expression of this influence in a noninstitutional way. In brief, political culture is a continuous dialogue between politics and reality, between various cultural forms and their intended audiences.

Indeed, the issues of audience and communication lie at the core of wartime discourse. Although this book examines the thoughts of a group of key resistance intellectuals—including dramatists Ouyang Yuqian and Tian Han, cartoonists Feng Zikai and Ye Qianyu, journalists Fan Changjiang and Cheng Shewo, writers Lao She and Lao Xiang—and their collective, conscious effort to use popular culture as a tool to counter the Japanese military onslaught, it is not really a book about intellectuals. It is a cultural study.[25] It looks at intellectuals as key agents in the transformation of popular culture and their role in reaching out to the people during the war.

Because spoken dramas, cartoons, and newspapers were intended for public consumption, they inevitably invited the participation of their audience, on whose approval their survival and effectiveness ultimately rested. Thus, although they were created not *by* the people but *for* the people, it would be erroneous to regard them as a mere imposition of elite values from above. In fact, a dynamic interaction was taking place between the intelligentsia and the people. Chinese resisters were, as Herbert Gans wrote with regard to America's mass media, "often engaged in a guessing game, trying to figure out what people want[ed], or rather, what they [would] accept."[26] What ordinary people thought and felt, and to what extent they accepted the new patriotic materials, were therefore key factors in the resistance campaign. Intellectuals' concern to bring their messages to the populace also brought them closer to the people, emotionally if not intellectually. Yet the art of persuasion was elusive and difficult to master. Writing in a language comprehensible to the largely illiterate general public proved a daunting and often frustrating assignment for Chinese intellectuals and artists.

This book draws on the ideas of art, literature, and journalism to provide as balanced and comprehensive a picture of the war as possible, within the constraints of the overall subject—that is, popular propaganda culture. It must be pointed out, however, that the focus on spoken dramas, cartoons, and newspapers leaves out two important genres of popular culture: songs and films. A brief explanation is in order. The sheer abundance of songs, coupled with my inadequate grasp of musical theory, makes it doubly difficult for me to treat this important subject thoroughly and convincingly. The growth and influence of wartime songs must therefore await a more capable chronicler. The history of wartime films is a different story. My initial plan was to include a chapter on cinema, but the task proved impossible owing to a scarcity of wartime films and the difficulties of obtaining those that do exist.[27] The eruption of the war brought most of the booming Shanghai film industry to an abrupt halt in 1937, and an acute shortage of film stock allowed few films (with the notable exception of government propaganda newsreels) to be made during the war. Many filmmakers, including Zhao Dan and Wang Ying, joined the spoken drama propaganda troupes that toured the interior. Systematic filmmaking did not resume until after the end of the Sino-Japanese War and the return of filmmakers to Shanghai. Thus, important productions such as *The Spring River Flows East* (*Yijiang chunshui xiang dong liu*, 1947 and 1948, in two parts) were made only in the wake of the war.[28]

This book deals largely with the Guomindang-controlled areas and the Communist-held border regions. It discusses little of the Japanese-occupied territories (except occupied Shanghai). Of course, resistance activities were not absent in the Japanese-controlled areas. The political and cultural issues involved, however, were so different that a separate study would be required to do justice to those complex regions. To be sure, the Guomindang-controlled territories and the Communist base areas differed with respect to the resistance campaign as well. While the cultural battle in the Guomindang-controlled hinterland was largely unsystematic and uncoordinated because of the factional infighting and often confusing policies of the government, in the Communist areas it was carefully orchestrated. Indeed, despite the fact that policies enacted at Yan'an, the headquarters of the Chinese Communist Party (CCP), were received differently in individual base areas, a general border-region culture, as chapter 6 argues, can still be discerned.[29] Such a culture was actively promoted by the Communists as the future of China.

The War of Resistance reshaped Chinese political culture. It created more than a military crisis: it precipitated a period of great uncertainty when fundamental traditional values about art and literature were questioned, intellectuals' roles were redefined, the social order was restructured, and popular culture took on new tasks and meanings. The widespread influence of popular culture in wartime China changed the attitudes of many conservative intellectuals toward this formerly ignored field and established popular culture as a valuable source for understanding popular behavior. More important, it caused the rapid fading of the urban, elitist character of Chinese culture and shifted the nation's attention to the countryside. This "ruralization" of Chinese culture was crucial to the success of the Communists following the war, for it helped to make their call for a rural revolution appealing and convincing. During the eight-year War of Resistance the Communists, not the Nationalists, emerged as the spokesmen of the rural hinterland—the bastion of China's resistance as well as its future.

1 The Rise of Modern Popular Culture

The battle of Shanghai, which began on 13 August 1937, ended swiftly in Chinese defeat in early November when the Japanese landed a surprise amphibious force in Hangzhou Bay, fifty miles southwest of Shanghai, and attacked China's leading metropolis from the rear. Despite their early heroic defense of the city, the GMD forces now withdrew westward to the capital of Nanjing, demoralized and in disarray. By the time Wuhan fell in October 1938, the Japanese effectively controlled some 10 percent of the territory in north and central China—mostly major cities and areas adjacent to the railway lines. If the Marco Polo Bridge Incident in early July signaled the beginning of China's resistance, the subsequent loss of Shanghai and other major cities made it clear just where this resistance would take place: in China's vast hinterland. The need for a new campaign to rally the support of the rural masses for the war cause thus became self-evident.

As was true elsewhere (such as Vichy France),[1] China's resistance movement was a coalition of various individuals and groups markedly different in political affinity, regional ties, and professional orientation. But willingly or unwillingly, they had a shared goal of resisting foreign aggression, and that tied their fates temporarily together. It became obvious that an unprecedented national crisis demanded unity and cooperation; internal difference and personal feuding had to be set aside. Despite debates over the exact course resistance should take, there seemed to be a consensus among Chinese intellectuals that certain forms of urban culture—particularly spoken dramas, cartoons, and newspapers—because of their popularity, could be of enormous value to facilitate communication and indoctrination in the rural hinterland. If carefully popularized and systematically disseminated, it was argued, these media could make a major difference in the outcome of the war. However, as the resisters soon found out, putting these urban forms to effective use in the rural interior was not to be an easy task. China's myriad problems—a backward hinterland, a primitive transportation system, high illiteracy, and extreme regional variation —constituted an enormous hindrance to any large-scale propaganda drive. If the resisters were to succeed, they would need more than courage and determination; they would have to mount a campaign comprehensible and convincing to the largely illiterate peasantry— a difficult job at best. The wartime popular culture campaign thus became the saga of transforming a host of urban culture forms into lucid vehicles able to rally support for the war cause among all Chinese, regardless of their educational or cultural background. To understand how these urban culture genres were refashioned into political tools and their subsequent impact, we need to examine their origin and rise in the cities in the early decades of twentieth-century China.

Treaty Ports and Shanghai

Before the war many Chinese cities, especially major treaty ports such as Shanghai and Tianjin, furnished a unique economic and social milieu within which myriad popular culture forms, including spoken dramas, newspapers, and cartoons, flourished.

The emergence of modern cities in China has been well studied.[2] By the early twentieth century China's treaty ports had developed into major commercial, industrial, and trade centers with a virtual monopoly on foreign trade.[3] Foreigners—British, French, and Japanese in particular—played a dominant role in shaping these cities' economic and political futures, largely as a result of certain privileges, such as low tariffs, special residential enclaves, and rights of extraterritoriality, accorded them in numerous treaties and agreements signed since the Treaty of Nanjing in 1842. On the eve of the Sino-Japanese War, the major treaty ports were characterized by their enormous population, social complexity, economic dominance, and cultural cosmopolitanism. In 1936, for example, Shanghai had 3.7 million inhabitants (of whom 57,000 were foreigners), while Tianjin had a population of 1.2 million (of whom 13,000 were foreigners).[4] Because of their role as trade and industrial centers, treaty ports drew scores of bankers, merchants, and entrepreneurs, native and foreign alike; they also attracted newcomers from China's countryside seeking a better life in a new environment. The cities thus hosted an ethnically diverse population, one often marked by deep intergroup antagonisms and regional biases.[5] In the cities, too, foreigners not only were a conspicuous presence because of their different appearance, language, and life-style, but with their new ideas they also created sharp cultural tensions.

Urbanization and industrialization quickened changes, precipitated anxieties, and bred social problems such as crimes and labor strikes. At the same time, material progress gave rise to a curious, acquisitive middle class that hankered for novelty and entertainment. Social life in the city was colorful and had a special hold on imagination. It was against this backdrop that a wealth of new urban culture forms emerged.

Perry Link has shown that cultural dilemmas and anxieties caused by a rapidly modernizing society, coupled with technological change (such as new methods of printing), the lower cost of such media as books and films, and rising literacy rates, all contributed to the rise of popular fiction in early-twentieth-century cities.[6] The emergence and popularity of spoken dramas, newspapers, and cartoon magazines in the cities can be attributed to these same reasons. But other factors came into play as well: a desire for novelty and sensationalism, cosmopolitanism, avant-garde attitudes, commercialism, professionalism, and decadence—all characteristics of modern urban society. Among major treaty ports, Shanghai set the agenda for these urban culture forms and decided their priorities.

Shanghai in the 1930s, with a population of over 3 million, was a place brimming with artistic achievement and a newfound sophistication. But it was also a city of sharp contradictions and contrasts, an oasis of modernity in a vast land of emerald rice fields and sleepy villages. With its foreign-ruled enclaves (the International Settlement and the French Concession), its booming commerce, its thriving film industry, and its numerous "street cars, neon signs, electric lights, and jazzy dances," as a *New York Times* reporter described it in 1931,[7] Shanghai was a city of opportunities and allure, an ideal world for young moderns to travel on the fast track and for businessmen to seal a lucrative deal. Shanghai drew artists, merchants, and dreamers like a magnet. Although Shanghainese might find little of interest in government intrigues, they could be easily aroused by the suicide of a movie star.[8] To many, Shanghai was the "Paris of the East."[9]

But Shanghai was not without its detractors. For some, the presence of so many unruly foreigners was a bitter reminder of China's humiliating past; in the eyes of many, moreover, the city's manifold temptations bred only greed and corruption. For the majority of residents, in fact, Shanghai was a world of Hobbesian brutes where mercilessness reigned supreme. The city was "like a monstrous hell . . . and a vassal state of foreign countries," bemoaned the well-known actress Wang Ying (1915–1974). "People dream of nothing else except gobbling up others all the time."[10]

Shanghai's contemptible process of cultural "commodification" provoked the wrath of traditional elites, especially the Beijingese. To the Beijingese, Shanghai was a metropolis of decadence and vice. Beijingese derided their southern cousins as nothing more than nouveaux riches—vulgar, profit-seeking people consumed by materialism and vanity—rootless and confused because of the influx of depraved Western ideas. The Shanghainese retorted that the Beijingese were simply out of touch with the times. Their old, genteel style belonged to a bygone era; they loved to savor vanished glory but refused to embrace necessary changes brought about by the advancement of civilization. Beijing (changed to "Beiping" by the Nationalists in 1928; the Communists reverted to its old name in 1949) might be the seat of power, they said, but Shanghai was the financial capital of the nation and the city of the future. It was here where the newest tastes were being shaped and opinions formed. The rivalry between the "Beijing style" (*Jing pai*) and the "Shanghai style" (*Hai pai*) was actually more than a difference in style. Similar to the rivalry between Moscow (the ideological home of the Slavophiles and the city linked to the past) and St. Petersburg (the modern city so loved by Westernizers) in nineteenth-century Russia,[11] it was also a confrontation between two opposing values—traditionalism and modernity—and a debate between two cultures—high and popular.[12]

In the 1930s, Shanghai had become the heart of China's intellectual avant-garde and the spawning ground for new ideas. The port city had nearly monopolized the country's learning and publishing, to an even greater extent than did Paris in France.[13] Predictably, there was no dearth of magazines and novelettes, which, like penny periodicals in Victorian England, thrived on themes of sex, crime, and thwarted love.[14] Yet Shanghai was also dotted with excellent bookstores and elegant theaters, in addition to its celebrated cafés and restaurants. The famous Fourth Road (Sima lu, officially known as Fuzhou Road)—the "Cultural Street" (Wenhua jie), as it was commonly called[15]—was the home of many nationally known bookstores, including Kaiming Bookstore, Beixin Bookstore, and World Bookstore (Shijie shuju), and vying for readers just around the corner were the legendary Commercial Press and Zhonghua Bookstore.[16] All this cultural activity encouraged scores of would-be writers and artists, not wishing to live a life of destitution and obscurity in the provinces, to come or send their works to this port city in search of money and fame. Shanghai might devour people, but to these aspiring artists it offered opportunities and held the promise of a better life. Consider the earlier success story of Wu Woyao (1866–1910), a Cantonese who came to the city in the late nineteenth century to work in newspapers and find a new life. He eventually made his name as a novelist by producing many highly acclaimed works, including *Strange Events Seen in the Past Twenty Years* (*Ershi nian mudu zhi guai xianzhuang*). In the mid-1930s, another Cantonese followed in his footsteps, though in a slightly different fashion. The cartoonist Liao Bingxiong (1915–) sent his works from Guangzhou to the well-known magazine *Modern Cartoons* (*Shidai manhua*) in Shanghai for publication. As a result of these opportunities Liao quickly established himself as one of the best talents in the field.[17]

Shanghai became a pacesetter of modern popular culture. This was particularly evident in the proliferation of drama clubs, cartoon magazines, and newspapers in the city, all urban culture forms with their own unique history.

A New Drama in Urban China

Chinese spoken drama (*huaju*, lit. "speaking play," a name used to distinguish it from traditional operas), a genre born out of the influence of Western drama, began as a marginal cultural activity in the opening years of the century. Because of its simplicity and flexibility, however, it grew quickly in popularity, ultimately occupying the center stage in China's cultural defense against the aggressors during the war.

In 1907 in Tokyo, the Spring Willow Society (Chunliu she), formed by the young Chinese theater enthusiasts Zeng Xiaogu, Li Shutong (1880–1942), and Ouyang Yuqian (1889–1962), staged *Chahua nü*, an adaption of *La dame aux camélias* by Dumas *fils*, and *Black Slave's Cry to Heaven* (*Heinu yutian lu*), based on the novel *Uncle Tom's Cabin* by Harriet Beecher Stowe.[18] These two plays, despite their performance by an all-male group of amateurs in a foreign land, marked the inception of Western-style drama by the Chinese.

The choice of *La dame aux camélias* and *Uncle Tom's Cabin* for the basis of these productions was not entirely accidental, for both had already gained enormous popularity in China through the elegant translations of Lin Shu (1852–1924).[19] The denunciation of racial prejudice in Stowe's novel found particularly strong resonance among young nationalistic Chinese. To the group of Chinese student dramatists who came to a more modernized Japan to acquire new knowledge that would strengthen their own country, the mistreatment of blacks in America aroused memory of the recent violence and discrimination Chinese laborers had experienced in the same country from the 1880s to the early 1900s. The anti-Chinese movement in America reminded them of the evils of racism and the impotence of the Qing government to protect its citizens abroad.[20]

The novelty of the new art form generated curiosity and drew many admirers. Nevertheless, the introduction of spoken drama into China must be understood within a larger context of rapid social and political change during the waning years of the Qing dynasty. This was an era when the old political hierarchy was crumbling and Confucian tradition eroding. The Manchu government's weakness and its inability to fend off any advances from the West aroused increasing criticism of traditional norms and caused youths to embrace new ways of thinking. Under the sway of nationalism, young Chinese dramatists yearned for their country to gain the strength to withstand oppression both at home (by the Manchus) and abroad (by the imperialist powers).

Ironically, the West also became a source of inspiration for Chinese youth. In the two decades after 1907, the plays of Shakespeare, Shaw, Wilde, Chekhov, Ibsen, and other Western masters were introduced,[21] joined by such native pieces as Hu Shi's (1891–1962) *The Greatest Event in Life* (*Zhongshen dashi*, 1919).[22] In the end, however, the new stage was used more as a pulpit to express radical social views and iconoclastic ideas than as a forum for artistic, theatrical experimentation. "In China," the writer Xiao Qian (1910–) observed, "Ibsen is looked upon as a social surgeon rather than as a playwright."[23] Indeed, young Chinese dramatists felt obliged with their art to reach a large audience and to shape social values. This sentiment was particularly evident in the manifesto of the People's Drama Society (Minzhong xijushe), founded in May 1921. It reads in part:

> The theatre occupies an important place in modern society. It is a wheel rolling society forward. It is an X-ray searching out the root of society's maladies. It is also a just and impartial mirror, and the standards of everybody in the nation are stripped stark naked when reflected in this great mirror. . . . This kind of theatre is precisely what does not exist in China at present, but it is what we, feeble though we are, want to strive to create.[24]

Such a commitment proved useful later, during the war, when dramatists turned their plays into political and educational vehicles for defending their nation against outside aggression.

The use of drama to educate an audience was, of course, not unique to China. The Greeks had a long history of using the theater to instruct citizens about communal values: Athenians went to the theater of Dionysus several times a year, to enjoy a popular traditional story and, in the process, receive reinforcement in an accepted ethic. In more recent times, Schiller expressed his view of the stage as a moral institution, an attitude echoed by Diderot; and playwrights from Ibsen to Shaw and Brecht all used the stage as a pulpit.[25] In Southeast Asia, too, the theater has long been used as an educational and political device. Wayang drama, for example, was the main vehicle by which Javanese and Balinese religion and philosophy were transmitted to the people.[26] What is notable about Chinese spoken drama, though, was the scope of its subsequent influence, the variety of its forms, and the energy that creators of spoken drama put into communicating with the masses during the war.

Young dramatists believed that the spoken drama heralded the dawning of a new age in Chinese art. They were drawn together by a common enthusiasm for something new and exciting. Yet their goal was not to mount an artistic endeavor per se; for them, rather, embracing something new was a way of breaking with the past. Unlike in the West, where the rise of realist dramas in the mid-nineteenth century was a conscious revolt against romanticism, Chinese spoken dramas targeted the spiritual ailments of the Confucian past. What appealed to young playwrights most about this new-style dramatic form was its ability to speak directly to the present—a far cry from its traditional counterpart. In their eyes, not only was the traditional theater hostile to new ideas, but its archaic language, techniques, and plots also bore little relevance to contemporary social and political issues. The old-style theater was a highly elegant art locked in time; embodying nothing more than a concoction of Confucian paragons and trite events, it had lost its ability to change. As one critic categorically stated, "It is a poison."[27] Many iconoclastic intellectuals echoed this opinion in the May Fourth era when they challenged traditional norms and sought to free the people's will from the confinement of the past. Hu Shi and Zhou Zuoren (1885–1967) both deemed old-style opera obsolete and called for its complete abandonment. This radical stand, in contrast to the more moderate view of Ouyang Yuqian and the drama critic Song Chunfang (1892–1938), who instead suggested far-reaching reform, gained the upper hand during the May Fourth drama debate.[28] During the war, however, even the radical view was tempered as the resisters embraced every possible means to combat the Japanese, including the previously condemned traditional operas.

Clearly, the revolt against tradition called for a different kind of art. It is true that in the early years of Chinese spoken drama, actors such as Ouyang Yuqian still relied heavily on the techniques of traditional opera for their interpretation; but the fact that this new performing art was Western-inspired gave it a novel look as well as a cosmopolitan flavor. In contrast to old-style opera with its standard repertoire of music and singing, formal character types, and established story lines, the spoken drama introduced naturalistic dialogue, curtains, and original plots. And more important, spoken drama allowed actors to portray realistic situations and enabled them to deliver their messages with unprecedented directness. Traditional opera's avoidance of tragedy was now corrected. For the first time in the history of Chinese theater, the stage was peopled with authentic characters reflecting life's contradictions and complexity: a mixture of good and evil, joy and sorrow, prosperity and privation. The new dialogue used in the plays was more down-to-earth and flexible, better equipped to mirror contemporary social problems and more open to artistic experimentation.

With the spoken drama came other innovations. More attention was paid to the details of setting and characterization, with the distinctiveness of individual characters being particularly emphasized. These innovations were exactly what Hu Shi had in mind when he wrote *The Greatest Event in Life*, a one-act play dealing with antitraditionalism, in 1919. The work ridiculed the old ways—embodied here in the twin evils of astrology and antiquated Confucian norms—that led the parents of a young woman to forbid her marriage to a well-educated young man she had met in Japan. The influence of Ibsen was readily apparent in Hu's play. Like the Norwegian master, whose influential play *A Doll's House* (1879) he translated into Chinese in 1918, Hu championed the ideals of individualism and a woman's right to arrange her own marriage. Moreover, both laid as much stress on the individual qualities of their characters as on the cause for which they argued.

Despite a promising start, Chinese spoken dramas in their first two decades remained amateurish, with few dramatic organizations to support production and limited audiences. Initial efforts to popularize the spoken drama thus proved difficult and frustrating. In this early period, Western-style theater fare was referred to as "new plays" (*xinju*) or "civilized plays" (*wenmingxi*)—so named because the term *wenming*, as Ouyang Yuqian noted, implied "progress."[29] Indeed, initially the new "civilized plays" strongly decried social ills, openly seeking to foster political reforms. Western drama "created a sensation when it reached Hankou," drama critic Xiong Foxi (1900–1965) wrote, recalling the early 1910s when he was a middle school student in this inland Yangzi River treaty port.[30] By the end of the next decade, however, "civilized plays" had degenerated into low-quality productions, filled with vulgar details, occasionally "to the extent of pandering to prurient interest."[31] Such plays, often lacking a unified plot, hastily composed, and performed on an impromptu basis, brought a negative notoriety to the new art. Even for those who were committed to mounting a respectable show, things were no easier: the majority of players were amateurs and their troupes poorly funded, if not already deep in debt.[32]

Worse still, the new art faced a formidable challenge from the traditional theater. Although many young dramatists ridiculed the usefulness and some even predicted the quick demise of old-style opera, it remained the favorite of most Chinese theatergoers, especially with the towering presence of such renowned actors as Mei Lanfang (1894–1961) and Cheng Yanqiu (1904–1958). To be sure, the new-style theater lacked actors of such elevated status. More important, however, was the fact that young dramatists were novices in a field long dominated by the Beijing opera and numerous other regional theaters. A new-style play could not be more alien to audiences accustomed to the traditional drama's familiar delivery and production—bare stage, structured rhythmic movements, standardized roles, magnificent acrobatics, and the unbridled noise in the theater.[33] Old-style theater devotees found the spoken drama's original plots, dialogue, absence of singing roles, and division into acts, with the accompanying curtains and intervals, unpalatable. They shunned the new theater. The debut of Shaw's *Mrs. Warren's Profession* in Shanghai in the spring of 1921, for example, proved a dismal failure despite heavy publicity. Audience reactions, which ranged from "totally incomprehensible" to "too many superfluous words," were a big disappointment to the sponsors.[34]

Despite the uncertain start of the new drama, young dramatists continued to fight for recognition in the mainstream theatrical world. Finally in the late 1920s spoken drama began to gain acceptance in urban areas, especially in cities like Shanghai, thanks largely to the efforts of a number of drama associations, particularly the People's Drama Society and the South China Society (Nanguo she).

The People's Drama Society was formed in 1921 in Shanghai by a heterogeneous group of thirteen people, including the actor Wang Youyou, the novelist Mao Dun (1896–1981), the literary historian Zheng Zhenduo (1898–1958), the drama critic Xiong Foxi, and Ouyang Yuqian. The name, inspired by Romain Rolland's People's Theater,[35] indicated the members' desire to bring the new art to the populace. Artistically, the society proposed creating all new sets and costumes—in short, rejecting the trappings of traditional opera. Intellectually, it advocated originality in production: rather than relying on translations of European works, the creation of native works was encouraged. "Only when we can produce a few plays that are comparable or even superior to their Western counterparts can we claim that they are genuine 'new plays,'" wrote Wang Youyou.[36] While the society's aim was to search out "the root of society's maladies," it never belittled the value of spoken drama as an entertainment medium. Indeed, the subtle blending of education with entertainment, they insisted, was required if spoken dramas were to gain wide acceptance. The society also issued a journal entitled *Drama* (*Xiju*), the first Chinese magazine devoted exclusively to the discussion and propagation of the new genre. Its brief existence notwithstanding (ten issues were printed from May 1921 to April 1922), the journal provided a much-needed theoretical justification for spoken drama.[37]

The South China Society was another major force in the early history of this new art form. Unlike the People's Drama Society, it had a charismatic leader: Tian Han (1898–1968), a gifted writer and also an erstwhile member of the renowned Creation Society. An early devotee of spoken dramas, Tian called himself "a budding Chinese Ibsen" when he was a student in Japan in 1920.[38] He was the first to coin the term *huaju* (spoken drama) in 1927, rechristening *xinju* (new plays) in order to emphasize the medium's use of dialogue and its nonmusical nature.[39]

Tian Han launched a new magazine, *South China Fortnightly* (*Nanguo banyuekan*), in January 1924 in Shanghai "to breathe a little bit of artistic fresh air into the depressed Chinese literary scene."[40] The journal became the first of many endeavors by Tian to promote spoken drama in China. In the summer of 1926, for instance, he established the South China Film and Drama Society (Nanguo dianying jushe; later renamed the South China Society). And in January 1928 he founded the South China Art Institute (Nanguo yishu xueyuan), artistic home to a score of future celebrated playwrights, including Chen Baichen (1908–).[41]

Tian Han's genius lay not so much in his role as an enthusiastic educator as in his determined spirit and his talent as a playwright. Within the eight-year period 1922–1930, he published sixteen spoken dramas, setting a high standard and giving the budding spoken drama movement an eloquent boost. Plays such as *Night Talk in Suzhou* (*Suzhou yehua*, 1927) and *Return to the South* (*Nan gui*, 1929), tinged with the familiar melancholy and sentimentalism of his earlier works, won high acclaim and brought the new-style drama wide recognition. Tian's productions suggested the influence of Ibsen, Strindberg, and Chekhov, but they were not without contemporary themes specific to China: the desire, however futile it might be, to reform the nation through art (as in *Night Talk in Suzhou*) and the longing for a bright new world (as in *Return to the South*).[42]

Inadequately funded, Tian struggled to secure enough financial resources to keep his organization afloat. But adversity only seemed to solidify his young followers' resolve. They were captivated by Tian Han's charm, his willingness to take risks in uncharted dramatic waters, and, above all, his single-minded devotion to art. Such devotion became the very model of artistic dedication, instilling a spirit of harmony in this group of idealistic youths.[43] Tian, a man sensitive to social ills and who gradually subscribed to the leftist ideology of his day (he helped found the League of Left-Wing Dramatists in 1930 and joined the CCP in 1932), encouraged his fledgling dramatists to embrace life with art. To bring his students into closer contact with the public Tian arranged a performing tour in 1929, which featured new plays and included such cities as Hangzhou, Nanjing, Guangzhou, and Wuxi. The tour proved a great success, and the warm reception that the group received was gratifying. As one female student put it after their performance in Nanjing, "Although we are still poor, nevertheless we have left a good impression in the minds of the Nanjing viewers."[44] The self-supporting principles preached by the society also helped to bond the group together. Chen Baichen summed it up thus in his recent memoirs: "We worked closely as a team."[45]

Spoken drama finally came of age in the 1930s when the Western devices that so marked the genre, such as realistic sets, stage curtains, the division of a production into acts, and the employment of both men and women actors (an idea first suggested by Hong Shen [1894–1955], a noted playwright and drama critic who was trained in the

United States),[46] finally gained acceptance among Chinese audiences. In that decade, sensational plays such as Cao Yu's (1910–) *Thunderstorm* (*Leiyu*, 1934) reaped instant success both in intellectual circles and at the box office. Professional drama troupes also emerged, such as Tang Huaiqiu's (1898–1954) China Traveling Drama Troupe (Zhongguo lüxing jutuan)—the first professional traveling group in China, established in 1933 in Shanghai.[47] Nevertheless, despite the genre's increasing status, spoken drama remained very much an urban phenomenon.

Even in the cities, the plots of the new drama were familiar only to the sophisticated few. Its artistic form simply did not fit well with traditional aesthetics. The fact that many companies continued to rely heavily on translations of foreign plays (such as Hong Shen's 1924 adaptation of Oscar Wilde's *Lady Windermere's Fan*) was alienating to the general public. Ticket prices were also formidable. An average theater seat generally cost from 20 to 40 *fen*, a better one from 60 *fen* to 1 *yuan*—the equivalent of almost a day's wages for a skilled worker.[48] Moreover, the cinema was growing in popularity during this time and competed with spoken drama in the cities as well.[49] As a consequence of these factors, the new drama attracted largely the elite, especially those who had come under the influence of the West. It was therefore the educated who nurtured the new drama with financial and moral support.

Limited audiences notwithstanding, spoken drama companies proliferated in major cities: in Beijing, there was the Venus Drama Society (Weina jushe); in Xi'an, the Chang'an Popular Drama Troupe (Chang'an minzhong jutuan); and in Tianjin, the famous Nankai School Drama Club, in which the future Communist leader Zhou Enlai (1898–1976) participated.[50] But it was in Shanghai that the new drama received the greatest attention. As the veteran playwright Xia Yan (1900–) recalled, that city in the 1930s was the indisputable capital of the new drama movement, becoming home to numerous professional and semiprofessional clubs and attracting flocks of young hopefuls.[51]

Before the Marco Polo Bridge Incident, numerous drama clubs sprouted in Shanghai, including the Great Way Drama Club (Dadao jushe, 1931) and the Virgin Land Drama Club (Xindi jushe, 1933).[52] Yet the formation in August 1930 of the League of Left-Wing Dramatists (Zuoyi jutuan lianmeng), which brought together a number of drama associations such as the Art Drama Association (Yishu jushe) and Modern Society (Modeng she), signaled a new twist: the growing radicalization of the art. The new drama now began to assume a more overtly political look, becoming a battleground on which the Communists and the Nationalists endeavored to settle their ideological differences.

The profusion of published articles on the spoken drama was another sign of the growing maturity of the art. New plays, essays, and debates about the genre appeared regularly in noted newspapers and journals, including "Unfettered Talk" ("Ziyou tan"), the literary supplement of the *Shanghai News* (*Shen bao*), as well as literary magazines such as *Modern Times* (*Xiandai*) and *Literature Monthly* (*Wenxue yuebao*). Scholars also proposed to establish spoken drama as a serious professional discipline by subjecting it to a judicious and timely review process.[53]

Nor was the new drama confined to professional or semiprofessional drama troupes, for it quickly took hold on school and university campuses—the locus of revolutionary ideas ever since the May Fourth era.[54] The spoken drama was looked upon by student activists as an ideal means for igniting social and political change. In June 1931 in Shanghai alone, a local magazine reported, there were over twenty university and middle school drama clubs. In that same year, the Ji'nan Drama Club (Ji'nan jushe) of Ji'nan University put on nineteen different plays, a mixture of translated works and originals that included Tian Han's *Seven Women in the Tempest* (*Baofengyu zhong de qige nüxing*), in which the growing nationalism following the Manchurian Incident of 18 September 1931 was a strong element.[55]

Sensing the increasing popularity of the new drama, more and more Shanghai theater owners—including the proprietors of the popular Gold (Huangjin daxiyuan) and Carlton (Kaerdeng xiyuan) theaters[56] —agreed to stage such productions, a decision deemed a financial risk but a short while before. The 1937 conversion of the Carlton from a cinema into a drama theater was, as A. C. Scott correctly notes, "a significant indication of the way the wind was blowing."[57] Prewar drama in Shanghai reached its zenith when a number of drama clubs jointly staged an unprecedented series of performances that spring at the Carlton Theater.[58]

As we have seen, before the war the emerging popularity of modern drama was confined to urban centers and the educated minority of the Chinese people. Even Tang Huaiqiu's China Traveling Drama Troupe performed almost exclusively in large cities.[59] All that changed when war broke out. Most significantly, the film industry in Shanghai collapsed, a circumstance that presented a unique opportunity for spoken drama. Not only did numerous screen actors join the traveling drama propaganda troupes in the interior, but in the absence of cinema, spoken drama became recognized as a particularly suitable vehicle for communicating with the people in a time of national crisis.

The Emergence of Chinese Cartoons

The term *manhua* (cartoon) was borrowed from Japan and first used in China by Feng Zikai (1898–1975) in May 1925,[60] though the art and its techniques were known as early as the late Qing era. As was the case with spoken drama, cartoons were very much an urban phenomenon before the war, their rise closely associated with the emergence of the urban press.

The Chinese periodical press emerged in the late nineteenth century from a blending of the styles of traditional periodicals such as the Beijing gazettes (known as *Jing bao*) and Western-style newspapers and magazines.[61] As the Western-style commercial newspapers arose in the treaty ports of late Qing China, a new type of political press was launched by such pioneers as Wang Tao (1828–1897) and Liang Qichao (1873–1929) to introduce new ideas and call for radical reforms.[62] Borrowing novel approaches from the West to enhance its prestige and sales, the Chinese press underwent various changes in both format and content. The fact that the Western press often supplemented articles with illustrations had a special impact.[63] Such a feature, as the editor of *The 1908 Pictorial* (*Wushen quannian huabao*) frankly admitted, "can greatly enhance the people's wisdom and broaden their horizons."[64] Within short order, illustrations began to appear in profusion in Chinese newspapers and magazines. Many, focusing on current events and drawing on popular sources for their appeal, had a distinct social and political overtone. Wu Youru's famous drawings in *Dianshi Studio Pictorial* (*Dianshizhai huabao*—the first Chinese pictorial, founded in 1884) were a case in point.[65] A visual record of the decay of Qing society and the political conflicts of the time, his work added a new and refreshing dimension to the Chinese press. Yet despite the pioneering quality of Wu's efforts, in the end his illustrations were, as cartoonist Ye Qianyu (1907–) pointed out, merely a kind of "recording picture" (*jilu hua*):[66] they portrayed current scenes in a realistic fashion and incorporated little of the exaggeration and satire commonly associated with cartoons today.

Like the English word *cartoon*,[67] the Chinese term *manhua* defies simple definition. Both before the war and since, it has been endowed with a wide range of meaning. To some, the *manhua* was a satirical graphic art form that used distortion and exaggeration to lay bare life's absurdities.[68] But to others, a cartoon was a kind of "social art" whose content related closely to the life of the common people.[69] Despite this ambiguity, however, cartoonists seemed to agree on three essential, albeit rather general, ingredients of the *manhua*. First, cartoons were a new graphic art form drawn with economy of line but replete with powerful ideas. Second, they typically featured exaggerated or ludicrous representations of events or persons. And finally, a cartoon's success lay in the thought it embodied, not artistic adroitness. As Feng Zikai put it, "To draw a cartoon, you must first have ideas, and then practice your brush."[70]

The rise of cartoons in twentieth-century China grew also from an older tradition, traceable to various unorthodox paintings of early times.[71] Yet cartoons' modern traits and distinctive techniques received their greatest inspiration from Japan and the West. Since the days of William Hogarth (1697–1764), James Gillray (1756–1815), and Honoré Daumier (1808–1879), cartoonists have taken on the task of recording major events of their time. For cartoonists are not only artists but also critical social observers and commentators, displaying in their works a great sensitivity to contemporary issues. Just as Daumier, the "Historian of the Bourgeois Government," for example, vividly depicted the decadent life of nineteenth-century French monarchists, clerics, and parvenus, so did Chinese cartoonists faithfully record the turmoils of their nation in the early twentieth century. Their drawings provide a remarkable social history of China during the waning days of the Qing, reflecting a deep national malaise brought on by government ineptitude and continuing foreign imperialism. Known by such names as "satirical drawings" (*fengci hua*) or "allegorical pictures" (*yuyi hua*),[72] cartoons were vociferous in their denunciations of the moribund Qing government (fig. 1).

With the publication of its first cartoon magazine, *Shanghai Punch* (*Shanghai poke*), in September 1918, China saw the art of the cartoon come of age. The magazine's founder and editor, Shen Bochen (1889–1920), was, along with Huang Wennong (1903–1934), one of the most influential cartoonists of his generation. A passionate and patriotic man, Shen used his cartoons to attack the warlord government and portray the social and political upheavals of the early Republican era.[73]

Chinese cartoons made great strides in the 1920s and 1930s. An array of specialized magazines such as *Modern Cartoons* (*Shidai manhua*; originally titled *Modern Sketch*) and *Independent Cartoons* (*Duli manhua*) thrived in Shanghai, and cartoons also began to appear

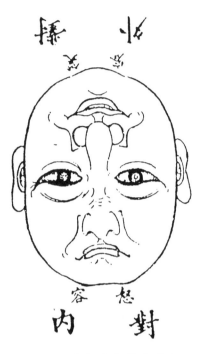

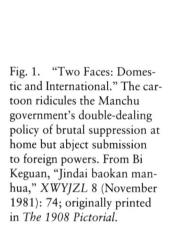

Fig. 1. "Two Faces: Domestic and International." The cartoon ridicules the Manchu government's double-dealing policy of brutal suppression at home but abject submission to foreign powers. From Bi Keguan, "Jindai baokan manhua," *XWYJZL* 8 (November 1981): 74; originally printed in *The 1908 Pictorial.*

in major general-interest journals, including the *Eastern Miscellany* (*Dongfang zazhi*), *Analects* (*Lunyu*), and *Cosmic Wind* (*Yuzhou feng*).[74] Newspapers added special cartoon sections, and magazines actively solicited submissions from their readers.[75] Simultaneously, in the mid-1920s a new breed of cartoonists began to emerge. The Cartoon Association (Manhua hui), China's first society dedicated to the art form, made its debut in the autumn of 1927 in Shanghai. Founded by Ding Song (1891–1972), Zhang Guangyu (1900–1964), Wang Dunqing (1899–), and Ye Qianyu, the association had eleven members initially, most of whom were novices who shared a common interest in trying a new technique and testing a new field. These young artists used their exuberant creative energy to establish caricature as an acceptable art form, hoping to gain recognition from the established art circle. Indeed, the launching of the Cartoon Association was an important event in the history of Chinese cartoons. Not only did the association nurture a certain esprit de corps among an otherwise loosely organized group of artists, but also, through its adoption of the term *manhua*, it sought to give its new craft a standard name, hoping to sweep away the various other terms that had been used for "cartoon."[76] By so doing, the association hoped to raise, in Wang Dunqing's words, "the standard of the cartoon art."[77] The Cartoon Association was the first of many such organizations to emerge in China before the war.[78] The rise in the 1920s and 1930s of many training classes and correspondence schools dedicated to the art of the cartoon, oriented to the next generation of artists, was a further reflection of interest.[79]

With the publication in 1935 of *Personal Essays and Cartoons* (*Xiaopinwen he manhua*), a special anthology commissioned by the respected literary journal *Venus* (*Taibai*) in Shanghai,[80] cartoons seemed finally to come into their own. Edited by Chen Wangdao (1890–1977; best known for his translation of Karl Marx's *The Communist Manifesto* into Chinese in April 1920) and with more than fifty contributors, the book was important to cartoonists in two respects. First, it recognized the cartoon as an important art form equal to that of the personal essay (*xiaopinwen*). Second, it attracted important writers like Lu Xun (1881–1936) and cartoonists like Feng Zikai to engage in thoughtful exchanges about what had formerly been regarded as an unworthy art. Lu Xun, long an avid advocate of such "lowbrow" art as woodcuts and serial illustrations, praised cartoons highly in his two articles for the anthology. Cartoons dealt with realistic aspects of life, Lu Xun said, "and because they are realistic, they are extremely powerful."[81]

The 1930s can be considered the golden age of Chinese cartoons. In the short span of less than three years from September 1934 to the eve of the Sino-Japanese War, nineteen cartoon publications sprang up in Shanghai.[82] Although many were relatively short-lived, lasting only one or two issues, cartoon magazines enjoyed increasing popularity. Often exquisitely designed or adorned with color covers (*Independent Cartoons*, for example), each vied with the others for readers and advertisers. The two best-known magazines were certainly *Modern Cartoons* and *Independent Cartoons*, edited respectively by Lu Shaofei (1903–) and Zhang Guangyu. The former lasted thirty-nine issues (January 1934–June 1937), becoming the longest-running cartoon magazine before the war. It enjoyed a national reputation, publishing works by cartoonists all over China.[83]

Like new spoken dramas, cartoons thrived in Western-influenced urban centers, providing a pleasant diversion for the acquisitive middle class. And as was true for spoken dramas, Shanghai became the center for Chinese cartoonists, attracting just about every aspiring talent in the country. In fact, very few cartoon magazines were published outside Shanghai, *Tianjin Cartoons* (*Tianjin manhua*) and Guangzhou's *Half-Angle Cartoons* (*Banjiao manhua*) being two well-known exceptions.[84] These publications, one cartoonist wrote in 1938, were directed at "*xiao shimin* [merchants, clerks, or urbanities in general] and intellectuals."[85]

Another sign of maturity of Chinese cartoons was the increasing emphasis among cartoonists on developing individual styles, both to gain recognition and to capture the public's attention. In the 1930s, many cartoonists—notably Ye Qianyu and Zhang Leping (1910–1992)—attempted to create their own unique styles through their fictional characters, endowing them with a new personality and placing them within a specific social context. Ye Qianyu's famous comic strip "Mr. Wang" ("Wang xiansheng"), for example, which debuted in *Shanghai Cartoons* (*Shanghai manhua*; originally titled *Shanghai Sketch*) in 1928, enjoyed enormous popularity. Mr. Wang and his foil Little Chen were typical middle-class Chinese who, living in a rapidly changing world, seemed to experience the whole gamut of sensations offered by the modern city life—luxury, gluttony, pleasure-seeking, even deceit (fig. 2).[86] Ye's equally famous sequel "The Unofficial History of Little Chen in Nanjing" ("Xiao Chen liu Jing wai-shi"), appearing in 1936, was a devastating exposé of a corrupt government.[87] In contrast to the work of Ye Qianyu, Zhang Leping's comic strip "San Mao" focused on the downtrodden. It depicted the woeful life of a vagrant urchin roaming the streets of Shanghai. Through this city boy's myriad mishaps, Zhang expressed the anguish of the common people caught in a morass of misfortune.[88]

The popularity of prewar cartoons climaxed when the First National Cartoon Exhibition was held in Shanghai in September 1936. The show, initiated by Lu Shaofei, Ye Qianyu, and Zhang Guangyu,

---

Fig. 2.   Ye Qianyu, "Avoiding Creditors at the New Year" (from "Mr. Wang"). Mr. Wang finds himself heavily in debt with the New Year approaching. To avoid his creditors, especially the biggest one, Little Chen, he and his wife decide to plant an advertisement in the newspaper. Issued in Mrs. Wang's name, the ad gives the impression that Mr. Wang has left home without a trace. When Little Chen departs after comforting Mrs. Wang, Mr. Wang emerges from his hideout, the sutra chanting room. From Ye Qianyu, *Ye Qianyu manhua xuan—sanshi niandai dao sishi niandai* (Shanghai: Renmin meishu chubanshe, 1985), pp. 1–2.

displayed well over six hundred cartoons from artists all over the country. The overwhelming success of the exhibition prompted the cartoonists to form a National Association of Chinese Cartoonists (Zhonghua quanguo manhua zuojia xiehui) in the spring of 1937. The association was intended to "unite all cartoonists in the nation, to promote cartoons as an art form, and to use them as an educational tool."[89] A few months later, however, the war brought a temporary halt to the blossoming cartoon movement.

As the specter of the Japanese invasion loomed ever larger in the early 1930s, cartoonists began to focus attention on the exact nature and role of their art. Should the cartoon be looked upon merely as a diverting commercial product of mass consumption? Or should it carry specific social messages, perhaps serving as a propaganda tool to resist outside aggression? Nowhere was this concern more evident than in the cartoonists' intensifying campaigns against what Lu Xun called "erotic cartoons" (*seqing manhua*).[90] In the 1930s, to meet the city dwellers' growing appetite for entertainment and pleasure, publishers came out with ever more drawings of women displaying their breasts and couples making love.[91] Low-cost books such as *Shanghai in Cartoons* (*Manhua Shanghai*), which portrayed numerous scenes of debauchery in that city, also gained popularity.[92] Even pioneers like Ye Qianyu and Lu Shaofei occasionally indulged in this genre in their early careers. Ye's piece "Snake and Woman" ("She yu furen"), for example, which appeared on the cover of *Shanghai Cartoons* in 1928, showed a naked, voluptuous woman caressing a python.[93]

As these erotic images began to flood the market, critics denounced them as a decadent art and began to call loudly for an end to pornography.[94] To many Chinese cartoonists, the burgeoning of erotic cartoons was indeed an alarming sign. This art, they felt, in openly preaching moral degradation and advocating sexual dalliance, was causing irreparable harm to society. Not only did these cartoons sully the integrity of artists, but they also corrupted the minds of the younger generation. At a time when the Japanese invasion seemed imminent, cartoonist Zhang E (1910–) wrote, instead of producing vulgar pictures (in his words, "displaying women's alluring thighs and soft bosoms") to satisfy the voyeuristic needs of readers, cartoonists should use their craft to portray the harsh social reality and expose the "imperialists' conspiracy to carve up China."[95] To Zhang E, a radical cartoonist who later went to Yan'an, the cartoon's main function was to enlighten, not to entertain.[96]

Erotic cartoons were not without their defenders, however. Wang

Dunqing, a pivotal figure in the early cartoon movement, was one of the few who questioned this campaign against so-called degenerate art. The obscenity charge, he said, was often exaggerated and inaccurate. Consider how much of Western art dealt with themes that were overtly or covertly erotic, Wang reminded his fellow artists. The Western tradition had produced many great painters of the nude. At a certain level, it was extremely difficult to distinguish between art and pornography. Moreover, "sex was part of natural human desire" and one should not feel ashamed to discuss it.[97] Yet Wang's voice, which echoed the May Fourth Movement's romantic glorification of subjective human passions, was soon drowned out by fervent demands that cartoons be put at the disposal of politics. Although the campaign against erotic cartoons came to an end when the war erupted in July 1937, the central issues raised in this debate—what was the role of a cartoonist and what was the purpose of cartoons—continued to occupy the minds of Chinese artists. And part of the answer came from the West.

The West and Japan clearly exerted a strong influence on the modern Chinese cartoon movement. Examples abound: Shen Bochen's Western-inspired works, drawn with a pen and in distinct black-and-white style, for one.[98] While Feng Zikai's lyrical cartoons are reminiscent of the drawings of such Japanese painters as Hokusai (1760–1849) and Takehisa Yumeji (1884–1934), Zhang Guangyu's hero was Miguel Covarrubias (1904–1957), Cai Ruohong (1910–) admired George Grosz (1893–1959), and Te Wei (1915–) named David Low (1891–1963) as his chief influence. A large array of Western cartoons began to appear in Chinese magazines and newspapers in the early decades of this century.[99] The editor of Shanghai's prestigious *Modern Cartoons*, Lu Shaofei, a man more noted for his organizing skill than for his craft, was tireless in introducing both Western cartoons and theories to his readers.[100] The publication of works by Francisco de Goya (1746–1828), Daumier, Käthe Kollwitz (1867–1945), Covarrubias, Low, and others—artists who, in addition to having innovative techniques, also held strong social and political views—spurred a Western craze among young Chinese artists.[101] It was a time of borrowing and assimilation, with aspiring cartoonists zealously imitating and identifying with individual Western masters. The result was a genuine transformation not only of their art but also of their way of looking at life and ultimately their method of presenting it.

Although young Chinese cartoonists were assiduous students of the West, they were by no means servile followers. In the 1930s,

motivated by a desire to be independent and sparked by growing nationalistic sentiments, they emphasized appropriation rather than blind
imitation. Many later emerged as distinguished artists themselves,
demonstrating a high degree of originality and ingenuity in their
blending of Eastern and Western traditions. These Chinese artists
also placed a high value on the social accountability of the Western masters they studied.

Francisco de Goya, for example, was more than a great Spanish
painter; he was also a resolute antiwar hero, a revolutionary artist
who used his craft to vent his wrath against the follies and cruelty of
mankind. Goya's work was introduced into China when the Japanese
invasion was looming. Understandably, therefore, it was not Goya the
successful court painter who drew the attention of his Chinese followers, but Goya the depicter of haunting images of senseless killing and
human misery in wartime.

Goya's most influential piece of work in China was unquestionably
The Disasters of War (1810–1820).[102] A set of eighty-two etchings
concerning Napoleon's invasion of Spain in 1808, *The Disasters of
War* is a masterpiece about death, destruction, and the violence of
warfare. In the eyes of Lu Xun and others, Goya was at his best when
depicting, through the use of visceral visual imagery, a world ruled by
terror and chaos.[103] Perhaps even more inspiring to them was the fact
that Goya, despite his numerous painful scenes in *The Disasters of
War*, was able to paint the defiant Spanish people mounting fierce resistance against the invaders. These heroic pictures (in which women
are often portrayed with greater valor than men) no doubt served as a
morale booster to the beleaguered Chinese people.[104]

"Goya's style was a model to be emulated," wrote art critic Chen
Yifan (Jack Chen, 1908–).[105] But it was the German artist Käthe
Kollwitz who related war to life and redefined the concept of art as a
tool for social change. Her work proved especially appealing to young
Chinese artists. While Goya depicted the tragedy of war, Kollwitz
dwelt on the plight of the common people suffering hunger, sickness,
and social wrongs. Influenced by Goya and like the great Spanish
artist, Kollwitz is not a cartoonist in the modern sense of the word.
Her major contributions lay in etching, lithography, and woodcuts,
and her influence in China during the war was primarily in the last
area. Such young woodcut artists as Li Hua (1907–) and Wang Qi
(1918–) count among the disciples of the German artist.[106]

Lu Xun first introduced Kollwitz's work into China in September
1931 when he published her woodcut *Sacrifice* in the journal *The Big*

Dipper (*Beidou*) to commemorate the death of Rou Shi (1901–1931), a young woodcut student and writer who had been executed by the GMD.[107] Lu Xun never hesitated to express his admiration for the German graphic artist. Not only did he share Kollwitz's ideas on war and peace, but he also felt the same frustrations at living in a society beset by political violence and social injustice. According to Lu Xun, Kollwitz's prints evinced a close emotional affinity with all those who were "being humiliated and persecuted."[108] Kollwitz's radical art and her advocacy for the victims of injustice won her wide admiration among left-wing artists. To them, Kollwitz's artistic achievement far surpassed that of Goya. After all, Goya never idealized the Spanish proletariat.[109]

Before and during the war, Chinese artists embraced the German cartoonist Grosz as a keen observer of society and a courageous opponent of fascism.[110] Grosz, whose drawings chronicle the crumbling of the Weimar Republic and the rise of Nazism, believed that the role of the artist was to depict societal and political problems as accurately as possible. His criticism of the resurgence of militarism in Germany and his blistering attacks on Nazism proved a great inspiration to Chinese cartoonists. His works were widely reprinted in Chinese magazines, including his famous piece *The White General* (1922), which portrays a vicious Nazi general brandishing his long sword and brutally slaughtering innocent people.[111] The cartoonist Zhang Ding (1917–) called Grosz "a patriotic rebel who dares to expose the evils of Nazism."[112]

Grosz had many followers in China, most notably Cai Ruohong and Lu Zhixiang (1910–1992). Using a scratchy pointed pen similar to Grosz's, both Cai and Lu combined simple, coarse, but powerful graphic lines to achieve a forceful composition. Cai's style resembled Grosz's so closely that he was nicknamed "China's new Grosz."[113] Yet Cai did have his own personal style. More than his German mentor, for example, he employed large areas of black hatching to give his cartoons a solemn, bitter tone. One of the few cartoonists who received traditional art training at the Shanghai Art School (Shanghai meishu zhuanke xuexiao), Cai came under the influence of socialism early in his life.[114] He joined the League of the Left-Wing Artists in 1930, and in 1939 he went to Yan'an to teach at the Lu Xun Academy of Art.

If Grosz taught a unique way to depict societal problems, David Low demonstrated how to produce biting cartoons about international events.[115] In both style and content, Chinese wartime cartoonists were perhaps more heavily influenced by David Low than by George

Grosz. His criticisms of fascism in general and the Nazi regime in particular certainly won Low world fame, as well as the special hatred of Adolf Hitler.[116]

Extolled by the cartoon critic Huang Mao (1918–) as "the world's greatest cartoonist," Low was introduced into China in the 1920s.[117] Yet it was not until the War of Resistance that "Dawei Luo" became almost a household name.[118] Low's impact in China was considerable. His art proved especially influential in a number of ways. First, Low focused primarily on international issues, a new area for Chinese artists and one for which they had few models. Second, a surprisingly large number of cartoons produced by Low during the war years (the "years of wrath," as Low called them) were about East Asia.[119] In particular, his vivid chronicle of Japanese brutality in China provided the tormented Chinese with much-needed psychological support, reminding them that their suffering did not go unnoticed by the rest of the world. Third, Low's bold black-and-white brushwork, combined with a simple yet assertive style, bore a close resemblance to the techniques of East Asian painting. Finally, Low was more than just a cartoonist: he was a cartoon theorist as well, one of the few artists who made people think seriously about caricature. His discussion of the close relation between literature and the cartoon bolstered Chinese cartoonists in their fight to elevate their art.[120] Perhaps what appealed to the Chinese most was Low's determination to impart new life into the cartoon, completely reshaping the nature of this important visual art. Like Grosz, Low had many followers in China, Te Wei being perhaps the best known.[121] Te Wei's forte was depicting international conflicts and Axis-camp barbarism, and his favorite targets were, predictably, Japanese militarists and Hitler.[122]

The Mexican artist Miguel Covarrubias offered something very different to his Chinese readers: a pure artistic style rich in variation and intensity. Covarrubias's caricatures, which bore the unmistakable imprint of both Pablo Picasso and other Cubists and the geometric motifs of Mexican Indian decorative arts, were introduced into China in the 1920s. To budding Chinese cartoonists, Covarrubias's work provided a refreshing contrast to that of Grosz and Low. His cartoons had a rich, flamboyant style rare in his generation. His portraits, always executed with great care, had a distinct three-dimensional, sculptural presence, providing an animated visual history of famous figures from around the world (as in his celebrated series "Impossible Interviews").[123] In sharp contrast to Grosz's sarcastic social commentary and Low's powerful political images, Covarrubias's pieces were elegant and graceful. They were looked upon by the Chinese, and correctly so, as a polished art form rather than as an instrument of political satire and social reform.[124] The fact that Covarrubias was the only noted Western cartoonist to have visited China (in the fall of 1933) made his impact even more immediate.[125] Young artists such as Zhang Guangyu, Ye Qianyu, and Liao Bingxiong were fascinated by Covarrubias's smooth, ornamental lines.[126]

Among Covarrubias's Chinese followers, none was more prominent than Zhang Guangyu. Indeed Zhang, who strove to elevate the cartoon to the rank of fine art in the 1920s and 1930s, was without question one of the most influential figures in the modern Chinese cartoon movement, founding cartoon magazines (such as *Shanghai Cartoons* in 1928) and establishing cartoon associations. Zhang initiated his own style by borrowing various ideas, including bright colors and sharply defined elements from Chinese folk art tradition and Covarrubias's geometrical abstraction.[127] Like the Mexican artist, Zhang effected a calculated quality in his work that one does not normally associate with caricature.

When the war with Japan erupted, Covarrubias-style cartoons, which had little political content, were immediately replaced by patriotic drawings. Covarrubias's effort to reestablish the cartoon as an art form rather than as political commentary thus failed miserably in China, a nation now engulfed by fervent nationalism. Chinese cartoonists thus turned for inspiration increasingly to political cartoonists in the West, who had much to teach about witnessing and depicting such horrors as were about to descend.[128]

The New Press and New Journalists

As has been mentioned, the rise of Chinese cartoons was tied closely to the emergence of the modern press. Chinese resistance intellectuals, convinced that the press was an efficient form of communication and that the printed word carried enormous weight, regarded newspapers as a weapon of immense value in spreading patriotic messages and politicizing public opinion.[129] The growing recognition in the 1920s of journalism as a respectable profession also contributed to its rising influence. To understand the effectiveness of the Chinese wartime press and the growing stature of journalists, we must briefly examine the earlier history of Chinese journalism.

The modern press in China had its origins in the Manchu court's humiliating defeat in the first Sino-Japanese War of 1895. From 1895 to the 1911 revolution, the Chinese press experienced a "Golden Period," with numerous new political magazines and daily papers clamoring for political and social changes.[130] This phenomenon was important not only in bringing pressure to bear upon the conservative, recalcitrant government officials, but also in helping usher in a new era of mass culture.[131]

The number of newspapers grew by leaps and bounds in the ensuing years. According to Rudolf Löwenthal, a professor of journalism at Yanjing University, there were 19 dailies nationwide in 1895; by 1912, the number had soared to 500; and by 1926, there were 628 daily newspapers.[132] Among major cities in 1926, Beijing topped the list with 125, followed by Hankou with 36, Guangzhou with 29, Tianjin with 28, and Shanghai with 23. The total number of dailies increased to 1,031 in April 1937. As with spoken dramas and cartoons in the same period, Shanghai had taken over as the center of newspaper publishing with a total of 50 newspapers; Beijing had 44, Tianjin 29, and Nanjing and Hankou each had 21.[133] While other cities would be proud to have one or two respectable newspapers, Shanghai had dozens, among them the *Shanghai News* (*Shen bao*), the *News* (*Xinwen bao*), and the *Eastern Times* (*Shi bao*). In 1933 both *Shen bao* (founded in 1872) and *Xinwen bao* (founded in 1893) had a daily circulation of 150,000, the largest in the country; two Tianjin newspapers—*Dagong bao* (*L'Impartial*, founded in 1902) and *Social Welfare* (*Yishi bao*, founded in 1915), a Catholic-sponsored journal—trailed distantly at 35,000 each.[134] The rise of *Shen bao* and *Xinwen bao* as the circulation giants of modern Chinese journalism reaffirmed the growing importance of Shanghai as the financial and cultural center of China.

Predictably, newspapers had a distinct flavor depending on their place of publication. While Beijing's newspapers excelled in political reportage and many were closely associated with particular political groups, Shanghai's gave the most comprehensive coverage on economic affairs. Furthermore, since many of Shanghai newspapers (including *Shen bao* and *Xinwen bao*) were located in the foreign concessions, they, unlike their Beijing and later Nanjing counterparts, enjoyed a large degree of political freedom.

In the 1920s, Shanghai's newspapers were diversified in content and not dominated by political affairs, unlike the traditional Beijing gazettes, which reported official news and served as a mouthpiece for the government. The new urban papers' commitment to news and adoption of the language of commercialism reflected a changing society where information was a valuable commodity in its own right and consumerism was increasingly seen to hold the keys to the national economy. News became a source of excitement and imagination. Although international events were covered with facts supplied by foreign news agencies like Reuters, it was local news that held center stage. In the case of *Shen bao*, for instance, news coverage in 1922 was 96 percent domestic and only 4 percent foreign.[135] Indeed, among Shanghai's established papers *Shen bao* was noted for its commitment to covering local events. The paper began to issue a special "local supplement" in February 1924, hiring staff reporters to cover local affairs and part-time correspondents in other major cities to file special stories. The supplement garnered much attention and became so popular that other major presses soon followed suit.[136] In sharp contrast to the traditional press, which faithfully transmitted official views, the urban newspapers were a public medium closely intertwined with the people. Not only did they fashion a new popular culture, but they also helped shape a shared universe in which the public sphere took on a new significance.

To draw more readers and increase its profitability, the modern press also instituted a number of new devices—special features, for example (such as educational news and financial reports)—to improve its contents.[137] The press also took a critical look at its distribution methods. Shanghai's major periodical publishers relied largely on the gradually improving postal system and railway networks to distribute their papers to other major cities.[138] In the mid-1930s, *Shen bao* took the step of acquiring its own delivery vehicles, which allowed papers to be sent to nearby cities such as Suzhou within hours after they came off the press.[139] This practice, however, was limited to Shanghai's vicinity. The great interior remained largely inaccessible, an impediment that proved a major challenge for the resisters when the war broke out.

Modern Chinese newspapers mirrored and reinforced the kaleidoscope of changing urban society. In general, the trend was toward more entertainment as the growth of illustrated material and entertainment news indicates. *Shen bao* issued a special "Pictorial Weekly" in May 1930. *Xinwen bao*, *Shen bao*'s chief rival, countered shortly thereafter with its own "News Pictures."[140] The public's thirst for more entertainment news and demand for stories of romance and martial arts also gave rise to a plethora of "mosquito newspapers" (*xiaobao*) in Shanghai, including *Crystal* (*Jing bao*) and *Diamond* (*Jingan zuan*).[141] Unlike newspaper giants such as *Shen bao*, which printed two to six big sheets (eight to twenty-four pages) per issue and was priced usually at 4 *fen*, mosquito newspapers issued one small sheet, or four pages, and cost only 1 *fen*. Catering to the general public, they contained serialized fiction and a mosaic of gossip and anecdotes. The publishers, embracing the notion that entertainment and sensationalism meant money, prided themselves not on accuracy but on diversity and amusement. In this they were certainly shrewd businessmen; as the journalist Zhao Junhao put it, they had a solid understanding of "mass psychology."[142] They watched changing tastes and moods with a keen eye and successfully exploited them. Besides mosquito newspapers, Shanghainese were also drawn toward the more visual, even titillating, medium of the pictorial publications such as *Good Companion Pictorial* (*Liangyou huabao*) and *China Pictorial* (*Zhongguo huabao*), which made their appearance in the 1920s in Shanghai. With current news photos and beautiful movie star portraits gracing their pages, they won a quick following in the booming publication industry.[143]

The modern Chinese press clearly had an influence on the intellectual ferment of China. This was particularly evident in the literary supplements (*fukan*) issued by major newspapers. *Shen bao*'s "Unfettered Talk," which began in August 1911, was one of the oldest and most prestigious of these supplements. Its preeminence as a bastion of new literature, however, did not actually begin until December 1932, when Li Liewen (1904–1972), a returned student from France, took the helm as editor from Zhou Shoujuan (1894–1968), a writer of the "Mandarin Duck–and–Butterfly School" known for producing romantic and sentimental entertainment fiction. Li's "Unfettered Talk" followed quite faithfully the distinguished tradition established earlier in the 1910s by the literary supplements of the Beijing *Morning News* (*Chen bao*) and Shanghai's *China Times* (*Shishi xinbao*).[144] Nonetheless, Li's supplement was unique in a number of ways. It was launched at a time when Shanghai was replacing Beijing as China's most exciting cultural center. In that period, too, the GMD was clamping down hard on dissension, which meant that left-leaning contributors such as Lu Xun and Mao Dun had to write under a wide variety of pen names to conceal their identities. As for Li Liewen, he was a liberal (he died in Taiwan in 1972) who strongly believed that different views should be aired and that ideas could thrive only in an uninhibited atmosphere. Thus he turned his literary supplement into one of the most exciting forums of the early 1930s for all men of letters, left and right alike.[145]

Predictably, the increasing popularity of the new medium and its growing circulation caught the eye of advertisers, and revenues from advertising soon became a major source of income for the press. Most newspaper advertisements were business-related (commercial transactions, finance, medical affairs). In the 1920s, for example, 51 percent of *Shen bao*'s pages were given over to business advertisements; Tianjin's *Yishi bao* was even higher, at 84 percent.[146] *Shen bao*'s chief rival, Shanghai's *Xinwen bao*, which was aimed specifically at businessmen, issued a special section on "economic news" to underscore its unique qualification to speak on that subject.[147] Though a relatively novel concept in Chinese journalism, advertising turned out to be a crucial factor in determining a newspaper's overall financial health, including such giants as *Shen bao*, *Xinwen bao*, and *Yishi bao*.[148] Still, there seemed to be few guidelines for what could be advertised. Newspapers were willing to print anything as long as the advertiser could pay. For instance, *Shen bao*'s "medical advertisements," which constituted the largest portion of business-related advertisements, abounded with quack doctors' unabashed claims of their ability to cure every conceivable venereal disease. Similar to the mass journalism of Joseph Pulitzer and William Randolph Hearst in late-nineteenth-century America, the 1930s Shanghai press was marked by an increasing commercialization, which was strongly reflected in the plethora of advertising.

For Chinese intellectuals, the unbalanced mix of commercialism and news was a cause for major concern. To them, the practice of selling advertising space on an indiscriminate, profit-only basis represented a lowering of the quality and even dignity of a newspaper. The press could easily lose its dedication to "transmit basic information," a purpose described by the journalism professor Xu Baohuang (1894–1930) as fundamental.[149] An even more alarming sign indicating the ascendancy of business interests over news reporting was the taking over of the front page by advertisers.

Commercial advertisement notwithstanding, the Chinese press drew a huge number of readers who considered newspapers a credible source of information and an inexpensive avenue of entertainment. This rising popularity of the press also coincided with the growing stature of the journalists, who, while trying to establish their own identity, became increasingly uncomfortable with what they considered the wrong direction of the modern Chinese press.

In the past, despite the potential influence of their occupation, journalists, or "kings without crowns" (*wumian huangdi*), enjoyed little social esteem.[150] In fact, journalism was generally condemned as "the miserable end of a literatus,"[151] and journalists, most of whom were unsalaried, were considered men without principles, whose views could be easily swayed. They parroted official policies, using journalism as a mere tool, a stepping stone on the path to officialdom. They were, in short, a loose group whose identity was ambiguous at best.[152] To improve this lowly image, many journalists in the 1920s and 1930s argued that a new identity had to be found. "We must try to establish the sacred, esteemed status of the Chinese reporter, so that when people utter the name 'reporter' [*xinwen jizhe*], they will do so with a sense of sincere admiration and great respect," Fan Changjiang (1909–1970), a noted reporter of *Dagong bao*, urged.[153]

To enhance their social status and engender respect for their craft, Chinese journalists in the 1920s and 1930s began to call for greater independence in their work and more objectivity in their reportage. Terms such as *zhiyehua* (professionalization), *zhuanmenhua* (specialization), and *keguan* (objectivity) began to take on new meaning, becoming synonymous with good journalistic practice.[154] Professionalization and specialization meant more than financial security; they meant a clear division of labor—news reporter, columnist, editor, and publisher: a far cry from old-style journalism, where generalists with broad but superficial knowledge of a variety of subjects reigned.[155] Objectivity meant reportage that was accurate, balanced, detached, and dispassionate.[156] These ideas of the new journalism stemmed in part from the increasing popularity and influence of newspapers as an information and entertainment medium, but also from the journalists' growing awareness of their craft as "a special occupation."[157]

The establishment of journalistic institutions was a major step toward professionalization. Inspired by the ideas of Walter Williams, dean of the University of Missouri School of Journalism, and Joseph Pulitzer, the American publisher whose $2 million endowment helped to build a journalism school at Columbia University in 1903,[158] journalism education officially began in China in 1918, when National Beijing University set up the Institute of Journalism (Xinwenxue yanjiuhui). Shao Piaoping (1884–1926), editor of the *Beijing News* (*Jing bao*), was hired as an instructor—among whose many students was a young man named Mao Zedong.[159] In 1920, the first department of journalism in China was founded at Shanghai's St. John's University. Yanjing University (1924) and Fudan University (1929) followed suit.[160] Yanjing University also hired foreign faculty, many recruited from Williams's program at Missouri. Vernon Nash, the head of the department at Yanjing, was an example. Other foreign experts included the journalist Edgar Snow and Rudolf Löwenthal, a German who specialized in comparative journalism.[161] Several newspapers also started their own training programs. The Beiping School of Journalism (Beiping xinwen zhuanke xuexiao), founded in 1933 by Cheng Shewo (1898–1991), then editor of Beijing's *World Daily News* (*Shijie ribao*) and Nanjing's *People's Livelihood News* (*Minsheng bao*), is perhaps the most notable example. Similar to a professional school, this institute provided workshop experience for young aspirants.[162] The inclusion of journalism in university curricula was important in at least two ways: it provided a regular setting for neophytes to learn the ropes, and, more important, it was a long-awaited sign of approval by the intelligentsia, who finally recognized this ignored field as a legitimate, worthy endeavor.[163]

The launching of professional associations and journals, which provided reporters with a common language and a certain esprit de corps, further elevated their social status and strengthened their new identity. One of the earliest reporters' associations was the Shanghai Reporters Club (Shanghai xinwen jizhe lianhuanhui), founded in late 1921.[164] By the 1930s, similar organizations had sprung up in almost every major city in China.[165] Along with the sprouting of professional associations came the proliferation of professional journals. Notable among them were *Journalism* (*Xinwen xuekan*, issued by the Beijing Journalism Association [Beijing xinwen xuehui]) in the mid-1920s and *Journalism Quarterly* (*Baoxue jikan*, the journal of the Shenshi News Agency in Shanghai) in the 1930s.

To further cement group solidarity and to win widespread social recognition, in August 1934 the Hangzhou Reporters Association (Hangzhou jizhe gonghui) proposed that September 1 be designated "Journalists' Day" (Jizhe jie), an idea that was enthusiastically embraced.[166] Fan Changjiang helped to launch the Chinese Young Journalists Society (Zhongguo qingnian xinwen jizhe xuehui) in Hankou in March 1938 and a "Reporters' Hostel" (Jizhe zhi jia) shortly thereafter. With these innovations he not only strengthened reporters' identity by giving them a place to gather and exchange ideas, but he also placed them at the forefront of the resistance movement against the Japanese—a position that would have a profoundly paradoxical impact on their professional role.[167] The society also launched an influential journal, *The Reporter* (*Xinwen jizhe*), in early April.[168]

Young journalists, in an effort to enhance their social role, also took great pains to distinguish between news (*xinwen*) and commentary (*pinglun*). "In our country," one journalist lamented, "the news is often a mixture of news and commentary. . . . Worse still, there is often a brief reporter's remark attached to the end of each piece. Such a piece can easily turn into a sensational statement."[169] Under the old tradition of "literati discussing politics" (*wenren lunzheng*), of which Liang Qichao and Huang Yuansheng (1885–1915) were two of the best-known practitioners, it had indeed been common practice to intermingle news reporting and commentary.[170] In this, both Liang and Huang closely resembled their counterparts in eighteenth-century Europe, where journalism was very much an adjunct of politics.[171] These men's semiclassical and semicolloquial style, however, was comprehensible only to the literate few.

News and commentary were not alike, young journalists insisted. Blending them confused the different function of each. Whereas news could be defined as "a most recent, accurately reported event that sparks the interest of readers," political or social commentary expressed nothing more than one's personal opinion.[172] News stories were detached and balanced records of facts; commentaries involved subjective attitudes and views.[173] "To gain the respect of our readers," one insisted, "we must make a clear distinction between the two."[174] In the face of national crisis, however, that goal grew ever dimmer; as China plunged into war and as reporters assumed the role of patriots, the line between objectivity and subjectivity blurred almost to the point of meaninglessness.

New journalists also repeatedly called for the independence of the press. When Zhang Jiluan (1888–1941), Hu Lin (Hu Zhengzhi, 1893–1949), and Wu Dingchang (1884–1950) took over the faltering Tianjin-based *Dagong bao* in September 1926, they issued a new editorial manifesto for the paper: "No partisanship, no dependence on outside commercial or political subsidies, no advancement of private interests through the newspaper, and no conformity at the expense of truth" (*bu dang, bu mai, bu si, bu mang*). These unorthodox ideals ushered in a new era of independent Chinese journalism.[175] For Zhang Jiluan and his associates, a newspaper was not an official party publication, and a reporter had little in common with the politician. Only independence of the press could guarantee nonpartisanship and an absence of ideological and political favoritism. Partiality was incompatible with honest journalism. The rapid rise of *Dagong bao* as a formidable force in journalism in the late 1920s was testimony to the public's acceptance of the newspaper as an unbiased medium of communication.

Increasingly, young journalists became more outspoken in their criticism of old-style Chinese newspapers. The new guard challenged established rules and proposed new formats, and in so doing breathed new life into what they regarded as the moribund journalistic tradition. Although Shanghai was the center of Chinese journalism, the new journalists charged that its newspapers and magazines exhibited some of the worst features of old-style journalism: elitism, sensationalism, and unreliability. The curt and detached narrative style of the old journalism, they argued, produced dull and superficial reports, which only alienated the people. By the same token, the old journalists' highbrow approach prevented them from understanding the everyday tribulations of the people, and it certainly was not conducive to fair and objective coverage. The so-called news, one critic pointed out, was nothing more than the daily accounts of politicians or profiles of movie stars and parvenus.[176] Gossip columns abounded, while hard news was neglected. Newspapers were filled with stories about sex and violent crime, accompanied by distasteful graphic descriptions, observed another critic.[177] Even Shanghai's influential *Shen bao*, Lin Yutang charged, printed irresponsible advertisements at the expense of important news.[178] Newspapers failed to inform the public and had become part of the daily entertainment of society, publishing only trivia to garner increasing profits. For many independent-minded journalists, such compromises were intolerable. To them, quality, integrity, and credibility had to be a paper's most valuable assets. It was imperative to find a new direction and establish a clear distinction between news and sensationalism.

As the reputation of journalism began to rise in the 1920s, journalists developed an ever greater awareness of the importance of their craft. Although both the Jeffersonian belief that the press should be valued above the government and the vast power of the modern American press ("In America the President reigns for four years, but journalism rules forever and ever," remarked Oscar Wilde)[179] were certainly foreign to Chinese journalists, they nonetheless began to realize that their work carried enormous influence. Compared to less public means of communication, the press was extremely effective in disseminating information to a wide audience, shaping their minds and swaying their emotions. It was a powerful instrument for spearheading social change and raising public consciousness. The "king" might still wear no "crown," but he now understood the power of his sword. Gradually journalism became something important: it brought excitement and promised its practitioners high visibility; it provided a front-row seat at important events and offered an avenue to power and prestige. The new journalists, however, were determined to do something quite different from their counterparts in the past. Not only were they interested in unlocking the corridors of political power and intrigue in Nanjing, but they also paid more attention to the larger social and economic forces that shaped the lives of most Chinese. In brief, they insisted that the press must be more responsive to public needs.

To establish a truly responsible and responsive press, new journalists argued, reporters must show concern for the general public and ground their stories in reality. Instead of using semiclassical language, they should address the mass audience by means of a new, simple, direct, personal style that relied heavily on eyewitness accounts and on-site investigations. "We must abandon obsolete journalistic practices," Fan Changjiang wrote. "We must do our best to experiment with new methods and to create new things."[180] "Let's educate the masses, guide the masses, and report about the masses," one journalist appealed.[181] In this way, young journalists redefined the role of a reporter. The new down-to-earth approach proved critical not only for gaining a better understanding of the life of the people, but also for inspiring support of the resistance cause. It is with this in mind that we now turn to a more focused discussion of the influence that spoken dramas (chapter 2), cartoons (chapter 3), and newspapers (chapter 4) had during the war.

2   Spoken Dramas

Spoken drama in prewar China remained the entertainment of an urban, educated minority. That all changed with the eruption of war, however. If the arts are considered useful tools of propaganda, spoken drama must rank as one of the most effective for the powerful impact it produces not only on the eyes and ears of its audiences, but also on their emotions.

Immediately after the war broke out in Shanghai in August 1937, a group of theater and cinema activists formed the Shanghai Theater Circle National Salvation Association (Shanghai xijujie jiuwang xiehui). Thirteen drama troupes were organized (figure 3) by such people as Song Zhidi (1914–1956) and Cui Wei (1912–1979) (Troupe 1), Hong Shen and Jin Shan (1911–1982) (Troupe 2), Zheng Junli (1911–1969) and Zhao Dan (1915–1980) (Troupe 3), and Yu Ling (1907–) (Troupe 12). With the exception of the tenth and twelfth companies, which remained in Shanghai, the other eleven, under the slogan "Spreading patriotic news to the countryside and to the battlefields," left sheltered city life and plunged into the remote villages of interior China to begin the ambitious task of rallying the Chinese people for the resistance movement.[1] On 1 August 1938, after a centralized propaganda effort was launched by the Third Section (literary propaganda, headed by Guo Moruo) of the Political Department, under the direction of the Military Affairs Commission, the thirteen Shanghai Theater Circle troupes were reorganized into ten Anti-Japanese Drama Companies (Kangdi yanjudui). Each comprising thirty members (who received 25 *yuan* per month in salary), these troupes were instructed to continue the task of spreading news and educating

Fig. 3.   Staging a street play in Wuhan, summer of 1938. The
partially covered sign reads, "Anti-Japanese Drama Troupe."
Courtesy of Lü Fu.

the masses about the war. The Nationalist general Chen Cheng
(1897–1965), director of the Political Department, aired his hope for
this ambitious undertaking: "These ten drama companies are tantamount to ten divisions of troops."[2]

Besides government-sponsored troupes, other drama groups such as
student propaganda teams, amateur drama clubs, children's traveling
drama corps, and local drama companies also sprang up, traveling to
different corners of China to awaken the peasants by means of plays
and songs.[3] This profusion of drama clubs grew so rapidly that by the
early 1940s more than 2,500 such units had appeared in China, involving more than 75,000 men and women.[4]

The war drastically changed the nature of modern Chinese drama.
Not only was the new drama that thrived during the eight-year War of
Resistance against Japan intensely political, but also, because so many
dramatists and actors migrated into the interior after the outbreak of
the war, it soon lost its elitist urban nature.[5] No longer a mere city-
oriented entertainment medium, the drama now became a primary
propaganda channel for communicating with broad masses of rural
people. And as the new theater redefined the limits of the stage experience and challenged the old norms, the center of attention shifted from
the play to the audience.

Popularization

Armed with poor and simple tools but full of enthusiasm and energy, young Chinese dramatists and student activists roamed the countryside to begin an unprecedented campaign of mass political education of the common people. It did not take long for them to realize that they were facing an audience very different from the one they were used to: less educated and less sophisticated peasants, living in a society still largely dependent on oral communication. The peripatetic nature of the dramatists' endeavor also meant that they had to adjust constantly to complex local cultures and dialects as they moved from one village to the next. The playwrights thus faced the problem of redesigning urban spoken drama to meet the needs of a rural population. Clearly, enlightenment of the masses could be achieved only if Chinese drama were popularized.

These twin wartime aims were by no means new. "Popularization" (*dazhonghua*) had long been a major concern of May Fourth intellectuals, who, under the slogan "Going to the people," sought simple but effective ways of enlightening the general public.[6] The enthusiasm continued unabated into the 1930s, while taking on an added political significance. The newly founded League of Left-Wing Writers, under the influence of Qu Qiubai (1899–1935), raised the banner of a "people's language," sparking heated debate among Chinese intellectuals.[7] In the end that debate reached far beyond language per se, to include the nature and the audience of Chinese theater.

Nor was the idea of using spoken drama to educate the peasants a wartime novelty. Already in the late 1920s, recognizing the potential of the modern drama to combat rural illiteracy and poverty, the National Association for the Advancement of Mass Education (Zhonghua pingmin jiaoyu cujinhui; NAAME), under the leadership of James Yen (Yan Yangchu, 1893–1990), had tested this new ground. Xiong Foxi, hired by James Yen to oversee the drama program, became the pivotal figure in the mass education and rural reconstruction campaign in Dingxian, Hebei province, in the period 1932–1937.[8] Xiong's early interest in using spoken drama to foster social change had led him in 1921 to cofound the People's Drama Society with Mao Dun and Ouyang Yuqian. Like many May Fourth iconoclasts, Xiong challenged established values and attacked old literary genres. He believed that traditional Chinese drama was an archaic, elitist form of entertainment, ill suited to meet modern challenges. New ideas and new techniques were needed to convey modern messages and to raise the literacy of the peasants. To him, spoken drama had unique virtues as a medium of communication, for it entertained and educated at the same time. As he put it, instruction came best under the guise of delight. Not surprisingly, "Education in entertainment" (*yu jiaoyu yu yule*) was the Dingxian drama workers' watchword.[9]

Championing the idea that spoken drama should serve society and reflect the struggle of life, Xiong was committed to mass education and firmly believed that "every genuine piece of art must be popularized."[10] During his stay in Dingxian, Xiong wrote scripts, many of which employed local dialects; designed open-air theaters; formed numerous peasant drama troupes (*nongmin jutuan*); and broke new ground in training peasants as actors. Such plays of his as *The Butcher* (*Tuhu*) and *Crossing* (*Guodu*), staged and acted entirely by peasants, enjoyed wide popularity among rural audiences.[11] By employing peasant actors, Xiong hoped to "blend the actors and audiences together,"[12] creating a sense of community and meshing what was happening on the stage with what went on in real life. His highly innovative efforts won him a reputation as "the pioneer of popular theater in China."[13]

Because Xiong Foxi's Dingxian experiments, innovative and fascinating though they were, were confined to a specific locality, they were never fully appreciated by his more urban-oriented colleagues. The war with Japan suddenly made Xiong's ideas, if not his actual work, important. Young Chinese students, filled with patriotic fervor, flocked to the countryside, plunging into "the jungle of the reality."[14] As they threw themselves into the patriotic cause, however, these zealous young propagandists encountered problems far beyond any they might have imagined. Most important, they discovered that good intentions were no match for harsh realities. Although the notion of bringing the patriotic message to rural areas was obvious, how to get there was just the first of many significant challenges. In 1939, George Taylor noted these telling statistics about one province in China: "Hopei [Hebei] is a province of 153,682 sq. km. in area and has less than 4,000 miles of motor road, of which less than 50 miles are paved."[15]

Apart from extreme hindrances to communication, young dramatists soon found that presenting a play comprehensible to the uncultured villagers could be a difficult, if not impossible, task. One actor recalled his frustrating experience:

> Rural plays are starkly different from urban ones. In fact, there are differences between a metropolitan play and a small city play, and a county play is not exactly the same as a village play.

During our six-month stay in Guilin, we rehearsed a few plays and staged them a couple of times. The audiences were mostly townspeople, educated, so the responses were quite good. We then thought that we would have a similar result if we put on a show in the rural areas. . . .

We first mounted two shows in a large village: *Little Compatriots in Shanghai* [*Shanghai xiao tongbao*] and *We Have Beaten Back the Enemy* [*Diren datui le*]. Some spectators raised the following questions: "What are you people doing up there on the stage? How come those young fellows act so recklessly up there? Why aren't there any gongs and drums [as in traditional opera]?" Our conclusion was that the country folk definitely needed a kind of play bustling with noise and excitement. . . .

We ran into snags when we staged another show in a different village. The villagers simply did not understand what we were performing. They didn't know what we were talking about [on the stage] and did not understand the play at all. They couldn't even recognize Japanese troops. We had to immediately cut short the dialogue and increase the action scenes, at the same time making it more comical. But all of this still fell on deaf ears: there simply was no response from the audience![16]

This was by no means an isolated incident. Similar complaints were voiced in all quarters.[17] The poor reception of spoken drama in the rural areas no doubt stemmed in part from the villagers' unfamiliarity with the new art form. In essence, though, the conflict was one between two different perspectives and sets of values: as urban playwrights projected their own views and tastes on the peasantry through this new art form, rural audiences demanded their accustomed music and plot in a traditional play. In his propaganda activities in rural Shandong in 1937, the drama activist Cui Wei was sensitive enough to recognize the problems and make a few adjustments:

Literacy among Shandong peasants is extremely low. If we tried to transplant urban plays to the rural areas, the peasants would not have understood them. Since there was no appropriate play, I decided to write a few myself. . . . My simple play [about Japanese brutality in Manchuria] was enthusiastically received. After the show, an old peasant stepped forward and spoke to us in tears. He told me that his son had been killed by the Japanese in Manchuria. [Since the villagers liked the play so much,] they insisted that we should stay, so we staged a revised play, *A Village Scene* [*Jiangcun xiaojing*], the same night. They wanted to give us money and went so far as to carry our baggage. We spent at least a week in this village [near Qingdao], putting on a few more newly revised plays. . . . [I found that] those artistic plays that moved urbanites to tears did not have much impact when staged in the villages. Perhaps only intellectuals could appreciate them, but they were certainly incomprehensible to the peasants.[18]

The task of bringing enlightenment and news to the masses—what young dramatists called "from Carlton [Theater] to the street" (*cong Kaerdeng dao jietou*)[19]—was indeed a challenge. But what was to be done? The transformation of modern urban drama from an elitist to a mass art, many believed, had to begin with its popularization. "When dealing with a rural population who have no idea of what the term 'Japanese imperialists' means," Hong Shen suggested, young performers should communicate with the peasants in simple language and by staging drama in the guise of storytelling.[20]

Indeed, the language issue was an important one. Drama critics often complained that the metaphors and abstract idioms of urban plays baffled peasant audiences and consequently dampened their interest in the drama. To communicate effectively with the masses, simple, colloquial language—what Hong Shen called "hometown language" (*xiangtu yu*)[21]—should be used. The use of dialects, in particular, was encouraged; dialects were usually down-to-earth and extremely lively and had the ability to convey the nuances of a locality and its inhabitants better than any other form of communication. "If we intend to go to the villages and win the acceptance of the rural folk," one playwright contended, "we have no choice but to use dialects."[22] Many dramatists (such as Hong Shen) did experiment with this idea, incorporating local sayings into their plays, for example. Yet mastering a dialect required time and dedication, not to mention a quick grasp of local sensibilities. And time was something young activists did not have as they hurried from one place to another to spread the patriotic gospel.

In the move to the countryside, playwrights and actors had to inject a sense of realism into their efforts, which included portraying the peasantry accurately. Realism, however, must finally be judged not by the style of a play, but by how comprehensible it was to its audience. An urban youth would naturally have difficulty playing the role of a humble peasant in a truly credible manner. Their life-styles were utterly different, and, as drama critic Zhou Gangming noted, their world outlooks were miles apart.[23] The best type of play, many drama critics argued, would be one in which peasants themselves acted. Thus Xiong Foxi's idea of "blending the actors and audiences together" received renewed attention during the war, the concept now imbued with a fresh political connotation. "For intellectuals to stage a play to entertain the common people is not as good as letting the people do it themselves," contended one dramatist.[24] Tian Han concurred: "If we wish to cause new drama to take root and sprout in the villages, we must foster the young peasants of that region as drama cadres to form themselves into healthy peasant companies."[25] By encouraging peasants to participate in their plays, young dramatists attempted to form a physical if not intellectual bridge between themselves and the illiterate.

Was enlisting peasants as actors a successful undertaking? In fact, apart from Xiong Foxi's prewar attempt in Dingxian, we have no sure evidence to suggest that such an idea was put into practice during the war. What scanty information there is indicates that it remained very much a paper resolution. Traditionally, rural China was largely impervious to outside influence. Even the basic goal of drawing peasants' attention to a new and unconventional type of play was at first a difficult problem for young dramatists. Deep-rooted notions of localism, combined with ignorance, more often than not prompted villagers to look with suspicion upon outsiders. "Because our troupe was composed of both men and women, sometimes we were [erroneously] charged by conservative local leaders with corrupting public morals and ended up in jail," one young participant angrily recalled.[26]

The Street Play Lay Down Your Whip

If young performers found mastering dialects a challenging task and bringing peasants into their plays remained a lofty dream, they were relatively successful in creating many ingenious dramatic forms to correspond to their itinerant life. These included:

1. Teahouse plays (*chaguanju*)—Actors would enter at a teahouse and intermingle with the customers. They would then perform a play in this setting, creating an atmosphere that conveyed the idea that the performed events actually occurred in the tearoom.
2. Parade plays (*youxingju*)—These would take place on festival days. Staging a play during a parade, actors distributed propaganda leaflets along the road.
3. Puppet plays (*kuileiju*)—Traditional puppets were used to portray patriotic events.
4. Commemoration plays (*yishiju*)—Plays such as *The Life of Dr. Sun Yat-sen* (*Guofu yisheng*) and *The Marco Polo Bridge Incident*

(*Lugouqiao*) commemorated influential political figures and historic incidents.

5. Newspaper plays (*huobaoju*)—Many of these were impromptu scenarios based on important news of the day, keeping the public abreast of recent happenings both at home and abroad.

6. Street plays (*jietouju*)—Short plays were staged on the street, with active audience response a key component.[27]

Despite their superficial differences, all these new plays shared certain characteristics: an informal setting, a current theme, simple language, and direct contact with the populace, the intent being to instill patriotism into the people. Instead of focusing on the text, these plays emphasized performance and action. Instead of resorting to fixed staging, they relied heavily on improvisation and creativity. And instead of displaying the skill of the actors, they stressed the importance of exchange with the spectators.

Among spoken drama forms, the newspaper play and the street play ranked as the two most popular and influential. Described as "living newspapers" (*huo de baozhi*),[28] newspaper plays reported recent armed conflicts, extolled heroic acts, exposed the enemy's brutalities, and related news and information, serving as a simple but much-needed communication channel for the common people. Local events and current news played an important role in the plays, part of the dramatists' effort to breed a stronger sense of realism and familiarity among local audiences.[29] As one actor recalled, many newspaper plays were written on the spot to depict very recent incidents, and members of the traveling troupes would often collect stories on the road, which they quickly turned into new plays.[30] This kind of improvised product, though rarely polished, gave the poorly equipped troupes added flexibility. Since one of their main purposes was to inform the public of the news, timeliness was considered of central importance.

The street play—defined by the literary critic Guangweiran (Zhang Guangnian, 1913–) as "a play that can be staged on the street in the quickest way, with the simplest equipment, and that can communicate in a most popularized format"[31]—was even more popular than the newspaper play. Like the newspaper play, the street play was relatively short (usually one act lasting less than thirty minutes), presented by a small group of four or five performers, and dealt largely, though not strictly, with current affairs.[32] The street play, however, had more complicated plots and was more flexible. Most important, street plays emphasized audience participation. Actors regularly disguised themselves as spectators, mingling with the crowd and then joining the play at a predetermined time as if the act were part of the audience's response; in this way they created a dramatic effect unmatched in other plays.

The popularity of the street play during the early phase of the war redefined the meaning of Chinese spoken drama in a time of national crisis. A street play was characteristically an improvised piece grounded in simplicity, flexibility, and interaction, unified by the theme of war, and serving as a rallying call for resistance. In contrast to an urban play, a street play had little, if any, scenery. Words were deemphasized while action was encouraged, the assumption being that words were often too sophisticated for the illiterate peasants to understand. Engaging facial expression and fist-clenching histrionics generated passions that high-sounding patriotic slogans like "Down with Japanese imperialism!" (*dadao Riben diguozhuyi*) simply could not. As one dramatist wrote, if the desire was to communicate effectively with the audience, "text [was] less important than performance."[33] Much of the language that remained in the street play was colloquial and direct; and instead of long didactic harangues, songs might be used to carry uplifting messages.

The novelty of the story and the unfamiliarity of characters in the spoken play challenged the audience's usual identification with the actor in a traditional play. Moreover, the fact that the audience, not the actor, lay at the core of a street play challenged the traditional division between the stage and the spectator as well as the notion of the audience as passive observers. It thrust the spectator into an active role, creating constant communication between the stage and the audience and, ultimately, a sense of community. Staging was not a display of individual talent, but a creation of what Richard Schechner called "relations" between actor and spectator.[34] In the end, the line between art and life was deliberately nullified, and theater became an act of exchange rather than a one-way communication.

Among numerous street plays, *Lay Down Your Whip* (*Fangxia nide bianzi*) was arguably the most popular (figure 4). A provocative piece written in 1931 by Chen Liting (1910–), then a primary schoolteacher in Nanhui, a county near Shanghai, *Lay Down Your Whip* underwent many transformations and assumed many forms during the war. It became the best-received and most influential street play in the early years of the wartime drama movement.[35] The piece, inspired by an earlier one-act play, *Lady Mei* (*Mei niang*) by Tian Han (who in turn drew his ideas from Goethe's *Wilhelm Meister*),[36] concerns two ref-

Fig. 4.   A traveling drama troupe staging the street play *Lay Down Your Whip* in 1937. From *Dongfang zazhi* 34.4 (16 February 1937): n.p.

ugees, an old man and his daughter, Fragrance (Xiang Jie), who escape flood, callous landlords, and oppressive government in their hometown. Destitute and homeless, they eke out a living as street performers. Though she is physically enervated, the old man pressures his daughter to perform acrobatics and sing on the street, particularly the popular melody "Fengyang Flower-Drum" ("Fengyang huagu"). Enraged by her poor performance, the old man raises his whip to punish the girl. A young worker (an actor in disguise) comes charging out from the crowd, shouting, "Lay down your whip!" He reproaches the old man for tormenting his own daughter. Surprisingly, Fragrance comes to her father's defense. She recounts her family's misfortune and the plight of her hometown folk, who suffer miserably under the tyrannical government. At the end, the young actor appeals to the now deeply moved spectators, calling on them to fight against government oppression: "We must resist those who coerce us to live a life of starvation and homelessness."[37] Because of these strong anti-Guomindang overtones, Chen did not put his name on the script for fear of government persecution.[38]

A failure when it debuted on 10 October 1931 in Nanhui, *Lay*

Down Your Whip had better luck in the following years, especially after the December Ninth Incident of 1935, when Japanese incursions into north China became more aggressive and when radical students increasingly demonstrated their dissatisfaction with the GMD government's policy of appeasement vis-à-vis Japanese imperialism.[39] The play rapidly assumed a new look: instead of running away from corrupt government and natural disasters, the old man and his daughter were now escaping the brutality of the Japanese occupation in Manchuria. Thus what was originally an anti-GMD play took on an increasingly anti-imperialist, anti-Japanese stand. Instead of treating a class struggle between landlords and peasants, the story now focused on a confrontation between two nations; and instead of appealing to his compatriots to resist oppressive and inept government, the young actor had a different message to offer: "If we do not unite quickly to defend ourselves against Japanese aggression, we will soon meet the same fate as our countrymen in Manchuria." The theme song was also replaced by the "September Eighteenth Melody" ("Jiuyiba xiaodiao"), which became an instant hit:

> The sorghum leaves are green, so green,
> On September 18th came the barbaric Japanese troops.
> They occupied our arsenals and seized our towns;
> They slaughtered our people and pillaged our land.
> Oh, they slaughtered our people and pillaged our land.
> Although our armed men numbered hundreds and thousands,
> They meekly surrendered the city of Shenyang.

The play's intensity and brevity were ideal for a propaganda piece. The simple yet well-wrought dialogue between father and daughter depicted a painful experience to which the audience could relate, and the passionate appeal of the young man spurred anger and sympathy. According to many eyewitness accounts, people responded with an outburst of emotions ranging from profound sadness to furious indignation, touching off waves of patriotic enthusiasm.[40] The play had an added meaning in concluding with an ominous warning of impending doom.

The popularity of such street plays as *Lay Down Your Whip* did not depend solely on the patriotic outburst. The large degree of flexibility the actors enjoyed with regard to content was also important, for it allowed them to improvise a plot that spoke to a particular location and a particular time. The father and daughter's place of origin in *Lay Down Your Whip*, for example, did not remain fixed; they came from Manchuria when it fell into the hands of the enemy, but when the Chinese capital of Nanjing was captured bloodily by the Japanese in December 1937 that city became their hometown. Any location devastated by Japanese troops served equally well. The theme song varied also. Besides the "September Eighteenth Melody," patriotic songs such as the "March of the Volunteers" ("Yiyongjun jinxingqu") and "Fight to Recover Our Homeland" ("Da hui laojia qu") graced some versions of the play.[41]

The peripatetic life of a traveling troupe added another dimension of flexibility to the street play. Actors were fairly free to move around—like an agile "light cavalry," as one described it[42]—and this allowed them to bring war news and patriotic messages to a host of places. If the task of Chinese dramatists, as one commentator suggested, was to wage "drama guerrilla warfare," the very core of the repertoire was street plays and newspaper plays.[43] It was important to get away from the urban nature of Chinese spoken drama, said the drama critic Liu Nianqu; Chinese dramatists should write plays closer to the life of the common people. In this way, not only would the urban youths of the traveling drama troupes gain a new perspective on life, but they would also have the opportunity to "sow seeds everywhere they visited." Someday these seeds would grow into trees all over China, Liu said.[44]

Clearly, Chinese wartime dramatists placed great emphasis on a play's audiences.[45] In contrast to the novel, drama is a shared experience that attempts to forge an instant bond with the audience, evincing, in the words of Susanne Langer, "immediate, visible responses of human beings."[46] As one writer insisted, "Actors must 'merge with the audience' [dacheng yipian]."[47] The audience issue, in fact, came to be accepted as the very key to a play's success or failure, to such a degree that other essential ingredients of a play such as the staging, acting, and mise-en-scène were considered relatively insignificant.

To stress the role of audiences is to underscore the importance of communication in drama. In *Lay Down Your Whip*, the interaction between performers and onlookers becomes the most dynamic aspect of the theater gathering. Signals and meanings are transmitted from stage to audience and back again. This reciprocity of the theater demands that the spectator not only respond but also participate, and ultimately empathize with the actors. Guangweiran pointed out that since the stage was often surrounded on all sides by spectators, a feeling of physical intimacy resulted that allowed the actor to hold the audience with maximum intensity.[48] The sudden appearance of an actor from among the onlookers also added a dramatic touch and an element of surprise. In *Lay Down Your Whip*, the young actor's entrance onto the stage defused an apparently dangerous situation and encouraged the audience to participate vocally and emotionally, eliminating the physical as well as the emotional gap between audience and characters. At the end, instead of applause there was patriotic shouting: "Down with the aggressor!" and "Recover our lost territories!"

Lay Down Your Whip, in large part because of its simple yet powerful plot, but also because of its combination of sorrow and fervent nationalism, became so popular during the early years of the war that it was staged throughout China.[49] One drama troupe performed it eighteen times in a single day in a remote Shandong village.[50] The play also appeared in different versions and under different titles. Cui Wei, for example, rewrote it, giving it a new name: *On the Starvation Line* (*Ji'exian shang*); two other writers called their versions simply *Fragrance* (*Xiang Jie*).[51] Although *Lay Down Your Whip* was unmistakably an anti-Japanese play, to a large extent it was also a political indictment of the GMD's ineffectual appeasement policy. Predictably, therefore, the play attracted the ire of the Nationalists, who banned it in the mid-1930s.[52] Yet right-wing dramatists, for their part, did not hesitate to turn this popular play around and use it to fuel anti-Communist sentiments. In their versions, the father-daughter team do not come from Manchuria; they flee from a notorious Communist-controlled area![53]

The tremendous success of *Lay Down Your Whip* helped usher in a new era of Chinese spoken drama. Street plays appeared in profusion during the war, creating a lasting impact on the minds of the people. Among the most popular were *Sanjiang hao* (literally, "How wonderful are the three rivers," referring to the Heilong, the Songhua, and the Yalu rivers), *The Last Stratagem* (*Zuihou yi ji*), and *March to the Front* (*Shang qianxian*).[54] *Sanjiang hao* portrays the wisdom and bravery of a resistance hero in the northeast, Sanjiang hao, who not only successfully eludes capture but also at the end persuades his pursuer to join him.[55] *The Last Stratagem* praises the shrewdness and the unyielding spirit of a patriot in his resistance against the Japanese.[56] These two plays were so enthusiastically received that they, together with *Lay Down Your Whip*, were collectively known as *Hao yi ji bianzi* (meaning literally "What a wonderful strategy, the whip"), a phrase combining the last words of the three titles.

Nevertheless, wartime street plays were not without their problems. Although constant travel was exciting for young performers, in practice it caused physical exhaustion and often proved dangerous. The pressure of the resistance campaign took its toll, with many actors contracting tuberculosis, heart disease, and stomach ailments, mostly from malnutrition and exhaustion; some died of these maladies,[57] while a few were killed by enemy gunfire at the front.[58]

In many ways, putting on a street play was an adventure into the unknown. An outdoor performance was vulnerable to such difficulties as unreliable location, unpredictable weather, and shifting groups of spectators whose actions could not be precisely anticipated. The blurring of the line between performers and audience meant a radical shift in command and control. The spectator had the potential for radically changing the play and leaving organizers and performers at a loss. The future became precarious, even hazardous. Incidents of verbal and physical assault against actors portraying collaborators and war profiteers were abundant.[59]

More important, one crucial issue was never fully addressed by young Chinese dramatists: the proper relation of performance and text. The street play's emphasis on collectively evolved performance as a better, more creative form of theater than one based on text conveyed an implicit yet unmistakable hostility toward literature and words. The majority of wartime street plays were impromptu pieces, unpolished and possessing little artistic value. The issue of immediate relevance around which the productions revolved rarely translated into long-lasting artistic excellence and more often than not failed to please the more cultured segment of the audience.

This deficiency partly explains why the street play began to wane in popularity two years into the war and why many began to call for a renewed focus on the text.[60] Yet to say that wartime street plays in general lacked artistic merit is not to say that they exerted little impact. On the contrary, particularly in rural areas their impact was enormous. In all this, it is important to recall that young drama activists did not just bring street plays to the remote villages; they also channeled news, held mini-exhibitions about the war, and taught basic civil defense to the peasants.[61] This novel experience was as important for the dramatists as for the peasants they performed for, providing them all with a sense of sacrifice and togetherness created under the constant fear that their country would soon be occupied by the enemy. The political crisis was unprecedented, as was the zest and the sense of mission that motivated thousands of young men and women to reach out to the masses. The great majority of them had no experience in mass political education. Street corners and temple fairs thus became schools for them as well as for their audiences. What gave meaning to their efforts and distinguished them from their predecessors, they believed, was that they backed up their words of commitment with practice and their lives. Although many drama troupes were short-lived owing to the perennial shortage of funds, the loose structure of most groups, and the mental and physical fatigue of the performers,[62] the sense of accord that these young people tried to create was intense and real. The war politicized and unified almost every aspect of life, and drama not least of all.

Despite the many difficulties encountered by the peripatetic dramatists, ample evidence shows that wartime newspaper and street plays had a significant impact on the common people, villagers and urbanites alike. American journalist Edgar A. Mowrer, for example, observed the following scene in Chengdu during the war:

> My friend Victor Hu . . . took my arm and urged me forward. But before we got close enough to see or hear much, the proceedings stopped and instead there went up from the crowd a roar of approval: "*Hao, hao*! (good, good)," which one may hear in any popular Chinese theater. . . .
> "What was it?"
> "It is called *The Death of General Wang Sze-chung* [*Wang Sizhong*] *at Tientsin* [*Tianjin*], a well known educational play."
> "And who are the players?"
> "High-school student propagandists. They travel all over the country and by their rather simple spectacles arouse the patriotism of the people and their indignation against the Japanese. There are a good many of these little theatrical troupes."[63]

Enthusiastic responses were recorded in rural areas, too, as one Chinese observer noted:

> They [the amateur dramatic organizations] go to small towns and neighboring villages where no spoken drama has ever been presented, where the peasants and the petty tradesmen see this new type of drama for the first time. It is frequently difficult, at first, for the country folks to understand the significance of the things presented on the stage. It is not always easy to keep order and quiet in the theatres, but generally as the performance goes on the audience becomes absorbed in the story and quiets down. Gradually the listeners grasp the meaning of the simple, educational plays and learn to hiss the villains, applaud the heroic deeds and victories of their own nationals working for the country's salvation, and by slow degrees begin to understand, even though super-

ficially, the meaning of the war that is raging through such an extensive area of the nation.[64]

But the resistance ideology was communicated not just through street plays on the sidewalks or in the teahouses. It found expression in a variety of other cultural forms as well, ranging from drama festivals (such as the unprecedented festival held in Guilin, Guangxi province, organized by Ouyang Yuqian and Tian Han in early 1944)[65] to historical plays with their strong symbols of feminine resistance.

Female Symbols of Resistance: Patriotic Courtesans and Women Warriors

The popularity of the street plays began to ebb in 1939 as the war with Japan entered a new phase of protracted struggle. With the excitement and the uncertainties of the early war years on the decline and more and more dramatists returning to the cities, the demand for a more structured, better staged, well-rehearsed drama increased. Chinese wartime dramas began to move away from pure propaganda to more subtle portrayals of the life of the people and of political intrigue. As a result, multi-act plays, especially ones based on historical themes, replaced simple improvised one-act plays as the most popular kind of spoken drama, especially in urban areas.[66] Historical plays in particular thrived in interior cities like Chongqing and Guilin.

Historical plays (*lishiju*; also known as costume dramas) did not spring up from nowhere. Their history stretched back to the 1920s, if not earlier. The genre was thus a familiar one, but it now had two new goals: cultivating political symbols in the fight against the Japanese invasion and spreading patriotic messages to a wider audience in the interior as well as in occupied cities like Shanghai. To realize these goals playwrights turned to heroes and heroines from the past. Two such historical figures were Yue Fei, the famed Southern Song general who resisted the invasion of the Jin,[67] and Hua Mulan, the legendary female warrior who donned man's garb to join the army in her ailing father's place.

Among the many ways in which Chinese dramatists sought to galvanize the people against the enemy, perhaps none was more visually appealing than the cultivation and exaltation of female resistance symbols. Symbols, according to Victor Turner, are "dynamic entities, not static cognitive signs"; they are "patterned by events and informed by the passions of human intercourse."[68] Female resistance symbols in wartime historical plays were just such dynamic entities. Designed to spark political fervor, they served many as examples for emulation. To determine what is new in these symbols, we must trace their origins to an earlier period.

Women's images underwent rapid changes in the 1910s and 1920s. A host of plays focusing on women appeared long before the outbreak of the Sino-Japanese War, including Guo Moruo's *Three Rebellious Women* (*Sange panni de nüxing*, 1926), which depicted the struggle of three legendary women, Zhuo Wenjun, Wang Zhaojun, and Nie Ying, against the constraints of the traditional marriage system; Ouyang Yuqian's *Pan Jinlian* (1926), describing the courageous love of a frustrated woman; and Song Zhidi's *Empress Wu* (*Wu Zetian*, 1937), published on the eve of the war, which sought to rehabilitate the tarnished image of the Tang dynasty female monarch. Of varying quality, many of these plays were marred by crude characterization and unsophisticated plots. Nevertheless, they faithfully exuded the prevailing May Fourth ethos: the fervent pursuit of romantic love and a constant yearning for individual emancipation. The intentions of the authors were clear. Song Zhidi, for example, confessed that his purpose in writing *Empress Wu* was "to depict women's resistance and struggle against a traditional, feudalistic, male-dominated society."[69] Among these plays, *Pan Jinlian* was no doubt the most innovative and controversial.

Ouyang Yuqian's *Pan Jinlian* is based largely on a famous episode in the Ming novel *The Water Margin* (*Shuihu zhuan*), later retold and expanded in another Ming novel, *Jin Ping Mei*. In the original story, Pan Jinlian, after committing adultery with a nouveau riche scoundrel, Ximen Qing, murders her dwarf husband, Wu the Elder. Wu's younger brother, the legendary bandit-hero Wu Song, avenges his brother's death by killing his unfaithful sister-in-law.

Despite superficial similarities, however, Ouyang's five-act play differs markedly from the original episode in both characterization and intention. In sharp contrast to the original Pan Jinlian, a nymphomaniac driven by insatiable sexual appetite and extreme cruelty, Ouyang's heroine is sensitive, passionate, and rebellious. Rather than being evil by nature, she is the victim of a society riddled with moral corruption and personal degeneracy. Her secret liaison with Ximen Qing is prompted more by her disenchantment with Wu Song's refusal to accept her love than by lust. It is also an act of defiance against the oppression of her husband, who behaves like a tyrant at home. Deeply depressed, she finds temporary comfort in the arms of Ximen Qing.

Far from being a traditional, submissive woman caught in domestic drudgery (in chapter 26 of *The Water Margin*, Pan Jinlian describes herself as "a crab without legs"), Ouyang's heroine is a modern, liberated woman in steadfast pursuit of romantic love. She is daring and fairly outspoken, lashing out at an unjust society in which women are stifled by inhuman social norms. By contrast, the famous hero-rebel Wu Song is portrayed as a paragon of morality in whom Confucian values maintain their stubborn hold. Though a superhero, he is surprisingly colorless and dull, a man insensitive to tender love and care. There is no doubt that Ouyang's sympathies lie with the heroine. To him, Pan Jinlian is a resolute woman, refusing to be "buried alive" by the oppressive social system.[70] The mere fact that she dares to stand against a decadent system deserves high praise. In the end, she chooses to die at the hand of Wu Song rather than live miserably in a world devoid of love.

Pan Jinlian was a resounding success when it was revised and staged as an opera in 1927. Pan's controversial new image no doubt contributed to the wide acclaim the production enjoyed. Perhaps just as important was the fact that the heroine was played by none other than the author himself. Ouyang Yuqian, one of China's most celebrated female impersonators, dazzled audiences with his remarkable skills.[71] The play became even more popular when the role of Wu Song was taken by an equally renowned actor, Zhou Xinfang (1895–1975), a master in the Southern school of Beijing opera.

The image of a modern, liberated woman seeking self-identity and struggling for genuine love was a marked departure from past depictions of women, who were bound by Confucian norms to an inferior status and forced to live in meek subservience to the male superiors in their families.[72] Moral issues aside, Ouyang Yuqian's Pan Jinlian epitomizes the hopes and frustrations of young Chinese women everywhere in the 1920s.

Women underwent another image change in spoken dramas during the war. As the conflict intensified, plays focusing on heroines appeared in profusion. The portrayal of strong women characters is of course not new in Chinese literature and performing arts. Chinese drama abounds with female warriors and strong-willed women. One notable example is *Women Generals of the Yang Family* (*Yangmen nüjiang*; among whom Mu Guiying is the most famous). Other heroines in traditional drama such as Hua Mulan, Liang Hongyu, and Qin Liangyu have also enjoyed enormous popularity.[73] Not surprisingly, many of these well-known characters resurfaced during the war.

Yet wartime plays that featured heroines were distinctive in several ways. For one thing, a truly extraordinary number of plays appeared in this category during this eight-year war period. Not only were familiar characters like Hua Mulan and Liang Hongyu resurrected, but a host of new names such as Ge Nenniang and Yang E emerged as well. The twin themes of unity of the people and determined resistance against the enemy were stressed in almost every play. And the fact that plays about a single character or event kept reappearing pointed to another feature of Chinese wartime dramas: whatever was recurrent was apt to be significant at a time of national crisis. One more departure from the past was that in these plays, wartime female symbols carried contemporary messages: condemnation of social injustice and a call for equality between the sexes, a continuation of the May Fourth assault against the Confucian tradition. Although wartime spoken dramas touched on a variety of themes, two recurrent subjects stood out: patriotic courtesans and female warriors.

Xia Yan's *Sai Jinhua* (1936), which appeared on the eve of the Japanese assault on China, was a pioneering work that set the tone for courtesan plays in the war years. Xia Yan based his characters on Zeng Pu's (1872–1935) famous late Qing novel *A Flower in a Sinful Sea* (*Niehai hua*), which follows the romance between a *zhuangyuan* (the highest-ranking examinee in the palace civil service examination), Jin Jun (modeled after Hong Jun [1840–1893]), and a charming courtesan, Fu Caiyun (modeled after Sai Jinhua [1874–1936]).[74] Unlike Zeng Pu's novel, however, which chronicled the long career of Jin Jun and a mosaic of events in various locations both in China and abroad, Xia Yan's play focuses on the legendary relationship between Sai Jinhua and the German field marshal Count von Waldersee, commander-in-chief of the allied occupation forces in Beijing during the Boxer Rebellion of 1900. It was largely through Sai's efforts and her unusual ties with the German commander, the legend says, that this erstwhile *zhuangyuan*'s wife saved many lives and forestalled further destruction of Beijing by occupying foreign troops.

In this play, Sai Jinhua is portrayed as a sensitive and kind-hearted woman. Acutely aware of China's impending doom, she openly displays her contempt for a declining government beset with rampant corruption. In act 1 of this seven-act play, when she is accused by an impudent official of defaming her deceased husband's name by returning to Beijing as a courtesan and of disgracing her nation by donning "outlandish dress" and "appearing like a calamity-causing monster in a doomed nation," Sai sarcastically responds: "Sir, I think you are joking. [What you have just said] implies that a nation's ruin is caused entirely by women's dress. . . . In a city like Beijing, there are simply too many 'monsters.'"

Xia Yan's Sai Jinhua represented a major change in how courtesans were portrayed. Chinese traditional literature, of course, abounds with stories about love affairs between handsome, gifted scholars (*caizi*) and beautiful, sentimental courtesans. Sai Jinhua, however, stands not for the past but for the present. She is clever, determined, capable of diffusing potentially explosive issues with wit, and, most important, she is intensely patriotic. Sai's behavior, her principles, and her emotions all belong wholly to the ethos and spirit of wartime China.

The play no doubt reflected the author's own bitter disillusionment with the political realities of the time. It is a devastating, if veiled, attack on a government incapable of dealing with the Japanese and on those who were ready to sell out China.[75] "The play was designed," as Xia Yan admitted many years later, "to satirize the government's humiliating foreign policy."[76]

Its polished style and vivid characterization, not to mention its ability to convey a painful sense of immediate reality, made the play an instant success when it debuted in 1936 to rave reviews and widespread public attention. The death of Sai Jinhua in December 1936 added a dramatic conclusion to the story. Needless to say, the play's popularity quickly aroused the suspicion of the GMD government, and it was not long before the play was banned. Xiong Foxi's lesser-known play bearing the same name was also banned, for "exaggerating the positive role of Sai Jinhua."[77]

If Xia Yan's *Sai Jinhua* reshaped the image of courtesans, Ouyang Yuqian's *The Peach Blossom Fan* (*Taohua shan*) gave an even more powerful voice to that persona. The play was originally written in the winter of 1937 as a Beijing opera script; it was subsequently revised as a spoken drama, playing to packed houses in the interior. Again, using the early Qing drama of the same title by Kong Shangren (1648–1718) as his model, Ouyang Yuqian infused his version with contemporary meaning.

The heroine of the play, Li Xiangjun, is a talented young prostitute living in an expensive Nanjing pleasure quarter. She is caught in a bitter struggle between, on the one side, Ming loyalists and gallant generals desperately trying to restore the crumbling Ming court and, on the other, evil advisers and sycophantic ministers who never hesitate to betray their country to the invading Manchus for personal gain. In order to weaken the loyalist Revival Club (an offshoot of the Donglin party, which stood for moral integrity and institutional reforms), the vicious scholar-official Ruan Dacheng conspires with his follower Yang Wencong, a talented poet and painter who maintains close ties with the Revival Club. The two men contrive to furnish a handsome trousseau to the brothel of Li Xiangjun, the purpose being to arrange a marriage between Hou Chaozong, a leading member of the Revival Club, and the courtesan. As a result, according to their scheme, Ruan and Yang will gain control over Hou.

The plan works. Hou Chaozong and Li Xiangjun happily marry. As a symbol of their love, Hou writes a love poem on Li Xiangjun's fan. In the second act, however, Ruan's secret plot is divulged, and Li, a virtuous woman with high personal integrity, flies into a rage. When news arrives that Ruan Dacheng has ordered the arrest of all Revival Club members because of their persistent refusal to cooperate with him, Li Xiangjun urges her husband to seek refuge in the camp of the loyalist Shi Kefa. Meanwhile, Ruan, together with his superior, Ma Shiying, supports the incapable Prince Fu as emperor in Nanjing. They corrupt the court with force and bribery. In the final act, which takes place in the second year of the new Manchu dynasty, we learn that Li Xiangjun has withdrawn to a nunnery but is anxiously awaiting the return of her husband, about whom she has heard a distressing rumor: that he has surrendered himself to alien rule by accepting an official title. Finally Hou Chaozong knocks at her door. Alas, he confesses that the rumors are indeed true. Li, heartbroken, returns the fan to Hou and commits suicide.

The Peach Blossom Fan must be ranked as one of Ouyang Yuqian's better pieces, in part because its dramatis personae are drawn with such compelling vividness. The play, of course, centers on three principal characters: Yang Wencong, Hou Chaozong, and Li Xiangjun. Yang is what Ouyang Yuqian described as a "double-dealer" (*liangmianpai*),[78] a man with no integrity and sordid morals who hides a villainous soul under a seemingly gentle demeanor. Straddling the political fence, he is ready to change his position in accordance with rapidly changing political tides. Strictly speaking, Hou Chaozong is no better than Yang. His submission to an alien dynasty marks the hypocritical Confucian scholar with ignobility. Effete and often wavering, he lacks moral direction. Li Xiangjun, exemplifying honor and uprightness, stands in direct contrast to Yang and Hou. She is a woman of enormous strength. Upon discovering that Hou's marriage to her was made possible by Ruan's money, she attacks Ruan, saying, "I would prefer death to wearing a villain's clothes and jewelry" (act 2, scene 1). When she parts with her husband, she asks him not to worry about her but to take care of himself "for the sake of the nation" (act 2, scene 2). In a confrontation with Ma Shiying, she bitterly accuses him of ruining the country by pillaging the poor and mercilessly killing honest officials (act 3, scene 1). At the end, when her husband succumbs to the new dynasty, she chooses death to show her bitter disappointment in his loss of integrity. In a period of crisis, honor and commitment become all the more precious and important.

Although the denouement in Ouyang Yuqian's play is different from that in Kong Shangren's original version (where both Li Xiangjun and Hou Chaozong enter a Daoist monastery), otherwise Ouyang followed Kong's plot quite faithfully. What is new about Ouyang's work is its message and the immediate relevance of that message to his time. The ruin of a nation, the play seems to suggest, is caused not by the enemy from without, but by the sometimes invisible enemy from within. The play's popularity made "Yang Wencong" into a common scornful epithet in wartime China. "Besides eliminating Ah Q," one writer wrote, "we still have to get rid of 'Yang Wencong.'"[79]

An ideal, patriotic woman, however, must not rely solely on her intellect; she must also maintain her capacity for action. The arrest of Sai Jinhua by her enemies at the conclusion of Xia Yan's play and the tragic end of Li Xiangjun in Ouyang Yuqian's work inevitably carried a dark sense of foreboding about the future. Their protest would be meaningless if no positive outcome were to follow. Thus, in addition to such tragic figures, a positive, hopeful, and forceful image was needed. During the war, a whole array of female warriors were created to serve this purpose, including Ge Nenniang, Yang E, Qin Liangyu, Liang Hongyu, and Hua Mulan.[80] Many versions of the same character appeared as well, indicating the popularity and influence of particular warrior symbols. Hua Mulan and Liang Hongyu, for example, both of whom were drawn from legends as well as from semihistorical sources, share certain outstanding traits: they are gifted in martial skills, exceptionally valorous, loyal, and endowed with charm and grace. And Ge Nenniang, the heroine in A Ying's (Qian Xingcun, 1900–1977) famous four-act play *Sorrow for the Fall of the Ming* (*Mingmo yihen*, 1939; also known as *Jade Blood Flower* [*Bixue hua*] and *Ge Nenniang*), is an interesting combination of the patriotic courtesan and female warrior.

Ge Nenniang, an enthralling beauty who lives in the Nanjing pleasure quarter, was trained in martial skills from childhood. Worrying about the increasing menace from the Manchus in the north, she constantly practices fencing in an attempt "to imitate Liang Hongyu," a female warrior of the Song who led a successful campaign against the invading Jin army. Ge's skills and courage win her high praise among her friends. "A truly unusual woman," one calls her. When news of the fall of Yangzhou and the tragic death of Shi Kefa reaches Nanjing, Ge Nenniang encourages her lover, Sun Kexian, to join Prince Tang's resistance force in Fujian, where she vows to meet up with him. Later the couple reunites in a defense post in the hills of Zhejiang province. The situation has become even more critical for the Ming. When the Ming general Zheng Zhilong refuses to lend troops to defend against the approaching Manchu forces despite the repeated remonstrances of his loyal son Zheng Chenggong (known to Europeans as Koxinga) and Ge Nenniang, the fall of the Ming seems inevitable. Zheng Zhilong subsequently surrenders to the Manchus. Ge and Sun, however, refuse to capitulate, and together with their troops (composed largely of peasant women) they fight on. In the final act, Ge and Sun are brought before the Manchu commander Boluo after their abortive attempt to break the siege. In an outpouring of wrath, Ge Nenniang condemns the Manchu general and the traitorous Chinese officials for their evil deeds. She slaps Boluo's face when he attempts to take liberties with her. As she is about to be taken out for execution, she bites her tongue and spits the blood on Boluo's face in a last gesture of defiance.[81]

Structurally, little in the plot of *Sorrow for the Fall of the Ming* could be considered sophisticated by Western standards. Thematically, however, the play communicates an urgent sense of poignancy. Through manipulation of a historical theme, A Ying, like Ouyang Yu-qian, filled his pages with powerful nationalistic sentiment. It is a play of patriotism devoted to exposing treacherous officials (Cai Ruheng and Ma Shiying), glorifying the courageous acts of loyal ministers (Sun Kexian and Shi Kefa), and praising the skills and courage of the heroines in the war (Ge Nenniang and her maid Mei Niang). Despite its late Ming setting, *Sorrow for the Fall of the Ming* clearly plays on modern passions. In lieu of a strong plot and striking events, A Ying placed heavy emphasis on the heroine's character and motives. Like Li Xiangjun, Ge Nenniang is upright and loyal to her country; but unlike Li, who commits suicide in the end, Ge Nenniang goes to her death by execution strong and defiant. Her death represents a tragic fulfillment of her unceasing devotion to her country.

Not only is she patriotic, but Ge is also portrayed as a warrior sensitive to the plight of women. "If men can charge ahead and take enemy positions on the battlefield," she asserts, "women can also defend their nation" (act 1). This acute awareness of women's equality with men is shared in the play by other female figures such as Lady Tian, Zheng Zhilong's wife. Indeed, equality of the sexes was a recurrent theme in Chinese wartime dramas, echoing an important struggle unleashed during the May Fourth era. For instance, Liang Hongyu, the heroine of Ouyang Yuqian's opera *Liang Hongyu*, rebuked her conservative husband, Han Shizhong, the famed Southern Song general, when he remarked contemptuously that "women should confine themselves to the kitchen and take care of domestic affairs"; she retorted, "[When a nation is in grave danger] there should be no distinction made between [the duty of] a male and a female" (act 3). In the story, Liang not only displayed her valor by beating the war drum to encourage her soldiers to fight, but she also saved her husband from many military blunders, proving to be the more capable and determined defender of an empire under attack. Such a portrayal of women was certainly consistent with the May Fourth spirit. In general, female characters in wartime spoken dramas demand equality with men. Indignant at being relegated to inferior roles defined by males, they refuse to be mere spectators who applaud men's bravery, or serve only as nurses who tend to the (male) wounded. They are in fact equal participants in the struggle against the aggressors.

Sorrow for the Fall of the Ming was a resounding success when it was first staged in Shanghai's International Settlement in late 1939. It quickly eclipsed all its predecessors in terms of popularity, playing to a packed house for thirty-five days straight and breaking all spoken drama records as the longest-running play in wartime China.[82] This reception was a sign of just how frustrated and enraged people had become over the Japanese invasion. Two years later, A Ying wrote *The Story of Yang E* (*Yang E zhuan*), another play set in the Southern Ming. Like *Sorrow for the Fall of the Ming*, this is a play about a sword-wielding heroine, who attempts to assassinate Wu Sangui (the renegade Ming general who helped the Manchus conquer China) to avenge the death of her husband and the Ming emperor Yongli.

Perhaps no female warrior better exemplifies the spirit of patriotism and resistance than Hua Mulan. The legend of this heroic woman has long been a favorite theme in the Beijing stage repertoire and continues to be popular today. During the war, of course, she was revived numerous times, including by Ouyang Yuqian in the film script *Mulan Joins the Army* (*Mulan congjun*). The film, released in 1939, was an instant success, catapulting its leading actress, Chen Yunshang, to stardom. The theme songs of the film also "were heard all over China."[83] Based on a famous ancient ballad, "Poem of Mulan"

(*Mulan shi*), by an anonymous writer of the fifth or sixth century A.D., Ouyang's play, built in turn on his film script, tells the story of a courageous woman who dresses up as a man to join the army in the place of her ailing father. The play, like the movie, was very popular during the war, playing to capacity audiences both in Shanghai and in the interior.[84]

Set in the Tang dynasty, the play opens with a hunting scene in which Hua Mulan demonstrates her superb martial skills by shooting down flying geese with pinpoint accuracy. When the empire is invaded by the northern Turks, the emperor orders a nationwide mobilization to defend the country. Hua Mulan's father, a veteran who is now in failing health, is ordered to rejoin the army. Worried over her father's well-being, Mulan proposes to join the army in his place. Her parents oppose the idea, but she finally persuades them by dressing up convincingly as a man and by demonstrating her unmatched martial ability. For twelve years she fights gallantly, her true identity undetected. Once she and a young army officer, Liu Yuandu, even disguise themselves as Turks to penetrate the enemy's encampment—he as a hunter and she as a woman! In act 6, Mulan foils a traitor's scheme and successfully lifts the siege of a city. She is promoted to major-general after the commander dies of an arrow wound. Upon defeating the enemy, Mulan returns to the capital in triumph. She refuses all the emperor's offers of reward, requesting simply a steed to carry her home. In the final scene, she surprises Liu Yuandu, with whom she has fallen in love, by revealing her true identity as a young maiden. The couple then marry and live happily ever after.

Ouyang Yuqian's play does not follow the original ballad very closely. With a little embellishment and imagination, he reshaped the image of Hua Mulan according to his own wartime vision. The love between Hua Mulan and Liu Yuandu, for example, is a new addition and, as Ouyang explained many years later in his autobiography, not part of his original plan: "I intended to write a tragedy portraying her [Mulan] as a woman fighting against feudalism. But in order to propagate the cause of resistance and to arouse the morale of the people, I stressed instead her courage and wisdom."[85] In the final analysis, *Mulan Joins the Army* is a disappointing piece. It is flawed by naive characterization and a crude plot, while many of the author's attempts to introduce new themes, such as romantic love, appear to be deliberate contrivances, lacking a sense of authenticity and artistry.

If Ouyang's play falls short of expectations, Zhou Yibai's (1900–1977) *Hua Mulan* is even less successful as an artistic endeavor. Based on the same theme but set in the earlier Sui dynasty, Zhou's 1941 play has a different ending. When Hua Mulan discloses her true identity in the imperial court, the notorious Emperor Sui Yangdi, enthralled by her beauty and skill, tries to force her to become his concubine. Adamant in her refusal, she is given a choice between decapitation and submission to the emperor's lechery. In the end, she narrowly escapes death when news about a new rebellion reaches the capital and she is assigned to lead an army to the trouble spot, after which, the emperor promises her, she will be allowed to return to her hometown.[86] This play, too, is marred by the absence of an integrated plot, an awkward conclusion, lifeless characterization, and inept efforts at creating dramatic tension. Critics' responses to Zhou's play were often unenthusiastic.[87]

Nevertheless, both Ouyang Yuqian's *Mulan Joins the Army* and Zhou Yibai's *Hua Mulan* captured the attention of Chinese audiences—not for their artistry, but because of the timeliness of their message. Strong anti-Japanese sentiments, presented in the guise of anti-barbarian themes, coursed through the two plays, as did loyalty to the nation and filial piety. Both the spirit and the subject matter were wholly contemporary: the perfidy of a traitor (in Ouyang's play, he is a high military officer in Mulan's camp) and the misleading advice of an evil minister (in Zhou's piece, he is the court official Yang Su) were chilly reminders that the most deadly enemies might be lurking in one's own camp. The notion of national unity, a strong theme in both plays, was thus placed in the spotlight.[88]

In wartime China, many Hua Mulan–type heroines appeared. In addition to plays and films, there were numerous cartoons, *kuaiban* (rhythmic comic talks to the accompaniment of bamboo clappers), and articles about the bold heroine.[89] If Nora symbolized liberated women in the May Fourth era, Hua Mulan effectively symbolized resistance in wartime China. Her strong character, as a symbol, played an important role in both the political and the military struggles against the Japanese.[90]

The female symbols of resistance received further reinforcement in real-life examples. Perhaps Xie Bingying (1906–) best personified the indomitability of Hua Mulan. Born into a gentry family in Hunan, Xie was a rebellious young woman who refused to have her feet bound when she was a child; she later broke tradition by entering a military academy in Wuhan at the age of twenty. Together with a group of women soldiers, she participated in the National Revolutionary Army during the Northern Expedition in 1927, an experience that she later described vividly in the popular book *Army Diary* (*Congjun riji*). Xie was equally active during the War of Resistance. After organizing a women's service corps in her home province, she then went to the Xuzhou front as a war correspondent, filing moving stories about the wounded soldiers and the enemy's atrocities. Her writings subsequently appeared in the books *Autobiography of a Woman Soldier* (*Nübing zizhuan*) and *Miscellaneous Essays in the Army* (*Junzhong suibi*), among others.[91] No mere flag-waving propaganda pieces about war, Xie's dispatches were often filled with tears and agony. Her genuine feelings and unusual courage won her many admirers across the nation. A lesser-known but equally determined woman was Hu Lanqi (1901–), who helped organize the Shanghai Women Frontline Service Corps in 1937. She visited the front to render medical service as well as to put on patriotic dramas to boost the troops' morale,[92] winning accolades as the "modern-day Hua Mulan."[93]

"Analyses of gender imagery in political rhetoric," suggests Joan Scott, "can reveal a good deal about the intentions of speakers, the appeal of such rhetoric, and the possible nature of its impacts."[94] Indeed, close examination of these female symbols sheds important light on the dynamics of wartime political culture. Although female warriors and patriotic courtesans have long been popular characters in Chinese theater, and although many Hua Mulan plays by intellectuals frustrated with China's inability to defend itself from foreign intrusions appeared in late Qing,[95] never before had such a large number of plays about female resistance fighters appeared. Among over six hundred Chinese plays published during the war, many have titles that mention patriotic courtesans and female warriors specifically.[96] Besides Ouyang Yuqian's and Zhou Yibai's works on Hua Mulan, for example, at least two other plays about this famed woman warrior were published.[97] And three plays dealt with Liang Hongyu.

Why Hua Mulan, Liang Hongyu, and Ge Nenniang? Did women portray the spirit of the resistance better than men? Were there special qualities in these female figures that best symbolized Chinese patriotism? Or were they merely historical accidents? For Chinese intellectuals, drama was seldom an arena for artistic creation per se but more a means of changing society. The female symbols conjured up by these plays were therefore of particular significance, for they reveal much about the political culture of the time. Although of varying aesthetic quality, wartime dramas were never short of patriotic appeal. Yang Cunbin's *Qin Liangyu*, for instance, a play about the late Ming female general who resisted the Manchu invasion in the north and quelled peasant rebellions at home, was dedicated "with passion to those intrepid soldiers who defend our motherland."[98] Moreover, patriotic calls were regularly interwoven with strong social ideas. Abandoning traditional, patriarchal conceptions of authority, playwrights placed responsibility for defending the nation on women's shoulders, thus continuing the assault on Confucian values set in motion during the May Fourth era. To cast women of humble social status as heroines was in itself an act of defiance. No longer presented as adoring, obedient complements to peremptory patriarchs, submissive, meek, and lacking in willpower, women were shown to be combative and, more important, to embody the noble ideals of patriotism.

Despite their common struggle against traditional values, the heroines of the wartime spoken drama differed from their May Fourth sisters in two significant ways. First, whereas May Fourth women championed individualism and subjectivism, wartime heroines expounded collective goals and devotion to the nation. Second, and similarly, whereas May Fourth women cherished romantic love and free marriage, the female warriors called loudly for love of country. Priorities were now reversed: instead of personal liberation, saving the nation from the Japanese became the overriding concern. The prevailing mood was to discourage self-interest and personal ambition and to cultivate a collective spirit of self-sacrifice. Resistance became a moral responsibility for every citizen, with personal causes submerged beneath the wave of patriotic fervor.

Female symbols also served the important function of personalization. For even the simplest peasant, war had real, immediate, and personal meaning: death, destruction, loss of home and livelihood were commonplace. The "nation," however, like "popular sovereignty" and "patriotism," is, as Victor Turner puts it, an "imageless concept," unable to "rouse and then channel the energies of the popular masses."[99] In a country overwhelmed by localism and widespread illiteracy, to transform patriotism—love of country—from an imageless concept into a heartfelt emotion was no easy task. If the patriotic resistance struggle could somehow be reduced to human terms, if it could be individualized as a *person*—a flesh-and-blood human being endowed with authentic feelings and experiences—then powerful nationalistic reactions among the people might be evoked.

The relationship between the play and the audience, as we have seen, was not unidirectional. Audiences were far from passive onlookers. Their ability to understand and identify with the female symbols presented to them, to feel that "she is one of us," was therefore crucial to the success of the play and to the creation of a sense of common heritage and purpose. For Chinese dramatists, Hua Mulan best personified the spirit they sought to instill in their audiences. As a symbol of loyalty, filial piety, youth, courage, sacrifice, and integrity, she surpassed all others. By presenting this familiar and powerful image, and by portraying her as a patriot, Chinese dramatists appealed to the people to identify their interests with those of the nation. Thus Hua Mulan became a symbolic medium for channeling political ideas, and her wide acceptance in that capacity gave her enormous political significance. As a historical figure, moreover, Hua Mulan also served as a tangible reminder of China's continuing struggle against invaders, providing a crucial element of psychopolitical continuity with the past.

Because a female warrior is more dramatic and striking in appearance than her male counterpart, she can be more effective in cultivating patriotism among the populace. Like the female knights-errant (*nüxia*) of traditional Chinese fiction, she is gentle, feminine, and blessed with unmatched beauty. Yet she is also brave and upright. Superbly skilled with the sword, she defies death on the battlefield. Her immense courage can easily unnerve the enemy. This juxtaposition of compassionate tenderness and military prowess makes for a most fascinating character. It titillates the audience, evoking a kind of awe and admiration much like that produced by female impersonators in traditional Chinese theater, whose ambiguous sexual identity seemed to bewitch seasoned theatergoers. In creating an effective resistance symbol, Chinese playwrights knew that they needed a character who was both visually attractive and smashingly entertaining. The female warrior's combination of feminine and masculine, coupled with her sexuality and emotional intensity, clearly did the trick.

Perhaps, too, the cultivation of female symbols reflected Chinese playwrights' unconscious assumption that valiant women warriors would shame male spectators, or at least stir traditional male pride, thus inspiring them to act. Another possibility is that the female warrior evinced the playwrights' own yearning for peace and postwar recovery. "There is a tradition," Jean B. Elshtain points out, "that assumes an affinity between women and peace," for they symbolize qualities—nurturance, humility, charity—that rebuff the barbarism of war and underscore social stability.[100]

But to what extent did the selfless, patriotic female symbols in the plays reflect the actual feelings and experiences of women in Chinese society? Did the war facilitate a liberation from economic and political constraints imposed by traditional sex roles? Although considerable research has been done on the significant role European and American women played during the two world wars,[101] the extent to which Chinese women contributed to the War of Resistance remains unclear. What information there is, however, points to a continued emphasis on the ideal of woman as wife and mother, not as equal partner of man.[102] The dramatists' overt assertions of feminine superiority in wartime plays, therefore, constituted a personal questioning of the existing patriarchal social structure; actual relations between the sexes were not necessarily reflected. Image and reality can be worlds apart. The fact that most of the female warrior plays were written by men makes them to a large extent men's literary idealizations.[103] Even so, that wartime dramas should show women with more latitude in their roles than was permitted in reality is not unprecedented; in the long Chinese literary tradition, women have often been portrayed in a more positive manner than true circumstances would allow, as in the two Qing novels *Dream of the Red Chamber* (*Honglou meng*) and *Flowers in the Mirror* (*Jinghua yuan*).

The conscious cultivation of symbolic females fighting an occupation force was of course not unique to China. In Vichy France, for example, French resistance fighters and patriotic educators fostered the image of Joan of Arc as a martyr and symbol of national unity in the struggle against the Germans.[104] Like Joan of Arc, Hua Mulan represented the ideal of nationalism, exuding determination and courage to defend her homeland. In wartime China, female warriors like Hua Mulan became the preeminent symbols of resistance. They were the embodiments of loyalty and strength and models for emulation. They exerted a strong influence on the minds and hearts of the Chinese people, providing them with a sense of unity at a time of profound crisis. A popular wartime slogan summed it up like this: "Women must learn from Hua Mulan and Liang Hongyu, and men from Yue Wumu [Yue Fei]."[105]

Historical Plays

Chinese wartime spoken historical dramas were of course not confined to plays about patriotic courtesans and women warriors. A wealth of other kinds of historical plays appeared to meet the voracious demand of theatergoers, touching on similar burning issues of the day—loyalty (for example, Gu Yiqiao's *Yue Fei* [1940]), internal unity in the face of an external threat (Yang Hansheng's *Chronicle of the Heavenly Kingdom* [*Tianguo chunqiu*, 1941]), and patriotism (Guo Moruo's *Qu Yuan* [1942]), to name just a few. Despite their enormous popularity, historical plays were not without their problems. What was a historical play (*lishiju*), after all? How *historical* were these plays? How effective were they in communicating with an audience and rallying them behind the resistance efforts? Were they better than realist plays (*xianshiju*) for reflecting the current conflict? These questions aroused passionate debate among wartime playwrights as they searched for an ideal way to blend fact and fiction in their political and artistic work.

During the war many dramatists used the term "historical play" with considerable latitude, and its exact connotation was never clearly defined. This confusion was evident in a lively but chaotic debate on the subject in a panel organized by the respected journal *Drama Annals* (*Xiju chunqiu*) in 1942 and involving such leading dramatists as Ouyang Yuqian, Tian Han, and Yu Ling, literary luminaries like Mao Dun, and scholars like Liu Yazi (1887–1958). Ouyang Yuqian first admitted his puzzlement over the nature of historical plays:

> In the past, I have edited some traditional plays and written a few spoken dramas. More than ten years ago I wrote *Pan Jinlian*. Whether this could be called a historical play I am not entirely sure. It was written in the general mood of the time. . . . Subsequently I wrote a few Beijing operas: *Liang Hongyu*, *The Peach Blossom Fan*, and *Mulan Joins the Army*. . . . I did not necessarily base my sources on history. . . . I added a few episodes, for example, to *Liang Hongyu*. I did the same thing to *The Peach Blossom Fan*. I hate people who sit on the fence, that's why I portray Yang Wencong in such a way. . . . I believe that the key to writing historical plays is to grasp the essential mood and issues of the time. As for minor details, we could allow some discrepancies. . . . [I think] historical plays and history are quite different.[106]

The most important issue about a historical play, it seemed to Ouyang Yuqian, was not whether it followed faithfully events in the past, but whether it served as an effective warning about past mistakes. Tian Han agreed, saying that historical plays served the useful function of "foreseeing the future by reviewing the past," but he also argued that historical truth could add a crucial element of credibility to a play. The more the playwright adhered to historical facts, he added, the more influential a play would become.[107] The novelist Mao Dun, however, expressed doubts about overemphasizing historical reality. Echoing Ouyang Yuqian, he warned of the danger of confusing artistic creation with history. A writer's task was significantly different from a historian's, he said. While a creative writer could dash off compositions on paper as his imagination dictated, a historian had to painstakingly support his arguments with convincing evidence. For Mao Dun, the success of a historical play depended not on its faithfulness to the past but on its relevance to the present.[108]

Liu Yazi, by contrast, took a hard line: for him, historicity was a cardinal rule in historical plays that should be strictly observed. Liu, the founder of the Southern Society (Nan she, 1909), a group that combined traditional literary practices with overtly radical, nationalistic sentiments, was an outstanding traditional poet and an expert on Southern Ming history. He repeatedly emphasized the importance of historical authenticity in writing costume dramas: "I for one would like to stress that we should preserve as much [historical] truth as possible, especially when we are writing about a historic personage about whom history has already reached a consensus on whether he was loyal or treacherous, good or bad."[109] Strictly speaking, in Liu Yazi's eyes Ouyang Yuqian must have been a serious "offender," for he frankly admitted that he had written many of what he himself called "revisionist plays" (*fan'an xi*).[110]

This exchange was one of many attempts to come to grips with the nature of the historical play during the war,[111] the abundance of such discussion underscoring the importance of the subject. Indeed, the debate over a play's historicity raised the crucial question of credibility. In 1939, when A Ying began to write what subsequently became known as the "Southern Ming Historical Plays Series" (*Sorrow for the Fall of the Ming* [1939], *Heroic Deeds of Zheng Chenggong* [*Haiguo yingxiong*, 1940], and *The Story of Yang E* [1941]), his friend Liu Yazi advised him to follow history closely in order to present a more believable picture to the audience. Heeding Liu's call, A Ying wrote detailed explanations, copious notes, long bibliographies, and numerous appendices in an effort to demonstrate the historical authenticity of his plays.[112] But he soon found that striking a balance between faithfulness to history and creative writing was extremely difficult, if not impossible. In his historical plays, he often had to reshape ancient characters, add new personalities, shorten or conflate events, and embellish plots to create necessary dramatic tension or to meet the requirements of the stage.[113]

The debate over historicity also raised an even more important question of communication: what was the most efficient and effective way of reaching out to the masses? Among wartime playwrights, Ouyang Yuqian was one of the most vocal advocates of bringing drama to the audience. A man of many talents—educator, director, drama historian—and a seasoned Beijing opera actor who played female roles, Ouyang was one of the pioneers in the Chinese spoken drama movement. Although he wrote many historical plays, Ouyang was less concerned with their historicity than with their artistry and impact on audiences. His early work *Pan Jinlian* was a bold, imaginative piece invested with contemporary emotions. For Ouyang, too much history could weaken a spoken drama, whose function was not to reflect the past but to serve the present. Many so-called historical plays, Ouyang wrote, were not based on the standard dynastic histories anyway; instead they drew freely from historical romances and anecdotal accounts of considerable literary range, the end product tending to be a fusion of legend, history, and imagination.[114] Even for standard histories, Mao Dun concurred, "their authenticity is far from certain."[115]

A historical play that faithfully followed the language of the past could also pose problems of comprehension to the audience, some critics argued. For instance, Wu Zuguang's (1917–) highly acclaimed *Song of Righteousness* (*Zhengqi ge*, 1940), a play about the heroic death of the Southern Song patriot Wen Tianxiang, was criticized for its archaic language, "incomprehensible to many," as one reviewer sneered.[116] Similar complaints were raised about costumes.[117]

Playwrights were hardly unanimous on whether costume dramas were the best dramatic form for presenting patriotic ideas in the first place. Among the critics of historical plays, Xia Yan was a powerful voice. One of the original founders of the League of Left-Wing Dramatists (established on 1 August 1930), Xia helped to radicalize Chinese spoken drama in the mid-1930s by investing it with revolutionary content and a high emotional charge. He was respected in literary circles not only as a gifted playwright but also as one of the best practitioners of historical plays before the war. Besides *Sai Jinhua* (April 1936), his *The Spirit of Freedom* (*Ziyou hun*, December 1936; also known as *The Biography of Qiu Jin* [*Qiu Jin zhuan*]), about a female martyr determined to overthrow the Manchu regime at the beginning of this century, also won critical acclaim. But Xia was never totally at ease with historical dramas. By the time he finished *The Spirit of Freedom*, the Japanese invasion seemed imminent. As a committed Marxist, he believed that the struggle against capitalists and imperialists had arrived; he also held that the downtrodden were the inheritors of history. Writing a play in contemporary time was important, he felt, for putting the class struggle in correct perspective. By 1937, Xia's prewar enthusiasm for historical plays had faded, and he had become increasingly critical of his own past work. When he published the realist play *Under Shanghai Eaves* (*Shanghai wuyan xia*) in 1937, his conversion from historical play to social drama was completed.[118]

A three-act play concerning poverty in a contemporary city and the conflict between two friends over a woman, *Under Shanghai Eaves* not only marked the beginning of Xia's new endeavor but also set the tone for future realist plays in wartime China. To Xia, because realist plays drew their inspiration from actual events, they could better express the joys and sorrows of the masses. In his preface to the play, Xia Yan admitted his past errors: "After *Sai Jinhua*, I gave my writing some serious thought. I decided to abandon the kind of 'writing-for-fun' attitude and resolved to learn how to write seriously in a realistic manner. . . . Although this [*Under Shanghai Eaves*] is my fourth play, it can very well be considered my first: it is the beginning of my search for realism in creative work."[119] For Xia Yan, the current struggle of the common people against evil, both domestic and foreign, was far more important than retelling stories from the past. *Under Shanghai Eaves* can therefore be seen as Xia Yan's manifesto for a new kind of spoken drama.

Xia Yan's view was echoed by left-wing drama critic Zhang Geng (1911–). Zhang contended that lessons from the past were often too remote to be directly relevant. Granting that historical plays did have value, Zhang argued that their effectiveness in a period of crisis could seldom be compared with that of "living plays" (*shenghuoju*).[120] The latter, based on incidents of contemporary life, rendered a sense of realism and relevance to the audience that was seldom matched by costume dramas.

Not everyone agreed with Xia Yan and Zhang Geng. Some playwrights preferred to draw on familiar characters and incidents from the past rather than to create new ones. Household names and well-known plots, deeply engraved in the popular tradition, almost unfailingly attracted an audience; contemporary events and personalities, by contrast, commanded no such attention. As writer Tang Tao (1913–1992) observed, "People who do not know of Wang Jingwei often are extremely familiar with [traitors like] Qin Hui (1090–1155)."[121] Although Ouyang Yuqian did not reject realist plays—indeed, he occasionally wrote in that genre himself—he considered historical drama a superior medium of communication precisely because of the familiarity factor.[122] Historical plays seemed best able to draw on common memories, which of course lay at the core of nationalism, and this fact served both the political and patriotic purposes of the resistance movement admirably. Quite naturally, at a time of national crisis, Chinese turned to their past for psychological and spiritual reassurance. And for people like Ouyang Yuqian, historical plays were an ideal tool of nationalism because they furnished their audiences with both a sense of pride about their past and a hopeful feeling about their future. A female symbol of resistance like Hua Mulan stirred emotion precisely because of its context: Chinese history. Again, China was not alone in invoking history to serve its contemporary needs in a time of national crisis. In Vichy France, the Friday evening broadcasts of René Payot from Switzerland recalled the greatness of France, and resisters constantly reminded their compatriots of how the Gauls steadfastly struggled against the Romans.[123] Like Joan of Arc, Vercingétorix stood out as a symbol of selfless patriotism.

The debate concerning the relative value of the two types of play had no clear winners. Indeed, if the controversy is examined from another angle, the differences between the two seem to fade. For in reality, a wartime historical play was a *contemporary* piece about the past. At the same time, it was a *realistic* play because of its current messages. Historical heroes or heroines were not abstract ideals or faceless models who lived in the remote past; they were familiar personages brought to life to comment on the present. This living reenactment is what gave historical plays their currency and forcefulness. "Whether a play is realistic or not cannot be determined or evaluated by its *historical* or *contemporary* subject matter," Guo Moruo observed. "It must be judged by its theme. Perhaps a historical theme can better reflect our present-day reality."[124] Time seemed a secondary factor in wartime historical plays; it opened up in both directions, flowing freely back and forth.

Despite their heated exchanges, wartime dramatists were not interested in drama theory per se. The two main issues involved in the debates on historical plays—the historicity of a historical play and the effectiveness of historical plays versus realist dramas—carried important practical weight. The question was not one of authenticity, but of how much a historical play had to say about the present and to what extent it was able to galvanize the support of the people in the face of the invaders. After all, wartime playwrights were not academic historians; they were writers who hoped to create political art with a pointed message. Their fascination with history sprang not from a love of the past but from their sensitivity to the unfolding crisis.

Ironically, the outcome of the debate over historical versus contemporary plays was not decided by their respective artistic merits, or by their audience reception, but by the political realities of the time. As the war dragged on, the GMD government, beset with rampant inflation, ineffectual rule, and official corruption, came under increasing attack. That and growing friction with the Communists after 1939 prompted the GMD to issue measures aimed at silencing all criticism.[125] After the New Fourth Army Incident of January 1941, which dealt a serious blow to the United Front strategy, Chinese dramatists were further handcuffed when Chongqing adopted what one playwright described as "two-scissor" censorship, in which both the text and the performance of a play were placed under close scrutiny.[126] In 1942, when the journalist Pan Gongzhan (1895–1975) was appointed to head the government's Central Censorship Committee on Books and Periodicals (Zhongyang tushu zazhi shencha weiyuanhui), intellectual surveillance and ideological control became even more suffocating. Playwrights had little choice but to select historical themes to camouflage their real intent. A case in point was Guo Moruo's *Qu Yuan* (January 1942), which focused on the legendary loyal Chu minister of the Warring States period and the infightings within the State of Chu to criticize the GMD's undermining of the United Front strategy. But Pan Gongzhan was quick to discern the play's real intent, and he banned it shortly after it debuted in Chongqing in April 1942.[127]

Nevertheless, historical plays remained a relatively safe channel for concealing political criticism within literary devices, and as a consequence costume dramas flourished after 1941. According to a 1946 study by Tian Jin, while historical plays represented only 14 percent of plays written between 1937 and 1941, that number jumped to 33 percent for the period 1941–1945.[128] Sophisticated theatergoers became attuned to looking for nuance of expression and seeking out allegorical messages in what was otherwise a fairly innocuous story.

The Southern Ming (1644–1662) was a favorite dynastic setting for historical drama—consider A Ying's famous plays, as well as Ouyang Yuqian's *Peach Blossom Fan*, Jiang Qi's *Chen Yuanyuan* (1940), and Shu Yan's *Dong Xiaowan* (1941). This interest in the Southern Ming was motivated not only by the intrinsic fascination of the period, but also by the unavoidable parallels between the seventeenth- and twentieth-century situations. Marking the former were atrocities committed by the invading Manchus from the north, the heroic resistance of the Ming loyalists, the chronic financial and political dislocations that so demoralized the government, and the scandalous behavior of disloyal ministers and generals—attributes too similar to those being experienced by contemporary China for writers to ignore. The call for unity in wartime China struck a particular chord when people recalled that the Southern Ming's resistance had failed owing largely to partisan wrangling among various resistance groups. It required little imagination to see that the ill-fated Ming empire closely resembled China under the GMD and that the invading Manchus implied none other than the Japanese. Playwrights had no trouble mining events from this tragic but familiar period that alluded to contemporary scenes. Suddenly, the bitter memories of "Yangzhou's ten-day massacre" and "Jiading's three butcherings" came alive, the atrocities committed by the Manchus in their conquest of the south three hundred years ago becoming linked to those of the Japanese troops in Nanjing in December 1937. A painful chapter from the past echoed in the present. There was simply too much inspiration to be drawn from the Southern Ming, the writer Tang Tao maintained.[129] Thus, while Chinese writers glorified Ming loyalists such as Shi Kefa for their heroic deeds in resisting the Manchus' encroachment, they castigated traitors like Ma Shiying and Ruan Dacheng for cooperating with the enemy.[130] The wrongs should be righted and the past mistakes should serve as a warning to the present.

But no two historical periods are exactly alike, and pushing the parallel too far could distort people's perception of reality. In fact, Zhou Li'an warned that the analogy between the late Ming and the contemporary crisis was far-fetched and potentially damaging to the resistance cause. The comparison, he said, could mask some very fundamental differences between these two periods. After all, whereas the late Ming ended in complete disaster, the struggle against Japan was just unfolding. Zhou warned that the tragic end of the Ming could easily instill a defeatist attitude in the general public. Worse still, it could be exploited by the traitors and the Japanese to weaken the spirit of the resistance.[131] In direct contrast to the sharply divided Southern Ming, Zhou argued, China was united. The war with Japan had created a wave of unprecedented patriotism and cooperation that had never before existed in China. "Today the situation is markedly different from that of the late Ming because the whole country is united in struggle [against the Japanese]."[132]

Traditional Dramas

Their general popularity notwithstanding, wartime historical plays remained largely an urban phenomenon, particularly in interior cities such as Chongqing, Changsha, and Guilin.[133] The plays' length, big

cast, elaborate props, and drawn-out preparation all made their performance difficult in the countryside. So what kind of impact did they
have on rural audiences? Perhaps very little. In another attempt to
bring patriotism to the villages, therefore, wartime dramatists turned
to a familiar performing art for help—traditional drama.

The inclusion of traditional drama in the resistance arsenal was not
without controversy. A series of questions had already been raised by
drama activists and government officials in the early phase of the war:
Could such popular traditional dramas as Beijing opera or other regional plays, which appealed equally to urbanites and villagers alike,
be used in service of the war cause? Or were they too archaic to be of
use in this critical time? If so, could they be reformed to channel patriotic messages to rural audiences? In other words, could new material
be put into old forms—a process known as "filling old bottles with
new wine" (*jiuping zhuang xinjiu*)?

As in the earlier May Fourth debate, heated exchanges over the nature and usefulness of this dramatic form were kindled among intellectuals and artists during the war. For some, including Xiong Foxi, the
highly unrealistic nature of Chinese traditional drama, with its structured staging and minimal emphasis on credibility, seriously limited its
usefulness as a political and educational tool.[134] As the writer Ding
Ling (1904–1986) pointed out, the extreme symbolism of Beijing
opera made it ineffective for propagating the resistance cause—though
that did not rule out the possibility that it could be changed.[135] Xiang
Peiliang disagreed. He argued that traditional Chinese theater remained remarkably persistent in its forms and content. Its formulaic
plots, controlled gestures, and standardized staging all made fundamental change difficult.[136] According to Xiong Foxi, form and content were mutually dependent, such that changing the content would
immediately affect the form. Xiong, an enthusiastic advocate of new
dramatic forms, maintained that the simple forms of traditional drama
could "hardly express the spirit of the time and can never satisfy the
psychological needs of the audience."[137]

But Tian Han, Hong Shen, and Ouyang Yuqian demurred.
Although Tian Han was a pivotal figure in the Chinese spoken drama
movement, he never abandoned traditional theater. He saw the two as
distinct artistic forms that not only could coexist but also were of
complementary value in China's propaganda war against the Japanese.
By the early 1930s Tian had turned his back on his sentimental past,
represented by such pieces as *Night Talk in Suzhou* (1927), and
embraced the Communist cause. As the war progressed, he looked at

the traditional theater with ever greater interest. Tian disputed Xiong Foxi's analogy of form and content, arguing that one could change the content without affecting the form. He believed that breathing new life into traditional drama was necessary and timely. To Tian and his friend Hong Shen, classical Chinese theater was more than an entertaining art; it was a rich treasure that could not be overlooked. Traditional theater was a popular art in which dance, song, and mime were meticulously blended to produce an expressive, rhythmic effect; most important, its plots were familiar to the common people. In sum, the classical theater provided an ideal social setting for spreading patriotic news.[138] During the war, Tian Han wrote and revised more than ten Beijing operas, including such famous pieces as *Yangzi Fishermen's Songs* (*Jiang Han yuge*, 1937), which portrayed the cooperation between the Song government and fishermen along the Yangzi River in their struggle against the invading Jin. In addition to patriotic language, most of the revamped plays resorted to classical allegory, harshly criticizing official corruption and ineffectual government.

Like Tian Han, Ouyang Yuqian was also a noted reformer of traditional opera. Despite such problems as inflexible rules and obsolete ideas in traditional dramas, Ouyang argued, with patience and ingenuity the medium could be transformed and resuscitated to meet present needs.[139] "[No one can deny that] there are excellent techniques and performing styles [in classical dramas]. Why can't we retain the valuable parts and put them to good use?"[140] Ouyang's position as director of the Guangdong Drama Institute (Guangdong xiju yanjiusuo) in 1929 and of the Guangxi Provincial Institute of Art (Guangxi shengli yishuguan) in 1939 provided him with a unique opportunity to launch drama reform in both provinces.[141] He added scenes, used curtains, installed lights, and even modified costumes to give plays a new look. "Adaptation," he wrote, "does not mean adding a word here or there; it is a thorough rewriting of the old pieces under new rules and in new formats."[142]

One common charge leveled against traditional dramas was that there were too many "feudalistic elements," a criticism that Ouyang Yuqian did not deny.[143] One such "poisonous weed," popular since the Qing dynasty, was *Silang Visits His Mother* (*Silang tan mu*), about a young Chinese Han general named Yang Silang who is taken captive by the invading barbarians. Though he is imprisoned, his talent impresses the empress dowager so much that she decides to give him her daughter in marriage. The rest of the play revolves around Silang's dangerous attempts to arrange a meeting with his mother, who is now leading a new campaign against the same barbarians. While traditional theatergoers were mostly intrigued by the spectacular casting of this Beijing opera (it has nine principal and four supporting roles), patriots in wartime China felt extremely uncomfortable about the theme of the play: the submission of a Chinese general to a barbarian state. The play was filled with what many called "a traitor's mentality."[144] Subsequently this play, together with others judged obscene or superstitious, was banned by the GMD government.[145]

True, playwright Ma Yanxiang admitted, there were unacceptable pieces like *Silang Visits His Mother*, and traditional plays abounded in emperors, kings, and talented scholars engaged in amorous intrigues, themes far removed from contemporary life; but to condemn traditional opera outright as feudal, obsolete, and unworthy of attention was to ignore the value of this rich genre. Ma argued that traditional dramas had not remained static. Like other forms, they had responded to change. Moreover, there was no dearth of plays in the traditional repertoire that expounded new ideas and endorsed progressive thoughts—plays such as *The Rebellion* (*Fan wuguan*), about soldiers who rebel against a tyrannical ruler, and *A Nun Seeks Worldly Pleasure* (*Sifan xiashan*), which portrays young nuns who free themselves from the cloistered life imposed on them by their parents.[146] Another notable example was *The Fisherman's Revenge* (*Dayu shajia*; also known as *Demanding the Fishing Tax*).[147] Popular since the mid–nineteenth century, this Beijing opera tells the story of a widowed man who, after abandoning the life of an outlaw, leads a simple life as a fisherman. Harassed by an insolent tax collector sent by a local landlord, and later unjustly flogged by the local magistrate when he files a complaint against the landlord, the old fisherman decides to take justice into his own hands. With the help of his daughter, he kills the landlord and his subordinates; together the old man and his daughter sail safely into the night to resume the life of outlaws. *The Fisherman's Revenge* is a powerful drama pitting the oppressed against the oppressors, fishermen against landlords, justice against inequity. The old man is certainly no heartless avenger: he is a righter of wrongs. Instead of succumbing to corrupt social and political forces, he retaliates and emerges triumphant. To many wartime dramatists this play was a potent reminder of the ongoing struggle between two opposing forces, promising that a bright future might lie not too far ahead. It was with such plays in mind that Ma Yanxiang called for a more objective and comprehensive evaluation of the traditional drama repertoire.[148]

Understanding that traditional operas could be turned into timely

political tools, the GMD government also became involved in the reform campaign. In 1939, under the supervision of the Ministry of
Education, a newly created Textbook Editorial Committee began to
draw up plans for revising traditional operas. Several years later it
issued a series of forty-eight revised Beijing operas whose values were
deemed congruous with "the pulse of the time."[149] Nevertheless, the
GMD effort seemed halfhearted, limited, and uncoordinated. In the
end, the government's preoccupation with military and financial
affairs left this crucial area of cultural propaganda almost entirely in
the hands of the Communists and their sympathizers. Indeed, the insufficient attention paid by the Nationalists to cultural propaganda
overall proved costly for them in their battle against the Communists.

It was in fact left-wing intellectuals like Tian Han, not government
officials, who played the most critical role in reforming traditional drama. Tian Han found classical plays, especially regional ones, ideal for
promoting interaction with rural audiences. Because of their enduring
popularity, long tradition, and rich variety, regional dramas already
commanded a huge and loyal following in various localities in China.
Tian Han thus urged that the genre be upgraded and promoted.[150] In
August 1938, Tian launched the famous Wartime Dramatist Class in
Hankou (Liu Han geju yanyuan zhanshi jiangxiban). The program involved seven hundred men and women, including performers from
such diverse dramatic forms as Beijing opera, Chu opera (*Chuju*,
popular in Hubei and Jiangxi), and Han opera (*Hanju*, popular in
Hubei and parts of Henan, Shaanxi, and Hunan), drum singers, and so
on.[151] The lecture class provided a rare opportunity for traditional
actors to gather together and learn from each other, as well as to
keep abreast of current developments in China.[152] Later that year in
Changsha, Tian Han initiated a similar program, in which some two
hundred traditional opera actors were involved.[153] Under the call of
resistance, various regional opera propaganda teams were formed,
including the Beijing Opera Propaganda Troupe (Pingju xuanchuandui)
and the Hunan Opera Propaganda Troupe (Xiangju xuanchuandui).
These troupes, like spoken drama traveling teams, provided the drama
movement with a greater degree of flexibility and mobility in the interior that it had otherwise not enjoyed.

Tian Han's programs were widely hailed for generating an unprecedented spirit of cooperation among a wide variety of performers and
providing, in one critic's words, an opportunity for traditional actors
to be "reeducated."[154] Others concurred, saying that traditional actors
had gained a much-needed psychological boost, for they now realized

that their contributions to the war effort were just as crucial as those of any other patriotic Chinese.[155] The drama reformers encouraged actors from the traditional theater to engage in a dialogue with their counterparts in spoken drama, to lessen mutual suspicion and to learn from one another. The inclusion of traditional artists in the cultural campaign against the enemy underscored the concept of unity. Instead of being buried, an old tradition was unearthed and revived for a pressing cause. The leitmotif of the traditional drama revival movement could now be discerned: national pride and cohesion.

During the war, Chu opera and Han opera were but two of the many regional dramas that underwent reform. Cantonese opera was another notable example that changed and as a result thrived anew. The famed Cantonese opera playwright Jiang Feng (Nanhai Shisanlang) leapt to the resistance cause, creating such new pieces as *Wu Sangui* and *Zheng Chenggong*, in which he ridiculed traitors and glorified patriots, respectively. Many actors heeded the call as well, Guan Dexing (stage name Xin Liangjiu) being perhaps the foremost representative. A well-known *wusheng* (military role) actor and a fervent patriot, Guan formed the Cantonese Opera Salvation Corps (Yueju jiuwang fuwutuan) during the war. He staged numerous performances in Guangxi, Hunan, and Guangdong, and traveled as far as Hong Kong, San Francisco, and the Philippines to raise large sums of money for war refugees. His acts won high acclaim in the drama world. "A truly remarkable man!" praised Ouyang Yuqian.[156]

Like the spoken drama traveling troupes, traditional opera actors carried their craft to the grass-roots level, which Ma Yanxiang considered crucial for reinvigorating the old performing art and keeping it in touch with the people.[157] The style and presentation of reformed traditional operas, in contrast to historical plays, were familiar to rural audiences, thus more accessible to them. And the fact that this endeavor relied heavily on preexisting regional opera troupes enhanced their chances of success among the villagers. But how effective were the reformed plays in actually speaking to the rural masses? The scattered data do indicate that they were popular among village audiences.[158] One report from a village in Zhejiang province gave this eyewitness account: "It is true that villagers are not very used to spoken dramas; but they all enjoy tremendously Beijing operas and other regional theater. . . . Based on this belief, we staged a play in Beijing opera style. . . . Its popularity even surpassed that of *Lay Down Your Whip*!"[159] Nevertheless, the limited number of regional troupes and actors suggests that whatever impact reformed dramas did have in the countryside during the war, it was not very great. Tian Han's traditional drama classes in Hankou and Changsha never involved more than a few hundred opera actors. And evidence shows that their activities (Guan Dexing's included) remained confined largely to small cities and towns in the interior.[160]

Limited influence in the rural area notwithstanding, the politicization and popularization of traditional dramas was a novel phenomenon during the war. The classical theater was no longer an entertainment filled with "decadent ideas and obsolete morality," one drama critic argued; rather, the war turned this old performing art into a noble vehicle for "national salvation."[161]

Unlike their May Fourth counterparts of twenty years earlier who took an iconoclastic stand against almost every aspect of traditional culture, repudiating it as worthless and harmful, wartime dramatists adopted a more moderate approach to the legacy of the past. To them, tradition was a potent defense against foreign invasion, and classical cultural forms were valuable assets. Ouyang Yuqian and Tian Han, while thoroughly modern in their outlook, plunged deep into the past in their search for solutions. They saw traditional drama not simply as an art form, but as an integral component of China's heritage, one that had now assumed a new political outlook and patriotic tone. Their attempt to rescue the traditional drama thus represented a search for an acceptable nationalist form (*minzu xingshi*) of art in a country under attack. "We must not let such a popular art form as traditional drama be separated from our resistance efforts," Ouyang Yuqian pleaded.[162]

This revival of traditional operas and the interest in historical plays were driven by Chinese playwrights' quest for a new meaning for their besieged culture. Their journey into the past was an intellectual as well as a sentimental one. Not only did these dramas affirm the present by reinforcing a sense of collective pride, but they also served as unparalleled psychological and intellectual defense against the invaders. Hua Mulan's devotion to her nation and Liang Hongyu's courage on the battlefield touched audiences far and wide. These historical heroines, reincarnated in the present, beckoned to their compatriots to join them.

As they did with spoken plays, Chinese playwrights politicized traditional dramas, writing on themes closely related to the everyday perils of the current war. The reform of traditional dramas was thus of more than nostalgic interest; it went beyond the intent of preserving China's heritage. It was a move of necessity to help keep patriotic sentiments alive among the populace. Still, the politicization of Chinese traditional dramas, like that of the street play, also made many productions artistically inferior. Yet that was a price many dramatists seemed willing to pay as long as it served the war cause.

From the start, wartime dramatists were keenly aware of the potential of spoken and traditional drama as a forceful tool of nationalism. To be politically effective in addressing the populace, however, they realized that their messages had to be both familiar and simple. Popularization thus lay at the heart of the drama resistance campaign. Abstract ideas such as "national salvation" (*jiuwang*) had to be translated into everyday language, and concepts of resistance would have little impact unless they were rendered into easily identifiable symbols like that of Hua Mulan. To popularize is to concretize and personalize the experience; all who saw *Lay Down Your Whip* certainly felt the poignancy and injustice of the ordeal suffered by Fragrance and her father as if at firsthand. Even though street plays, historical dramas, and traditional theater were different in artistic legacy and dramatic technique, and granted that their impact varied depending on their venue, whether urban or rural, several common threads linked them together: the popularization, politicization, and dissemination of the drama.

3   Cartoons

The resistance political culture was not confined to the cultivation of female symbols, staging of street plays, or rewriting of costume dramas. It also included the creation of simple but powerful images of the war by Chinese cartoonists. Rather than using past events or historical allusions to present a contemporary message, political cartoons commented directly on the present. They became an indispensable medium of communication during the war, swaying the attitudes and beliefs of the mass audience. The ideas underlying them might be complicated, but as pictures they were unambiguous and potent.

The struggle against the aggressors, many resistance intellectuals argued, must be waged not only on the battlefield, but on every conceivable front—including the field of cartoons. In an influential article published in the inaugural issue of *National Salvation Cartoons* (*Jiuwang manhua*) in September 1937, the cartoonist Wang Dunqing raised the banner of what he called "cartoon warfare" (*manhua zhan*) urging his fellow artists to join hands "to score the final victory against the Japanese."[1]

The National Salvation Cartoon Propaganda Corps

Like other patriotic Chinese, cartoonists responded with enthusiasm to the government's call for national defense. Perhaps more than others, though, they realized that they possessed a unique weapon: a brush capable of producing powerful graphic images. Such a weapon, if used with skill and ingenuity, could have enormous impact in a land of widespread illiteracy. The cartoonists' increasing awareness of the importance of their craft crystallized in the founding of the Shanghai

National Salvation Cartoon Association (Shanghai manhuajie jiuwang xiehui) soon after the Marco Polo Bridge Incident in early July 1937. To bring patriotic messages to the people through a host of drawings, the association formed a propaganda team, known officially as the National Salvation Cartoon Propaganda Corps (Jiuwang manhua xuanchuandui), and published the journal *National Salvation Cartoons*. In September, after a brief period of intense activity, the corps, led by Ye Qianyu and including such figures as Zhang Leping, Te Wei, and Hu Kao (1912–), left for Nanjing. It soon moved to Hankou, where it joined the Third Section under the Military Affairs Commission of the GMD government. Using newspapers, posters, and other media, cartoonists continued to wage an art offensive throughout the war. From 1937 to 1945, in fact, cartoons, like spoken dramas, were more than an art form: they were an effective educational tool and a potent agent for political indoctrination. They also served as a major chronicle of the age, bearing witness to a devastating conflict. Of all forms of propaganda, the cartoon can be the most persuasive.

When the National Salvation Cartoon Propaganda Corps left Shanghai and headed for the interior in September 1937, its leader, Ye Qianyu, and the other seven members had little idea what lay ahead. But as work got under way, their task became increasingly clear: to drive home to every citizen the urgency and importance of resistance and to raise the soldiers' morale at the front.[2] The War of Resistance, destructive as it was, seemed to give those involved inner strength and a sense of mission. This saga of "cartoon warfare" created a new chapter in the history of Chinese popular culture.

Like the drama propaganda campaign, the process of spreading patriotic sentiments to the people and bringing issues into focus through cartoons was a complicated one, both physically exhausting and emotionally taxing. But it also proved to be intellectually invigorating, involving constant movement and the creation of visual images comprehensible to country folk. Xuan Wenjie, a member of the corps, years later recalled the experience:

> The corps left Shanghai in September and headed west. On our way to Nanjing, we joined hands with the drama corps to stage propaganda shows on the streets of Zhenjiang. The simultaneous appearances of cartoon shows and street plays created a furor in this centuries-old city on the banks of the Yangzi River.
> From Shanghai to Nanjing, the enemy planes tailed us and bombed trains and people, leaving seas of fire and a land of moaning. I will never forget these terrifying, tragic scenes. Zhang

Ding and Lu Zhixiang joined us in Nanjing. We worked day and night to draw propaganda cartoons on pieces of huge cloth, recording enemy brutality that we had just witnessed. We put on "Anti-Japanese Cartoon Exhibitions" despite constant air raid sirens. These exhibits were received with enthusiasm, drawing a large crowd and reflecting people's interest [in cartoons] and their confidence [in us]. Despite enemy planes hovering overhead, they were engrossed in each and every cartoon on display.

When the Japanese troops occupied Nanjing in December 1937 we withdrew to Wuhan. . . . During our stay in Wuhan we concentrated on the following: First, drawing a large number of big propaganda cartoon posters and showing them in Hankou, Wuchang, and Qiaokou. This was our major assignment. . . . We also mobilized citizens to donate gold and money to help the war cause. Second, designing printed materials for anti-enemy propaganda. Many of us were involved, and the results were considerable. . . . Third, editing *Resistance Cartoons* [*Kangzhan manhua*]. The magazine, which was the official publication of the corps, published a total of twelve issues in Wuhan (three more issues came out in Chongqing, making fifteen issues in all). Besides paying tribute to the people's heroic resistance effort and hammering away at enemy brutality, a large number of pages were devoted to reporting resistance movements in other parts of the country.[3]

The corps left for Changsha when Chinese troops evacuated Wuhan in the fall of 1938, and soon headed for Guilin when Changsha was threatened. In Guilin, the corps decided to form two teams in order to reach more people. One team, with Zhang Leping as its leader, went to the southeastern battlefronts. The other, headed by Te Wei, stayed behind in Guilin. Te Wei's group arrived in Chongqing in early 1939. They put on street shows and held exhibits in nearby villages.[4] But the Nationalist government now viewed their activities with increasing suspicion, believing they were under the ideological sway of the Communists. In 1940, when the GMD reshuffled the Third Section and forced Guo Moruo out, it also discontinued funds to the Cartoon Propaganda Corps. The corps was soon disbanded, and its members scattered to various cities in the interior, especially Chongqing. "In its more than three years of existence [1937–1940]," recalled one member, "the corps traveled to places like Nanjing, Wuhan, Changsha, Guilin, Chongqing, Tunxi, Shangrao, held more than one hundred exhibits, edited numerous magazines and journals, and produced thousands of cartoons."[5]

The corps was of course not the only such group engaged in anti-Japanese campaigns. Other cartoon propaganda teams were active in the Guangzhou and Xi'an areas, for instance,[6] and numerous shows were mounted by local artists.[7] Provincial officials also launched their own exhibits, including a highly successful one held at a Confucian temple in Liancheng, Fujian province, in the spring of 1940.[8]

In 1938, the National Association of Chinese Cartoonists, which was formed before the war in Shanghai and whose members included artists from the Cartoon Propaganda Corps, resumed its work in Wuhan, setting up a special committee to coordinate different kinds of propaganda drives throughout the nation. A flurry of activities followed: cartoonists established training classes in Guilin and Xi'an, held individual exhibitions (such as those of Ding Cong [1916–] in Chengdu and Zhang Wenyuan [1910–] in Kunming), and launched various magazines, including *Cartoon and Woodcut* (*Manhua yu muke*) in Guilin and *Anti-Enemy Pictorial* (*Kangdi huabao*) in Xi'an.[9] In south China, Guangzhou became an active cartoon center; a host of talents gathered there to form a regional branch of the National Association of Chinese Cartoonists, with Yu Feng (1916–), Zhang E, and Huang Mao as its leading members. When the city fell into the hands of the Japanese troops in late 1938, Hong Kong replaced Guangzhou as the leading cartoon center in the south.[10]

When the First National Cartoon Exhibition was held in Shanghai in November 1936, China boasted about two hundred cartoonists.[11] The number increased during the war—to some five to eight hundred, according to Hu Kao.[12] Though the figure is not large given a population of 460 million, Chinese cartoonists nevertheless played a key role in the wartime propaganda movement.

To be politically productive, cartoons had to be capable of rapid production and dissemination. A variety of methods were used. Besides putting on numerous shows, for instance, cartoonists joined hands with dramatists to put on exhibits.[13] They also produced a deluge of images, which appeared on posters and in newspapers, pamphlets, books, and leaflets. When zinc plates were unavailable owing to supply shortages, artists resorted to woodcuts to produce cartoons in newspapers, establishing a new genre known as "woodcut cartoons" (*muke manhua*).[14] Cartoonists used street corners, signboards, poles, walls, huge banners, or whatever visible spots they could find to display their patriotic sentiments in drawings. They also painted pictures on huge white cloth banners, which were more durable and made transportation less difficult. They showed these repeatedly, explaining them to their audiences—a popular mode known as "picture storytelling" (*jiehua*).[15] Magazines such as *Resistance Cartoons* also enjoyed enormous popularity. In essence, cartoons became one of the most effective rallying tools for the war cause.

Patriotism notwithstanding, cartoonists did not blind themselves to the government's failings. As the GMD became increasingly mired in bureaucratic disarray and corruption in the later phases of the war, the cartoonists—most notably Ding Cong, Zhang Guangyu, and Liao Bingxiong—began to aim their barbs in that direction. Under the watchful eye of the censor, however, the criticisms tended to remain veiled and allegorical.

Images of War

In the West, war cartoons and etchings have a long history, dating back to before the days of medieval woodcuts. Goya's *Disasters of War*, for instance, was preceded by the terrifying scenes of Jacques Callot's (1592–1635) famous *Miseries of War* (1633). Later, during World War I, the Dutchman Louis Raemaekers (1869–1956) conveyed the outrages of that conflict through the use of cartoons, and Käthe Kollwitz, as we have seen, produced remarkable portraits of the anguish of wartime misery and hunger by means of various graphic arts techniques.

Chinese war cartoons have a shorter history. They began to appear sporadically in the late 1910s and early 1920s, at a time when conflicts between China and foreign powers were intensifying. Shen Bochen's "Qingdao, Shandong province" (1919) (fig. 5), for example, depicts Japan's imperialist intentions in China: while a skull with a rising-sun emblem on its forehead is ready to gobble up Qingdao City and Shandong province, the Chinese people fight gallantly to save their land. The cartoon reflects foreign aggression on the one hand and the soaring nationalist fervor in China on the other. Indeed, it accurately expressed the feelings of the young May Fourth generation, who, on that memorable Sunday of 4 May 1919, took their anger to the streets of Beijing to protest foreign encroachment on China's sovereignty and the ineptness of the Beijing warlord government. Predictably, Chinese war cartoons did not appear in profusion until the formal conflict between China and Japan erupted in mid-1937, but then they started streaming forth, forming a powerful visual narrative of modern Chinese history.

Chinese wartime cartoons relied heavily on directness and common imagery to achieve their effect. Like David Low's devastating exposés

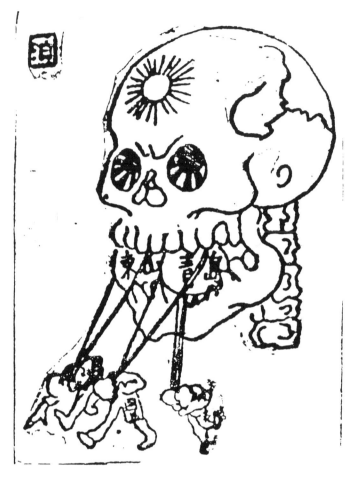

山东 · 青岛 (1919) 沈泊尘

Fig. 5. Shen Bochen, "Qingdao, Shandong province." From Bi
Keguan and Huang Yuanlin, *Zhongguo manhua shi* (Beijing:
Wenhua yishu chubanshe, 1986), pl. 66.

of fascism, Chinese wartime cartoons focused not on the abstract in-
humanity of war, but on the physical concreteness of the crisis. In
both cases, the images were solid and the lines sure, leaving no doubt
about who the villain was. But there were distinct differences between
Western and Chinese cartoons as well: while the former occasionally
delivered their message with a light touch, Chinese cartoons were
deadly serious. They also tended to be simpler in design and less fluent
in artistry; the novelty of the craft in China and the exigency of the

time precluded sophistication. As a result, one saw few bold symbols like the American cartoonist Daniel Fitzpatrick's (1891–1969) tumbling swastika,[16] nor did one encounter the exquisitely delineated details of the Polish artist Arthur Szyk's (1894–1951) anti-Nazi drawings.[17] What they lacked in artistic subtlety and refinement, however, they more than made up for in their robust vitality and compelling images.

The power of images in art has been much studied.[18] The image—or what it represents—can easily arouse anger, sympathy, desire, or myriad other emotions. Very often cartoon images communicate ideas that are too abstruse for verbal expression. But for images to be effective, they must be grounded in concreteness: they must have their source in real life. Unlike fine art, which tends to have a relatively complex and layered motivation, political cartoons by definition are simplistic and very often combative. They rely on popular sources for their appeal, and their context is often overlaid with rich emotive signs; this gives them a strong sense of familiarity and directness. Like their Western counterparts, Chinese cartoonists were concerned primarily with political and psychological expression. "In comparison with literature, which uses abstract language to express ideas," observed Feng Zikai, "the propaganda effect of the cartoon is definitely faster and more powerful."[19]

To have the maximum impact, many Chinese cartoonists argued that they had to carefully compose appropriate images and present them creatively and systematically, with participation from both artists and audiences. But could cartoons, a modern urban art, command universal appeal? Or should different types of cartoons be addressed to different people? Liao Bingxiong warned that illiterate peasants did not necessarily understand cartoons. Formerly an elementary school teacher, Liao was particularly concerned with how to communicate with the less educated. Although a member of the Cartoon Propaganda Corps, Liao criticized his fellow artists for failing to present simple enough images to the masses. "Their works were not popularized enough," he said.[20]

Since individual pieces with complicated artistic designs could be confusing, "picture storytelling" might help. But what if no one was around to explain the cartoon? Like Hong Shen with spoken drama, Liao suggested that images were most compelling if presented in a serial story format. As such, they were coherent, featuring sequences of simple, realistic pictures and facts interspersed among the stories. A Cantonese who came under the influence of storytelling and other folk arts in his early years, Liao believed that cartoonists could use the mode of traditional storytelling to establish a rapport with the people, and then allow the images to work their magic. Such a combination of a traditional performing art and modern drawing was one of many ingenious tactics advanced during the war. Liao's highly popular wartime cartoon serials, including "The War of Resistance Is Bound to Be a Victory," certainly bore this fact out.[21]

Although the cartoon changed during the war in terms of technique and imagery, its themes and messages remained remarkably the same. In general, Japan was depicted as an aggressive beast, a culture turned barbaric and committing atrocities on its neighbor from whom it once borrowed invaluable cultural and intellectual treasures. The frequent repetition of certain motifs suggested not a rigidity of approach but the desire to create a lasting impression on viewers. Japan's thrust into China, for example, might be portrayed as a venomous snake forcing its way through the Great Wall (fig. 6). But it was the Nanjing Massacre in December 1937 that truly shocked the world. The enemy's behavior in this notorious incident was partly captured by Li Keran's (1907–1989) "Killing Contest" (fig. 7), based on an actual incident in which two Japanese soldiers engaged in a "friendly contest" to cut off the heads of 150 Chinese.

Among thousands of cartoons produced during the war, several important themes emerge. First is the forced separation of mother and child. In a cartoon entitled "Feeding on Blood" (fig. 8), which bears an unmistakable Groszian imprint in technique, Cai Ruohong depicts a scene after Japanese planes have bombed a Chinese city: a baby sucking at his dead mother's breast, her body, still bleeding, lying amid the rubble. A bundle wrapped in cloth just beside the woman's body indicates that she is a refugee, her attempt to flee the war having proved futile. The child is cradled in her left arm, suggesting the poor mother's desperate effort to protect her baby before her death. Meanwhile the infant, innocent and incapable of knowing the terrible fate that has befallen his mother, sucks hungrily for nourishment. In its dramatic portrayal of the moment when death abruptly severs the intimate bond between mother and child, leaving the infant unprotected and helpless, Cai's cartoon, based on an actual Japanese air raid in Shanghai in the fall of 1937, is one of the most shocking images of Japanese wartime violence. It was widely reprinted and left an indelible impression on all those who saw it.[22]

In an equally forceful cartoon, Feng Zikai presents a similar but even more graphic scene: a mother meeting a horrible death while nursing her baby (fig. 9). Feng Zikai accompanied this frightening scene, which occurred in 1937 in Jiaxing, Zhejiang province, with a moving *ci* poem:

> In this aerial raid,
> On whom do the bombs drop?
> A baby is sucking at its mother's breast,
> But the loving mother's head has suddenly been severed.
> Blood and milk flow together.[23]

In this cartoon, images and words blend to register a most appalling sight. Unlike the Western practice, where the commentary is printed either below a drawing in caption form or coming out of the mouths of the subjects in balloons, Feng Zikai's method here was to use a conventional Chinese form: poetry. A silent poem describes the incident with great poignancy and yet speaks loudly of the artist's pain and anger. Although such a juxtaposition of visual representations and poetry is familiar in Chinese art, Feng's technique—the cartoon—is new and his messages contemporary.

The separation of mother and child was, however, but a small part of the larger human tragedy that was unfolding. There were other incidents: reducing villages to ashes, ravishing women (in Hu Kao's "Japanese Soldiers' Bestiality," fig. 10), committing random massacres, and torturing prisoners—"rape, obscenity, looting, and slaughter," as Lu Zhixiang summed it up.[24] For Chinese cartoonists surveying the Japanese destruction, indiscriminate killings were perhaps the most condemnable. Scenes of enemy planes dropping bombs on innocent people were abundant in Chinese cartoons (as in Zhang Leping's "Basic Training for the Enemy Air Force").[25] In "Bombing" (fig. 11), Feng Zikai paints a picture of impending doom: a school for the blind and the mute is about to be hit by bombs. No one inside the school will be spared; but more appalling is the fact that these handicapped students have no way of knowing about the imminent catastrophe.

With their villages devastated, loved ones killed, and property lost, those who narrowly escaped death managed to grab a few belongings and flee the yoke of Japanese occupation. The result was endless treks of refugees—another perennial theme in wartime cartoons. Ye Qianyu, for example, tells the story of one family's ordeal in "Living for Vengeance" (fig. 12).

Japanese cruelties were regarded as so gruesome that they could be compared only to the acts of beasts. Cai Ruohong's "Eastern Pirate's Specialty" depicts Japan as a monstrous ape mutilating innocent Chinese people and then devouring them (fig. 13). Reptiles were another common negative image (see fig. 6), for in Chinese folklore the

蜿蜒南下 穆一龍作

Fig. 6. Mu Yilong, "A Viper Wriggles South-ward." From Bi Keguan and Huang Yuanlin, *Zhongguo manhua shi*, pl. 183.

殺人比賽（漫畫）　　　　李可染作

Fig. 7. Li Keran, "Kill-ing Contest." From *Wenyi zhendi* 2.6 (1 January 1939): n.p.

Fig. 8. Cai Ruohong, "Feeding on Blood." From *Fenghuo* 1 (5 September 1937): n.p.

Fig. 9. Feng Zikai: A mother's head severed. From *China Weekly Review* 88.6 (8 April 1939): 177.

Fig. 10.   Hu Kao,
"Japanese Soldiers'
Bestiality." From *QGXJ*,
p. 85.

日寇的獸行

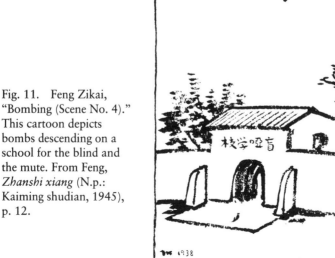

Fig. 11.   Feng Zikai,
"Bombing (Scene No. 4)."
This cartoon depicts
bombs descending on a
school for the blind and
the mute. From Feng,
Zhanshi xiang (N.p.:
Kaiming shudian, 1945),
p. 12.

Fig. 12. Ye Qianyu, "Living for Vengeance." From W. H. Auden and Christopher Isherwood, *Journey to a War* (New York: Random House, 1939) (reproduced by permission of the publisher).

Fig. 13. Cai Ruohong, "Eastern Pirate's Specialty." The bodies on the ground are labeled "people." From *QGXJ*, p. 84.

snake is regarded as "clever but wicked and treacherous"[26]—an adequate description of the invading Japanese. Cartoonists also portrayed Japanese soldiers as pigs and dogs, animals that behaved in a most deplorable way.[27] The use of bestial imagery, of course, is common in wartime propaganda.[28] In Charles Press's words, as a form of psychological warfare it is "meant to be cruel and to hurt. . . . The hate shines through, uncontrolled and slightly insane."[29] By dehumanizing the enemy, propagandists could justify the armed resistance as a crusade against barbarism and evil. By the same token, the Chinese were themselves depicted as lions or tigers, symbols of courage, pride, and steadfastness. The imposing presence of the majestic big cats expressed the country's resolve to resist and to win, thus stimulating the flagging spirit of the Chinese people.[30] Such an approach set up an opposition of subhuman and human, evil and good, in which the viewer was clearly aligned with the latter.

The root cause of the war lay in Japanese militarism, and it was at that militarism that Chinese cartoonists directed their heaviest attacks. Wartime cartoons showed Japan as a nation stymied by internal conflict and mired in economic and political crises. But the major threat to Japan's welfare, as the cartoonists correctly suggested, came from the military. In general, they assumed that aggression occurred when internal checks were absent and the military was allowed to overwhelm the civilian government. Japan faced just such a dilemma. The country, wartime cartoons tell us, was the victim of unbridled military power. Its emperor had become powerless, and the high officers of the army and navy, like a colossal monster, manipulated Prime Minister Konoe Fumimaro.[31]

Japan was also portrayed as a nation that showed little respect for international law. Zhang Ding, for example, pictures a Japanese soldier disemboweling a woman with his bayonet (fig. 14) to satirize Japan's unilateral abrogation in 1938 of the Nine-Power Pact (signed sixteen years earlier at the Washington Conference). In addition to their routine defiance of the international community, the Japanese had more ominous designs abroad. The military leaders presented themselves deceptively as men of peace, proffering an olive branch to make "cooperation" between China and Japan palatable, or promoting cordial understanding between Japan and its Asian neighbors with its "Greater East Asia Co-Prosperity Sphere." This was a huge ruse, cartoonists warned, nothing but a dangerous trap. Japan, Gao Longsheng (1903–1977) cautioned, was like a two-headed man: one half held out a gun while the other half toasted with a glass of champagne; his ultimate intention, however, was clear for all to see (fig. 15).

But Japan was not the only country with malicious designs. As another cartoon by Gao Longsheng showed, Japan together with Hitler formed an awful alliance aimed at conquering the world (fig. 16). The image of a mask, a familiar motif in Western and Soviet art,[32] was now adopted by Chinese cartoonists. Zhang E's "A Nazi Soldier," for example, depicts a trooper with a swastika on his helmet removing a mask labeled "Peace" from his aggressive face. The German invasion plan, Zhang cautioned, included annexing Austria and attacking the Soviet Union.[33] The emphasis was thus not on Japan's invasion of China alone, but on the danger of the spread of fascism throughout the world and its threat to civilization and peace. Like Low and Fitzpatrick, Chinese cartoonists warned that Japanese fascism was no local phenomenon; it was part of an international conspiracy that threatened the very survival of the human race.

Chinese artists also made careful attempts to distinguish between the Japanese people and their aggressive military leaders. The assumption was that war was created by the machinations of ambitious warlords, who dreamed of foreign aggrandizement and military glory. Like the Chinese under enemy occupation, the Japanese people at home faced coercion. Their leaders extorted money from them and compelled them to submit to harsh labor so that the militarists could maintain their war machine abroad, continuing their dream of conquering China. Zhang Ding, in a cartoon entitled "Unbearable" (fig. 17), portrayed this exploitation, which was pushing the nation to the brink of social and economic ruin, as being like loading a heavy cannon on the back of an emaciated donkey. Of course, the idea that the Japanese army did not enjoy popular support at home overlooked a strong right-wing, militaristic sentiment in that country. Nevertheless, the portrayal of a powerful military was correct: in the late 1930s it indeed controlled the government and every facet of society.

The threat to China's stability and survival as a nation came not only from outside, but also from within. The killing and plundering by Japanese troops required accomplices in China. Hence the War of Resistance was more than just a defense against outsiders; it was also a civil war against China's internal enemies, the *hanjian* (traitors). By clearly differentiating between patriots and *hanjian*, the intellectuals in a sense affirmed their own morality. Attacking *hanjian* thus became a ritual of self-justification, an act that reassured upright citizens about

Fig. 14.   Zhang Ding: The destruction of the Nine-Power Treaty. The characters on the woman read, "Nine-Power Treaty." From *JWMH* 10 (5 November 1937): 3.

Fig. 15.   Longsheng (Gao Longsheng), "United." From *Yue bao* 1.3 (15 March 1937): 474.

Fig. 16. Gao Longsheng, "'De' bu gu, bi you lin." The original quote from *Analects* (IV, 25) means "Virtue never dwells in solitude, it will always attract neighbors." Here, however, the term *de* stands for "Germany" (*Deguo*) rather than the original "virtue" (*de*). The cartoon depicts Hitler holding a head labeled "Austria." The characters on the skull held by a Japanese general read, "Puppet organization." From *QGXJ*, p. 61.

Fig. 17. Zhang Ding, "Unbearable." The cartoon is labeled "military expenses for China invasion"; the donkey is the "Japanese people," and the man is identified as "Japanese warlord." From *QGXJ*, p. 39.

the correctness of their behavior and conferred honor upon those who embraced the same view.[34] Like the Yang Wencong type in Chinese wartime dramas, the *hanjian* is ubiquitous in Chinese cartoons, diminutive, cringing, outrageously shameless, and despicable in his obsequiousness. In the eyes of Liao Bingxiong, an early follower of Covarrubias who later became known for his distinctively original and thought-provoking works, a traitor is willing to do anything for his foreign masters (fig. 18). Liao used dramatic geometric lines and distortion to portray a most ignominious act: a master, with a glass of champagne before him and his muscular right hand under his chin, glows with delight and pride as his lackey, kowtowing at his feet, offers up his most precious belonging—his head.

When Wang Jingwei became head of a puppet government in Nanjing in March 1940, he instantly emerged as the embodiment of base servility. As the news of his submission to the Japanese spread, cartoonists wasted no time in unleashing a barrage of scathing attacks on China's Number One Traitor. To them, the capitulation of Wang, the former disciple of Dr. Sun Yat-sen (Sun Yixian, 1866–1925) and an erstwhile revolutionary leader, was repugnant and intolerable. In the eyes of Te Wei, the setting up of a new government under Japanese aegis was nothing more than a farce played to its fullest extent.[35] And indeed, Wang's regime was precisely as Feng Zikai's cartoons depicted it: "a monkey show," an ignominious puppet performance that cost untold lives.[36] Still, Chinese collaborators were not confined to political figures like Wang Jingwei. As Gao Longsheng and Lu Zhixiang pointed out, a collaborator could be any one of any number of people—warlords, frustrated politicians, spineless men of letters, coldblooded youths, or hatchet men.[37] The image of the treacherous, furtive traitor was so prevalent in Chinese wartime cartoons that it served as a constant reminder to the people that they must always be on the alert: the evil ones could destroy them if they allowed their defenses to slip.

According to Chinese wartime cartoons, however, the greatest danger to the nation's survival was neither the ferocity of the enemy and their military superiority, nor the havoc caused by traitors, but a weak will to resist. War could easily spread despair and create disorientation among the people. To win the war, and ultimately to save the nation, the Chinese people had to be transformed from unconcerned onlookers to active participants.

In Ye Qianyu's "Abandon the Civilian Life, Join the Army" (fig. 19), the famous cartoon character Mr. Wang (see fig. 2) has assumed a

才 奴 準 標

Fig. 18. Liao Bingxiong, "A Typical Lackey." From Bi Keguan and Huang Yuanlin, *Zhongguo manhua shi*, pl. 184.

Fig. 19. Ye Qianyu, "Abandon the Civilian Life, Join the Army." From *Xin dongxiang* 2.10 (30 June 1939): 751.

new identity. No longer a petty bourgeois indulging in a decadent life in a corrupt city like Shanghai, Mr. Wang has donned a military uniform. He is wearing a helmet, carrying a gun, and marching to the battlefront. The transformation of Mr. Wang from a typical middle-class Philistine to a resolute patriotic soldier worked as a compelling call to arms, underlining the urgent need for every citizen's participation in the struggle against the Japanese. The ultimate strength of the resistance lay at the grass-roots level: a successful war against Japan could only be a people's war. The heroic struggle waged by common civilians against the invaders is vividly captured by Liang Baibo in "Let's Hand the Enemy an Even More Deadly Blow Following the Victory in Southern Shandong" (fig. 20). A man, filled with anger and standing upright like Hercules, is about to focus all his might on pounding a Japanese soldier with his mallet. The aggressor, defeated and fallen to the ground, shakily raises his crooked, blood-stained sword as he looks helplessly at impending doom. The gigantic stature of the hero contrasts dramatically with the diminutive villain. The outcome of the battle, as this cartoon clearly tells us, is decided not by the type of weapon used, but by the people's determination to fight. The first critical acts of resistance are therefore shown to be those of individuals, common men and women who dare to stand up and fight.

The people's power can be awesome, Lu Shaofei pointed out. In his "The Strength of the Armed People" (fig. 21), Lu depicts a Japanese soldier surrounded by raging peasants, who are determined to use every conceivable means to crush the invader. Again, the vivid contrast between the immense size of the Chinese resisters and the smallness of the intruder has a far greater impact on the audience than would subtle nuances. Such a device, of course, enjoys a long tradition in the West—consider James Gillray's famous series of cartoons about Napoleon, which ridiculed Bonaparte ("Little Boney") as a dwarf in military attire, or pieces by cartoonists such as Daniel Fitzpatrick during World War II. And as we have seen, it was also put to vigorous use by various Chinese artists. Part of the effectiveness of the device lies in its suggestion of Chinese superiority, spiritually if not militarily—though ironically, when the enemy was presented as the beastly aggressor, it was he who was huge and towering; only when the focus was on the valiant resistance of the Chinese people did he appear as diminutive and petrified.

In Lu Shaofei's piece, the sheer number of the Chinese people involved in the battle was shown to be a deciding factor in the final outcome. To defeat the enemy, the Chinese people must unite together.

And the unity of the will to resist, as Te Wei's cartoon indicates, is just like building an iron wall that will hold back the enemy's incursion (fig. 22). Besides symbolizing unity, the wall stood for something tangible: hard labor and war bonds. The contrast between the one (a lone Japanese soldier) and the many (a multitude of Chinese), along with the opposition of high (Chinese on top) and low (Japanese at the bottom), conveyed the same kind of optimism about the outcome of the war. The title with its familiar phrasing, "Mass will forms an impregnable wall" (*zhong zhi cheng cheng*), appealed directly to patriotic sentiment. To ignore the strength of the masses or to fail to mobilize them would be the gravest mistake that any government could make. If the masses were left unattended, as Zhang Ding's cartoon "The Abandoned and Unorganized Masses" cautioned, the country would face grave consequences: there would be no logistic support to soldiers at the front, hooligans and local tyrants would betray their country because of lack of internal constraint, and women and children would be molested and slaughtered by the enemy troops.[38] Zhang's piece served as a somber admonition to the government.

Women and intellectuals also figured prominently in wartime cartoons. Like Hua Mulan in spoken dramas, the women depicted in cartoons display not only beauty and charm, patience and care, but also valor and resolve, virtue and strength.[39] "I hope that every baby girl born will grow up like Hua Mulan," Feng Zikai said, thereby expressing his hope and admiration for the woman warrior (fig. 23).[40] But unlike Hua Mulan, who joined the army on behalf of her ailing father (thus not totally of her own will) and whose identity was concealed until the very end, the modern-day Hua Mulan went to the battlefront voluntarily and had the full support of both her family and her country. With the revival of the Hua Mulan image in cartoons, a familiar experience of the past was given a new visual interpretation and a new context.

Two women cartoonists were particularly well placed to capture the thoughts and sensibilities of women in wartime China. In her "Sharing Equal Responsibility" (fig. 24), for instance, Liang Baibo shows how women assumed a multitude of important roles during the war—as nurses, as suppliers of munitions and medical aid, as members of the "battlefront visiting teams," and as soldiers. Against the background of a huge national flag, the young women in the cartoon exhibit confidence and optimism: their gaze focused, their heads held high and expression animated, they display utmost determination. Like the female symbols of resistance in the spoken drama, the figures

跟着「魯南勝利」給敵人以更大打擊

白波作

Fig. 20. Baibo (Liang Baibo), "Let's Hand the Enemy an Even More Deadly Blow Following the Victory in Southern Shandong." Chinese soldiers scored a victory against Japanese troops in Taierzhuang, Shandong province, in April 1938. From *QGXJ*, p. 26.

魯少飛作

武裝民衆的力量

Fig. 21. Lu Shaofei, "The Strength of the Armed People." From *QGXJ*, p. 100.

Fig. 22. Te Wei, "Mass Will Forms an Impregnable Wall." The cargo is labeled "war bonds." From *JWMH* 8 (25 October 1937): 3.

Fig. 23. Feng Zikai, "I Hope That Every Baby Girl Born Will Grow Up Like Hua Mulan." From Feng, *Zhanshi xiang*, p. 5.

in Liang's piece remind us that in comparison to men, women can contribute just as much, if not more, to their country. Yu Feng's "Let the Gunfire of National Salvation Smash This Pair of Shackles," portraying a woman breaking off her handcuffs in a battle (fig. 25), is an even more forceful statement. The piece, though lacking in artistic refinement, nevertheless evoked a passionate response. To Chinese women, the War of Resistance may have meant more than just defeating the enemy; it also meant liberation from all kinds of suppression, including Confucianism, which relegated women to an inferior status. The title of the piece plays on this sentiment: it is a call to resist all oppression, be it foreign or domestic.

What about the role of intellectuals? More than any other citizens, cartoonists argued, Chinese intellectuals should assume a greater burden of responsibility in time of war. As guardians of moral rectitude and social truth, as well as the embodiment of knowledge and wisdom, they served as important role models for the common people. The catastrophe that had engulfed the nation demanded immediate action. Failure to take a stand was not just a sign of weakness; it was a disgrace and a moral crime. When the survival of a nation is at stake, neither passivity nor dispassionate inquiry should be tolerated. "Let's Change into New Uniform," Ye Qianyu urges, calling on his comrades to join the resistance movement (fig. 26).

Like their civilian countrymen, Chinese soldiers were portrayed as selfless and valorous. They were professional men who were ready to take up arms to defend their homeland. Chinese cartoons, however, featured no individual soldier heroes like Bill Mauldin's (1921–) "Willie and Joe"; neither did they carry the satirical and critical tone of Mauldin's pieces.[41] Mauldin prowled World War II foxholes to uncover a realistic, personal picture of war, his unshaven and sunken-eyed American GIs summing up the predicament of battle-weary infantryman. Chinese cartoonists, however, penned their soldiers in a more idealistic and abstract fashion—as heroic and resolute, always ready to lay their lives on the line. Zhang Ding's "Recover Lost Territory" (fig. 27) is a case in point. Depicted again in colossal size, the soldier stands upright, holds his head high, grasps his gun and sword firmly, and, exuding an air of self-confidence, calls on his countrymen to join hands to recover lost territory. The Great Wall reemerges not only as the ultimate line of defense but also the starting point for recovering land from the enemy. Besides bravery, the idea of self-sacrifice, of dying a heroic death, was also frequently invoked.[42]

Images in that vein, though, represented not the grim reality of the battlefield, but the imaginations and wishful thinking of patriotic artists. It is therefore not surprising that much of wartime art was exhortatory.

Nevertheless, to present a convincing picture, images must be grounded in real-life events. The Battle of Taierzhuang (April 1938) provided a rare opportunity to do so in a positive manner. That battle was the first major victory registered by Chinese forces since the outbreak of the war. After repeated defeats and humiliation at the hands of a better-equipped Japanese army, the victory could not have come at a better time. It was more than a morale booster: it shattered once and for all the myth of the invincibility of the Japanese war machine. Predictably, the victory quickly found its way into pictures and images. Te Wei, for example, recorded the euphoria in his "Warriors at Taierzhuang" (fig. 28): a soldier, a grenade in his left hand and a bloodstained sword in his right, charges fearlessly toward the enemy's encampment, followed by his comrades.

Without downplaying the importance of conventional warfare, Chinese cartoonists also placed increasing emphasis on guerrilla warfare, especially after the second alliance between the GMD and the CCP was announced. Perfected by Mao Zedong, guerrilla warfare is characterized by surprise and deception, together with extreme mobility of troops. Liao Bingxiong's "Guerrillas"[43] and Ding Cong's "How Come I Still Haven't Met an Eighth Route Army Soldier?" (fig. 29) reflected this strategy well. The increasing recognition that cartoonists accorded guerrilla warfare reflects the approval that Chinese artists in general felt for Mao's unique military approach.[44] Indeed, the Communist tactics won the praise even of Western cartoonists, including David Low.[45]

The second alliance between the GMD and the CCP, in 1937 in the wake of the Xi'an Incident (December 1936), was hailed by most Chinese as an epoch-making event. It was, in fact, a crucial step toward reunifying China after decades of chaos and incessant civil war. Pushed by the political exigencies of the time, warring factions resolved to set aside their differences and face their common foe. Continued partisan wrangling, both sides realized, would only paralyze the country further, presenting the enemy with an easy prey. Cai Ruohong's cartoon "A Sacred Handshake" (fig. 30) perhaps best expressed the sentiments of the time: a strong desire to end the bitter civil war and to see a grand alliance between the GMD and the CCP—

Fig. 24. Baibo (Liang Baibo), "Sharing Equal Responsibility." From *QGXJ*, p. 8.

你救们　　释解的匀均任责

Fig. 25. Yu Feng, "Let the Gunfire of National Salvation Smash This Pair of Shackles." From *QGXJ*, p. 103.

！吧铐镣这了毁摧火炮的放解族民让

—凬郇—

Fig. 26. Ye Qianyu, "Let's Change into New Uniform." From *T'ien Hsia Monthly* 7.4 (November 1938): n.p.

Fig. 27. Zhang Ding, "Recover Lost Territory." From *JWMH* 3 (30 September 1937): 3.

and against the invaders—finally materialize. The alliance, however, turned out to be short-lived, and the two parties soon renewed their old animosity.

To instill an optimistic spirit, Chinese cartoonists presented a bright future: the War of Resistance might be protracted and bitter, but if the Chinese people could join together as a single unit, they would triumph in the end. Such a notion was repeatedly cultivated. Cai Ruohong's famous cartoon "Surges of National Resistance," for instance, depicts the whole nation under arms: like roaring waves, the Chinese people will drown the invaders in the sea (fig. 31). Japan's penetration into China's interior, this cartoon also shows, is like sinking deeper and deeper into a quagmire. It is doomed to failure. The China quagmire became one of the most popular images used in Chinese wartime cartoons.[46]

In sum, wartime cartoon images were nationalistic, emotional, and idealistic. Using visual rhetoric, they portrayed a besieged nation fighting not merely for survival, but for justice and peace. The majority of cartoons were strong and spirited political statements, resting on the simple assumption that the current conflict was caused by Japan's unbridled imperialism—a theme designed to rekindle the bitter memories of repeated foreign encroachment on China in the past century. To repel the invaders and to rebuild China, nothing short of total unity was required. Unity was thus the cartoonists' battle cry.

For many cartoonists, the decision to participate in the resistance movement was an act of patriotism and a realization of their role as responsible citizens. But patriotism did not mean blind loyalty to the government. In fact, as the war progressed, cartoonists became increasingly critical of the GMD.

By the early 1940s, the excitement and high morale of the early war years had eroded as the economy was ravaged by inflation and the political climate became more oppressive. Initial support for the Nationalists had given way to alienation and disillusion. Cartoons critical of the government began to appear, mostly of an allegorical sort. For example, such images as "A Rich Man's Air-Raid Shelter" in Ye Qianyu's series "Wartime Chongqing" (1941), behind their humorous façades, condemned the extreme inequality that existed in the wartime capital.[47] And Ding Cong's (Xiao Ding) "The Social Phenomenon" (1944) painted a gloomy picture of society plagued by social ills and economic dislocation.[48] In Ding's piece, Guomindang society was a world populated by ruthless officials, profiteers, and penniless intellectuals. Liao Bingxiong's "A Professor's Meal" (1945) spoke

台 兒 莊 的 壯 士

特
偉

Fig. 28.   Te Wei, "Warriors at Taierzhuang." From *QGXJ*, p. 19.

further of the intellectuals' ordeal: dressed in tatters and with empty
bowls, an enervated teacher and his family are eating his Western
book to fill their empty stomachs.[49] The scene was an embarrassment
to the teacher, but more important, it was a disgrace to the Nationalist
government, for it pointed out its inability to feed the Chinese people.
Zhang Guangyu's colorful series "Journey to the West" ("Xiyou manji," 1945) made similar charges; here we find the pilgrimage of Tripi-
taka and his three disciples from the Ming novel being used as a
backdrop,[50] though instead of monsters and deities, the pilgrims now
encounter bribery and government demoralization on their journey to

Fig. 29. Ding Cong: Japanese invader says, "How come I still haven't met an Eighth Route Army soldier?" From *JWMH* 8 (25 October 1937): 4.

Fig. 30. Cai Ruohong, "A Sacred Handshake." The characters on the left read, "Chinese Communist Party," and on the right, "Chinese Nationalist Party." (According to the artist, the question mark after the title "Sacred Handshake" was a misprint; letter to the author, 26 July 1992.) From *QGXJ*, p. 17.

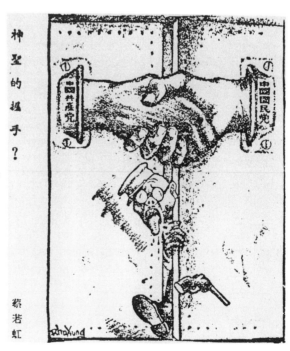

Fig. 31.   Cai Ruohong, "Surges of National Resistance." The characters in the middle read, "United resistance." From *JWMH* 1 (20 September 1937): 1.

Fig. 32.   Liao Bingxiong, "Mouse Bribery." The characters on the document read, "Passed." From Liao, *Bingxiong manhua* (Guangzhou: Lingnan meishu chubanshe, 1984), n.p.

the Buddha's paradise. Cartoon criticism intensified during the civil war period. Liao Bingxiong's "The Cat Kingdom" ("Maoguo chunqiu," 1945–1946), a devastating series on the dictatorial rule and corruption of the Guomindang, set the tone for what would follow in the ensuing years. In "Mouse Bribery," Liao painted a cat bearing the GMD emblem being plied lavishly with fish; in return he allows the mice's smuggling activities to continue unrestrained (fig. 32).[51] This visual assault no doubt further undermined the public support for the government.

A New Form of Art

The wartime cartoon movement brought both artistic innovation and political radicalism to China. This campaign made concerted use of visual propaganda addressed to the common audience. But to Chinese cartoonists, the cartoon was more than a transient propaganda tool; it was a subtle blending of genuine art and pressing politics. The men and women who joined the cartoon movement before and during the war struggled to combat the Japanese with their drawing pens. They also wished to make a strong statement about the importance of their new craft, one condemned by traditional-style artists as inelegant. Thus another theme of central importance in the modern cartoon movement emerged, focusing on the tension between modernism and traditionalism in Chinese art.

For many cartoonists, the War of Resistance marked a radical departure from the past. Not only did it inspire a search for new means of expression to rally support, but it also triggered an intellectual quest for a new identity. "The war," one artist argued, "is a turning point in the history of Chinese painting. . . . [The new art] reminds us of the urgency of national survival, registers protests, and insists on [the necessity of patriotic] education."[52] The war created a sense of transition that inspired innovation, and it offered cartoonists an opportunity to see China in a new light and to reflect upon the meaning of their art. Cartoonists dismissed conventional painting as obsolete. For them, making art was not a mere act of combining color and form, but a social and political activity with an immediate powerful impact on reality. Cartooning was not a solitary exercise, but a constant dialogue with life. Wartime cartoonists consciously sought liberation from the prevailing academic constraints, seeking instead a more open, bold, realistic, mass art geared not to a select few but to the common people at large. Their new art called into question all kinds of old forms and traditions, and ultimately the theoretical and moral justifications behind them. Thus began what they called the "New Art Movement" (*Xin meishu yundong*).[53] Woodcut artist Lai Shaoqi described three significant changes that characterized this new trend in art: an end to vulgar, erotic drawings (or what Lai bluntly called the art of "women's butts"); a shift toward realism; and an unprecedented unity among Chinese artists.[54] The war not only made old ideas obsolete, but it also demanded a fresh look at the meaning of art.

The potential for conflict with established art circles became apparent as soon as young cartoonists began to show their work, attempting at the same time to redefine the conception of art. Predictably, traditional-style artists had harsh words for the young cartoonists. In their eyes, cartoonists were unwelcome intruders who not only borrowed arbitrarily from the West, but also willfully challenged established artistic standards of good and bad. Conservative painters dismissed the cartoon as "lowbrow," "vulgar," and too "plebeian" to qualify as art; at best it was a form of casual drawing (*manbi*), lacking substantial content, and "not even worthy of being hung on the wall."[55] As for cartoonists, they were shoddy artists who indulged in crass commercialism and lacked any individual creativity. To traditional painters, wartime posters and mass graphic art were nothing more than tasteless "advertisement art" (*guanggao hua*).[56] One old-style artist even went so far as to condemn cartoonists as the "scum of art" (*yishu de bailei*).[57]

The condescension with which conservatives approached cartoons received a speedy rebuttal. Such charges as the traditional-style artists were making, the cartoonists said, revealed nothing but their deep-rooted biases and their utter ignorance of the spirit of the times. Here again, the Western tradition came to the cartoonists' aid. As Hu Kao noted, "The fact that the work of the great German cartoonist Grosz is included in *The Complete Works of World Art* attests to the importance of the cartoon in Western society."[58] Grosz, of course, was not the only cartoonist in the West to be awarded such respect: the French cartoonist Daumier, another art critic added, enjoyed celebrity status in France's academic circle just like Victor Hugo.[59] The contrast between the West's tribute to the art of the cartoon and China's contemptuous treatment of cartoonists was, Chinese cartoonists believed, a clear indication of the narrow-mindedness and conservatism of Chinese art circles. They argued that the cartoon was a serious and opportune art whose value should be accorded the highest respect. "Wartime art wields enormous influence," one claimed.[60]

For young cartoonists, the West was an important resource, helping them both to defend their art and to escape the restrictions of tradition. But the West also created problems of identity. In the 1930s cartoonists enthusiastically imitated foreign masters, whom they believed to be the best models for their art. But did their passion for all that was new and foreign go too far? The undiscriminating introduction of Western concepts, some critics charged, was tantamount to blind worship of foreign ideas. It had a deleterious effect on Chinese art because it caused artists to abandon tradition altogether; as a result, their works were unoriginal if not totally uninspiring. Te Wei's cartoons, for instance, were criticized as being "too Europeanized" (*tai Ou hua*), lacking a clear identity and therefore "difficult for Chinese readers to accept."[61] If cartoonists relied wholly on the West, one observer warned, "the [new art] movement was doomed to failure" because "it was not rooted in the soil."[62]

Soon a heated debate on "national form in painting" erupted in Chinese cartooning circles. The war, as we have seen, created a wave of nationalism in China. And cartoonists were not immune to this upsurge of emotion. No longer content to view everything through a Western lens, cartoonists attempted to establish a distinctly Chinese style. As ardent nationalists, many now felt a strong desire to defend their Chineseness. Good cartoons, they argued, like literature or any other art form, must be closely linked with China's own culture and its people's life; they must be "sinicized" (*zhongguohua*), as Shen Zhenhuang (d. 1944) suggested,[63] the goal being what Huang Shiying called a unique form of "national cartoon" (*minzu manhua*).[64] But how could Western methods be blended with unique, Chinese conditions? How could cartoonists develop what one critic called "an artist's true self"?[65] And what exactly *was* "a national cartoon" or "a sinicized cartoon"? Huang Mao attempted an answer:

> The sinicized cartoon . . . does not disregard the merits in
> Chinese traditional painting. . . . We must retain the marvels of
> brush and ink in Chinese art. But we also lack a scientific
> approach to drawings and are short of basic sketching tech-
> niques. By combining these with Western perspective devices
> and the art of human anatomy, we can create a new style. In
> brief, Western techniques must be expressed through our nation-
> al forms. . . . If we can blend Chinese reality with our national
> forms, sinicized cartoons [*zhongguohua de manhua*]
> will emerge.[66]

There is no question that Chinese cartoonists were profoundly influenced by Western techniques. The rich black-and-white contrast of pen and ink was a hallmark of Shen Bochen's and Huang Wennong's works, and Western perspective devices were commonly used by Te Wei and others (see figs. 28 and 33). Perhaps the most visible Western impact, however, was in the area of figure drawing. In general, although Chinese painting has a long tradition of human subjects, it is weak in subtle facial and bodily expression. Both Daumier's rich repertoire of figure drawings and Kollwitz's acute grasp of pose and gesture proved deep inspirations to young Chinese artists, cartoonists and woodcut artists alike. The cruelty of war could never be captured if human suffering and agony were not rendered fully. Often a simple facial expression or stance can reveal human folly in its most painful and tragic way. In opposition to traditional landscape painting, which championed abstract ideals and was commonly associated with a small group of literati or eccentrics, Ye Qianyu argued that a new national cartoon art must be established based on human sketches, which could convey a powerful sense of "strength" and "realism" to its readers.[67]

The late 1930s saw a move away from the old emphasis on foreign influence to a cultivation of a native style of art. That move, however, should not be interpreted as a turning away from the West. Rather, it was an effort on the part of Chinese cartoonists to develop their own sense of style and to raise national consciousness. Exposure to foreign contacts kept them abreast of new developments in the Western art world; it also forced them to reflect upon their own role as *Chinese* cartoonists. The concern for sinification thus symbolized their increasing awareness that this largely Western-inspired art form would not be fully accepted by the Chinese unless it was very carefully transplanted into Chinese soil. It also revealed the deep sensitivity of many Chinese cartoonists and their desire to demonstrate to their Western mentors that the transplanted art not only had come of age, but it had also developed a distinct personality of its own. Sinification did not mean exclusion of the West, cautioned Huang Mao. On the contrary, "To successfully create a national style, we must work Western ideas into our art."[68] The emphasis was thus on creative adaptation, as opposed to blind imitation. Ding Cong's use of the traditional handscroll for his cartoons (for example, "The Social Phenomenon")[69] is a case in point. Zhang Guangyu was successful in blending Western techniques with Chinese traditional decorative art in his works, especially "Journey to the West." And Liao Bingxiong integrated folk arts smoothly into his provocative drawings, notably the "Cat Kingdom" series. Liao, a great lover of Cantonese songs and folk arts, had a knack for adorning his works with local rhymes and idioms.[70] Thus, although their techniques might be Western, the meaning they wished to convey was definitely Chinese. Perhaps the best-known practitioner of this hybrid art is Feng Zikai, who used a traditional Chinese brush to paint some of the most memorable cartoons in modern Chinese history.

The wartime cartoon movement owed much of its spiritual élan to its skirmish with revered conventions. In their attempt to find a new direction for their art, young cartoonists came to view detachment from reality and abstraction in art with considerable distrust. The feeling that they were not welcome within the art establishment only added to their discontent—and was perhaps added to by a sense of inferiority resulting from the fact that few cartoonists had proper artistic training. In their eyes, traditional-style artists with their outdated practices offered little guidance for China's future; excessive emphasis on high art at the expense of other areas of visual culture, moreover, nurtured a marked insensitivity to change. Huang Mao put it bluntly: "Among all kinds of intellectuals, traditional-style painters probably make up the one group that remains the most detached from the people." Worse still, Huang Mao continued, old-fashioned artists regarded themselves as "talented scholars" (mingshi), looking contemptuously on the people and "indulging in constant self-admiration in their ivory towers."[71] Because of their stubborn adherence to archaic ideas and strict rules, they tended to produce mediocre, uninspired pieces, devoid of creativity and timeliness. According to cartoonists, the traditional landscape and flower-and-bird paintings, painted for and comprehended by only a select few, induced insensitivity, invited escape from social realities, and dampened the revolutionary ardor so needed in this critical time. As one put it, "[At a time of national crisis], the great masters of traditional schools are still wrapping themselves up in their 'literati painting' [wenren hua], leisurely enjoying their flowers and birds. Do they remember what Goya, an aging nationalistic Spanish painter, did a hundred years ago?"[72] In the eyes of young cartoonists (with but a few exceptions such as Zhang Shanzi [1882–1940], Xu Beihong [1895–1953], and Guan Shanyue [1912–]),[73] the majority of the traditional-style painters—or what one young artist sarcastically dubbed "aloof painters" (chaoran huajia)[74]—had withdrawn into a small world of resignation and cynicism.

To move from the margin to the mainstream of Chinese art, however, cartoonists had to do more than criticize the traditionalists and sinicize Western influences. They had, in a word, to revolutionize the meaning of art by bringing it to the people. This new breed of artist believed that cartoons were a special form of expression that faithfully reflected the rhythm of the people's life and related art to struggle. Thus cartoonists were laying the groundwork for a future great Chinese art—easily accessible, stylistically vivid, and socially responsible. Their works extended beyond an interest in painting and drawing to include commitment and participation. This conception signified a fundamental change in the way artists lived, a recognition that the arts had to align themselves with reality if they were to prosper.

These ideas were fully evident in cartoonists' efforts to formulate a new theory. Many artists felt that a new technique, no matter how good, should be grounded in a sound theoretical framework. Cartoonists were eager to prove that their craft was more than just a visually exciting medium, that it was a superb art with profound intellectual implications and strong involvement in life as it is lived.

The search for a theory, to be sure, did not begin during the war. *Modern Cartoons* is a showcase of some earlier energy spent on the topic. Throughout its existence from 1934 to 1937, the influential Shanghai cartoon magazine devoted pages to discussion of the nature of the cartoon. Japanese and Western theories (such as those of Kuriyagawa Hakuson [1880–1923] and William Gropper [1897–1977]) were introduced and debated.[75] A cartoon, the new artists maintained, might appear simple in technique, but it was never short of artistry and was always rich in aesthetic appeal. To strengthen their position, cartoonists painstakingly tried to clarify the term for cartoon, *manhua*, and the nature of their craft. Lu Shaofei contended that although the word *man* singularly could mean "romantic" as in the term *langman*, the term *manhua* (cartoon) meant something entirely different, incorporating spontaneity and playfulness, a kind of free-flow drawing that nevertheless demanded mastery of sophisticated technique.[76] Lu Shaofei also reiterated a point made by Lu Xun in an article written in 1935, namely, that it would be a grave mistake to interpret the character *man* to mean "casual jottings" (as in *manbi*), like the writings of the traditional literati.[77] A good cartoon, Lu Xun and Lu Shaofei both contended, could easily display a level of artistic adroitness equal, if not superior, to any other polished art. "Looking at cartoons is like sipping good wine or enjoying a cigarette: it brings a sense of excitement," Huang Miaozi added.[78] Yet the novelty and value of the cartoonist's craft came mainly from its rich contents and unique purpose. A good cartoon never failed to convey the artist's sincerity and was capable of providing a sense of immediacy to readers. "Cartoons are not jokes," one cartoonist wrote. "They are not designed to curry favor or seek laughs unrelated to life. On the contrary, they strive to reflect life. They are the life sketches of the people, revealing their pressing needs and desires."[79] It was this new realism that set cartoonists apart from traditional-style painters, they insisted.

The cartoon, argued Wang Dunqing, "is rich in propaganda value and can promote social change. It is a much superior tool [to traditional-style painting] in expressing ideas."[80] "Cartoons," Hu Kao echoed, "must be in close communication with the common people. They must merge with them."[81] The fact that Wang Dunqing and Hu Kao did indeed define their art partly on the grounds of its propaganda value rekindles the old debate over the precise nature of the cartoon as an art form. Does propaganda art, for example, have intrinsic value? Should it be considered a worthy endeavor, as cartoonists claimed? Or were the traditional artists correct when they disparaged the cartoon as a "vulgar" form? It is true that propaganda art, which tends to be time-specific and politically motivated, usually has little lasting value. It is also true that many wartime artists, trapped by the official line, lacked originality and subtlety. Most of the drawings produced during the war were hastily dashed off and technically rudimentary, hence of short-lived interest. Still, it would be erroneous to assume that all wartime cartoons were simply one prolonged cliché. Many, such as those of Ye Qianyu and Liao Bingxiong, showed considerable ingenuity and poignancy. More important, the strong emphasis Chinese cartoonists placed on bringing their art to the people made their undertaking unique. Cartooning, as Hu Kao and others argued, was no longer an individual activity; it was a joint venture involving both the artist and the audience. This audience-oriented perspective lay at the heart of wartime popular culture.

To Hu Kao, cartoons were an effective political vehicle that could sway public opinion.[82] The force of a cartoon, echoed the artist Xinbo, was just like "a silent bomb," which, if detonated at the right time, could have an enormous effect.[83] In the early years of the war, as young propagandists roamed the countryside attempting to arouse patriotic feelings among the country folk, it became clear that cartoons, posters, and other graphic media reached the audience more easily, quickly, and far more widely than books or other types of printed material. One artist related his own experience in late 1937:

> As a member of the Sixth National Salvation Drama Propaganda Team, I spent a whole month doing propaganda work in more than ten villages in Zhejiang province. Everywhere we visited we

used songs, dramas, speeches, and drawings as our main propaganda tools. But no matter where we were, the only thing that could draw a large peasant crowd and really arouse their interest was the huge drawings we brought along!

Although songs could also interest them, a large portion of the songs were not popularized enough. Furthermore, we sang in Mandarin, which was largely incomprehensible to them.

Staging dramas also proved problematic. First, it was often difficult to find an ideal location to put on the show. Second, audiences did not always behave in an orderly fashion. They talked and yelled freely so that actors' lines were largely inaudible.

As for making speeches, often because of the unpolished oratorical skill of the speaker, the talk quickly became dull and dry, and many listeners left halfway through. . . . Among the four [propaganda methods], the one that proved most understandable to and welcomed by the peasants was drawings.[84]

Clearly, relatively simple materials and speed of production were beneficial in making cartoons widely available. The best type of wartime cartoon for stirring up patriotic feelings, according to Hu Kao, was what he called a "reportage picture" (*baodao hua*), an easily reprinted drawing that employed simple brushstrokes and described real happenings.[85] To reach as many people as possible, Huang Mao proposed that political cartoons appear in different forms and in every conceivable place: exhibitions (including indoor, street, mobile, and window displays), huge banners hung across the streets, signboards, wall posters, mimeographed material, magazines, packaging, postcards, and touring cars.[86]

To produce maximum impact, cartoonists often reduced the complex issues to a number of readily identifiable visual signs. The slogan "Japanese imperialism," as many resistance intellectuals had pointed out, was too abstract for peasants to understand. But the image of a snake was not: it was an ominous sign of catastrophe. Cartoonists also employed polarized stereotypes to stress the differences between Chinese and Japanese. The enemy was identified as a torturer, rampantly insensitive to suffering and death. The Chinese, by contrast, were victims, which made their armed resistance a justifiable act. Killing for them was a means of survival, the only way to restore order and peace. The invaders were also portrayed as loners, whose deplorable acts were condemned not only by the invaded but also by their own people and the world community at large. The Chinese resisters, meanwhile, appeared in abundance and in different forms. The quantity and variety indicated more than just a large, diverse population: it signified the will of the majority and unity against aggression.

The impact of an image, however, tended to be instantaneous and fleeting; cumulative results were in no way guaranteed. Here Liao Bingxiong's suggestion proved most useful: a storytelling format had the best chance of turning a visual representation into an unforgettable icon. Nonetheless, there were other problems, the most serious being the ambiguity of images. A visual sign, no matter how simple, can be invested with a variety of meanings. Messages can also be decoded by readers in ways different from what the cartoonist originally intended. As Cao Bohan observed, not every peasant understood cartoons, and many came away with conflicting interpretations.[87] The ambiguity could be resolved by supplying the cartoon with a simple text. While Feng Zikai's poems were no doubt too literary for the general public to grasp, the majority of cartoons used simple, direct language to achieve three key functions: summation, anchorage, and relay.[88] That is, the text sums up, usually in a very few words, a particular situation depicted in the picture; it then directs viewers to read the visual image and steers them to grasp the intended message. Cartoonists also frequently used easy-to-understand titles or proverbs—such as "The mass will forms an impregnable wall" (*Zhong zhi cheng cheng*) and "Bogging down in the quagmire" (*Ni zu shen xian*)—to make their points even clearer.

Chinese cartoonists called on fellow artists to get involved, to "open their eyes to see the real society."[89] Young artists were urged to forsake their sheltered city life and go to the villages and battlefronts to paint the lot of common peasants and foot soldiers. Shen Yiqian (1908–1944) and Zhao Wangyun (1906–1977) heeded the call. Shen was the first Chinese cartoonist to go directly to the front to record the war. After first visiting the northern front (the Chahar-Suiyuan area) when the war erupted, he later formed a battlefield artist team and traveled from one battlefront to another, capturing the bravery of Chinese soldiers and the horrors of the war in his works.[90] But the artist who perhaps best symbolized a new type of traveling cartoonist was Zhao Wangyun.

Coming from a poor peasant family in Hebei province, Zhao first made his name as an illustrator for the Tianjin-based *Dagong bao*. His early paintings such as *Countryside Sketches* (*Nongcun xiesheng ji*, 1933) provide a rare, intimate look into the life and people of a northern Chinese rural community—a peasant relaxing after a demanding day of work, a night soil man, and a sweating ox laboring in the fields.[91] His friend General Feng Yuxiang (1882–1948) and his colleague Xiao Qian hailed him as one of the few artists whose works genuinely reflected the hardships of the people.[92] Although Zhao's early pieces showed many unsettling scenes of the deteriorating rural community, his cartoons after the eruption of the war presented an even grimmer picture of peasant life. Filled with patriotic passion and what journalist Cao Juren (1900–1972) called "a rare feeling of sincerity,"[93] Zhao traveled from one village to another, producing some of the most disturbing pictures of a countryside suffering from war and governmental ineptitude: houses on fire after air raids, refugees running away from war-torn villages.[94] Zhao used traditional Chinese landscape painting techniques in his cartoons, breathing life and pain into the scenes he portrayed. But what made his paintings unique was his emphasis on rural China, on the painful life of peasants and their struggle against disintegration and total disillusion. Ye Qianyu sums up his work well: "From Zhao's brush, Chinese peasants—the symbol of China's sufferings—emerge."[95]

Like many of his contemporaries, Zhao's wartime cartoons exude the people's determined spirit to fight against foreign aggression. In "Country Warriors" (fig. 33), for example, an old peasant stands with majesty in the foreground, his eyes glaring fiercely and his hands grasping a tasseled spear: he is ready to take on the enemy. And he is not alone. In the background, in a unified phalanx, stand equally determined countrymen eager to join him in battle. The picture clearly conveys the determination and enormous strength of rural China. Their weapons might be obsolete, but their spirit is definitely new. Likewise, though the idea of close peasant ties and community spirit was old, the emphasis on military heroism was not.

Zhao Wangyun's focus on country life and the spirit of the peasantry was more than an expression of personal style: it was another indication of how urban popular culture assumed a new look during the war. In a country marked by broad illiteracy, a visual propaganda tool relying on simple images and easily learned slogans could play an important role in garnering peasants' support for the war effort. Like dramatists, cartoonists were fully aware that China's countryside was an untapped source of resistance force. As the cartoon critic Shen Zhenhuang put it in 1939:

> The mainstay of a protracted war of resistance lies in the villages. But the strength must be nurtured early so that it can grow and yield positive results. In the countryside, where illiteracy is

作雲望趙　　民間的戰士

Fig. 33.   Zhao Wangyun, "Country Warriors." From *KDD* 10 (16 May 1938): n.p.

widespread, cartoons can play a crucial role in disseminating ideas and educating the people. They are not just an effective propaganda weapon but also an ideal tool for organizing the peasants. . . . Let's sincerely call on cartoonists. . . . Go to the front! Go to the villages![96]

This appeal reflected a new direction in the art of cartoons. No longer was the targeted audience the urban middle class; rather, cartoonists now made a conscious effort to reach the peasantry specifically, to encourage their participation in the resistance movement. Zhao Wangyun's "Country Warriors" (fig. 33) and Lu Shaofei's "The Strength of the Armed People" (see fig. 21) are but two of many examples of such works.[97] Zhao's "Country Warriors," for one, no doubt sparked more recognition and excitement among peasants than Ye Qianyu's new Mr. Wang, who was now in uniform (see fig. 19). Moreover, cartoon magazines were no longer published to entertain urbanites or for artistic experimentation; they now had the clear goal of inculcating the rural masses. *National Mobilizers Pictorial* (*Guojia zongdongyuan huabao*) is a case in point. Edited by Lu Shaofei and Zhang E in Guangzhou in 1938, the magazine was carefully designed to serve as a mass propaganda tool. Huang Miaozi wrote:

> Unlike previous cartoon publications published in the cities and geared to the taste of the petty bourgeoisie and intelligentsia, this pictorial was launched to bring pictures to the masses as propaganda messages. It concerned practical topics, and its styles are both realistic and easily comprehended. And because of its unique distribution network, the whole endeavor was such a big success that it had to change from publishing every five days to every three. It circulated throughout Guangdong province and developed a cordial bond with the people. Total sales ran as high as fifty to sixty thousand copies. It was truly unprecedented![98]

Ye Qianyu summed up this important shift of cartoons thus: "During the war, . . . cartoons moved from magazines to banners and street walls, and from printings to street exhibitions."[99]

But what impact did political cartoons have on the populace? How far did they actually reach into the countryside? These questions are difficult to answer. Wartime cartoon magazines were certainly few in number (not more than a dozen) and mostly limited in circulation.[100] Many of them were also short-lived. *Resistance Cartoons*, for example, lasted only fifteen issues. The cartoon exhibitions, though enormously popular, were largely confined to interior cities like Guilin and

Changsha and their suburbs. And the small number of cartoonists involved would seem to suggest a meager impact. Yet political cartoons appeared not only in cartoon magazines, but also in profusion in newspapers and literary magazines throughout the war years; many were also widely reprinted, as in the case of Feng Zikai's depiction of a mother meeting a tragic death (see fig. 9).[101] As a visual art and through various printed media, therefore, cartoons were able to reach a wider audience than spoken dramas.

Not every cartoonist was happy treating cartoons as a propaganda art. Feng Zikai, China's foremost philosophical cartoonist of his time, was among the dissenters. Feng saw cartoons as a pure art form; but more important, his strong concern with human fate took precedence over his interest in art. He succeeded in raising his art to a level of universality and timelessness unparalleled in his generation.

War and Peace in the Cartoons of Feng Zikai

Unlike many of his fellow cartoonists, Feng Zikai viewed the War of Resistance with mixed feelings. He realized that the war was a matter of survival for his country. A nation under siege and occupation had every right to defend itself and ultimately to defeat the enemy and reestablish peace. But war inevitably led to untold human suffering and death—a direct assault on Feng's own firmly held Buddhist beliefs. His wartime cartoons vividly reveal his ambivalence: even as he appeals to his fellow countrymen to resist the enemy's aggression, at the same time he presents a powerful indictment of the senseless waste of human lives. It is not violent death and the desolation of the survivors alone that make his cartoons memorable and thought-provoking. Underneath them lie more fundamental philosophical questions: Why should there be war? Why can't humans stop killing one another? And why is there so much suffering in life?

Feng Zikai, a multitalented artist and scholar, towers above his contemporaries as a first-rate cartoonist by virtue of his imaginative power and warm touch.[102] A native of Shimenwan (Tongxiang county, Zhejiang province), Feng received his training in Japan and was well informed about both Asian and Western art. He produced some of the most influential works on art theory in China in the 1920s and 1930s.[103] His superb personal essays (*xiaopinwen*), characterized by a blending of human warmth, poetic beauty, and philosophical touches, won high praise among literary luminaries of his time.[104] Feng was also a musician, calligrapher, and religious artist. Under the influence of his famous high school mentor, the artist-turned-teacher Li Shutong (who later took the tonsure to become the monk Hongyi), Feng produced several volumes of religious cartoons entitled *Paintings on the Preservation of Life (Husheng huaji)*, dealing with the Buddhist teaching of nonkilling and releasing life.[105] Indeed, Buddhist thought is a constant undercurrent in Feng's cartoons.

Feng's numerous contributions to Chinese art notwithstanding, he is best remembered for his role in the modern Chinese cartoon movement. One of the three most influential cartoonists in the Republican era (the other two being Ye Qianyu and Zhang Guangyu), Feng almost single-handedly established cartoons as a respected art form in China. It was he who first introduced the term *manhua* from Japan in 1925; and it was he who first contributed cartoons regularly to such esteemed literary journals as *Short Story Monthly (Xiaoshuo yuebao)* and influential newspapers as Shanghai's *Shen bao*.[106] Feng, along with such men as Huang Mao and Wang Dunqing, was also one of China's few cartoon theorists. His pioneering book *Cartooning Methods (Manhua de miaofa*, 1943) outlines the technical aspects of the cartoon and provides a detailed, sophisticated theoretical justification of its importance in Chinese art.

Feng Zikai initially gained acclaim as an artist with his series of cartoons of lovable, mischievous children. Like many of his contemporaries, Feng had a rather romantic view of children.[107] He believed that a child's mind is innocent and sincere, neither constrained by worldly conventions nor driven by evil thoughts. Only children, according to Feng, seem able to comprehend the fundamental Buddhist belief that life should be filled with love and hope rather than prejudice and hypocrisy.[108] Feng spent a large part of his early career drawing children, often using his own offspring as models. His children are always innocent, happy, enchanting, and sometimes mischievous (as in "When Father Is Away," 1926).[109] Feng's drawings of children reveal the unmistakable imprint of the work of Takehisa Yumeji, a noted Japanese painter and poet known for his portrayals of children and women.[110] Like Yumeji, Feng captured charmingly both the movements and feelings of children. Also like Yumeji, he often accompanied his drawings with a song or verse, giving them a distinctly poetic flavor uncommon in his generation. Despite these influences, Feng developed a style and approach all his own by combining traditional Chinese brush strokes with contemporary social settings, often lacing them with humor and religious purport. This original look set Feng apart from such contemporaries as the political cartoonists Cai Ruohong and Te Wei, whose works are strongly reminiscent of the Western satirical caricature.

Although the cartoon is a modern urban phenomenon, Feng's early work seems curiously traditional, in mood if not in content. Steeped in classical literature, he had a predilection for adorning cartoons with famous poems from the Tang and Song dynasties. Consider, for example, his collection *Old Poems in New Paintings* (*Gushi xinhua*).[111] Using a traditional brush and modern cartoon techniques, Feng painted a series of smooth, lyrical pieces, but ones that often convey a melancholic, pathetic mood. Thus "How Wonderful Is the Setting Sun" (fig. 34, from the poem "Mounting Leyouyuan" ["Deng Leyouyuan"] by Li Shangyin of the Tang) is tinged with a sadness at the passing of time, underscoring the Buddhist notion that impermanence is the inexorable law of all existence. Far from being satirical and entertaining—two characteristics of many modern-day cartoons —Feng's works were often thought-provoking and illuminating. His philosophical touch elevated his cartoons to a religious level unique in his generation.

Feng Zikai was no traditionalist, however. He was inspired more by the mood and rich symbolism of classical poetry than by its outmoded ideas or its strict rules of prosody. Feng's artistic outlook was thoroughly modern, inspired by direct observation of the world around him. "My drawings are closely related to my life," he once said. "As in the keeping of accounts, I record only what I feel in my daily life."[112] Feng was also highly critical of traditional-style painters for painting only "recluses and ancient beauties" but not "workers and rickshaw men."[113] True to his words, Feng himself focused on the people he saw and met in the streets and on events happening around him, portraying a kaleidoscope of activities in Chinese society, both urban and rural. His cartoons, as he put it, are like being on a train, for they detail the myriad events that unfold in "compartment society."[114]

Unlike Cai Ruohong or Hu Kao, Feng Zikai was neither a satirist nor an activist who wished to use his cartoons to foster social change. His prewar work had been largely apolitical: he merely recorded what he saw and heard in his life, painting with a gentle, sympathetic touch. The Buddhist ideas of nonaggression and withdrawal that appear in his work also made him seem more like an aloof observer than an active participant. This attitude did not sit well with activists who believed that artists should take a positive, involved role in reforming society and focusing readers' attention on current political problems,

Fig. 34.   Feng Zikai, "How Wonderful Is the Setting Sun."
From Feng, *Gushi xinhua* (N.p.: Kaiming shudian, 1945), p. 68.

especially at a time of potential outside aggression. For some critics, Feng's subjects were "far removed from China's reality," failing to inform the public about the seriousness of the national crisis.[115] Feng's style, Huang Mao complained, exhibited a detached, elegant mood totally divorced from real life.[116]

The war, however, changed Feng's attitude toward art profoundly. He quickly became active in the resistance movement and began to draw patriotic cartoons, using them to arouse nationalistic passion; yet remarkably, his faith in humanity did not waver—indeed, it may have been strengthened by adversity.

In late November 1937, after his hometown, Shimenwan, had been attacked in Japanese air raids, Feng and his family fled into the interior, starting a long and painful ordeal as refugees. Following brief sojourns in places like Guilin, Liangjiang, and Zunyi and enduring all kinds of hardships, the family finally settled in Chongqing, where they stayed until the end of the war. Feng was never a detached loner; he was foremost a family man, pleased when his children surrounded him and when his wife greeted him at the door as he returned from work. But the war uprooted his family and brought ruin and destruction to his country, causing him to change his artistic focus dramatically. Even before the war erupted, Feng saw the impending catastrophe. Before he fled his hometown, appalled by the rapidly spreading chaos, he decided to recount the turmoil and misery in a series of drawings to be entitled *Cartoons on Japan's Invasion of China* (*Manhua Riben qin Hua shi*). Japanese air raids, however, aborted his plan. As the war dragged on, he became more involved. In March 1938 he added his name to the newly founded All-China Resistance Association of Writers and Artists and joined the editorial board of *Resistance Literature and Art* (*Kangzhan wenyi*), the official publication of the association. His drawings on war began to appear widely not only in that journal, but also in various magazines and newspapers, condemning Japanese brutality in China.

There is no question that Feng Zikai was bitter about the war. "For eight years," he wrote in 1947, "I have been wandering constantly on the road in Guizhou, Guangxi, Sichuan, and Shaanxi provinces. As I gaze into the distance in the direction of Jiangnan, I am truly heartbroken. I pray to heaven, wishing that China can turn defeat into victory."[117] His family was uprooted, his livelihood threatened, and his beloved Yuanyuan Studio, where he drew his cartoons and stored his precious books and other mementos, including the monk Hongyi's calligraphy, burned down. In a moving article called "Commemorating the Spirit of the Yuanyuan Studio," Feng poured out his anger against the enemy.[118] Feng Zikai now argued that some things were more important than life itself, "not to become a conquered people" being one of them.[119] Although the Chinese people had long been accused of behaving like "a heap of loose sand," lacking the necessary unity to resist outside aggression, Feng contended that the War of Resistance was like a sandbag that bound together all Chinese.[120] As an artist, Feng now believed that art could and should play a major role in saving China.[121] When the survival of a nation is at stake, Feng repeatedly argued, every citizen should heed the call to fight—an attitude that won Feng praise within the literary circle.[122]

On the surface, Feng Zikai's wartime cartoons resembled the work of many of his contemporaries. Determined to record the bestialities of aggression and the ensuing human suffering, he portrayed Japanese brutality (see figs. 9, 11), ridiculed traitors, depicted soldiers leaving for the front, showed the ruins of war, and demonstrated the people's determination to defend their nation.[123] In his wartime cartoons, even the innocence of his beloved children had disappeared. Like adults, children are now painted as patriotic and strong-willed in their desire to help defend the country, donating money to the war cause (fig. 35), forming the "Youth National Salvation Army,"[124] and writing patriotic slogans even in occupied territory.[125] Feng's children have "grown up"; they live in a cruel world where killing is common and where survival depends solely on one's determination to fight back. Children are not ill-natured nor aggressive; they are simply self-defensive.

Feng Zikai also had a knack for using symbols in his works. He could create powerful images with a few deft lines, skillfully summing up a complicated situation. Two cats playing havoc with objects on top of a desk implies Japan's repeated tramplings on China's culture.[126] The notion of giving one's life for one's country is symbolized with blood and flowers: "From the Pool of Blood Grows the Flower of Freedom,"[127] and "Let the Blood of the Martyrs Nourish the Flower of Freedom" (fig. 36). The images are familiar and the message simple: without sacrifice there can be no liberation. Feng was confident that his country would eventually prevail. China was like a tall tree, Feng wrote; although it had been chopped down by the enemy, when the spring came, new buds would emerge (fig. 37). A tall tree was an important sign of hope and vitality. "It symbolizes today's China as a single entity," and with constant rejuvenating efforts China would become an even stronger country.[128]

The difference in tone and mood between his prewar drawings and his wartime cartoons is striking. Unlike his lyrical and graceful pieces of the early 1930s, many of which praised common and modest things, Feng's later cartoons were highly passionate and permeated with strong nationalist sentiment as he urged his compatriots to rally behind the government. Feng became an ardent patriot who believed that the best way he could contribute to the war effort was by drawing cartoons and recording faithfully the scenes of destruction and atrocity caused by invading troops.

今朝不喫糖將錢去救國
雖只一分錢多少有補益

Fig. 35. Feng Zikai: "Today I am not going to have any candy, / The money will be donated to our government. / Although it is a small sum, / Every bit will certainly help." The collection box is labeled "National Salvation Fund." From Feng, *Zhandi manhua* (Hong Kong: Yingshang buliedian tushu gongsi, 1939), n.p.

灑將忠烈血，栽培自由花。

Fig. 36. Feng Zikai: "Let the Blood of the Martyrs Nourish the Flower of Freedom." The vase is labeled "Freedom," and the watering can, "Martyr." From Feng, *Zhandi manhua*, n.p.

大
樹
被
斬
伐
生
機
並
不
絕

春
來
怒
抽
條
氣
象
何
蓬
勃

Fig. 37. Feng Zikai: "A tree has been chopped down, / But its instinct for life never dies. / When spring comes again, / It will grow and thrive." From Feng, *Zhandi manhua*, n.p.

Yet despite his numerous patriotic pieces, Feng Zikai was never fully comfortable with what he had painted. To Feng, wartime cartoons were mostly expedient tools of propaganda; they could hardly be described as genuine art. When the war broke out, some suggested that he should burn his *Paintings on the Preservation of Life* because of the book's theme. Feng retorted:

The purpose of *Paintings on the Preservation of Life* is to admonish people to treasure their lives and to refrain from killing so that we can cultivate benevolence and love and promote peace. . . . When I ask an urchin not to trample on ants, it is not because I cherish ants, or because I want to provide food to sustain them; it is because I am afraid that this little cruelty [if it remains unchecked] will turn into aggression in the future, using planes to carry heavy bombs to kill innocent people.[129]

Feng Zikai divided cartoons into three categories: reflective, satirical, and propaganda. The first are cartoons that come from the artist's heart. Unlike satirical cartoons, they are not intended to criticize or express an opinion, and unlike propaganda cartoons, they are not calculated to attain results. They are painted to touch a common chord between artist and reader. A good example, according to Feng Zikai, is his "The Instinct for Life" (fig. 38), which depicts a sprout struggling to survive on a brick wall. The ability of a sprout to survive against all odds is, in Feng's words, "an astounding phenomenon."[130] A reflective cartoon, according to Feng, can only be appreciated by a genuinely thoughtful mind. "It is the most artistic type of all cartoons."[131]

In contrast to reflective cartoons, satirical cartoons are designed to raise criticisms against unreasonable social phenomena. They do not point out problems directly; instead, they often resort to analogy. Finally we come to propaganda cartoons, which are used to instigate action. This type of cartoon, according to Feng, thrives in a conflict-ridden society. However, Feng warned,

> conflicts are an abnormality of human society. It is not its normal state. The basic ideals and intentions of human beings are for peace and happiness, living harmoniously together. Who would like to live in a world full of conflicts? But when others invade us, I have no choice but to resist and to fight to end the conflict. This is using struggles to end struggles. . . . It is therefore clear that conflicts are the abnormality of human life, just like propaganda cartoons are the abnormality of the cartoon; . . . we must be fully aware that they are not the essence of the cartoon. The essence of the cartoon is art.[132]

Feng was preoccupied with the irreconcilability of art and propaganda throughout the war. Intellectually, he was reluctant to create propaganda cartoons; but emotionally he realized that they were effective in galvanizing the people's support for the government. If conflict was inevitable and defensive measures were needed, Feng wanted to remind his readers: "We are using killings to end killings, and using benevolence to overcome cruelty."[133] The subject of most concern to Feng was not the war, however much it occupied his mind, but the human suffering associated with manmade destruction. This reflective mood sets him apart from his contemporary cartoonists, including Ye Qianyu and Cai Ruohong.

Feng's distinct humanistic style won him wide respect and enormous popularity during the war. His work appeared regularly in major journals, including *Cosmic Wind* and *Resistance Literature and Art*; his exhibitions were received with enthusiasm, winning him new fans and providing him with income to support his family during those difficult war years.[134] His cartoons were also widely reprinted, including some that, to the artist's chagrin, were reissued for profit without his permission. One such collection of twenty-five drawings was *Battlefield Cartoons* (*Zhandi manhua*), published in Hong Kong in 1939.[135]

Feng Zikai did not join the Cartoon Propaganda Team. In fact, there is little evidence to suggest that he maintained any contact with the group. He was first and foremost a devoted family man. When his family was uprooted by the war, he felt a strong responsibility to bring all of them to safety; this is seen in many of his wartime writings, such as *A Teacher's Diary* (*Jiaoshi riji*), which he wrote in 1938 while seeking refuge in Guilin. When war broke out in 1937 he was almost forty, well established in his field, and much older than many other cartoonists (Ye Qianyu was thirty and Hu Kao only twenty-five). It would have been difficult both emotionally and physically for him to join the team. Moreover, Feng frankly admitted that he was not a sociable type.[136] He abhorred the idea of serving in the government, preferring instead to live a simple life like that of Tao Yuanming (365–427), the famous Jin dynasty recluse who resigned from the government to return to his village so that he could be in close touch with nature.[137]

Because of his fundamental aversion to conflict and his dislike of propaganda art, Feng Zikai might not even rate his own wartime cartoons highly, at least as art. Compared to his prewar works, it is true, many of his wartime cartoons were artistically crude. But it would be a mistake to overlook their philosophical value. W. A. Coupe argues that a cartoonist is concerned primarily with the creation and manipulation of public opinion;[138] yet Feng Zikai's works, even those that qualify as propaganda, tend to be highly personal. They are thoughtful statements suggesting deep truths about human existence. Appalled by the sheer magnitude of the tragedy China was experiencing, Feng

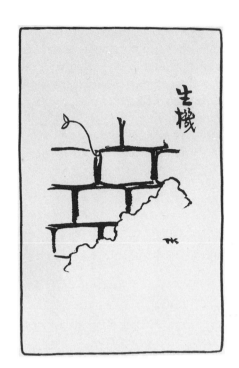

Fig. 38.   Feng Zikai, "The Instinct for Life." From Feng, *Husheng huaji* (reprinted Taibei: Chunwenxue chubanshe, 1981), 1:50.

Fig. 39.   Feng Zikai, "War and Music." (The date "1925" in the cartoon is incorrect. This is one of the sixty-four drawings printed in Feng's *Zhanshi xiang*, all of which, according to Feng, were "drawn during the war when I was a refugee." See Feng, *Zhanshi xiang*, preface, p. 2.) From Feng, *Zhanshi xiang*, p. 18.

Fig. 40. Feng Zikai: "I want to become an angel, / Soaring high in the sky, / Following the enemy planes, / And grabbing their bombs." From *Jianwen* 1 (1 August 1938): 2.

Fig. 41. Feng Zikai: "In this world, / I hope there will be no more war. / Weapons turn into ploughs, / And bombshells can be flower vases." From Feng, *Zhandi manhua*, n.p.

sought constantly for an answer to humanity's infinite capacity for blunder and aggression. Perhaps more than any of his fellow cartoonists, he imparts to his wartime work a powerful conviction that mutual hostility must cease, simply because it is against basic human nature. Feng's wartime cartoons are thus not merely extraordinary pictorial documents of their time, epitomizing all the savagery of a bitter conflict; more important, they are condemnations of war as an irremediable crime against humanity.

This forceful humanistic current provides a unified framework for all his work, prewar and wartime alike. In sharp contrast to Goya's graphic scenes of torture and violence in *The Disasters of War*, Feng's wartime cartoons, with but few exceptions, do not show the ferociousness of Japanese brutality directly; rather, their barbaric acts tend to be implied.[139] Perhaps by focusing on the consequences of Japanese actions rather than on the deeds themselves he made the people's ordeal even more painful and unforgettable. Interestingly enough, while most of his fellow cartoonists concentrated on the grisly aspects of the calamity, Feng attempted to show that there was a *humane* side to this tragedy as well. A soldier, putting aside his rifle, picks up a musical instrument and plays, enjoying temporary peace of mind in the midst of a bitter war (fig. 39). To Feng Zikai, these peaceful activities were far more meaningful than the battle itself. By emphasizing culture over bloodshed, music over war, he communicated through his drawings a unique sense of peace and tranquillity.

Feng would never have agreed with Gibbon's dictum that history is "little more than the register of the crimes, follies, and misfortunes of mankind." For Feng, history was an unending search for the meaning of life and peace, and his wartime cartoons represent that search in a chaotic world. A major theme in his work is the contrast between war and peace: one is destruction, the other prosperity; one causes death, the other celebrates life; one is ugliness, the other beauty. The juxtaposition of guns and music is not to promote war but to elicit peace. Feng argued that unlike an aggressive war, the War of Resistance was fought for neither power nor glory, but simply to repel the enemy and to end all conflicts. He wrote: "In this war, our mission is not only to repel the invasion and to subdue the enemy, but also to spread justice all over the world, to arouse those who love peace and support humanity. Together we will eradicate ruthlessness, inhuman devils, and establish a foundation of everlasting peace and happiness for all mankind."[140]

Fig. 42.   Feng Zikai, "War and Flower." From Feng, *Manhua de miaofa* (Shanghai: Kaiming shudian, 1948), p. 21.

Feng frequently envisions a world of peace, and he presents his hope earnestly in his works. In Feng's ideal world, angels will stop deadly bombs from falling on civilians (fig. 40) and artillery shells will be used not as implements of war but as flower vases (fig. 41)— echoing Isaiah's hope that warriors would "beat their swords into plowshares, and their spears into pruning-hooks." Feng's peace cartoons may be simple, but their message is profound and sincere.

Behind Feng's quest for peace lies a deep philosophical and religious outlook that emphasizes the sanctity of life. His works, in the end, were motivated more by moral than by artistic concerns. Cartoons to him were not merely a sincere art form; they were an effective means of affirming life. Thus one sees an unflagging optimism permeating his work. This unique attitude toward art makes him one of the most original and philosophical cartoonists of his time. "The Instinct for Life" tells us that every creature in the world, no matter how small, will fight for its existence. Life is indomitable. Perhaps nowhere is the struggle between life and death more evident than in "War and Flower" (fig. 42), in which a soldier gazes at a flower he has picked at the battlefront. This picture, Feng said, "reveals a major contradiction in life: the contrast between war and the flower demonstrates the mighty contention between ugliness and beauty, cruelty and peace, death and life, and human affairs and heaven's will."[141] Feng was optimistic about the outcome, however. China would prevail in the war, just as the mutilated tree would survive and thrive when spring came. It was not victory on the battlefield but the instinct for life that held the promise of the future. As Feng wrote, "In this world, we might suffer natural disaster and manmade calamity, or experience temporary setbacks, but if the instinct for life has not been extinguished, then someday things will take a turn for the better."[142]

4   Newspapers

Like spoken dramas and cartoons, newspapers were turned into a propaganda and educational tool during the war. The journalist Cheng Shewo (1898–1991) described the power of the press vividly in his influential article "'Paper Bullets' Can Also Annihilate the Enemy" published in 1938. It would be a grave mistake, Cheng wrote, to belittle the influence of the press, for it was a weapon that could stir up national consciousness and wage political war against the invaders. Like bullets, newspapers "killed," Cheng claimed.[1] If spoken dramas created heroic symbols of resistance, and cartoons conjured up terrifying images of war, then newspapers waged a different kind of battle against the Japanese: a battle of words.

It was during the War of Resistance that China saw its first generation of war correspondents (*zhandi jizhe*) come of age. Notable names include Fan Changjiang, Qiujiang (Meng Qiujiang, 1910–1967), Xu Ying (1912–), and his wife Zigang (Peng Zigang, 1914–1988), all of *Dagong bao*; Lu Yi (1911–), of the *The New China Daily* (*Xinhua ribao*); Cao Juren, of the Central News Agency (Zongyang tongxun-she); and Huang Zhenxia, of the *Great Evening News* (*Dawan bao*), to mention just a few.[2] Together they represented a new type of correspondent who challenged traditional journalistic practices, redefined the role of a reporter, created a new language, and, most important, like dramatists and cartoonists, attempted to reach a wide audience. Because of the enormous influence of the press during the war, war correspondents were some of the most important shapers of modern Chinese history.

Wartime Dispatches

The idea of frontline reporting did not come to China from the West. William Howard Russell of the London *Times*, whose coverage of the Crimean War marked the beginnings of war reportage in Europe, was an unknown name in China. So were other celebrated Western correspondents such as James Creelman of the *New York Journal*, who reported the Japanese massacre at Port Arthur during the Russo-Japanese War, and Herbert Matthews of the *New York Times*, who covered the Abyssinian War. Chinese war correspondents like Fan Changjiang and Lu Yi (fig. 43) were homegrown and products of their time. After the incident of 28 January 1932, when Japanese troops attacked Shanghai to divert international attention from their aggression in Manchuria, Lu Yi, then a young reporter for Shanghai's *Xinwen bao*, was in fact one of the first correspondents to head for the battle zones. He volunteered to go to Zhabei the next day to gather news, thus beginning a distinguished career as one of China's best war correspondents.[3]

The ensuing conflict with Japan awakened a voracious appetite for information. As public demand for stories about the war grew, newspapers such as *Dagong bao* and *Shen bao* began to send their own men and women to the front. The Battle of Taierzhuang in April 1938, for example, drew an unprecedented twenty war correspondents.[4] Unlike old-style reporters, they were young (90 percent were under thirty years of age)[5] and daring, with great curiosity and a keen sense of adventure. The new assignment allowed them to watch the military drama at first hand and demanded that they report what really happened with directness and urgency. Suddenly, through the printed page, distant battles in strange places seemed to unfold before one's eyes, as if the thunder of cannons was nearby. War correspondents sent home thrilling accounts of skirmishes and moving stories of bravery—as George Mosse puts it, they were "domesticating the war experience."[6] At the same time, they delivered the hometown news to the front,[7] thus narrowing the physical as well as the emotional gap between the two worlds. The power of the "paper bullet" was now beyond doubt. Indeed, coverage of the Japanese invasion by China's war correspondents was the best and fullest in the history of Chinese journalism. As the circulation of newspapers (especially local newspapers) soared during the war,[8] well-known war correspondents became a selling point for newspapers, and their new style and vivid stories captivated millions of readers. So popular did the war news be-

Fig. 43. Fan Changjiang (front row, far right) and Lu Yi (front row, second from right) visited the front in Ruichang, Jiangxi province, in September 1938. Courtesy of Lu Yi.

come, in fact, that even respected literary journals like *Cosmic Wind* began to solicit frontline reports from its readers.[9]

Wartime reporting, however, was a difficult and perilous assignment, requiring physical stamina as well as mental readiness. A good war correspondent, said Liu Zhuzhou, "must have the ability to endure every conceivable kind of exhaustion and pain."[10] Physical exhaustion was nothing, however, compared to the enormous danger war correspondents faced. Frontline reporting was an endeavor that required reporters to be ever ready to lay their lives on the line. In his *The Struggle of Shanghai's Journalists*, Zhao Junhao gave frightening accounts of how reporters in occupied Shanghai were gunned down by the Japanese and by Wang Jingwei's secret agents.[11] The fortunes of war did not always smile on those correspondents who ventured to the battleground.

Like cartoons, wartime dispatches focused on several themes: the brutality of the Japanese, the heroism of Chinese troops, the endless lines of refugees, and the importance of grass-roots support. Unlike cartoons, wartime dispatches were mostly eyewitness accounts written in a concise narrative format. They unfolded the drama sequentially, often providing a sense of coherence and completeness. While cartoons sought to create a certain immediacy, wartime dispatches strove for a more lingering effect. In "The City of Hanyang in Flames," written in the summer of 1938, Zigang of *Dagong bao* depicted this gruesome picture after a Japanese air raid:

> No sooner was the siren turned off than the Wangjiaxiang Dock was packed with people who wanted to board the ferry [and leave]. We all knew that the city of Hanyang was bombed. It was a scorching day, people were sweating and feeling heavy at heart. . . .
>
> Passengers on board the ferry were anxious to reach the other shore of Turtle Hill. Black clouds mingled with smoke billowing from below and drifted away, as if devils had darkened the city with poisonous black powder.
>
> "Nanzheng Street was hit," someone wailed. Those who had just returned from the bombed area were awash with grief and could not utter a word.
>
> People streamed in and out of narrow Nanzheng Street. As in a funeral procession, many burst into tears. . . .
>
> The section of Kuixin Lane from No. 23 to No. 36 was totally demolished by bombs. This was what the Japanese did best: in the twinkling of an eye, houses and lives were reduced to nothing. In many instances the entire family was lost, so no relatives remained to mourn the dead. Rescuers had no choice but to put their house number plate atop their coffins to identify the victims. A certain Yang Xindan, who was both the leader of the street section and a rescuer himself, was killed. His mother, dumbstruck, used a fan to cool off the body, which lay quietly on a bamboo bed, as if he could still feel the heat. . . .
>
> A section of houses near the bank of the river was leveled. I was told that there were many people gathered at the ferry. [Then suddenly] bombs and machine-gun fire rained down from above, killing almost one hundred people both on the dock and aboard the ferry . . .
>
> Wuchang and Hanyang added eight hundred new ghosts. They died with an intense grudge.
>
> To avenge the deaths of many who were killed during the Japanese invasion of Wuhan, we must unite to defend the city.[12]

Such accounts were common in wartime reportage, the images of Japanese atrocities familiar. But instead of relying on pictures, the dispatch gave a concrete account of the destruction left in the wake of a

Japanese air raid. Zigang, one of the few female reporters during the war (the other notable women were Yang Gang [1905–1957] and Pu Xixiu [1910–1970]) was known for her candid reports and moving stories of human suffering, mostly in the interior.

Wartime dispatches were full of reports of Chinese dignity and heroism in which, predictably, men in uniform figured prominently. Generals and commanders were portrayed as calm, determined, and professional men who marched to the front in high spirits and performed their duty with extraordinary skill and courage. Most important, they exuded confidence and optimism at a time when confusion and uncertainty reigned. Such enthusiastic descriptions of Chinese commanders were common in the early days of the war, for they served an important propaganda purpose. Consider this account by Cao Juren, a reporter for the Central News Agency:

> In a very relaxed atmosphere, I met a few commanders [at the front]. They gathered around a table and looked at the maps. As though playing chess, they calmly discussed various plans of operation. I had not seen Commander A for a few months; he looked a bit tired from campaigning. He gave me a very satisfactory answer [about the future of the war] by firmly stating, "Only one word: fight!"
>
> [Suddenly] we heard artillery and the roar of guns outside; the situation must have become tense at the front. Commander A left in a hurry. . . . I told the deputy commander and the chief of staff that over one hundred thousand refugees in Shanghai were standing in the pouring rain anxiously waiting for the news of victory to arrive. . . . The deputy commander replied with a slow but sure voice: "War is certainly not a fashionable thing. . . . What we know is that we will fight. The War of Resistance is a struggle to save our nation. We will wage total resistance against the enemy. To score a final victory, we must be patient." . . . The commanders wanted us to relay these messages to the people, so that they could take realistic measures to work for the cause of the resistance. [Indeed,] we civilians must have patience!
>
> The men in uniform take only concrete steps. They think only of practical issues.[13]

If commanders appeared to be cool-headed and full of confidence in mapping out strategies, they were also courageous and selfless on the battlefield. Fan Changjiang of *Dagong bao* described the bravery of Chinese soldiers in an early battle during the Japanese advance southward from Beijing in 1938:

In a small village about one or two miles from the Little Bengbu, we [reporters] met Brigade Commander Dou and Regiment Commander Liang. . . . On the 8th [of February], when enemy troops overran Little Bengbu, over half a battalion of Liang's regiment was lost. When Commander Dou and his men mounted a counterattack, the enemy across on the southern bank of the Huai River detected them and started to bombard them with artillery. Dou was forced to lie down in the mud. Seven or eight of his men were either wounded or killed. When we met him on the night of the 9th, the mud on his clothes and shoes was still there. Dou, Liang, and their troops had no food for two days and nights, not to mention sleep. . . . One company commander and his men had twice engaged in hand-to-hand combat with the enemy. They annihilated all the Japanese at the end. [I was told that] some soldiers' bellies were ripped open by the enemy's bayonets, and sections of their intestines oozed out. The soldiers pushed them back into their abdomens and smiled contentedly at the enemy's bodies lying along the banks of the Huai River. . . .

The Chinese soldiers hated the Japanese army bitterly. [Near Linhuaiguan,] once three Japanese soldiers were chasing after seven Chinese women on the south bank of the Huai River. Our soldiers on the north bank tried desperately to find a way to rescue them, but to no avail. They finally took aim and shot and killed those three animals. According to a fifty-year-old woman, she had already been repeatedly raped. . . . [14]

The victory, however, turned out to be short-lived—the Japanese were soon reinforced and in a few days overran the Chinese army. Fan's vivid accounts nonetheless presented a moving story of the bravery of the Chinese soldiers.

Fan Changjiang and the Rhetoric of War

Among a host of war reporters, Fan Changjiang, already well known even before the outbreak of the war, was a particularly dominant presence. In 1936, Fan published *The Northwest Corner of China* (*Zhongguo de xibei jiao*), a collection of articles written in 1935 and 1936 when Fan was traveling in the relatively unknown territories of the northwest as a roving reporter for the famous Tianjin newspaper *Dagong bao*. This was a time when Japan was intensifying its penetration into Inner Mongolia. Fan, distressed by the political unrest at home and concerned over Japanese aggression in the north, decided to investigate the situation firsthand.[15] He began his long and hazardous journey in Chengdu, Sichuan province, and over the next ten months he traveled extensively across Gansu, Ningxia, and Inner Mongolia. Meandering through the shifting sands of the northern desert and scaling the forbidding peaks of the Qilian Mountains, Fan visited remote border regions and sent back sensational reports about the life and customs of the frontier people, the grim reality of political and economic chaos, and racial inequality in China, especially the GMD government's discriminatory policies regarding minority nationalities—ominous signs, Fan warned, of a brewing social and political crisis.

Published when Fan was twenty-seven, this landmark book signaled the rise of the journalist as a social critic and the emergence of a new, witty, personal style in Chinese journalism. It became an instant bestseller, reaching its eighth printing and selling thousands of copies within just a few months.[16] The book's popularity and authority quickly established Fan Changjiang as one of the most influential journalists of his time.[17] To be sure, Fan's book was not the only one about the border regions to appear in the 1930s.[18] Yet his book was definitely the most original as well as the most compelling. Its lucid style, its exotic contents, its firsthand reports, and its fervent plea for a solution to the worsening nationality problem all combined to make *The Northwest Corner of China* a tour de force in journalistic writing.

Although Fan Changjiang's early work made him widely known as a brilliant reporter, it was his frontline dispatches during the early phase of the War of Resistance that earned him an international reputation as "China's most famous war correspondent."[19] In 1936 and 1937 he was sent by *Dagong bao* to cover the fighting between Prince De, who led a combined Manchukuo-Mongol force in rebellion, and the Nationalist government. He was the first reporter to enter Xi'an in early February 1937 after the historic Xi'an Incident, and that same month he was the first Chinese reporter from outside to visit Yan'an. He described vividly his night-long interview with Mao Zedong in his celebrated piece "A Trip to Northern Shaanxi."[20] All these sensational reports subsequently appeared in another best-selling book, *Journeys on the Frontier (Saishang xing)*, published in 1937.

In July 1937 Fan was sent to report on the Marco Polo Bridge Incident. The next month he covered the fall of Beijing and the fierce fighting at the Nankou Pass in central Hebei. And in early 1938 he covered the bloody battles of Taierzhuang and Xuzhou. From the battlefields, Fan sent back eyewitness reports that won him a devoted audience, the praise of his colleagues, and the enmity of the government, for Fan did not hesitate to report on the incompetence and corruption within the Guomindang army. Many of his wartime columns subsequently appeared in book form: *Battles on the Western Front* (*Xixian fengyun*, November 1937), *The Fall of Beiping and Tianjin* (*Lunwang de Ping-Jin*, January 1938), and *From the Marco Polo Bridge to Zhang River* (*Cong Lugouqiao dao Zhanghe*, September 1938), to name but a few.[21] All were extremely popular during the war.

In reportage about the fighting between the Chinese and Japanese, dramatic and tragic stories abounded. Many correspondents risked and lost their lives, and others established their reputations, filing numerous excellent pieces.[22] Qiujiang's "Outflanking the Enemy at the Nankou Pass," for example, easily ranks as one of the best stories to come out of wartime China.[23] Nevertheless, Fan Changjiang was unique among his contemporaries in his grasp of background information and above all in his incisive, insightful commentary.[24] Perhaps more than any other reporter, he provided an intimate look at the war; as one colleague put it, Fan "creat[ed] a sensation throughout the country."[25]

Fan often filed dispatches describing emotional victories, but he was noted for bringing home the cruel images of the war and stories of common soldiers struggling to survive on the battlefield. Indeed, Fan Changjiang was at his best when depicting the human agony of the war:

> Recently, Japanese planes have flown over Baoding almost every day. They have machine-gunned people down below, wounding many. Only those barbaric Japanese soldiers would not hesitate to shoot at unarmed, innocent civilians. . . . To avoid mass slaughter, the only outlet for the defenseless people has been to flee. As a result, trains leaving Baoding for the south have been jammed with people, especially women and children. . . . Their peaceful life disrupted, they had to be parted amid much sadness. On the train I saw a middle-aged Cantonese woman who was sobbing as she bade farewell to her husband. Her two girls and a boy were also in tears, incessantly calling out for their father. Outside the train window was a middle-aged man and a young fellow who looked like his oldest son, gazing morosely at their loved ones. The train started to move, the crying inside and outside the train became more intense and bitter. The men ran after the train, waving. Not until those outside the train could no longer be seen did the mother turn and start to comfort her three children.[26]

The war with Japan left a lasting impression on those who reported it. Three themes kept reemerging in Fan's and other war correspondents' dispatches: the brutality of the Japanese, the omnipresence of Chinese collaborators,[27] and the endless suffering of refugees. Even more tragic than the indiscriminate killing of civilians, burnings, bombings, and rapes by the Japanese, Fan Changjiang wrote, was the number of collaborators abetting the enemy in these crimes. Yet always, the sorrowful scene of refugees was the most telling reminder of the terror of the war. A sudden increase of beggars, Fan observed, could be interpreted as signaling the worsening picture at the front.[28]

Yet the war, brutal and inhuman as it was, had its occasional uplifting moments. Fan captured one such scene:

> On the morning of 31 January [1938], the train moved slowly into Xuchang station [Henan province]. In a third-class car were two elderly waiters engaged in heated discussion about the future of the war. The bald-headed fellow, speaking in pure Beiping accent, insisted that he would soon be able to return to Beiping. According to him, the war had finally eliminated regionalism [in China], and everyone was now willing to unite under the banner of the central government—a truly unprecedented phenomenon! "China is a big country," he said. "If everyone can join together, our strength will be awesome!" He went on to make a witty remark: "In fighting against the Japanese, we must not score a quick victory. Doing so would have two serious consequences. First, China will not have enough time to undergo thorough reconstruction, and then more troubles lie ahead. Second, the best strategy against the Japanese is 'wearing them down' [*hao*]. Without completely wearing them down, our victory cannot be considered final. Japan is like a candle: the longer we wait, the more damage [we can inflict on them]. This is because in wartime, Japan's industry and commerce cannot operate normally. For a country like Japan, which relies so much on industry and commerce [to survive], how can they withstand 'wearing down'? As for us Chinese, we can rely on farming. No matter how much land is occupied [by the enemy] and how many battles we lose, we can still survive. Based on this general principle, Japan will be defeated!" Everyone listened with rapt attention. To show his respect [for the speaker], one passenger even went over to pour him a cup of tea.[29]

The narrative is simple and moving. It portrays vividly the common people's confidence in the positive outcome of the war. Yet it is hardly an objective style. Like Zigang and Cao Juren, Fan wrote as a patriot who hated the Japanese invaders and sought to rally the people for resistance.

If cartoons used forceful images to convey patriotic messages, wartime dispatches utilized a vivid and emotional vocabulary to report on the armed conflict and to recount legends of heroism on the battlefield (such as stories of Commander Yao Ziqing and Airman Yan Haiwen, both killed in the early phase of the war). Here words were more than just a form of communication: they were weapons of politics. Carefully chosen expressions in combination with facts could turn tired propaganda slogans into poignant exhortations or painful reminders of the country's collective fate. This new style of reporting that came to life during the Sino-Japanese War had an internal textual unity based on a simple reality: China's future was at stake. Covering an array of events—scenes of combat, victory, retreat, and so on—the frontline reports were unabashedly patriotic. They were also gripping as historical reports and on occasion attained distinction as excellent literary prose, presenting a refreshing contrast to the stereotypical and platitudinous writing of the past.

In general, Chinese war correspondents told simple but uplifting stories, preferring to speak concretely about what really happened at the front. Whenever possible, names of victims were given (as in Zigang's piece) to elicit readers' empathy. Yet this down-to-earth approach did not preclude the frequent use of high-sounding slogans and phrases to make a passionate appeal. To reporters, the War of Resistance was more than a contest of weaponry: it was a battle of different ideals, a confrontation between the forces of order and of evil. The war therefore had to be addressed at a high moral level if the complete picture was to be gained.

Realizing the power of words to arouse people, war correspondents created a host of new words and descriptions that served as political weapons. Theirs was a language of combat, a charged rhetoric intended to heighten the Chinese people's sensitivity to the unfolding crisis. This new political language was more than just a reflection of the realities of war or a departure from the past; it also went beyond the Durkheimian notion that language is a carrier of cultural integration. Rather, it was "an instrument of political and social change"[30] and a means for political integration, a tool that was used to shape public opinion in a time of national crisis.

Fan Changjiang belonged to a new generation of reporters who were dissatisfied not only with traditional journalistic practices but also with the traditional use of language. In their view, most reports in the established press were stilted and dull. The traditional journalistic language was often too sophisticated for common people to understand. It showed little variation of vocabulary, syntax, and style, and its descriptions of battle were monotonous and uninspiring, devoid of human sensitivities. Worse still, it could not adapt quickly to the changing demands and responses of audiences. As a result, Chinese newspapers were riddled with what the young journalists called "eight-legged news essays" (*xinwen bagu*)[31]—in which clichés such as "the ultimate victory belongs to us" and "our troops scored a resounding triumph" were repeated ad nauseam—which could render the newspaper unreadable, thus destroying its value as a vehicle of communication.[32] Thus the new generation of reporters aspired to create a language that would speak to the masses and to intellectuals alike, a common tongue that could unite a country divided by regional and cultural differences. The trend was away from elegant prose and toward facts and figures, but with a personal touch. An excellent reporter, these reformers argued, should captivate readers both with his or her knowledge and with exciting, well-written stories. Fan's book *The Northwest Corner of China* and his wartime dispatches were models to be emulated. His delivery, paired with imaginative titles such as "Mourning Datong" and "Recalling the Battlefield at Night," evoked both anger and sadness among his readers and won him quite a few followers. Pieces by Qiujiang like "Outflanking the Enemy at the Nankou Pass" and "Lament for Zhangjiakou" bore the unmistakable imprint of Fan.[33]

The wartime political vocabulary comprised a small number of emotionally charged and timely words and phrases. This was a new journalistic language that bore little resemblance to that of the past. Its effectiveness depended on a vivid use of metaphors and the ability to render complicated national issues in simple and memorable terminology. Chinese journalists took advantage of popular sayings of the time, and they often embellished their rhetoric with familiar military imagery. The channeling of news to the frontline was itself compared to a military campaign. The journalist Gao Tian (1917–), for instance, called on reporters to establish "cultural war stations" (*wenhua bingzhan*) to communicate vital information to the soldiers at the front and launch what he called "a total cultural attack against the enemy."[34] Putting this idea into practice, in 1938 the Chinese Young Journalists Society established a "Battlefront Newspaper Supply Team" (Zhandi baozhi gongyingdui), which brought newspapers and magazines to the front. This "spiritual supply line" (*jingshen bujixian*), as Gao Tian called it, created a unique bond between soldiers at the front and the people at home.

Others stated, "Wartime journalists must not 'fight in isolation' [*gujun zuozhan*]."[35] The importance of unity was repeatedly stressed. Memorably, as we have seen, Cheng Shewo described newspapers as "paper bullets": tools that could not only channel vital news to every village but also score a propaganda victory against the enemy.[36] The juxtaposition of *paper* and *bullet* was striking, for it reminded people of the power of words and the ability of the press to achieve something extraordinary. The press, in other words, was more than a vehicle of communication; it was a weapon that could inflict heavy damage on the enemy.

To emphasize the importance of propaganda work behind enemy lines, the correspondent Shi Yan proposed that a kind of "journalism guerrilla warfare" (*xinwen gongzuo de youjizhan*) be waged. "Let's call upon those hundreds and thousands of courageous, determined journalists to go behind Japanese lines to establish dailies, rural wall papers, and mobile journals" that would constitute "a network of cultural battle lines" (*wenhua huoxianwang*).[37] Although it is not known how many of these "guerrilla" newspapers were established in those territories, or where, the repeated call for their creation indicated the seemingly limitless forms that resistance could take.

The call for journalists to wage "guerrilla warfare" against the invaders underscored the importance of their involvement in the resistance movement. The search by reporters for a new role in turbulent times and a new vocabulary to describe the armed conflict created an original rhetoric couched in military phraseology, which in turn shaped public knowledge about the war, providing a feeling of actual participation. The war of words could be as important to success as actual combat on the battlefield. Journalists were no longer mere bystanders. In interesting juxtaposition to the intellectual in Ye Qianyu's cartoon "Let's Change into New Uniform" (fig. 26), journalists were combat troops dressed in civilian clothes.

The War Correspondent

Wishing to be accurate, involved, and responsible, Chinese war correspondents employed a writing style drastically different from anything in the past. They used simple language, registered personal observations, recorded statements verbatim to provide a more intimate sense of reality, and, above all, wrote with feeling. "In filing a wartime dispatch," wrote Fan Changjiang, "we must invest it with emotion."[38] It was precisely this ingredient of emotion that brought force and passion to wartime journalism.

Yet to be a good war correspondent was not easy, Fan Changjiang warned, and in this he was echoed by numerous reporters looking for a more effective role.[39] Could a war correspondent be accurate and objective yet patriotic at the same time? Could a story written in a highly emotionally and personal style even claim to be objective? Was there a difference between propaganda and honest reporting? What was the role of a reporter vis-à-vis the government? Should reporters be independent critics, or should they collaborate with their news sources?

In an interview with Fan Changjiang and Lu Yi in July 1938, Edgar Snow, who shortly before had achieved celebrity status in China with his book *Red Star over China* (1937), pointed out three serious threats to the objectivity and independence of a wartime report: poor observation, resorting to stereotyped accounts, and use of unreliable information. Such shoddy practices, Snow warned, could easily undermine the credibility of the press.[40]

Snow's concerns were not entirely new; in fact, they had already been intensely debated within the Chinese Young Journalists Society (CYJS). The founding of the society in March 1938 was certainly a high point in the history of modern Chinese journalism, in part because it came at a time when the left and right were still talking to each other in the name of national unity, before ideological differences split them asunder. The society comprised a host of distinguished reporters, editors, and politicians, including Shao Lizi (1882–1967), the former director of the Guomindang Central Publicity Department; Xiao Tongzi (1895–1973), director of the Central News Agency; and Guo Moruo, head of the Third Section of the Political Department in charge of literary propaganda. From the beginning, it stressed that in the face of mounting Japanese pressure it was imperative for journalists to coordinate their activities and share the nation's limited publication resources.[41] Fan Changjiang and Lu Yi, the central figures of the society, saw the CYJS as a location where professional knowledge could be learned and experience shared, and where camaraderie could be promoted in a time of adversity. The feeling of solidarity was reinforced by the establishment of a "Reporters' Hostel" in Hankou in September 1938, providing peripatetic reporters with a temporary abode and a place to share views about the crisis.[42] In addition to launching an influential journal, the *Reporter*, the society also published *A Primer for Wartime Journalism*, the most exhaustive discussion of the subject to appear during the war. The book examined in great detail various aspects of wartime journalism: its theory and practice, the distribution of newspapers, and above all, "the cultivation and learning of a war correspondent."[43] The *Reporter* did essentially the same thing. Besides soliciting support for the correspondents' endeavor, the journal's major function was to provide a forum for reporters to define their own role. "How to be a good war correspondent" became a topic of major concern.

To Fan Changjiang, poor observations by a reporter—the first of Snow's concerns—stemmed from a lack of knowledge and proper training. True, a good war correspondent needed to have "courage, solid military knowledge, a knack for careful attention, objectivity, and an excellent writing technique," as his friend Qiujiang suggested;[44] but to acquire these qualities required painstaking effort and constant practice. Fan suggested that novices start with the fundamentals, then continue to study, and ultimately pursue specialized learning—a process of what he called "self-cultivation."[45] This approach stood in sharp contrast to that of old-style journalists, who, Fan maintained, spread themselves too thin as generalists. Professionalization, he argued, meant having thorough knowledge of the event one wants to write about and a solid command of the facts. To be topnotch, therefore, war correspondents had to possess at least basic, up-to-date military information. "Accurate and wide knowledge," Fan wrote, "is the supreme authority of life."[46] Fan practiced what he preached.[47] His *The Northwest Corner of China* demonstrated a remarkable command of the history and geography of the remote lands,[48] and his wartime dispatches only bolstered the impression of solid observation and possession of the facts.[49]

To be a good reporter, one must also master writing and learn how to communicate effectively in the simplest way. Formalistic, stereotypical writing—Snow's second concern—rendered news coverage uninteresting and uninspiring. Besides making conscious use of a new political vocabulary, war correspondents paid particular attention to the art or craft of writing. For the journalist Bu Shaofu (1909–), a good reporter was someone who took writing skills seriously, who considered the style of a dispatch as important as the subject matter. A good report, according to Bu, should exhibit the following qualities: concreteness, vividness, depth, and pithiness.[50] Such qualities would allow a war correspondent to present his story in the most direct and realistic way possible, so that it, in turn, could exert a powerful impact on its readers. Again among Chinese war correspondents, Fan

Changjiang stood out as one of the best writers of his generation. He frequently opened his pieces with a brief but forceful line. In his "Beside the Marco Polo Bridge," for instance, he began: "China's repeated minor conflicts with foreign powers [particularly Japan] are a good indication of how this country is raising its head every day;"[51] and in "Marching to the Western Front" he started out on an equally upbeat note: "It's hard to express my feelings, but every time I reach the front, hope fills my heart."[52] These short lead-ins each introduced an intricate political and military story. For Fan and others, approaching the topic in this personal and emotional manner was the best way to grasp the reader's attention. If brevity and interest were paramount in a dispatch, Fan believed, then each word must be direct and forceful.

Good writing also included choosing a good title—in the journalist Zhang Youluan's (1904–1990) words, this was the "most important [aspect] of the editorial process,"[53] for it brought out the essentials of a story and captured the imagination of readers at first glance. A good title could hold the key to a story's success. We have seen some of Fan Changjiang's and Qiujiang's titles; Xiao Fang's (Fang Dazeng of *Dagong bao*) "The Bloody Battle at the Juyong Pass" ("Xiezhan Juyongguan") was another memorable example. Such a dramatic style, it need hardly be stated, had little in common with traditional journalistic practice.

Perhaps the most serious problem facing war correspondents was inaccurate or false information—the third concern raised by Snow. To be fair and accurate, it was argued, reporters should seek out the news exhaustively and approach a story from many different angles, especially that of the common people. In this view, to file a report about a military clash without taking its larger context into full consideration was to present a partial and perhaps distorted picture. The journalist and educator Xie Liuyi (1898–1945), for instance, charged that Shanghai's newspapers often ridiculed refugees and failed to present an accurate picture of their plight.[54] The same inaccuracy occurred in war reporting, Shi Yan observed. He pointed out that in the past, coverage of wars tended to be dull and shallow—straightforward, factual accounts of military campaigns, interviews with commanders, details about the enemy's brutality. Such an approach, he said, hardly did justice to the complexity of war. Instead he proposed a new "three-dimensional" (*litihua*) method: it encouraged reporters to look beyond government briefings, which could color one's stories, and seek out unofficial sources and ask more questions. In a war, reporters should make use of such channels as common foot soldiers, for example, and probe into the hidden meaning "behind the news," Shi Yan suggested.[55] The nature of a battle could be comprehended fully only by independently examining socioeconomic conditions and political factors. A good reporter would therefore base his or her reports on exhaustive, objective, on-the-spot investigation; it was this that would make a story credible. "Even a refugee or a prisoner-of-war will tell us something about the war," Liu Zhuzhou said.[56] Gao Tian elaborated: "Horizontally, the coverage of the war should especially include information about the crucial supporting force behind the campaign— the mobilization of the common people. . . . Vertically, the reporter should gather information not only from commanders, but also from the rank and file."[57] "The closer you get to the rank and file," Liu Zunqi (1911–) echoed, "the richer the material."[58]

Shi Yan's and Liu Zunqi's proposal pointed to a fundamental truth of journalism: the one-source story is not only bad but potentially dangerous. More important, their approach underscored the importance of independence in journalism. The gathering and dissemination of information had to be freely conducted by those who were specially trained, whose minds were unclouded by biases and stereotypes, and who could make use of reliable sources. As the newspapers became more and more politicized, reporters' personalities took on increasing significance. Because of their unique profession, Fan Changjiang warned, reporters were natural targets for special interest groups who would seek every opportunity to influence them to write something in their favor. Sometimes pressure was exerted, other times monetary rewards were given. A reporter's integrity was at stake. "Political or military subsidies," warned Fan, "carry deadly poison that can easily ruin the career of a promising reporter."[59]

How objective *were* Chinese wartime dispatches? There is no question that many war correspondents, as professionals, made a conscious effort to maintain a high standard of accuracy and thoroughness in their articles. Yet reporting human emotion is the most difficult kind of writing. Clear documentation of battles and scenes of refugees was one thing, describing intangible feelings another, with excessiveness, hysteria, and vindictiveness too often the result. Striking a balance between heart and mind was no easy task.

For this reason, the highly personal and emotional language style of Chinese war correspondents had its share of critics. As the veteran journalist Zeng Xubai (1895–) pointed out, news reporting was frequently confused with literature. Yet "good literature," he wrote, "is not necessarily good reporting; and the reverse is also true. . . . Literary works can be subjective, whereas news reports must be absolutely objective."[60] To Zeng, wartime news reports were long on personal sentiment but short on dispassionate observation. Lu Yi agreed, arguing that in contrast to literature, which is a product of the imagination or a blending of fact and fiction, wartime dispatches must contain three distinct ingredients: authentic news, actual observation by the reporter, and timeliness. "It would be a mistake to label Qiujiang's report on the Battle of the Nankou Pass as literature, because it was an eyewitness account," he added.[61] But by creating a new, personal rhetoric, wartime journalists committed themselves to a literary language that too readily allowed exaggeration, impaired judgment, and colored the stories presented.

In the end, it was not the fairness and balance of their stories that made China's war correspondents influential, but the liveliness, passion, and easy-to-read language of their reports. Reporters like Fan Changjiang and Qiujiang seemed to believe that a frontline dispatch could be both objective and involved at the same time. But in time of war, when not only the reporter's own survival but the survival of his or her nation was at stake, maintaining journalistic objectivity was difficult, perhaps not even desirable. Objectivity is certainly not the best description for Fan's and Qiujiang's writings when they used the press as "paper bullets." The War of Resistance called for commitment; journalistic detachment could be interpreted as avoidance of responsibility. The calamity of the war compelled reason to give way to strong emotion—pain, anger, and patriotism. With the nation's fate at stake, Fan Changjiang wrote emphatically in 1938, "we must place national interest above everything else."[62] As the Chinese press became ever more involved in the campaign against the Japanese invasion, many journalists found it extremely difficult to follow Walter Lippmann's advice and keep a "certain distance" from their subjects, assuming instead an overtly political and patriotic outlook.[63]

The Journalist as Critic

During these dire times, new journalists like Fan Changjiang and Qiujiang, despite earlier efforts to maintain reportorial objectivity, often followed their predecessors' lead and wrote without making a clear distinction between news and commentary. Many journalists' wartime dispatches thus resembled personal views more than news reports as they simultaneously played the dual role of fair-minded news reporter and conscientious social critic. "A reporter must serve society," wrote

Zhang Jiluan.[64] "He must be both a critic and a guide to society," affirmed the veteran journalist Chen Bosheng (1891–1957).[65] Hu Zhengzhi, Zhang's colleague and the general manager of Dagong bao, echoed these views.[66] Such an assertion went beyond the notion of journalism as a profession, for it demanded in addition social commitment and frowned on apathetic withdrawal. The line between a reporter and a commentator hence remained nebulous.

The image of intellectuals as social critics is an ancient one. In the Confucian tradition, intellectuals were the enlightened few who concerned themselves with important matters. Refusing to close their eyes to social and political ills, they acted as the conscience of society, responsible for righting wrongs through either moral suasion or active participation in social reform. Journalists, by casting themselves in a role similar to that of the scholar-official, took over that tradition. To remain independent of political interest was in any event almost impossible at this time of national struggle against an invasion and continued strife between the Nationalists and the Communists. As emotions took control, reporters easily turned into critics, and newspapers became a voice for social justice.

As the war progressed, many journalists were appalled by the poor discipline and low morale of the GMD army. True, there were those who displayed great valor on the battlefield, but there were also many soldiers who acted ignominiously. Government troops, underpaid and undernourished, often resorted to indiscriminate looting. Worse still, they did not hesitate to commit violence against Chinese civilians. "It is our own troops who were the first to make the lives of the people miserable," Fan Changjiang lamented.[67] Growing disappointment with the Guomindang turned Fan and many other reporters into vocal critics of the government.

War correspondents soon discovered that problems in the military were not confined to the rank and file, but extended far up the hierarchy. Higher levels were plagued by corruption, incompetence, and insubordination. Many officers were negligent of their troops; they embezzled funds and made fortunes by selling surplus grain to profiteering merchants. Clearly, winning the war required the coordination and support of all military units, yet many, instead of fighting the Japanese, jealously guarded their own territories. Perhaps the most notorious case was that of Liu Ruming (1895–1975). Liu, commander of the Twenty-ninth Army, was assigned to guard Zhangjiakou, a strategic position northwest of the Nankou Pass between Inner Mongolia and Beijing. During the critical Battle of the Nankou Pass in

August 1937, Liu, fearing casualties to his men and thus a weakening of his own position, intentionally delayed reinforcing the Second Army Corps, commanded by General Tang Enbo (1899–1954), which guarded the pass. The underarmed and undermanned Tang troops fought gallantly against three much stronger, mechanized Japanese divisions in one of the bloodiest battles of the war. In the end, the pass fell quickly to the Japanese when a Japanese unit attacked Tang's troops from the rear. The tragic loss of the Nankou Pass—described most vividly in Qiujiang's famous report "Outflanking the Enemy at the Nankou Pass"—prompted Fan Changjiang to call for the "execution of Liu Ruming."[68] If the Cantonese Nineteenth Route Army, which valiantly resisted the Japanese in Shanghai in 1932, was an apt symbol for the bravery and heroism of Chinese soldiers, then Liu Ruming represented cowardice, insubordination, and defeat.[69]

Underneath the corruption and incompetence of the military, many journalists charged, lay the grim reality of politics in faction-ridden Chongqing. Before the war, journalists' criticisms of the government, if any, were veiled. In *The Northwest Corner of China*, for instance, Fan Changjiang described how the once-fertile Chengdu Plain in Sichuan province had been reduced to poverty. The villages were devastated, and starving peasants lay dying along the roadsides. "Who caused this, and what made it happen?" Fan asked rhetorically.[70] During the war, however, the criticism became more direct and open.

The war exposed China's ills, Fan Changjiang wrote in 1938, and no ill was more serious than the ineffectiveness and demoralization of the government.[71] To Fan, in short, China's woes stemmed not so much from the worsening economy or growing social unrest, but from the ineptitude of the GMD regime. This view was of course shared by many, including such foreign journalists as Theodore White.[72]

Shortly after the war erupted, Fan Changjiang and other reporters issued a scathing indictment of the government's lack of a comprehensive war plan and its failure to prepare its citizens for Japanese aerial attack. "Not only did the people not know how to avoid air raids," Xiao Fang said after a raid on Zhangjiakou in 1937, "they even gathered naively in the middle of the street to look up at the enemy planes."[73] The lack of preparedness resulted in the avoidable loss of numerous lives. Worse still, people were frequently forced to evacuate without any warning, which not only caused panic and confusion but also provided ample food and supplies to the approaching enemy troops, Qiujiang charged.[74] The transportation system was in such a shambles that food and fuel could not be moved from one place to the other when they were urgently needed. Wounded soldiers perhaps fared the worst because of this situation, combined with a general unavailability of medical care. Fan Changjiang described a perennial scene during the war:

> There were only a few paramedics, and ambulances were in acute shortage. As a result, when the number of wounded soldiers suddenly increased, they jammed the road and no help was given to them. . . . Those suffering lesser injuries stumbled miserably along the roads, still bleeding. Those left with one leg managed to hobble forward with the help of staves. And those unable to walk lay trembling on the roadsides, moaning incessantly.[75]

Qiujiang reported this depressing scene on the streets of Taiyuan in Shanxi province in late 1937:

> A wounded soldier, like a frog badly hurt by an oxcart, managed to crawl and find protection from the wind and lie down. Half of his left thigh had been blown away by a shell. Another, his left hand severed, huddled like a hedgehog. In the frigid temperature, they managed with difficulty and in pain to reach Taiyuan in the dark, and then they found that there was no hospital. They could do nothing except wander helplessly through the streets.[76]

Fan Changjiang lamented: "The soldiers devoted their lives to defending their country, yet after they were wounded we could not even provide them with sufficient medical care. . . . Our country and people had indeed let them down!"[77] The agony of the wounded also greatly concerned Western journalists, who issued blistering attacks against the government's deplorable medical service.[78]

But to Fan Changjiang and Qiujiang, the most serious wartime problem was the government itself, which, pursuing what Fan called an "obscurantist policy" (*yumin zhengce*), deliberately kept the people in the dark.[79] This practice, Fan suggested, stemmed from the government's deep-rooted mistrust of its own people. Because the GMD regarded any popular movement as Communist-inspired, it viewed grass-roots action with trepidation and suspicion. The government's disastrous policy of conscripting civilians as coolies in the war resulted in people fleeing en masse (known in those days as "escaping to the mountains," *taoshan*).[80] The gap between the government and the people was only widening, Xiao Fang warned, and this could bring disaster in the future. "It was a grave mistake to dub any [grass-roots] resistance movement reactionary," he wrote.[81] The war against Japan,

Fan Changjiang and Xiao Fang argued, was not just a government's or a soldier's war, but a people's war. If China was going to defeat Japan, the common people needed to be awakened, the peasants needed to be organized.[82] Denying the strength of the people was the gravest mistake that any government could make.

Like many of his friends, Fan championed a united front policy against the Japanese. In his view, Jiang Jieshi, by turning his guns against the domestic "threat" rather than joining the Communists to force the invaders out, was pursuing a wrong course that would bring ruin and humiliation to China. "Resisting the Japanese is the top priority" (*Kang-Ri gao yu yiqie*), Fan proclaimed, repeating a popular slogan of the time.[83] "We must place national interest, the War of Resistance, and people's livelihood at the top of our priorities."[84]

As Chinese journalists became more openly critical of the government's war effort, the Chongqing government immediately clamped down on them. Any material unpalatable to those in power was to be suppressed. "Seditious literature" (such as subjects related to communism) and criticism of the government (for internal corruption, for example) were censored. If such stories were printed anyway, newspapers were confiscated and their editors incarcerated.[85] The political climate grew so oppressive that the truth was scarcely to be found, Fan Changjiang lamented. What actually appeared in the newspapers were dull government propaganda announcements. "People rush to buy newspapers, but nobody believes what is printed."[86] The restrictive Chinese press law (issued in 1937), Fan pointed out, would not only undermine the credibility of the press, but it would also further tarnish the image of the government, and this at a time when it desperately needed the press to reach the people. "Today's slogan in China should be 'Resisting the Japanese is everything, fighting is everything, and victory is everything.' Anything else should be considered secondary. . . . Anyone should have the right to criticize any action that contradicts our national interest."[87] In times of conflict, he continued, "I feel that we journalists must uphold a certain standard, simply because the most influential things in the war are newspapers. . . . Realizing this potential impact, we must always take a responsible attitude!"[88] This strong statement reflected Fan's belief in the critical role of the reporter, and it served as pointed criticism of the government.

Not surprisingly, Fan's writing won few friends in Chongqing. It also caused uneasiness and anxiety at *Dagong bao*. By the time the war broke out, in fact, Fan may have already developed an ideological, if not personal, conflict with Zhang Jiluan, editor-in-chief of the paper.

Zhang, despite his avowedly independent stand, generally sympathized with the Nationalist cause and was more or less tolerant of the government's censorship. He was also highly respected by Jiang Jieshi. Zhang insisted that in a time of national crisis, every citizen must support the government.[89] This position Fan found unacceptable,[90] and he warned against "political subsidies," whether financial or symbolic. To him, Zhang's virtual adoption of the official line ran counter to the original editorial manifesto of *Dagong bao*: "No partisanship."

The gap between Fan and the *Dagong bao* editors widened as the war continued.[91] By 1938, Fan discovered that his dispatches were occasionally being rejected and that portions of articles critical of the government were being deleted. Infuriated, he left the newspaper in the fall of that year. In September 1941, in an article memorializing Zhang, Fan referred in passing to their differences: "He [Zhang] was one of the few who made an earnest effort to teach me. Later we disagreed on a number of major issues; I therefore left *Dagong bao* at the time of the Battle of Wuhan [October 1938]."[92]

Fan's fervent nationalism and disillusionment with the Chongqing government drove him gradually to the left. Persistent chaos and the continuing ideological battle between the Nationalists and the Communists led him increasingly to believe that the press was in fact inseparable from political interests. It would be naive, he argued in January 1939, to say the press could even function independently.[93] As he put it, "Lacking a proper understanding of politics [on the part of journalists] is like sailing a ship without a compass."[94] Fan moved further to the left, and in May 1939 he joined the CCP, reportedly through the introduction of Zhou Enlai.[95]

In the 1920s and 1930s, Chinese journalists clearly sought to professionalize their craft, thereby making their work more respected, elevating their social status, and freeing the press of vested interests. Reporters' associations were established, professional journals launched, and journalistic ethics debated. Such laudable efforts came to an end for many journalists when they declared their allegiance to a political party. Fan Changjiang, of course, did not shy away from social and political commentary even in his early years as a journalist. But for most of his career, such commentary was made in light of the higher ideal that the press should be free from political influence and journalists should struggle to obtain objectivity. He condemned "political subsidies" and embraced knowledge, which he thought to be the best defense against bias and stereotypes. As an ardent patriot, his political writings before 1939 were inspired more by his strong nationalism and his earnest hope for a united front against the Japanese invasion than by any commitment to the communist cause. But the war, the ills of the GMD government, and the harsh censorship policy called his early journalistic beliefs into question, and ultimately caused him to turn to communism. Even here, though, his decision was prompted not so much by his embrace of socialist ideas, but largely by his patriotism and his deep dissatisfaction with the GMD government.

The road to an independent press in modern China was a twisted and painful one. Although young journalists started out by attempting to break the traditional bond between the press and politics and establish their occupation as a respected field, when their country came under attack they realized that they were Chinese first, and journalists second. Ironically, they became unabashed patriots in a profession that increasingly played down open emotion as undermining the principle of objectivity. Given their personal and often emotional language and style of writing, it is clear that their main contribution to modern Chinese journalism does not lie in their role as unbiased observers, which remained an unrealized ideal. Rather, their contribution lies in their role as active promoters of the patriotic cause, which was strengthened immeasurably by their firsthand reporting, passionate language, and simple prose.

Dissemination and Decentralization

Wartime reporters did not concern themselves only with creating a new journalistic language or participating in the resistance movement; they were also involved in deciding how best to spread the news in a land plagued by illiteracy and poverty. Together with the dramatists, that is, they faced the issue of popularization and dissemination. Cheng Shewo put it this way:

> Even though our country is in grave danger of being subjugated [by a foreign power], many people are still living in the dark. . . . The reason the people are so ignorant and uninformed is largely because they never read newspapers. We journalists must take the most responsibility for this unfortunate situation. Our newspapers never pay any attention to mobilizing the people, to making them understand the importance of their nation, their role as citizens of this country, and the danger facing China today.[96]

Modern social scientists have demonstrated the vital link between mass media and national development. Wilbur Schramm, for example, argues convincingly for the power of modern communication (newspapers, radio, television) to promote rapid change and reshape social values in traditional villages, and Herbert Passin shows the influential role the press played in disseminating information and winning public support for reforms in some Asian countries in the early decades of the twentieth century.[97] In China, the dissemination issue became particularly acute with the eruption of war. Before July 1937, Chinese newspapers remained highly concentrated in major cities (see chapter 1). Moreover, of the eighty-two radio broadcasting stations registered in 1936, sixty-five were found in Jiangsu (47), Zhejiang (10), and Hebei (8); only a few could be heard in the rest of China, and only the Nanjing station was of international significance.[98] The Chinese press, according to Rudolf Löwenthal, faced three major obstacles: low circulation, small size, and insufficient income. He estimated in 1936 that "every person in China on the average obtains two copies of a newspaper annually."[99] In another study conducted in the mid-1930s, Löwenthal and his colleague Vernon Nash concluded that "only one person out of 800 to 1,000 receives a copy of a newspaper daily in the rural districts."[100]

The paucity of local newspapers as well as the lack of other effective communication tools posed a formidable obstacle to the whole mobilization campaign. In the provinces, news of the conflict was inevitably slow to arrive. When it did filter through, local presses, if they existed at all, printed it faithfully. Should more regional newspapers be launched at a time of extreme paper shortage and financial difficulties? Should regional papers devote more space to news about their own localities, or should they print more national news? These issues aroused passionate discussion among journalists and politicians alike.

The clustering of the press in the cities has been a problem in many developing countries.[101] But in China the issue was complicated by a number of factors. The backwardness of the transportation system in such a vast nation was one major barrier to the flow of information. In a short but revealing article, "Newsreels and Newspapers," published in 1935, the dramatist Hong Shen warned that the overconcentration of newspapers in the urban centers would severely hinder the flow of information, thus thwarting the development of the country. Few journalists, Hong Shen lamented, were willing to venture beyond the city limits to report on remote rural areas, "where many things were happening that might affect our life."[102]

Rudolf Löwenthal, Vernon Nash, and Hong Shen were by no means the only ones to comment on the urban concentration of Chinese newspapers. In the mid-1930s, with the Japanese military threat looming ever larger and the coastal cities seeming particularly vulnerable to attack, many journalists began to realize the urgency of spreading newspapers to rural areas. The respected *Journalism Quarterly*, for instance, in 1935 published a special issue entitled "How to Develop Newspapers in the Interior and the Border Regions."[103] Journalists also called for closer cooperation between the cities and the interior generally, and between urban and border-region newspapers more specifically. This would lessen the gap between the city and the hinterland, one reporter wrote, and arouse the patriotic sentiments of the frontier people, now increasingly under threat from "imperialist aggression."[104] Stressing the importance of spreading literacy to the interior, and possibly anticipating an imminent Japanese attack, the journalist Tang Ren'an warned that it would be a serious mistake to put too much emphasis on "foreign concession culture" and "urban culture." Instead he called for moving Chinese culture "away from the concession area and the city to the village."[105]

The distribution of newspapers to the interior was one important issue; another was the popularization of the press.[106] While the former focused on locality and quantity, the latter stressed the importance of simple language and efficient communication. Dissemination and communication—those were the keys to the resistance movement. And the principal voices stressing these points were Cheng Shewo and Zou Taofen (1895–1944).

In the early 1930s, Cheng Shewo voiced his concern over the unhealthy trend of what he called the "elitism" of the press in China. The majority of newspapers, he said, aimed not at serving the public, but at catering to the special interests of the rich and powerful. Cheng charged that newspapers had become "nothing more than charts of official promotion, records of the daily life of the famous, and entertainment features about the wealthy."[107] And he devoted his whole life to trying to correct this tendency.

Cheng was born in Nanjing in 1898. Like many young patriotic Chinese in the early years of the Republic, he was captivated by the ideals of a republican form of government, taking part in the second revolution against Yuan Shikai's restoration of monarchy. Inspired by the rising influence of the press, Cheng began to think seriously about becoming a journalist when he was a student at National Beijing University in 1918. He paid for his education by working as an editor for Tianjin's *Yishi bao*. In 1924, he founded his first paper, *World Evening News* (*Shijie wanbao*) in Beijing. But it was not until he launched the highly successful *World Daily News* the following year in the same city that he won national prominence. In 1927 he inaugurated the equally successful newspaper *People's Livelihood News* (*Minsheng bao*) in Nanjing. His critical and uncompromising stance often incurred the wrath of both warlords and GMD leaders (such as Wang Jingwei); indeed, he was jailed several times.[108] Yet he felt strongly that China needed an independent, mass-oriented press, and these ideas exerted a lasting influence on the history of modern Chinese journalism.

A man committed to modernization, Cheng Shewo saw the potential of the press for bringing about public enlightenment and fostering social reforms. But they would be useless unless they could be purchased and read by the general public. Besides condemning urban newspapers for emphasizing sensationalism and rumors at the expense of serious reportage, Cheng argued that their high price prohibited them from reaching a wider readership. An average Shanghai daily newspaper, for example, was priced at 3 to 4 *fen*, which amounted to more than 1 *yuan* per month; yet an average worker's daily wage was only about 30 to 60 *fen*. This was far more expensive, relatively speaking, than in England, for instance, where newspapers generally cost one penny apiece, or only about one-hundredth of a worker's daily income.[109] Because of a shortage of advertising revenues, papers had to raise prices to cover the cost of publication. The high price also covered the cost of newsprint, almost all of which was imported (mainly from Canada and the United States) and therefore quite expensive.[110] In any event, Cheng thought, Chinese newspapers wasted newsprint by printing far more pages than necessary. The "principle of economical editing" (*jingbian zhuyi*) was what Chinese newspapers needed.[111] An ideal paper, he suggested, would be in tabloid size, sell at a reduced price, and reach as many people as possible.

But how could a newspaper be truly mass-oriented? Cheng was not naive; he realized that money played an important role in determining the fate of a newspaper. Nevertheless, he argued that the ownership of a newspaper should not be placed in the hands of "a few selfish capitalists." Rather, it should be in the hands of those who actually put the newspaper together, including the publisher, editors, and typesetters.[112] Cheng, of course, was not a socialist. What he had in mind was simply an "affordable newspaper" (*pingjia bao*) with a focus "directed toward the people"[113]—in brief, a people's paper rather than a commercialized, elite press.

Cheng realized his dream by founding *Stand-up Journal* (*Li bao*) in Shanghai in 1935.[114] *Stand-up Journal* was a tabloid (*xiaoxing bao*), smaller than a regular newspaper (in quarto format rather than folio) and priced at only 1 *fen*. More important, it was distinctly different in character from Shanghai's entertainment-oriented "mosquito papers" such as *Crystal* and *Diamond*, which featured popular fiction, sensational news, and scandalous gossip.[115] Under the slogans of "popularization of the press" and "fair-mindedness," *Stand-up Journal* printed concise hard news using simple language in a fresh new layout. It also created a few highly acclaimed columns, including "Little Teahouse," edited by Sa Kongliao (1907–1988), which contained articles about, in Sa's words, the "blood and sweat" of the workers.[116] The result was a spectacular success: *Stand-up Journal* soon rivaled the two largest Shanghai newspapers, *Shen bao* and *Xinwen bao*, in popularity, and its circulation quickly soared, reaching an unprecedented 200,000 on the eve of the Sino-Japanese War.

Cheng Shewo, naturally, was not alone in recognizing the importance of a more popularized press geared to the majority of the people rather than to a tiny few.[117] Zou Taofen was perhaps equally vocal on the subject. Born in Fujian, Zou studied English at St. John's University in Shanghai. He became a well-known name in journalism when he assumed the editorship of *Life Weekly* (*Shenghuo zhoukan*) in 1926, promptly turning it from a vocational education journal into a popular forum for discussing political and social concerns. "In this publication," Zou declared, "we want to avoid the esoteric writings of the elite and utilize the plain and simple writings of the people."[118] In addition to introducing cartoons and printing articles of interest to the readers, he created a special "Brief Discussions" column oriented toward contemporary social issues and instituted a highly popular "Letter Box" section, printing readers' letters together with his replies on a mosaic of daily concerns—marriage, family, jobs. The weekly enjoyed enormous popularity, its circulation soaring to 150,000 in 1932, a record in the history of Chinese journal publications.[119] As time went on, Zou drew the ire of the Guomindang by becoming ever more outspoken on government corruption and the official policy of appeasement toward the Japanese. He joined the China League for the Protection of Civil Rights in 1933. Predictably, the GMD put pressure on the magazine and finally ordered it to close in December 1933.

Like Cheng Shewo, Zou's main concern was how to reach a wide audience through publications catering to the interests of the majority. His principles were straightforward: Zou insisted that the issues addressed relate to the masses, that ideas be kept simple, and that the language be direct and easy to understand. After *Life Weekly* was forced to shut down, he continued to publish highly popular magazines according to these principles. In November 1935 he started *Life of the Masses* (*Dazhong shenghuo*) in Shanghai, whose circulation soon surpassed even that of its predecessor, reaching a new record of 200,000 (it was banned by the government the following year);[120] and in June 1936 he launched *Life Daily* (*Shenghuo ribao*) in Hong Kong, for which he wrote: "I hope my 450 million compatriots will look at this daily as a public property."[121] The theme of serving the interests of the general public was familiar, but, told with sincerity and zest by Zou, it continued to draw readers. All three of Zou Taofen's major publications bore the word *life*, which to him meant the daily tribulations of the common people. Unlike Cheng, Zou was sympathetic to the socialist cause. He moved even more to the left in his final years, especially after visiting the Communist-held areas of northern Jiangsu in late 1942. On his deathbed he expressed his wish to join the CCP; it was granted by the Communists two months after his death in July 1944.

The eruption of war lent new meaning and urgency to the idea of "popularization of the press." But how could journalists spread patriotic values among a largely illiterate population? What kind of information should newspapers transmit? What kind of language was most appropriate?

Like dramatists, wartime journalists were concerned not only with the idea of "popularization," but also with how it might be achieved. Transportation was a major problem, to be sure, but illiteracy was an even bigger one, and at the time no one knew how to tackle either. Xie Liuyi nevertheless believed that journalists had certain options for making newspapers more accessible to their readers. For one thing, he proposed that the number of written characters used in newspaper articles be limited, which also meant that journalists should avoid using difficult words. In the case of local correspondence, reporters should make the widest possible use of dialects.[122] These proposals, however, were problematic. How many characters were appropriate for a newspaper? What were the drawbacks of using dialects in an article? Without disputing Xie's views, the leftist journalist Liu Shi (1903–1968) proposed a more realistic approach. To enhance a paper's readability, Liu recommended the inclusion of popular songs: ballads such as "Anti-Japanese Mountain Songs" ("Kang-Ri shan'ge"), extremely popular in Hunan, Hubei, and Shanxi, and pieces like "Along the Songhua River" ("Songhuajiang shang") and "Ballad of the Great Wall" ("Changcheng yao"), which were winning hearts and minds all over China.[123] Moreover, writings could be more easily digested if illustrations accompanied them. The combination of cartoons, pictures, and simple essays was put to good use by Zou Taofen in his wartime magazines, especially *War of Resistance* (*Kangzhan*) and its successor, *United Resistance* (*Quanmin kangzhan*). The down-to-earth approach and striking graphic covers gave the magazines a special appeal.

Another notable name in the popularization of journalism was Li Furen (1899–1958). Li, a Communist since October 1937 but working under the guise of the Democratic League,[124] was educated in Japan and was a great lover of Chinese folk songs and proverbs. In November 1937, as a teacher at the Xi'an Normal School, he launched a successful and influential weekly, *The Common Folk* (*Laobaixing*). The contents and candid language made the publication unique. Like Zou's magazines, *The Common Folk* proposed all-out resistance to the Japanese invasion. But unlike Zou's, it catered to the rural population in the interior and touched on a variety of rural subjects: planting, sanitation, epidemic prevention. Its language was plain and sometimes inelegant, to the point of including common profanity. Li Furen made no bones about his anti-Japanese stand, nor did he intend to polish his language. Since common people themselves used unrefined expressions, he pointed out, any embellishment or refining would distort the real picture, rendering it hypocritical and unnatural. "He uses people's language to talk about their ups and downs," one of his friends said about him.[125]

Li Furen's style was unorthodox and imaginative. He did not shy away from controversial subjects, and his skillful use of folk songs and proverbs gave his ideas a natural forcefulness. The circulation of *The Common Folk* climbed to ten thousand by its first anniversary in 1938, with copies reaching as far as Xinjiang province.[126] As a Communist, Li Furen was of course critical of the Nationalist government. Like Zou Taofen, he attacked the corruption and weakness in Chongqing, and he supported the GMD-CCP alliance against the Japanese. And like Zou Taofen's magazines, *The Common Folk* drew the suspicion of the Guomindang and was ordered to close down in April 1940.

Li Furen apparently found the right formula for a magazine acceptable to commoners, and *The Common Folk* proved a success. But how influential was it? In May 1938, one of Xi'an's newspaper reported: "*The Common Folk* enjoyed great popularity here. Although the majority of the peasants cannot read, they pay special attention to the weekly. They enjoy the weekly when others read it to them. Therefore, as soon as the paper is out, they snatch it up."[127] Li Furen's diary entry for 31 March 1938 noted: "Today there are more subscribers. It's a good feeling."[128] Based originally at Xi'an Normal School, the paper had another advantage over other periodicals: students, after they graduated from the school and went on to serve as teachers in various parts of the province, could spread the journal to villages far removed from Xi'an. This kind of person-to-person connection was important in rural China, where the communication process was intimately related to personal ties. However, although one source claims that in its two and a half years of existence *The Common Folk* had subscriptions surpassing ten thousand, and, with a total of 113 issues, over a million copies were printed,[129] its influence was still very much restricted to the northwestern corner of China, especially Shaanxi.

While popularization of the press made some strides before the war, in reality it remained largely a theoretical ideal. Despite their enthusiasm for establishing a closer link between the cities and the interior, Cheng Shewo's and Zou Taofen's publications stayed in cities like Shanghai and Nanjing and were aimed largely at urbanites rather than rural people. Although it is impossible to know just where the readers of the *Stand-up Journal* lived, there is no reason to believe that this successful paper had a distribution far beyond metropolitan Shanghai.

Dramatic change came only after the eruption of the war. Fleeing from Japanese occupation, journalists headed for the interior, taking their newspapers with them. The Japanese step-by-step advance forced newspapers to move from place to place. The famous Tianjin-based *Dagong bao* is a case in point. In 1936, when the Japanese military presence in north China became too strong to ignore, Zhang Jiluan and Hu Zhengzhi, the guiding spirits of the *Dagong bao*, decided to divert parts of their investment to south China. The *Dagong bao* Shanghai edition made its debut on 1 April 1936, and the paper's main office in Tianjin was closed down when the Japanese army occupied the city in early August 1937. A week later, Shanghai's stability was again threatened when Japanese forces opened their southern front. Undaunted, Zhang and Hu launched a Hankou edition of *Dagong bao* on 18 September 1937. Subsequently, a Hong Kong (13 August 1938), a Chongqing (1 December 1938), and a Guilin (3 March 1941) edition were published successively as Japanese troops flooded into China proper, forcing the GMD government to withdraw into Sichuan.

The nomadic moves of the *Dagong bao* give an idea not only of the uncertain footing on which the press rested, but also of the enormous personal danger that journalists faced. Those who stayed in the

Japanese-occupied areas lived a life of fear. Even those who remained in the so-called Orphan Island (Gudao) in Shanghai, where newspapers registered under foreigners' names in the concession areas were free of direct enemy control for several years, could expect to be harassed by Japanese soldiers, and subsequently by Wang Jingwei's secret agents. Many journalists were murdered in broad daylight, their bodies tossed onto the streets, for publishing articles critical of the occupation force and Wang's puppet government.[130] As a result, it was not uncommon for journalists to flee to the interior, and there the idea of dispersion of the press was put into practice, by choice or not, thus changing the course of the Chinese press.

Local Newspapers

The distribution of newspapers to the interior provinces was only part of the pressing problem of wartime journalism. As the hinterland became the bastion of China's resistance, an equally urgent issue began to draw attention: how to develop local newspapers (*difang baozhi*) to further the national cause. In " 'Paper Bullets' Can Also Annihilate the Enemy," Cheng Shewo proposed that a small local paper—which he called a "people's edition"—be set up in every county not yet under Japanese occupation.[131] The value of the local press during the war was quite apparent to journalists. In a country where regionalism prevailed and the lack of communication channels often thwarted national campaign efforts, promoting local newspapers seemed the only viable course of action. But to wartime journalists, the local press was more than a mere vehicle of communication; it was also a window onto the outside world, a forum for contemporary politics and society, and a tool to break regional barriers. In other words, it was crucial to national unity. Feng Yingzi (1915–), a member of the Chinese Young Journalists Society and an enthusiastic advocate of local newspapers, argued that China's size and the backwardness of the transportation system, together with urban papers' sophisticated language and high price, rendered such publications ineffective in advancing local reforms and mobilizing the people in the interior. A local paper, by contrast, printed hometown news with a sensitive touch and conveyed a sense of intimacy to the readership. It had few distribution problems because it was printed locally, and it cost less. Because it worked within customary linkages and organizations, Feng noted, the local paper wielded enormous influence in the immediate area.[132]

But local newspapers should be careful lest they succumb to parochialism, warned Liu Shi. He argued that for a local press to be effective, its editors had to have a broad vision. They must encourage their readers to extend their imaginations beyond their own communities, helping them to gain a bigger picture of the world. The resistance movement demanded a large degree of national awareness; regional self-interest was not the goal. In Liu Shi's eyes, therefore, the local press should act as a vital link between local people and the central government.[133] As another commentator put it, it should "function like a postman," forming an information bridge between the outside world and the interior.[134]

Fan Changjiang went a step further in elaborating the importance of the local press. Not only were local newspapers an important means of communication, he said; they were also a key vehicle in fostering social and political change. As a journalist, Fan believed that the local press had a greater social impact than other media because it was a better and more regular news channel. And its role kept growing as China concentrated its resources in the interior in the battle against the Japanese. In an article entitled "The Movement to Unite Journalism and Journalists in the New Era" published in 1939, Fan contended that the vast majority of China's human and natural resources lay not in the coastal cities, but in the countryside. If these resources were to be fully developed, he continued, effective means must be found—and what better way than by using local presses? Like Hong Shen, Fan criticized the overconcentration of newspapers in urban areas. However, the breakdown of local power and traditional norms during the war, he noted, offered new opportunities and hope for journalists to address the imbalance in newspaper distribution. Newspapers should no longer be concentrated in major cities; instead they should be spread to "the counties and villages in the vast interior."[135]

Fan made an appeal to the high officials in Guangxi during a trip to this southwestern province in April 1939. "Guangxi today is a resistance stronghold in South China. Strengthening Guangxi's local newspaper network would not only benefit this particular province, but also set a good leadership example for other southern provinces to follow." Then, even though parts of Guangxi might fall into enemy hands in the future, "we still can form a powerful link with the Guangxi people based on this previously established network." The more regional newspapers there were, the better future national reconstruction would be, he said. "Once this cornerstone is solidly laid, it will become a potent tool for promoting popular culture after Japan is defeated."[136]

But how should journalists proceed with the task? Fan proposed an ambitious plan: the entire province could be subdivided into many microregions, each with a local newspaper (to be supported by local funds) under the supervision of the Guilin-based and government-funded *Guangxi Daily* (*Guangxi ribao*), the largest newspaper in the province. Because of the acute shortage of newsprint and modern printing presses, editors could substitute handmade paper (*tuzhi*) and rely on mimeograph machines. As far as staff was concerned, a number of young journalists could first be trained in a central training program. Each graduate would in turn train a new group of local reporters when he or she was sent down to the county or village to work. News sources could come partly from radio and partly from the *Guangxi Daily*, which would gather, analyze, and then distribute national and international news to local branches. Local news could then be added, to produce a finished, readable product.[137] Underlying Fan's proposal was a genuine professional desire to bring newspapers to the grass roots. The notion resonated in many corners of the journalistic field. An article in the influential *Reporter*, for example, urged correspondents to "go to the countryside" in order to establish a "rural communication network."[138] Fan's local newspaper scheme was in fact one of the most comprehensive projects advocated by any journalist during the war, and it fell on receptive ears: top-level Guangxi officials responded with enthusiasm. In October, Governor Huang Xuchu (1892–1975) initiated a series of concrete plans to develop local newspapers in his province, which yielded considerable results.[139]

Activities in the rest of interior China were equally impressive. True, the war had either ruined or bankrupted more than six hundred newspapers in its first year and destroyed newspaper communication in the coastal cities.[140] In the interior, however, the newspaper industry managed to survive and even flourish. The arrival of many journalists in the hinterland, including such influential men as Fan Changjiang, Zhang Jiluan, and Cheng Shewo, contributed to a remarkable period of vitality and growth. Also important was the multiplication of a single newspaper into many—"breaking the whole into parts" (*hua zheng wei ling*), as one scholar later described it.[141] The Tianjin-based *Dagong bao*, which proliferated into Shanghai, Hankou, Hong Kong, Chongqing, and Guilin editions, was but one of many such examples. The GMD's military paper, *Mopping Up News* (*Saodang bao*), originally based in Hankou, was soon appearing in Chongqing and Guilin editions. Similarly, the *Central Daily* (*Zhongyang ribao*), the GMD's party paper, multiplied into Chongqing, Kunming, Guiyang, and Hunan editions; subsequently more than thirty editions were printed. Even the Communist *New China Daily*, after moving from Hankou to Chongqing, appeared in two additional editions: North China (Huabei) and Guilin.[142]

The tabloid presses flourished during the war as well, appearing in various forms: as local newspapers, the frontline press, and occupied-area news. In Zhejiang, for example, although at the outbreak of the war 28 newspapers were closed down, two years later over 185 papers had emerged, two-thirds of them mimeographed tabloids. In Shanxi, 11 newspapers were destroyed in 1937, but close to 100 tabloid papers had emerged in the same province by 1939.[143] Even in provinces as far removed as Guizhou and Yunnan, the number of newspapers increased: from 6 and 10 in prewar years to 14 and 22 respectively for these two provinces.[144] Moreover, whereas in the past most newspapers were located in urban centers, now they could be found all over the country. Jiangxi's newspapers, for example, had been clustered in Nanchang, its provincial capital, before the war, but after 1937 they spread to places like Ji'an, Taihe, and Suichuan.[145]

The rise and diffusion of local newspapers in China's hinterland during the war must be analyzed with caution, however. Local presses differed from their urban counterparts not only in location, but also in size and production. The shortage of newsprint and modern printing presses meant that a large proportion of local newspapers were tabloids. They were smaller in size (usually a single sheet as against four sheets in a prewar urban paper, and the smaller quarto format as against the folio), mimeographed in form, and limited in circulation (fewer than three thousand copies).[146] Although newspaper publishers were encouraged to seek local funding, the insolvency of the rural economy due to war and heavy taxation made extra money unavailable. Insufficient government funding further complicated the issue.[147] To save newsprint, publications might be reduced from daily to semiweekly or even weekly. Their quality was uneven. Regular correspondents, if any, were poorly trained. And the news was often hopelessly out of date and monotonous, gleaned largely from the government-controlled Central News Agency.[148] The absence of an efficient distribution system and a high rural illiteracy rate further obstructed the flow of information. Furthermore, the government's attitude was frequently ambiguous. While GMD officials proposed dispersion of the press to minimize the impact of enemy attacks and endorsed the idea of launching more newspapers to spread the resistance cause,[149] they also feared that the Communists might initiate their own newspapers to spread socialism and undermine the government's authority.[150]

Continued rivalry between the Guomindang and regional military powers also cast doubt on the government's sincerity in wishing to promote local presses in such provinces as Guangxi, which was under the control of General Li Zongren and General Bai Chongxi (1893–1966). The fierce competition for readership between the GMD-controlled *Central Daily* and the Guangxi faction's *Guangxi Daily* was a well-known story in the war.[151]

Despite numerous impediments, local newspapers did thrive in China's hinterland. But did they actually reach the grass roots? How influential were they really? We should not forget that Chongqing, the wartime capital, was the de facto center of journalism during this period. By 1939, most of the major prewar national newspapers had relocated to that city, among them *Dagong bao* and the *Central Daily*. At one time, twenty-two newspapers and twelve news agencies clustered in the capital.[152] Nevertheless, the printed media flourished in provincial cities and towns as well. Not only major inland cities such as Chengdu (Sichuan) and Hengyang (Hunan), but also medium-size towns like Dushan (Guizhou) and Yongchun (Fujian) experienced a journalistic boom.[153] Nor was the circulation of local newspapers confined to cities and towns: it reached down to the villages as well, though just what impact these publications had is difficult to assess. Many, apparently, were brought by young activists who read aloud to the illiterate peasants.[154] The quality of these local newspapers was no doubt uneven; still, it is hard not to be impressed by the extent of this local journalistic activity and the sincere effort that so many made to reach the rural masses.

The dispersal of the Chinese press and the exodus of journalists into the interior underlined the shift of cultural activity from the urban toward the rural. This change would have a profound impact both during and after the war. Wartime journalists such as Fan Changjiang and Cheng Shewo repeatedly argued that the clustering of newspapers in major cities like Shanghai and Beijing could severely impede social advancement, breeding mutual mistrust and animosity between urbanites and villagers and furthering cultural and social imbalance—all detrimental to China as a united country. Their appeal to focus on the interior no doubt reflected an interest in the press as a resistance tool; but it also showed journalists' intent to use it as an instrument of national integration. The general assumption among reporters was that a heightened flow of information would lessen regional division and bring the country together, transforming discrete voices into collective action. In the eyes of Fan Changjiang and Liu Shi, the press was also an ideal agent of social change. Newspapers could introduce new knowledge, break down class barriers, and encourage literacy. Such views, of course, represented the hopeful aspirations of young journalists. These aspirations inevitably collided with the harsh realities of the war.

The thriving of local newspapers during the war did, however, raise hopes that China might one day come together. Even with irregular quality and limited circulation, more and more local newspapers were launched. Many journalists observed this change with excitement and anticipation. In 1941, Fan Changjiang described his feelings:

> [In the past three years] while urban newspapers fell behind, interior newspapers advanced with great strides. Formerly, people living in Shijiazhuang and Baoding considered only Beiping and Tianjin newspapers worth reading. Shanghai newspapers gained a respectable market in Nanjing. And if people in Guangzhou and Wuzhou missed reading Hong Kong newspapers, they would think that they had lost touch with current political reality. All these cases apparently stemmed from the fact that as far as information sources, reporters' abilities, business profits, printing facilities, transportation systems, and sources of newsprint are concerned, urban newspapers were in a far superior position [than papers in the interior]. But what about now? . . . Interior newspapers have made great advances. This is no doubt crucial for mobilizing every Chinese citizen. . . . It [also] indicates that the cultural level in the interior has been substantially raised. . . . These interior newspapers will no doubt be an important component in China's future journalism.[155]

5　New Wine in Old Bottles

In May 1938, the All-China Resistance Association of Writers and Artists held an informal meeting in Hankou to discuss a pressing question: how to compile popular reading materials for the soldiers at the front. Although a direct Japanese attack on this Yangzi River city was growing ever more likely, a sense of hope and enthusiasm permeated the discussion. With Tian Han, Lao Xiang (Wang Xiangchen, 1901–1968), An E (1905–1976), Wang Pingling (1898–1964), and others in attendance, President Lao She (Shu Qingchun, 1899–1966) called the meeting to order. He reminded those assembled that when the association was founded two months earlier, on 27 March, the members had decided to publish a total of one hundred different kinds of popular literary works designed to meet the needs of the soldiers and the masses. "A discussion today about this issue," Lao She noted, "will perhaps help us to better prepare for this challenge."[1] A lively debate ensued, with several important questions raised: What kind of books should be written? Based on what sources? Should distinctions be made between materials aimed at soldiers and those intended for the general public? And should old cultural forms be used to serve the present needs? It was the last question, or what Lao She called "the question of pouring new wine into old bottles," that generated the most spirited exchanges:

> An E: I think we should be selective in using old forms. Consider folk ditties. Some of them portray people's lives, expressing their emotions, but others are licentious and immoral. We should promote the former but discard the latter. It is important to note that things that are popular among the populace are not necessarily beneficial to them. We have the responsibility to educate

the masses. It is unwise to use harmful materials to cater to the needs of the people.

Lao She: Old and new forms are both acceptable. The important issue is to be careful about the choice of words. Some new words are certainly beyond the comprehension of the general public. Consider the following: "Lao She's eyes cast like an arc, arousing a trace of sentimentality." (*Laughter*) I doubt even a junior high school student could understand its meaning completely. So we must be careful in using certain words and expressions.

Wang Pingling: If we want to use "old bottles," we must first determine whether or not they are suitable for current use. We can indeed compose new materials based on old *dagu* [drum singing] verses. But we cannot do so with "Eighteen Touches" ["Shi ba mo"—an erotic song]. In short, it is a matter of whether the wine is good or bad, regardless of the age of the bottle.

Lao Xiang: I remember a story: A car salesman goes to the village to tout his products. He asks those gathered around whether they understand the wonders of the automobile. You know what happens? A peasant counters with a question: Without an ox to pull the car, how can it run?

Tian Han: Because we are intellectuals, we like to write in an elegant style. It seems that we never feel completely satisfied unless we do so. In Changsha, I saw some [anti-Japanese] slogans written in artistic calligraphy. How could the country folk understand them when they can't even understand those written in regular script?

The plan to publish one hundred different kinds of popular books for soldiers, however, never materialized owing to lack of funds and lukewarm support from the government (an issue that will be pursued later in this chapter).[2]

The discussion of "pouring new wine into old bottles" in popular literature was reminiscent of an earlier, similar debate regarding traditional drama. In both cases, the question was how best to communicate with the largely illiterate populace to win support for the war cause. In both cases, too, resistance intellectuals looked to native culture to accomplish the task. Only the medium had changed, with the focus now on popular literature rather than theater.

To the resisters, the call "Literature must go to the countryside! Literature must join the army!" (*wenzhang xiaxiang, wenzhang ruwu*), one of the most popular slogans coined by the ACRAWA,[3] would remain forever a lofty and useless dream unless they could determine what kind of literature should be written, how it should be sent to the countryside, and in what way it could be presented to the peasantry. Intellectuals and writers should not engage in wishful thinking, Lao Xiang warned, but should "study the immediate needs of the people."[4] To Lao She and Lao Xiang, the best way to satisfy the needs of the people was through the use of "popular literature and art" (*tongsu wenyi*), already a strong thread in the fabric of Chinese society.

Although the Chinese folk culture movement made its debut during the May Fourth era, its importance was not universally recognized until after the outbreak of the war. Before the Japanese invasion, the movement championing folk values and culture, despite its importance in modern Chinese cultural and intellectual history as a reaction against Confucian tradition, was very much a scholarly endeavor limited to a few intellectuals (such as Liu Fu [1891–1934] and Zhou Zuoren) and confined to a small number of university campuses.[5] The war suddenly thrust folk literature onto center stage, arousing enormous public interest, especially among politicians and propagandists. But the renewed interest in folk literature had shifted its focus—from the literary and romantic value of the plebeian culture, and toward politics and nationalism. During the war popular and folk literature were mixed to form a hybrid resistance culture, the distinctions between them becoming blurred and insignificant, in practice if not in theory. In many instances, the two types of literature were used by resistance intellectuals interchangeably.

The Use of Popular Literature

The ability of popular literature and art to shape people's minds and feelings is well documented. English chapbooks in the seventeenth century and Russian *lubki* (popular prints) in the nineteenth century formed the staple of lower-class reading in those two countries and had an enormous impact on the peasants' literacy and attitudes.[6] These were commercial in intent, however, whereas Chinese wartime popular literature and art was strictly political. It was a common assumption among resistance intellectuals that no attempt to repel the enemy would succeed in the long run unless ordinary people were willing to act together. One effective way to galvanize the disparate individual groups was by means of "popular literature," an easily comprehensible and beloved cultural form deeply rooted in the life of all Chinese people.

The writer Wang Pingling described a familiar rural scene: in villages in southern China, whenever there was a temple fair or a festival, scores of itinerant book peddlers would appear, touting a host of chapbooks for customers. Most of the books were slim volumes of small cost, ranging from popular songbooks to familiar tales such as *The Story of Yue Fei (Yue zhuan)*. "For the great majority of people," Wang noted, "these books served as major sources of information about Chinese history. Villagers could be equally captivated [by these books as] by a story of bandit-heroes avenging cases of injustice told by a professional storyteller in a country teahouse."[7] Echoing Wang Pingling, Lao Xiang saw a bright future for popular literature in China's bitter struggle against the invaders. According to Lao, stories from popular novels such as *The Romance of the Three Kingdoms*, including accounts of the brilliant strategy of the wise man Zhuge Liang and the bravery of Guan Yu, not only remained enormously popular with Chinese readers but also continued to shape their worldview, and thus could be valuable for educating the public in the cause of the resistance. In fact, popular culture proved to be far more influential than its elite counterpart. As Lao Xiang put it, "There were more of Guandi's [Guan Yu] temples in China than of Confucius's."[8] But what exactly *is* "popular literature"? Does it refer only to popular novels like *The Romance of the Three Kingdoms* and *The Story of Yue Fei*? Or does it include something more? And what are the differences between "popular literature" and "elite literature"?

Ironically, although the term *popular literature* was widely used during the war, its contents and its underlying assumptions remained vague. The term defied simple definition in part because it was a catch-all expression, diffuse and pluralistic in nature, and in part because its meaning changed over time. At the beginning of the war it referred loosely to anything that was not considered elitist—that is, literary forms other than such recognized genres as poetry and lyrics. Subsequently the term was often used interchangeably with *folk literature (minjian wenyi)*, literature or art such as folk songs and legends believed to be orally transmitted and collectively composed by the common people.

The search for a definition of "popular literature and art" provoked heated debates within intellectual circles. Some rated the quality of popular literature quite low, especially the old genres. Zheng Boqi (1895–1979), a former member of the Creation Society, a May Fourth literary association, was one such critic. He argued that "popular literature" meant two types of literary products: first, "feudal relics" inherited from the past such as *Setting Fire to the Red Lotus Temple (Huoshao Hongliansi)* and tales of adventure, superheroes, and spectacular sword fights; and second, shoddy and often shameless modern works scribbled by mediocre writers whose sole intent was financial gain. Detective novels, "Mandarin Duck–and–Butterfly fiction," and stories of romantic triangles and sadism fit into the latter category. Zheng denounced these as "poisonous products," intended to promote ideas of hedonism, espousing fantasy, and corrupting people's minds.[9]

The writer A Ying saw similar problems with popular songbooks produced in Shanghai. As a Communist, however, he adopted a more political outlook. A Ying observed a substantial increase in songbooks after the incident of 28 January 1932. Many of the songs bore patriotic titles, condemning foreign invasion and advancing nationalism. But in reality, A Ying said, they were crass commercial products that espoused "archaic ideas of fatalism and retribution." He attributed this phenomenon to the erroneous views of "feudalistic song writers" who, in his words, intended to "drug the laboring masses, leading them down the road of destruction."[10] A Ying's criticism clearly reflected his own political view: the booming popular songbook publishing industry represented a society marred by greed and exploitation. Marxist clichés notwithstanding, his criticism addressed a common concern of intellectuals: not all popular literature was useful. In fact, much of it was deemed harmful to the cause of the war.

The historian and folklorist Gu Jiegang (1893–1980), however, looked on Chinese popular literature with a more sympathetic eye, stressing its positive influences rather than its detrimental impact. Gu, a nationalist and a brilliant scholar whose monumental multivolume work *Critical Discussions of Ancient History* (*Gushi bian*, 1926–1941) had permanently reshaped Chinese historiography, enthusiastically embraced the theory of "pouring new wine into old bottles." His meticulous study of ancient Chinese history convinced him that it was the very presence of the past that determined China's present and future. The nation's enduring legacy should be carefully examined and accorded due respect, for anything that could remain virtually unchanged over thousands of years must have great intrinsic value. Hence, unlike Zheng Boqi, Gu affirmed a host of traditional cultural forms. In an important article from 1938, "How to Write Popular Literature," Gu argued that popular literature encompassed the following: novels such as *The Water Margin*, storytelling, drum singing, regional drama, folk songs, *xiangsheng* (comic dialogue), *shuanghuang* (a two-man act with one singing or speaking while the other acts out the story), *la yangpian* (a still-picture show viewed through a magnifying lens), New Year pictures (*nianhua*), and so on.[11] His list, which covered a wide range of topics, was the most detailed and comprehensive one proposed during the war. Significantly, it combined works written by the educated (such as novels) and those produced by illiterate people (such as folk songs and New Year pictures). In this sense it thus underscores a significant development in wartime China: the merging of popular and folk literature in the campaign being waged by Chinese intellectuals against the Japanese.

But why were these old and to some extent outmoded cultural forms such as storytelling and comic dialogue valuable? How could they be resurrected to serve present needs? Like the dramatist Ouyang Yuqian, Gu Jiegang believed that tradition was a vital part of China's wartime culture. His celebrated study of the legend of Lady Meng Jiang had already in the 1920s demonstrated how China's folk heritage continued to shape the hearts and minds of contemporary Chinese. But he was equally sensitive to the urgent needs of the time. Gu argued fervently that popular traditional forms should not be misinterpreted as the products of a merely conservative impulse. Rather, they were the accumulated wisdom of the folk, embodying the people's thoughts and feelings. Given their long historical roots and enduring popularity, they were potent weapons for rallying the masses.

To be sure, Gu Jiegang held a rather romantic view of the common people.[12] Even so, he was correct in stressing the potential use of folk and popular literature in a period of national crisis. The advantages of such forms were many: they used a rich array of common sayings drawn directly from the people's experience and thus would be familiar and understandable to the peasantry; their straightforwardness would allow intellectuals to reach the masses swiftly and sincerely; and if music were involved, because its tones were simple and easy to learn, an instant rapport could be established between intellectuals and the commoners.[13]

Lao Xiang echoed Gu Jiegang's views. Besides popular novels like *The Romance of the Three Kingdoms*, Lao Xiang argued, well-loved detective stories such as *The Cases of Lord Peng* (*Penggong an*) and *The Cases of Lord Shi* (*Shigong an*) could be placed under the same rubric of popular literature. They were works of great merit that should not be brushed aside as inelegant or unworthy. The mere fact that they were extremely popular attested to their importance in the life of the common people. Studying them would yield valuable information about the attitudes of the reading public.[14] In the past, such popular stories were usually considered too insignificant to warrant any attention. Lao Xiang, however, considered this censure to be presumptuous. Although popular works were predictably uneven in quality, they often exhibited a profound understanding of life, on top of being highly entertaining and rich in imagination. Popular literature, Lao Xiang warned, should not be confused with things "vulgar" or "shallow."[15]

What impressed Gu Jiegang and Lao Xiang most was the sense of realism inherent in popular literature and its simple and lively language, which seldom fell victim to embellishment and pretentious punditry. Often witty and down-to-earth, popular stories faithfully mirrored social reality and the people's life. Both folk and popular literature, Gu observed, used language naturally and effectively, and both expressed ideas with a sense of colloquialism. The writer Fang Bai agreed. Folk literature was a treasure trove of insights that could provide unlimited inspiration to resistance intellectuals. Illiteracy, Fang noted, was so widespread in China that it would be naive to think that sophisticated works such as Lu Xun's *Call to Arms* (*Nahan*, 1923) or Mao Dun's *Midnight* (*Ziye*, 1933), however well received by critics, would be comprehensible to the general public. The hidden symbols and rich allegories in these books were simply alien to most people's lives. Something simpler, though no less forceful, was needed. Folk literature such as common sayings and proverbs could help, Fang suggested,[16] thus reiterating a familiar proposal voiced earlier by Liu Fu and Zhou Zuoren during the May Fourth Movement. But now the argument was politicized, for it was the practical function, rather than the intrinsic value, of folk literature that drew these intellectuals' attention. And the argument was not used to reject traditional elite culture, as Liu Fu and Zhou Zuoren had done, but to spur the country to national consciousness.

Although Gu Jiegang and Lao Xiang stressed repeatedly the importance of popular and folk literature,[17] they did not overlook its less attractive aspects. These old cultural forms, they agreed, were full of violence and superstition, and many were the products of booksellers who cared not about cultural values but about profits.[18] But like the drama reformers Ouyang Yuqian and Tian Han, Gu and Lao proposed reform rather than complete rejection. Gu argued that an extensive review process was needed to select the useful works and discard the undesirable ones. The old forms must be transformed and given a new life. He suggested some fundamental changes: replacing "feudal mentality" with "national consciousness," and "lewd songs" with music that portrayed the reality of life.[19] In the writing and publishing of good popular literature, Gu recommended a wide range of topics:

national leaders' speeches, the mobilization of the people, conscription, wounded soldiers, guerrilla warfare, the atrocities of the Japanese troops, and national heroes. Since most people had little interest in theory, the ideas introduced must be simple and related to their life. Intellectuals, he said, should approach the subject of popular culture with understanding, sensitivity, and respect, not with condescension or abstraction. Their efforts to awaken the masses would yield results only if they paid sufficient attention to the people's practical needs and emotions. In these views Gu was supported by Lao She and Lao Xiang.

Lao She and Lao Xiang

Lao She and Lao Xiang were pivotal figures in the popular culture drive, for they put ideas into practice. As the president of the ACRA-WA, Lao She played a particularly crucial role in promoting popular literature. As a widely acclaimed writer in his own right, he lent the art a much-needed sense of legitimacy and mapped out a strategy for its dissemination. Lao She's nonpartisan stand and his unassuming character not only earned him wide respect among his peers, but it also seemed to underscore the sincerity of the work he was sponsoring.

Born in Beijing and of Manchu origin, Lao She first burst onto the literary scene in the mid-1920s with his novels *The Philosophy of Old Zhang* (*Lao Zhang de zhexue*) and *Zhao Ziyue*. Like his contemporary Shen Congwen (1903–1988), Lao She was noted for championing simple values and human integrity in his works. But unlike Shen, who focused especially on soldiers, peasants, and remote rural life, Lao She's characters are mostly urbanites caught in a world of corruption and deceit.[20] Lao She felt strong sympathy for the underprivileged. Nowhere was this more evident than in his treatment of the tragic hero Camel Xiangzi, the protagonist and title character of his masterpiece written on the eve of the Sino-Japanese War. Xiangzi is a kind-hearted, indefatigable country lad who is determined to eke out a living in Beijing by sheer hard work. But his repeated attempts to own a rickshaw and live an independent life are thwarted by evil forces all around him: the unruly military, the atrocious secret police, and the ugly daughter of his rickshaw boss. In the end, this honest man is destroyed by a rapacious and depraved society. His fate seemed to point to the futility of individual effort and the need for concerted action, an idea that became a reality for Lao She as he joined the collective campaign against the Japanese when the war broke out.

Throughout the war years, Lao She continued to write novels. But none quite matched the brilliance and sophistication of his earlier works. Perhaps realizing spoken drama's potential to reach a wide audience, Lao She also tried his hand at writing plays, producing a number of them, including *The Nation Above All* (*Guojia zhishang*, coauthored with Song Zhidi) and *The Problem of Face* (*Mianzi wenti*). As a whole, however, the plays are mediocre at best, devoid of artistry and visual appeal and lacking originality and insight into character. "Because he is a novelist," drama critic Tian Qin remarked politely, "his plays seem to retain the wit of a novel"[21]—a shortcoming that Lao She frankly admitted later when he confessed that he did not understand the distinctions between writing scenes in a play and chapters in a novel.[22] Arguing that everything must serve the war cause, Lao She imbued his plays with a distinct patriotic fervor.[23] *The Nation Above All*, for example, tells the story of a stubborn Moslem who, realizing that China cannot win the war against Japan unless people join together with a single will, decides to put aside ethnic and religious differences and join hands with his fellow countrymen.[24] Yet what Lao She lacked in artistic refinement in his wartime novels and spoken dramas, he made up for by his robust promotion of popular literature.

Lao She left Ji'nan in Shangdong province for Hankou in late 1937. En route he was robbed several times, which were bitter and traumatic experiences.[25] Fortunately, he was able to find temporary solace at the home of Feng Yuxiang, the famous Christian general, whom he had known earlier when he was a lecturer at Qilu University in Ji'nan in the early 1930s. General Feng, a passionate man with an imposing presence, received Lao She with open arms and enthusiastically supported his work in popular culture. Despite Feng's colorful public image, he lived a simple life and participated in arduous maneuvers with his troops. Like other patriots, he was also extremely critical of the GMD government's conciliatory policy toward the Japanese, and so drew the ire of Jiang Jieshi. In his early years, Feng had used simple songs (many of them his own compositions) and plays to inspire his troops and teach them such virtues as bravery and patriotism, an unorthodox method in his day.[26] During the war, Feng promoted the resistance cause, inviting folk artists to join the movement and lecturing and writing voluminously on Japanese aggression; he was especially known for his simple, down-to-earth, nationalistic songs called *qiuba shi* (soldiers' poems).[27] More important, Feng was an enthusiastic champion of popular culture and a staunch supporter of the ACRA-

WA. He lent his prestige to the organization from the start, serving as a director and contributing money when it was badly needed.[28]

In Hankou, with the support of Feng and together with Lao Xiang and He Rong (1903–1990), Lao She helped to launch the magazine *Resisting Till the End* (*Kang dao di*), a bastion for popular literature in the early phase of the war.[29] When the ACRAWA was founded in March 1938 in Hankou, Lao She, widely respected by left and right alike, was elected its president. He vowed to turn the organization into "a new mechanized force,"[30] a martial phrase reminiscent of the language of wartime journalists. He remained in that post throughout the war years, helping to set the nation's cultural and literary agenda.

Lao She's mild and charming manner masked an iron will: he was resolute in pushing what he believed in. Like Gu Jiegang and Lao Xiang, he viewed popular culture as an ideal propaganda weapon. In his early career, he already demonstrated an enormous interest in a variety of traditional cultural forms. As a child growing up in the capital, Lao She had developed an enduring interest in the folk arts and local customs of old Beijing. He frequented the theaters and the teahouses, enjoying Beijing opera and listening to the storytelling and comic dialogues of local artists. The performing skills that he inadvertently picked up in these rather unconventional places later added a theatrical touch to his classroom lectures, earning him a reputation as a lively teacher in his Qilu University days.[31]

Lao She was never an iconoclast. Unlike his May Fourth contemporaries, who vehemently attacked Chinese tradition as fusty and backward, Lao She had strong feelings of nostalgia toward the past. What he cherished, however, was not the Confucian elite culture, but the old customs and manners that still thrived among ordinary people. "I was born in Beijing," Lao She once wrote, "and I know well its people, its events and scenery, its atmosphere, the cries of peddlers selling plum juice and almond tea. As soon as I close my eyes, the city appears before me like a vivid, richly colored painting. This gives me the courage to describe it."[32] Lao She's genuine love for popular culture in general and old Beijing in particular is evident in his works, which contain a wealth of information about lower-class people and their life in that ancient city. Many of his stories seem to conjure up an old, forgotten China brought back out of memory. He was particularly noted for his lively use of Beijing dialect (as in *The Philosophy of Old Zhang*).

Thus when Lao She came to promote popular culture during the war, he was already an expert in and great admirer of this art. To him, popular cultural forms not only possessed superior intrinsic value, but they also embodied certain essential ingredients of China's rich cultural legacy. The war, instead of undermining his emotional and spiritual ties with the past, only strengthened his love for his country's multifaceted traditions. Echoing Xiong Foxi's notion of "education in entertainment," Lao She embraced popular culture as an educational tool. His childhood experience constantly reminded him that "inelegant" places like theaters and storytelling houses were as important as academic settings in providing the general public with knowledge of life's realities. "They were," he said, "tantamount to people's schools."[33]

To plead a convincing case for popular culture, Lao She realized that he had to dispel the myth that it was low and worthless. Like Lao Xiang and Gu Jiegang, he argued that popular culture forms were often moving and entertaining. "Their fresh and pure words resemble newly picked vegetables from the garden. Their vocabulary comes from the people, representing their thoughts and imagination. On this point alone, perhaps, popular culture contains more new blood than the classics and the new vernacular literature."[34]

Lao She's comment, which seemed to echo the views of such May Fourth folklorists as Liu Fu and Zhou Zuoren, was certainly romantic and exaggerated. To him, folk tradition was a pastoral landscape not yet trampled by the evils of urbanization and modernization, and popular culture forms were a potent source for cultural rejuvenation. Yet Lao She also gave the most detailed and convincing argument on why writing popular literature was such a difficult task for intellectuals, and in so doing he brought respect to the genre. Lao She believed that writers encountered three difficulties when composing such popular pieces: namely, the writing must be comprehensible, entertaining, and pleasing to the ear (*yue'er*)—a difficult task at best.[35] But before writers could begin to solve these riddles, they needed to ask an even more fundamental question: For whom was the writing intended? To Lao She, the answer was very clear: "We must aim at the common people."[36] In an influential article from 1938, "The Difficulty of Writing Popular Literature," Lao She offered the following advice:

> First, forget that you are a man of letters. In other words, forget Shakespeare and Du Fu, and turn yourself into a country storyteller.
>
> Second, discard highly specialized sociological and economic terms. If you can change descriptions such as *modeng nüxing*

[modern ladies] to *xiao jiaoniang* [young women], it would be even better.

Third, in portraying characters, black and white must be contrasted sharply. It must be simple and forceful.

Fourth, put your story into a familiar, easily recognizable setting.

And finally, use dialect.[37]

In suggesting dialects as a useful vehicle in writing popular literature, Lao She was raising a difficult question long debated by May Fourth intellectuals. The folklorist Liu Fu, for example, recognized the value of dialect literature as a genuine folk product coming from the illiterate peasantry, and the leftist writer Qu Qiubai valued dialects as essential components in his ideal "mass language."[38] Like Qu, Lao She criticized the new vernacular literature as being a kind of elitist writing focusing on "college professors, bank managers, dancing girls, and politicians" and thus separate from the life of real people. "Popular literature," Lao She wrote, "must use the language of the folk and write about the life of the people." Nevertheless, the dialect issue was a controversial one, for its full realization could lead to parochialism, which would contradict the original goal of fostering a national consciousness.

For Lao She, those who could best master "the language of the folk" were folk artists such as storytellers and drum singers. "They are the ones who live among the people, while we intellectuals are no doubt far removed from them," he lamented.[39] Lao She therefore heartily applauded General Feng Yuxiang's move to invite folk artists to join the resistance camp. In his view, that act was more than a proper recognition of an underrated art; it was a true confession on the part of intellectuals that they were inferior to folk artists when it came to using popular cultural forms as a resistance tool.

Since the majority of the people were illiterate, simplicity of content was essential to make popular literature influential, Lao She argued. Subtlety, sophistication, and finesse had no place in such works. He particularly advocated the use of rhymes to reach as wide an audience as possible, pointing out that popular literature was not just a written form of artistic expression, it was "oral persuasion" (*koutou xuanchuan*). "Beside paying special attention to the common vocabulary and their simple meanings, we must make sure that popular literature exudes beautiful melodies," he wrote.[40] His friend He Rong agreed: "Rhymes are the main ingredient of popular literature." Without a basic understanding of rhyme patterns and their implementation, a writer could hardly claim that he had mastered the essence of popular literature.[41]

By stressing the importance of rhymes, Lao She showed his unique understanding of the nature of popular performing arts. He was in fact one of the few resistance intellectuals to note the actual performance effect of popular literature. His theatergoing experience made him realize that the composition of an audience and the conditions of performance were just as important as the work itself in deciding its success or failure. The effect of a piece of popular literature, in other words, came not from its latent possibility but from its realization.

The effectiveness of a piece of popular literature relied heavily on the circumstances under which it was performed, including the personalities involved. A seasoned performer such as the famous Beijing drum singer Liu Baoquan could easily bring the audience to its feet, but a less experienced performer might have just the opposite effect.[42] Since writing popular literature was by no means easy, and since most of the writers in this endeavor were amateurs, Lao She suggested that they study the folk singers and traditional storytellers for ideas and techniques. "Learn from experts [*neihangren*]!"[43] Practicing what he preached, during the war Lao She cultivated a close friendship with a father-daughter Beijing drum singing team, the Potato (Shanyaodan, whose real name was Fu Shaofang) and Big Blossom (Fuguihua, whose real name was Fu Shu'ai), learning their techniques. He also sought advice from Bai Yunpeng, another acclaimed Beijing drum singer.[44] Lao She's sincere respect for folk artists and his repeated emphasis on the conditions of performance underscored his strong aversion to grandiose theorizing. The power of a piece of popular literature, he firmly believed, lay not in its text, but in its ability to communicate directly with the audience. This view reflected the general determination among resistance intellectuals to translate abstract issues into personal and concrete statements.

Lao She created works in a variety of areas during the war, including drum songs, comic dialogues, *shulaibao* (rhythmic storytelling to the accompaniment of clappers), and Henan *zhuizi* (ballad songs popular in Henan province). Some of them—three drum songs, four traditional operas, and one old-style novel—were published in his popular literature collection entitled *San si yi* (*Three, Four, One,* 1939). They were produced, Lao She wrote in the preface, according to the formula of "pouring new wine into old bottles."[45] Among a score of Lao She's drum songs, "Wang Xiao Drives a Donkey" ("Wang Xiao gan lü," 1938) is one of the best known. A short piece that touches directly on the issues of patriotism and sacrifice, it describes how Wang Xiao, a peace-loving and hardworking young man who takes care of donkeys as a living, decides to join the army after China is invaded by the Japanese. Shocked by the brutality of the invaders, Wang Xiao resolves:

> I shall go enlist in the army.
> I am a man of indomitable spirit,
> To die for my country I feel no regret,
> It is better than living as a slave under the bayonets of the enemy.

After bidding farewell to his widowed, ailing mother, Wang Xiao sets off on his journey to the front:

> As he turns around and looks at his home again,
> He sees his mother standing stiffly at the doorstep.
> Choosing between being a loyal citizen and a filial son is hard,
> But [at last] he stamps his feet and leaves his hometown.[46]

"Wang Xiao Drives a Donkey" was certainly one of Lao She's better pieces.[47] Despite its predictable ending, the song nevertheless bursts with emotion, a general call to arms issued in a familiar folk art form. Other of his drum songs such as "The Second Phase of the War of Resistance" ("Erqi kangzhan," 1938) and "A Eulogy to the Wartime Capital" ("Peidu zan," 1942) exude similar confidence and fervent nationalism, attempting to instill a sense of optimism amid a climate of uncertainty and fear.

Lao She was concerned more with patriotic value than with artistic sophistication. This can be seen in his "Classic for Women" ("Nü'er jing," 1938), a *kuaiban* piece (rhythmic comic talk to the accompaniment of bamboo clappers), where he praises women warriors:

> They are women, but as courageous as men.
> Patriots who won't live with a false peace.
> Hardworking, they never dress up,
> They donate their savings to the nation
> And deliver winter clothing to the barracks. . . .
> Full of courage, they take up their guns.
> They are heroines like Hua Mulan. . . .
> Women of a new era, their arms hold up the sky.
> And the names of the heroines spread far and wide.[48]

The theme was familiar, but by using the popular *kuaiban* format, which is particularly effective in creating both drama and tension in a performance, Lao She clearly sought to heighten audience emotions. Again, the actual performance was of primary concern.

Enthusiasm and versatility notwithstanding, Lao She's works in the domain of popular literature can hardly be rated as artistically superior. Many were mediocre pieces that paled in comparison with his more celebrated prewar novels. But Lao She was a humble man (he called himself a "foot soldier") and a patient learner, and he frankly admitted that, despite his attempts, he remained an amateur in writing popular literature. Still, he never had any doubt about the value of this powerful tool. "If *War and Peace* only lies on the sofa, whereas drum songs are widely read by soldiers and the people, I certainly [feel] no regret for writing drum songs and not coming out with *War and Peace*," Lao She wrote in 1939.[49] China, after all, was living in troubled times, and he was willing to sacrifice artistic refinement for practical needs.

Like his friend Lao She, Lao Xiang avidly promoted popular literature during the war. He was also an accomplished practitioner, producing a prodigious number of works in a short span of time. A graduate of Beijing University's Chinese literature department, Lao Xiang first made his name as a fine essayist noted for his wit and humor. But he was by no means a pure stylist. He often invested his writings with passion and, more important, with a strong dose of social commentary on current rural problems.

Born in a small town in southern Hebei, Lao Xiang considered himself very much a country man with a heritage deeply rooted in the Chinese soil.[50] He firmly believed that the roots of China's problems lay in the countryside, a vast area long ignored or misunderstood by intellectuals. According to Lao Xiang, one of the gravest shortcomings of Chinese education was its indifference toward the peasantry. Consider school textbooks: they were filled with decorated mansions and sumptuously dressed women, representing a life-style far beyond the comprehension of humble peasants. Lao Xiang had long toiled against illiteracy. "Education," he wrote, "must be designed to meet the challenges of real life." He criticized government officials and teachers who were blind to the fact that "the real national resources of China are not coal or iron, but the 300 million reticent peasants."[51]

Not surprisingly, one of Lao Xiang's favorite essay topics was the countryside. His two most popular books, *The Yellow Mud* (*Huangtu ni*) and *The Countryside* (*Minjian ji*)—both collections of essays that first appeared in such journals as *This Human World* (*Renjian shi*) and *The Analects* (*Lunyu*)—chronicled a myriad of rural activities, ranging from "a water pump" to "offering sacrifices to the kitchen god," and were variegated and entertaining. Lao Xiang's prose was always down-to-earth, displaying his profound capacity for realism. No aloof observer, Lao Xiang was a participant as well. His concern for rural problems such as illiteracy, superstition, and hygiene prompted him to devote a large portion of his early career to improving the living conditions of country folk. He spent the early 1930s, for example, in Dingxian as an active member of the Mass Education Movement headed by James Yen, trying to eliminate illiteracy in the countryside. For Lao Xiang, education was more than formal training: it involved changing the minds of the people and exposing problems so that remedies could be found. This concern was the main thrust of his essays during this period. He went to Dingxian to teach, an act described by his friend the writer Sun Fuyuan (1894–1966) as a kind of "homecoming."[52] Indeed, Lao Xiang's knowledge of and love for rural China was rare among other writers of his generation. Another friend, Qu Junong, summed it up best: "In the past, articles about peasants' lives were often the results of intellectuals' dreams, fanciful and unsympathetic. Lao Xiang's pieces, however, are microcosms of rural China. They are real!"[53]

Lao Xiang was in Beijing when that city fell to the Japanese in late July 1937. Life under the occupation was both humiliating and frightening.[54] He managed to flee to the south, later joining the ACRAWA in Hankou. Although there is no direct evidence that Lao Xiang participated directly in the Dingxian mass education group's efforts to collect a large amount of folk literature, notably *yangge* plays and narrated stories, he spoke enthusiastically about this famous endeavor led by his friend Sun Fuyuan, the director of the "Popular Literature Section" in Dingxian.[55] Lao Xiang's thorough acquaintance with rural life (in Dingxian and elsewhere) and his interest in peasant culture proved to be extremely valuable during the war when he began to refashion a host of traditional popular and folk literature forms into what he called "powerful educational tools."[56] His dream was realized when he took center stage of the popular literature campaign by assuming the editorship of *Resisting Till the End* in January 1938. The semimonthly, supported and financed by Feng Yuxiang, was one of but a few publications dedicated entirely to the advocacy and dissemination of popular literature during the war. Now Lao Xiang was in a key position to influence the course of that movement, which he did with zeal.

Vowing to "use ink as blood and to turn words into weapons,"[57] Lao Xiang transformed the journal into a major force for popular literature. The journal's appeal lay in its rich array of popular literary forms (ditties, comic dialogues, and drum songs), cartoons (Zhao Wangyun, a friend of Feng Yuxiang's, was a major contributor), patriotic stories, and articles on "pouring new wine into old bottles." For all their variety, the pages displayed a strong nationalist current. Even the title of the journal was an obvious call to arms. *Resisting Till the End* was a fresh breeze in the publishing world in part because no magazine had ever before placed so much emphasis on popular culture, and in part because of the devotion and energy of its staff (which included Lao She and He Rong—who later replaced Lao Xiang as editor of the journal).

Priced at 8 *fen* (later increased to 10), *Resisting Till the End* lasted twenty-six issues, from January 1938 to November 1939. Its impact is difficult to gauge, since circulation data for the journal are scanty, but it seems to have been well received by educated and semiliterate readers. In the eyes of Lao Xiang, the journal played a crucial role in arousing people's nationalistic sentiments by encouraging them to write: "One more word," he noted, "is one extra resistance effort."[58] In his view, this sense of engagement alone was enough to have far-reaching consequences. Besides *Resisting Till the End*, Lao Xiang helped launch another journal, *Resistance Pictorial* (*Kangzhan huakan*), with Lao She and Zhao Wangyun, also financed by Feng Yuxiang.[59]

Perhaps more than any other resistance intellectuals (Lao She included), Lao Xiang experimented with different types of popular culture and excelled in many of them.[60] One area in which he shone was children's song writing. "Collecting Winter Clothing" ("Mu hanyi," 1940) is a good example:

> The snow is dancing,
> The lone crow is crying.
> I am making a fur hat for the soldier.
> Where can I find furs?
> I ask help from a fox.
> The fox runs into the grass.
> Oh fox, oh fox, please don't run.
> Can you lend me a big fur coat?
> I won't wear it,
> Nor will he,
> We are sending it to the soldier at the front.

> It feels so warm,
> It looks so good,
> We're sure to beat those Japanese.[61]

This piece is in the best tradition of Chinese children's songs. It begins with the familiar description of a natural phenomenon, then the human emotion it arouses. But Lao Xiang was not interested in rhetorical devices. He wished to carry a contemporary message: the importance of supporting the soldiers on the battlefield. Structurally, the song is simple, down-to-earth, and lively, yet its meanings are serious and its mood sanguine. Death is a subtext here, but is treated in an instructional, patriotic manner. The metamorphosis of a dead fox into a fur hat is more than a physical change: it is a transformation of values. Killing revives life, a victory will soon be in sight if the soldiers are well clothed, and many lives will be saved in the end. The image is not of death, but of life and triumph.

Another of Lao Xiang's songs, "A Small Swallow" ("Xiao yanzi," 1939), touches on a different but related theme of war: the bitter experience of a refugee living an uprooted life.

> A small swallow,
> Atop the roof beam.
> Fled from home at seven or eight,
> She misses her father,
> And misses her mother,
> She thinks about her beloved hometown.
> What a wonderful place!
> A place that's good!
> Thinking of home, she hates the Japanese.
> Oh, the Japanese devils,
> Came to her town,
> Killing and burning everything.
> She lost her father,
> She lost her mother.
> She sobs bitterly by the road.
> Do not weep,
> Do not whine,
> If we don't take revenge, we'll be worse than swine.[62]

Again, despite the defeats and suffering that the song describes, it ends on a note of determination and hope.

Besides children's songs, Lao Xiang composed drum songs, comic dialogues, *shulaibao*, and *kuaiban*. All were written with a gusto that the reader could not miss. But perhaps his most successful piece was a revision of the *Three-Character Classic* (*Sanzi jing*), a telling case of "pouring new wine into old bottles."

Indeed, Lao Xiang's *Anti-Japanese Three-Character Classic* (*Kang-Ri sanzi jing*) was one of the most popular texts penned by a resistance intellectual. But why the traditional *Three-Character Classic*? To explain his reasons, Lao Xiang recalled two shabby, almost deserted bookstores he had known in Dingxian before the war. Contrary to his expectation that the bookstores were on the verge of closing, their business continued. The secret of their survival, he later learned, was that they were regional wholesale dealers of a number of "outmoded books," including the *Three-Character Classic*, the *Thousand-Character Classic* (*Qianzi wen*), and the *Hundred Names* (*Baijia xing*)—books that had dominated traditional elementary education in China from Song times on.[63] These texts remained enormously popular among the general public, even in an age of airplanes and telephones. When Lao Xiang later found that few, if any, soldiers or common people understood the contents of resistance magazines like *Resisting Till the End*, he turned to these "outmoded books" for help.

Lao Xiang published his *Anti-Japanese Three-Character Classic* in *Resisting Till the End* in March 1938. As he put it, "Since the *Three-Character Classic* is such influential reading material among the Chinese people, by pouring 'anti-Japanese new wine' into this old bottle, perhaps the people can accept [this literature] more easily."[64] Yet besides superficial similarities such as title and format (both books used three-character couplets), the two versions were markedly different in content and ideas. Lao Xiang's new version was longer (1,428 words versus about 1,100 in the traditional work, which was available in many versions), and its tone was patriotic rather than didactic. The differences between the two are immediately apparent in their respective opening lines. The traditional *Three-Character Classic* begins:

> Men at their birth are naturally good.
> Their natures are much the same; their habits become widely different.
> If foolishly there is no teaching, the nature will deteriorate.
> The right way in teaching is to attach the utmost importance to thoroughness.[65]

Lao Xiang's version begins:

> Men at their birth are naturally loyal and persistent.
> Loving their nation is instinctive.

When the nation falls, the family cannot survive.
Protecting the nation is the first concern [for everyone].[66]

In the place of the traditional version's call for filial obedience, Lao Xiang emphasized patriotic duty and paid tribute to generals who sacrificed their lives in defense of the nation. And instead of providing historical anecdotes from the Chinese past, the new version chronicled the recent conflict with Japan. Lao Xiang, of course, presented no paragons of morality like Huang Xiang of the Han, who as a young boy warmed his parents' bed in winter before they went to sleep; nor did he exalt the Confucian ideals of benevolence and righteousness. Instead he praised sacrifice and unity, and urged perseverance and contribution to the war cause. Descriptions in the new version were not about past sages and their admirable deeds but about contemporary heroes and Japanese brutality; the emphasis was not on persistent learning but on armed resistance. While the traditional *Three-Character Classic* ends by advising, "Diligence has its reward; play has no advantages. Oh, be on your guard, and put forth your strength," the new version concludes with a call for revenge and for the recovery of lost territory.

Lao Xiang's piece was an overwhelming success. Not only was it widely reprinted in other magazines, but it sold more than fifty thousand copies in offprints during the first month of issue—a rare achievement at a difficult time in China.[67] Critics hailed it as a virtuoso work that could only have sprung from the author's deep understanding of the resistance movement and his delight in writing it.[68] Part of the reason for its phenomenal success was its low price of 1 *jiao* (10 *fen*). The vivid illustrations by Zhao Wangyun, Gao Longsheng, and others also helped. But the main reason was its familiar format—a confirmation of Lao Xiang's own belief that no recipe was more effective in combating the Japanese than the use of traditional forms.

Despite its success, the *Anti-Japanese Three-Character Classic*, though well organized and written with passion, was by no means a superior artistic achievement. It could not, for example, match the vividness and charm of the same author's children's song "Collecting Winter Clothing." It was longer than its traditional counterpart, its language was more difficult, and its messages utterly familiar, even stale. How ironic that its success was due largely to the perennial influence of an ancient Confucian text that new intellectuals had fought so hard to repudiate since the May Fourth era.

Lao Xiang, of course, was not the first modern writer to use the *Three-Character Classic* for a purpose other than Confucian education. The Taipings, for instance, realizing the prestige of that earlier work, had used it to render Christianity comprehensible to the masses in the mid–nineteenth century.[69] Christian missionaries in the waning years of the Qing dynasty had also reshaped it into religious tracts.[70] Lao Xiang, then, in writing both this tract and a less successful sequel, the *Anti-Japanese Thousand-Character Classic* (*Kang-Ri qianzi wen*),[71] was following a long tradition of literary borrowing.

Drum Singing and Other Popular Culture Forms

Among a rich variety of popular culture forms, drum singing was one of the most prevalent during the war. Lao She, who, as we have seen, wrote the drum song "Wang Xiao Drives a Donkey," enjoyed the genre so much that he wrote a novel about it. *The Drum Singers* (*Gushu yiren*), based on his real-life friendship with the Potato and his daughter, Big Blossom, portrays the bitter life of an exiled drum-singing family in Chongqing from 1938 to 1945. Most Chinese readers, however, had gotten their first glimpse of this art in Liu E's (1857–1909) famed description of a performance of Pear Blossom drum singing by two sisters in his late Qing novel *The Travels of Lao Can* (*Lao Can youji*): "They were unparalleled songs sung by two beautiful women," marveled the author at the virtuosity of the singers Dark Maid and Fair Maid.[72]

Dagu is a collective term for a host of drum singing styles performed in north China, especially in Shandong province. Originating in the Qing,[73] drum songs are accompanied by a small drum and a stringed instrument. Beyond that, certain variations define the different styles. Their names identify them as to either the type of additional musical instruments used (Pear Blossom drum songs [*Lihua dagu*], for example, use two pieces of iron hit together as their primary instrument) or the region where they are popular (for example, Beijing drum songs [*Jingyun dagu*] or Leting drum songs [*Leting dagu*]).[74] Extremely flexible in rhymes and varying in length (they range from eight lines to a few hundred, though the common length is between one and two hundred), traditional drum songs drew their subject matter from such popular stories as *The Romance of the Three Kingdoms* and *The Water Margin*. They were immensely popular in north China, attracting large audiences in cities and villages alike. Virtuoso performers like the great Beijing Drum Singing School masters Liu Baoquan and Bai Yunpeng commanded a wide following before the war. Liu Baoquan's piece "The Battle of Changsha," an episode taken from *The Romance of the Three Kingdoms*, always played to packed houses wherever he performed.[75]

The popularity of drum singing continued unabated during the war and caught the attention of Lao She, Lao Xiang, and Zhao Jingshen (1902–1985), a scholar of folk literature and performing arts.[76] Drum songs with a contemporary viewpoint soon began to appear in profusion, becoming one of the most widely used forms of popular art for political purposes. The Popular Reading Publishing House (Tongsu duwu biankanshe), founded by Gu Jiegang, issued drum song pamphlets like *Fierce Battle at the Marco Polo Bridge* (*Xuezhan Lugouqiao*). Newspapers and magazines also featured them prominently.

Like their predecessors, wartime drum songs often began with opening lines like "Let's talk about" (*biao de shi*), "You fellows" (*lie wei*), and "If you asked me" (*ruo wen*). These phrases are rooted in the storytelling tradition, and they established an instant rapport with the audience. In content and length, however, wartime drum songs differed substantially from their forerunners. As Lao She's "Wang Xiao Drives a Donkey" demonstrates, the new works naturally placed considerable emphasis on the current conflict with the Japanese. And while the old ones often ran to more than a hundred lines, the new versions were substantially shorter. Two pieces by Zhao Jingshen are good examples. "The Pass at Juyong" ("Juyongguan," 1937), about the battle at the Nankou Pass in August 1937, has only sixty-five lines, and "The Pass at Pingxing" ("Pingxingguan," 1937), hailing a successful military maneuver by the Communist Eighth Route Army against the Japanese at the Pingxing Pass on the Great Wall in September 1937, is even shorter, with forty-six lines.[77]

Like newspaper articles and cartoons, the thrust of wartime drum songs was patriotism. They abounded with tragic war scenes and stories of the valiant Chinese troops. In "The Pass at Pingxing," which appeared in *National Salvation Daily* the month after the battle occurred, Zhao Jingshen describes the surprise attack on the Japanese with hyperbole:

> When he heard about the arrival of the Eighth Route Army,
> Commander Itagaki [Itagaki Seishirō] was alarmed and panicky.
> "Damn! I have heard of the brilliance of the Red Army's guerrilla
>   warfare for a long time,
> We sure are facing grave danger!"
> Let's not talk about how frightened the Japanese troops had
>   become,

But spend a few words on our courageous Red Army.
A battalion of them was sent to encounter the enemy.
They lured the Japanese into the precipitous pass pretending they
    were being beaten.
When the enemy saw us retreat,
They gleefully poured into the pass in hot pursuit.
At the right time, with a big shout,
Our troops in ambush
Attacked the enemy on both sides.
They encircled them day and night.
And inflicted heavy casualties on the enemy. . . .
How gallant were our Big-Sword Teams!
How like frightened babies were the invaders!
We annihilated them in hundreds and thousands,
Their bodies lying all over the mountain pass.[78]

Another example was the Battle of Taierzhuang—also the sub-ject of a cartoon by Te Wei (fig. 28)—which was given a new inter-pretation in Lao Xiang's famous piece "The Resounding Victory in Southern Shandong" ("Lunan dasheng," 1938). Instead of detailing the battle scenes, Lao Xiang presented a vivid picture of the men at the front, especially General Li Zongren, the commander in charge of the campaign:

If you asked me how General Li dressed,
I am happy to give you a full description:
In gray trousers and gray coat,
He is even more modestly clad than a commoner.
But humble apparel has nothing to do with ability on the
    battlefield.
Resisting the Japanese does not rely on good clothing.
Let's not mention clothing,
And let me tell you something about his looks.
A man of strong physique,
He certainly can shoulder national affairs.
Born to be a great general who guards our land,
His eyes glare like a tiger's,
And he loves his people.
He sets strict rules for his troops,
But he speaks gently with a kindly face.[79]

Lao Xiang's piece was a classic drum song both in its use of rhyme and in technique. Even his description of General Li was reminiscent of the familiar portrayal of heroes in classical novels and storytelling:

a brilliant warrior who is not only gifted in military affairs but also charming as a person. The piece thus presents a unique intimate look that contrasts sharply with the haunting reality of war.

While Lao Xiang was adroit in furnishing the human dimension of the war, Zhao Jingshen, as demonstrated in his "The Pass at Pingxing," focused on heroic battle scenes. As an avid promoter of folk literature in the 1920s,[80] Zhao Jingshen was certainly no novice when it came to "pouring new wine into old bottles," and he produced a string of highly successful drum songs in the early phase of the war. Like others, Zhao idealized his heroes: generals are brilliant strategists, and soldiers are vigorous, robust fighters with enormous confidence. But the fact that he wrote about real people (such as the air force hero Yan Haiwen)[81] and the stories were authentic, he believed, lent his pieces credibility. Surely Zhao recognized these drum songs as propaganda works; but he thought highly of this unique performing art because of its flexibility and enduring popularity.[82]

Drum singing was but one of the many popular "old bottles" filled with "new wine" during the war. Other forms were used as well, such as folk songs, *tanci* (storytelling to the accompaniment of stringed instruments), and local ballads.[83] Folk songs were especially popular, enjoying a surge of renewed interest in the late 1930s. Wartime intellectuals again found ways to make them work as political instruments. "Let us edit them and turn them into a new popular wartime art," one writer proposed.[84] And Chen Yiyuan did exactly that. In his 1938 "Anti-Japanese Mountain Song," he used the traditional *duige* (love duet) format to express his feelings. The first few verses are as follows:

> (*Woman*) Magpies flutter under the eaves,
> My loved one has finally arrived.
> Oh! My love, you bring along an umbrella,
> And you carry a bag on your back.
> Are you going away on a long trip?
> (*Man*) I am prepared to enlist in the army,
> I want to become a soldier to fight against the Japanese.
> When the enemy is defeated
> And I return in two or three years,
> Our love will be reunited.
> (*Woman*) You are such a dumb fellow.
> Haven't you heard that "good men never enlisted"?
> Maybe there is another woman out there?
> Has she stolen your heart?
> And you have forgotten our pledge.

(*Man*) I will never be a heartless man.
But love and loyalty are two different things.
Now our country is under siege,
I must put my love aside for the moment.
But in the future we will have a long time together.[85]

Chen's love song (also known as a "mountain song") is an excellent piece, lighthearted yet serious, endearing yet solemn, weaving lyrical evocations of love with the militant celebration of armed struggle. The love duet style and the juxtaposition of contrasting feelings that it allows create a particularly dramatic impact. Instead of the amorous love of traditional love songs, Chen's song lauds the idea of devotion to one's country. There is no question of the outcome when it comes to choosing between love and patriotism.

The continuing popularity of the folk song tradition and its extreme flexibility, in fact, made it a favorite vehicle for many resistance writers to show their support for their country. The dramatist Ouyang Yuqian, for instance, wrote a song praising the heroic deeds of Chinese women in the war effort.[86] And Bao Tianxiao (1876–1973), the Butterfly fiction writer turned patriot, wrote an equally compelling piece accusing the Japanese troops of numerous atrocities during their 13 August 1937 attack on Shanghai. "I hope this song will spread far and wide among the Chinese people," Bao wrote.[87]

As we have seen, the dramatist Cui Wei furnished new words to the "September Eighteenth Melody" when staging *Lay Down Your Whip*, and many wartime song writers did likewise. The revised "Thirteen Months" ("Shisan yue," 1938), for example, begins:

> January is the first month of the year,
> Our leader is Generalissimo Jiang.
> He is determined to defend our nation,
> And he is China's Great Wall of Iron.

The song continues for eleven more stanzas, each referring to a particular month or seasonal change and describing either a famous battle or a celebrated general, including Feng Yuxiang, Chen Cheng, and Zhu De (1886–1976), commander in chief of the Chinese Communist forces. The piece ends on an upbeat note:

> The thirteenth month is a leap month.
> The whole nation is united into one.
> We are determined to resist till the end;
> The final victory no doubt will be ours for sure.[88]

Such popular love songs as "Seeing My Loved One Off" ("Song dage") and "Embroidering a Purse" ("Xiu hebao") also were given a new patriotic content.[89]

But individual efforts, no matter how original and well articulated, were generally limited to specific localities. Thus resistance writers launched collective campaigns to try to shape public consciousness, invoking the devices of popular literature to stimulate civilian morale. In early May 1937, two months before the conflict actually broke out, the Shanxi Provincial Sacrifice and National Salvation Alliance (Shanxi xisheng jiuguo tongmenghui) in Taiyuan, in addition to issuing a series of drum songs and *tanci* about the war, invited over 160 local folksingers and storytellers to stage a variety show. The event incorporated a number of patriotic items, including a story entitled "United to Resist," a *shuanghuang* called "The May Thirtieth Incident" (about an anti-imperialist demonstration in Shanghai on 30 May 1925 during which many Chinese students were killed), and a Henan *zhuizi* entitled "The Japanese Invasion of 18 September 1931." The performers were reportedly warmly received by the audience.[90]

The organizers, however, were not content to stage the performance only in the city; they wanted to see the campaign bear fruit in the countryside as well. A reporter gave this eyewitness account of the reaching-out campaign:

> To spread this national salvation storytelling drive into the villages, several men went down to Taigu county [about thirty miles south of Taiyuan] and set up a teahouse. Storytelling and drum singing were performed and created a great sensation. Even the county magistrate offered his help to make the show work. Each performance easily drew four to five hundred people. Not only did this kind of performance bring the patriotic message to the countryside, but it also attracted country folksingers and performers to Taiyuan in order to learn more about nationalist songs and stories.[91]

Organizers clearly realized the importance of a concerted crusade. A variety show helped to bring people together, coalescing their individual experiences into a collective one. Perhaps nothing was so effective as providing the audience with entertainment that was both familiar and well loved. The show was designed to recruit new patriots and establish a firm grass-roots base in line with the ideal of "every citizen a participant" (*quanmin dongyuan*). The effort was successful, at least for the early years of the war, when collective enthusiasm remained high; only later, as the conflict turned into a protracted one, did the energy start to wane.[92]

Popular Reading Materials

To mount an effective campaign against the Japanese, the government and the public at large had to join hands and work side by side, that much was clear. Yet in the eyes of many resistance intellectuals, the government was not doing enough. The ACRAWA, for instance, was founded largely on the initiative of individual writers, with little assistance from the government. The mere fact that the organization was chronically short of funds was an indication of the government's lukewarm support. The tentative plan to publish one hundred different kinds of popular literary works never materialized, largely because there was never enough money; even coming up with the rent for the organization's headquarters in Hankou was a constant headache for Lao She and other association officers. Its meager income from the membership fee (which ranged from one to five *yuan* per person annually) hardly sufficed; as a result, the association had to rely heavily on the generous though intermittent donations of such prominent figures as Feng Yuxiang and Shao Lizi.[93]

To be sure, the war did open the eyes of some government officials, inducing them to play a role in the popular culture effort. The publication and dissemination of certain popular reading materials was one task they took on. Notable examples include the pamphlet series "Air Battles" ("Kongjun dazhan"), issued by the Central Propaganda Department, and "Donating Money to Save Our Nation" ("Shucai jiuguo"), put out by the Department of Education.[94] The Logistics Section of the Military Council also published a "Resistance and Reconstruction Popular Series" ("Kangjian tongsu wenku"); using a variety of popular culture forms, this series contained a plethora of titles, including "The Monks on Mt. Wutai Participate in the Resistance" ("Wutaishan heshang kangzhan"), a drum song, and *Counterespionage (Fanjian ji)*, a spoken drama, to name but two. As the products of a government agency, these items—such as the drum song booklet *Generalissimo Jiang's Address to the Army and the People on the Second Anniversary of the War (Jiang weiyuanzhang kangzhan liangzhounian gao junmin)*—predictably voiced support for the GMD.[95] Another organization, the Disabled Soldiers Vocational Training Center (Rongyu junren zhiye xunliansuo), also published a series of patriotic songbooks. One of them was entitled *Smashing Little Japan (Da xiao Riben)*. In four sections and in simple language, this booklet begins with a familiar admonition, but it goes on to offer a specific way to disseminate patriotic ideas in the neighborhood:

> This is a little songbook.
> Despite its plain language and colloquial expressions,
> Every word in it is true and sincere.
> I hope you fellow readers will read it with great care,
> So that the exact nature of the Sino-Japanese War becomes crystal clear.
> With evil intention, the Japanese want to conquer China.
> We can no longer endure any more provocation;
> We will become a subjugated people unless we stand up and fight.
> It is easy to sing using a songbook,
> But to save a nation is far more difficult.
> Unless we Chinese join hands together
> Our nation will never be strong.
> If you can gather all your neighbors together,
> Be they young or old.
> Sing this song to them
> And follow with explanation.
> This will be a great contribution [to your nation].[96]

The language in this songbook series was neither difficult nor exquisitely crafted; there were no artistic turns of phrase or rhymes. It was specifically designed for people at a very low level of education and, like the folk songs "Thirteen Months" and "Seeing My Loved One Off," was meant to be sung in a group and in public, so that emotions could be shared and hearts touched.

The government's effort was unsystematic, however. Apparently the Guomindang had no overall plan to publish and distribute popular reading materials, and little coordination among different government agencies can be detected. Given the popularity and effectiveness of these materials, the lack of official support is perplexing. Was the government short of funds, or unable to find qualified authors? Did government officials hold an elitist view and place popular reading materials low on their agenda? Or did the inaction reflect the GMD's continued suspicion of the popular movement in general as Communist-inspired, a point raised earlier by journalists Fan Changjiang and Xiao Fang?

There is no question that the Nationalists considered the mobilization of all human and material resources for the war effort as their top priority. But their conservatism and distrust of the masses contradicted and ultimately undermined their policies and original objectives. A case in point is the National Spiritual Mobilization Movement, a campaign initiated on 12 March 1939 to rally people behind the government. The movement, as Lloyd Eastman puts it, "encouraged people to swear to a 'Citizens Pact,' all twelve articles of which were negatives—'Not to act contrary to the Three People's Principles,' . . . 'Not to participate in traitorous organizations,' etc."[97] Instead of issuing positive instructions to gain public support, the entire campaign seemed more like a warning to the people about the serious consequences of wrongful political affiliations. Like the earlier New Life Movement (1934), it soon ended in failure.

The conservative nature of the government's activities was particularly evident in the realm of higher education. Under the direction of Chen Lifu (1899–), China's wartime minister of education, the government continued to stress the importance of what Chen called "character education" in an attempt to reintroduce Confucian values of filial piety and loyalty into university curricula.[98] Such a program, however, was incongruous with the harsh realities of the war and met strong opposition from students.[99]

As the war progressed, the GMD leaders' suspicions regarding the political loyalties of artists and dramatists grew, particularly those involved in the drama propaganda traveling troupes. The belief that many propaganda troupes were heavily infiltrated by the Communists led to the curtailment of funds to these groups and ultimately forced them to shut down—as occurred with the Cartoon Propaganda Corps in late 1940, for example. This concerted nonsupport further alienated independent-minded artists like Ye Qianyu, who viewed it as oppressive.[100] The removal of Guo Moruo as the head of the Third Section of the Political Department in the fall of 1940 was undoubtedly meant to curtail the Communists' influence in the propaganda arena. But the man who replaced him, Huang Shaogu (1901–), a GMD loyalist, lacked the vision and charisma to lead a forceful campaign. More important, the Guomindang's culture policy in general remained, as the literary historian Liu Xinhuang (1915–) put it, "perfunctory and passive."[101] The party's preoccupation with military and administrative affairs left its entire cultural propaganda program in a state of neglect.

In sharp contrast to the Nationalists, the Communists were serious about launching and coordinating different kinds of popular movements, including directing a well-orchestrated popular literature campaign in the border regions. The results of the two groups' efforts, in the end, were very different from each other, even though popularization and politicization of popular culture occurred in both Guomindang and Communist areas during the war. As will be discussed in the next chapter, the differences in outcome were not just a matter of the Communists succeeding and the Guomindang failing in their efforts. Rather, at issue was the fact that the Guomindang helped to start the campaign but then failed to capitalize on it.

Also in contrast to the government was the private sector, which actively published popular reading materials in the form of pamphlets, an effective format that the novelist Bao Tianxiao called "the culture shock troops" against the Japanese military.[102] Two key presses were the Three Households Publishing House (Sanhu tushu yinshuashe) and the Popular Reading Publishing House (Tongsu duwu biankanshe). Founded by Feng Yuxiang in Hankou in early 1938, the Three Households Publishing House drew its name from a famous episode in *Records of the Grand Historian* (*Shi ji*, first century B.C.) in which the Master Nan of Chu said, "Be there but three houses [*sanhu*] left in the state of Chu, still Chu will finally destroy Qin" (chapter 7). The name had a distinctly modern ring when it was revived during the war. The pamphlets published by the Three Households Publishing House, including Feng's own *The Great Masses in the War of Resistance* (*Kang-Ri de weida minzhong*), were inexpensive, ranging between 8 to 45 *fen* apiece.[103]

The history of the Popular Reading Publishing House went back even further, having been established by Gu Jiegang in Beijing right after the Manchurian Incident in September 1931. It was quite successful, publishing, as the name implied, a wide variety of booklets and magazines for the general reader. Each booklet cost between 2 and 4 *fen* and averaged eight pages in length (a reflection in part of the limited paper supply). With over four hundred titles published, this press "penetrated deep into the countryside of north China," as one source put it.[104] When Beijing fell into the hands of the Japanese, the Popular Reading Publishing House moved southwest to Taiyuan, on to Xi'an, and then to Wuhan. Despite the shaky circumstances, it continued to turn out popular drum song pamphlets such as *Five Hundred Soldiers Die Martyrs' Deaths at Xifengkou* (*Wubai dadaodui zhansi Xifengkou*), glorifying the heroism of common foot soldiers, and *Commander Hao Mengling Dies a Hero's Death* (*Hao Mengling kangdi xunguo*) about how Commander Hao gave his life to defend the city of Taiyuan against the Japanese in October 1937.[105] As in wartime cartoons, collaboration with the enemy was another dominant theme; an example is *Capturing Bai Jianwu Alive* (*Huozhuo Bai Jianwu*), which describes the arrest and execution of a notorious collaborator in Hebei. Most of these pamphlets could be sung "either in drum singing or Henan *zhuizi* style." Many were also designed to be read aloud to the public.

The Three Households Publishing House and the Popular Reading Publishing House were two of many privately funded organizations that disseminated simple, inexpensive pamphlets to the populace. Life Bookstore (Shenghuo shudian) also published a series of popular readings, and the National Association for the Advancement of Mass Education, headed by James Yen, likewise issued a famous series of booklets entitled "Peasant Resistance" ("Nongmin kangzhan congshu"). Both these series, like those of the Popular Reading Publishing House, skillfully employed traditional popular literature styles. For instance, *Eight Hundred Heroic Men Defend Zhabei to the End* (*Babai haohan sishou Zhabei*), by Zhao Jingshen, was written as a traditional drum song, and *War Songs* (*Zhan'ge*), by Yang Cunbin, was a spoken drama. And once gain, patriotism permeated the writings. Xi Zhengyong's eighteen-page *Ban Chao Pacifies the Western Region* (*Ban Chao ding Xiyu*), for example, tells the famous story of the Eastern Han general Ban Chao's (32–102) successful campaign against the nomadic Xiongnu people, with which he brought about a long peace on China's western flank. Ban Chao is described in the booklet as a patriot who, realizing the country is being threatened, decides to abandon his study for a military career. He is a man of commitment who firmly believes in the old saying "Every man has a share of responsibility for the fate of his country" (*guojia xingwang, pifu youze*). The book concludes with an admonition on the current crisis: "Now the enemy warplanes are hovering above us, and their artillery moves ever closer. To avoid destruction we must march to the front. It is time for old scores to be settled and foreign aggression repelled. Let's abandon our studies and join the army, and let's learn from the courageous Ban Chao who stamped his name on a foreign land."[106]

Although James Yen's mass education campaign in Hebei was abruptly interrupted by the Japanese attack, he continued to be active in the resistance movement after he moved NAAME to Changsha in 1937. While fighting hard to keep the association's education activities afloat in the interior, Yen also turned NAAME into a propaganda agency, producing, under the supervision of the dramatists Xiong Foxi and Yang Cunbin, a series of popular patriotic plays, among other things.[107]

Resistance intellectuals' communication with the populace did not, of course, rely only on booklets. Cao Bohan, an expert on propaganda, suggested a host of different kinds of activity. In his 1938 book *A Reader for Propaganda Techniques* (*Xuanchuan jishu duben*), Cao discussed an array of methods for reaching the populace: woodcuts, cartoons, wall pictures, postcards, parades, regional dramas, and dialect plays, to name just a few.[108] Collectively, these media contributed to what Liu Qun called "artistic propaganda." Most of them were simple in form, requiring no elaborate planning or technical expertise to produce.[109] Old-style Spring Festival couplets (*chunlian*), for example, because of their visibility and popularity at the New Year festival, could be easily reshaped into an anti-Japanese tool, the editors of *National Salvation Daily* reminded their readers.[110] Wall newspapers (*bibao*) could also be used to great effect despite their less than elegant appearance, Cao Baohan observed. They were easy to produce and could be pasted on the wall with relative ease; since they were handwritten, the complication of printing could be avoided; their articles were generally brief and timely; and their authors were local residents who were in close touch with their immediate surroundings. They were thus ideal vehicles for spreading military knowledge and teaching patriotic songs.[111]

The mass production of a great variety of popular literature was an important development in wartime China, to be sure. But through what channels were they passed along to the general public? Who actually read them? To what extent were these publications influential? Realizing the difficulty of spreading information, Lao Xiang and He Rong suggested that perhaps old country bookstores could be used to help distribute materials in the rural areas;[112] the unreliability of the network and the scarcity of country bookstores were limitations to this scheme, but they might be surmountable. Maybe the government could play a more active role, they suggested. In any event, to reach the widest possible readership, Lao Xiang argued, traditional, orthodox methods of communication no longer sufficed. Every possible means should be used and new channels explored. Books and pamphlets could be displayed at public places like temple fairs, village offices, and teahouses, and "book vendors, soldiers, students, and folk artists could also help to promote them."[113] Yet despite numerous ingenious proposals, the distribution issue was never satisfactorily resolved, owing to the government's lack of supervision and coordination and the uncertainty of the times.

But had popular literature actually gone down "to the country," as Lao She and many others had so passionately urged? Chen Yiyuan's answer was an emphatic no: "Not only has literature not reached the countryside; it has not even reached the county level. It remains in a few large cities."[114] The root cause, He Rong insisted, lay in the intellectuals' stubborn urban mentality. They never could fully identify with country folk. Their city-oriented attitude and effete life-style produced disappointing results when they attempted to bring popular literature to the masses. "You certainly would be an eyesore to the villagers if you went down to the countryside dressed in Western-style clothing and leather shoes," he wrote critically.[115] Such a lack of understanding led to shoddy products and empty slogans, agreed Xiang Linbing, a literary critic who wrote extensively on this subject.[116] To Xiang, the vocabulary of this wartime popular literature was limited, literary, and embellished, never truly becoming "the language of the folk."[117]

Such admonishments notwithstanding, a large amount of wartime propaganda literature was in fact produced, suggesting that some activists viewed it as an ideal tool to motivate the general public. And as a whole, these works did exert considerable influence at the grassroots level, forging an emotional, if not intellectual, bond between intelligentsia resisters and the illiterate.[118] Through small, relatively inexpensive wartime pamphlets, a communication channel was built that allowed interacting, persuading, and learning experiences to take place: intellectuals swayed the attitudes and beliefs of the mass audience, and in turn the commoners exerted an influence on the educated—teaching them, among other things, how to speak in a language comprehensible to the masses.

True, much of the popular literature from the war years was superficial and dull. Most of these writings, after all, were propaganda items, pure and simple. Every piece, be it folk song or comic dialogue, seemed the same, clinging to a nationalistic formula that no one dared abandon. This is not to say, however, that they were entirely devoid of artistic value. Many of Lao Xiang's pieces, such as "Collecting Winter Clothing" and "A Small Swallow," were respectable literary achievements, and Lao She's "Wang Xiao Drives a Donkey" was excellent. For Lao She and Lao Xiang, not only did propaganda literature draw huge audiences, but it also could yield fine products if approached with care and a sincere heart. In the end, though, the actual attempt by intellectuals to reach out to the public was just as important as what they produced.

Despite the resistance intellectuals' attempt to make the popular literature movement a collective effort, most of the works were individual undertakings, connected, perhaps, by the common sense of shared patriotism. Questions of subject matter, technique, audience, and purpose continued to divide creative individuals into separate camps. As mentioned earlier, A Ying derided writers for producing what he described as "feudalistic" popular literature to poison the people. And the leftist writer Liu Shi boldly declared that the popular culture movement was "an anti-imperialist, antitraitor movement."[119] To the leftists, the War of Resistance was not just a struggle against Japanese militarism: it was a battle between two social systems— socialism versus capitalist imperialism. In the GMD-controlled territories, where feuding factions and inconsistent, uncoordinated policies wreaked havoc on solidarity movements, the ultimate purpose of popular literature was at times far from clear. In the Communist areas, by contrast, a coherent political philosophy and unified approach to popular literature gradually developed. Nevertheless, this policy, directed as it was from above and not by the artists themselves, dictated content and methods of expression that aroused a bitter sense of anxiety among intellectuals. The result was an atmosphere unconducive to creativity.

6 Popular Culture in the Communist Areas

The profound political and social changes that took place in the Communist-controlled areas during the war cannot be fully understood without a careful analysis of the use and spread of popular culture. There is no question that Communist leaders were superb craftsmen in utilizing a rich array of popular culture forms to wage war against Japan, to win public support, and, most important, to spread revolutionary ideas and socialist reforms. The Communists experimented with and carefully manipulated various forms of popular culture, including dramas, cartoons, and newspapers. These forms became propaganda tools as well as political symbols, championing the cause of a socialist revolution. The Yan'an years (1937–1947) were a dynamic period during which fundamental changes occurred. Ironically, the new age also had a crippling effect on Chinese culture. To forge a unified front on both political and intellectual grounds, the CCP imposed strict guidelines on literature and art beginning in 1942, seriously limiting if not completely stifling artistic creativity and intellectual debate.

In the areas under their control, Mao Zedong and his associates tried to instill hope, optimism, and a sense of uniqueness by means of popular culture. Using drama and art, the Communists illustrated the very different outlooks and futures of people living in Japanese-occupied China, the Guomindang-controlled areas, and the Communist border regions. While people in the occupied sector lived under constant intimidation, and those in the Guomindang areas were "full of complaints and frustration," the people in the Red areas, it was shown, enjoyed a life of happiness and promise.[1] The idea that the border-region culture was the future culture of all China was one of

221

the most persistent themes in the Communist propaganda effort. Portraying a backward countryside undergoing an exciting social transformation, the Communists painted rustic Yan'an as the center of China's future hope.

The popular culture activities in the Yan'an period, however, must be examined within the larger political ambience of the 1920s and 1930s. The Communist campaign, namely, did not develop independently; it was inspired in large part by the popular culture efforts first seen in the Guomindang regions. There were, it is true, some drama activities and folk song singing in Communist-controlled territories during the Jiangxi Soviet period (1931–1934)[2]—such as the August First Drama Troupe (Bayi jutuan), established in 1932, which performed periodically in local villages in Jiangxi.[3] But large-scale and systematic undertakings—most significantly, newspapers and cartoons—did not commence until the Yan'an years. The arrival in 1938 of such talents as the dramatist Cui Wei and the cartoonist Hu Kao, former members of the Drama Propaganda Troupe and the National Salvation Cartoon Propaganda Corps, respectively also added momentum to the Communists' popular culture drive.

As we will see in this chapter, Mao's articulation of popular art and literature was a product of the times. The fact that the Communist experiment was initiated largely after Mao's Rectification Campaign (*Zhengfeng*) of 1942 allowed the leadership to benefit from what had already transpired in the GMD areas; they simply adapted existing forms to promote their message with single-minded determination. In the end, the fact that the popular culture drive in the Communist border regions was more effective than its counterpart in the Guomindang areas had more to do with centralization and coordination—or lack thereof—than with the actual tools used.

The Village Drama Movement

The Communist drama movement in the Yan'an era was in many ways distinct and ingenious not because it created new types of dramatic forms, but because it rejuvenated the old, infusing them with new ideas. For the Communists, the stage was an ideal political platform from which to enlighten the masses, and spoken drama was a powerful agent for socialization. These new dramas revealed the profound transformation of ideology, attitudes, and beliefs that had occurred in the Red areas. Through their widespread influence and subtle mix of symbolic idiom and stark realism, a new peasant political culture was created.

When Edgar Snow made his historic trip to the blockaded Communist area in Shaanxi in 1936, he witnessed a unique drama movement still in the process of developing:

> People were already moving down toward the open-air stage, improvised from an old temple, when I set out with the young official who had invited me to the Red Theatre. . . .
>
> Across the stage was a big pink curtain of silk, with the words, "People's Anti-Japanese Dramatic Society," in Chinese characters. . . . The programme was to last three hours. . . .
>
> The first playlet here was called *Invasion*. It opens in a Manchurian village, in 1931, with the Japanese arriving and driving out the "non-resisting" Chinese soldiers. In the second scene, Japanese officers banquet in a peasant's home, using Chinese men for chairs, and drunkenly making love to their wives. . . . In the end, of course, all this proves too much for the villagers. Merchants turn over their stands and umbrellas, farmers rush forth with their spears, women and children come with their knives, and all swear to "fight to the death" against the *Erh-pen-kuei* [*Riben gui*]—the "Japanese devils." . . .
>
> Another unique and amusing number was called the "United Front Dance," which interpreted the mobilization of China to resist Japan. . . .
>
> What surprised me about these dramatic clubs, however, was not that they offered anything of artistic importance to the world . . . but that, equipped with so little, they were able to meet a genuine social need. They had the scantiest properties and costumes, yet with these primitive materials they managed to produce the authentic illusion of drama. The players received only their food and clothing and small living allowances, but they studied every day, like all Communists, and they believed themselves to be working for China and the Chinese people. . . .
>
> The Reds write nearly all their own plays and songs. . . . There is no more powerful weapon of propaganda in the Communist movement than the Reds' dramatic troupes, and none more subtly manipulated.[4]

Snow was sympathetic to the Communist drama movement. But it was a performing art still in its infancy. It soon developed into a full-scale and mature force laden with peasant idealism, though frequently couched in patriotic language.

Contrary to Snow's claim that "the Reds wrote nearly all their own plays," famous pieces such as Cao Yu's *Thunderstorm*, Ouyang Yuqian's *The Death of Li Xiucheng* (*Li Xiucheng zhi si*), and foreign works like Gogol's *The Inspector General* and Ostrovsky's *The Storm* dominated the early theater in Yan'an and the other border areas.[5] The staging of these plays—dubbed "big plays" (*daxi*) or "famous plays" (*mingxi*) by critics, often with a disparaging tone[6]—stemmed partly from the shortage of scripts and partly from a fascination with accomplished works. It seemed natural and practical for those dramatists who had just arrived in Yan'an (for example, Cui Wei and Zhang Geng, both of whom came to the Red capital in 1938) to stage familiar pieces rather than to attempt something from scratch at short notice. Putting on a new play was both time-consuming and full of uncertainties. Nevertheless, Communist dramatists soon found that although these well-known pieces were popular with the cadres, they produced little resonance among the peasants. With soldiers and peasants "doz[ing] off in the middle of a famous play," as one critic observed,[7] city-oriented works came increasingly under fire. Artistic merit was not at issue; rather, political questions were now paramount. "These plays were completely divorced from reality," Zhang Geng later recalled.[8] Spending large sums of money on majestic and imposing sets in this barren and poverty-stricken land, another critic charged, was extravagant and nothing more than an ostentatious ploy on the part of the dramatists to show off their talent.[9]

Putting on an urban-oriented or foreign play became even more controversial with the launching of the Rectification Campaign in early 1942, a thought-remolding push directed against party cadres and intellectuals that subsequently established Mao Zedong's ideological preeminence in the CCP. Mao's decision to build a new China with the Shaan-Gan-Ning (Shaanxi-Gansu-Ningxia) Border Region (which centered on Yan'an) as his testing ground implied sweeping changes in all aspects of Chinese life. Old ideas, he proclaimed, should be discarded and new ones introduced. Thorough reform was possible only with a correct political viewpoint and careful implementation of the "mass line." As is now well understood, Mao's rural background and the realities of the Shaan-Gan-Ning Border Region allowed him to emphasize the peasantry. His concept of the mass line, however, was more than a class notion; it was a romantic belief in the masses (especially peasants) as the font of virtue and struggle. In comparison with Lenin and Stalin, Mao attributed to the masses a more critical role in fostering revolution and changing history. The CCP could not exist without learning from the masses, he said. In his famous directive of June 1943, Mao explicitly stated: "All correct leadership is necessarily from the masses, to the masses."[10] Intellectuals should learn from and become members of the masses through self-criticism and thought reform.

For Mao and his associates, a "big" or "famous play" production was more than a display of artistic arrogance: it was a sign of political insensitivity toward the needs of the people. Might "big plays" help to raise the standard of Communist dramas? Perhaps, but as Zhang Geng argued, one must never be divorced from the masses merely for the sake of raising the standards of drama. "We understand too little about China," he wrote in August 1942. "What we need to understand now is the life of the workers and peasants."[11] Besides being a misplaced exercise in elitism, an "imported" production could also be interpreted as casting doubts on the ability of homegrown talent, definitely an insult to the wisdom of the folk.

The harsh criticisms against urban and foreign plays resulted in few, if any, of them being performed in Yan'an after 1942.[12] General Nie Rongzhen (1899–1992), commander of the Jin-Cha-Ji (Shanxi-Chahar-Hebei) Border Region, perhaps detecting that the pendulum had swung too far, aired a rare difference of opinion in August 1942. While admitting that drama should be "popularized" to serve the people, Nie nevertheless insisted that "putting on a great foreign play like Gorky's *Mother* once a year can certainly raise our artistic standards."[13] But Nie's voice belonged to the minority. The bone of contention now was not whether or not Gorky and Ostrovsky were great, conscientious writers; the mere fact that they were foreigners was enough to raise eyebrows among nationalistic drama critics in the Communist areas.

This controversy over foreign plays must be viewed within a wider perspective. For it was not simply a debate over the value of foreign literary forms. Rather, it reflected Mao's attempt to undermine the influence of Wang Ming and the International Faction, known commonly as the "returned Bolsheviks." Wang, namely, following Stalin's instruction, favored a resistance policy centering on the Guomindang, while Mao advocated a more independent line for the Chinese Communists, and hence avoidance of further subordination to the will of Moscow.[14]

The dispute over foreign plays also reflected Mao's drive to forge a new revolutionary experience based squarely on Chinese soil, which necessarily included the sinification of foreign ideas in general and Marxism in particular. In a report to the Sixth Plenum of the Sixth Central Committee in November 1938, Mao wrote:

There is no such thing as abstract Marxism, but only concrete Marxism. What we call concrete Marxism is Marxism that has taken on a national form, that is, Marxism applied to the con-crete struggle in the concrete conditions prevailing in China, and not Marxism abstractly used. . . . Consequently, the Sinification of Marxism—that is to say, making certain that in all of its manifestations it is imbued with Chinese peculiarities, using it according to these peculiarities—becomes a problem that must be understood and solved by the whole Party without delay. . . . We must put an end to writing eight-legged essays on foreign models; there must be less repeating of empty and abstract re-frains; we must discard our dogmatism and replace it by a new and vital Chinese style and manner, pleasing to the eye and to the ear of the Chinese common people.[15]

As a Communist, Mao fully endorsed the need for international class struggle. Yet China and the interests of the Chinese people remained his top priority. Internationalism and patriotism were not in conflict, he told Agnes Smedley in 1937, "for only China's indepen-dence and liberation will make it possible to participate in the world Communist movement."[16] The sinification of Marxism was thus more than the simple adaptation of a foreign political ideal to meet China's needs; it was also a definite manifestation of nationalism. For Mao, the sinification of Marxism was a defense against decadent Western bourgeois ideas, on the one hand, and a reassertion of national pride, on the other hand. The great tradition of China's past and the nation's bitter experience in the previous hundred years, he noted, should be brought to bear in the current struggle against imperialism. Hence, at the core of the Maoist-style socialist revolution lay not only the mass line, but also nationalism. In practice, nationalism often overrode Communist ideology when it came to making political or artistic deci-sions. Mao, of course, maintained that there was no inherent contra-diction between the universality of Marxism as a political doctrine and China's peculiarities; indeed, their union was a sine qua non for a suc-cessful socialist revolution in China. The Yan'an experience led him to believe that the two blended well together.

The debate over foreign plays also underscored the desire of dramatists and party officials to find the artistic style best suited to the rural environment. In 1943, the Communist writer Zhou Libo (1908–1979) charged that students in Yan'an were drawn excessively to for-eign classics, to the extent that some dramatists were captivated even by "the eyelashes of Anna Karenina"—an ominous sign of what he called "book poisoning."[17] Zhang Geng voiced a similar concern. He warned against "blindly adopting foreign methods," pointing specifically to the Stanislavsky System, a drama training method popular among urban Chinese dramatists in the 1930s that emphasized every detail of speech and gesture and the actor's profound psychological characterization.[18] Following Western styles, Zhang cautioned, would mean falling victim to "foreign dogmatism" (*yang jiaotiao*) and ignoring China's harsh rural realities.[19] Of course Zhang, an early participant in the left-wing drama movement of the early 1930s and a member of the drama propaganda troupe in 1937, did not belittle the contribution of the legendary founder of the Moscow Art Theater. He did, however, believe that Chinese dramatists, rather than imitating a foreign model, should create their own style to address problems in the countryside.

Although Communist playwrights agreed that a new kind of drama was necessary, few in 1937 had a clear idea of what it should be. Yet they wasted no time in looking for a new formula that would meet rural needs. To be sure, the search was not a new undertaking; the CCP had been involved in the field of drama since the mid-1920s when Mao turned his eyes away from the city to look for revolutionary change in the countryside. Realizing the potential to reach a wide audience, the Communists intended to turn the theater not just into an entertainment center, but into a lecture hall. By 1938, therefore, a fledgling village drama movement was already in evidence in north China.

The founding of the Lu Xun Academy of Art (Lu Xun yishu xueyuan; commonly known as "Luyi") on 10 April 1938 marked a turning point in the Communist drama movement. Headed by the dramatist Sha Kefu (1905–1961), Luyi comprised four departments: literature, music, art, and drama. With Zhang Geng as the director of the drama section and experienced teachers like Cui Wei as instructors, the academy (which became known as "the art center of the northwest")[20] immediately emerged not only as the cradle of experimentation in art, but also as the headquarters of a full-scale drama campaign. A year later it was followed by the establishment of the All-China Resistance Association of Dramatists, Border Region Branch (Zhonghua xijujie kangdi xiehui bianqu fenhui) and other regional drama associations.[21]

Early Yan'an dramas brimmed with patriotic fervor. Even urban-centered productions or foreign pieces were often staged with an unmistakable intention of unifying people to resist foreign aggression.

When the Northwest Front Service Corps (Xibei zhandi fuwutuan), organized by the writer Ding Ling in 1937, traversed remote villages to spread the news about the war, it brought along emotion-charged short plays like "Joining the Guerrilla Forces" and "Arresting Traitors."[22] The same was true of the famous Shaan-Gan-Ning Border Region Popular Drama Troupe (Bianqu minzhong jutuan). The troupe, founded in 1938 and headed by the poet Ke Zhongping (1902–1964), spent a lengthy period traveling through numerous counties to spread patriotic news, earning the endeavor the accolade of a "Small Long March."[23] From the beginning, however, it was clear that the Communists were not content merely to wage an anti-Japanese campaign. The proletarian cause was never far below the surface of the resistance battle. According to Mao and his associates, for a revolutionary struggle to be truly meaningful, it must embrace a larger cause. China needed profound social and political transformation if feudalism and imperialism—the twin evils that Mao believed underlay the nation's problems—were to be vanquished. And this transformation must start with the countryside, where the majority of Chinese lived and where the sufferings of the people were most acutely felt.

Chinese Communist leaders firmly believed that the creation of a unified ideology required systematic coordination and careful planning from the top down. Even before Mao's famous "Yan'an Talks" of 1942, therefore, the Communists took steps to facilitate dramatic activities in the villages. Besides Luyi, they set up several regional art training centers to provide basic lessons to local cadres and artists (many of these also commemorated Lu Xun, the preeminent Chinese writer and a strong advocate of the leftist cause in his final years).[24] Well-reputed drama clubs such as the Northwest Front Service Corps and Mt. Taihang Drama Club (Taihangshan jutuan) organized rural cadre training classes, teaching peasant activists and theater enthusiasts basic directing, makeup, and singing techniques, thereby producing scores of trained or semitrained personnel for grass-roots activities.[25] "Model drama troupes" were simultaneously established in different border areas, charged with the task of teaching the peasants performing techniques, helping the village drama clubs to train directors and actors, and supervising their performances.[26] In addition, dozens of special teams were created to print basic drama materials for distribution throughout the border regions. The results were remarkable: in the Mt. Taihang Region, for example, more than 100 village drama clubs had been organized by the summer of 1940;

in Central Hebei, 1,700 by 1942; and in Beiyue (western Hebei and northeastern Shanxi), 1,400 by the same year.[27]

The numbers can be deceiving, however. The majority of the newly founded drama clubs were loosely organized, and many were relatively short-lived, lacking the managerial skills and firm ideological commitment required to sustain themselves. Worse still, as Sha Kefu pointed out, "the direction [of the drama movement] was unclear. . . . There was no mention of reforming art on the original basis of the peasants' tradition, and some cadres still retained a condescending attitude toward traditional folk artists and their crafts."[28] Although cadres and intellectuals were encouraged to go the villages to make contact with the peasants, many never took the assignment seriously. "[The assignment] was treated as if they were just 'taking a bath' [*xigezao*]," lamented one critic.[29] Direction finally came from the top in 1942, when the CCP took on the role of arbiter of the arts.

As is now well known, in his historic "Talks at the Yan'an Forum on Literature and Art" in May 1942—part of the newly initiated Rectification Campaign—Mao stated explicitly and forcefully the basic party canon for literature and art. The Party was to oversee all cultural activities, and literature and art should unswervingly serve revolutionary causes. It was the task of writers and artists, Mao pronounced, simultaneously to "popularize" their products and "raise the standards" of the people. Although Mao's specific concern was with political issues, his "Talks" were all-embracing and stipulated a new direction for all kinds of literature and art, popular culture included. Mao called on intellectuals and cadres to serve the interests of "the broadest masses," to present their ideas in simple language comprehensible to all, to praise the bright side rather than to expose the dark facets of socialist reality, and to go to the countryside "to observe, experience, and study." He continued:

> Our specialists in drama should pay attention to the small
> troupes in the army and the villages. Our specialists in music
> should pay attention to the songs of the masses. Our specialists
> in the fine arts should pay attention to the fine arts of the masses.
> All these comrades should make close contact with comrades
> engaged in the work of popularizing literature and art among
> the masses.[30]

Mao's "Talks" effectively consolidated the CCP's ideological ground and provided guidance to intellectuals and party cadres embroiled in heated debates over literary policy. Studying Chairman Mao's

"Talks," one dramatist recalled years later, was "like a sick person suddenly discovering the right medicine."[31] Although the "Yan'an Talks" reached different border areas at different times and were not officially published until 19 October 1943,[32] they nevertheless had a profound impact on the course and nature of the rural drama movement. Perhaps no effect was more visible than the renaissance of the traditional *yangge*.

Yangge (rice-sprout songs) was a song-and-dance form of folk entertainment from north China. Performed during the lunar New Year in villages and cities alike, it was beloved by all the people. Although *yangge* dances varied from place to place—the northern Shaanxi version, for instance, was performed with considerable rhythmic freedom, whereas the Jin-Cha-Ji type was more rhythmically controlled[33]—each generally involved a troupe of twenty to thirty male performers, with men playing women's roles. Led by an actor known as *santou* (the umbrella), who in fact did carry an umbrella to guide the troupe's movement, performers, sometimes in pairs, twisted and danced according to a set of prescribed steps accompanied by drums and gongs. Clowning was also an integral part of the dance. One of the most popular folk entertainments, *yangge* dances were always tumultuously received by the audience. Colorful and gaudy costumes made the procession exceptionally attractive, and erotic moves and flirtation during a dance often drew resounding applause.[34]

A long history notwithstanding, *yangge* were not widely known to the Chinese intellectual world until the Mass Education Movement headed by James Yen made a serious effort to collect them in Dingxian, Hebei in the mid-1920s. The Dingxian researchers, motivated as they were by their anti-illiteracy campaign, discovered that these well-liked *yangge* dances and plays, an orally transmitted art, if carefully reformed could be an ideal tool to promote education. A valuable collection of *yangge* plays entitled *Dingxian yangge xuan* (*Dingxian Plantation Songs*) was published in 1933 to record their findings.[35]

Inspired in part by the Dingxian reformers, years later the Communists in Yan'an turned this popular folk art into a political and social medium to promote socialism.[36] A certain folk artist, Liu Zhiren, is said to have been the first in Shaanxi to incorporate political content into the old *yangge* as early as 1937,[37] but systematic *yangge* reform did not occur until 1943, when Luyi began to experiment with a series of new *yangge* plays.[38] Needless to say, the new type of *yangge* that would soon emerge was radically different from its predecessor.

In sharp contrast to what the Communists repudiated as old-fashioned and harmful "flattery *yangge*" (*saoqing dizhu*), which focused on deplorable servility to landlords, a new type of "struggle *yangge*" (*douzheng yangge*) emerged,[39] aimed, as one writer asserted, "at reshaping the mind of the people."[40] Marked changes were made: the troupe leader's umbrella was replaced by a sickle and a hatchet, symbolizing the dawning of a new age; the clowns and clowning acts were discarded because, the critics maintained, they defiled the image of the common people; erotic gestures and love dances were likewise eradicated in favor of heroic stories of unstinting patriotic service to the nation. In the popular *Brother and Sister Clear Wasteland* (*Xiongmei kaihuang*), a play that commends tireless production and cherishes the spirit of cooperation, the original cast of husband and wife was changed to brother and sister—to avoid, said Zhang Geng, presenting "a wrongful image of flirtation."[41]

Yangge plays appeared in abundance in 1943 and 1944, a time when the resistance war was suffering a stalemate. Although there was no dearth of anti-Japanese struggle in the new *yangge* plays, the emphasis had shifted to something quite different: building a new society with a new political philosophy. Besides two old mainstays—glorifying production and condemning the oppression of the landlords—Communist *yangge* plays manufactured a host of new themes to paint a bright society bursting with energy and joy: sexual equality (*Twelve Sickles* [*Shi'erba liandao*]); female model workers (*A Red Flower* [*Yiduo honghua*]); anti-illiteracy campaigns (*Husband and Wife Learn to Read* [*Fuqi shizi*]); the founding of the new peasant associations (*Qin Luozheng*); local elections: an indication of democracy at work at the grass-roots level (*A Red Flower*); rural hygiene (*An Old Midwife Enters the Training Class* [*Laoniangpo zhu xunlian*]); the harmonious relationship between the Red Army and the people (*Niu Yonggui Is Wounded* [*Niu Yonggui guacai*]); and the correct leadership of Mao Zedong and the Communist Party (*An Honor Lamp* [*Guangrong deng*]).[42]

At the same time, a wealth of rich symbols—like the sickle and the bright lamp—were carefully incorporated into the plays to create striking new perceptions. Colloquial language was used, and the inclusion of popular tunes drawn from *Meihu* (the local opera of Shaanxi) provided a familiar indigenous flavor. The plays' ever-present optimism helped to portray the border region, though backward and impoverished, as a society full of promise and vigor. Indeed, the fact that the majority of these new *yangge* plays (such as Ma Ke's [1918–1976] *Husband and Wife Learn to Read*) drew inspiration from local culture made them all the more significant: it showed that Mao's "learning from the masses" campaign was yielding political fruits.

To add authenticity, many new pieces relied heavily on actual events. *Zhong Wancai Starting from Scratch* (*Zhong Wancai qijia*) is a case in point. Zhong Wancai, a native of northern Shaanxi, was a sluggard and an opium addict—a type of social outcast known in the border areas as *erliuzi* (a bum). But thanks to the unceasing persuasion of the party cadres, Zhong finally gave up opium and became a model worker. He even earned himself the title of propaganda chief in the county, teaching others how to increase their food production. The dramatic turnaround of Zhong Wancai was singled out for praise by the Party as one of many similar success stories under the new government.[43] Zhou Yang (1908–1989), the cultural commissar, proudly declared that in this new society "people are no longer being treated as clowns. They are emperors!"[44]

While the Communist dramatists painted a rosy picture of the border region, they were unrelenting in their denunciations of the Guomindang government. As relations between the CCP and the GMD deteriorated during the last phase of the war, scathing attacks against Jiang Jieshi became increasingly common in the *yangge* plays. In *An Honor Lamp*, for example, Jiang is openly referred to as "a traitor, who sold China to American financial cliques."

This burst of creativity stemmed largely from the CCP's strong endorsement of the *yangge* form and from efforts made by such touring drama troupes as Luyi's Work Team (Luyi gongzuotuan), headed by Zhang Geng.[45] By 1944, numerous *yangge* troupes had sprung up. In two northern Jiangsu counties (Maji and Jiaoxiang) in central China alone, for instance, more than thirty female teams emerged.[46] Three *yangge* plays—*Brother and Sister Clear Wasteland*, *A Red Flower*, and *Niu Yonggui Is Wounded*—were even staged in Chongqing in the spring of 1945 under the auspices of the *New China Daily*.[47]

The Communist village drama movement, however, involved more than just the production of *yangge* plays. Based on *yangge* and utilizing Western operatic techniques, a new type of drama known as "new opera" (*xingeju*) emerged. The phenomenal success of *The White-haired Girl* (*Baimaonü*, 1945)—the story of a servant girl who, after being forced by a tyrannical landlord to flee to the mountains where her hair turns white, returns to take her revenge with the help of the Red Army—contributed to the popularity of this new opera type and reaffirmed Mao's notion of developing a new national form of art.

As in the Guomindang-controlled areas, traditional Beijing operas and regional dramas, their enduring popularity too obvious to be ignored, were revived and promoted as well. Beginning in the late 1930s, the Communists set up drama societies to remodel folk plays in the light of the current social and political struggle.[48] Perhaps the most famous effort was the Beijing Opera Study Society (Pingju yanjiuhui), established in Yan'an in October 1942 and having two major aims: "to propagate the resistance cause and to carry on a distinguished tradition." In the early 1940s, determined to overcome what it called "the outdated idea that Beijing opera has nothing to do with revolution,"[49] the society unleashed a series of reforms and infused the old dramatic form with new political content. Among others, two highly successful pieces appeared. *Driven up Mt. Liang* (*Bi shang Liangshan*, 1943), the first opera to emerge from this new endeavor, is based on a famous episode from Mao Zedong's own favorite, *The Water Margin*. It is a story about a military officer, Lin Chong, who, after being pursued by corrupt government agents, decides to join a group of bandit-heroes on Mt. Liang. The new opera, however, instead of focusing on Lin's personal adventure and individual heroism, praises the awesome force of the common people—for it is only when Lin Chong joins hands with the protesting masses that he is able to defeat the pursuing troops and begin a new life.[50] The second equally successful piece, *Three Attacks at Zhu Mansion* (*San da Zhujiazhuang*, 1944)—also based on a story from *The Water Margin*—describes the familiar theme of popular revenge against a landlord and the power of peasant uprisings.[51]

This outburst of drama activity in the Communist areas did not go unnoticed by the outside world. Gunther Stein, reporting for the *Christian Science Monitor*, was fascinated by *yangge* plays when he was allowed to visit this blockaded land in the spring of 1944. He reported enthusiastically: "Each time I saw [the play] performed I was under its spell like everybody around me. . . . A good *yangko* [*yangge*] party goes on for hours with several shows, in a gay and happy community atmosphere such as I have never seen elsewhere in the Orient."[52] The artist Jack Chen was equally impressed by the seemingly exuberant spirit and the profusion of artistic productions in this border region.[53] And Huang Yanpei (1878–1965), one of the representatives of the People's Political Council who visited the Communist capital in early July 1945, lauded *Three Attacks at Zhu Mansion*, which he saw presented at Yan'an, as "a truly powerful weapon [in winning the hearts and minds of the people]."[54] These observations, superficial though they are, reflect well the buoyant atmosphere of success and hope created by the Communists.

Art for Politics' Sake

There is some evidence to show that already in the early days of the Chinese Communist Party, leaders like Mao recognized the potential of art as a propaganda medium. While serving as director of the Peasant Movement Training Institute (Nongmin yundong jianxisuo) in Guangzhou in 1926, for instance, Mao is said to have introduced courses on peasant art to its curriculum.[55] In his "Report on an Investigation of the Peasant Movement in Hunan" (1927), Mao reminded people that "simple slogans, cartoons and speeches have produced such a widespread and speedy effect among the peasants that every one of them seems to have been through a political school."[56] A certain amount of artistic activity was also apparent in the Jiangxi Soviet period.[57] Such efforts, however, were scattered and unorganized. It was not until the Yan'an era that a coherent ideology embracing various forms of art was constructed, one that came to occupy a strategic position in the political education of the people. The influx of artists from the Guomindang areas breathed new life into the Communist art crusade.

In comparison with most Guomindang publications, such as the *Central Daily* with its unappealing layout and poor use of visual effects, Communist publications employed a variety of art forms to produce a more dramatic and striking appearance. During the war, a host of pictorials were printed and distributed in the border regions—even despite the acute paper shortage[58]—and in them Communist artists demonstrated a real knack for using art to spark patriotic fervor in China. As early as 1937, the *National Salvation Daily*—first published in Shanghai and subsequently moved to Guangzhou and later Guilin, with the prominent left-wing writers Guo Moruo and Xia Yan as its publisher and editor, respectively—had devoted considerable space to patriotic cartoons.[59] But that was not enough: beginning on 15 January 1938, a special weekly "National Salvation Art Section" was added, indicating the enormous significance cartoons carried for the Communists.[60]

The Yan'an cartoon campaign gained new momentum with the arrival of such artists as Hu Kao, Zhang E, Cai Ruohong, Hua Junwu (1915–), and Zhang Ding in the late 1930s and early 1940s. Many of them—Cai Ruohong, for instance—had been affiliated with the

League of Left-Wing Artists. Others, such as Hua Junwu, were disillusioned with the Guomindang rule and made the trek to the Communist capital to seek a new life and fulfill a new dream.

Hua Junwu was already a veteran cartoonist when he arrived in Yan'an in late 1938 at the age of twenty-three, but predictably his style became more political. Revealing the influence of the German artist E. O. Plauen, creator of the cartoon strip "Vater und Sohn" (Father and Son), and the Russian cartoonist Sapajou, who worked for the British-owned Shanghai newspaper *North China Daily News*, Hua's early works were a bleak chronicle of urban life, depicting the chaos, hedonism, and alienation of modern society, especially in Shanghai—though without the bitterness and sarcasm that so marked Cai Ruohong's works.[61] Hua found a new life in Yan'an. Moved by the mission of emancipating the proletariat and fascinated by the vision of a worker's paradise, Hua joined the CCP in 1940.

Realizing the enormous political potential of cartoons, Hua Junwu and his fellow cartoonists began to offer classes at Luyi.[62] In 1941 Hua, together with Jiang Feng (1910–1982), set up an art workshop to promote cartoons and other artistic designs.[63] He also designed a cartoon cloth banner (which he called a "wall paper") for public display.[64] Cartoons began to appear everywhere. They could be found in pictorials such as Yan'an's *Resistance Pictorial* (*Kangdi huabao*) and Jin-Cha-Ji Border Region's *Shanxi-Chahar-Hebei Pictorial* (*Jin-Cha-Ji huabao*). The work of Hua Junwu, Zhang E, and Cai Ruohong also became a constant feature in Yan'an's *Liberation Daily*, the CCP's official newspaper.[65] The *New China Daily*, which was published in Guomindang-controlled Hankou and later in Chongqing, gave this powerful art even more prominence, frequently devoting its front page to biting cartoons. Hu Kao's "Japanese People Under the Oppression of the [Japanese] Warlords," which appeared in the 24 January 1938 issue of the *New China Daily*, heralded a new pictorial format for this Communist paper.[66] In addition to promoting cartoons, Zhang E, art editor of the *New China Daily*, also labored hard to bring a variety of other art forms like woodcuts and comic strips to this influential newspaper, blending forceful messages with simple images. Yan'an and Chongqing, of course, were not the only places where cartoons were thriving. In the Jin-Cha-Ji Border Region the political cartoons of Li Jiefu (1913–1976) and Ding Li (1916–) also reaped critical acclaim.[67]

The Yan'an wartime cartoons drew the attention of the Communist leaders, especially Mao Zedong. In the eyes of Mao, however, the early Yan'an drawings had some serious shortcomings. They focused too heavily on problems existing within the CCP, paying insufficient attention to the Communists' political struggle against external foes. In short, as one modern Communist art critic put it, the artists had failed to realize that there were *two* major enemies: "the national enemy [Japan] and the class enemy [the Guomindang]."[68]

For Mao, nowhere was this deficiency more evident than in the famous "Three Man Satirical Cartoon Show" (Sanren fengci manhua zhan) held in Yan'an in February 1942. In their introduction to this exhibition, Hua Junwu, Zhang E, and Cai Ruohong declared their purpose in holding such a show: "We have seen the beauty and radiance of the new society. But we have also witnessed its ugly and dark sides, which are inherited from the past. These archaic dregs cling to the new society and are gradually corrupting us. Our responsibility as cartoonists is to root them out and bury them."[69]

True to these words, the well-publicized show focused mainly on exposing the social and political problems that the three artists saw in Yan'an. Hua Junwu's "Modern Decoration," for example, criticized the casual attitude of party cadres in learning Marxism-Leninism, treating it as nothing more than "an ornament." Zhang E's "I Am No. 6 in the World" described the insolence of these same cadres, who consider themselves on top of the world—ranked right next to Marx, Engels, Lenin, Stalin, and Mao.[70] The show was an overwhelming success, creating a sensation in Yan'an because of both its novelty and its boldness in pinpointing problems within the Party. The three artists' attack on the arrogance, insensitivity, and incompetence of party cadres no doubt struck a chord among the audience. "Like a scalpel, satirical cartoons cure the sickness," hailed one critic.[71]

But exposing the Party's weaknesses also touched a sensitive nerve among party officials. Unhappy with what he saw, Mao summoned the three artists to his residence for a discussion late one steamy summer afternoon. Over dinner, he criticized them for their incorrect attitude. Granted that the Party had its shortcomings, Mao said, one should not dwell on its demerits without simultaneously pointing out its merits.[72] More serious still, the artists' attitude was also at variance with, if not totally contradictory to, the views Mao expressed in his "Talks": "For revolutionary writers and artists the targets for exposure can never be the masses, but only the aggressors, exploiters and oppressors and the evil influence they have on the people."[73] In short, the three artists had committed a grave error by lumping friends and foes together and by turning their criticisms against their own people rather than their enemies.

The significance of Mao's meeting with Hua Junwu, Zhang E, and Cai Ruohong can be understood only within the context of the Rectification Campaign. It was, in essence, a reaffirmation of what Mao called "concrete Marxism." Different forms of art, according to Mao, must be channeled or refashioned to meet the current needs. And in this task, the CCP had a responsibility to take command. He once again asserted the Party's authority to dictate the direction of art in the Communist areas. In a socialist revolution, he said, the political purpose had to be solved before the aesthetic: art was not to be judged by its quality, but by its intention. In reflecting CCP policy, art in turn reaffirmed ideological certitudes. The building of a new society, in the end, would follow radically restructured aesthetic principles that adhered to socialist ideals. Mao's meeting with Hua Junwu, Zhang E, and Cai Ruohong demonstrated once again that the Party was the final arbiter of right and wrong in art, and that artists had no choice but to show active support for the Party. Thus Mao instilled a rigid formalism in the artistic world that left little room for individual expression.

The style and content of cartoonists' work underwent a series of adjustments after Mao's "Talks." Instead of focusing on party cadres, cartoons now targeted "the aggressors, exploiters, and oppressed," and artists took pains to reach a wider audience through a closer and more realistic portrayal of the people's life (the practice of "popularization" that Mao stipulated). While Cai Ruohong, a diehard Marxist, was so affected by Mao's criticism that he admitted his past ideological errors and almost completely abandoned cartooning,[74] Hua Junwu took a more positive step: as Communist dramatists had done with their foreign models, he relinquished the style of Sapajou and Plauen from his Shanghai days and attempted to "sinicize" his art, incorporating folk idioms (such as proverbs) into his cartoons to present a more familiar look to the peasants. He and Zhang E also turned their drawing pens against the Guomindang.

As the relationship between the CCP and the GMD continued to deteriorate, especially after the New Fourth Army Incident of January 1941, criticism of the Guomindang government mounted. Cartoonists depicted the ruling party as a corrupt regime that failed to take measures to improve the lot of the people. It is here that the Communist cartoonists left their strongest mark. Hua Junwu's memorable piece "Bumper Harvest" (1944, fig. 44) paints an anthropomorphic locust

豐　收　　　華君武作　　曹國興刻

Fig. 44.   Hua Junwu, "Bumper Harvest" (cartoon by Hua Junwu, woodcut by Cao Guoxing). The sack is labeled "rice." From *JFRB*, 3 November 1944, p. 1.

who, atop a bulging rice sack, sits comfortably with Jiang Jieshi and Kong Xiangxi (1880–1967), the minister of finance and Jiang's brother-in-law. Before them is a starving man delivering his last grain—a biting image of exploitation. Zhang Ding's "The Warlock 'Leader'" (1945, fig. 45) portrays another cruel aspect of Guomindang rule: a blatant breach of democracy. Here Jiang Jieshi is depicted as a wizard who holds up a wooden placard inscribed "Jiang's Democracy" as he mercilessly whips a crying, bound woman who embodies the people in the areas under Guomindang control. In another piece, "Close Resemblance," Hua Junwu compares the Guomindang's secret police with the Gestapo, and the Nationalist labor camps with Nazi concentration camps. "If European fascism meets its end, will its Chinese counterpart be far behind?" he asks.[75]

The critical bite of Communist art was further enhanced by another powerful medium: the woodcut. During the war, if Communist cartoons excelled at painting the Guomindang as villains, woodcuts took a fresh course: they, like *yangge*, were at their best portraying the bright future China would enjoy under Communist rule. Woodcut art

Fig. 45. Zhang Ding, "The Warlock 'Leader.'" The placard in Jiang's left hand is marked, "Jiang's democracy," and the characters on the woman read, "People in the interior." From *JFRB*, 1 April 1945, p. 4.

became extremely well loved in the Communist border regions, surpassing even the cartoon as the most innovative and forceful form of popular art. Not only did woodcuts draw the attention of millions of Chinese throughout China; they also earned Chinese artists international recognition when foreign magazines such as *Life* (9 April 1945) reproduced patriotic works to illustrate the combatant spirit and artistic ferment in that war-torn country. Indeed, the eight-year war against Japan has been called "the golden age of Chinese woodcut."[76] For Communist artists, the cartoon and woodcut were twin developments that provided mutual nourishment and affirmation in a period of crisis.

In October 1942, after visiting a woodcut exhibition of left-wing artists from the Communist-controlled areas in Chongqing, the painter Xu Beihong made an interesting observation: "There is no doubt that right-leaning people never go near woodcuts—a peculiar phenomenon in China."[77] Xu's statement was no doubt exaggerated, for he overlooked woodcut artists like Fang Xiang (1920–) who were sympathetic to the Guomindang cause.[78] Nevertheless, it is true that the woodcut circle was dominated by left-wing artists. The reason lies in the origin of the Chinese woodcut movement.

Although the art of engraving has a long history in China, the woodcut did not come on the scene until the 1930s.[79] Its motivating force was Lu Xun, "the father of the Chinese woodcut movement." In the late 1920s and early 1930s, at a time when he felt strong sympathy for the CCP and helped to launch the League of Left-Wing Writers, Lu Xun avidly introduced the work of Käthe Kollwitz, the Russian engraver Vladimir A. Favorsky (1886–1964), and the Belgian woodcut artist Frans Masereel (1889–1971) to China. He mounted woodcut exhibitions, published graphic art collections, and drew a group of devoted young followers, whom he urged to use their newly acquired craft to portray social ills and to represent the voice of the lower orders. To him, woodcut art, like the cartoon, should never be confined to the ivory tower. Instead it should be used to foster social change and promote political reforms.[80]

Under Lu Xun's influence and inspired by the work of such Western masters as Kollwitz, a new generation of Chinese woodcut artists made their appearance: Li Hua (1907–), Yefu (Zheng Yefu, 1909–1973), Chen Yanqiao (1911–1970), and Li Qun (1912–), among others, became key figures in introducing this powerful art to a wider audience. Numerous woodcut associations were founded, including the influential Eighteen Society (Yiba yishe) and MK Woodcut Study Association (MK muke yanjiuhui, "MK" coming from the Chinese characters for woodcut, *muke*). Most of these organizations, however, were ephemeral. The government quickly suppressed them because of their close ties to Lu Xun and the League of Left-Wing Writers, and also because of the radical, sometimes subversive, content of their art. On the eve of the Sino-Japanese War, therefore, the young Chinese woodcut movement, despite its thorny start, had already assumed a revolutionary outlook, and this tradition continued with added fervor in Yan'an.

Communist woodcut art made great strides after the artists Hu Yichuan (1910–), Jiang Feng, and Wo Zha (1905–1974) arrived in Yan'an in the late 1930s.[81] Luyi began to offer systematic courses in the subject, later producing such prized students as Gu Yuan (1919–), a young virtuoso whom Xu Beihong praised as "the great artist in the Chinese Communist Party."[82] The institute also sent woodcut teams to other areas to teach the techniques.[83]

The potential of the woodcut medium was recognized early. "Relying only on black and white and no other colors," one art critic observed in 1933, "woodcuts can present the most moving and vivid pictures."[84] To Communist artists, the woodcut was a convenient propaganda tool with endless possibilities. Its distinct, simple lines seemed austere and were well suited, as the German graphic artist

Max Klinger (1857–1920) once argued, to portraying the agony and sufferings of the people.[85] Cheap and quick to produce, woodcut prints were readily available for low prices—a most economic mode of popularization. "It was the most convenient and the most combatant form of propaganda weapon [in the border regions]," one Communist artist later recalled.[86] Even cartoonists, owing to the acute shortage of zinc plates and the high availability of wood in Yan'an, came to rely heavily on woodcut artists to prepare their work for publication in the newspaper.[87] Many of Hua Junwu's pieces in the *Liberation Daily* were the result of help from woodcut artists, including his classmate and friend Gu Yuan.[88]

The enthusiasm for woodcuts was apparent from the start of the Yan'an period. Woodcuts appeared in practically every newspaper, magazine, and book published by the Communists. The *New China Daily* even created a special "Woodcut Front" beginning on 11 February 1942. Their ease of production allowed soldiers in the New Fourth Army to turn out a deluge of woodcuts about the war.[89]

Though their techniques might be largely foreign, the artists' work was rooted firmly in China's present. Like cartoons, Communist woodcuts had a strong anti-Japanese spirit. Li Shaoyan's "Struggle," for instance, shows an unarmed peasant woman's fierce resistance against a Japanese soldier.[90] An overwhelmingly large number, however, depicted a new society undergoing rapid change. Negative anti-Japanese slogans were often overshadowed by effusive praise of the CCP and its wise leaders, and tributes to devoted, unselfish cadres in turn led to repeated condemnation of the hopelessly corrupt and faction-ridden Chongqing government. Zhang Wang's (1916–) piece depicting "two different worlds" (fig. 46) employed a familiar technique of contrast: in the great interior, people's lives were miserable, under constant threat from the tyrannical Guomindang police; in the border areas, by contrast, peasants enjoyed a life of peace and abundance.[91] The importance of production, land reform, the caring relationship between soldiers and the people, and a democratic government were perennial themes. Wo Zha's "The Eighth Route Army Helps the People at the Wheat Harvest" (fig. 47), for example, reinforces the good nature of the Communist troops, whose job it was not only to fight the invaders, but also to aid the humble masses in every conceivable way. Niu Wen's (1922–) "Measuring Land" (fig. 48) describes a happy and just social order under Communism where land has been distributed and landlordism eliminated. It is a society in which peasants no longer suffer; on the contrary, poor people who

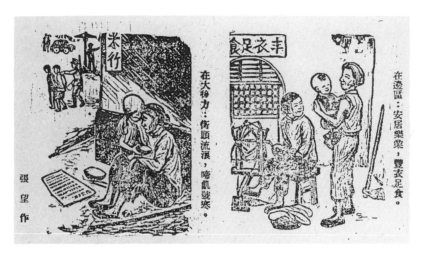

Fig. 46. Zhang Wang: Two different worlds—In the great interior: a life of destitution, homelessness, hunger, and fear. In the border regions: a life of plenty, peace, and contentment. From *JFRB*, 22 July 1943, p. 4.

Fig. 47. Wo Zha, "The Eighth Route Army Helps the People at the Wheat Harvest." From *Jin-Cha-Ji huabao* 4 (20 September 1943): n.p.

Fig. 48.   Niu Wen, "Measuring Land." From *Jin-Sui jiefangqu muke xuan* (Chengdu: Sichuan renmin chubanshe, 1982), p. 38.

were denied learning in the past can now study during the winter off-season (Li Qun's "Attending Winter School"),[92] and they are eager to contribute to the public good for a noble cause (Li Qun's "Delivering Public Grain").[93]

What made Communist woodcuts especially effective is that their themes were simple and drawn directly from local experience, and, most important, they were presented in a framework of optimism.[94] Gu Yuan was a master at presenting this sense of vivacity under Communist rule. A Cantonese who arrived in Yan'an in January 1939 and became a student at the newly established Luyi, Gu Yuan was trained entirely under the new Communist artistic doctrines. Such early pieces as "A Cartload of Straw," "A Flock of Sheep," and "Home" (all 1940) showed a world in which people lived close to the soil, simple yet buoyed by confidence and joy. Subsequently, to portray a society full of promise, Gu Yuan turned to clearer lines and patterns to give a more optimistic appearance. This change can be seen well in "A Divorce Suit." While the 1941 version (fig. 49b) bears the unmistakable influence of Kollwitz with its dark shading and solemn air, two years later a simpler background and a brighter outlook convey a completely different message (fig. 49a); in this piece, the artist acknowledges his indebtedness not to the West, but to Chinese folk art.[95] To Gu Yuan, more than a change in technique was at issue; rather, his new

Fig. 49a–b.   Gu Yuan, "A Divorce Suit." The book is labeled "divorce registry." From Gu, "Chuangzuo suibi," *Banhua yishu* 1 (June 1980): 8.

approach was a testimony to Mao's call for the sinification of Western art. Although their world might seem idyllic, his work proclaimed, the peasants earned a good living through sheer hard work and determination. Gu Yuan "is a singer of the border region," lauded the poet Ai Qing (1910–).[96] On the surface, Gu Yuan's pieces were simple and apolitical, yet they raised a fundamental political question: what made this cheerful life possible in a time of crisis?

Optimism was equally evident in other forms of popular art: comic strips (*lianhuantu*), wall paintings (*qianghua*), New Year pictures, and papercuts (*jianzhi*).[97] The New Fourth Army even unleashed a "Wall Painting Campaign" to gain support for the CCP.[98] Long popular in rural China, New Year pictures employed the bold lines and bright colors characteristic of Chinese folk art.[99] Now, though, instead of traditional designs of heroes, gods, and good-luck charms, the pictures celebrated the glory of joining the Red Army, the jovial image of a hardworking peasant ready to devote his life to the Communist Party, and a multitude of boisterous rural activities centering on the collective goal. Such notions were applied also to door pictures, where fierce-looking generals from the past were replaced by soldiers carrying loaded rifles and standing side by side with peasant volunteers, exuding determination in defending their land against outside invaders.[100]

Newspapers and a New Language

Newspapers were the most convenient carrier of cartoons and woodcuts to the people and a powerful channel for explaining the views of the CCP. Realizing their enormous influence, the Communists issued a large number of newspapers in their Yan'an years. "Combine the barrel of a gun with the barrel of a pen" became a rallying cry of journalists.[101] In the three Communist-controlled northern border regions alone—Jin-Cha-Ji, Jin-Sui (Shanxi-Suiyuan), and Jin-Ji-Lu-Yu (Shanxi-Hebei-Shandong-Henan)—an incomplete survey revealed that 120 newspapers were in publication in 1940.[102] By 1945, 101 publications of various types were recorded in central China: 51 newspapers, 27 magazines, and 23 others.[103] Although few of the newspapers were actually typeset, and most of them were mimeographed, they became, as one writer claimed, "the collective guiding force for the unity of the military, the government, and the people."[104]

This "guiding force" did not, however, appear instantly. The Communist newspaper campaign in fact ran a twisted course as a formula for this powerful printed medium was sought. At the beginning, international news was routinely given front-page treatment, followed by events from the Guomindang areas. News in the border areas was generally given the lowest priority, appearing in the last pages of the paper and amounting to no more than one-eighth of the total space. Newspapers also followed *Pravda* and *Dagong bao* in having one editorial each day, a practice described by critics as lacking flexibility and identity. Worse still, as the propaganda chief Lu Dingyi (1906–) pointed out, in giving Guomindang news prominent coverage, publishers committed the grave mistake of not distinguishing between "enemies and friends."[105] One commentator charged that most newspapers had "the four diseases"—deafness, blindness, muteness, and feebleness: they were unheedful of the people's suggestions, inattentive to the welfare of the general public, incompetent to explain CCP policy, and incapable of standing firm against the enemy.[106] Mao sounded a similar alarm in March 1942.

In the history of the Chinese Communist press, Mao's March 1942 speech to a group of journalists concerning the style and format of the *Liberation Daily* ranks as a particularly important outline of policy. Delivered a month after the official launch of the Rectification Campaign and three months before his "Talks," the speech reiterated the rectification theme of combating "subjectivism, sectarianism, and stereotyped party writing (commonly known as the 'party eight-legged essay' [*dang bagu*])." The press would play a central role in educating the masses about this policy, Mao insisted. Although his speech repeated the standard slogans of resistance against Japan, its main thrust was to assert the role of the Party in dealing with erroneous tendencies on the part of editors and writers. "Unless we act together and march in unison, [this campaign] will never succeed. . . . Through newspapers [such as the *Liberation Daily*] we can pass along experience from one section to others, thereby facilitating reform."[107]

Like Lenin, Mao viewed the newspaper as "a collective propagandist, agitator, and organizer";[108] but more than the Soviet leader, he paid particular attention to the peasant readers whom the Party was trying to reach. In the past, he charged, the newspaper had proceeded in a wrong direction; its editors ignored local news and paid little attention to actual happenings in China. The fact that two reports about Mao's Rectification Campaign appeared on page three of the *Liberation Daily* (2 and 10 February 1942) instead of being given front-page coverage enraged him. Furthermore, Mao argued, the paper's editors and reporters too often spoke in a language incomprehensible to the masses. They failed both to understand and meet the needs of the people.

Mao's criticism of the editorial policy of the *Liberation Daily* was a direct attack on Bo Gu (Qin Bangxian, 1907–1946), the paper's chief editor and a member of Wang Ming's International Faction. The faction pursued what Mao called the erroneous policies of "ignoring rural revolution" and "surrendering the independence of the Chinese Communist Party to the Guomindang." Still, the dispute reflected more than a power struggle for party leadership or a simple move away from Stalin's policy of close cooperation with the Guomindang. It was, rather, Mao's affirmation of what he believed to be the correct policy for building a socialist China. The effectiveness of a newspaper, in Mao's view, depended largely on its editors' ability to communicate with the masses, by drawing examples from everyday life and addressing their readers' immediate concerns. Mao suggested that the Party and the party newspaper should work together; in that way, serious mistakes could be corrected and a proper perspective restored.

Despite Mao's emphasis on the masses as the source of wisdom and experience, the need for a tightly organized party on the Leninist model was never far from his mind. As at his subsequent discussion with the cartoonists Hua Junwu, Zhang E, and Cai Ruohong, Mao reaffirmed the CCP's paramount role in deciding policy. "Let the whole party run the newspapers" (*quan dang ban bao*) became a slogan in Communist journalism.[109]

The speech to the *Liberation Daily* reporters yielded instant results. On 1 April 1942, the paper assumed a new look: party instructions were now printed on the front page, and reports about activities in the Communist regions increased dramatically in number. At the same time, international news was given less coverage. The paper also became increasingly critical of the Guomindang in general and Jiang Jieshi in particular, partly through the use of cartoons and woodcuts. The primary responsibility of the press was not to discuss, but to explain and justify the policies of the Party. Chairman Mao's speech, one journalist later said, "made us realize that every word, every sentence, even a punctuation mark, must be responsible to the Party."[110]

Mao's directive was of course not limited to the *Liberation Daily*. Newspaper editors in other border areas were bound by it as well. In a September 1942 telegram to general Chen Yi (1901–1972), acting commander of the New Fourth Army, Mao made this clear: "Please pay close attention to newspapers and magazines in northern Jiangsu. Make sure that they serve the Party in propagating its current policy."[111] But could opposing viewpoints be printed? Perhaps they could in the Communist newspapers printed in the Guomindang-controlled territories. In a March 1942 telegram to Zhou Enlai, who supervised the publishing of the *New China Daily* in Chongqing, Mao stressed that "non-Party members' viewpoints should be included."[112] Yet despite this apparent openness, those viewpoints that appeared in the *New China Daily* were definitely sympathetic to, if not supportive of, Communist policy. Openness did not mean permissiveness, and inclusion of outside views did not rule out screening and bias.

Mao in fact tolerated no dissent in his own backyard. In the border regions, the press and the Party had to speak with one voice; and Communist journalists' self-censorship became a form of party devotion. Underlying Mao's speech was also a promotion of Chinese over foreign ideas. Rather than covering foreign events that took place in remote corners of the world, often in the form of exotic intrigues far beyond the comprehension of humble peasants, the press must address local problems and write about the joys and sufferings of the country folk. The battle against excessive "foreignism" received widespread support among party officials and intellectuals alike. The blind borrowing of "foreign eight-legged essays" (*yang bagu*) could sound the death knell of Chinese literature, Zhou Yang stated.[113]

The result was a dramatic increase in newspaper coverage of local issues. The CCP instructed cadres to lend a hand in the production of local papers, supplying information and contributing articles whenever possible. Such tasks, as the Party's directive made clear, "should be regarded as part of your regular, important work."[114] The *Shanxi-Suiyuan Daily* (*Jin-Sui ribao*, later renamed the *Resistance War Daily* [*Kangzhan ribao*]) adopted a policy of "localization and popularization" in 1942, devoting three-fifths of its space to coverage of regional events.[115] Mao, in his meeting with a representative from the *Shanxi-Suiyuan Daily* in December 1944, made his argument even more explicit: "In the newspaper layout, local news is the most important, followed by national, and then international. . . . You are not running the newspaper for the New China News Agency [in Yan'an]," he told the representative, "you are publishing it for the people in the Shanxi-Suiyuan Border Region."[116] The presence of these local editors and reporters, be they professional or amateur, had a double significance: practically, it represented an important link between the Party and the peasantry; symbolically, it reaffirmed Mao's commitment to address China's issues at their most basic level.

"Localization," however, was by no means the only issue confronting Communist journalists. Finding a proper newspaper language became an equally challenging task. The early Communist newspapers used a language laden with elegant phrases and high rhetoric, which hardly evinced an emotional affinity with rural readers. Seemingly aware of these dangers, Deng Tuo (1912–1966), editor of the *Shanxi-Chahar-Hebei Daily* (*Jin-Cha-Ji ribao*), urged his fellow journalists to restrict their vocabulary to combinations of no more than 3,000 characters.[117] Literary essays interlaced with esoteric terms and opaque expressions, he warned, could form a wall between the writers and the people. For Deng, establishing direct contact with the people was more important than writing style. Political ideas and values were meaningful, after all, only if they could be comprehended and eventually assimilated. "It does not matter if the term is native or foreign; so long as it is understood by the people, it is a good term," he once said.[118] The smaller number of Chinese characters used in his newspaper also met a practical need: flexibility. Given the constant threat of enemy attack, a "guerrilla-type" press needed to be developed for easy mobility. Simple printing equipment could be rapidly mounted on donkeys or mules and make a swift and safe retreat when enemy troops were approaching. This kind of operation earned the *Shanxi-Chahar-Hebei Daily* the sobriquet "The Paper Published on the Back of Eight Mules" (*Batou luozi banbao*).[119]

Small newspapers appeared in profusion in the Communist areas, their target being semiliterate and illiterate villagers. While it is difficult to gauge their impact, the outpouring of such publications suggests that they commanded a wide readership in the countryside. In 1945, according to one survey, the border areas boasted more than seventy tabloids.[120] Among these small newspapers, perhaps the *Border Region People's Press* (*Bianqu qunzhong bao*), launched on 25 March 1940, was the most famous; as its editor, Hu Jiwei (1916–), put it, the goal was that "those who know a few words can read it; and those who are illiterate can understand it when it is read to them."[121] Although both the *Liberation Daily* and the *Border Region People's Press* were official party papers (the former for the Central Committee of the CCP, the latter for the local committee), they targeted different audiences—on the one hand, cadres, especially middle- and high-level officials, and on the other, the general public. As the principal party paper, the *Liberation Daily* adopted a more traditional hard-news approach; the *Border Region People's Press*, by contrast, covered a broader range of lively topics. Its articles were relatively short, often less political, and written in a vivid style. The paper concentrated on concrete economic and social issues, such as raising literacy in the countryside, improving local sanitation, and increasing agricultural yield; thus it served as an information channel as well as a classroom for the peasants. To broaden its appeal, the paper also incorporated *yangge*, folk songs, riddles, and *kuaiban*.[122] By addressing day-to-day problems, the *Border Region People's Press* reduced the general campaign of a socialist revolution to its most concrete and effective terms.

To many Communist intellectuals, "popularization" meant finding an ideal language with which to communicate with the villagers. Ai Siqi (1905–1966), author of the popular book *Philosophy for the Masses* (*Dazhong zhexue*, 1934), argued vehemently that a basic understanding of "the people's language" was essential in reaching both the heart and mind of the country folk.[123] To the Communists, language was not simply a vehicle of communication; it was an essential ingredient in the shaping of a new political reality and hence a new social order. In many ways, politics in Yan'an became an unending search for a "people's language" capable of stirring up the masses and galvanizing their support.

The significance of language in driving a revolution is paramount. Political upheavals produce new vocabulary, rituals, and symbols that work together to shatter old political structures and renounce tradition while affirming new values or establishing a new community. François Furet has argued, for example, that during the French Revolution the political vacuum created by the French monarchy between 1787 and 1789 was filled by a new political language that attempted to redefine reality: "Language was substituted for power, for it was the sole guarantee that power would belong only to the people, that is, to nobody."[124] Similarly, Mona Ozouf contends that speeches at revolutionary festivals were aimed at establishing a new national identity based on space and time.[125] In an unstable and transitional period, language becomes a symbol of power, and politics turns into a competition for words. New political language wields enormous power. It signals a new era and can be crucial in justifying the legitimacy of the event.

The Chinese Communists used language for just these purposes. But in contrast to a complex plural society where, in J.G.A. Pocock's words, people speak "a complex plural language,"[126] Mao and his associates adopted a political language marked by both precision and force. There was little room for ambiguity in the Chinese Communist system. As a result, the language evolved not through consensus, but by being imposed from above. It was a powerful tool able to shape people's perceptions, carefully contrived to appeal to their emotions as well as their minds. In the hands of the Communists, language took on the Marxist function of an instrument for class struggle, fostering social change and revolutionary reform. It was also used in the Durkheimian fashion as a vehicle of cultural integration, pulling disparate elements together to face the common task of establishing a new order. To create a collective feeling in the Communist border regions, new political terms were created and old ones rejuvenated, all invested with lofty political ideals and high emotion. Clichés took on new life when the Communists used them to explain new social circumstances. Indeed, Mao and his associates had an astonishing flair for reducing complex ideas to a few simple, powerful slogans.

The aim in adopting a new political language was not only to signal a break with the past, but also to transfer individual loyalty to a collective goal. Nowhere is this notion better demonstrated than in the specific names given to an array of magazines and newspapers. The terms *qunzhong* (the masses), *dazhong* (the people), *laobaixing* (the common folk), and *nongmin* (the peasants) were widely used. In southwestern Shanxi, for example, one found the *Common Folk* (*Laobaixing*), *The Peasant* (*Nongmin*); in the Shanxi-Suiyuan Border Region, the *Shanxi-Suiyuan People's Press* (*Jin-Sui dazhong bao*); in western Hebei, the *Common Folk's Press* (*Laobaixing bao*); and in northern Jiangsu, *Yan-Fu People* (*Yan-Fu dazhong*).[127]

None of these terms, of course, was exactly new. But each was infused with a strong sense of righteousness and a fresh political connotation. Thus the old forms took on new vigor, and clichés became battle cries for a new social order. The terms were also intended to create a feeling of sharing: everyone was included, and all were working toward a common goal. Only through continuous struggle and numerous hardships could they bring about the painful birth of the new order. The fact that political terms like *laobaixing* and *qunzhong* were being used over and over again only added to their symbolic significance. The new community in Yan'an was therefore a *laobaixing*'s community, a *dazhong*'s world, radically different from past societies where kings and generals ruled, and completely at odds with a capitalist society, where personal gain and fame reigned supreme. In a socialist country, a community was not made up of "individuals"; rather, it was a community of "us," belonging to the common people. The term *dazhong* became so prevalent that *Literature and Art Attack* (*Wenyi tuji*), a well-known publication in the Shaan-Gan-Ning Border Region, was renamed *People's Literature and Art* (*Dazhong wenyi*), shedding its former belligerent image and becoming, as its editors claimed, "a magazine that truly belongs to the people."[128]

But revolutionary language did more than just create a sense of belonging. The Communists used it as an instrument for political and social struggle. For them, revolutionary language was a means of empowerment, allowing the masses to feel control over their own destiny. The term *fanshen* (freeing oneself, standing up, turning over) is a good example of this rhetoric. In his book of the same name, William Hinton gives a good description of the term:

> Literally, it means "to turn the body," or "to turn over." To China's hundreds of millions of landless and land-poor peasants it meant to stand up, to throw off the landlord yoke, to gain land, stock, implements, and houses. But it meant much more than this. It meant to throw off superstition and study science, to abolish "word blindness" and learn to read, to cease considering women as chattels and establish equality between the sexes, to do away with appointed village magistrates and replace them with elected councils, it meant to enter a new world.[129]

Although Hinton's book treats dramatic social and political changes in a northern Chinese village in the late 1940s, the term *fanshen* had already gained currency in the Jiangxi Soviet period.[130] In sharp contrast to most political vocabulary, which tends to be quite abstract, *fanshen* is highly specific and concrete. Like the term *jiefang* (liberation, as in *Liberation Daily*), it is a vivid metaphor that evokes an intense response. It is also a rhetorical exercise replete with potent political implications.

To be effective, the anthropologist Robert Paine argues, rhetoric must come across in such a way that listeners believe their interests are shared and reflected in what is said.[131] Chinese Communists showed political acumen in fostering such a "we are together" feeling. They portrayed themselves as the representatives of oppressed people, fighting against a common enemy and sharing the same historical destiny. Used in opposition to *shou yapo* (oppressed), *fanshen* represents a new beginning, a new life free of oppression. And like all successful political terms, *fanshen* conjures up a vivid image: that of a new society, divorced from the past, in which humble people finally are capable of "turning" over. No longer at the bottom of the social hierarchy, they are masters of a new order.

While wartime newspaper vocabulary such as "paper bullets" inspired determination and patriotism, Communist political language had a different purpose: it provided a unifying political symbol for the common struggle ahead. *Fanshen* thus functioned as a tool of political integration and social transformation. It became a catch-all phrase, appearing in songs, folk tunes, novels, dramas, and *yangge* plays. Examples abound: the poet Tian Jian's (1916–1985) famous series "Songs of Turning Over" ("Fanshen ge") specifically praised the achievements and wise guidance of the CCP;[132] organizations with names like "Fanshen Drama Club" ("Fanshen jutuan") sprang up everywhere;[133] and comic strips using *fanshen* in their titles were not at all uncommon.[134] The writer Zhao Shuli's (1906–1970) 1945 short story "Meng Xiangying Turns Over" ("Meng Xiangying fanshen"), allegedly based on a true story, depicts a poor peasant woman in the Jin-Cha-Ji Border Region who finds new life by joining the local Communist committee. In the end, she is selected as a model peasant in her county.[135]

The passion for *fanshen* often ran high, especially when it concerned a sea of disgruntled peasants who had been aroused by Communist political suasion. A song from the *yangge* play *Qin Luozheng* reflects this strong political sentiment: "Like a sudden roar of spring thunder, the 'turning over' of the peasants has shaken heaven and earth." The term *fanshen* was more than a mere political slogan. It underlined, as Hinton rightly points out, a cultural transformation as well. The Communists argued that a profound cultural change should begin with basic education. Learning now belonged to everyone, no longer to a privileged few. Ma Ke's *Husband and Wife Learn to Read*, for example, depicts a peasant couple, Liu Er and his wife (curiously, her name is never mentioned, perhaps indicating a certain bias of the author) striving to become literate. Ultimately, their hard work yields positive results:

> *Liu Er (singing)*:
> We know nothing if we don't study.
> In the past, when you were uneducated,
> You were subjected to humiliation without even understanding why.
> *Liu Er and his wife (singing together)*:
> Now, we finally are "turning over"!
> The suffering people have become the masters.
> How can an illiterate person [*zhengyan de xiazi*] walk?
> Learning to read is the most urgent task.
> Oh, the most urgent task.

Fanshen kept appearing in *yangge* plays such as *Twelve Sickles* and *An Honor Lamp*, a compelling assertion that the peasants had finally stood up after centuries of being oppressed by evil gentry and ruthless landlords. It was an attack against the Guomindang, certainly; but even more it was a paean to Mao and his followers.

Creating a New Society

The notion of a new society undergoing thorough, exciting change and a land peopled by men and women pursuing a noble dream was reinforced by other popular culture forms. Many of these forms were brought to life through the familiar technique of "filling old bottles with new wine." Again, the *Three-Character Classic* was a favorite subject.

One of the earliest Communist *Three-Character Classics* to appear was a block-printed *Workers and Peasants Three-Character Classic* (*Gong nong sanzi jing*), issued in 1930 by the soviet government in Xingguo county, Jiangxi province. Instead of the familiar moral tone in the opening sentences in the Confucian version—"Men at their birth are naturally good / Their natures are much the same; their habits become widely different"—the new text, predictably, carries a strong political message from the outset:

> In this world,
> Human beings are the cleverest.
> Among them,
> Workers, peasants, and soldiers are the creators.[136]

Perhaps inspired by the popularity of Lao Xiang's *Anti-Japanese Three-Character Classic*, the Communists in the Shaan-Gan-Ning Border Region also came out with a work bearing the same name in 1940. At first glance, it seems to be filled with the same anti-Japanese rhetoric and passion as Lao Xiang's; but closer scrutiny reveals the party line running strongly through the Communist *Anti-Japanese Three-Character Classic*. Glorifying the Chinese Communist Party in its unswerving struggle against the Japanese, the 180-line propaganda piece is a glowing encomium to Mao's correct and wise leadership, including his theory on "protracted war."[137]

The majority of the Communist *Three-Character Classics* were short, ranging from 130 to 260 lines. They became increasingly anti-Guomindang in tone after 1945 and seemed to inflame public feeling in the border regions. In 1944, the blind storyteller Han Qixiang turned the *Anti-Japanese Three-Character Classic* into a story. "It was warmly welcomed by listeners," he recalled later in his autobiography.[138]

The political intention of the Communist *Three-Character Classics* was obvious. So was that of street poetry. Inspired by traditional Chinese wall poems and the work of the Soviet poet Vladimir Mayakovsky (1893–1930), a Futurist turned socialist, Tian Jian and Ke Zhongping introduced a new kind of "street poetry" (*jietoushi*) in Yan'an in August 1938. According to Tian Jian, a street poem was "a short, popular, rhymed poem intended for propaganda and agitation purposes." Written on the wall or handed out on a sheet of paper, it had to be brief yet potent in meaning. It acted, said Tian, "like a bayonet on the battlefield." It was with this combatant spirit in mind that the two poets launched the first "Street Poetry Day" on 7 August 1938. "Instantly," as Tian recalled years later, "city walls and street corners were packed with street poems."[139]

As the name indicates, street poems were meant to encourage poets and writers to go to the streets, to merge art with reality. In Tian Jian's mind, a poet had to devote his pen to the service of the armed struggle against the Japanese and the capitalist system. His "A Volunteer" (1938) is a case in point:

> Along Mt. Changbai [in Northeastern China],
> Chinese sorghum thrives glowingly in the blood.
> Amid wind and dust,
> A volunteer soldier
> Astride a horse passes through his hometown.
> He has returned:
> With an enemy's head
> Dangling from his gun.[140]

This poem carries powerful symbols and strength. Mt. Changbai, which fell into enemy hands in the early days of the Sino-Japanese War, evoked bitter memories in the minds of the Chinese; yet life and struggle, like the hardy sorghum, continued to flourish in the occupied northeastern China. A volunteer's valor and an enemy's defeat promised hope for the future. "A Volunteer" was one of the best street poems and, together with other equally passionate pieces, earned Tian Jian a reputation, in the words of the poet Wen Yiduo (1899–1946), as "the drummer of our age."[141]

The majority of street poems, however, were more direct in approach, devoid of the visual effect and rich symbols of Tian Jian's masterpiece. The following is an example:

> A magpie cries on the branch,
> A yellow dog wags its tail.
> With the arrival of the New Fourth Army,
> People sing and hail.[142]

In reality, then, street poems were propaganda slogans dressed in poetic form. To send street poetry to the people, Tian Jian formed poetry groups and called on others to "let art and the people merge together."[143]

But how could art and the people truly merge together? Should literary creation come from the people instead of from poets like Tian Jian and Ai Qing? Ai Qing, aware of this dilemma, answered the question this way: "New poets must come from the masses. What about us [intellectuals]? We are no more than a midwife."[144] As a writer who enthusiastically embraced the Maoist cause, Ai Qing seemed perfectly willing to play a subordinate role to the common people. But to many the idea of playing "midwife" was unpalatable, not to mention easier said than done. Intellectuals soon found that learning from the masses was a difficult and often frustrating experience.

If writing street poetry was still essentially an intellectual exercise, perhaps a better approach to learning from the masses, some argued, was to collect folk songs and the stories of folk artists. While the latter effort proved quite challenging, the gathering of folk songs turned out to be relatively unproblematic.

As was true with other forms of popular and folk culture, folk song collecting became a highly visible campaign in the Communist areas. Such an undertaking, of course, was by no means new, having been pursued in the early decades of the twentieth century by such intellectuals as Gu Jiegang and Liu Fu.[145] But here again, the Communists sought to create an alternate mass culture based on a radical philosophy. Moreover, they paid special attention to local particularities. According to Jia Zhi, a veteran folklorist, interest in folk songs was evident during the Jiangxi Soviet era,[146] but systematic collecting did not begin until the Communists were fully in control several years later in northwest China. And understandably, interest only grew after Mao's "Talks."

Folk songs, already one of the most popular forms of folk entertainment, became a basic ingredient in many new *yangge* plays, as the appearance of the popular tune "Embroidering a Purse" ("Xiu hebao") in *Zhong Wancai Starting from Scratch* demonstrates. More important, the Communists now began to collect folk songs systematically and on a large scale. Tian Jian and Li Ji (1922–1980) were two particularly avid collectors. One product of their labors was a published compendium of folk songs acquired by Tian Jian in the Jin-Cha-Ji Border Region in 1945.[147] Li Ji's efforts were even more ambitious and successful. Li was particularly interested in a type of northern Shaanxi folk song known collectively as *shuntianyou* (literally, "follow-heaven-roam," also known as *xintianyou*), which, inspired by Mao's "Talks," he roamed the countryside to collect. "The more I collected," he exclaimed, "the more fascinated I became by them."[148] *Shuntianyou*, one of the three most popular two-sentence folk song types in northern China,[149] proved an ideal tool for the Communists to inculcate socialist passion, for by stringing the (generally rhymed) couplets together, the *shuntianyou* performer can spin a narrative story. It was with this narrative nature in mind that Li Ji wrote his famous long poem "Wang Gui and Li Xiangxiang" (1945), based on the *shuntianyou* form.

"Wang Gui and Li Xiangxiang" concerns the familiar confrontation between the avaricious landlord Second Master Cui and the poor peasant Wang Gui. It also tells of the romance between Wang and the peasant girl Li Xiangxiang, a well-loved theme in the Chinese folklore tradition. At the end of the story, Wang Gui, helped by the Communist guerrilla forces, defeats the evil landlord, and Wang and Li live happily ever after. Li Ji's poem received widespread attention, partly because of the many interesting twists and turns in the story and partly because of its heavy dose of revolutionary romance. What made Li Ji's composition unique, Guo Moruo rightly observed, was not his technique but his message. The poem was fraught with what Guo called "people's consciousness." "This is a piece that signals the 'turning over' [*fanshen*] of literature and art."[150] Though Guo's comment had a political focus, the true explanation for the popularity of "Wang Gui and Li Xiangxiang" must be Li Ji's adroit use of the popular *shuntianyou* style of folk song. So impressed was Li Ji with *shuntianyou*, in fact, that he went on to publish a fine collection of them entitled *Two Thousand Follow-heaven-roaming Songs* (*Shuntianyou er qian shou*, 1950).

For Li Ji and his comrades, folk song collecting was more than an artistic exercise. It was overwhelmingly a social and political activity. Consider *Selected Folk Songs of Northern Shaanxi* (*Shaanbei min'ge xuan*), a famous collection compiled by the Luyi in 1945, for example. Though this compendium might seem to bear superficial resemblance to the earlier one initiated by Lu Fu and Gu Jiegang at Beijing University, He Qifang (1912–1977), a poet and the head of the literature department at Luyi, was quick to point out that the two differed substantially both in methods of collecting and in content, and hence had different results. He Qifang argued that while the earlier collection assembled mainly children's songs gathered from urban university students and high school teachers, the Yan'an project sent students to the remote countryside to collect genuine folk songs from farmers, porters, and peasant women. The songs were received, therefore, from the mouths of the people rather than through the memories of intellectuals. "They [the Luyi students] went down to the countryside in northern Shaanxi, established a friendly relationship with the people, lived with them . . . and listened to their songs [before they recorded them]."[151] For He, this project linked students and the folk together. To be scientific, the collectors were instructed to record exactly what they heard. The result was an uncommonly reliable record of folk songs of northern Shaanxi.[152] Nevertheless, despite the inclusion of some traditional love songs and erotic songs, or what the editors called "old folk songs," their emphasis was unmistakably on new examples.

The juxtaposition of old and new songs was intended, as the editors admitted, "to mirror past and present life in the Shaan-Gan-Ning Border Region."[153] Thus the collection bore a strong political stamp. Indeed, the contrasts between the old and the new are stirring. "Contracted Laborer's Song," for example, tells a painful story of the past:

> A contracted laborer's life is full of bitterness,
> Oh, what a painful life!
> Beginning in January and ending in October,
> My life is as hard as that of an ox or horse,
> And my food is as bad as a pig's or a dog's.

Under a new government, however, the future holds enormous promise, as the first part of "The Four-Season Production Song" tells us:

> Peach blossom blooms in spring.
> A new government directive has just arrived:
> Mobilize the masses for production!
> Everyone is full of exhilaration.
> Peasants labor hard and long,
> Becoming model heroes and
> Spreading their names.
> Being showered with accolades and songs.

The folk song drive was later turned into a political attack against the
Nationalists as the relations between the CCP and the GMD deteriorated after the war, with the Communists denouncing Jiang Jieshi for
everything from operating a police state to bankrupting the nation's
economy.[154]

The folk song collecting campaign in the Communist areas was important not so much for what it accomplished as for what it symbolized: a major commitment by intellectuals to go to the people and
record their feelings and thoughts—an example of how Mao's "mass
line" concept actually bore tangible results. This kind of commitment
also spilled over into the storytelling campaign. But here it involved a
different set of questions: How could traditional storytellers be
brought into the Communist camp? Should their old repertoire be
modified? What was the role of intellectuals vis-à-vis folk artists?

While intellectuals in the Guomindang-ruled territories used drum
singing to fire patriotic passion, the Communists relied instead on
storytelling. The value of this folk art form, which had a long and
popular tradition in China,[155] was recognized officially at a meeting of
Communist writers in Yan'an in September 1944.[156] As an instrument
of propaganda, however, storytelling paled in comparison to *yangge*,
for it was never as organized and well orchestrated by the Party. Yet it
had a few distinct advantages. While *yangge* were performed only at
festival times or in the New Year to celebrate the beginning of a new
cycle, stories could be told anyplace and at any time. Moreover,
whereas a *yangge* troupe required at least three to four and often
twenty to thirty members to stage a show, storytellers could perform
alone, traveling around the countryside to charm crowds with their individual talents. Finally, while a *yangge* performance necessitated extensive preparations and substantial props, a storyteller was normally
accompanied by nothing more than a simple three-stringed plucked

instrument (*sanxian*). "To a certain extent," the writer Zhou Erfu (1914–) contended, "the simple nature of storytelling meets the needs of the common people far better than *yangge*."[157]

The popularity and high mobility of storytelling made it an ideal tool for mass education. And the abundance of storytellers made it an even more effective means for reaching obscure corners of the country-side. A casual survey in northern Shaanxi in 1941 revealed that Yan-chang and Yanchuan counties had more than ten storytellers each, while Suide topped the list with ninety.[158] Many of these performers were peripatetic blind singers who, armed with a broad repertoire of stories, made their living by bringing laughter and excitement to re-mote villages and towns where peasants otherwise endured a rather monotonous life. Before the Communists could make wide and thor-ough use of this popular folk art, however, they insisted on revamping it thoroughly, infusing it with new spirit and new content. For them, many traditional stories were filled with what they called "poisonous ideas," propagating harmful Confucian notions and encouraging fatal-ism. "Well-wishing Storytelling," (Ping'an shu), for example, preached superstition and servility. "They were active promoters of feudal thoughts," Zhou Erfu charged.[159]

The reform began in earnest after 1944. First storytelling training classes were set up to assemble folk artists. In 1945, a Storytelling Group (Shuoshu zu) was formed under the direction of the Cultural Federation of the Shaan-Gan-Ning Border Region. This group co-ordinated the reform movement, establishing a tie between the story-tellers and the Party and serving as a school where socialist ideals and revolutionary thought could be transmitted to traditional storytellers. A series of recordings was also made to preserve this art.

Perhaps the most successful case to emerge from the reform was Han Qixiang (1915–1989), an illiterate and blind storyteller who be-came the most celebrated young folk artist in the border area. A man with a phenomenal memory, Han could recite with ease more than seventy stories and sing fifty different kinds of folk tunes.[160] In 1940, at the age of twenty-five, Han arrived in Yan'an from his native town of Hengshan in northern Shaanxi. The Communist revolution moved him deeply. Under the guidance of the Storytelling Group, Han aban-doned his old repertoire and began to compose new stories, producing twenty-four between July 1944 and December 1945—more than 200,000 words.[161] Although storytelling was an oral tradition of col-lective creativity, Han was able to stamp his works with a distinctive, individual flavor. He based his stories partly on actual events and partly on fiction, but optimism for a new socialist system knit them together as a coherent whole. Endowed with local flavor and full of propaganda rhetoric, Han's stories painted the picture of a backward border area vibrant with life and happiness. Among his many "new storytelling" works, "The Reunion of Liu Qiao" ("Liu Qiao tuanyuan," 1945) and "Zhang Yulan Participates in the Election" ("Zhang Yulan canjia xuanjuhui," 1946) are the most famous.

Based on a local Shaanxi drama, "The Reunion of Liu Qiao" tells of the hardworking, beautiful young woman Liu Qiao who, tricked by her avaricious father, breaks her arranged engagement with her impoverished fiancé, Zhao Zhu, whom she has never met. When her father forces her to marry a wicked, wealthy middle-aged shop owner instead, she escapes unscathed with the help of a friend. Later, Liu Qiao accidentally runs into her fiancé, now a labor hero, and realizes that she had been fooled by her father. Finally, with the help of the local Communist government, justice prevails. The young couple is happily reunited, and Liu's father repents and promises to start anew. The story comes to a happy end for everyone, concluding, just as it began, with an enlivening melody:

> Plucking a three-stringed instrument hear my song,
> I roam the countryside all year long.
> Telling stories has an unmistakable objective:
> Promoting culture and entertaining common folks.
> Oh! Our border region is such a marvelous place,
> Men ploughing and women weaving all day long.
> Everyone is well clothed and properly fed,
> Practicing democracy and celebrating new days.[162]

While "The Reunion of Liu Qiao" condemns the feudal tradition of treating marriage as a business transaction, "Zhang Yulan Participates in the Election" emphasizes the right of women to take part in politics. Set in the northern Shaanxi area, this story portrays an old-fashioned, jealous husband, Feng Guangqing, who refuses to allow his politically active and strong-willed wife, Zhang Yulan, to attend political meetings held by the local Communist government. A stubborn man but without much confidence, he never hesitated to beat his wife to exert his traditional male authority. Undaunted, Zhang Yulan, instructed by Communism, firmly believes in the equality of the sexes. She not only takes part in meetings, but also speaks out against the wrongdoings of the county head, winning wide applause from the audience. Her husband is at first enraged by her "unruly" behavior but later admits his own mistakes. This story, too, ends happily with the couple enthusiastically participating in the election meeting together. It concludes with the following ditty:

> The border region is bursting with democracy and peace,
> Practicing democracy is for the sake of the people.[163]

If these stories appear crude and simplistic, their political messages are nevertheless direct and powerful. Both tell their listeners that the remarkable achievements in the remote, backward border areas were brought about by the selfless efforts of the Communists under the wise leadership of Chairman Mao. The Guomindang regime, by contrast, is condemned as insensitive to the needs of the people, corrupt, and incompetent. An old man vents his grievances during a political meeting in "Zhang Yulan Participates in the Election":

> In 1942,
> A terrible drought hit Hengshan.
> The Guomindang demanded food and money,
> Forcing our family to flee![164]

Han Qixiang also berated the Nationalist regime, dismissing it as oppressive and downright dishonest, in other works such as "A Current Affair" ("Shishi zhuan").[165] This harsh criticism of the Guomindang contrasted sharply with the unreserved praise he showered on the new Yan'an government.

Han Qixiang, of course, was not the only folk storyteller to be recruited and reformed by the Communists. Other well-known storytellers included Yang Shengfu and Gao Yongchang. Each came out with his own version of praise for the arrival of the new social order.[166]

Communist officials encouraged intellectuals to help old storytellers like Han Qixiang immerse their work in the socialist ideal. In essence, intellectuals were asked to act as a bridge between the Party and the folk artists. At the same time, they were also advised to integrate with the masses. A number of writers (notably Lin Shan [1910–] and Gao Minfu [1905–1975]) were assigned to help Han Qixiang write his stories.[167] Gao Minfu played an important role in the shaping of "The Reunion of Liu Qiao," for instance, and he also assisted Yang Shengfu in editing that blind storyteller's works. Yet overall, the encounter of these two worlds was far from harmonious.[168] Although Gao Minfu said that he was pleased with his collaboration with Han Qixiang and believed there was a great future for what he described as "the close collaboration between intellectuals and folk artists,"[169] others were less optimistic. Zhou Erfu was frank enough to admit that intellectuals approached old-style storytelling in two ways: either they belittled it as unworthy, or else they called outright for its abolishment.[170] The notion that peasants were hopelessly backward and notoriously superstitious country bumpkins prevailed among certain intellectuals; the fact that many storytellers were also fortune-tellers (Han Qixiang included)[171] only added fuel to the fire. At the beginning, in fact, Han was referred to by Communist cadres as "Mr. Fortune-Teller" ("Suanming xiansheng")—hardly a sign of respect.[172]

Conversely, folk artists were not entirely happy with the intrusion of outside intellectuals into their territory. For them, a Shanghai highbrow who knew nothing about rural China yet posed as an expert on local folk forms was unacceptable. Some, in fact, did not hesitate to offer a few suggestions to their urban mentors. One such case was Liu Zhiren, the *yangge* innovator and an early collaborator with intellectuals whom we met before. He made several recommendations for the *yangge* movement, including using youngsters to perform because "their movements are more supple and attract the viewer."[173] Ellen R. Judd, in her study of the subject, suggests that the conflict between folk artists and Communist intellectuals also stemmed from their different conceptions of art. While the former thrived on performance, the latter were more interested in the political content of the reformed text.[174] A fruitful collaboration required a thorough transformation on both parts, a process which would take years to accomplish.

While the elite-folk relationship was less than harmonious, the relationship between the government and folk artists was completely different, for it was built on neither collaboration nor willingness, but on obedience. Compliance became a test of one's loyalty and commitment to the Party. Disobedience was a crime that few dared to commit. The setting up of a Storytelling Group in 1945 by the Yan'an government was thus more than a means to facilitate artistic reform; it was a way to ensure the success of a socialist experiment with a popular folk art. As in the case of *yangge* plays, cartoons, and newspapers, the Communists believed that without supervision from the top, the reform of storytelling would go awry. The Party, especially after 1942, tolerated no public dissent from its followers.

The Border Region Culture

The change of Zhong Wancai from an opium addict to a model worker in the new *yangge* play *Zhong Wancai Starting from Scratch* conjures up visions of a new society full of reformed *erliuzi*, people determined to abandon their disgraceful past and embrace a new life. But what the Communists were really trying to promote in these stories was the positive, purposeful attitude of characters like Zhang Yulan. Indeed, heroes and heroines were an all-important component of the Communists' efforts to inspire men and women with the socialist cause. The new Communist social order should be peopled by new citizens, different from their predecessors in actions as well as in thought. These "labor heroes" (*laodong yingxiong*), as they were called, represented the future of China.

In the vast, backward countryside, Chinese proletarians were simply nonexistent. Thus peasants became the pathbreakers, the "model workers," exuding fortitude and boundless energy in their reconstruction of a moribund society. In sharp contrast to the backward, submissive, ignorant peasant promulgated in the works of Confucian scholars, the new peasants of Communist popular literature were dedicated, intelligent, and politically active. Hardworking and selfless men and women who had finally "turned over" (*fanshen*), their first allegiance was to the collective. They acted in the service of the community, never hesitant to sacrifice themselves for the people. And they were no longer victimized by predatory capitalists or tyrannical landlords. Popular culture was a primary means of announcing the arrival of these "new men and women."

Among the many peasant heroes promoted by the Communists during the Yan'an years, perhaps none was more celebrated than Wu Manyou. Wu, a peasant refugee who once had to sell his three daughters to avoid starvation, moved to Yan'an from northern Shaanxi in the mid-1930s to eke out a living. On land allotted to him by the Communists, and by means of hard work, determination, ingenious cultivating methods such as deep ploughing, and sound management, Wu was able to increase his cultivated land manyfold, raise sheep and cattle, and live a comfortable life. In April 1942, the *Liberation Daily* launched a "Learning from Wu Manyou Movement." It lasted a considerable time, filling the newspapers with articles about the enormous achievement of Wu and his devotion to the collective.[175] In its 11 January 1943 editorial, the *Liberation Daily* counseled the people to study Wu's spirit: "[Wu's] direction is the direction for all the peasants in the border areas."

Heeding the Party's call, Ai Qing added his voice to this well-publicized campaign, writing a long nine-part poem for the *Liberation Daily* in early March 1943. In sharp contrast to his early, pre-Yan'an poems, which were mostly melancholic in mood, Ai Qing's long "Wu

Manyou" evoked enthusiasm and strong passion. Using simple but emotionally charged language, the poet describes how Wu's bitter life takes a dramatic turn only with the arrival of the Communist revolution. In Ai Qing's portrait, Wu Manyou is a poor peasant who has a keen sense of right and wrong. What makes him special is his boundless love of the border region and his total devotion to a just cause. Wu Manyou's world is a world of liberation and happiness:

> The world has now completely changed. . . .
> Today the poor people are masters of this world.
> They eat what they have planted,
> They wear what they have woven.
> They are not laboring for the warlords,
> Nor are they working for government officials.[176]

To render his peasant hero Wu Manyou realistically, Ai Qing visited Wu and recited his work to him, in order, as the poet put it, to "observe his reactions." Wu, in turn, never hesitated "to suggest additions or corrections."[177] The visit to Wu's home may have added a convincing touch to the finished piece. But perhaps even more important, it demonstrated that Ai Qing was responding affirmatively to Mao's call for intellectuals to learn from the masses.

Ai Qing's celebrated poem represented but one of many ways in which the Communists elevated the image of a model peasant. Gu Yuan's woodcut "Emulate Wu Manyou" (fig. 50), which appeared in the *Liberation Daily* of 10 February 1943, presented an even more vivid picture of this erstwhile refugee. In the bold strokes of Chinese folk art design, Gu Yuan paints a smiling, contented Wu Manyou surrounded by bumper harvests and fat livestock. Well fed and well clothed, he is living proof of the success of the Communist revolution. What Gu Yuan's piece lacks in subtlety and elegance it more than makes up for with its robust vitality. This woodcut, proclaimed Lu Dingyi, "blends art and propaganda skillfully together"; it was a lively example of "sending culture down to the village" and "a great achievement of the Rectification Campaign."[178]

The "Learn from Wu Manyou" campaign spread the peasant's name far and wide.[179] Yet Wu was not the only peasant to be singled out for praise. Communist publications abounded with heroic stories of selfless and energetic peasants who were willing to struggle for a new life. More important, they showed that the poor no longer needed to rely on the generosity of others. A glance at the *Liberation Daily* for a single year (from early 1943 to early 1944) reveals numerous heroes,

向吳滿有看齊

XIANG WU MANIOU KAN KI

古元作

Fig. 50. Gu Yuan, "Emulate Wu Manyou." From *JFRB*, 10 February 1943, p. 4.

including Zhao Zhankui, Zhang Chuyuan, and others.[180] A certain model peasant named Yang Chaochen, whose achievements were said to "rival" those of Wu Manyou, vowed to "challenge" Wu Manyou in a "friendly competition" centered on production.[181] To generate more enthusiasm, local party committees selected regional heroes and showered them with accolades. For example, Shanxi's Wen Xiangshuan was not only an excellent peasant, but he also helped organize village dramas in service of the revolution.[182] The climax of this campaign came in the fall of 1943, when 180 "model workers" were publicly honored in the First Shaan-Gan-Ning Border Region Labor Hero Meeting held in Yan'an. Twenty-five of them were named "special model workers," with Wu Manyou topping the list. Their woodcut portraits were prominently displayed on the front page of *Liberation Daily* (19 December 1943). The government also showered them with material rewards: each received a hefty prize of 30,000 *yuan*.[183]

The significance of promoting "model peasants" and "new men and women" through a variety of popular culture forms can be understood in the larger context of the Communists' attempt to create what they called "village literature and art" (*xiangcun wenyi*). This new peasant culture proved to be markedly different from that of the past, though its roots were still firmly planted in Chinese soil.[184] This "village culture" represented nothing less than the future of China. In the eyes of the Communist party ideologues, their May Fourth predecessors had bequeathed a gloomy, tragic picture of a crumbling rural China; the Communists, however, viewed the countryside from a different perspective. Mao steadfastly argued that China must look to the primitive countryside for its future, and not to the urban centers where corruption and decadence ran rampant. Reshaping Chinese society would depend largely on a correct understanding of the life and thoughts of the peasants. Not surprisingly, therefore, the Communists made a dogged and enthusiastic effort to create a new village political culture suited to answer the pressing problems of rural decline and a ruined economy. This effort gained new momentum with the unleashing of the Rectification Campaign in 1942.

In many ways, Communist intellectuals equated this "village culture" with what they called "border region culture" (*bianqu wenhua*).[185] In the border regions, people lived a harsh, guerrilla-like life under ceaseless attack from the Japanese and the Guomindang, yet in the process they won both the hearts and minds of the rest of the Chinese people. "The border area is more than the center of the anti-Japanese struggle," Sha Kefu proudly declared; "it is the fortress of new culture and new art."[186] Pride in the border regions seemed to be everywhere. *Brother and Sister Clear Wasteland*, for example, starts with an upbeat song:

> Loudly cries the rooster,
> The bright red sun rises.
> A robust young man,
> How can I sleep late and be sluggish?
> Carrying a hoe on my shoulder,
> I march into the fields.
> Atop the hill I look around,
> Oh, what a wonderful sight!
> The higher I stand, the farther I can see:
> Our border region has now become such a marvelous place.

The border region culture and spirit as the keys to China's future were stressed repeatedly in all manner of Communist popular culture forms. These were in essence political and propaganda works full of the promise of salvation through class struggle and hard work. The pervasive emotion associated with the border area was optimism. There was no place for doubt or melancholy. People performed their assigned tasks with the utmost energy and enthusiasm. Through its well-coordinated and relentless campaign, the Party drove home the need to defend the collective entity and the marvels of Communism.

The image of Yan'an as a Spartan but happy land undergoing unprecedented transformation, of the CCP as the incarnation of China's future, and of Mao as a patriotic leader—a man who desired peace with his nemesis Jiang Jieshi but refused to yield an inch of land to the Japanese—was conveyed to the people outside the border regions through a variety of channels. Supplementing the official *New China Daily*, for example, Zhou Enlai brought woodcuts celebrating the life of the border area to Chongqing for display in the "National Day Festival Woodcut Show" in October 1942, and new *yangge* plays were staged in Chongqing in 1945. Despite the Nationalists' blockade, information about the border regions was filtered out by both Western and Chinese journalists,[187] especially in the waning years of the war.[188] Most Western reporters, if not all, were impressed by Yan'an's resistance policy, educational reforms, economic independence, equality of the sexes, leaders' sincerity, and, above all, its "air of gaiety."[189] In comparison with the Guomindang, a regime wracked by corruption and internal turmoil and that had lost virtually all momentum in its reform efforts during the early 1940s, Mao and his Party presented a refreshing, even hopeful, alternative for China's future. The sociologist

Fei Xiaotong (1910–) made an incisive observation in May 1945: "To the ordinary layman who has never been to Yenan [Yan'an] and who has never had the opportunity to read reports on activities in the Red capital, the 'Border Region' is a land of mystery. Those who are dissatisfied with the reality surrounding them tend to regard Yenan as a romantic paradise."[190] It was among those "dissatisfied with the reality," who desired a positive and forceful change, that Mao's message found the most receptive ears.

Within the border regions proper, however, the totality of Yan'an culture that the Party tried to impose did not meet with unqualified acceptance. The passage of time began to reveal many points of tension in the relationship between the Party and the intelligentsia. On the one hand, the search for a new ideal was emotionally appealing and morally gratifying; on the other hand, total submission to the Party aroused a sense of foreboding about the future of literature and art. The case of Wang Shiwei (1900–1947), who found the restrictions imposed from above unpalatable, is now well known. His "Wild Lilies" incident was but one of the few examples of open opposition to the party line. Ding Ling's criticism of the fate of women in Yan'an and Xiao Jun's (1907–1988) attack on party cadres fell under the same category.[191] A lesser-known but equally significant case was Mo Ye's story "Liping's Distress" ("Liping de fannao"). Appearing in *Northwestern Literature and Art* (*Xibei wenyi*) in the Shanxi-Suiyuan Border Region in 1942, this story depicts an unhappy marriage between Liping, an educated patriotic young woman (who once played the role of Fragrance in *Lay Down Your Whip*), and an old-fashioned, middle-aged army cadre. Insensitive, extremely jealous, and clinging to the obsolete idea that "wives must obey their husbands," he demands his wife's submission, hoping that she will stay home and give birth to a son. The differences in education, temperament, and background between the two results in divorce. Mo Ye, a female Fujianese author, had once been a member of a drama propaganda troupe and a student in Luyi's literature department. She delved into the dark side of the border region, uncovering loneliness, unhappy marriages, and the unruly behavior of party cadres.[192] Her work provoked bitter condemnation from official critics. One charged that Mo Ye had tried to use "bourgeois intellectual thoughts to corrupt the revolution." The work, he said, was tantamount to an anti-Party act.[193] Like Ding Ling's "In the Hospital" ("Zai yiyuan zhong," 1941), Mo Ye's piece touched on the sensitive issue of the fate of women under the socialist system. And like Ding Ling, she was chastised for voicing a dissenting opinion unacceptable to the Party. When the Communists launched their official rectification campaign in the Shanxi-Suiyuan Border Region in 1943, "Liping's Distress" was singled out for particularly vehement attack. In 1947, Mo Ye was criticized again and was imprisoned for a few months.[194]

These bitter cases, of course, were not in line with the joyful image the Communists were trying to portray through a host of popular culture forms during the Yan'an years. But such incidents were the exception rather than the rule. The appeals and ideals of a bright socialist country were simply too powerful for most individuals to ignore. Despite their occasional brushes with Communist officials and unpleasant encounters with folk artists, intellectuals and artists in the border regions were not the victims of party coercion. On the contrary, most of them were willing participants in this new, carefully orchestrated political experiment, firmly believing that popular culture would help them realize their socialist dreams. Ding Ling, for example, soon admitted her "erroneous thoughts" about women and joined the Party in denouncing Wang Shiwei.[195] She went on to support the revolution with great loyalty.

Thus in the use of popular culture as in so many other ways, the Communist border regions were significantly different from the areas under Guomindang control. While the Guomindang employed popular culture largely as a patriotic tool, the Communists used it as a political vehicle to promote socialism and to politicize the people's life. Mao and his followers seemed to believe that symbols and pictures were more potent than mere words, and they made sure that the script of this political campaign was carefully written and screened not by individuals, but by the Party, thus allowing little room for dissension. The Rectification Movement, therefore, can be viewed as a deliberate attempt by the Party to create a new political culture. The popular culture campaign in the Communist areas aimed not at abstractions or highbrow symbolism but at simple realism. Although it undoubtedly benefited from the efforts made earlier in the Guomindang areas, it was not an urban-oriented drive; instead, it delineated vividly a rural base undergoing profound revolutionary changes, and it painstakingly projected this culture as the future of China. The campaign proved vital in the subsequent victory of the Communist Party in 1949.

7 A New Political Culture

The Sino-Japanese War was a conflict of extreme violence and cruelty and a period of immense cultural change in China. The Japanese invasion caused massive destruction, snuffed out numerous lives, and brought intense suffering to the Chinese people. According to some estimates, civilian casualties stood at between eight and ten million, more than three million Chinese troops were killed or wounded, and there were incalculable property losses.[1] Such a scale of destruction was unprecedented in Chinese history. Among the many Japanese atrocities, the December 1937 "Rape of Nanjing" would be remembered as a particularly notorious example of human brutality.

In this tragic conflict, however, China, though badly battered, was unbowed. Despite renewed Japanese attacks in the later phase of the war, including the devastating "Three-all" ("Burn all, kill all, loot all") mopping-up campaign of 1941–1943 against the Communist-held border regions in the north and the destructive Ichigō offensive of 1944 against the Nationalists' defensive lines in the south, the nation as a whole never lost its will to resist. By the time the war ended in 1945, China had tied down 1.2 million of a total 2.3 million Japanese overseas armed forces, thus making a significant contribution to the Allied victory.[2]

Despite chaos and ruins, the war marked a turning point in modern Chinese cultural and political history. This book has proposed that we consider the Sino-Japanese War not simply as a military confrontation between China and Japan or a period of economic upheaval and governmental disarray, but as an event that marked the emergence of a new political culture. We have explored several major changes that occurred in the eight-year war period: the intellectuals' move to the

270

hinterland and their attempt to reach out to the people and galvanize public support for the war cause; the dissemination and politicization of a host of popular culture forms, especially spoken dramas, cartoons, and newspapers, from urban centers like Shanghai to the rural interior; and the Communists' skillful use of these forms in their crusade to foster socialism and create a new China. The war shifted the momentum of cultural development to the rural hinterland, a reorientation that added importance and legitimacy to the Communists' rural revolution. At the same time, the Nationalists' failure to capitalize on this momentous change, together with their militaristic rule and their failure to provide a remedy to the worsening economy, meant their downfall in the civil war.

Intellectuals and Participation

"War," as Clausewitz wrote, "is an act of force and there is no logical limit to the application of that force."[3] But ironically, war is not just about force and destruction; it is also about commitment, expectation, and reconstruction. The Sino-Japanese War caused loss, fear, and uncertainty among some Chinese intellectuals, but among others it raised hopes for a new social and political order, propelling them to action. The conflict created an unprecedented wave of patriotism in China and, in its early phase, allowed a colossal release of frustrated feelings. Many claimed that after decades of foreign exploitation and years of thwarted efforts in bringing about a stable political system, the moribund nation had a new lease on life.

For intellectuals like Zheng Zhenduo, a literary historian and bibliophile who stayed in Shanghai throughout the war years, war was purely an act of destruction—not only of people, but of culture and history as well. When Japanese troops attacked Shanghai in August 1937, over ten thousand volumes of Zheng's priceless collection housed in the Kaiming Bookstore, many of them original Yuan and Ming editions, were lost in a fire.[4] "Those masterworks, which took numerous writers and scholars infinite pains to produce, could not withstand a single fire lit by the barbaric invaders," Zheng lamented.[5] Nevertheless, Zheng, prompted by patriotism and his love of books, launched a personal crusade to save many rare works from possible annihilation.[6] Under extremely difficult conditions, he managed to search out valuable items in bookstores all over Shanghai and reprint many rare Chinese texts, among them a multivolume *History of Chinese Prints* (*Zhongguo banhuashi tulu*, 1940–1947). He also moved many precious volumes to safety in the hinterland. Appealing in

1940 to the Nationalist government in Chongqing to help him and his friends in Shanghai set up a committee to preserve historical and literary documents,[7] he implored: "Let's protect our culture from destruction and occupation."[8]

In contrast to Zheng, who viewed the Japanese invasion as a crime and a cultural disaster, the Communist writer Guo Moruo saw it as a conflict between civilization and barbarism and an opportune time for intellectuals to make a commitment. As he wrote in September 1937, it was a "war between reason and bestiality, a war between evolution and retrogression, and a war between civilization and barbarism."[9] China's raising of arms in self-defense was thus justified, if in fact war could be justified. To Guo, then, war was more than an armed conflict; it was a cultural confrontation between two markedly different sets of values: good and evil, reason and madness.[10] Guo and many others seemed to believe that war, brutal as it was, promised to unleash a powerful energy of rejuvenation.

War was a sweeping change carried out by violent means. It eroded antiquated and harmful norms and promised to bring forth a new society. Many intellectuals, no doubt thinking of the years of internal chaos and ineffectual Guomindang rule, believed that China had reached a dead end, had lost its ability to renew itself. The conviction that the sick nation could not be rejuvenated until it experienced a major trauma was widespread among resisters, left and right alike. The correspondent Fan Changjiang, who took an increasingly critical stand against the Nationalist government as the war progressed, expressed this sentiment well in 1938: "War is the biggest destructive force, but at the same time it is also the most constructive. Only in a war can we destroy age-old evils and spur the growth of new life."[11] And Bu Shaofu, a journalist sympathetic to the Nationalists, wrote: "The War of Resistance propels everything in China forward."[12] When full-scale war between China and Japan finally erupted in July 1937, therefore, Chinese intellectuals experienced great excitement and euphoria. Guo Moruo registered his exhilaration in a poem, "Ode to the War of Resistance," after the conflict broke out in Shanghai in August 1937:

> When I heard the rumble of guns above Shanghai,
> I felt nothing but happiness.
> They are the auspicious cannons announcing the revival of our
>   people.
> And our nation has determined to resist till the end.[13]

Guo was not alone in his excitement. "We welcome war," Zang Ke-jia echoed. "It announces that we [Chinese] finally stand up."[14] True, China had now entered a difficult period of fighting for its own surviv-al. "But tragedy," the dramatist Xiong Foxi stated emphatically, "is good for rousing the spirit."[15] This mixed sentiment perhaps reflects the old saying, "Life thrives in adversity, but perishes in comfort and pleasure" (*Sheng yu youhuan, si yu anle*). Suffering would enable men and women to rise spiritually and to understand the need for sacrifice. "Only when one is willing to sacrifice oneself for the country can Chi-na survive forever," wrote historian Gu Jiegang.[16]

A shared feeling that a new era was dawning prevailed among intel-lectuals. The early resistance movement seemed to eliminate discord, break down barriers, and unite feuding factions. In the face of a fear-some enemy, for the first time in many years political parties, including the Nationalist government and the Communist Party, agreed to bury their ideological differences. The country brimmed with hope. China's victory in the war would not just signify the triumph of order over chaos; it would mean a long-divided country had again found its soul.[17]

But how was this unification to be realized? Guo Moruo believed that "the rumble of guns" had awakened intellectuals and "summoned them into the streets, to the front, to the countryside."[18] To dramatists and artists like Ouyang Yuqian and Ye Qianyu, the formation of drama traveling troupes and the Cartoon Propaganda Corps was more than just a new course for the resistance campaign: it was a call for intellectuals' commitment and action. Vividly reflecting this new trend were two popular wartime slogans: "Go to the street" (*Dao jietou qu*) and "Literature must go to the countryside! Literature must join the army!" (*Wenzhang xiaxiang, wenzhang ruwu*).

The term *jietou* (street) first gained currency in the mid-1930s with the publication of Liu Shi's *Street Talks* (*Jietou jianghua*) and Xu Maoyong's *Street Essays* (*Jietou wentan*).[19] Both authors were left-wing writers, and both intended, in Liu Shi's words, to "talk about common social knowledge with people on the street."[20] This objective echoed the earlier search by left-wing writers for a "people's lan-guage," an idea first proposed by Qu Qiubai, one-time Communist Party general secretary and a prominent figure in the League of Left-Wing Writers. Qu's vision of a language of the masses was aptly ex-pressed in the title of his posthumously published book *Collection of Street Essays* (*Jietou ji*).[21]

But the word *jietou* has a distinct urban ring; indeed, in Qu

Qiubai's case it referred specifically to city-dwelling proletarians, not to rural peasants. That connotation underwent a transformation during the war, acquiring added significance, and in a non-Marxist sense. Instead of being a class-related concept, *jietou* now referred to a patriotic fulfilling of one's obligation. Most resisters, in other words, associated the term less with the left-wing cause than with nationalism.[22] Reality, it seemed to say, could not be reduced to abstraction, and China could be saved only when resisters took action to the populace—specifically, to the countryside. Thus the term acquired a more rustic flavor. The drama slogan "From Carlton [Theater] to the street" reflected this new rural vision, and street plays like *Lay Down Your Whip* were products of the shift.

This move from the city to the countryside and the importance of participation was reflected even more clearly in the slogan "Literature must go to the countryside! Literature must join the army!" First used by the All-China Resistance Association of Writers and Artists, this was a call for intellectuals to build a broad base of support among the rural masses for the resistance cause. Like the slogan "Go to the street," "Literature must go to the countryside" expressed criticism of academic pursuits. The precariousness of everyday existence in the crisis not only "forced [writers and artists] into a confrontation with the concrete,"[23] but, more important, it also compelled them to examine their role in relation to their country. Indulgence in lofty ideals now drew fire from practically every corner. Esoteric talk had suddenly become a luxury, and perhaps even a moral crime, for it conveyed an air of apathetic indifference. The mood of the time stressed sacrifice *and* action. Getting involved helped intellectuals abandon their doubt and disillusionment and reaffirmed their traditional role as cultural spokesmen. Cultural nationalism—pride in China's heritage—and hope for the country's rebirth certainly played a role here; but feelings of individual responsibility and belief in freedom from foreign oppression were equally compelling motivations.

Slogans such as "Literature must go to the countryside" and the related "Drama must go to the countryside" (*xiju xiaxiang*)[24] affirmed intellectuals' participatory role in the war, yet they also marked a shift in cultural orientation toward the rural interior for which the resisters were ill prepared. General Feng Yuxiang offered specific advice: "Take off your mandarin jacket and change your clothes [into something compatible with the people]."[25] Ye Qianyu's hero in his cartoon "Let's Change into New Uniform" (fig. 26) did exactly that, the determined look on the young man's face unmistakable. The picture implied a radical reorientation of value and an endorsement of action. As a leader of the National Salvation Cartoon Propaganda Corps, Ye Qianyu himself was a living testament to this metamorphosis from scholar to soldier. If a middle-class Philistine like Mr. Wang could change into a patriotic foot soldier (fig. 19), should not intellectuals do the same?

Granted that much of what resistance intellectuals were now advocating seemed to echo the May Fourth ideal of "going to the people,"[26] the new campaign had several novel aspects. This time the goal was far more focused, the number of participants greater, the methods of delivery new, and the area of coverage vast. The May Fourth's slogan of "going to the people," after all, never ventured far beyond the academic wall. Ironically, it took a war to drive this noble message home and put it into practice.

But did the resisters manage to shed their elitism in reaching out to the masses? Despite its unprecedented scope, after all, the wartime popular culture campaign was still largely an intellectual drive to educate the peasants and mobilize them to fight for a collective goal. Most intellectuals, however, did recognize that the resistance could be effective only if a genuine dialogue was established between the participants and their audiences. The harsh reality of the war dictated that success required the active commitment and participation of the masses. Hence, the resisters kept their audience—the ways in which people thought and talked about politics—very much in mind. The urge of intellectuals to communicate, indeed *interact*, with the people was sincere and fully evident, and they displayed great sensitivity to the people's responses and needs. This development represents a significant change in both attitude and method from the earlier May Fourth era.

The Dissemination of Urban Popular Culture Forms

The slogan "Literature must go to the countryside," was more than just an affirmation of action on the part of intellectuals. It also directed attention to the vast interior, which rapidly became China's stronghold of defense against the invaders. The resisters realized that the success of the anti-Japanese campaign required more than merely the will to fight; it also required an efficient propaganda effort to inform and win over the masses.

The crisis caused by the Japanese invasion saw the emergence of a new political culture. The various urban culture forms that were called into play in the resistance effort were highly politicized and popu-

larized during the war, ultimately to be transformed into a key vehicle
of persuasion targeting the general public. Together with rejuvenated
rural genres such as drum singing and storytelling, these refashioned
urban forms created a sociopolitical coherence by cultivating compelling images and invoking shared symbols, which in turn helped shape
the way people saw, felt, and thought about the Sino-Japanese conflict. What gave this political culture its cohesion was nationalism.
Street plays brought the idea of unity to the grass roots, and patriotic
symbols drove home the message of resistance. Historical figures like
Hua Mulan and Liang Hongyu made China's past come alive in a
vivid and personal way, in the process concretizing the ideal of patriotism. Similarly, the use of beasts and snakes to demonize the
Japanese troops worked effectively to provoke public fury.

Political language offers another fascinating arena in which to study
wartime popular culture. Like symbols and images, inflamed rhetoric
and slogans abounded during the war.[27] They were never couched in
abstract terminology, nor were they complex in connotation. Instead
they tended to be simple, emotionally charged, and laced with gritty
imagery. They dominated wartime discourse, appearing in newspapers, magazines, leaflets, and daily conversation. Clearly, the resisters were keenly aware of the manipulative functions of language, including political oratory and rhetoric. Wartime political language was
never a static *product*; it was a *process* in which Chinese resisters and
their audiences were carrying on an intense conversation. Political pro-
nouncements appealed to shared feelings.[28] Charged slogans such as
"The country is supreme! The people are supreme!" (*Guojia zhishang,
minzu zhishang*) produced a collective sense of excitement and created the emotional bonds that tied people together, thus serving the
function of social and national integration in the Durkheimian
fashion. Designed to be spoken aloud, these slogans emphasized oral
transmission; this made their impact on the illiterate possible and
effective, hence adding a new dimension to the close relationship between politics and language.

The destruction of war seemed to demand a stringently political
approach to everything, including the production and appreciation of
literature and art. The fact that literature and art were so systematically used for a single cause and aimed at the entire population was truly
unprecedented in Chinese history. Politics came to dominate everyday
existence. In these troubled times, resistance intellectuals believed, art
and literature could not afford to be mere entertainment; they had to
serve the war. As a result, not only did the distinction between politics

and art become blurred, but politics became the ultimate yardstick of literary and aesthetic value. This homogenization and overpoliticization of culture, however, had damaging effects: wartime literature and art often produced bland and banal products, devoid of imagination and artistry—as the critics' epithet *kangzhan bagu* (eight-legged essay of the War of Resistance) indicated.[29]

Under the banner of "propaganda first, art second,"[30] anything irrelevant to the war was condemned as unpatriotic and perhaps even disloyal. In December 1938, Liang Shiqiu (1903–1987), a critic and the editor of the literary supplement of the Guomindang-controlled *Central Daily*, stated that he welcomed articles related to the War of Resistance, "but," he added, "those which are unrelated will also be accepted if written with genuine lucidity and grace."[31] Liang's proposition drew immediate fire from practically every corner, especially from the left, whose representatives accused him of insensitivity and irresponsibility.[32] Granted that the attack on Liang was launched in the early phase of the war when emotions ran high, and was prompted by his perceived ties with the Nationalists, the denunciation nevertheless reflected an oftentimes stifling climate of absolute intolerance to things deemed unpatriotic or pessimistic. This rigidity and excessively politicized view produced many unfortunate casualties; Liang was only its first and perhaps best-known victim.

Such a narrow political view, though loud and insistent, was not without its detractors. The independent writer Shen Congwen, for example, argued that things not directly related to the war—such as scientific research—might benefit the nation in the long run and so were worth writing about.[33] The linguist and writer Wang Liaoyi (Wang Li, 1900–1986) was even more blunt in confessing an aversion to the overpoliticized atmosphere. He wrote, "To be frank, the reason that I wrote [these] miscellaneous essays was not for the benefit of the reader, but for myself. . . . The essays might appear uninspiring to others, but to me they are like a cool and refreshing drink."[34]

But was such "self-interest" really bad? As the patriotic idealism of the early phase of the war began to wane and a military stalemate set in, the need for easy avenues to forget the present troubles became apparent. Some literature and art began to resume its prewar flavor of escapism, and the public in the hinterland as well as in occupied Shanghai turned increasingly toward light comedy and other seemingly frivolous entertainments. When Qin Shouou's (1908–) *Begonia* (*Qiu Haitang*), a sentimental play about the unfortunate life of a Beijing opera performer, opened in Shanghai in late 1942, it was an immediate success, running for 135 days and breaking every existing record, including that of *Sorrow for the Fall of the Ming.*[35]

Notwithstanding that too much politics proved dull and suffocating, the dynamics and complexities of the war were intimately connected to the political world, especially its culture. As we have seen, the Sino-Japanese War was a time of extraordinary ferment in political culture, with spoken dramas, cartoons, and newspapers taking the lead in shaping public consciousness. The war also "publicized" artistic behavior. Drawing a cartoon or writing a play was no longer a solitary, private exercise; it had become a public act of enlightening the masses. In many ways, China's wartime political culture was a culture of popular media, for it attempted to institute new values by transforming an elitist and urban popular aesthetic into a rural one. As such, it marks an important shift in the collective consciousness of the time.

But what impact did the various politicized popular culture forms have in the interior provinces, especially in the Guomindang-held territories? True, we cannot know for sure. Yet contrary to Chen Yiyuan's argument that popular culture remained restricted to a few large cities during the war,[36] ample evidence suggests that newspapers and cartoons did penetrate to small cities and towns in the interior provinces, if not necessarily to the deep countryside—a pattern far different from their prewar concentration in a few coastal metropolises. Street plays in fact reached many rural corners and often met with considerable success, as in the case of *Lay Down Your Whip*, though again, such activity was confined largely to the early phase of the war. Some forms of communication, of course, spread more successfully than others; political cartoons, for example, which appeared in the print media, could reach far more people than performances of spoken drama or drum singing. Nevertheless, there is no question that popular culture as a whole was an effective mobilizing tool. Never before in Chinese history had young dramatists roamed the countryside in such numbers to spread the gospel of patriotism, nor had political publications so flooded the interior to encourage the people to stand up against aggression. Newspapers and spoken dramas would be like "cultural cars" (*wenyi che*), as one literary magazine hopefully described them in 1942, delivering much-needed messages to the people.[37]

Yet the popular culture drive in the Guomindang-held territories was never well coordinated. The government's directive was half-hearted and unclear, and its urban-elitist distrust of mass movements debilitated this cultural campaign. Further, the Nationalists' rule over a wide and disparate area with deep regional differences and old factional rivalries undermined their ability to mount a consistent cultural propaganda effort. The same was not true of the Communists, who managed to conduct a well-organized, carefully orchestrated crusade in their border regions.

Village Culture

The success story of the Communist popular culture drive likewise owes much to the reorientation of Chinese culture toward the rural interior during the war. As the resistance momentum shifted rapidly to the countryside when the coastal cities fell into the hands of the Japanese early in the war, the dramatist Zhou Yan expressed a prevailing sentiment: "China is an agrarian country. To achieve nationwide mobilization and to sustain protracted war, educating peasants is ten or one hundred times more important than educating other groups of people."[38] To repel the enemy, intellectuals and policy makers dreamed of a country unified as an organic whole in defending itself.

Wartime intellectuals used the term *hinterland* (*houfang*) rather loosely to refer to the expanse of China unoccupied by the Japanese: interior cities, towns, and rural areas. But the term was also used specifically to refer to the countryside (*nongcun*). In the course of eight years, the hinterland/village culture came to dominate the minds of Chinese intellectuals. The assumption here was that the countryside, not the cities, was the mainstay of national defense against the Japanese invasion; it stressed the resistance potential of the vast peasant masses; and it argued not only that peasants were numerically significant (at least four-fifths of a total population of 460 million in 1936) but also that their culture—folk songs, *yangge*, drum songs, storytelling—should be accorded proper respect, both because of its intrinsic artistic value and because of its potency as a propaganda tool. The arrival of twentieth-century urban culture forms in the countryside during the war forced a reassessment of these traditional cultural genres and their new patriotic meaning. This new awareness and the repeated emphasis on village China marked a critical shift in Chinese consciousness: the "ruralization" of Chinese culture had commenced. Literature and art rapidly lost their urban, highbrow orientation and increasingly acquired a rustic flavor.

The interest in rural life, of course, has a long tradition in China. For centuries, Daoist ideals of a tranquil, idyllic world have fascinated Chinese scholars and artists. In the early decades of the 1900s, Chinese folklorists also developed a strong romantic attachment to rural culture forms such as folk songs and legends, prompting them to hurry to the villages to collect what they regarded as unduly ignored but now rapidly vanishing folk products.[39] A deeply rooted appreciation of nature in its most pristine aspects has likewise played a central role in the cultural and spiritual life of China. Many in the past idealized the countryside as a society bound by communal solidarity and harmonious relationship; it was a world in which honest peasants toiled on their land and children were raised with simple values and abundant love. In this primitive Daoist setting, conflicts were few and harmony reigned supreme.

This romantic image of an eternal China of hardworking peasants, sleepy villages, and slow-moving river boats was rapidly replaced in the late 1930s by a more realistic and painful understanding of the countryside. As writers and students rushed to the villages to spread patriotic news, for the first time they looked closely at the harsh rural reality: poverty, backwardness, ignorance, and a parochialism manifested most vividly in the peasants' deep-rooted suspicion of outsiders. Yet the young activists, despite the challenges, set to work educating the largely illiterate peasants about patriotism and pulling vastly disparate regions together, for there was little doubt about where the center of resistance activity should be—it was reflected succinctly in two popular slogans: "To the countryside" (*Dao nongcun qu*) and "To the hinterland" (*Dao neidi qu*).[40]

Literature and art about rural China gained instant popularity during the war. There was a craze for things rural. Of the three major themes in the fiction of the 1930s—the rural situation, intellectuals, and anti-Japanese patriotism—the rural situation topped the list as the most written about subject,[41] indicating a shift from the May Fourth emphasis on subjective sentiments to nationalist goals and from urban culture to life close to the soil. That shift in emphasis was universal. The powerful images of burned-down hamlets and armed peasants came to dominate wartime art (as in the cartoons of Zhao Wangyun and Lu Shaofei), and the disquieting pictures of a rural society undergoing rapid transformation formed the core of the works of Ai Wu (1904–1992), Ding Ling, Sha Ding (1904–), Wu Zuxiang (1908–), and others.[42] Fan Changjiang's call for more local newspapers and Ye Qianyu's suggestion that cartoons be moved from magazines to street walls reflected the shift as well. Similarly, the arrival of new urban forms such as cartoons and newspapers in the interior spurred a new awareness of the potential of the traditional rural genres for the future of China. In brief, the contents of this new political culture were oriented dramatically to matter rural, not urban. Intellectuals' prewar preoccupation with cities now gave way to exploration of the unfamiliar rural hinterland.

It was not easy for the urban intelligentsia, at home in Shanghai cafés and movie theaters, to endure the discomforts of the long journey to the hinterland and then to acclimatize themselves to the utter strangeness of peasant life. Many were psychologically unprepared to depict their newfound rural brethren. Although Hong Shen and Ding Ling, for example, claimed a certain emotional affinity with the peasants, their descriptions of the countryside seldom demonstrated a highly observant eye, and they lacked compelling realism and freshness. Moreover, the fact that they were writing in haste because of their itinerant life frequently resulted in shoddy products. But what they lacked in artistic subtlety they more than made up for in an effusive display of nationalism. The pressing question for these writers was not whether their work was artistically superior, but whether it could function effectively as a political device to arouse the spirit of the peasants. The road now led to the countryside. "In the early days of the war," wrote drama critic Tian Qin in 1944, "many regarded staying long in the city to launch a drama campaign a most shameful act."[43]

In the past, the left-wing drama critic Ge Yihong (1913–) contended, Chinese drama was one-sided, focusing on coastal cities to the exclusion of the vast hinterland. The same was true of the more recent spoken dramas. The war changed all that. Said Ge, "The center for drama has now moved from the urban area to the countryside."[44] Hong Shen concurred: "If the main force of the resistance is to come from the vast hinterland, dramas must center on rural China."[45] Signs of change were visible as early as the mid-1930s, when the specter of open conflict with Japan loomed on the horizon. In the inaugural issue of *Drama Times* (*Xiju shidai*), published in Shanghai in May 1937, several prominent playwrights called on their students and friends to direct their energy and talent toward the important but ignored hinterland. Anticipating a bitter war, one member of the group made a passionate appeal: "Dramas that people urgently need now are not necessarily those staged in majestic theaters, but are those performed in the dilapidated playgrounds and in the gloomy trenches. My fellow nationalist dramatists, let's work toward these goals."[46] Fan Changjiang and Cheng Shewo pleaded in a similar vein as they independently called for the dispersal of the press from cities to the hinterland.

To be sure, the decentralization of culture from coastal cities to the interior was propelled by the war. The process gained momentum when the Nationalist government moved its capital to Chongqing in late 1937 and as propaganda teams began to penetrate into rural areas. Ironically, what began as a military retreat yielded considerable cultural fruits. This dramatic cultural shift, one critic argued, corrected the past mistake of the "radiation" (*fushere*) effect, in which major cities served as centers to spread ideas to other parts of China.[47] Coastal cities now no longer monopolized resources and talents, and the countryside began to benefit from its newly arrived urban visitors with the development of art and literature and ultimately new ideas.

The arrival of urban intellectuals benefited the hinterland in more than one way. Regional newspapers, for one, began to thrive, and the dissemination of knowledge to different parts of China accelerated. Withdrawing its headquarters from Shanghai after the war broke out, the famous Life Bookstore (Shenghuo shudian) established nearly thirty branch outlets throughout the country. Kaiming Bookstore and Beixin Bookstore followed suit, broadening their distribution networks and increasing their publications even despite paper shortages and financial uncertainties.[48] In so doing, new thoughts spread to interior towns and small cities. "Owing to the development of the resistance war, the cultural center has now moved to regional towns," one observer declared.[49] It is, of course, problematic to argue that the popular culture campaign permanently altered the political consciousness of the rural masses; but for eight years it certainly fueled the flames of the national salvation movement in China. Similarly, granting that cultural activities remained largely concentrated in cities and towns in the hinterland and less in the countryside, and granting that the momentum was halted when most bookstores and newspapers returned to coastal cities after the war, the wartime impact of the popular culture movement should not be underestimated.

The shift of Chinese culture from urban to rural areas during the war benefited Mao Zedong's conception of a rural-based revolution, indirectly if not directly. If nothing else, the war suddenly made the countryside central to China's survival and to everyone's concern. By denouncing the Nationalists as the mouthpiece of capitalism and imperialism and proposing that the countryside provided a systematic antidote to China's myriad problems, Mao emerged as the true spokesman of rural China.

In his writings, Mao consistently portrayed his party as the incarnation of nationalism and the embodiment of China's hope, always with rural China as its foundation. He cultivated the image of himself not only as a liberator from foreign oppression and the fetters of China's past, but also as a prophet of rural woes. Although resistance intellectuals might not share Mao's deeply ingrained anti-urban bias (he believed strongly that cities, especially former treaty ports, were corrupted by predatory foreign influence and decadent bourgeois values)[50] and his faith in the spontaneous revolutionary creativity of the peasants, many of them did agree that the future of China lay in the countryside and that the peasants were pivotal in the resistance effort. Chinese Communists equated the "border region culture" with the "village culture." Although economically backward, the base area was depicted as politically active and full of promise. It was from here that a new revolution would be unleashed, with peasants as its loyal troops, delivering China from past sorrows. While the Nationalists ruled over a divided territory, were plagued by internal bickering, and lacked a coordinated propaganda effort, Mao and his associates were able to launch a concerted and controlled cultural campaign to realize their plan.

In waging war against the Japanese from their barren and poverty-stricken bases, the Chinese Communists did not abandon their dream of building a new socialist China. To this end they introduced a new discourse based on demolishing capitalistic and feudalistic norms, on the one hand, and extolling Marxist-Leninist-Maoist ideals, on the other. The proliferation of socialist rhetoric in the base areas attested to such an ideological undertaking, which became more systematic with the launching of the Rectification Campaign in 1942.

New socialist rhetoric dominated the Communist border regions. Language in these areas was employed in two ways: as an anti-Japanese weapon and as a systematic propaganda tool to refashion social order. Chinese Communists were ingenious at inventing new words and giving old phrases fresh meaning. Like the French revolutionaries who coined the term *ancien régime* to dismiss an antiquated social and political order,[51] the Chinese Communists were determined to create a different world with a new rhetoric. The Communists' attack on "semifeudalism and semicolonialism"—Mao's famous characterization of China—is now familiar. Other terms were equally provocative, including "new society" (*xin shehui*) and "labor" (*laodong*). For Mao and his followers, China's "old society" (*jiu shehui*) stood for oppression and corruption. When the old one was completely discarded, a new society (*xin shehui*) would emerge, in which "those who had suffered hardships" (*shoukuren*) in the past would rise to the top, fully "in charge of their own fate" (*dangjiaren*). These were the peasants who tilled the land and prided themselves on labor and production (*shengchan*). And most important of all, they supported the Eighth Route Army and the Chinese Communist Party.[52] The Yan'an language was dense with hagiographic references to Mao and his associates as the force behind this moral and political regeneration.[53]

Chinese Communist rhetoric bore witness to the unfolding socialist transformation in Yan'an and other border regions. It was a language that demanded a change in consciousness, because it spoke enthusiastically of class struggle and with an air of certainty about the future. The political sayings in the Communist border regions did not just mirror radical social changes taking place in those areas; they were the very force that would realize those changes. The repeated and emotional use of the term *fanshen* (freeing oneself, turning over) bore this out. *Fanshen* was capable of magical effects, symbolizing as it did the peasants' awakening from centuries of oppression, bursting their chains, crying for revenge, and rising up to take control of their own fate. Similarly, *qunzhong* (the masses), like *fanshen*, was lauded as the cornerstone of a new society. *Qunzhong* were not just ordinary country folks; they were politically active patriots, the driving force in bringing about a new order. By putting the common people on center stage, Chinese Communists glorified the power of the masses while belittling that of the elite. The "people" now replaced the "rich and powerful" in making history, and villages, not urban areas, were where the dramatic transformation would occur. According to the Communists, the future of China lay not in the coastal cities, but in the interior, in villages—most specifically, in the border regions. And they used newspapers, cartoons, woodcuts, and *yangge* to drive this message home.

The rise of the Communist movement during the war was a complicated phenomenon. The social and economic reforms in the Shaan-Gan-Ning Border Region and the Party's organizational strength certainly contributed to their ascent.[54] But the history of the Communists' rise during the war will be incomplete and even incomprehensible if we fail to consider the vibrant political culture that they created. The Communist revolution was to a certain extent an experiment in new socioeconomic programs and a party-imposed rectification reform. Perhaps more important, it was also a careful and systematic effort to use powerful visual imagery (joyful life under the Communist rule), symbols (labor heroes), and language (terms such as *fanshen* and *qunzhong*). The socialist revolution launched by Mao was a battle of words and images fought for hearts and minds. Cartoons, woodcuts, *yangge*, and newspapers were its strongest weapons. The war was waged on the battleground as well as on the popular culture front. Of the two, the latter posed a bigger victory for the Chinese Communists. Mao's strategy of wrapping socialism in the banner of national salvation and in a multitude of popular culture forms was of vital importance in the rising influence of the Chinese Communist Party.

The War of Resistance witnessed the enormous potential of popular culture. It also created a new political culture that shifted China's attention to the countryside. This shift provided a historic opportunity for the Communists to make their cause visible and appealing.

Appendix:
Persons Interviewed

Name	Profession	Place	Date
Cai Ruohong (1913–)	cartoonist	Beijing	29 Sept. 1989
Chen Baichen (1908–)	dramatist	Nanjing	5 Dec. 1989
Chen Jiying (1908–)	journalist	Xindian, Taiwan	26 July 1990
Chen Liting (1910–)	dramatist	Shanghai	17 Nov. 1989
Chen Mengyin (1910–)	journalist	Alameda, Calif.	22 Aug. 1989
Chen Yifan (Jack Chen, 1908–)	cartoonist, writer	El Cerrito, Calif.	12 Dec. 1987, 25 Mar. 1988
Cheng Shewo (1898–1991)	journalist	Xindian, Taiwan	2 Aug. 1990
Ding Cong (1916–)	cartoonist	Beijing	25 Sept. 1989
Fang Meng (1923–)	journalist	Beijing	8 Oct. 1989
Fang Xiang (1920–)	woodcut artist	Taibei	30 July 1990
Feng Huazhan (1924–) (son of Feng Zikai)	professor	Shanghai	3, 11 Dec. 1989
Feng Yingzi (1915–)	journalist	Shanghai	20 Nov. 1989

Name	Profession	Place	Date
Ge Yihong (1913–)	drama critic	Beijing	28 Sept., 20 Oct., 4 Nov. 1989
Gu Yuan (1919–)	woodcut artist	Beijing	6 Oct., 4 Nov. 1989
He Xin (1922–) (son of He Rong)	journalist	Taibei	25 July 1990
Hu Kao (1912–)	cartoonist	Beijing	25 Sept. 1989
Hua Junwu (1915–)	cartoonist	Beijing	23 Sept., 15 Oct. 1989
Huang Mao (1918–)	art critic	Hong Kong	13 Sept. 1989
Ke Ling (1909–)	writer	Shanghai	26 Nov., 8 Dec. 1989
Li Hua (1907–)	woodcut artist	Beijing	12 Oct. 1989
Liao Bingxiong (1915–)	cartoonist	Guangzhou	3, 4 Jan. 1990
Lu Shaofei (1903–)	cartoonist	Beijing	26 Oct. 1989
Lu Yi (1911–)	journalist	Shanghai	16 Nov., 10 Dec. 1989
Lü Fu (1914–)	dramatist	Beijing	24 Oct. 1989
Qian Xinbo (1923–)	journalist	Beijing	8 Oct. 1989
Shu Yi (1935–) (son of Lao She)	scholar, writer	Beijing	11 Oct. 1989
Tang Tao (1913–1992)	writer	Beijing	12 Oct. 1989
Tao Diya (1910–)	journalist, writer	Taibei	1 Aug. 1990
Wu Qiang (1910–1990)	writer	Shanghai	29 Nov. 1989
Wu Zuguang (1917–)	dramatist	Minneapolis	5 Nov. 1987
Wu Zuxiang (1908–)	writer	Beijing	4 Nov. 1989
Xia Yan (1900–)	dramatist, journalist	Beijing	16 Oct. 1989

Name	Profession	Place	Date
Xiao Qian (1910–)	journalist, writer	Beijing	3 Oct. 1989
Xie Bingying (1906–)	writer	San Francisco	20 Nov. 1988, 21 Aug. 1989
Xu Zhucheng (1907–1991)	journalist	Shanghai	24 Nov. 1989
Ye Qianyu (1907–)	cartoonist	Beijing	27 Sept. 1989
Yu Ling (1907–)	dramatist	Shanghai	23 Nov. 1989
Zeng Xubai (1895–)	journalist	Taibei	5 Aug. 1990
Zhang E (1910–)	cartoonist	Beijing	30 Sept. 1989
Zhang Foqian (1908–)	journalist	Taibei	28 July 1990
Zhang Geng (1911–)	drama critic	Beijing	14 Oct. 1989
Zhang Leping (1910–1992)	cartoonist	Shanghai	19 Nov., 10 Dec. 1989
Zhang Xiluo (1918–)	journalist	Beijing	7 Oct. 1989
Zhong Jingwen (1903–)	folklorist, essayist	Beijing	5, 22 Oct. 1989
Zhu Jiefan (1911–)	folklorist	Taibei	5 Sept. 1989, 27 July 1990

Notes

INTRODUCTION

1. Robert E. Bedeski argues that the Guomindang achieved some degree of success in recentralizing its power on the eve of the war; see "China's Wartime State," in *China's Bitter Victory: The War with Japan, 1937–1945*, ed. James C. Hsiung and Steven I. Levine (Armonk, N.Y.: M. E. Sharpe, 1992), pp. 33–49.

2. Besides *Defend the Marco Polo Bridge*, other noted titles bearing the name of the bridge include Tian Han's *The Marco Polo Bridge* (*Lugouqiao*), Hu Shaoxuan's *The Marco Polo Bridge* (*Lugouqiao*), and Zhang Jichun's *Shedding Blood for the Marco Polo Bridge* (*Xuesa Lugouqiao*). See ZGHJYD 2:98–104; GM 3.4 (25 July 1937): 260–267; XWXSL 2 (February 1979): 27.

3. A feeling of loss and alienation was particularly evident among college students. See Wen-hsin Yeh, *The Alienated Academy: Culture and Politics in Republican China, 1919–1937* (Cambridge, Mass.: Council on East Asian Studies, Harvard University, 1990), p. 229.

4. In his *Economic Growth in Prewar China* (Berkeley and Los Angeles: University of California Press, 1989), Thomas G. Rawski argues that China's economy did not stagnate but grew substantially before the war. See esp. chap. 6.

5. GM 3.4 (25 July 1937): 213–214.

6. Zang Kejia, "Chule kangzhan shenme dou mei yiyi," in *Kangzhan song*, ed. Tang Qiong (Shanghai: Wuzhou shubaoshe, 1937), p. 37.

7. Mu Mutian, "Yong zhanzheng huida zhanzheng," in ibid., p. 52.

8. Xiang Zhongyi, "Yujiu Zhongguo bixu kaifa minzhong yundong," *Xin zhanxian* 3 (1 January 1938): 75–76.

9. In recent years, Japanese scholars have been paying increasing

attention to this incident. See, for example, Hora Tomio, ed., *Nitchū sensō Nankin daizangyaku jiken shiryō shū*, 2 vols. (Tokyo: Aoki shoten, 1985); Hata Ikuhiko, *Nankin jiken* (Tokyo: Chūō kōronsha, 1990); Furuya Tetsuo, ed., *Nitchū sensōshi kenkyū* (Tokyo: Yoshikawa kōbunkan, 1984); and Ienaga Saburō, *Taiheiyō sensō*, 2d ed. (Tokyo: Iwanami shoten, 1990), pp. 230–232. Ienaga, for one, argues that the Japanese military commanders should bear the responsibility of the atrocities committed during the incident.

10. For a brief history of the early war years, see Hsi-sheng Ch'i, *Nationalist China at War: Military Defeats and Political Collapse, 1937–45* (Ann Arbor: University of Michigan Press, 1982), chap. 2; and Lloyd E. Eastman, "Nationalist China During the Sino-Japanese War, 1937–1945," in *Cambridge History of China*, vol. 13: *Republican China, 1912–1949*, pt. 2, ed. John K. Fairbank and Albert Feuerwerker (Cambridge: Cambridge University Press, 1986), pp. 547–580.

11. The literature on popular culture is abundant, a recent offering being Chandra Mukerji and Michael Schudson, eds., *Rethinking Popular Culture: Contemporary Perspectives in Cultural Studies* (Berkeley and Los Angeles: University of California Press, 1991). Other influential works include Peter Burke, *Popular Culture in Early Modern Europe* (London: Temple Smith, 1978); Herbert Gans, *Popular Culture and High Culture: An Analysis and Evaluation of Taste* (New York: Basic Books, 1974); C.W.E. Bigsy, ed., *Approaches to Popular Culture* (Bowling Green, Ohio: Bowling Green University Popular Press, 1976); and Leo Lowenthal, *Literature, Popular Culture, and Society* (Palo Alto, Calif.: Pacific Books, 1961). Two important books on this subject in the China field are David Johnson, Andrew J. Nathan, and Evelyn S. Rawski, eds., *Popular Culture in Late Imperial China* (Berkeley and Los Angeles: University of California Press, 1985); and Perry Link, Richard Madsen, and Paul G. Pickowicz, eds., *Unofficial China: Popular Culture and Thought in the People's Republic* (Boulder, Colo.: Westview Press, 1989).

12. See Natalie Z. Davis, "The Historian and Popular Culture," in *The Wolf and the Lamb: Popular Culture in France*, ed. Jacques Beauroy, Marc Bertrand, and Edward T. Gargan (Saratoga, Calif.: Anma Libri, 1977), p. 11. I am indebted to Davis for her discussion of these two approaches, which she dubbed "anthropological" and "literary-sociological" (see esp. pp. 9–12), though I think the term *literary-cultural* is better and more inclusive than *literary-sociological*.

13. *Oxford English Dictionary*, 2d ed. (Oxford: Clarendon Press, 1989), 12:124–125, s.v. *Popular*, definitions 4 and 6.

14. This is demonstrated clearly in Johnson, Nathan, and Rawski, eds., *Popular Culture in Late Imperial China*.

15. See Chang-tai Hung, *Going to the People: Chinese Intellectuals*

and Folk Literature, 1918–1937 (Cambridge, Mass.: Council on East Asian Studies, Harvard University), chap. 1.

16. See Bigsy, ed., *Approaches to Popular Culture*, chap. 1; and Lowenthal, *Literature, Popular Culture, and Society*, chap. 2.

17. David Welch, "Introduction," in *Nazi Propaganda: The Power and the Limitations*, ed. David Welch (London: Croom Helm, 1983), p. 2.

18. Symbols represent many things, and their meanings can be interpreted differently in different contexts. Symbols, as the anthropologist Michael Herzfeld puts it, "do not stand for fixed equivalences but for contextually comprehensible analogies" (quoted in Robert Darnton, "The Symbolic Element in History," *Journal of Modern History* 58.1 [March 1986]: 219).

19. For a concise discussion of image, see Susanne K. Langer, *Mind: An Essay on Human Feeling*, vol. 1 (Baltimore: Johns Hopkins Press, 1967), pp. 59, 67–68.

20. Clifford Geertz, *The Interpretation of Cultures* (New York: Basic Books, 1973), pp. 5, 89.

21. See Burke, *Popular Culture in Early Modern Europe*, esp. chap. 7; Natalie Z. Davis, *Society and Culture in Early Modern France* (Stanford: Stanford University Press, 1975), esp. chap. 6; and Johnson, Nathan, and Rawski, eds., *Popular Culture in Late Imperial China*, esp. chaps. 5 and 6.

22. Of course, the Geertzian interpretive method is not without its problems. Although Geertz's theory offers historians a unified framework within which to study human experiences, how these experiences change over time is not addressed. His emphasis on the deciphering of meaning tends to ignore causal laws of explanation and diachronic analysis, a disadvantage when it comes to understanding the evolution of political culture in wartime China. Moreover, the assumption of a unified cultural system ignores conflicting interests and appropriations by the people involved. Thus, a more objective interpretation of wartime culture is possible only when change and conflict are taken into account. Chapter 6, on the Communists' experiment in creating a new social order in the territories under their control, is an attempt to address some of the differences and conflicts in this period.

23. Victor Turner, *Dramas, Fields, and Metaphors: Symbolic Action in Human Society* (Ithaca: Cornell University Press, 1974), p. 140.

24. See Keith M. Baker, "Introduction," in *The French Revolution and the Creation of Modern Political Culture*, ed. Keith M. Baker, vol. 1 (Oxford: Pergamon Press, 1987), pp. xi–xviii.

25. This book therefore differs from works that focus heavily on

the political and diplomatic history of the period, for example John H. Boyle's *China and Japan at War, 1937–1945: The Politics of Collaboration* (Stanford: Stanford University Press, 1972) and Lloyd E. Eastman's *Seeds of Destruction: Nationalist China in War and Revolution, 1937–1949* (Stanford: Stanford University Press, 1984). Japanese historical studies on the China war, though few for political and emotional reasons, likewise center largely on military and political aspects, as in the case of Hora Tomio's *Nankin daigyakusatsu* (Tokyo: Gendaishi suppankai, 1984). It is only in recent years that historians and students of literature have begun to study the complex intellectual changes and cultural upheavals of these turbulent years. Notable works in this area are Edward M. Gunn's *Unwelcome Muse: Chinese Literature in Shanghai and Peking, 1937–1945* (New York: Columbia University Press, 1983) and John Israel's "Chungking and Kunming: Hsinan Lienta's Response to Government Educational Policy and Party Control," in *Kangzhan jianguoshi yantaohui lunwenji* (Taibei: Institute of Modern History, Academia Sinica, 1985), pp. 343–376. Scholars in Taiwan and mainland China have independently developed a similar interest. The 1987 publication in Taiwan of a three-volume set of materials on wartime literature (comprising Qin Xianci, ed., *Kangzhan shiqi wenxue shiliao*; Li Ruiteng, ed., *Kangzhan wenxue gaishuo*; Su Xuelin, et al., *Kangzhan shiqi wenxue huiyilu*, all published by Wenxun Monthly Magazine [Wenxun yuekan zazhishe] in Taibei), for example, indicates a growing fascination with this period. The scholarly activities in mainland China are even more visible and vigorous, including studies on wartime drama and fiction by such scholars as Liao Quanjing (*Dahoufang xiju lungao* [Chengdu: Sichuan jiaoyu chubanshe, 1988]) and Wen Tianxing (Wen, *Guotongqu kangzhan wenxue yundong shigao* [Chengdu: Sichuan jiaoyu chubanshe, 1988]), and the publication of a twenty-volume set entitled *Zhongguo kang-Ri zhanzheng shiqi dahoufang wenxue shuxi* (Chongqing: Chongqing chubanshe, 1989). Encouraging as this research is, so far it has been limited in focus and conventional in approach.

26. Gans, *Popular Culture and High Culture*, p. ix.

27. Just how many wartime films actually survive is still a mystery. In the past few years I have made several attempts to secure China's wartime films through official as well as personal channels in mainland China, Taiwan, and Hong Kong, including a visit to the Chinese Film Archives (Zhongguo dianying ziliaoguan) in Beijing in October 1989. But the effort proved unproductive and frustrating.

28. It is now widely known that, although Cheng Jihua, Li Shaobai, and Xing Zuwen discussed wartime films in detail in their two-volume *History of the Development of Chinese Film* (*Zhongguo dianying fazhanshi*) (Beijing: Zhongguo dianying chubanshe, 1963),

they based their research largely not on actually *seeing* the films but on *reading* the printed materials (such as scripts and reviews) published at that time.

29. Recent works focusing on Communist base areas other than the Shaan-Gan-Ning Border Region (where Yan'an is located) and on local specificities have warned against looking at those regions as a homogeneous entity. See, for example, Yung-fa Ch'en, *Making Revolution: The Communist Movement in Eastern and Central China, 1937–1945* (Berkeley and Los Angeles: University of California Press, 1986); also Lyman Van Slyke, "The Chinese Communist Movement During the Sino-Japanese War, 1937–1945," in *Cambridge History of China*, vol. 13, pt. 2, pp. 609–722.

1. THE RISE OF MODERN POPULAR CULTURE

1. See H. R. Kedward, *Resistance in Vichy France: A Study of Ideas and Motivation in the Southern Zone, 1940–1942* (Oxford: Oxford University Press, 1978), pp. 229–248.

2. See, for example, G. William Skinner, ed., *The City in Late Imperial China* (Stanford: Stanford University Press, 1977); Mark Elvin and G. William Skinner, eds., *The Chinese City Between Two Worlds* (Stanford: Stanford University Press, 1974); Rhoads Murphey, *Shanghai: Key to Modern China* (Cambridge, Mass.: Harvard University Press, 1953); and William Rowe, *Hankow: Conflict and Community in a Chinese City, 1796–1895* (Stanford: Stanford University Press, 1989). Few of these works, however, deal with urban cultural activities.

3. See Rhoads Murphey, "The Treaty Ports and China's Modernization," in Elvin and Skinner, eds., *Chinese City*, pp. 17–71.

4. *China Handbook, 1937–1943*, comp. Chinese Ministry of Information (New York: Macmillan, 1943), p. 2; and *China Year Book, 1936*, ed. H.G.W. Woodhead (Shanghai: North China Daily News, 1936), pp. 382, 456.

5. For example, Emily Honig, in *Sisters and Strangers: Women in the Shanghai Cotton Mills, 1919–1949* (Stanford: Stanford University Press, 1986), pp. 4–5, has demonstrated that there were divisions and antagonisms between workers from Subei and those from Jiangnan.

6. Perry Link, *Mandarin Ducks and Butterflies: Popular Fiction in Early Twentieth-Century Chinese Cities* (Berkeley and Los Angeles: University of California Press, 1981), pp. 40, 79.

7. George E. Sokolsky, "China and America: A Study in Tempos," *New York Times Magazine*, 2 August 1931, p. 8.

8. A case in point was the tragic death of actress Ruan Lingyu on 8 March 1935. Ruan's funeral drew tens of thousands of worshippers

and spectators, and even the noted literary magazine *Taibai* (Venus) devoted a special section to her death. See *Taibai* 2.2 (5 April 1935): 74–88.

9. See, for example, Wu Zuguang, *Wu Zuguang lunju* (Beijing: Zhongguo xiju chubanshe, 1981), p. 211.

10. Wang Ying, "Wang Ying xie gei Yingzi de xin," *XWXSL* 30 (22 February 1986): 34.

11. See Sidney Monas, "St. Petersburg and Moscow as Cultural Symbols," in *Art and Culture in Nineteenth-Century Russia*, ed. Theofanis G. Stavrou (Bloomington: Indiana University Press, 1983), pp. 26–39.

12. Articles on the difference between *Jing pai* and *Hai pai* abounded in the 1930s and 1940s. See, for example, a series of discussions on the subject in *Shen bao*, January–March 1934; also *Taibai* 2.4 (5 May 1935): 165–166.

13. According to Rudolf Löwenthal of Yanjing University, writing in the 1930s, "practically all the [book] publications are printed in the six cities: Shanghai, Nanking [Nanjing], Peiping [Beiping], Tientsin [Tianjin], Canton [Guangzhou] and Hankow [Hankou]. Only 0.6 percent of the titles or 1.1 percent of the volumes; i.e., 1.4 percent of the aggregate value, are issued in other places. Shanghai's predominance is shown by the fact that there have been issued in that city alone 92.5 percent of the titles or 91.8 percent of the number of volumes, representing 85.3 percent of the aggregate value. The six leading publishing houses of China, all of which are located in Shanghai, control approximately 30 percent of the whole market representing 40 percent of the value" ("Public Communications in China Before July, 1937," *Chinese Social and Political Science Review* 22.1 [April–June 1938]: 43). See also Link, *Mandarin Ducks and Butterflies*, chap. 3.

14. An unofficial guide to Shanghai, for example, boasted of over one thousand female dancers from the southern province of Guangdong, describing vividly how these women were willing to perform any sexual service for their customers; see *Amorous Shanghai* (*Shanghai fengqing*) [N.p.: Lantian shubao zazhishe, n.d.], p. 22. And the *Mysterious Guide to Shanghai* (*Shanghai shenmi zhinan* [Shanghai: Datong tushushe, n.d.]) gave details of the city's notorious brothels and dance rooms.

15. See Zhang Jinglu, *Zai chubanjie ershinian* (Hankou: Shanghai zazhi gongsi, 1938), p. 3. See also *Shanghai shenghuo* (Shanghai life), 3.5 (17 May 1939): 5.

16. Zhang Jinglu, *Zai chubanjie ershinian*, pp. 111–116, 122–128.

17. Interview with Liao Bingxiong, 3, 4 January 1990, Guangzhou. See also Huang Mengtian (Huang Mao), "Liao Bingxiong jiushi," *Dagong bao* (Hong Kong), 17 September 1983, p. 6.

18. See Ouyang Yuqian, "Huiyi Chunliu," in *ZGHJYD* 1:13–46.

19. For Lin Shu's translation of *La dame aux camélias*, see discussion in Leo Ou-fan Lee, *The Romantic Generation of Modern Chinese Writers* (Cambridge, Mass.: Harvard University Press, 1973), pp. 44–46.

20. Ouyang Yuqian, "Huiyi Chunliu," p. 14.

21. According to a survey conducted by drama critic Tian Qin during the war, 387 translated titles of foreign plays were published in China from 1908 to 1938. Among the countries represented, France topped the list with 132, followed by England (127), Japan (84), Russia (70), the United States (43), Germany (42), and others. Shakespeare came in first on the individual authors' list with 20, followed by Chekhov (14), Shaw (12), and Ibsen (9). See Tian Qin, *Zhongguo xiju yundong* (Shanghai: Shangwu yinshuguan, 1946), pp. 105–143, esp. pp. 105–107.

22. Hu Shi, of course, was not the first Chinese to write a modern play. Other attempts were made earlier, especially by the Nankai Middle School (after 1919, Nankai University) in Tianjin, which had an unusually early interest in Western-style plays. Among its distinguished graduates was the well-known playwright Cao Yu. See Wang Weimin, "Introduction," in *Zhongguo zaoqi huajuxuan*, ed. Wang Weimin (Beijing: Zhongguo xiju chubanshe, 1989), pp. 1–12.

23. Hsiao Ch'ien (Xiao Qian), *The Dragon Beards Versus the Blueprints: Meditations on Post-War Culture* (London: Pilot Press, 1944), p. 16.

24. Hong Shen, "Introduction," in *Zhongguo xinwenxue daxi*, ed. Hong Shen, vol. 9 (Shanghai: Liangyou tushu yinshua gongsi, 1935), p. 23; translation quoted from William Dolby, *A History of Chinese Drama* (London: Paul Elek, 1976), p. 205.

25. For a survey history of modern Western drama, see J. L. Styan, *Modern Drama in Theory and Practice* (Cambridge: Cambridge University Press, 1981), esp. vol. 1.

26. See James R. Brandon, *Theatre in Southeast Asia* (Cambridge, Mass.: Harvard University Press, 1967), esp. chap. 17.

27. Quoted from Hong Shen, "Introduction," in Hong Shen, ed., *Zhongguo xinwenxue daxi* 9:24.

28. Ibid., pp. 16–23.

29. Ouyang Yuqian, "Tan wenmingxi," in *ZGHJYD* 1:48.

30. Xiong Foxi, "Wo de wenyi xizuo shenghuo," *Wenyi chunqiu* 4.2 (15 February 1947): 132.

31. Ibid., p. 135. For the decline of "civilized dramas," see also Hong Shen, "Introduction," in Hong Shen, ed., *Zhongguo xinwenxue daxi* 9:14–15.

32. See Hong Shen, "Introduction," in Hong Shen, ed., *Zhongguo*

xinwenxue daxi 9:14–15; Xu Banmei, *Huaju chuangshiqi huiyilu* (Beijing: Xiju chubanshe, 1957), p. 28.

33. For detailed discussions of the traditional theater, see Tao-Ching Hsu, *The Chinese Conception of the Theatre* (Seattle: University of Washington Press, 1985).

34. Hong Shen, "Introduction," in Hong Shen, ed., *Zhongguo xinwenxue daxi* 9:33–34.

35. Ibid., p. 27.

36. Quoted from Ge Yihong, ed., *Zhongguo huaju tongshi* (Beijing: Wenhua yishu chubanshe, 1990), p. 50.

37. Hong Shen, "Introduction," in Hong Shen, ed., *Zhongguo xinwenxue daxi* 9:23–33. See also Ge Yihong, ed., *Zhongguo huaju tongshi*, pp. 47–54.

38. See Tian Han's 1920 letter to Guo Moruo, in Tian Han (Tian Shouchang), Zhong Baihua, and Guo Moruo, *San ye ji* (Shanghai: Yadong tushuguan, 1923), pp. 80–81.

39. See Ouyang Yu-chien (Ouyang Yuqian), "The Modern Chinese Theatre and the Dramatic Tradition," *Chinese Literature* 11 (November 1959): 103–104. See also Xu Banmei, *Huaju chuangshiqi huiyilu*, p. 124. A recent study, however, suggests that it was Hong Shen who first proposed the term *huaju* in March 1928 in Shanghai during the celebration of the hundredth anniversary of the birth of Ibsen; see Ge Yihong, ed. *Zhongguo huaju tongshi*, p. 119.

40. Tian Han, "Women de ziji pipan," in *Tian Han zhuanji* (N.p.: Jiangsu renmin chubanshe, 1984), p. 28.

41. For a history of the South China Society, see Tian Han's own account, "Nanguo she shilüe," in *ZGHJYD* 1:111–135.

42. See Constantine Tung's analysis, "Lonely Search into the Unknown: T'ian Han's Early Plays, 1920–1930," *Comparative Drama* 2.1 (Spring 1968): 44–54.

43. *ZGHJYD* 1:136–143; Chen Baichen, *Shaonian xing* (Beijing: Sanlian shudian, 1988), pp. 136–205; interview with Chen Baichen, 5 December 1989, Nanjing.

44. See *ZGHJYD* 1:142.

45. Chen Baichen, *Shaonian xing*, p. 185.

46. See *ZGHJYD* 1:216.

47. See Liu Cunren, "Jin shinian lai woguo huaju yundong de niaokan," *Dafeng* 92 (20 June 1941): 3075–3076. See also Ge Yihong, ed., *Zhongguo huaju tongshi*, pp. 151–155.

48. For the ticket prices, see *ZGHJYD* 1:176. See also *Xiju gangwei* 1.1 (15 April 1939): 31; and Ge Yihong's letter to the author of 12 September 1991. A skilled worker in a Shanghai electricity company in 1929 earned between 1.2 to 2 *yuan* a day. A study in 1939 listed the average annual income of a four-member household at 252

yuan, or about 21 *yuan* per month, of which 64.3 percent was spent in food; 9.5 percent on clothing; 16.7 percent on rent; and the remaining 9.5 percent for miscellanies. See Tang Zhenchang, ed., *Shanghai shi* (Shanghai: Shanghai renmin chubanshe, 1989), p. 755. A female spinner earned about 0.327 to 0.432 *yuan* a day between 1931 to 1935, whereas a male packing worker's daily wages were 0.557 to 0.689 *yuan* during the same period; see Honig, *Sisters and Strangers,* p. 55.

49. According to Rudolf Löwenthal, by 1937 "there [were] some 300 cinema theatres in China with a seating capacity of about 300,000." The vast majority of them were located in Shanghai, Nanjing, Beijing, Tianjin, and Guangzhou. See Löwenthal, "Public Communications in China," pp. 47–48.

50. For the Venus Drama Society, see Ge Yihong, ed., *Zhongguo huaju tongshi,* pp. 107–108. For Chang'an Popular Drama Troupe, see *ZGHJYD* II, pp. 84–85. For the Nankai School Drama Club, see Lai Xinxia, ed., *Tianjin jindai shi* (Tianjin: Nankai daxue chubanshe, 1987), p. 318; see also *Tianjin wenshi ziliao xuanji* (Selected literary and historical materials on Tianjin) (Tianjin: Renmin chubanshe, 1985), esp. pp. 197–198.

51. Xia Yan, *Lan xun jiu meng lu* (Beijing: Sanlian shudian, 1985), p. 159.

52. See Gao Lihen, "Tan jiefang qian Shanghai de huaju," in *Shanghai difangshi ziliao,* vol. 5 (Shanghai: Shanghai shehui kexueyuan chubanshe, 1986), pp. 124–147. See also Zhao Mingyi, "Wei zuoyi juyun kaipi dadao—ji 'Dadao jushe,'" *Wenyi yanjiu* 2 (25 April 1980): 69–71.

53. See, for example, Tian Qin, *Zhongguo xiju yundong,* chap. 1.

54. See Chow Tse-tsung, *The May Fourth Movement* (Cambridge, Mass.: Harvard University Press, 1960); and Vera Schwarcz, *The Chinese Enlightenment: Intellectuals and the Legacy of the May Fourth Movement of 1919* (Berkeley and Los Angeles: University of California Press, 1986).

55. See Ge Yihong, ed., *Zhongguo huaju tongshi,* p. 131; and Qianli, "Zhongguo xiju yundong fazhan de niaokan," *Beidou* 2.2 (20 January 1932): 52–54. Tian Han's *Seven Women in the Tempest* was not published as a separate work until mid-1932; see *Wenxue yuebao* 1.1 (10 June 1932): 43–77.

56. See *ZGHJYD* 1:9, 2:5. See also Ge Yihong, ed., *Zhongguo huaju tongshi,* pp. 164–165; and Hong Shen, *Kangzhan shinian lai Zhongguo de xiju yundong yu jiaoyu* (Shanghai: Zhonghua shuju, 1948), pp. 147, 152, 160, 161.

57. A. C. Scott, *Literature and the Arts in Twentieth-Century China* (New York: Anchor Books, 1963), p. 44. See also *XJSD* 1.1 (16 May 1937): 22.

58. A Ying, "Shanghai ge huaju jituan chunji lianhe gongyan wenxian jiyao," *XJSD* 1.1 (16 May 1937): 243–254.

59. See, for example, Zhao Huishen's account, "Zai Zhongguo lüxing jutuan," *Juchang yishu* 6 (20 April 1939): 20–25.

60. Feng Zikai first used the term *manhua* in May 1925 when his "Zikai's Cartoons" ("Zikai manhua") appeared in *Wenxue zhoubao* (Literary weekly); the title was apparently suggested to him by Zheng Zhenduo, editor of the journal. See Zheng Zhenduo's preface to Feng's *Zikai manhua* (Shanghai: Kaiming shudian, 1931), pp. 3–5. The Chinese term *manhua* is a direct translation from the Japanese *manga*, which, according to Feng, was first used by the Tokugawa *ukiyo-e* painter Hokusai; see Feng, *Manhua de miaofa* (Shanghai: Kaiming shudian, 1948), p. 7.

61. See Ge Gongzhen, *Zhongguo baoxue shi* (reprinted Taibei: Xuesheng shuju, 1964); and Zeng Xubai, ed., *Zhongguo xinwen shi*, 2 vols. (Taibei: Guoli Zhengzhi daxue xinwen yanjiusuo, 1966).

62. For a discussion of Wang Tao and his time, see Paul A. Cohen, *Between Tradition and Modernity: Wang T'ao and Reform in Late Ch'ing China* (Cambridge, Mass.: Harvard University Press, 1974). For Liang Qichao, see Lai Guanglin, *Liang Qichao yu jindai baoye* (Taibei: Shangwu yinshuguan, 1968).

63. The West had a long tradition of using illustrations such as cartoons in periodicals and newspapers. By the 1830s, for example, cartoons with strong political connotations were appearing regularly in French daily newspapers. See Irene Collins, *The Government and the Newspaper Press in France, 1814–1881* (London: Oxford University Press, 1959).

64. Quote from Bi Keguan, "Jindai baokan manhua," *XWYJZL* 8 (November 1981): 69. Illustrations, of course, were nothing new in China; Chinese publications often contained meticulous, colorful illustrations, but they differed from modern cartoons in style and content. See Zheng Zhenduo, "Chatu zhi hua," *Xiaoshuo yuebao* 18.1 (10 January 1927): 1–20.

65. See *Dianshizhai huabao*, 10 vols., preface dated 1884; also *XWYJZL* 10 (December 1981): 149–181. Other well-known pictorials include *Xiaohai yuebao* (Child's monthly), first published in Shanghai in May 1875, and *Qimen huabao* (Primer pictorials), launched in Beijing in June 1902. See *XWYJZL* 30 (April 1985): 191–203 and 31 (July 1985): 168–175.

66. Qianyu (Ye Qianyu), "Manhua de minzu xingshi," *Huashang bao*, 1 October 1941, p. 3.

67. For a discussion of the meaning of the cartoon, see John Geipel, *The Cartoon: A Short History of Graphic Comedy and Satire* (Newton Abbot, Eng.: David & Charles, 1972), chap. 1: "What Is a

Cartoon?"; also Edward Lucie-Smith, *The Art of Caricature* (Ithaca: Cornell University Press, 1981), pp. 7–19.

68. Lin Jianqi, "Zhongguo de manhua yu muke," *Yue bao* 1.2 (15 February 1937): 453.

69. See Liu Zhenqing, *Manhua gailun* (Changsha: Shangwu yinshuguan, 1939), p. 3.

70. Feng Zikai, *Manhua de miaofa*, p. 37.

71. Lu Xun had argued that certain traditional Chinese paintings bore a close resemblance to modern cartoons—for example, the series by Luo Pin (Luo Liangfeng, 1733–1799), "The Delights of the Ghosts" ("Gui qu tu"). Luo, one of the eight famous "Yangzhou Eccentrics," used these eight ghost paintings to ridicule the absurdities of life and to satirize social corruption. See Lu Xun, "Mantan 'manhua,'" in *Xiaopinwen he manhua*, ed. Chen Wangdao (Shanghai: Shenghuo shudian, 1935), p. 10.

72. Bi Keguan, "Jindai baokan manhua," p. 69.

73. See Bi Keguan and Huang Yuanlin, *Zhongguo manhua shi* (Beijing: Wenhua yishu chubanshe, 1986), chaps. 2–4.

74. See, for example, *Dongfang zazhi* 21.19 (10 October 1924) and 21.22 (25 November 1924); *LY* 20 (1 July 1933): 722, and 22 (1 August 1933): 808; and *YZF* 2 (1 October 1935): 94; 4 (1 November 1935): 172.

75. See, for example, "Tougao guiyue" (Rules for submission), *Taibai* 1 (20 September 1934).

76. The term *manhua* was by no means universally accepted by Chinese artists. Other terms, such as the transliterated *katun*, were being used even as late as the mid-1930s. See, for example, *LY* 20 (1 July 1933): 722, and 22 (1 August 1933): 808.

77. Quote from Huang Mao, *Manhua yishu jianghua* (Shanghai: Shangwu yinshuguan, 1947), p. 26.

78. Another such group, for example, was the Cartoon Study Association (Manhua yanjiuhui), founded by Ye Qianyu, Zhang Guangyu, and Hu Kao. See *SDMH* 23 (20 November 1935): 37.

79. For cartoon training classes, see Bi and Huang, *Zhongguo manhua shi*, pp. 164, 175. There were a few cartoon correspondence schools, the two most famous being the China First Art School (Zhongguo diyi huashe) and the China Cartoon Correspondence School (Zhonghua manhua hanshou xuexiao). See *Liangyou* 37 (July 1929): 38; also *Duli manhua* 4 (10 November 1935): 23, and 6 (10 December 1935): 40. At the China Cartoon Correspondence School, for one, it took six months to complete the entire training course. Some cartoonists, such as Lu Shaofei, Wang Dunqing, and Ye Qianyu, also offered private classes. See their advertisements in *SDMH* 17 (20 May 1935) and 18 (20 June 1935).

80. Chen Wangdao, ed., *Xiaopinwen he manhua*, esp. "Preface."

81. Lu Xun, "Mantan 'manhua,'" p. 12. The other article, "Manhua er you manhua," was published under his pen name, "Qiejie," in Chen Wangdao, ed., *Xiaopinwen he manhua*, p. 152.

82. See Bi and Huang, *Zhongguo manhua shi*, p. 94.

83. For example, *Shidai manhua* received contributions from Hangzhou, Guangzhou, Nanjing, and Tianjin, among other places; see 20 (20 August 1935), 22 (20 October 1935), and 35 (20 February 1937).

84. See Bi and Huang, *Zhongguo manhua shi*, p. 93. *Banjiao manhua*, edited by Ye Yinquan, was launched on 6 December 1929. Because of more advanced publishing technology in Hong Kong, the magazine was printed in Hong Kong and then distributed in Guangzhou. It cost five *fen* per issue. See *Ming bao*, 22 September 1987 (Hong Kong ed.), p. 22.

85. Huang Miaozi, "Kangzhan yilai de Zhongguo manhua," Preface to *QGXJ*, p. 4.

86. Huang Yao's "Niubizi" (Mr. Ox Nose), resembling Ye Qianyu's "Mr. Wang," and Lu Shaofei's "Tao Ger" (Little Tao), similar to Zhang Leping's "San Mao," were other memorable characters created at this time. For "Niubizi," see, for example, *Duli manhua* 1 (25 September 1935): 29; for "Tao Ger," see *Liangyou* 36 (31 March 1929): 37.

87. This comic strip also appeared in a number of places, for example *Liangyou* 130 (July 1937): 56, and 132 (December 1937): 38. See also Ye Qianyu, *Ye Qianyu manhua xuan—sanshi niandai dao sishi niandai* (Shanghai: Renmin meishu chubanshe, 1985).

88. Interview with Zhang Leping, 19 November 1989, Shanghai. See also Zhang Leping, "San Mao," *Duli manhua* 3 (25 October 1935): n.p.; *SDMH* 26 (20 February 1936): n.p. Although Zhang's comic strip "San Mao" appeared before the war, it did not become famous until after the war was over. See Zhang Leping, *San Mao liulangji quanji* (Beijing: Renmin meishu chubanshe, 1984). "San Mao" also made it to the silver screen, released in 1948 as *The Wanderings of San Mao* (*San Mao liulangji*) by the Kunlun Film Studio; see *Dazhong dianying* (Popular film) 21 (11 November 1953): 18–19.

89. Bi and Huang, *Zhongguo manhua shi*, p. 134.

90. Quoted in ibid., p. 125.

91. See, for example, *SDMH* 23 (20 November 1935): 25.

92. See Xiao Jianqing, *Manhua Shanghai* (Shanghai: Jingwei shuju, n.d.).

93. Ye Qianyu, "She yu furen," *Shanghai manhua* 4 (12 May 1928): cover.

94. See *Duli manhua* 4 (10 December 1935): 2–3; and *Manhua he shenghuo* 1.3 (20 January 1936): 34–36.

95. Zhang E, "Wo hua manhua de jingguo," in Chen Wangdao, ed., *Xiaopinwen he manhua*, pp. 146–147.

96. Interview with Zhang E, 30 September 1989, Beijing.

97. Wang Dunqing, "Seqing manhua de zanyang," *SDMH* 26 (20 February 1936): n.p.

98. See Liu Zhenqing, *Manhua gailun*, pp. 27–28.

99. See, for instance, *LY* 2 (1 October 1932): 13; *Yue bao* 1.1 (15 January 1937): 44–51; and *YZF* 67 (1 May 1938): 32.

100. Interview with Lu Shaofei, 26 October 1989, Beijing.

101. For Covarrubias, see *SDMH* 2 (20 February 1934); for Daumier, *SDMH* 18 (20 June 1935); and for Goya and Low, *SDMH* 30 (20 September 1936). Interview with Lu Shaofei, 26 October 1989, Beijing.

Goya, Daumier, Kollwitz, Grosz, Low, and Covarrubias were of course not the only cartoonists and painters to have been introduced into China before and during the war. Other familiar figures included the Soviet cartoonist Boris Efimov, America's Daniel Fitzpatrick and Carey Orr, and Germany's Henrich Zille, to name just a few. On Efimov, see Ye Qianyu, "Lüetan Zhongguo de manhua yishu," *Renwen yikan*, 12 December 1948, p. 30; and *Yue bao* 1.4 (15 April 1937): 719; 1.6 (16 June 1937): 1163. On Fitzpatrick and Orr, see *Yue bao* 1.4 (15 April 1937): 719; and *China Weekly Review* 85.6 (8 October 1938): 191. On Zille, see *YZF* 91 (1 January 1940): 214. See also *Ou Mei manhua jingxuan*, ed. Qian Gechuan (N.p.: Zhonghua shuju, 1943).

102. See, for example, *SDMH* 30 (20 September 1936): n.p.

103. See Lu Xun, "Mantan 'manhua,'" p. 12; and Huang Mao, *Manhua yishu jianghua*, pp. 3, 50.

104. See *Huashang bao*, 5 November 1941, p. 3.

105. See comments by Chen Yifan (Jack Chen) in Shen Qiyu, "Zhongguo manhuajia cong Sulian dailai de liwu," *GM* 1.9 (10 October 1936): 572.

106. See Lu Xun, "Tan muke yishu," *Wenlian* 1.1 (5 January 1946): 5–6; Li Hua, "Kangzhan qijian de muke yundong," *Xin Zhonghua* 4.8 (16 September 1946): 36–40; Wang Qi, *Xin meishu lunji* (Shanghai: Xin wenyi chubanshe, 1951), pp. 93–94, 137, 144; and Yu Feng, "Yong yanshe poxiang Faxisi," *Huashang bao*, 16 July 1941, p. 3. See also Shirley Hsiao-ling Sun, "Lu Hsun and the Chinese Woodcut Movement, 1929–1936" (Ph.D. diss., Stanford University, 1974).

107. Lu Xun, "Kaisui Kelehuizhi muke 'Xisheng' shuoming," in *Lu Xun quanji*, vol. 8 (Beijing: Renmin wenxue chubanshe, 1981),

p. 312; and Shirley Hsiao-ling Sun, *Modern Chinese Woodcuts* (San Francisco: Chinese Culture Foundation, 1979), pp. 18–21.

108. Lu Xun, "Kaisui Kelehuizhi banhua," *Zuojia* 1.5 (15 August 1936): 1224–1227. Keenly aware of the prints' potential as a propaganda tool, the ailing Lu Xun, with the assistance of Agnes Smedley and Mao Dun, published *Selected Prints of Käthe Kollwitz* (*Kaisui Kelehuizhi banhua xuanji*) in July 1936, three months before his death. See Smedley, *Battle Hymn of China* (New York: Alfred A. Knopf, 1943), p. 81.

109. When Kollwitz died in 1945, *Liberation Daily*, the official newspaper of the CCP in Yan'an, paid her a great tribute by printing a number of commemorative articles. See, for example, *JFRB*, 2 July 1945, p. 4.

110. See, for example, Qiejie (Lu Xun), "Manhua er you manhua," p. 152; and Hu Kao, "Xiwang yu manhuajie," *Qianqiu* 15 (1 January 1934): 7–8. Grosz's cartoons appeared in such journals as *Tuohuang zhe* (Pioneer) 1.1 (10 January 1934) and *Taibai* 1.3 (20 October 1934).

111. *Huashang bao*, 3 September 1941, p. 3. See also Te Wei, "Faxisi he yishujia," *Huashang bao*, 16 July 1941, p. 3.

112. Zhang Ding, "Manhua yu zawen," *JFRB*, 23 May 1942, p. 4.

113. See Bi and Huang, *Zhongguo manhua shi*, p. 130. During my interview with Cai Ruohong (29 September 1989, Beijing), Cai admitted his artistic debt to Grosz.

114. Cai's cartoons appeared in such magazines as *Shidai manhua* (e.g., 22 [20 October 1935]: n.p.) and *Manhua shenghuo* (Cartoon life), among others.

115. In a letter (25 November 1988) to the author, Cai also admitted his debt to David Low.

116. Nothing linked to fascism was immune from Low's acerbic attack; see Low, *Autobiography* (New York: Simon & Schuster, 1957), p. 254.

117. Huang Mao, *Manhua yishu jianghua*, p. 4; and interview with Huang Mao, 13 September 1989, Hong Kong. On the introduction of Low to China, see, for example, *Dongfang zazhi* 22.16 (25 August 1925): 11.

118. Low's cartoons were widely reprinted in such journals as *Shijie zhishi* (e.g., 3.9 [16 January 1936]: cover), *Guowen zhoubao* (e.g., 14.24 [21 June 1937]), and *Huashang bao*, 20 July 1941, p. 3. See also Huang Mao, *Manhua yishu jianghua*, pp. 4, 50.

119. David Low, *Years of Wrath: A Cartoon History, 1931–1945* (New York: Simon & Schuster, 1946); and idem, *A Cartoon History of Our Times* (New York: Simon & Schuster, 1939), pt. 3.

120. See *Huashang bao*, 2 July 1941, p. 3; also *Zazhi* 7.5 (20 June 1940): 32–34.

121. On Low's influence on Te Wei, see Xinbo, "Wusheng de zhadan," *Huashang bao*, 7 May 1941, p. 3; and *Huashang bao*, 29 October 1941, p. 3.

122. See, for example, *SDMH* 35 (20 February 1937): n.p.; and *JWRB*, 5 January 1938, p. 4.

123. For a discussion of Covarrubias's work, see Beverly J. Cox and Denna Jones Anderson, *Miguel Covarrubias Caricatures* (Washington, D.C.: Smithsonian Institution Press, 1985).

124. See, for example, *LY* 8 (1 January 1933): 265, and 14 (1 April 1933): 483–484. See also Marc Chadourne, *China*, illustrated by Miguel Covarrubias (New York: Covici Friede, 1932), passim.

125. Covarrubias was on his way to Bali for anthropological fieldwork, which later blossomed into an important second career. The Mexican artist was warmly received by his young admirers. Ye Qianyu (*Hua yu lun hua* [Tianjin: Renmin meishu chubanshe, 1985], p. 234) admits that he learned his famous sketch techniques largely from Covarrubias when he met the artist in Shanghai in September of that year.

126. See Huang Mao's discussion in *Manhua yishu jianghua*, p. 30; and in Huang Mengtian (Huang Mao), *Huajia yu hua* (Hong Kong: Shanghai shuju youxian gongsi, 1981), pp. 67, 170.

127. Zhang's celebrated series "Folksongs of Love" ("Minjian qingge"), which appeared in *Shidai manhua* and *Duli manhua* in the early 1930s, was strongly marked by Covarrubias-esque geometrical abstraction. See, for example, *SDMH* 1 (20 January 1934); and *Duli manhua* 1 (25 September 1935): n.p.

128. See, for example, the work of the American cartoonist Daniel Fitzpatrick in *JWMH* 3 (30 September 1937): 4.

129. Chinese resisters were naturally not alone in realizing that the press could play a critical role in shaping public opinion. Their foes also utilized the press to their own advantage, cultivating the press and magazines as a channel of disinformation and a means of silencing discontented Chinese. Information about newspapers in Japanese-occupied areas abound but has not yet been systematically studied. For example, the Japanese purchased Tianjin's *Yong Post* (*Yong bao*); they also published several newspapers in Nanjing in 1939, including the *New Nanjing Daily* (*Xin Nanjing bao*); and they of course ran numerous dailies and magazines in Manchuria. See *Baoren shijie* 7 (April 1937): 5–9; and *KZWY* 5.2–3 (10 December 1939): 36–37, 53.

130. Lin Yutang, *A History of the Press and Public Opinion in*

China (Chicago: University of Chicago Press, 1936), p. 94.

131. See Leo Ou-fan Lee and Andrew J. Nathan, "The Beginning of Mass Culture: Journalism and Fiction in the Late Ch'ing and Beyond," in Johnson, Nathan, and Rawski, eds., *Popular Culture in Late Imperial China*, pp. 360–395.

132. Quoted from Lin Yutang, *History of the Press*, p. 146.

133. *China Handbook, 1937–1943*, p. 697.

134. See Lin Yutang, *History of the Press*, p. 145; also Hu Daojing, *Xinwenshi shang de xin shidai* (Shanghai: Shijie shuju, 1946), p. 103.

135. Ge Gongzhen, *Zhongguo baoxue shi*, p. 277.

136. Hu Daojing, *Xinwenshi shang de xin shidai*, p. 94; Yuan Changchao, *Zhongguo baoye xiaoshi* (Hong Kong: Xinwen tiandishe, 1957), p. 80.

137. Other new methods were introduced to improve newspapers' quality. For example, more white space was used to avoid uniformity and denseness, and different types of headings furnished an artistic touch. Some of the techniques, as Zeng Xubai, editor of Shanghai's *Great Evening News* (*Dawan bao*), admitted, were inspired by the Japanese; see *Zeng Xubai zizhuan*, vol. 1 (Taibei: Lianjing chuban shiye gongsi, 1988), p. 111.

138. For the distribution of newspapers through the postal system, see Lin Yutang, *History of the Press*, p. 147.

139. Zeng Xubai, ed., *Zhongguo xinwen shi* 1:386.

140. See Hu Daojing, *Xinwenshi shang de xin shidai*, pp. 95–96; Zhao Junhao, *Zhongguo jindai zhi baoye* (N.p.: Shangwu yinshuguan, 1940), pp. 21–22.

141. See Yao Jiguang and Yu Yifen, "Shanghai de xiaobao," *XWYJZL* 8 (November 1981): 223–244; Link, *Mandarin Ducks and Butterflies*, pp. 119–124; and Zhao Junhao, *Zhongguo jindai zhi baoye*, pp. 101–111.

142. Zhao Junhao, *Zhongguo jindai zhi baoye*, p. 103.

143. Ibid., pp. 102–103.

144. The supplement format went back to the turn of the century. See Hu Daojing, "Lun fukan" (On the supplement), in *Xinwenshi shang de xin shidai*, pp. 77–79.

145. Li Liewen during his tenure (1932–1934), for example, initiated over twenty debates, one of the most memorable being a discussion of the superiority of the "Shanghai style" versus "Beijing style." See *Shen bao*, January–March 1934.

146. Ge Gongzhen, *Zhongguo baoxue shi*, pp. 286, 291.

147. Zeng Xubai, ed., *Zhonggo xinwen shi* 1:335–336.

148. Ge Gongzhen, *Zhongguo baoxue shi*, p. 292. Huang Tian-

peng indicated that the monthly advertising income for *Shen bao* was about 150,000 *yuan* in 1930, but since the annual budget and profit of the newspaper are not known, the exact meaning of this figure is unclear. Advertisement revenues at *Xinwen bao*, according to Huang, were "even higher," but he gave no figure. See Huang, *Zhongguo xinwen shiye* (Shanghai: Xiandai shudian, 1932), p. 138.

149. Xu Baohuang, "Xinwenxue dayi," in Xu Baohuang and Hu Yuzhi, *Xinwen shiye* (Shanghai: Shangwu yinshuguan, 1924), p. 1.

150. The term "a king without a crown" (*wumian huangdi*) was used commonly in reference to reporters. See, for example, *Baoxue jikan* 1.3 (29 March 1935): 124; and *Xinwen zazhi* 1.10 (25 September 1936): 45. For the low status of the journalists, see Huang Tianpeng, ed., *Xinwenxue lunwenji* (Shanghai: Guanghua shuju, 1930), p. 61.

151. Xu Zhuchang, *Jiuwen zayi* (Hong Kong: Sanlian shudian, 1982), p. 169.

152. Liu Zucheng, "Guangyu xinwen jizhe zhiye diwei queli wenti," *Baoxue jikan* 1.1 (10 October 1934): 59; Changjiang, "Zhanshi xinwen gongzuo de zhenyi," *XWJZ* 1.6–7 (10 October 1938): 18.

153. Changjiang, "Jianli xinwen jizhe de zhengque zuofeng," *XWJZ* 1.2 (1 May 1938): 5.

154. Wu Guanyin, "Xinwen zhiyehua yu kexuehua," in *Xinwenxue minlunji*, ed. Huang Tianpeng (Shanghai: Shanghai lianhe shudian, 1930), pp. 97–98; see also *XWJZ* 2.10 (16 March 1941): 24; and *Xinwen zazhi* 1.20 (20 February 1936): 1.

155. See Zhang Jinglu, *Zhongguo de xinwen jizhe yu xinwenzhi* (Shanghai: Xiandai shuju, 1932), pt. 1; pt. 2, sec. 4; and Huang Tianpeng, ed., *Xinwenxue lunwenji*, esp. pp. 45–62.

156. Xu Baohuang, "Xinwenzhi yu shehui zhi xuyao," in *Baoxue congkan*, ed. Huang Tianpeng, vol. 1, no. 2 (Shanghai: Guanghua shuju, 1930), pp. 2–3; Huang Tianpeng, ed., *Xinwenxue lunwenji*, pp. 17–18.

157. Changjiang, "Jianli xinwen jizhe de zhengque zuofeng."

158. See *Xinwen zazhi* 1.20 (20 February 1937): 1. Walter Williams had twice visited China, and his work "The Journalist's Creed," a Hippocratic oath for journalists, became a required text for Chinese journalism students.

159. Edgar Snow, *Red Star over China* (New York: Random House, 1938), p. 135.

160. Ge Gongzhen, *Zhongguo baoxue shi*, chap. 6, sec. 13; Yuan Changchao, *Zhongguo baoye xiaoshi*, chap. 11. See also "Xinwen jiaoyu jiguan gaikuang," *Baoxue jikan* 1.2 (1 January 1935): 117–127 and 1.3 (29 March 1935): 147–150.

161. Zhao Junhao, *Zhongguo jindai zhi baoye*, pp. 122–123, 126; Ge Gongzhen, *Zhongguo baoxue shi*, pp. 276–277; "Xinwen jiaoyu jiguan gaikuang," *Baoxue jikan* 1.2 (1 January 1935): 119–122.

162. See "Xinwen jiaoyu jiguan gaikuang," pp. 122–124.

163. Chinese journalism education continued to thrive, and by the 1930s it was having a major influence on the newspaper industry. More and more journalists were being trained in academic institutions, then going on to work as correspondents and editors in newspapers, magazines, and news agencies all over China. See "Xinwen jiaoyu jiguan gaikuang."

164. Zhang Jinglu, *Zhongguo de xinwen jizhe yu xinwenzhi*, pt. 1, p. 78.

165. See *Baoxue jikan* 1.3 (29 March 1935): 151–152.

166. "Qingzhu 'Jiuyi' jizhe jie," *Xinwen zazhi* 1.8–9 (5 September 1936): 1, 23; interview with Zhang Xiluo, 7 October 1989, Beijing.

167. Fan Changjiang, *Tongxun yu lunwen* (Chonqing: Xinhua chubanshe, 1981), pp. 263–273; Lu Yi, "Ji Zhongguo qingnian jizhe xuehui de chengli dahui," *XWJZ* 1.2 (1 May 1938): 17–18; and interview with Lu Yi, 16 November, 10 December 1989, Shanghai.

168. The founding of the Chinese Young Journalists Society was a particularly high moment in the history of modern journalism. It came at a time when the left and the right were still talking to each other in the name of national unity; their ideological differences soon split them asunder.

169. Huang Tianpeng, ed., *Xinwenxue lunwenji*, p. 38. See also Xu Baohuang, "Xinwenzhi yu shehui zhi xuyao," pp. 1–4.

170. While Liang Qichao, one of modern China's foremost intellectual leaders and a skilled publicist, used his many journals (*New Fiction* [*Xin xiaoshuo*] included) as political forums in support of constitutional monarchism, Huang, a star reporter for Shanghai's *Shishi xinbao* and *Shen bao* in the 1910s, unearthed melodramas of political intrigue in Beijing in order to expose the corruption of the warlord government. Huang championed republicanism and was a severe critic of Yuan Shikai's plan for restoring the monarchy. For Liang Qichao, see Lai Guanglin, *Liang Qichao yu jindai baoye*; for Huang Yuansheng, see Huang, *Yuansheng yizhu*, 4 vols. (Shanghai: Shangwu yinshuguan, 1924).

171. See Jack R. Censer and Jeremy D. Popkin, eds., *Press and Politics in Pre-Revolutionary France* (Berkeley and Los Angeles: University of California Press, 1987).

172. Zhao Kunliang, "Xinwen jiujing shi shenme?" *Baoxue jikan* 1.4 (15 August 1935): 47–51.

173. Xu Baohuang, "Xinwenzhi yu shehui zhi xuyao."

174. Huang Tianpeng, ed., *Xinwenxue lunwenji*, p. 38.

175. *DGB* (Tianjin), 22 May 1931, p. 1; Chen Jiying, *Baoren Zhang Jiluan* (Taibei: Wenyou chubanshe, 1957), p. 5; idem, *Hu Zhengzhi yu Dagong bao* (Hong Kong: Zhanggu yuekanshe, 1974), pp. 96–97; Howard L. Boorman, ed., *Biographical Dictionary of Republican China*, 4 vols. (New York: Columbia University Press, 1967–1971), 1:21.

176. Dong Sheng, "Fengjian shili zai baozhi shang," in Zheng Zhenduo, *Haiyan* (Shanghai: Xin Zhongguo shudian, 1932), pp. 139, 142.

177. Xie Liuyi, *Bai longmenzhen* (Shanghai: Bowen shudian, 1947), pp. 27–28.

178. Lin Yutang, "Suo wang yu *Shen bao*," YZF 3 (16 October 1935): 115–116; idem, "*Shen bao* de yiyao fukan," YZF 18 (1 June 1936): 270–271.

179. Quoted in William L. Rivers, *The Opinionmakers* (Boston: Beacon Press, 1965), p. 71.

180. Changjiang, "Zenyang fa zhanshi dianxun yu xie zhandi tongxun," *XWJZ* 1.4 (1 July 1938): 5.

181. Liu Zucheng, "Guanyu xinwen jizhe zhiye diwei queli wenti," p. 59.

2. SPOKEN DRAMAS

1. See, for example, Hong Shen, *Kangzhan shinian lai*, pp. 4–7; *KZWYYJ* 8 (1983): 24–32, and 9 (1983): 68–78; and *ZGHJYD* 1:218–241.

2. See Hong Shen, *Kangzhan shinian lai*, p. 12.

3. See Liang Bing, "Kaifeng jiuwang juyun de yipie," *JWRB*, 27 April 1938, p. 3; *Dongfang huakan* (The eastern pictorial) 1.4 (July 1938): n.p.; *ZGHJYD* 1:261–269; *KZWYYJ* 11 (1983): 69–74, 49, and 13 (1984): 86–97; Guo Moruo, *Hongbo qu* (Hong Kong: Yixin shudian, n.d.), pp. 44–45, 93. Many children's traveling drama corps were formed during the war, including the Xiamen Children's National Salvation Drama Corps (Xiamen ertong jiuwang jutuan), which traveled to Guangdong, Guangxi, and Vietnam to perform. See *Zhandi tongxun* (Battlefront correspondence) 3.8 (16 April 1940): 8–10.

4. The exact number of drama clubs and people involved is not known. According to one estimate, as many as 130,000 people took part; see Wang Yao, *Zhongguo xin wenxue shigao*, 2 vols. (Shanghai: Shanghai wenyi chubanshe, 1982), 2:488. Tian Han estimated that in 1942 there were about 2,500 dramatic clubs in China, each with some thirty members on average, which amounted to approximately 75,000 participants in this movement; see *ZGHJYD* 1:231. These figures, of course, are rough estimates.

5. See Ge Yihong, *Zhanshi yanju zhengce* (Shanghai: Shanghai zazhi gongsi, 1939), p. 23; Zheng Junli, *Lun kangzhan xiju yundong* (N.p.: Shenghuo shudian, 1939), p. 12.

6. See Chang-tai Hung, *Going to the People*, esp. chap. 7.

7. See Wen Zhenting, ed., *Wenyi dazhonghua wenti taolun ziliao* (Shanghai: Shanghai wenyi chubanshe, 1987); also Qu Qiubai, *Qu Qiubai wenji*, 4 vols. (Beijing: Renmin wenxue chubanshe, 1953–1954), esp. 2:853–916.

8. Xiong Foxi detailed his experiment in Dingxian, especially in the villages of Dongbuluogang and Dongjianyang, in his books *Xiju dazhonghua zhi shiyan* and *Guodu ji qi yanchu*, both published by Zhengzhong shudian (n.p.) in 1947.

9. Tian Qin, *Zhongguo xiju yundong*, p. 88.

10. Xiong Foxi, "Zhengzhi, jiaoyu, xiju, sanwei yiti," *Xiju gangwei* 1.1 (15 April 1939): 3–5.

11. See Xiong Foxi, *Xiju dazhonghua zhi shiyan* and *Guodu ji qi yanchu*. See also Yang Cunbin's account in *Yue bao* 1.3 (15 March 1937): 667–674.

12. Xiong Foxi, "Zenyang zuoxi yu zenyang kanxi," *Yue bao* 1.4 (15 April 1937): 896.

13. Liu Cunren, "Jin shinian lai woguo huaju yundong de niaokan," p. 3074.

14. See Wang Yao, *Zhongguo xin wenxue shigao* 2:362.

15. George E. Taylor, *Japanese-sponsored Regime in North China* (New York: Garland, 1980), p. 38.

16. Zhang Junxin, "Zai xiangxia yanju," in *Kangzhan de jingyan yu jiaoxun*, ed. Qian Jiaju, Hu Yuzhi, and Zhang Tiesheng (N.p.: Shenghuo shudian, 1939), pp. 190–191.

17. See, for example, Liu Jian, "Ruhe shi huaju shenru dao nongcun qu," *Kangzhan xiju* 2.2–3 (May 1938): 80–81.

18. See "Yidong yanju yundong teji," *GM* 3.3 (10 July 1937): 189–190.

19. *Baqian li lu yun he yue—Yanju jiudui huiyilu*, ed. Yanju jiudui duishi bianji weiyuanhui (Shanghai: N.p., n.d. [epilogue dated 1988]), p. 37.

20. Hong Shen, "Kangzhan shiqi zhong de xiju yundong," *Xiju kangzhan* 1.1 (16 November 1937): 2–4, esp. p. 4.

21. Hong Shen, *Kangzhan shinian lai*, p. 33.

22. See *GM* 2.12 (25 May 1937): 1561.

23. Zhou Gangming, "Lun xian jieduan de yanju yishu," *Wenyi zhendi* 5.1 (16 July 1940): 64–76.

24. Quoted in Hong Shen, *Kangzhan shinian lai*, p. 91.

25. Quoted in Colin Mackerras, "Theater and the Masses," in

Chinese Theater: From Its Origins to the Present Day, ed. Colin Mackerras (Honolulu: University of Hawaii Press, 1983), p. 153.

26. See, for example, Lin Jing, "Zai xiangcun zhong yanju de liangzhong zaoyu," in Qian, Zhu, and Zhang, eds., *Kangzhan de jingyan yu jiaoxun*, pp. 252–253.

27. Hong Shen, *Kangzhan shinian lai*, pp. 17–18.

28. The origin of the terms *huo de baozhi* and *huobao* (both mean "living newspaper") is not clear. It might have come from the Soviet Union in the early 1930s. See David Holm, *Art and Ideology in Revolutionary China* (Oxford: Clarendon Press, 1991), p. 25.

29. See *Kangzhan sanrikan* 6 (6 September 1937): 11–12, esp. p. 11.

30. *ZGHJYD* 1:257.

31. Guangweiran, "Lun jietouju," *Xin xueshi* 2.2 (25 October 1937): 86.

32. Interview with Lü Fu, 24 October 1989, Beijing. See also Chen Yongliang, "Xiezuo jietouju zhi guanjian," *Zhongyang ribao*, 23 September 1938, p. 4; Zhao Qingge, *Kangzhan xiju gailun* (Chongqing: Zhongshan wenhua jiaoyuguan, 1939), p. 28.

33. Ma Yanxiang, ed., *Zuijia kangzhan juxuan* (Hankou: Shanghai zazhi gongsi, 1938), p. 194.

34. Richard Schechner, *The End of Humanism: Writings on Performance* (New York: Performing Arts Journal Publications, 1982), p. 119.

35. The authorship of the play has long been disputed, though Chen Liting is now widely recognized as the original author. Interview with Ge Yihong, 20 October 1989, Beijing; and with Lü Fu, 24 October 1989, Beijing. Because many people had a hand in rewriting it, however, the play often appears listed as a "collective work."

36. See Tian Han's own account in his "Zhongguo huaju yishu fazhan de jinglu he zhanwang," in *ZGHJYD* 1:6–7. See also Chen Baichen, *Shaonian xing*, p. 145. Chen was Tian Han's student.

37. Materials about this play are abundant. See, for example, *GM* 2.10 (25 April 1937): 1407–1413; *ZGHJYD* 1:7, 228–229, and 2:107–108. Photographs of a performance appear in *Dongfang zazhi* 34.4 (16 February 1937); and *Wenxian* 4 (10 January 1939): A1.

38. Interview with Chen Liting, 17 November 1989, Shanghai. See also Ding Yanzhao, "*Fangxia nide bianzi* dansheng, liuchuan he yanbian," *Shanghai xiju* 101 (28 April 1986): 30–31.

39. Ibid.

40. Interviews with Xie Bingying, 21 August 1989, San Francisco; Chen Liting, 17 November 1989, Shanghai; and Lü Fu, 24 October 1989, Beijing. Many actors had performed in *Lay Down Your Whip*,

but the memorable performances of drama activist Cui Wei as the old man and the popular actress Zhang Ruifang (1918–) as the distressed Fragrance, at Fragrant Hill (Xiangshan) in Beijing in April 1937, were best remembered. See *GM* 2.10 (25 April 1937): 1407–1413.

41. You Jing (Yu Ling), ed., *Dazhong juxuan* (Hankou: Shanghai zazhi gongsi, 1938), pp. 21–22.

42. Liang Guozhang, "'Yanju qingqidui' chuanguo le zhandi," *XJCQ* 2.1 (25 May 1942): 62–64.

43. Baoluo, "Zhankai xiju de youjizhan," *Kangzhan xiju* 1.1 (16 November 1937): 6–9.

44. Liu Nianqu, "Wo xiang liudong yanjudui jianyi," *Kangzhan xiju* 1.2 (1 December 1937): 39–40.

45. For one of many articles on this subject, see Lin Fei, "Yanju yu guanzhong," *JWRB*, 28 April 1938, p. 4.

46. Susanne K. Langer, *Feeling and Form* (New York: Charles Scribner's Sons, 1953), p. 306.

47. Chen Yongliang, "Yanchu jietouju ersan shi," *Zhongyang ribao*, 7 October 1938, p. 4.

48. Guangweiran called this a "natural stage"; see his "Jietouju de yanchu fangfa," *DGB* (Hankou), 17 December 1937, p. 4.

49. The play's popularity extended to other media as well, notably photographs; see, for example, *Dongfang zazhi* 34.4 (16 February 1937): cover inside page; *Kangzhan xiju* 1.1 (16 November 1937): back cover. In 1940 the celebrated painter Xu Beihong captured vividly the performance of Fragrance on his canvas, using actress Wang Ying as his model. Wang Ying even brought the famous street play to the White House at the invitation of President Franklin D. Roosevelt when she toured the United States in 1942, creating quite a sensation in a foreign land. See the subsequent report in *Dianying yu xiju* 1 (January 1947): 32. There are numerous eyewitness accounts and reports about the enormous success of *Lay Down Your Whip* during the war. A few examples will suffice: interviews with Ge Yihong, 28 September, 20 October 1989, Beijing; and with Lü Fu, 24 October 1989, Beijing. See also *Dongfang zazhi* 40.8 (30 April 1944): 58.

50. Wang Yao, *Zhongguo xin wenxue shigao* 2:364.

51. Ding Yanzhao, "*Fangxia nide bianzi* dansheng, liuchuan he yanbian," p. 31. See also *XWXSL* 13 (22 November 1981): 216–227, esp. p. 223.

52. See Yang Hansheng, *Fengyu wushinian* (Beijing: Renmin wenxue chubanshe, 1986), p. 181.

53. I did not see the script; Chen Liting (interview, 17 November 1989, Shanghai) and Yu Ling (interview, 23 November 1989, Shanghai) mentioned this version to me.

54. See Shen Xiling et al., *Jietou yanju* (N.p.: Guofang xiju yanjiuhui, 1938); A Ying, ed., *Kangzhan dumuju xuan* (N.p.: Kangzhan duwu chubanshe, 1937); and Ma Yanxiang, ed., *Zuijia kangzhan juxuan*.

55. The play, which was based on Lady Gregory's *The Rising of the Moon*, was written collectively by Lü Fu, Shu Qiang, Wang Yi, and Xu Zhiqiao. See *Baqian li lu yun he yue*, p. 462; also interview with Lü Fu, 20 October 1989, Beijing.

56. *The Last Stratagem* is said to be based on a foreign play, but I have been unable to trace its origin. The play was reportedly rewritten by Qu Baiyin (1910–); see *Zhongguo kang-Ri zhanzheng shiqi dahoufang wenxue shuxi*, 20 vols. (Chongqing: Chongqing chubanshe, 1989), 17:2242. Hong Shen and Xu Xuan also rewrote the play and gave it a new title, *Sili qiusheng* (From the jaws of death); see esp. p. 1 of the published version (N.p.: Shenghuo shudian, 1938).

57. *ZGHJYD* 1:7, 237; *XJCQ* 2.3 (10 September 1942): 4; *Baqian li lu yun ye yue*, passim.

58. See Lü Fu, "Kangdi yanjudui wushi zhounian zuotanhui qianyan," unpublished paper, 5 October 1988, Wuhan, pp. 8–9.

59. See, for example, a report in *Zhandi* (Battlefront) 4 (5 May 1938): 114–115. See also Shen Xiling et al., *Jietou yanju*, p. 40.

60. See, for example, "Editorial," *Wenxue chuangzuo* 1.6 (1 April 1943), and p. 119.

61. Interview with Lü Fu, 24 October 1989, Beijing. See also *Kangzhan sanrikan* 2 (23 August 1937): 9.

62. Liu Jian, "Ruhe shi huaju shenru dao nongcun qu," p. 80.

63. Edgar A. Mowrer, *The Dragon Wakes: A Report from China* (New York: William Morrow, 1939), pp. 166–167.

64. Karl Chia Chen, "The Undeclared War and China's New Drama," *Theatre Arts* 23.12 (December 1939): 899.

65. *ZGHJYD* 2:168–201. See also *XJSD* 1.2 (1 January 1944): 8.

66. Interview with Ge Yihong, 20 October 1989, Beijing; and with Lü Fu, 24 October 1989, Beijing. See also Tian Qin, "Zhongguo zhanshi xiju chuangzuo zhi yanbian," *Dongfang zazhi* 40.4 (29 February 1944): 53–57, esp. p. 56.

67. The literature on male warriors in wartime dramas is abundant, but a comprehensive picture necessitates more research.

68. Turner, *Dramas, Fields, and Metaphors*, p. 96.

69. Song Zhidi, "Xiezuo *Wu Zetian* de zibai," *GM* 3.1 (10 June 1937): 44.

70. Ouyang Yuqian, *Pan Jinlian* (Shanghai: Xindongfang shudian, 1928), pp. 3–4.

71. *ZGHJYD* 1:119–120.

72. What is stated here is the prevailing attitude toward women that persisted in Chinese culture from Confucian times well into the twentieth century. The present author is well aware that various, and often conflicting, images of women were held in traditional China. One finds, as Margery Wolf and Roxane Witke point out, "evidence for a Chinese conception of women as weak, timid, and sexually exploitable *as well as* dangerous, powerful, and sexually insatiable" (Wolf and Witke, eds., *Women in Chinese Society* [Stanford: Stanford University Press, 1975], p. 2).

73. Ouyang Yuqian, *Huaju, xingeju yu Zhongguo xiju yishu chuantong* (Shanghai: Shanghai wenyi chubanshe, 1959), p. 12; Yang Hansheng, "Zhongguo xiju zhong de xinjiu nüxing," *Wencui* 1.6 (13 November 1945): 18–21.

74. In addition to Zeng Pu's novel, Liu Fu's famous interview with Sai, as well as other sources, inspired Xia Yan's play. See Xia Yan, "Sai Jinhua," *Wenxue* 6.4 (1 April 1936): 590.

75. See *GM* 2.7 (10 March 1937): 1263–1264.

76. Xia Yan, *Lan xun jiu meng lu*, p. 328.

77. *GM* 2.12 (25 May 1937): 1546–1550.

78. Ouyang Yuqian, *Taohua shan* (Beijing: Zhongguo xiju chubanshe, 1957), p. 5.

79. Wen Zaidao et al., *Biangu ji* (Shanghai: Yingshang wenhui youxian gongsi, 1938), p. 248.

80. A Ying, *Bixue hua* (Beijing: Zhongguo xiju chubanshe, 1957); idem, *Yang E zhuan* (Shanghai: Chenguang chuban gongsi, 1950); Bi Yao, "Qin Liangyu," in *Guofang xiju xuan* (N.p.: n.p., n.d.); Yang Cunbin, *Qin Liangyu* (N.p.: Sichuan shengli xiju jiaoyu shiyan xuexiao bianzuan weiyuanhui, 1940); Gu Zhongyi, *Liang Hongyu* (Shanghai: Kaiming shudian, 1941); Zhou Jianchen, *Liang Hongyu* (N.p.: Xinyi shudian, 1940); Zhou Yibai, *Hua Mulan* (Shanghai: Kaiming shudian, 1941); Ouyang Yuqian, "Mulan congjun," *Wenxian* 6 (10 March 1939): F1–F31; idem, *Liang Hongyu* (Hankou: Shanghai zazhi gongsi, 1938).

81. See also Edward Gunn's analysis of this play in *Unwelcome Muse*, esp. chap. 3.

82. See Hong Shen, *Kangzhan shinian lai*, pp. 156–157. See also *Zazhi* 10.6 (10 March 1943): 92. Among the many enthusiastic reviews of the play was *Shanghai shenghuo* (Shanghai life), 3.11 (17 November 1939): 30.

83. Jay Leyda, *Dianying: An Account of Films and the Film Audience in China* (Cambridge, Mass.: MIT Press, 1972), p. 141.

84. See Hong Shen, *Kangzhan shinian lai*, p. 161; also *ZGHJYD* 2:183; and Ying Sun, "Guanyu *Mulan congjun*," *Wenxian* 6 (10 March 1939): F32–F35.

85. Ouyang Yuqian, *Dianying banlu chujia ji* (Beijing: Zhongguo dianying chubanshe, 1962), p. 36.

86. Zhou Yibai, *Hua Mulan*, esp. act 4. See also Edward Gunn's description in *Unwelcome Muse*, pp. 125–126.

87. *Zazhi* (Magazine) 15.5 (10 August 1945): 103–105.

88. The unity and the strength of the people is again stressed in such plays as Gu Zhongyi's *Liang Hongyu*, esp. act 4.

89. Other plays on the same theme include Zhao Ming's *Mulan congjun ji* (*Mulan Joins the Army*), mentioned in *Baqian li lu yun he yue*, pp. 383–384, 463; and in Shui Hua's *Mulan congjun* (*Mulan Joins the Army*), in *ZGHJYD* 2:213, 226. For more information, see Chang-tai Hung, "Female Symbols of Resistance in Chinese Wartime Spoken Drama," *Modern China* 15.2 (April 1989): 149–177, esp. p. 174, n. 5. An example of a cartoon on the theme is Feng Zikai's "A Modern-Day Hua Mulan," *YZF* 71 (16 July 1938): 230. And for a *kuaiban*, see Lao She, "Nü'er jing," in *Lao She wenji*, 14 vols. (Beijing: Renmin chubanshe, 1980–1989), 13:55. An interesting article on the subject concerns a Hunanese girl, Tang Guilin, who disguised herself as a male soldier during the war; surprisingly, her identity was not discovered until a few years later. See Cao Juren, "Xiandai Mulan Tang Guilin de ceying," *Zazhi* 5.1 (16 June 1939): 56.

90. Although patriotic courtesans and female warriors were the two major types of female symbols of resistance created during the war, they were by no means the only ones. Guo Moruo's Nie Ying, for example, belongs to neither category. A protagonist in Guo's five-act play *Devoted Siblings* (*Tandi zhi hua*, 1942), Nie Ying is a righteous woman of the Warring States period. She and her brother Nie Zheng together sacrifice their lives for the cause of unity in opposition to the tyranny of the Qin. There is definitely a contemporary ring in Guo's presentation.

91. Interview with Xie Bingying, 20 November 1988, 21 August 1989, San Francisco.

92. Hu Lanqi, *Hu Lanqi huiyilu*, vol. 2: *1936–1949* (Chengdu: Sichuan renmin chubanshe, 1987), esp. pp. 27–28.

93. See Hu Lanqi, ed., *Zhandi ernian* (N.p.: Laodong funü zhandi fuwutuan, 1939), p. 8.

94. Joan W. Scott, "Rewriting History," in *Behind the Lines: Gender and the Two World Wars*, ed. Margaret R. Higonnet et al. (New Haven: Yale University Press, 1987), p. 30.

95. Ying Sun, "Guanyu *Mulan congjun*."

96. A total of 627 titles with known publication dates are said to have been published during the war. In addition, there were 36 titles whose publication dates are unknown. Many titles, however, are collections of plays, and some titles appeared in more than one edi-

tion. See Qin Xianci, ed., *Kangzhan shiqi wenxue shiliao*, pp. 170–203. About 30 of these titles bear the names of patriotic courtesans, past female warriors, and modern women fighters. Another account gives the total number of plays produced as 989; this tally includes those that appeared in journals and magazines, but unfortunately no titles are given. See *Zhongguo kang-Ri zhanzheng dahoufang wenxue shuxi* 17:2244.

97. There were other Hua Mulan plays that did not appear in print, such as those by Zhao Ming and Shui Hua (see above, n. 89).

98. Yang Cunbin, *Qin Liangyu*, "Preface."

99. Turner, *Dramas, Fields, and Metaphors*, p. 106.

100. Jean Bethke Elshtain, "Women as Mirror and Other: Toward a Theory of Women, War, and Feminism," *Humanities in History* 5.2 (Winter–Spring 1982): 31–32.

101. There are many studies on European and American women's active role during the two world wars, especially the second. See, for example, Margaret Weitz, "As I Was Then: Women in the French Resistance," *Contemporary French Civilization* 10.1 (1986): 1–19; Leila Rupp, *Mobilizing Women for War: German and American Propaganda, 1939–1945* (Princeton: Princeton University Press, 1978); and Higonnet et al., eds., *Behind the Lines*. Feminist scholarship has been particularly active in studying the relationship between the politics of gender and the politics of war. Feminist scholars argue that the two world wars provided opportunities for women to assume roles previously reserved for men. But since women were excluded from public power and combat roles in the military, the "changes in women's material conditions and cultural image seem ephemeral" (Higonnet et al., eds., *Behind the Lines*, p. 32). In America, Leila Rupp claims that World War II created only a temporary change in women's status.

102. As in the West, the status of women changed little in wartime China. See Kay Ann Johnson, *Women, the Family, and Peasant Revolution in China* (Chicago: University of Chicago Press, 1983), esp. chap. 2; Honig, *Sisters and Strangers*; and Ono Kazuko, *Chinese Women in a Century of Revolution, 1850–1950*, ed. Joshua A. Fogel (Stanford: Stanford University Press, 1989).

103. For a discussion of the relationship between the image and reality of women in Chinese literature, see Anna Gerstlacher et al., eds., *Woman and Literature in China* (Bochum, W. Ger.: Brockmeyer, 1985).

104. For a comparison of the symbol of Joan of Arc and that of Hua Mulan, see Chang-tai Hung, "Female Symbols of Resistance."

105. Wang Ping, "Tian Han zai 'feixu shang,'" *Juchang yishu* 9 (20 July 1939): 14.

106. "Special Issue on Historical Plays," *XJCQ* 2.4 (30 October 1942): 40–41.

107. Ibid., p. 41.

108. Ibid.

109. Liu Yazi participated in this panel discussion but did not respond to the questions directly. He agreed to write a separate article addressing issues related to the discussion. This article appeared in the same issue of *XJCQ*. See Yazi (Liu Yazi), "Zatan lishiju," *XJCQ* 2.4 (30 October 1942): 49.

110. *XJCQ* 2.4 (30 October 1942): 46.

111. For other discussions, see, for example, He Fangyuan, "Lishiju lunzhan," *Zazhi* 13.2 (10 May 1944): 153–156; and *Zazhi* 12.5 (10 February 1944): 159–161.

112. Wei Ruhui (A Ying), "*Bixue hua* renwu bukao," *Wanxiang* 1.1 (1 July 1941): 41–43. See also Liu Yazi, "Zatan A Ying xiansheng de Nan Ming shiju," *Wenxue chuangzuo* 1.2 (15 October 1942): 52–57.

113. A Ying, *Yang E zhuan*, p. 16.

114. Ouyang Yuqian, *Huaju, xingeju yu Zhongguo xiju yishu chuantong*, p. 9.

115. See *XJCQ* 2.4 (30 October 1942): 41. Playwrights often found it difficult to authenticate characters and events in a historical play. *Mulan Joins the Army* is a case in point. Accounts of Hua Mulan's life are flimsy at best and perhaps even fabricated. She may have lived during the Tang dynasty or in the earlier Northern and Southern dynasties, as the famous "Poem of Mulan" suggested. Although we have sufficient evidence to prove that the Mulan legend had become quite popular by the Tang, the exact time when this legend started and how it grew are still not known.

116. He Fangyuan, "Lishiju lunzhan," p. 153.

117. See *Zazhi* 12.5 (10 February 1944): 159–161, esp. p. 160; *Wenyi xianfeng* 2.4 (20 April 1943): 5

118. Interview with Xia Yan, 16 October 1989, Beijing.

119. Xia Yan, "*Shanghai wuyan xia* houji," in Hui Lin et al., *Xia Yan yanjiu ziliao* (Beijing: Zhongguo xiju chubanshe, 1983), p. 178.

120. Zhang Geng, "Muqian juyun de jige dangmian wenti," *GM* 2.12 (25 May 1937): 1493.

121. Tang Tao, *Touying ji* (Shanghai: Wenhua shenghuo chubanshe, 1940), p. 164.

122. See Ouyang Yuqian, *Huaju, xingeju yu Zhongguo xiju yishu chuantong*; and idem, "Zaitan jiuxi de gaige," *Shen bao zhoukan* 2.7 (21 February 1937): 139–142; 2.8 (28 February 1937): 166–167; 2.12 (28 March 1937): 257–258.

123. Kedward, *Resistance in Vichy France*, p. 211.

124. Guo Moruo, "Tan lishiju" (On historical plays), quoted in Su Guangwen, *Kangzhan wenxue gaiguan* (Chongqing: Xinan shifan daxue, 1985), p. 166.

125. On GMD censorship, see Lee-hsia Hsu Ting, *Government Control of the Press in Modern China, 1900–1949* (Cambridge, Mass.: East Asian Research Center, Harvard University, 1974); see also Yiqun, "Yijiusier nian Yu Gui ge zhanqu juyun pingshu," *Wenxue chuangzuo* 1.6 (1 April 1943): 119–125.

126. Tian Jin, "Kangzhan banian lai de xiju chuangzuo," *Wenlian* 1.3 (5 February 1946): 27.

127. See Lan Hai, *Zhongguo kangzhan wenyi shi* (Ji'nan: Shandong wenyi chubanshe, 1984), p. 252.

128. Tian Jin, "Kangzhan banian lai de xiju chuangzuo," p. 27. Chen Baichen gave slightly different statistics: historical plays composed 16 percent of all plays in the first period, and 34 percent in the second. See Wang Xunzhao et al., eds., *Guo Moruo yanjiu ziliao*, 3 vols. (Beijing: Zhongguo shehui kexue chubanshe, 1986), 1:364.

129. Tang Tao, *Touying ji*, p. 166.

130. For one of numerous articles on Shi Kefa, see Wen Zaidao et al., *Biangu ji*, pp. 221–222. On Ma Shiying and Ruan Dacheng, see Tang Tao, *Duan chang shu* (Shanghai: Nanguo chubanshe, 1947), pp. 124–126, 155–170; interview with Tang Tao, 12 October 1989, Beijing.

131. For Zhou Li'an's argument, see Wen Zaidao et al., *Biangu ji*, p. 198.

132. Zhou Li'an, *Huafa ji* (Shanghai: Yuzhou feng she, 1940), p. 32.

133. Interview with Wu Zuguang, 5 November 1987, Minneapolis.

134. Xiong Foxi, *Foxi lunju* (Shanghai: Xinyue shudian, 1931), p. 148.

135. Ding Ling, "Lüetan gailiang Pingju," *Wenyi zhendi* 2.4 (1 December 1938): 496.

136. Xiang Peiliang, "Lun jiuju zhi buneng gailiang," *Shen bao*, 6 September 1935, p. 20.

137. Xiong Foxi, "Wo duiyu chuangzao xingeju de yidian yijian," *Yicong* 1.2 (July 1943): 6.

138. For Tian Han's argument, see, for example, Tian Han, *Tian Han zhuanji* (N.p.: Jiangsu renmin chubanshe, 1984), pp. 155, 163. See also Hong Shen, *Kangzhan shinian lai*, chap. 5; and Ouyang Yuqian, *Huaju, xingeju yu Zhongguo xiju yishu chuantong.*

139. Ouyang Yuqian, "Zaitan jiuxi de gaige."

140. Ouyang Yuqian, "Mingri de xingeju," *XJSD* 1.1 (16 May 1937): 70.

141. *Ouyang Yuqian yu Guiju gaige*, ed. Guangxi yishu yanjiuyuan and Guangxi shehui kexueyuan (Nanning: Guangxi renmin chubanshe, 1986), esp. "Introduction," pp. 1–27.

142. Ouyang Yuqian, "Zaitan jiuxi de gaige," p. 141.

143. Ouyang, "Zaitan jiuxi de gaige."

144. Ma Yanxiang, "Ruhe renshi difangju," *Renmin wenyi* 1.3 (15 March 1946): 60.

145. See Hong Shen, *Kangzhan shinian lai*, p. 27.

146. Ma Yanxiang, "Ruhe renshi difangju"; idem, "Duiyu jiuju de zai renshi," *Beida banyuekan* 6 (1 June 1948): 13–14, 17.

147. See discussion in *GM* 1.8 (25 September 1936): 520.

148. Ma Yanxiang, "Ruhe renshi difangju," pp. 60–61.

149. Hong Shen, *Kangzhan shinian lai*, pp. 34–36.

150. See ibid., chap. 5. See also Huang Zhigang, "Zenyang liyong difangxi zuo kangdi xuanchuan," *Kangzhan yishu* 1 (1 September 1939): 1–7.

151. Hong Shen, *Kangzhan shinian lai*, pp. 40–41.

152. Guo Moruo, *Hongbo qu*, p. 100.

153. Tian Han, *Yingshi zhuiyilu* (Beijing: Zhongguo dianying chubanshe, 1981), p. 54.

154. Hong Shen, *Kangzhan shinian lai*, p. 38.

155. See *GM* 3.3 (10 July 1937): 202.

156. See Hong Shen, *Kangzhan shinian lai*, pp. 31–33. Even before the war broke out, Guan had donated his only property—an automobile—to the government on the fiftieth birthday of Generalissimo Jiang Jieshi. See "The Patriotic Actor Mr. Kuan Teh-shing [Guan Dexing]," *Dongfang huakan* (The eastern pictorial) 2.7 (October 1939): 32–33; and "The Kwangtung Dramatic Corps in the Philippines," *Dongfang huakan* 4.1 (April 1941): 32–33.

157. Ma Yanxiang, "Jiuju kangzhan," *KZWY* 1.10 (25 June 1938): 127.

158. Li Gongpu, "Yige zhanxin de gejudui," *Quanmin kangzhan* 69 (5 May 1939): 988–989.

159. Li Puyuan, "Guanyu xiju de yige shiyan," *Minyi zhoukan* 9 (9 February 1938): 12.

160. See Tian Han, *Yingshi zhuiyilu*, p. 54.

161. *XJCQ* 2.3 (1 September 1942): 16–17.

162. Ouyang Yuqian, "Gaige Guixi de buzhou," in *Ouyang Yuqian yu Guiju gaige*, p. 6.

3. CARTOONS

1. Wang Dunqing, "Manhua zhan," *JWMH* 1 (20 September 1937): 1.

2. See Huang Mao, *Manhua yishu jianghua*, p. 36.

3. Xuan Wenjie, "Kang-Ri zhanzheng shiqi de manhua xuanchuandui," *Meishu* 6 (25 July 1979): 37–38.

4. Ibid., p. 39.

5. Ibid.

6. Zhang Wenyuan, "Zhongguo manhua yundong de huigu yu qianzhan," *Wenchao yuekan* 2.3 (1 January 1947): 606.

7. A successful cartoon show was held in Beiping (Beijing) in July 1937; see *DGB* (Tianjin), 7 July 1937, p. 15. Such shows were also held in the provinces. See, for example, the woodcut artist Li Hua's report from Nanning, Guangxi province, in *JWRB*, 12 January 1938, p. 3.

8. See *Zhandi tongxun* 3.11 (1 June 1940): 23–24.

9. For the above information, see Bi and Huang, *Zhongguo manhua shi*, pp. 168–176. See also Zhang Wenyuan, "Zhongguo manhua yundong de huigu yu qianzhan," pp. 606–608.

10. Bi and Huang, *Zhongguo manhua shi*, pp. 176–180.

11. Ibid., p. 96.

12. Hu Kao, "Zhanshi de manhuajie," in *Kangzhan yu yishu* (Chongqing: Duli chubanshe, n.d.), p. 8.

13. Interview with Zhang Leping, 19 November, 10 December 1989, Shanghai.

14. Cartoons were closely associated with woodcuts during the war. See, for example, the "Cartoons and Woodcuts" column in the *Jiuwang ribao* (National salvation daily), which began on 1 November 1939 (p. 4); and the "Woodcuts and Cartoons" column in the *Xinhua ribao* (New China daily), 21 August 1943, p. 4. See also Ji Zhi, "Guanyu 'muke manhua,'" *Xinhua ribao*, 19 March 1942, p. 4; Liao Bingxiong, "Guanyu manmu hezuo," *JWRB*, 22 February 1940, p. 4.

15. Interview with Zhang Leping, 19 November, 10 December 1989, Shanghai.

16. Daniel Fitzpatrick called the swastika "the tumbling engine of destruction" (*As I Saw It* [New York: Simon & Schuster, 1953], p. 10). For his anti-Nazi drawings, see ibid., esp. pp. 40, 43, 51, 87. Although Fitzpatrick's crayon-on-grained-paper technique found few imitators in China, his anti-Hitler works did make a strong impression on Chinese artists, especially his "Piece by Piece," which depicts a Japanese soldier using a bayonet to divide China into different occupied spheres, marking them with Japanese flags. See *JWMH* 3 (30 September 1937): 4.

17. For Szyk's anti-Nazi cartoons, see, for example, "New Order" and "A Madman's Dream," in his *The New Order* (New York: G. P. Putnam's Sons, 1941), n.p. Szyk also attacked Japanese militarists; see "Aryan Ally" in ibid.

18. David Freedberg, for example, has explored the role of images in religious controversies in European history, particularly in the wake of the Protestant Reformation; see *The Power of Images: Studies in*

the History and Theory of Response (Chicago: University of Chicago Press, 1989). R. W. Scribner uses broadsheets to examine the importance of images in the spread of the evangelical movement during the first half-century of the Reformation in Germany; see *For the Sake of Simple Folk: Popular Propaganda for the German Reformation* (Cambridge: Cambridge University Press, 1981).

19. Feng Zikai, Preface to *Ou Mei manhua jingxuan*, p. 1.

20. Interview with Liao Bingxiong, 3, 4 January 1990, Guangzhou.

21. For Liao's cartoons, see, for example, *JWRB*, 11 May 1939, p. 4, and 2 January 1940, p. 4. See also Liao, *Bingxiong manhua* (Guangzhou: Lingnan meishu chubanshe, 1984).

22. This cartoon first appeared in *Fenghuo* (Beacon-fire) 1 (5 September 1937). It was reprinted in *Wencong* (Literature) 1.6 (20 April 1938). For its influence, see Hu Feng's comments in *Jian, wenyi, renmin* (Shanghai: Nitu she, 1950), p. 89. The cartoon was shown during a touring cartoon exhibition; see Xuan Wenjie, "Kang-Ri zhanzheng shiqi de manhua xuanchuandui," p. 37. Other information is from Cai's letter to the author, 25 November 1988; and interview with Cai, 29 September 1989, Beijing.

23. This cartoon was subsequently redrawn and reprinted by Feng Zikai in a number of places. See, for example, Feng, *Zhanshi xiang* (N.p.: Kaiming shudian, 1945), p. 10; and *China Weekly Review* 88.6 (8 April 1939): 177. See also Feng's own description about this 1937 incident in his *Feng Zikai sanwen xuanji* (Shanghai: Shanghai wenyi chubanshe, 1981), pp. 171–172. In an accompanying piece, Feng portrayed another scene from Guangzhou: that of a child's head severed in an enemy's bombing attack. He accompanied the cartoon with another *ci* poem: "When the mad bombing begins / A mother, carrying her baby on her back, starts running / But before reaching the air raid shelter / The baby's tiny head is thrown into the air / Hot blood gushes out like a raging torrent" (*Zhanshi xiang*, p. 11; *YZF* 76 [1 October 1938]: 154; *China Weekly Review* 88.7 [15 April 1939]: 207).

24. In *QGXJ*, pp. 86–87.

25. Ibid., p. 88.

26. Wolfram Eberhard, *A Dictionary of Chinese Symbols: Hidden Symbols in Chinese Life and Thought* (London: Routledge & Kegan Paul, 1986), p. 268.

27. In *QGXJ*, pp. 14, 68. See also Zhang E's piece "Fengkuang de yeshou" (A wild beast), *Quanmin kangzhan* 88 (16 September 1939): cover.

28. The British, for example, called Hitler the "Mad Dog of Europe"; see Anthony Rhodes, *Propaganda* (New York: Chelsea House, 1976), p. 113. The use of bestial imagery is of course loaded with racism; see John Dower, *War Without Mercy: Race and Power*

in the Pacific War (New York: Pantheon Books, 1986), esp. pp. 181–200, 234–261.

29. Charles Press, *The Political Cartoon* (New Brunswick, N.J.: Associated University Presses, 1981), pp. 76–77.

30. Hu Kao, for example, portrayed China as a lion (*QGXJ*, p. 55); traditional-style painter Zhang Shanzi compared China to a tiger (see *Wenxian* 3 [10 December 1938]: n.p.). Painters such as Gao Qifeng of the Lingnan School of Painting had also used lions to convey similar messages in the early decades of the Republican era; see Ralph Croizier, *Art and Revolution in Modern China: The Lingnan (Cantonese) School of Painting, 1906–1951* (Berkeley and Los Angeles: University of California Press, 1988), pp. 40–41, 88–91.

31. See Dou Shi's cartoon "Hijacking the Young and Ignorant Prime Minister," in *QGXJ*, p. 48. Prince Konoe was of course no bystander in the war: he sided with the army and played an active role in promoting Japan's interests in Asia. See the discussion in James Crowley, *Japan's Quest for Autonomy: National Security and Foreign Policy, 1930–1938* (Princeton: Princeton University Press, 1966), esp. chap. 6, "The China War."

32. See, for example, Rhodes, *Propaganda*, pp. 57, 103; and Stephen White, *The Bolshevik Poster* (New Haven: Yale University Press, 1988), p. 17.

33. See *QGXJ*, p. 62.

34. For one of numerous articles on *hanjian*, see Qian Junrui, "'Zhun hanjian' lun," *Xin xueshi* 2.3 (10 November 1937): 110–111.

35. See Te Wei's cartoon "The Coronation of the Renegade Wang Jingwei," on the cover of *Quanmin kangzhan* 118 (13 April 1940).

36. See Feng's "Putting on a Farce" and "A Puppet Show," in his *Zhanshi xiang*, pp. 33, 36.

37. See *QGXJ*, pp. 42, 82.

38. Ibid., p. 90.

39. One example is Hu Kao's cartoon of four women in uniform and its accompanying poem summing up their aspirations: "My second sister is a caring nurse / The youngest one fights the enemy on the battlefront / Their accomplishment is by no means inferior to that of men / A platoon of women warriors marches to the front" (*QGXJ*, p. 113).

40. The legendary heroine was one of Feng Zikai's favorite archetypes during the war; see also his cartoon "Like Hua Mulan, a woman warrior is leaving home to join the army," in *Zhandi manhua* (Hong Kong: Yingshang buliedian tushu gongsi, 1939), n.p.

41. Mauldin's famous aspirin cartoon is a good example of the satirical type; see Mauldin, *Up Front* (Cleveland: World, 1945), p. 133, and pp. 27, 112, 214 for other examples.

42. As in Hu Kao's "A Badly Wounded Warrior," in *QGXJ*, p. 31.

43. See Bi and Huang, *Zhongguo manhua shi*, pl. 207.

44. See, for example, Lu Shaofei's piece on guerilla warfare in *QGXJ*, p. 43.

45. See Low's "Do you smell something burning?" (1938) in his *Cartoon History of Our Times*, pp. 64–65.

46. See, for example, Cai Ruohong's "The Quagmire of Japan's Future," in *QGXJ*, p. 16; Jiang Mi's "Japan's Quagmire," in Bi and Huang, *Zhongguo manhua shi*, pl. 215; Li Fanfu"s "Sink Deeper and Deeper into the Quagmire," in *QGXJ*, p. 46. David Low used a similar image in his piece "Further and Deeper"; see *A Cartoon History of Our Times*, pp. 60–61.

47. Ye Qianyu, *Ye Qianyu manhua xuan*, pp. 118–154, esp. p. 150.

48. Ding Cong, *Zuotian de shiqing* (Beijing: Sanlian shudian, 1984), pp. 2–3 (reprinted in *Fortune*, August 1945, pp. 118–119).

49. Liao Bingxiong, *Bingxiong manhua*, n.p.

50. See Zhang Guangyu, *Xiyou manji* (Beijing: Renmin meishu chubanshe, 1983), esp. chaps. 2, 4, and 9.

51. See Liao Bingxiong, *Bingxiong manhua*, n.p. A detailed analysis of cartoons during the civil war period is beyond the scope of this book; for a discussion, see my article "The Fuming Image: Cartoons and Public Opinion in Late Republican China, 1945 to 1949," *Comparative Studies in Society and History* (forthcoming).

52. See *Huashang bao*, 14 August 1941, p. 3.

53. Ning, "Xin meishu yundong," *Huashang bao*, 19 June 1941, p. 3; Jianxun, "Xin meishu yundong zhankai zhong—wo de jidian yijian," *Huashang bao*, 6 August 1941, p. 3; Te Wei, "Lian ren dai yi," *Huashang bao*, 13 November 1941, p. 3.

54. Lai Shaoqi, "Manhua yu muke," in Qian, Hu, and Zhang, eds., *Kangzhan de jingyan yu jiaoxun*, pp. 15–17.

55. Quoted in Xinbo, "Wusheng de zhadan," p. 3.

56. Zhang Guangyu, "Guonei meishujie de qingzhuang," *Huashang bao*, 25 June 1941, p. 3.

57. Zhu Xingyi, "Wo suo xiji yu manhuajie de," *Duli manhua* 4 (10 November 1935): 3.

58. Hu Kao, "Xiwang yu manhuajie," p. 7.

59. Feng Yi, "Manhua Zhongguo jin bainian xuelei shi," *Zazhi* 6.2 (20 January 1940): 36.

60. Tang Yifan, "Kangzhan yu huihua," *Dongfang zazhi* 37.10 (16 May 1940): 27.

61. See Xinbo, "Wusheng de zhadan," p. 3; see also *Huashang bao*, 29 October 1943, p. 3.

62. Chen Chin-yun, "Art Chronicle," *T'ien Hsia Monthly* 11.3 (December–January 1940–1941): 270.

63. Shen Zhenhuang, "Duiyu manhua xuanchuan gongzuo de yijian," in Qian, Hu, and Zhang, eds., *Kangzhan de jingyan yu jiaoxun*, p. 224.

64. Huang Shiying, "Manhua gailun," in Chen Wangdao, ed., *Xiaopinwen he manhua*, p. 143.

65. See *YZF* 91 (1 January 1941): 214–215, esp. p. 215.

66. Huang Mao, *Manhua yishu jianhua*, p. 64.

67. Qianyu (Ye Qianyu), "Manhua de minzu xingshi." Ye, however, disagreed with others that China lacked a strong tradition of figure drawing.

68. Huang Mao, "Huihua Zhongguohua tanxie," *JWRB*, 12 May 1940, p. 4.

69. Ding Cong, *Zuotian de shiqing*, pp. 2–3.

70. Interview with Liao Bingxiong, 3, 4 January 1990, Guangzhou. See also Liao, *Bingxiong manhua*, passim.

71. Huang Mao, *Du hua suibi* (Hong Kong: Renjian shuwu, 1949), pp. 3–4.

72. Quoted in Huang Mao, *Manhua yishu jianghua*, p. 51.

73. See "Art Chronicle," *T'ien Hsia Monthly* 9.1 (August 1939): 83 and illustrations; *Huashang bao*, 23 July 1941, p. 3; *Wenxian* 3 (10 December 1938): n.p.

74. Xinbo, "Xiang Sulian ji shijie jinbu de huajia xuexi," *Huashang bao*, 30 July 1941, p. 3.

75. On Kuriyagawa Hakuson, see *SDMH* 10 (20 October 1934): n.p.; on William Gropper, see *SDMH* 22 (20 October 1935): n.p.

76. Lu Shaofei, "Kangzhan yu manhua," *Dikang sanrikan* 15 (6 October 1937): 9.

77. Lu Xun, "Mantan 'manhua,'" p. 10.

78. Huang Miaozi, "Tan manhua," *Manhuajie* 7 (5 November 1936): n.p.

79. Ling He, Preface to *Manhua he shenghuo* 1.3 (20 January 1936): 3.

80. Wang Dunqing, "Manhua de xuanchuan xing," *SDMH* 17 (20 May 1935): n.p.

81. Hu Kao, "Jianli kangzhan manhua de lilun," *Zhandi* 2 (5 April 1938): 35.

82. Hu Kao, "Xiwang yu manhuajie," p. 7.

83. Xinbo, "Wusheng de zhadan," p. 3.

84. Li Qun, "Xuanchuanhua zai nongcun," *Dikang sanrikan* 17 (13 October 1937): 8.

85. Hu Kao, "Baodao hua", *Huashang bao*, 3 December 1941, p. 3; idem, "Jianli kangzhan manhua de lilun," p. 35.

86. Huang Mao, "Manhua de xuanchuan fangshi," *Kangjian tongsu huakan* 2.2 (1 July 1942): 18–19.

87. Cao Bohan, *Xuanchuan jishu duben* (N.p.: Shenghuo shudian, 1938), pp. 74–75.

88. I am indebted to R. W. Scribner (*For the Sake of Simple Folk*, p. 244) for the terms *anchorage* and *relay* and their explanation.

89. Huang Miaozi, "Wo de manhua lilun," in Chen Wangdao, ed., *Xiaopinwen he manhua*, p. 61.

90. See *T'ien Hsia Monthly* 7.2 (September 1938): 207; also *Dongfang huakan* 3.11 (February 1941): 11, inter alia. Shen's earlier pieces, mostly filled with patriotic sentiments, appeared in *Shida manhua* and *Manhuajie*—for example, *Shida manhua* 24 (20 December 1935): n.p.; *Manhuajie* 6 (5 September 1936): cover.

91. Zhao Wangyun, *Zhao Wangyun nongcun xiesheng ji* (Tianjin: Dagong bao she, 1934). For a discussion of Zhao's drawings, see *YZF* 12 (1 March 1936): 588–589. Zhao's sketches also appeared in *YZF*, January 1937–June 1937.

92. Feng Yuxiang, Preface to Zhao Wangyun, *Zhao Wangyun nongcun xiesheng ji*, p. 3; Xiao Qian, *Wei dai ditu de lüren—Xiao Qian huiyilu* (Hong Kong: Xiangjiang chuban gongsi, 1988), p. 96.

93. Cao Juren, "Ping Zhao Wangyun *Nongcun xiesheng ji* ji qi tishi," *Shen bao*, 30 January 1934, p. 15.

94. See *QGXJ*, p. 108.

95. Ye Qianyu, *Hua yu lun hua*, p. 174.

96. Shen Zhenhuang, "Duiyu manhua xuanchuan gongzuo de yijian," pp. 222–223.

97. There were many wartime cartoons on armed peasants. In addition to the two mentioned above, see, for example, *JWRB*, 29 January 1938, p. 4.

98. Huang Miaozi, "Kangzhan yilai de Zhongguo manhua," pp. 4–5.

99. Ye Qianyu, "Lüetan Zhongguo de manhua yishu."

100. On the number of wartime cartoon magazines, see Bi and Huang, *Zhongguo manhua shi*, pp. 152, 160, 176–177. With the exception of *National Mobilizers Pictorial*, which printed about 50,000 to 60,000 copies per issue (see *QGXJ*, p. 5), the circulation of other wartime cartoon magazines is not clear. But according to Lu Shaofei, the majority printed only "a few thousand copies per issue" (interview, 26 October 1989, Beijing).

101. This piece was widely reprinted. See, for example, *China Weekly Review* 88.6 (8 April 1939): 177; and Xu Wancheng, *Kangzhan banian Chongqing huaxu* (Tidbits of Chongqing during the eight-year War of Resistance) (Shanghai: Longwen shudian, 1946), cover.

102. For a general discussion of Feng's cartoons, see Christoph Harbsmeier, *The Cartoonist Feng Zikai: Social Realism with a Buddhist Face* (Oslo: Universitetsforlaget, 1984); and Shuen-shuen Hung, "Feng Tzu-k'ai: His Art and Thought" (M.A. thesis, Michigan State University, 1986). Feng's cartoons became so popular in the 1930s that many others attempted to imitate his work. A certain "Feng Zikai the Second" (Cikai) even appeared. See *YZF* 10 (16 July 1939): 452–454.

103. Feng wrote a score of books on art theory; most notable among them are *Yishu gailun* (An introduction to art, 1928), *Xiandai yishu shier jiang* (Twelve talks on modern art, 1928), and *Yishu conghua* (Miscellaneous talks on art, 1935).

104. See, for example, Zhao Jingshen, "Feng Zikai he tade xiaopinwen," *Renjian shi* 30 (20 June 1935): 14–16.

105. Feng Zikai, *Husheng huaji*, 6 vols. (reprinted Taibei: Chunwenxue chubanshe, 1981). See Feng Yiyin et al., *Feng Zikai zhuan* (Hangzhou: Zhejiang renmin chubanshe, 1983), for detail.

106. Feng's cartoons began to appear regularly in *Xiaoshuo yuebao* in the mid-1920s—for example, 17.1 (10 January 1926): inside title page, 12; 17.3 (10 March 1926): inside title page. For *Shen bao*, see 24, 25 May 1934 et seq.

107. For a general discussion of how children are perceived in modern China, see Chang-tai Hung, *Going to the People*, chap. 5.

108. In Feng's famous article "Cong haizi dedao de qishi" (Inspiration that I received from children), he argued that an adult's world is one of corruption, endless cravings, vanity, and fame; but when children look at the world, they see only beauty, innocence, peace, and joy. See Feng, *Yuanyuantang suibi* (Shanghai: Kaiming shudian, 1948), pp. 39–40. For a discussion of Feng's views on children, see Chang-tai Hung, "War and Peace in Feng Zikai's Wartime Cartoons," *Modern China* 16.1 (January 1990): 39–83.

109. Feng Zikai, *Ertong xiang* (N.p.: Kaiming shudian, 1945), p. 22.

110. Takehisa Yumeji, who illustrated a large number of newspapers and magazines during the late Meiji and Taishō eras, was one of Feng's favorite Japanese painters; see Feng, *Yuanyuantang jiwai yiwen*, ed. Ming Chuan (Hong Kong: Wenxue chubanshe, 1979), p. 1. See also, for example, Takehisa Yumeji, *Kodomo no sekai* (Tokyo: Ryuseikaku, 1970).

111. See Feng Zikai, *Gushi xinhua* (N.p.: Kaiming shudian, 1945).

112. Feng Zikai, *Chexiang shehui* (Shanghai: Liangyou tushu yinshua gongsi, 1935), p. 227.

113. Feng Zikai, *Yishu quwei* (N.p.: Kaiming shudian, 1946), pp. 93–94.

114. See Feng Zikai, *Chexiang shehui*, esp. pp. 1–9.

115. Fang Zhizhong, "Minzu ziwei yu manhua," *Manhua he shenghuo* 1.3 (10 January 1936): 11.

116. Huang Mao, *Manhua yishu jianghua*, p. 49.

117. Feng Zikai, Preface to *Jieyu manhua* (Shanghai: Wanye shudian, 1947).

118. In Feng Zikai, *Yuanyuantang jiwai yiwen*, pp. 90–99, esp. p. 99.

119. Feng Zikai, "Fo wu ling" (Buddha has no magic power), in *Yuanyuantang jiwai yiwen*, p. 111.

120. Feng Zikai, "Sansha yu shadai" (Loose sand and sandbags), in ibid., p. 117.

121. Feng Zikai, "Yishu bineng jianguo," *Yuzhou feng yikan* 2 (16 March 1939): 52–53, esp. p. 53.

122. Ke Ling, "Kangzhan zhong de Feng Zikai xiansheng," in Wen Zaidao et al., *Biangu ji*, pp. 354–362.

123. See Feng Zikai, *Zhanshi xiang*, pp. 16, 28, 40.

124. See Feng Zikai, *Zhandi manhua*, cartoon no. 4.

125. Feng Zikai, "In the Occupied Territory," in *Zhanshi xiang*, p. 43.

126. See Feng Zikai, "Ruining [Chinese] culture," *Zhoubao* 8 (27 October 1945): cover.

127. See Feng Zikai, *Kechuang manhua* (Guilin: Jinri wenyishe, 1943), p. 11.

128. Feng Zikai, "Zhongguo jiu xiang ke dashu," *Yuzhou feng yikan* 1 (1 March 1939): 6.

129. Feng Zikai, "Ze wu hui zhi yi" (Do not burn it), in *Yuanyuantang jiwai yiwen*, pp. 115–116.

130. Feng Zikai, *Manhua de miaofa*, pp. 23–24.

131. Ibid., p. 24.

132. Ibid., pp. 35–36.

133. Feng Zikai, "Ze wu hui zhi yi," in *Yuanyuantang jiwai yiwen*, p. 116.

134. See Feng Zikai's letter in *Wanxiang* 3.7 (1 January 1944): 67.

135. Feng Zikai, *Zhandi manhua*. See also Feng, *Kechuang manhua*, "Preface."

136. See Feng, "Yanhui zhi ku" (The agony of attending dinner parties), in *LY* 132 (1 July 1947): 621–622.

137. See Feng Huazhan's (Feng Zikai's son) account in Preface to *Feng Zikai sanwen xuanji*, p. 19.

138. W. A. Coupe, "Observations on a Theory of Political Caricature," *Comparative Studies in Society and History* 11.1 (January 1969): 82.

139. As in his piece "In Panic," which portrays the plight of refugees—that is, the consequences of the Japanese actions. See Feng, *Zhanshi xiang*, p. 24.

140. Feng Zikai, "Tan kangzhan gequ," *Zhandi* 4 (5 May 1938): 100.

141. Feng Zikai, *Manhua de miaofa*, pp. 21–22.

142. Feng Zikai, "Shengji," in Feng, *Yuanyuantang zaibi* (N.p.: Kaiming shudian, 1948), p. 23.

4. NEWSPAPERS

1. Cheng Shewo, "'Zhidan' yi ke jiandi," *DGB* (Hankou), 13–15 May 1938.

2. For a list of war correspondents during the 1930s and 1940s, see Bu Shaofu, *Zhandi jizhe jianghua* (Guiyang: Wentong shuju, 1942), pp. 5, 10–11. See also Zeng Xubai, *Zeng Xubai zizhuan*, pp. 123–124.

3. For more on the early history of war correspondence, see Bu Shaofu, *Zhandi jizhe jianghua*, p. 5. For information on Lu Yi, see his *Zhandi pingzong* (Beijing: Renmin ribao chubanshe, 1985), pp. 3–5; some of the present material was also gotten from an interview with Lu Yi on 16 November and 10 December 1989 in Shanghai. China, of course, had journalists reporting its armed conflicts with foreign countries at least as early as the Sino-Japanese War of 1894–95 (see Li Liangrong, *Zhongguo baozhi wenti fazhan gaiyao* [Fuzhou: Fujian renmin chubanshe, 1985], p. 11), but they were not full-time, formal war correspondents in the modern sense of the word.

4. Bu Shaofu, *Zhandi jizhe jianghua*, p. 109.

5. Ibid., p. 10.

6. George L. Mosse, "Two World Wars and the Myths of the War Experience," *Journal of Contemporary History* 21.4 (October 1986): 492.

7. The journalist Gao Tian called for the founding of numerous "cultural war stations," designed specifically to channel the news to the frontline and thus establishing what he called a reliable "spiritual supply line" ("Pubian jianli 'wenhua bingzhan,'" *XWJZ* 1.9–10 [10 December 1938]: 12). According to Lu Yi (interview, 16 November, 10 December 1989, Shanghai), journalists frequently carried newspapers and other reading materials to the front during the war.

8. In 1921, there were 550 daily newspapers in China (not including local papers); in 1926, 628; in 1937, 1,031; and in 1948, 1,372 (see *China Handbook, 1937–1945*, comp. Chinese Ministry of Information [New York: Macmillan, 1947], p. 506; and *China Handbook, 1950*, comp. China Handbook Editorial Board [New York: Rockport Press, 1950], p. 678).

9. See *YZF* 108 (1 November 1940): 381, and 110 (1 December 1940): 459.

10. Liu Zhuzhou, "Zenyang zuo zhandi jizhe," *Xinwen zhanxian* 2.2–3 (16 May 1942): 16.

11. Zhao Junhao, *Shanghai baoren de fendou* (N.p.: Erya shudian, 1944), esp. chaps. 2 and 3.

12. Zigang, "Yanhuo zhong de Hanyang," *DGB* (Hankou), 12 August 1938, p. 2.

13. Cao Juren, "Zhandi guilai," in Tian Han et al., *Zhandi guilai* (Shanghai: Zhandi chubanshe, 1937), pp. 16–17.

14. Changjiang, ed., *Huaihe dazhan zhi qianhou* (N.p.: Jiangsheng shushe, 1938), pp. 62–64.

15. Changjiang, *Zhongguo de xibei jiao* (Tianjin: Dagong bao, 1937), pp. 307–308.

16. On the popularity of the book, see Zhou Fei, "Zhongguo de xibei jiao," *Guowen zhoubao* 13.39 (5 October 1936): 41–43; *YZF* 64 (21 March 1938): 153–154; and Kong Xiaoning, "Fan Changjiang xinwen de tese," *XWYJZL* 23 (January 1984): 2. Fan's book was even used as a reference text in university geography courses; see *XWYJZL* 1 (August 1979): 89–91, esp. p. 91.

17. Ironically, Fan Changjiang did not set out to be a journalist. Born into a declining gentry family in Neijiang county, Sichuan province, Fan (whose original name was Fan Xitian), overwhelmed by the revolutionary tide in the early Republican period, became a student activist in his youth. Forced to leave Chengdu in 1927 after participating in student demonstrations against Sichuan warlords, he joined the army in Wuhan. In 1928, Fan attended Nanjing's Central Political Institute, a GMD-sponsored academy. Disappointed with the GMD's passive policy against the Japanese, he left in 1931 for Beiping (Beijing). In the fall of 1932 he entered National Beijing University as a student of philosophy. To help pay his tuition, he began to freelance for Beijing's *Chen bao* and Tianjin's *Yishi bao*, writing mostly on cultural and educational affairs. In 1934 he became a regular reporter for the *Dagong bao*. Fan returned home to Sichuan during the summer of 1935. He wrote to Hu Zhengzhi, manager of the *Dagong bao*, saying that after visiting his hometown he would like to travel to western Sichuan and write reports about his trips. Hu concurred. Thus began Fan's famous trip to the northwest. For a biography of Fan's life, see Fang Meng, *Fan Changjiang zhuan* (Beijing: Zhongguo xinwen chubanshe, 1989); see also *XWYJZL* 1 (August 1979): 72–110 (a special issue on Fan Changjiang); and *XWYJZL* 11 (May 1982): 74–78. For a discussion of Fan's journalistic style, see Chang-tai Hung, "Paper Bullets: Fan Changjiang and New Journalism in Wartime China," *Modern China* 17.4 (October 1991): 427–468.

18. Other books about the frontiers included Liu Wenhai, *Xixing jianwen ji* (Journeys to the west) (Shanghai: Nanjing shudian, 1933);

Chen Yan, *Shaan-Gan diaocha ji* (Survey of Shaanxi and Gansu provinces), 2 vols. (Beiping: Beifang zazhishe, 1936–1937); and Chen Gengya, *Xibei shicha ji* (A tour of the northwest) (Shanghai: Shen bao, 1936). Chen Gengya's trips might have been prompted by Fan's highly rated reports. As a reporter for Shanghai's *Shen bao*, the *Dagong bao*'s main competitor, Chen was specially assigned to cover the border regions. His works were less successful than Fan's, however. See Xu Zhucheng, *Zhadan yu shuiguo* (Hong Kong: Sanlian shudian, 1983), p. 208.

19. Israel Epstein, *The Unfinished Revolution in China* (Boston: Little, Brown, 1947), p. 147.

20. Fan Changjiang, "Shaanbei zhi xing," in *Saishang xing* (Tianjin: Dagong bao, 1937), pp. 311–338. Fan was the first Chinese reporter to visit Yan'an (see ibid., p. 330). The first reporter ever to visit the Red capital, of course, was Edgar Snow, who went to the blockaded Red area in June 1936, staying there for four months. See Snow, *Red Star over China.*

21. With the exception of *Huaihe dazhan zhi qianhou,* most of these books—which also included reports by fellow correspondents such as Qiujiang (Meng Qiujiang) and Xu Ying—were edited by Fan.

22. Many Chinese reporters lost their lives during the war. See *XWJZ* 1.6–7 (10 October 1938): 21; and Zeng Xubai, ed., *Zhongguo xinwen shi* 2:418–419.

23. Qiujiang, "Nankou yuhui xian shang," *DGB* (Hankou), 3–4 October 1937. The article also appears in Changjiang, ed., *Xixian fengyun* (Shanghai: Dagong bao, 1937), pp. 55–68.

24. It is interesting to compare the writing of Fan Changjiang with that of Ernie Pyle (1900–1945), widely acclaimed as America's greatest war correspondent during the Second World War. See my article "Paper Bullets," esp. p. 462, n. 9.

25. Chen Jiying, *Hu Zhengzhi yu Dagong bao,* p. 287.

26. Changjiang, "Baoding qianfang" (At the Baoding front), in *Cong Lugouqiao dao Zhanghe* (Hankou: Shenghuo shudian, 1938), p. 30.

27. See, for example, Changjiang, ed., *Lunwang de Ping-Jin* (Hankou: Shenghuo shudian, 1938), 83–86, 110–114; and Changjiang, *Cong Lugouqiao dao Zhanghe,* pp. 22–24.

28. Changjiang, ed., *Huaihe dazhan zhi qianhou,* p. 12.

29. Ibid., pp. 9–10.

30. I am indebted to Lynn Hunt for this idea; see her *Politics, Culture, and Class in the French Revolution* (Berkeley and Los Angeles: University of California Press, 1984), esp. p. 24.

31. For the term "eight-legged news essay," see Liu Wenqu,

"Chuangzao xinwen xiezuo de xinxing," *Xinwen zhanxian* 2.2–3 (16 May 1942): 24–25.

32. See *Zhanshi xinwen gongzuo rumen* (N.p.: Shenghuo shudian, 1940), pp. 72, 112, 200, 257.

33. For Fan Changjiang's pieces, see Changjiang, "Diao Datong," in Changjiang et al., *Xixian xuezhan ji* (N.p.: Zhanshi chubanshe, n.d.), pp. 38–45; and "Yi ye zhanchang," in Tian Han et al., *Zhandi guilai*, pp. 35–42. For Qiujiang, see "Nankou yuhui xian shang"; and "Ketong de Zhangjiakou," in Changjiang, ed., *Xixian fengyun*, pp. 23–42.

34. Gao Tian, "Pubian jianli 'wenhua bingzhan,'" p. 12.

35. See *XWJZ* 2.7 (1 June 1940): 5.

36. Cheng Shewo, "'Zhidan' yi ke jiandi," 13 May 1938, p. 3.

37. Shi Yan, "Xinwen gongzuo de zhuanxingqi," *XWJZ* 1.9–10 (10 December 1938): 6.

38. Changjiang, "Zenyang fa zhanshi dianxun yu xie zhandi tongxun," p. 6.

39. See *Zhanshi xinwen gongzuo rumen*; Bu Shaofu, *Zhandi jizhe jianghua*; and Liu Zhuzhou, "Zenyang zuo zhandi jizhe."

40. See Lu Yi, "Tan dangqian de zhandi xinwen gongzuo," *XWJZ* 1.6–7 (10 October 1938): 17.

41. Lu Yi, "Ji Zhongguo qingnian jizhe xuehui de chengli dahui." See also *XWJZ* 1.2 (1 May 1938): 23–24; and a special issue on the Young Journalists Society, *XWYJZL* 7 (December 1981): 26–75.

42. See Fan Changjiang, *Tongxun yu lunwen*, pp. 263–273.

43. *Zhanshi xinwen gongzuo rumen*, esp. sec. 2. The majority of the articles in this book appeared first in the *Reporter*.

44. Qiujiang, "Zenyang zuo zhandi xinwen jizhe," *XWJZ* 1.6–7 (10 October 1938): 20.

45. Changjiang, "Jianli xinwen jizhe de zhengque zuofeng."

46. Changjiang, "Yige xinwen jizhe de renshi," in Qian, Hu, and Zhang, eds., *Kangzhan de jingyan yu jiaoxun*, p. 85.

47. See Feng Yingzi, "Huiyi Changjiang," *XWYJZL* 28 (December 1984): 150; interview with Lu Yi, 16 November, 10 December 1989, Shanghai.

48. See, for example, Changjiang, *Zhongguo de xibei jiao*, pp. 16–17, 64–65, 100–101, 134, 137–138, 252–253.

49. For example, when he wrote about his visit to the town of Wanping in July 1937, he gave the reader a feeling of the past by invoking the legend of the nearby Marco Polo Bridge. See Fan Changjiang (Changjiang), *Tongxun yu lunwen*, p. 8.

50. Bu Shaofu, *Zhandi jizhe jianghua*, pp. 114–118.

51. Changjiang, "Lugouqiao pan," *DGB* (Tianjin), 23 July 1937, p. 3.

52. Changjiang, *Xixian fengyun*, p. 1.

53. Zhang Youluan, *Zhanshi xinwenzhi* (Chongqing: Zhongshan wenhua jiaoyuguan, 1938), p. 19.

54. Xie Liuyi, "Zhanshi de xinwen jizai," *Kangzhan* 5 (3 September 1937): 10.

55. Shi Yan, "Litihua de zhandi caifang," *XWJZ* 1.6–7 (10 October 1938): 14–15.

56. Liu Zhuzhou, "Zeyang zuo zhandi jizhe," p. 19.

57. Gao Tian, "Zhandi tongxun de xin dongxiang," *XWJZ* 1.6–7 (10 October 1938): 16.

58. Liu Zunqi, "Zhandi jizhe de yixie yinxiang," in Qian, Hu, and Zhang, eds., *Kangzhan de jingyan yu jiaoxun*, p. 21.

59. Changjiang, "Jianli xinwen jizhe de zhengque zuofeng."

60. Xubai (Zeng Xubai), "Wenxue zuopin yu xinwen zuopin," *XWJZ* 1.1 (1 April 1938): 9.

61. Interview with Lu Yi, 16 November, 10 December 1989, Shanghai.

62. Changjiang, "Zhanshi xinwen gongzuo de zhenyi."

63. Walter Lippmann's advice, as quoted in David S. Broder, *Behind the Front Page* (New York: Simon & Schuster, 1987), p. 356. See also the discussion in Lippmann's *Public Opinion* (New York: Harcourt, Brace, 1922).

64. Zhang Jiluan, "Xinwen jizhe genben de genben," in *Baoren zhi lu*, ed. Wang Wenbin (Shanghai: Sanjiang shudian, 1938), pp. 6–7.

65. Chen Bosheng, "Zuo xinwen jizhe de jige yuanze," *XWJZ* 1.1 (1 April 1938): 6.

66. Hu Zhengzhi, "Xinwen jizhe zui xuyao you zerenxin," in Wang Wenbin, ed., *Baoren zhi lu*, pp. 8–11.

67. Changjiang, "Diao Datong," p. 44.

68. See Changjiang et al., *Xixian xuezhan ji*, pp. 22–30.

69. See Qiujiang, "Tuishou Yanmenguan," *DGB* (Hankou), 30 September 1937, p. 2. See also Changjiang et al., *Xixian xuezhan ji*, p. 51. Liu Ruming gave a different version of the incident in his memoirs, accusing Fan Changjiang of "sowing discord" among Guomindang troops; see *Liu Ruming huiyilu* (Taibei: Zhuanji wenxue chubanshe, 1966), pp. 115–116.

70. Changjiang, *Zhongguo de xibei jiao*, p. 5.

71. Changjiang, ed., *Huaihe dazhan zhi qianhou*, pp. 54, 82–84.

72. See Theodore H. White and Annalee Jacoby, *Thunder Out of China* (New York: William Sloane, 1961). For an account of American journalism in China in the 1930s and 1940s, see Stephen R. MacKinnon and Oris Friesen, *China Reporting: An Oral History of American Journalism in the 1930s and 1940s* (Berkeley and Los Angeles: University of California Press, 1987).

73. Xiao Fang, "Baoding yi nan," in Changjiang, ed., *Cong Lugou-qiao dao Zhanghe*, p. 65.

74. Qiujiang, "Ketong de Zhangjiakou," p. 42; also idem, "Dazhan Pingxingguan," *DGB* (Hankou), 7 October 1937, p. 2.

75. Changjiang, "Yi ye zhanchang," p. 40.

76. Qiujiang, "Tuishou Yanmenguan," 2 October 1937, p. 2.

77. Changjiang, "Yi ye zhanchang," p. 40.

78. Agnes Smedley, for example, was highly critical of the government's medical service, calling it "negligent" and "careless." See *XWJZ* 1.5 (1 August 1938): 23; and Smedley, *Battle Hymn of China*. See also Mowrer, *Dragon Wakes*, chap. 6.

79. Changjiang, ed., *Xixian fengyun*, pp. 93, 96.

80. See Shi Yan, "Litihua de zhandi caifang," p. 14.

81. Xiao Fang, "Baoding yi nan," pp. 62–63.

82. Xiao Fang, "Cong Niangziguan dao Yanmenguan," in Changjiang, ed., *Xixian xuezhan ji*, p. 47; see also Changjiang, ed., *Huaihe dazhan zhi qianhou*, p. 9.

83. Changjiang, ed., *Xixian fengyun*, p. 76.

84. Changjiang, "Zhanshi xinwen gongzuo de zhenyi."

85. Li Mo et al., "Guomindang fandongpai chajin baokan mulu," in *Zhongguo xiandai chuban shiliao*, ed. Zhang Jinglu, vols. 3–4 (Beijing: Zhonghua shuju, 1956–1959), 4:153–176. See Ting, *Government Control of the Press*, pp. 18–19 and chap. 6.

86. See Fan Changjiang, *Tongxun yu lunwen*, p. 32.

87. See Changjiang, ed., *Xixian fengyun*, p. 76.

88. Ibid., pp. 2, 6.

89. See Zhang Jiluan, *Jiluan wencun* (Tianjin: Dagong bao, 1947), esp. 2:77–79, 82–85, 175–178.

90. See Fang Meng, *Fan Changjiang zhuan*, pp. 207–212; also Chen Jiying, *Hu Zhengzhi yu Dagong bao*, pp. 300–312.

91. Fan may even have developed a personal conflict with Wang Yunsheng (1901–1980), an editor well known for his multivolume work on the history of Sino-Japanese relations. See Cao Juren, *Caifang waiji* (Hong Kong: Chuangken chubanshe, 1955), pp. 79–80.

92. Changjiang, "Dao Jiluan xiansheng," *Huashang bao*, 8 September 1941, p. 3.

93. See Changjiang, "Zenyang xue zuo xinwen jizhe" (How to learn to be a reporter), in *Tongxun yu lunwen*, p. 214.

94. Ibid., p. 290.

95. Fang Meng, *Fan Changjiang zhuan*, p. 258; interview with Fang Meng, 8 October 1989, Beijing.

96. Cheng Shewo, "Wo suo lixiang de xinwen jiaoyu," *Baoxue jikan* 1.3 (29 March 1935): 112.

97. Wilbur Schramm, *Mass Media and National Development:*

The Role of Information in the Developing Countries (Stanford: Stanford University Press, 1964); Herbert Passin, "Writer and Journalist in the Transitional Society," in *Communications and Political Development*, ed. Lucian W. Pye (Princeton: Princeton University Press, 1963).

98. Rudolf Löwenthal, "Public Communications in China," p. 57.

99. Rudolf Löwenthal, "The Tientsin Press: A Technical Survey," *Chinese Social and Political Science Review* 19.4 (January 1936): 557.

100. Vernon Nash and Rudolf Löwenthal, "Responsible Factors in Chinese Journalism," *Chinese Social and Political Science Review* 20.3 (October 1936): 423.

101. See the discussion in Schramm, *Mass Media and National Development*, esp. chap. 3.

102. Hong Shen, "Xinwen dianying yu baozhi," *Baoxue jikan* 1.2 (1 January 1935): 24.

103. *Baoxue jikan* 1.2 (1 January 1935): 57–93.

104. Chen Qiancun, "Bianjiang neidi yu dushi de xinwen xiezuo," *Baoxue jikan* 1.1 (10 October 1934): 78–79.

105. Tang Ren'an, "Difang baozhi," *Baoxue jikan* 1.1 (10 October 1934): 36.

106. The popularization of the press was a major concern of journalists during the war; see discussion in Zeng Xubai, ed., *Zhongguo xinwen shi* 1:416.

107. Cheng Shewo, "Wo suo lixiang de xinwen jiaoyu," p. 111.

108. See Cheng's own biographical sketches in his *Baoxue zazhu* (Taibei: Zhongyang wenwu gongyingshe, 1956), pp. 118–159. For a solid account of Cheng's life, see Cheng Cangbo, "Zhongguo ziyoushi shang yiwei duli de jizhe—Cheng Shewo xiansheng," *Baoxue* 2.1 (June 1957): 6–8. *People's Livelihood News* was closed down by Wang Jingwei in 1934 for printing highly critical articles about the Executive Yuan, of which Wang was the president. Cheng was incarcerated for some forty days.

109. Cheng Shewo, "Wo suo lixiang de xinwen jiaoyu," p. 111.

110. See *China Handbook, 1950*, p. 680; also Rudolf Löwenthal, "Printing Paper: Its Supply and Demand in China," *Yenching Journal of Social Studies* 1.1 (June 1938): 107–121.

111. Cheng Shewo, "Zhongguo baozhi zhi jianglai," *Wenhua yuekan* 2 (March 1934): 77.

112. Ibid., p. 76.

113. Cheng Shewo, "Women xuyao 'pingjia bao,'" *Dongfang zazhi* 39.9 (15 July 1943): 24–27.

114. *Stand-up Journal* was not the first tabloid founded by Cheng Shewo. He had earlier started *People's Livelihood News*, but it was never as influential and popular as *Stand-up Journal*.

115. For a brief account of mosquito papers, see Yao Jiguang and

Yu Yifen, "Shanghai de xiaobao"; see also Perry Link, *Mandarin Ducks and Butterflies*, chap. 3.

116. Quoted in *Xinwen daxue* (Journalism university), 14 (August 1987): 64–66.

117. See, for example, Xiang Shiyuan, "Ruhe shi xinwen shiye zhenzheng minzhonghua," *Baoxue jikan* 1.3 (29 March 1935): 93–97.

118. Zou Taofen, "Benkan yu minzhong," in *Taofen wenji*, vol. 1 (Shanghai: Sanlian shudian, 1956), p. 6.

119. For a discussion of Zou's years as the editor of *Life Weekly*, see Margo S. Gewurtz, "Tsou T'ao-fen: The *Sheng-huo* Years, 1925–1933" (Ph.D. diss., Cornell University, 1972); for the circulation numbers of the weekly, see p. 40.

120. Zou Taofen, *Huannan yushengji* (Beijing: Sanlian shudian, 1980), p. 32.

121. Zou Taofen, "*Shenghuo ribao* de chuangban jingguo he fazhan jihua," in *Renmin de houshe* (Fuzhou: Fujian renmin chubanshe, 1980), p. 157.

122. Xie Liuyi, "Dazhongyu he baozhi," *Shehui yuebao* 1.5 (15 October 1934): 14–16.

123. Liu Shi, "Difang ribao qikan bianji yaodian shangque," *XWJZ* 1.2 (1 May 1938): 8–9. See also Shou Ming, ed., *Kangzhan gequji*, vol. 2 (Hankou: Shenghuo shudian, 1938), esp. Tian Han's preface.

124. Jiang Shuchen, "Li Furen," *Xinwenjie renwu* 8 (April 1987): 65. See also *JFRB*, 24 July 1946, pp. 1, 4.

125. See Li Furen, ed., *Laobaixing shelunji* (Xi'an: Laobaixing biankanshe, 1940), p. 5. I am indebted to Zhu Jiefan for providing me with this text.

126. *JFRB*, 24 July 1946, p. 1; Jiang Shuchen, "Li Furen," pp. 69, 73, 77, 104; interview with Zhu Jiefan, 5 September 1989, Taibei.

127. Quoted in Jiang Shuchen, "Li Furen," p. 77.

128. Ibid.

129. Ibid., p. 69.

130. See, for example, Zhao Junhao, *Shanghai baoren de fendou*.

131. Cheng Shewo, "'Zhidan' yi ke jiandi," 14 May 1938, p. 3.

132. Feng Yingzi, "Fuzhi difang xinwenzhi," *XWJZ* 1.4 (1 July 1938): 23–24; see also idem, "Jianli difang baozhi he dihou baozhi," *Minzu gonglun* 1.6 (20 February 1939): 118–123.

133. Liu Shi, "Difang ribao qikan bianji yaodian shangque."

134. Zai Mu, *Lun kangzhan qizhong de wenhua yundong* (Shanghai: Shenghuo shudian, 1937), pp. 51–52.

135. See Fan Changjiang, *Tongxun yu lunwen*, p. 226.

136. Changjiang, "Zenyang tuijin Guangxi difang xinwen gong-

zuo," *Jianshe yanjiu* 1.2 (15 April 1939): 33.

137. Ibid., pp. 33–34.

138. Fan Tong, "Nongcun tongxun de pinruo," *XWJZ* 2.10 (16 March 1941): 28–29.

139. See *XWYJZL* 28 (December 1984): 168. On the local press in Guangxi, see also *XWYJZL* 9 (November 1981): 177–201.

140. Zeng Xubai, ed., *Zhongguo xinwen shi* 1:407.

141. Ibid., p. 408.

142. Ibid.

143. Ibid. See also Changjiang, "Liangnian lai de xinwen shiye," *XWJZ* 2.2 (1 August 1939): 2.

144. Cheng Qiheng, *Zhanshi Zhongguo baoye* (Guilin: Mingzhen chubanshe, 1944), pp. 78, 81.

145. Ibid., pp. 63, 66.

146. Even a large local newspaper such as Nanning's *Guangxi Daily* had a circulation of less than 3,000; see *XWYJZL* 9 (November 1981): 178.

147. See Zeng Xubai, ed., *Zhongguo xinwen shi* 1:409.

148. Ibid., pp. 409–410.

149. Cheng Qiheng, *Zhansi Zhongguo baoye*, pp. 74–75. See also Zeng Xubai, ed., *Zhongguo xinwen shi* 1:411.

150. See Xia Yan, *Baitou jizhe hua dangnian* (Chongqing: Chongqing chubanshe, 1986), esp. sec. 1.

151. See *XWYJZL* 9 (November 1981): 177–201, and 21 (September 1983): 140–160. See also *Dazhong xinwen* (Public News) 1.9 (1 October 1948): 20. On the conflict between the GMD government and the provinces, see Eastman, *Seeds of Destruction*, esp. chap. 1.

152. See Cheng Qiheng, *Zhansi Zhongguo baoye*, p. 5.

153. See *XWJZ* 1.6–7 (10 October 1938): 24; *XWJZ* 1.8 (1 November 1938): 24; and Cheng Qiheng, *Zhansi Zhongguo baoye*, pp. 81, 95.

154. Cheng Qiheng, *Zhansi Zhongguo baoye*, pp..62, 107, 109. See also Su Xingzhi, "Kangzhan zhong de woguo baozhi," *Dafeng* 91 (5 June 1941): 3039–3041; and *Xinzhi banyuekan* 3.6 (25 January 1940): 35–37.

155. Changjiang, "Tuibu yu jinbu," *XWJZ* 2.10 (16 March 1941): 2.

5. NEW WINE IN OLD BOTTLES

1. "Zenyang bianzhi shibing tongsu duwu," *KZWY* 1.5 (21 May 1938): 34–36. The quotations that follow have been abridged from the same source.

2. See Lao She, "Guanyu Wenxie," *YZF* 73 (16 August 1938): 38–40, esp. p. 39.

3. See Lao She, "Wo zenyang xie tongsu wenyi," in *Lao She quyi wenxuan* (Beijing: Zhongguo quyi chubanshe, 1982), p. 33.

4. Lao Xiang, "Tongsu wenyi gailun," in Lao She et al., *Tongsu wenyi wujiang* (Chongqing: Zhonghua wenyijie kangdi xiehui, 1939), p. 3.

5. For a history of the Chinese folk literature movement, see Chang-tai Hung, *Going to the People*.

6. See Margaret Spufford, *Small Books and Pleasant Histories: Popular Fiction and Its Readership in Seventeenth-Century England* (Cambridge: Cambridge University Press, 1981); and Jeffrey Brooks, *When Russia Learned to Read: Literacy and Popular Literature, 1861–1917* (Princeton: Princeton University Press, 1985), esp. chap. 3.

7. Wang Pingling, "Tongsu wenxue zai shangdui," *Wenhua xianfeng* 1.14 (1 December 1942): 3.

8. Lao Xiang, "Tongsu wenyi de liliang," *Wenhua xianfeng* 1.14 (1 December 1942): 11.

9. Zheng Boqi, "Xin tongsu wenxue lun," *GM* 2.8 (25 March 1937): 1268; see also idem, "Shenme shi xin de tongsu wenxue," *Xin Zhonghua zazhi* 5.7 (10 April 1937): 90.

10. A Ying, "Shanghai shibian yu dazhong gequ," in *Xiandai Zhongguo wenxue lun*, ed. Qian Xingcun (Shanghai: Hezhong shudian, 1933), esp. pp. 145, 151, 159.

11. Gu Jiegang, "Women zenyang xiezuo tongsu duwu," *KZWY* 2.8 (29 October 1938): 116–117.

12. See Chang-tai Hung, *Going to the People*, esp. pp. 166–168.

13. Gu Jiegang, "Women zenyang xiezuo tongsu duwu," pp. 116–117.

14. Lao Xiang, "Tongsu wenyi de liliang."

15. Lao Xiang, "Tongsu wenyi gailun," pp. 3–4.

16. See Fang Bai, "Tongsu wenyi jiqiao tan," *KZWY* 4.2 (25 April 1939): 48–49.

17. Other wartime intellectuals agreed with them; see, for example, Wen Zongshan, "Tongsu wenyi yu tongsu xiju," *Wanxiang* 2.5 (1 November 1942): 135.

18. Lao Xiang, "Kangzhan sinian lai de minzhong duwu," *Wenyi yuekan* 11.7 (7 July 1941): 34–36.

19. Gu Jiegang, "Women zenyang xiezuo tongsu duwu," p. 117.

20. For a discussion of Lao She's works, see Ranbir Vohra, *Lao She and the Chinese Revolution* (Cambridge, Mass.: East Asian Research Center, Harvard University, 1974).

21. Tian Qin, *Zhongguo xiju yundong*, p. 59.

22. Lao She, "Xianhua wode qige huaju," *Kangzhan wenyi xuan-*

kan 1 (April 1946): 26.

23. See Li Ruiteng, ed., *Kangzhan wenxue gaishuo*, p. 99.

24. See Lao She's preface and epilogue in Lao She and Song Zhidi, *Guojia zhishang* (Shanghai: Xinfeng chuban gongsi, 1945).

25. See Li Ruiteng, ed., *Kangzhan wenxue gaishuo*, p. 59.

26. See discussion in James Sheridan, *Chinese Warlord: The Career of Feng Yu-hsiang* (Stanford: Stanford University Press, 1974), pp. 86–89.

27. During the war, Feng's poems appeared in a variety of magazines. See, for example, *Kangzhan sanrikan* 5 (3 September, 1937): 9; and *Dikang sanrikan* 13 (29 September 1937): 10. A collection of his wartime poems can be found in his *Feng Yuxiang kangzhan shige xuan* (Shanghai: Nuhou chubanshe, 1938). Feng wrote profusely during the war period. In *Kang-Ri de weida minzhong* (Guilin: Sanhu tushu yinshuashe, 1938), p. 1, he wrote: "In order for 'literature to go to the country' and 'literature to join the army,' we must take off our long gowns and mandarin jackets and change our clothes, so that we won't feel out of place with the villagers."

28. For Feng's financial contributions and support to the association, see, for example, *KZWY* 1.3 (10 May 1938): 23; 3.7 (28 January 1939): 112; 4.1 (10 April 1939): 2.

29. Feng Yuxiang helped to launch the magazine. He had close ties with the All-China Resistance Association of Writers and Artists. For details see Yu Zhigong, "Feng Yuxiang xiansheng yu wenyijie," *XWXSL* 19 (22 May 1983): 245–246.

30. Lao She, "Ru hui shici" (Inauguration oath), in *Lao She wenji* 14:114.

31. See Hu Jinquan, *Lao She he tade zuopin* (Hong Kong: Wenhua shenghuo chubanshe, 1977), p. 82.

32. Quoted in Wang Xianzhong, "Beijing Folk Customs in the Works of Lao She," *Chinese Literature*, Summer 1985, p. 202.

33. Lao She, "Tongsu wenyi de jiqiao," *KDD* 25 (1 August 1939): 2.

34. Ibid.

35. Ibid., p. 3.

36. Lao She, "Zhizuo tongsu wenyi de kutong," *KZWY* 2.6 (15 October 1938): 90.

37. Ibid., pp. 91–92 (paraphrased and abridged).

38. For Liu Fu's interest in dialect literature, see Chang-tai Hung, *Going to the People*, pp. 62–64. For a discussion of Qu Qiubai's ideas, see Paul G. Pickowicz, *Marxist Literary Thought in China: The Influence of Ch'ü Ch'iu-pai* (Berkeley and Los Angeles: University of California Press, 1981), chap. 9.

39. See Lao She, *Lao She quyi wenxuan*, p. 44.

40. Lao She, "Tongsu wenyi de jiqiao," pp. 4–5.

41. He Rong, "Tongsu yunwen qianshuo," in Lao She et al., *Tongsu wenyi wujiang*, pp. 59–86.

42. See Lao She, *Lao She quyi wenxuan*, pp. 175–176.

43. Lao She, "Duo xi duo xie," *Wenhua xianfeng* 1.14 (1 December 1942): 9.

44. For Lao She's close friendship with the Potato and Big Blossom, see the preface by Hu Xieqing (Lao She's wife) to the Chinese retranslated edition of *Gushu yiren* (Beijing: Renmin wenxue chubanshe, 1980). The original English version was translated from the Chinese by Helena Kuo and published in 1952 by Harcourt, Brace. In the absence of a Chinese original, this English version was translated back into Chinese for publication in 1980. For his ties with Bai Yunpeng, see Lao She, *Lao She quyi wenxuan*, p. 33.

45. Lao She, Preface to *San si yi* (N.p.: Duli chubanshe, 1939).

46. Lao She, "Wang Xiao gan lü," *Wenyi zhendi* 1.3 (16 May 1938): 77.

47. For additional comments, see Mu Mutian, "Wenyi dazhonghua yu tongsu wenyi," *Wenyi zhendi* 2.8 (1 February 1939): 642. Lao She seemed to prefer this piece over any of his other drum songs; see his preface to *San si yi*.

48. Lao She, "Nü'er jing," p. 55.

49. Lao She, "Da ke wen—wenyi zuojia yu kangzhan," *Yuzhou feng yikan* 2 (16 March 1939): 55.

50. For a brief autobiographical account of Lao Xiang, see *YZF* 3 (16 October 1935): 160–161; 4 (1 November 1935): 201; 5 (16 November 1935): 244–245.

51. Lao Xiang, "Xiandai jiaoyu babi," *LY* 62 (1 April 1935): 683.

52. Sun Fuyuan, Preface to Lao Xiang, *Huangtu ni* (Shanghai: Renjian shuwu, 1936), esp. p. 1.

53. Qu Junong, "Miaoxie nongcun shenghuo de wenzhang," *YZF* 40 (1 May 1937): 168.

54. See *YZF* 46 (1 August 1937): 455–457.

55. See *Renjian shi* 27 (5 May 1935): 5, and 34 (20 August 1935): 8–11.

56. Lao Xiang, "Kangzhan sinian lai de minzhong duwu," p. 34.

57. See "Fakan ci" (editor's opening statement), *KDD* 1 (1 January 1938): 1.

58. Ibid.

59. See Yu Zhigong, "Feng Yuxiang xiansheng yu wenyijie," pp. 245–246; and Ye Qianyu, *Hua yu lun hua*, p. 176.

60. See, for example, Lao Xiang's work in *YZF* 68 (16 May 1938): 114–115; also *KZWY* 1.10 (25 June 1938); and *KDD* 7 (1 April 1938): 12–13.

61. Lao Xiang, "Mu hanyi," *YZF* 109 (16 November 1940): 416.

62. For "Xiao yanzi," see Lao Xiang, "Kangzhan geyao," *YZF* 78 (16 May 1939): 268.

63. Lao Xiang, "Guanyu *Kang-Ri sanzi jing*," *KZWY* 1.7 (5 June 1938): 19. For a discussion of these classics, see Evelyn S. Rawski, *Education and Popular Literacy in Ch'ing China* (Ann Arbor: University of Michigan Press, 1979), esp. chap. 2.

64. Lao Xiang, "Guanyu *Kang-Ri sanzi jing*."

65. See *San Tzu Ching: Elementary Chinese*, trans. and annot. Herbert A. Giles (reprinted Taibei: Literature House, 1964), pp. 1–5.

66. Lao Xiang, "Kang-Ri sanzi jing," *KDD* 5 (1 March 1938): 2.

67. Lao Xiang, "Guanyu *Kang-Ri sanzi jing*." See also the advertisement, *KDD* 8 (16 April 1938): 22. Lao Xiang later rewrote the text and changed it to *Anti-Japanese Four-Character Classic* at the suggestion of Zhang Daofan (1896–1968), director of the GMD Central Propaganda Bureau. Zhang thought that "those with less education will find the four-character couplet format easier to read." See Lao Xiang, Preface to *Kang-Ri qianzi wen, sizi jing* (N.p.: Zhengzhong shuju, 1938).

68. Sha Yan, "Ping *Kang-Ri sanzi jing*," *KDD* 11 (1 June 1938): 19–20.

69. See Xiang Da et al., eds., *Taiping Tianguo* (The Heavenly Kingdom of Great Peace) (Beijing: Shenzhou guoguang she, 1953), 1:223–228.

70. See Evelyn S. Rawski, "Elementary Education in the Mission Enterprise," in *Christianity in China: Early Protestant Missionary Writings*, ed. Suzanne Wilson Barnett and John King Fairbank (Cambridge, Mass.: Committee on American–East Asian Relations of the Department of History in collaboration with the Council on East Asian Studies, Harvard University, 1985), pp. 146–151.

71. Lao Xiang, "Kang-Ri qianzi wen," *KDD* 20 (16 January 1939): 7–9.

72. Liu E, *Lao Can youji* (The travels of Lao Can) (Beijing: Renmin wenxue chubanshe, 1983), pp. 14–18; English translation by Harold Shadick, *The Travels of Lao Ts'an* (Ithaca: Cornell University Press, 1952), pp. 23–26 (paraphrased).

73. The exact origin of drum singing is still a matter of great dispute among scholars. According to Li Jiarui, for example, drum singing began in the Qianlong era (1736–1795). Zhao Jingsheng, however, believed drum singing was a more recent phenomenon, starting only in the Tongzhi period (1862–1874). See Li Jiarui, *Beiping suqu lüe* (Beiping: Lishi yuyan yanjiusuo, Academia Sinica, 1933), p. 4; idem, "Tan dagushu de qiyuan," *Renjian shi* 31 (5 July 1935): 24; and Zhao Jingshen, "Shuo dagu," *Renjian shi* 21 (5 February 1935): 20.

74. See Li Jiarui, *Beiping suqu lüe*, p. 6. In "Peking Drumsinging"

(Ph.D. diss., Harvard University, 1973), p. 137, Catherine Stevens points out that "there are ordinarily four musical instruments used in performing a Beijing Drumsong. There are two percussion instruments, the clapper and the drum, which are played by the singer. The two stringed instruments, the three-stringed guitar and the four-stringed fiddle, are played by two accompanists." For the life of a female Beijing drum singer, see Zhang Cuifeng, *Dagu shengya de huiyi* (Taibei: Zhuanji wenxue chubanshe, 1967); translated into English as "My Life as a Drum Singer" by Rulan Chao Pian, *CHINOPERL Papers* 13 (1984–1985): 12–99. Zhang was a gifted disciple of master Beijing drum singer Liu Baoquan.

75. See Zhang Cuifeng, *Dagu shengya de huiyi*, pp. 21, 29, 123–202; see also report in *Dagong bao* (Tianjin), 11 June 1937, p. 15.

76. Another drum song advocate was Mu Mutian (1900–1971), a member of ACRAWA and a former associate of the Creation Society. See Mu Mutian, *Kangzhan daguci* (Hankou: Xinzhi shudian, 1938). See also *KDD* 5 (1 March 1938): 8–11.

77. Zhao Jingshen, "Juyongguan," *JWRB*, 12 October 1937, p. 4; and idem, "Pingxingguan," *JWRB*, 14 October 1937, p. 4.

78. Zhao Jingshen, "Pingxingguan."

79. Lao Xiang, "Lunan dasheng," *YZF* 68 (16 May 1938): 114. It is said that Lao Xiang's praise of General Li Zongren incurred the wrath of General Chen Cheng, Li's rival and one of Generalissimo Jiang Jieshi's most trusted subordinates. According to Chen, Lao Xiang's piece was tantamount to propaganda for an individual general. See Guo Moruo, *Hongbo qu*, pp. 56–57.

80. See Chang-tai Hung, *Going to the People*, pp. 86, 123, 131.

81. Zhao's drum songs appeared mostly in *National Salvation Daily* in 1937. They later were published as *Zhanshi daguci* (N.p.: Zhanshi chubanshe, 1938). For the piece on Yan Haiwen, see pp. 4–7 in *Zhanshi daguci*.

82. Zhao, Preface to *Zhanshi daguci*, p. 1.

83. See Bo Han, "Shangbing daoqing," *Quanmin zhoukan* 1.11 (19 February 1938): 174; Huo Gong, "Kangdi *zhuzhici*," *Kangdi zhoubao* 1 (18 September 1937): 5; and Hong Shen, *Kangzhan shinian lai*, p. 24.

84. Zhou Wen, "Gaibian min'ge de yidian yijian," *KZWY* 3.8 (4 February 1939): 126.

85. Chen Yiyuan, "Kang-Ri shan'ge," *Quanmin zhoukan* 1.13 (5 March 1938): 196.

86. Ouyang Yuqian, "Shan'ge," *JWRB*, 10 October 1937, n.p.

87. Bao Tianxiao, "Ba yue shisan," *JWRB*, 15 October 1937, p. 4.

88. "Shisan yue," in *Kang-Ri Shibeicha* (Wuchang: Tongsu duwu biankanshe, 1938), p. 2.

89. Ibid., pp. 3, 4–5.

90. Mai Dong, "Taiyuan de jiuwang shuci yundong," *Shen bao zhoukan* 2.25 (27 June 1937): 564.

91. Ibid.

92. See, for example, *Wenyi zhendi* 1.4 (1 June 1938): 107–108.

93. See "Huiwu baogao" (Association reports), *KZWY* 1.9 (18 June 1938): 112; 1.11 (2 July 1938): 144; 2.10 (12 November 1938): 160; 4.1 (10 April 1939): 2–3. The total income from membership fees amounted to about 300 *yuan* between March 1938 and March 1939 (see *KZWY* 4.1 [10 April 1939]: 2). These reports were written mostly by Lao She.

94. Lao Xiang, "Kangzhan sinian lai de minzhong duwu," p. 34.

95. For a list of titles, see *Fanjian ji* (N.p.: Junshi weiyuanhui houfang qinwubu zhengzhibu, 1939), inside cover page.

96. *Da xiao Riben* (N.p.: Rongyu junren zhiye xunliansuo, n.d.), pp. 1–2 (abridged).

97. See Eastman, "Nationalist China During the Sino-Japanese War, 1937–1945," p. 603.

98. See Chen Lifu, *Zhanshi jiaoyu fangzhen* (N.p.: Zhongyang xunliantuan junshizhengzhibu jiaoguan yanjiuban, 1939), pp. 11–14; see also idem, *Four Years of Chinese Education (1937–1941)* (Chungking: China Information Committee, 1944), p. 17.

99. See John Israel, "Chungking and Kunming," p. 357.

100. Interview with Ye Qianyu, 27 September 1989, Beijing.

101. Liu Xinhuang, *Xiandai Zhongguo wenxue shihua* (Taibei: Zhengzhong shuju, 1971), p. 755.

102. Bao Tianxiao, "Wenhuajie de xijidui—xiao cezi," *JWRB*, 17 October 1937, p. 4. Bao published quite a few patriotic articles during this period. See, for example, *JWRB*, 15 October 1937, p. 4; 29 October 1937, p. 4.

103. See *KDD* 5 (1 March 1938): 30; Yu Zhigong, "Feng Yuxiang xiansheng yu wenyijie," pp. 245–246; Feng Yuxiang, *Kang-Ri de weida minzhong*. See also the book advertisement in *KDD* 10 (16 May 1938): 30.

104. See "Jieshao Tongsu duwu biankanshe jianshi ji gongzuo," *KZWY* 1.4 (14 May 1938): 32. According to this source, "over a million copies from the series were printed." I have no way of verifying the number, but I believe this is greatly exaggerated.

105. Li Ke, *Hao Mengling kangdi xunguo* (Wuchang: Tongsu duwu biankanshe, 1938).

106. Xi Zhengyong, *Ban Chao ding Xiyu* (Changsha: Zhonghua pingmin jiaoyu cujinhui, 1938), pp. 17–18.

107. See *DGB* (Hankou), 4 December 1937, p. 4; 6 December 1937, p. 4; *Kangzhan xiju* 1.1 (16 November 1937): 20. See also

Yang Cunbin, *Zhan'ge* (Changsha: Zhonghua pingmin jiaoyu cujinhui, 1937). For the NAAME's mass education activities during the war, see Charles W. Hayford, *To the People: James Yen and Village China* (New York: Columbia University Press, 1990), pp. 183–203.

108. Cao Bohan, *Xuanchuan jishu duben*, pp. 74–88.

109. Liu Qun, *Zhanshi de xuanchuan gongzuo* (Shanghai: Shenghuo shudian, 1937), pp. 26–28.

110. See *JWRB*, 1 February 1938, p. 2.

111. Cao Bohan, *Jietou bibao* (Shanghai: Shenghuo shudian, 1937), pp. 4, 16–19.

112. Lao Xiang, "Tongsu wenyi gailun," p. 10. See also He Rong, "Zenyang shi wenzhang xiaxiang," *KDD* 10 (16 May 1938): 18–19.

113. Lao Xiang, "Kangzhan sinian lai de minzhong duwu," p. 38.

114. Chen Yiyuan, "Wenzhang xiaxiang," *Quanmin kangzhan* 64 (10 April 1939): 909.

115. He Rong, "Zenyang shi wenzhang xiaxiang," p. 17.

116. Xiang Linbing produced a number of rather influential essays on the nature of popular literature. See, for example, "Kangzhan yilai tongsu wenyi yundong de fazhan yu quexian," *Dushu yuebao* 1.1 (1 February 1939): 6–8; and "Xian jieduan tongsu wenyi de quexian ji qi kefu," *KZWY* 4.4–5 (10 October 1939): 127–129.

117. Xiang Linbing, "Xian jieduan tongsu wenyi de quexian ji qi kefu"; and especially "Kangzhan yilai tongsu wenyi yundong de fazhan yu quexian," pp. 6–7.

118. See Mai Dong, "Taiyuan de jiuwang shuci yundong"; and *Wenyi zhendi* 1.4 (1 June 1938): 107–108. Both accounts describe the enthusiastic reception that peasants gave popular propaganda materials.

119. Liu Shi, "Dazhong wenhua yundong yu minzu jiefang," *Dushu shenghuo* 3.9 (10 March 1936): 392–393.

6. POPULAR CULTURE IN THE COMMUNIST AREAS

1. See *Shanxi wenyi shiliao*, vol. 2 (Taiyuan: Shanxi renmin chubanshe, 1959), p. 187.

2. See *ZGHJYD* 1:180–194, esp. pp. 183–184; also Akiyoshi Kukio, *Kōsei Soku bungaku undō shiryō shū* (Tokyo: Tōkyō daigaku Tōyō bunka kenkyūjo, 1976), pp. 141–155.

3. See Zuo Lai and Liang Huaqun, *Suqu "Hongse xiju" shihua* (Beijing: Wenhua yishu chubanshe, 1987), chap. 3, esp. p. 36. See also Holm, *Art and Ideology*, pp. 23–30.

4. Snow, *Red Star Over China*, pp. 100–105.

5. See *KRZZY* 1:456–457, 2:68, 89; and *ZGHJYD* 3:26, 73; and *Jin-Cha-Ji huabao* (Shanxi-Chahar-Hebei pictorial) 1 (7 July 1942): n.p.

6. *KRZZY* 1:229, 2:90, 3:116.

7. See *KRZZY* 3:66.

8. Zhang Geng, "Huiyi Yan'an Luyi de xiju huodong," in *KRZZY* 1:457.

9. See *KRZZY* 1:133.

10. Quoted in Stuart R. Schram, *The Political Thought of Mao Tse-tung*, rev. ed. (New York: Praeger, 1969), p. 316.

11. Zhang Geng, "Lun bianqu juyun he xiju de jishu jiaoyu," *JFRB*, 12 September 1942, p. 4.

12. For a list of dramas staged in Yan'an from 1938 to 1945, see *ZGHJYD* 3:211–218.

13. See *KRZZY* 2:115–124, esp. p. 124.

14. For a brief discussion of the Mao Zedong–Wang Ming conflict, see Van Slyke, "The Chinese Communist Movement During the Sino-Japanese War," pp. 615–619.

15. Mao Tse-tung, *Selected Works of Mao Tse-tung*, 4 vols. (Peking: Foreign Language Press, 1967), 2:209–210. I use Stuart Schram's translation, *The Political Thought of Mao Tse-tung*, pp. 172–173. In Mao's "Reform Our Study" (May 1941), he reiterated the same theme. See Mao, *Selected Works* 3:19–21.

16. Quoted in Stuart Schram, *Mao Tse-tung* (Harmondsworth, Eng.: Penguin Books, 1967), p. 201.

17. Libo (Zhou Libo), "Houhui yu qianzhan," *JFRB*, 3 April 1943, p. 4.

18. For the popularity of the Stanislavsky system in China, see, inter alia, *Juchang yishu* (Theater arts monthly), 2 (20 December 1938): 1–4; and *Xiju yu wenxue* (Drama and literature), 1.1 (25 January 1940): 131–146.

19. Zhang Geng, "Huiyi Yan'an Luyi," p. 458.

20. See "Art Chronicle" in *T'ien Hsia Monthly* 9.1 (August 1939): 85.

21. See *KRZZY* 1:445–450, 2:511.

22. See Ding Ling and Xi Ru, eds., *Xibei zhandi fuwutuan xiju ji* (Hankou: Shanghai zazhi gongsi, 1938).

23. Hou Weidong, "Ke Zhongping lingdao Bianqu minzhong jutuan," *XWXSL* 18 (22 February 1983): 146–151.

24. One of these was the Lu Xun Academy of Art and Literature in southeastern Shanxi (Lu Xun wenxue yishuyuan, est. 1939, with Li Bozhao [1911–1985] as its president). For others, see Ai Qing, "Jiefang qu de yishu jiaoyu," in *Zhonghua quanguo wenxue yishu gongzuozhe daibiao dahui jinian wenji* (N.p.: Xinhua shudian, 1950), pp. 235–238.

25. Sha Kefu, "Huabei nongcun xiju yundong he minjian yishu gaizao gongzuo," in ibid., p. 348.

26. Li Bozhao, "Dihou wenyi yundong gaikuang," in *KRZZY* 2:304.

27. Sha Kefu, "Huabei nongcun xiju yundong," p. 349.

28. Ibid.

29. See *KRZZY* 3:89.

30. Mao Zedong, "Talks at the Yan'an Forum on Literature and Art," in *Selected Works* 3:69–97, esp. p. 84.

31. See *ZGHJYD* 3:101.

32. The news of Mao's "Talks" reached northwestern Shanxi around June or July 1942. Not long after, the document itself was brought by dramatist Ouyang Shanzun (1914–); see *Shanxi wenyi shiliao*, pp. 8–9. It reached Shandong in early 1943; see *KRZZY* 3:166.

33. Ha Hua, *Yangge zatan* (Shanghai: Huadong renmin chubanshe, 1951), p. 27.

34. See, for example, Ai Siqi et al., *Yangge lunwen xuanji* (N.p.: Xinhua shudian, 1944); Zhou Erfu et al., *Yanggeju chuji* (Chongqing: Xinhua ribao, 1944); and Hu Sha, "Shaanbei yangge," *Beifang wenhua* 1.6 (16 May 1946): 28–31. For a detailed discussion in English, see Holm, *Art and Ideology*.

35. See Li Jinghan and Zhang Shiwen, eds., *Dingxian yangge xuan* (N.p.: Zhonghua pingmin jiaoyu cujinhui, 1933), esp. the Preface.

36. According to David Holm (*Art and Ideology*, p. 122), the Communists in the 1940s were familiar with the Dingxian *yangge* work, and "Dingxian was particularly significant because there was a direct link between the Dingxian project and the Jin-Cha-Ji [Border Region] cultural workers."

37. See Zhou Yang, Xiao San, and Ai Qing et al., *Minjian yishu he yiren* (Zhangjiakou: Xinhua shudian, 1946), pp. 1–10.

38. See Zhang Geng, "Huiyi Yan'an Luyi"; and idem, "Luyi gongzuotuan duiyu yangge de yixie jingyan," *Xiju yu yinyue* 1 (1 March 1946): 1; 2 (1 April 1946): 3–5.

39. Zhang Geng, "Huiyi Yan'an Luyi," p. 461.

40. See *Shanxi wenyi shiliao*, p. 99.

41. Zhang Geng, "Huiyi Yan'an Luyi," pp. 460–461.

42. It goes without saying that a *yangge* play can include more than one theme. For example, besides the idea of equality of the sexes, *Twelve Sickles* stresses the harmonious link between soldiers and the people. For a series of *yangge* plays, see Zhang Geng, ed., *Yanggeju xuan* (Beijing: Renmin wenxue chubanshe, 1977).

43. See *JFRB*, 19 March 1944, p. 4.

44. Quoted in Ai Siqi et al., *Yangge lunwen xuanji*, p. 15.

45. For a firsthand look at this troupe's work to spread new *yangge* plays throughout northern Shaanxi, see Zhang Geng, "Luyi gongzuotuan."

46. See *KRZZY* 3:266.

47. See *XYXSL* 4 (August 1979): 301.

48. The Folk Drama Study Association (Minjian xiju yanjiuhui) in northwestern Shanxi was one such example. See Li Bozhao, "Dihou wenyi yundong," p. 310.

49. See *KRZZY* 1:520–521.

50. See the discussion of Liu Zhiming, director of the Yan'an Beijing Opera Study Society, in *Bi shang Liangshan*, ed. Pingju yanjiuhui (N.p.: Xinhua shudian, 1945), pp. 94–95 (app.).

51. Li Lun, Wei Chenxu, Ren Guilin et al., *San da Zhujiazhuang* (Beijing: Zhongguo xiju chubanshe, 1957), pp. 206–208.

52. Gunther Stein, *The Challenge of Red China* (New York: Whittlesey House, 1945), pp. 219–220.

53. Jack Chen (Chen Yifan) visited the Shaan-Gan-Ning Border Region twice, in 1938 and again in 1947; interview with Jack Chen, 12 December 1987, 25 March 1988, El Cerrito, Calif. See also Jack Chen, "Folk Art and Drama in North-West China To-day," *Our Time*, May 1946, pp. 213–214.

54. Huang Yanpei, *Yan'an guilai*, in *Bashinian lai* (Beijing: Wenshi ziliao chubanshe, 1982), p. 144.

55. Huang Fengzhou, "Huiyi 'Nong jian suo,'" *Meishu* 5 (25 September 1977): 10–11. See also *Meishu* 5 (25 September 1977): 11–13.

56. Mao, *Selected Works* 1:48.

57. See *Meishu yanjiu* 12 (15 November 1959): 62–64.

58. See *XWYJZL* 18 (March 1983): 153–164.

59. See, for example, *JWRB*, 10 October 1937, n.p.

60. See, for example, *JWRB*, 15 and 22 January 1938, p. 4 for both.

61. See, for example, *LY* 46 (1 August 1934): 1034, and 69 (1 August 1935): 1031; *YZF* 9 (16 January 1936): 456, and 43 (16 June 1937): 310.

62. Li Qun, Preface to *Jin-Sui jiefangqu muke xuan* (Chengdu: Sichuan renmin chubanshe, 1982). The other art subject offered at Luyi was making woodcuts.

63. See the brief report in *Huashang bao*, 21 May 1941, p. 3.

64. Interview with Hua Junwu, 23 September, 15 October 1989, Beijing.

65. See, for example, *JFRB*, 5 September 1942, p. 3; 18 September 1942, p. 2; 6 February 1943, p. 3.

66. Woodcuts appeared even earlier in *New China Daily*. Hu Kao's piece "Unite Together! Resist Till the End!" appeared in the inaugural issue of the newspaper on 11 January 1938, p. 1. At that time

woodcuts were printed regularly. See, for example, the issues of 12 and 13 January 1938, p. 1.

67. See *Jin-Cha-Ji huabao* 1 (7 July 1942) and 4 (20 September 1943).

68. Huang Yuanlin, "Kangzhan shiqi jiefangqu de manhua," *KZWYYJ* 13 (15 May 1984): 67.

69. See *JFRB*, 15 February 1942, p. 4.

70. Zhang E, "I am No. 6 in the World," *JFRB*, 6 April 1943, p. 4.

71. Jiang Feng, "Guanyu 'fengci huazhan,'" *JFRB*, 15 February 1942, p. 4.

72. Interview with Hua Junwu, 23 September, 15 October 1989, Beijing.

73. Mao, "Talk at the Yan'an Forum," in *Selected Works* 3:91.

74. Interview with Cai Ruohong, 29 September 1989, Beijing. Cai drew few cartoons after his meeting with Mao. Two examples may be found in *JFRB*, 6 February 1943, p. 3, and 18 August 1945, p. 4. Cai did not resume active cartooning until after the war. In 1948 he produced *Ku cong he lai* (Shanghai: Chenguang chuban gongsi, 1948), a series of cartoons on political dislocation and social ills under GMD rule.

75. Hua Junwu, "Xiangcha buduo," *JFRB*, 2 August 1943, p. 4.

76. See, for example, Fang Xiang, "Kangzhan, muke yu wo," in Li Ruiteng, ed., *Kangzhan wenxue gaishuo*, p. 205.

77. Xu Beihong, "Quanguo muke zhan," reprinted *JFRB*, 16 March 1943, p. 4.

78. Interview with Fang Xiang, 30 July 1990, Taibei. See also Fang Xiang, "Kangzhan, muke yu wo"; and idem, *Fang Xiang muke xuanji*, 2 vols. (Taibei: Gongtong yinshuachang, 1956).

79. For a history of Chinese engraving, see Zheng Zhenduo, *Zhongguo banhua shi tulu*, 20 vols. (Shanghai: Zhongguo banhuashi she, 1940–1947). On the Chinese woodcut movement, see Lu Di, ed., *Zhongguo xiandai banhua shi* (Beijing: Renmin meishu chubanshe, 1987).

80. Lu Xun's role in the Chinese woodcut movement was pivotal. On 8 October 1936, in his final days, the ailing writer attended the Second National Woodcut Exhibition in Shanghai. He died eleven days later. Materials on Lu Xun's role in promoting Chinese woodcut are numerous. See, for example, Chen Yanqiao, "Lu Xun xiansheng yu banhua," *GM* 1.12 (25 November 1936): 780–783; Li Hua, "Lu Xun xiansheng yu muke," *Minzhu shijie* 3.8 (1 November 1946): 23; and Shirley Sun's "Lu Hsun and the Chinese Woodcut Movement." The important volume *Kangzhan banian muke xuan* (Woodcuts of wartime China, 1937–1945), edited by the China Woodcut Associa-

tion and published in 1946 by Shanghai's Kaiming Bookstore, was dedicated to "the late Mr. Lu Hsun [Lu Xun]: the Arch-Sponsor of Woodcutting in China on the Occasion of the Tenth Anniversary of His Death."

81. Li Qun, "Xizhanchang shang de muke yundong," *Wenyi zhendi* 4.5 (1 January 1940): 1377; Lu Di, "Muke zai baozhi shang de zhendi," *XWYJZL* 10 (December 1981): 185–186. See also Akiyoshi Kukio, *Kahoku konkyochi no bungaku undō* (Tokyo: Hyōronsha, 1976), pp. 205–206.

82. Xu Beihong, "Quanguo muke zhan."

83. Hu Yichuan, "Huiyi Luyi muke gongzuotuan zai dihou," *Meishu* 5 (October 1961): 45–48.

84. Xu Baishi, "Tan muke," *Shen bao,* 2 December 1933, p. 21.

85. Quoted in Mina C. Klein and H. Arthur Klein, *Käthe Kollwitz: Life in Art* (New York: Schocken Books, 1975), p. 20.

86. Yu Da, "Cong qiangtou hua dao tu dianying," *Meishu* 11 (15 November 1958): 40.

87. See, for example, *JFRB,* 21 and 22 August 1943, p. 4 (both issues). See also Ji Zhi's discussion, "Guanyu 'muke manhua.'"

88. See, for example, *JFRB,* 21 August 1943, p. 4. Interviews with Gu Yuan, 6 October, 4 November 1989, Beijing; and with Zhang E, 30 September 1989, Beijing.

89. See Yang Han, ed., *Xinsijun meishu gongzuo huiyilu* (Shanghai: Shanghai renmin chubanshe, 1982), esp. pp. 63–66.

90. See *JFRB,* 17 October 1942, p. 4.

91. Gu Yuan used a similar technique in his "Duizhao zhi xia" (A comparison), *JFRB,* 17 July 1943, p. 4.

92. Li Qun, "Attending Winter School," in *Jin-Sui jiefangqu muke xuan,* p. 10.

93. Li Qun, "Delivering Public Grain," in ibid, p. 6.

94. See Hu Man, "Kangzhan banian lai jiefangqu de meishu yundong," *JFRB,* 19 June 1946, p. 4.

95. Interview with Gu Yuan, 6 October, 4 November 1989, Beijing; and letter from Gu Yuan to the author, 16 July 1990.

96. See Ai Qing, "Di yi ri," *JFRB,* 18 August 1941, p. 2.

97. See *Meishu yanjiu* 12 (15 November 1959): 49–58. For papercuts, see Gu Yuan, "Minjian jianzhi," *Beifang wenhua* 2.1 (1 June 1946): 44–45; Ai Qing and Jiang Feng, eds., *Xibei jianzhi ji* (Shanghai: Chenguang chubanshe, 1949).

98. Yang Han, ed., *Xinsijun meishu gongzuo huiyilu,* pp. 99–101, 137–139.

99. A Ying, *Zhongguo nianhua fazhan shilüe* (Beijing: Zhaohua meishu chubanshe, 1954), pp. 29–31. See also *JFRB,* 18 May 1945, p. 4.

100. See Huang Mao, *Manhua yishu jianghua*, p. 46; also *Meishu yanjiu* 12 (15 November 1959): 49–53, esp. p. 51.

101. Chang Zhiqing, "Zai *Jin-Sui ribao* de niandai li," in Zhang Jinglu, ed., *Zhongguo xiandai chuban shiliao* 4:206.

102. Liu Yunlai, "Huabei dihou geming baokan de chuangjian," *XWYJZL* 29 (February 1985): 95.

103. Lu Zipei, "Huazhong jiefangqu baozhi zazhi yilan," in Zhang Jinglu, ed., *Zhongguo xiandai chuban shiliao* 3:380.

104. Liu Yunlai, "Huabei dihou geming baokan de chuangjian," p. 95.

105. Lu Dingyi, "Tan Yan'an *Jiefang ribao* gaiban," *XWYJZL* 8 (November 1981): 1–8, esp. p. 6. See also Yang Fangzhi, "*Jiefang ribao* gaiban yu Yan'an zhengfeng," *XWYJZL* 18 (March 1983): 1–5, esp. pp. 2–4. The Guomindang news was given considerable attention. For example, on 12 February 1942 *Jiefang ribao* gave front page coverage to Generalissimo Jiang Jieshi's warm reception by the Indian people during a visit to that country.

106. See Liao Jingdan, "*Kangzhan ribao* de zhandou suiyue," *XWYJZL* 29 (February 1985): 61.

107. Mao Zedong, "Zai *Jiefang ribao* gaiban zuotanhui shang de jianghua," in *Mao Zedong xinwen gongzuo wenxuan* (Beijing: Xinhua chubanshe, 1983), pp. 90–91.

108. Quoted in Alex Inkeles, *Public Opinion in Soviet Russia: A Study in Mass Persuasion* (Cambridge, Mass.: Harvard University Press, 1950), p. 135. Lenin's famous saying was quoted in a *JFRB* editorial on 1 April 1942, front page.

109. See *XWYJZL* 22 (November 1983): 15.

110. Yang Fangzhi, "*Jiefang ribao* gaiban," p. 2.

111. Mao Zedong, "Zengqiang baokan xuanchuan de dangxing," in *Mao Zedong xinwen gongzuo wenxuan*, p. 96.

112. Telegram from Mao to Zhou Enlai, 14 March 1942; in *Mao Zedong xinwen gongzuo wenxuan*, p. 93.

113. Zhou Yang, "Yishu jiaoyu de gaizao wenti," in *KRZZY* 1:210.

114. See "Xibeiju guanyu *Jiefang ribao* jige wenti de tongzhi" (Circular of the Northwestern Bureau concerning issues related to *Liberation Daily*), *JFRB*, 30 March 1943, front page.

115. Chang Zhiqing, "Zai *Jin-Sui ribao* de niandai li," pp. 209, 212.

116. Mao Zedong, "Zenyang ban difang baozhi," in *Mao Zedong xinwen gongzuo wenxuan*, p. 120. See also Liao Jingdan, "*Kangzhan ribao* de zhandou suiyue," p. 62.

117. See Liao Mosha et al., *Yi Deng Tuo* (Fuzhou: Fujian renmin chubanshe, 1980), p. 19; also *Kang-Ri zhanzheng shiqi de Zhongguo*

xinwenjie, ed. Zhongguo shekeyuan xinwen yanjiusuo (Chongqing: Chongqing chubanshe, 1987), p. 145.

118. See Liao Mosha et al., *Yi Deng Tuo*, p. 81.

119. Ibid., pp. 75, 86, 89. See also *Kang-Ri zhanzheng shiqi de Zhongguo xinwenjie*, p. 145.

120. Ding Dong, "Bianqu ji jiefangqu de xiaoxingbao," *JFRB*, 17 May 1945, p. 4.

121. Hu Jiwei, "Ban yizhang renmin qunzhong xiwen-lejian de baozhi," *XWYJZL* 30 (April 1985): 4.

122. See, for example, *Bianqu qunzhong bao*, 5 March 1944, p. 1; 12 March 1944, p. 1; 16 April 1944, p. 1; 14 May 1944, p. 1. The paper also issued a series of booklets, including the highly popular *Ditties* (*Xiaoquzi*, 1944), a collection of sixteen songs.

123. See Ai Siqi et al., *Yangge lunwen xuanji*, p. 6.

124. François Furet, *Interpreting the French Revolution*, trans. Elborg Forster (Cambridge: Cambridge University Press, 1981), p. 48.

125. Mona Ozouf, *Festivals and the French Revolution*, trans. Alan Sheridan (Cambridge, Mass.: Harvard University Press, 1988).

126. J.G.A. Pocock, *Politics, Language, and Time: Essays on Political Thought and History* (New York: Atheneum, 1973), p. 22.

127. Liu Yunlai, "Huabei dihou geming baokan de chuangjian," pp. 97–98; *Kang-Ri zhanzheng shiqi de Zhongguo xinwenjie*, p. 267; *KRZZY* 2:49, 3:150–158; Zhang Jinglu, ed., *Zhongguo xiandai chuban shiliao* 3:382. These newspapers, of course, were not restricted to the Communist areas; Li Furen's *The Common Folk*, for instance, originated in Xi'an (see chap. 4).

128. Editor's notes; see *KRZZY* 1:544.

129. William Hinton, *Fanshen* (New York: Vintage Books, 1968), p. vii.

130. See, for example, *Jiangxi Suqu wenxueshi*, ed. Jiangxi shifan daxue zhongwenxi, Suqu wenxue yanjiushi (Nanchang: Jiangxi renmin chubanshe, 1984), pp. 63, 76, 94.

131. Robert Paine, "When Saying Is Doing," in *Politically Speaking: Cross-cultural Studies of Rhetoric*, ed. Robert Paine (Philadelphia: Institute for the Study of Human Issues, 1981), pp. 10–11.

132. Tian Jian, *Shici* (Shanghai: Xinwenyi chubanshe, 1953), sec. 9.

133. See *ZGHJYD* 3:123.

134. See *Zhonghua quanguo wenxue yishu gongzuozhe*, p. 504.

135. Zhao Shuli, *Zhao Shuli wenji*, vol. 1 (Beijing: Gongren chubanshe, 1980), pp. 195–210.

136. See *Xin minzhu zhuyi geming shiqi gongnongbing sanzi jing xuan*, ed. Zhongguo geming bowuguan bianxiezu (Beijing: Wenwu chubanshe, 1975), p. 14.

137. Ibid., pp. 24–27.

138. Han Qixiang, *Han Qixiang yu Shaanbei shuoshu*, ed. Shaanxi sheng quyi shouji zhengli bangongshi, Shaanxi sheng qunzhong yishuguan (N.p.: n.p., 1985), p. 83.

139. Tian Jian, "Tian Jian zishu," *XWXSL* 25 (22 November 1984): 109–110; 29 (22 November 1985): 120–121.

140. Tian Jian, "Yiyongjun," in *Shici*, p. 7.

141. Wen Yiduo, "Shidai de gushou—du Tian Jian de shi," in *Wen Yiduo quanji*, ed. Zhu Ziqing et al., vol. 3 (Hong Kong: Nam Tung Stationery, n.d.), pp. 233–238.

142. See *KRZZY* 3:237.

143. Tian Jian, "Tian Jian zishu," *XWXSL* 29 (22 November 1985): 120.

144. Ai Qing, "Zhankai jietoushi yundong," *JFRB*, 27 September 1942, p. 4.

145. See Chang-tai Hung, *Going to the People*, chap. 3.

146. Jia Zhi, "Lao Suqu de min'ge," *Minjian wenyi jikan* 1 (1950): 46–57. See also Liu Yun, "Hongjun de geyao," *Dafeng* 4 (5 April 1938): 106–109.

147. See *KRZZY* 2:181–182.

148. Li Ji, ed., *Shuntianyou er qian shou* (Shanghai: Shanghai zazhi gongsi, 1950), p. 263; and idem, "Wo shi zenyang xuexi min'ge de," in *Li Ji yanjiu zhuanji* (Fuzhou: Haixia wenyi chubanshe, 1985), p. 104.

149. The other two are *pashan'ge* (mountain climbing songs), popular in western Inner Mongolia, and *shanqu'er* (mountain melodies), popular in northwestern Shanxi. For a discussion of these songs, see Chen Ziai, "Woguo min'ge de tishi yu gelü," *Kanshou zhidao* 38 (1988): 33–36.

150. Guo Moruo, Preface to Li Ji, *Wang Gui yu Li Xiangxiang* (N.p.: Shenghuo, Dushu, Xinzhi, 1949), pp. ii–iii.

151. He Qifang, "Cong souji dao xieding," in *He Qifang wenji*, vol. 4 (Beijing: Renmin wenxue chubanshe, 1983), p. 148.

152. Ibid. See also the Preface to *Shaanbei min'ge xuan*, ed. Lu Xun wenyi xueyuan (N.p.: Xinhua shudian, 1949).

153. *Shaanbei min'ge xuan*, p. 1.

154. See, for example, Miao Peishi, ed., *Geyao congji* (N.p.: Taofan shudian, 1947), esp. appendix, "The People's Voice from the Guomindang-ruled Territories."

155. For a history of Chinese storytelling, see Jaroslav Průšek, "Urban Centers: The Cradle of Popular Fiction," in *Studies in Chinese Literary Genres*, ed. Cyril Birch (Berkeley and Los Angeles: University of California Press, 1974); V. Hrdličková, "The Chinese Storytellers and Singers of Ballads," *Transactions of the Asiatic Society of Japan*, 3d ser., 10 (August 1968): 97–115.

156. Zhou Erfu, "Postscript," in Han Qixiang, *Liu Qiao tuanyuan* (N.p.: Shenghuo, Dushu, Xinzhi, 1949), p. 142. Lin Shan, however, gave an earlier date, saying that the Yan'an county government began to discuss the importance of storytelling in July 1944; see Lin Shan, "Gaizao shuoshu," *JFRB*, 5 August 1945, p. 4.

157. Zhou Erfu, "Postscript," in Han Qixiang, *Liu Qiao tuanyuan*, p. 140.

158. Lin Shan, "Gaizao shuoshu."

159. Zhou Erfu, "Postscript," in Han Qixiang, *Liu Qiao tuanyuan*, p. 141. See also Lin Shan, "Gaizao shuoshu."

160. Zhou Erfu, "Postscript," in Han Qixiang, *Liu Qiao tuanyuan*, p. 144; Wang Lin, "Ji Han Qixiang shuoshu," *Beifang wenhua* 2.6 (16 August 1946): 52–53, 47. See also *JFRB*, 5 August 1945, p. 4. For Han's own account, see his autobiography, *Han Qixiang yu Shaanbei shuoshu*. For a full discussion of Han Qixiang and his work, see Chang-tai Hung, "Reeducating a Blind Storyteller: Han Qixiang and the Chinese Communist Storytelling Campaign," *Modern China* 19.4 (October 1993): 395–426.

161. Zhou Erfu, "Postscript," in Han Qixiang, *Liu Qiao tuanyuan*, pp. 144–146.

162. The 1949 version of the story is slightly different from the original one recorded in 1946. I followed the later version. See *Liu Qiao tuanyuan* (Shanghai: Shenghuo, Dushu, Xinzhi, 1949), p. 98.

163. Han Qixiang, *Zhang Yulan canjia xuanjuhui* (N.p.: Xinhua shudian, 1946), p. 50. This version is again slightly different from the original one (see *JFRB*, 28 November 1945, p. 4).

164. Han Qixiang, *Zhang Yulan canjia xuanjuhui*, pp. 20–21.

165. Han Qixiang and Wang Zongyuan, *Shishi zhuan* (N.p.: Xinhua shudian, 1946), esp. pp. 6–14, 17–21.

166. Lin Shan, "Gaizao shuoshu."

167. See *JFRB*, 7 August 1945, p. 4; 28 November 1945, p. 4; Lin Shan, "Gaizao shuoshu." See also Gao Minfu, Preface to Han Qixiang, *Liu Qiao tuanyuan* (N.p.: Xinhua shudian, 1946), pp. 4–9.

168. Ellen R. Judd, "Cultural Articulation in the Chinese Countryside, 1937–1945," *Modern China* 16.3 (July 1990): 269–308.

169. Gao Minfu, Preface to Han Qixiang, *Liu Qiao tuanyuan* (1946 ed.), p. 8.

170. Zhou Erfu, "Postscript," in Han Qixiang, *Liu Qiao tuanyuan*, p. 141.

171. Hu Mengxiang, *Han Qixiang pingzhuan* (Beijing: Zhongguo minjian wenyi chubanshe, 1989), p. 275.

172. He Jingzhi, "Wei renmin yishujia lizhuan," *Quyi* 207 (15 October 1989): 5.

173. Paraphrased in Judd, "Cultural Articulation in the Chinese Countryside," p. 287.

174. Ibid.

175. See, for example, *JFRB*, 30 April 1942, p. 1; 13 August 1942, p. 4; 1 March 1943, p. 1.

176. Ai Qing, "Wu Manyou," *JFRB*, 9 March 1943, p. 4.

177. Ibid.

178. Lu Dingyi, "Wenhua xiaxiang—Du 'Xiang Wu Manyou kanqi' yougan," *JFRB*, 10 February 1943, p. 4.

179. See, for example, *Bianqu qunzhong bao*, 19 March 1944, p. 3; 16 April 1944, p. 1.

180. For Zhao Zhankui, see *JFRB*, 2 September 1943, p. 1; 14 January 1944, p. 1. For Zhang Chuyuan, *JFRB*, 2 February 1944, p. 3. For others, see *JFRB*, 10 February 1944, p. 2.

181. See *JFRB*, 28 February 1943, p. 4.

182. See *Shanxi wenyi shiliao* 2:82–83.

183. To be sure, Chinese Communists were not the first to use workers as models. The Russians had already set a precedent by repeatedly honoring "Heroes of Socialist Labor." But the Yan'an experience was unique in that its heroes were poor peasants rather than urban workers. And while Stalin's Stakhanovites enjoyed special privileges, developing in later years into a new labor aristocracy, Yan'an's Wu Manyou and his comrades received far fewer material incentives from the Party. Chinese Communists thus presented a better image of a group of "model peasants" working for the common good.

184. See *KRZZY* 2:153–157, 164–169.

185. Ibid., pp. 4–6, 38–41, 41–51, 52–56, 256–257.

186. Sha Kefu, "Huigu yijiusiyi nian zhanwang yijiusier nian bianqu wenyi," in ibid., p. 94.

187. See, for example, Zhao Chaogou, *Yan'an yiyue* (Nanjing: Xinmin bao she, 1946).

188. See Haldore Hanson, *Fifty Years Around the Third World* (Burlington, Vt.: Fraser, 1986), p. 75; Stein, *Challenge of Red China*; and Harrison Forman, *Report from Red China* (New York: Henry Holt, 1945). See also Warren W. Tozer, "The Foreign Correspondents' Visit to Yenan in 1944: A Reassessment," *Pacific Historical Review* 41.2 (May 1972): 207–224, esp. pp. 211, 221.

189. Hanson, *Fifty Years*, p. 75.

190. Fei Hsiao-tung (Fei Xiaotong), review of *Yan'an yiyue* by Chao Chao-kuo (Zhao Chaogou), in *Pacific Affairs* 18.4 (December 1945): 391–393, esp. p. 392.

191. For details of the dissenting views, see Merle Goldman, *Literary Dissent in Communist China* (Cambridge, Mass.: Harvard University Press, 1967), chap. 2.

192. Mo Ye, "Liping de fannao," in *Shenghuo de bolan* (Xi'an: Shaanxi renmin chubanshe, 1984), pp. 80–101.

193. See *Shanxi wenyi shiliao* 2:142–156, esp. pp. 144, 146, 157–163.

194. See the author's own bitter recollection, *Shenghuo de bolan*, pp. 109–112.

195. See *KRZZY* 1:385–389.

7. A NEW POLITICAL CULTURE

1. See Xu Zhuoyun (Hsu Cho-yun) and Qiu Hongda (Chiu Hongdah), eds., *Kangzhan shengli de daijia* (Taibei: Lianjing chuban shiye gongsi, 1986), pp. 16, 185. And Dick Wilson, *When Tigers Fight: The Story of the Sino-Japanese War, 1937–1945* (Harmondsworth, Eng.: Penguin Books, 1983), p. 1.

2. Quoted from Immanuel Hsu, *The Rise of Modern China*, 4th ed. (New York: Oxford University Press, 1990), p. 611.

3. Carl von Clausewitz, *On War*, ed. and trans. Michael Howard and Peter Paret (Princeton: Princeton University Press, 1976), p. 77.

4. Zheng Zhenduo, "Shao shu ji," in *Zheju sanji* (Shanghai: Shanghai chuban gongsi, 1951), p. 48; see also Zheng, "Shi shu ji," *Fenghuo* 9 (31 October 1937): 1–2.

5. Zheng, "Shi shu ji," p. 2.

6. Zheng described this morally and intellectually exhilarating experience in his book *Jie zhong de shu ji* (Shanghai: Gudian wenxue chubanshe, 1956).

7. See Chen Fukang, *Zheng Zhenduo nianpu* (Beijing: Shumu wenxian chubanshe, 1988), p. 286. The proposal, which was sent by Zheng and others like Zhang Jusheng of the Commercial Press in early January 1940, received endorsement from the Nationalists, but predictably with no promise of financial assistance from the government.

8. Yuanxin (Zheng Zhenduo), "Baowei minzu wenhua yundong," *Wenyi zhendi* 5.1 (16 July 1940): 3. Zheng's efforts earned high praise among his friends. See *Wenchao yuekan* 1.3 (1 July 1946): 161.

9. Guo Moruo, "Lixing yu shouxing zhi zhan," *Wenhua zhanxian* 1 (1 September 1937): 7.

10. Such an argument is certainly not new. European history is full of similar analogies. War was often portrayed as a cosmic drama, a battle between life and death, a clash between the Apollonian spirit and the irrational, destructive Dionysian force. See Modris Eksteins, *Rites of Spring: The Great War and the Birth of Modern Age* (Boston: Houghton Mifflin, 1989); and Sam Keen, *Faces of the Enemy: Reflec-

tions of the Hostile Imagination (San Francisco: Harper & Row, 1986), p. 122.

11. Changjiang, "Jianli xinwen jizhe de zhengque zuofeng."

12. Bu Shaofu, *Zhandi jizhe jianghua*, p. 12.

13. Guo Moruo, "Kangzhan song," *Kangzhan sanrikan* 1 (19 August 1937): 3.

14. Zang Kejia, "Chule kangzhan shenme dou mei yiyi," p. 37. Zang described his joy when he heard about the coming of the war.

15. See *Wenxue chuangzuo* 1.3 (15 November 1942), "Editorial" (paraphrased).

16. Gu Jiegang, "Xisheng," *Dazhong zhishi* 1.3 (20 November 1936): 15.

17. Such euphoria was similar to the enthusiasm with which many European intellectuals greeted the outbreak of the war in 1914. See Robert Wohl, *The Generation of 1914* (Cambridge, Mass.: Harvard University Press, 1979), pp. 216–217.

18. Quoted in Dryden L. Phelps, "Letters and Arts in the War Years," in *China*, ed. Harley F. MacNair (Berkeley and Los Angeles: University of California Press, 1946), p. 409.

19. Liu Shi, *Jietou jianghua* (N.p.: Shenghuo shudian, 1936); Xu Maoyong, *Jietou wentan* (1936; Shanghai: Guangming shuju, 1946).

20. Liu Shi, *Jietou jianghua*, pp. ii, 3.

21. Qu Qiubai, *Jietou ji* (Shanghai: Xia she, 1940). Qu Qiubai was critical of the vernacular language advocated by May Fourth scholars such as Hu Shi. Ridiculing it as too "Europeanized," he believed this vernacular language to be too sophisticated, its meanings and vocabulary too foreign to be comprehended by the general public. A new proletarian "common language," he said, based partly on traditional popular literature such as storytelling and historical novels but largely on the language of the working class, should be created to meet the demands of the general population. This language was the language of the street. Qu's experimentation with this "new" language resulted in a series of storytelling-type popular essays written mostly in the early 1930s, which were published in 1940 as *Jietou ji*. Qu's idealistic goal was never realized, however, because nobody, including Qu, spelled out exactly what this new language should be, how it should be written, and what it should include. Nevertheless, the search for a language comprehensible to the masses continued to occupy the minds of many left-wing intellectuals.

22. For example, Cao Bohan suggested launching a "Street Culture Movement" (*Jietou wenhua yundong*), a large-scale grass-roots education campaign to teach the populace patriotic songs and basic defensive techniques against the Japanese. See Cao, *Jietou bibao*, pp. 16–19, esp. p. 19.

23. This quotation was borrowed from James Wilkinson; see his *The Intellectual Resistance in Europe* (Cambridge, Mass.: Harvard University Press, 1981), p. 263. The situation in Europe was in many ways highly reminiscent of that in China, as this quotation shows.

24. See Hong Shen, *Kangzhan shinian lai*, pp. 21, 93; and Tian Qin, *Zhongguo xiju yundong*, p. 89.

25. Feng Yuxiang, *Kang-Ri de weida minzhong*, "Preface."

26. See Chang-tai Hung, *Going to the People*, esp. chap. 7.

27. See, for example, Guo Moruo, *Zhanshi xuanchuan gongzuo* (N.p.: Zhongyang lujun junguan xuexiao, 1938), pp. 29–30; Mao Dun, "Dazhonghua yu liyong jiu xingshi," *Wenyi zhendi* 1.4 (1 June 1938): 121; *Wenxue chuangzuo* 1.3 (15 November 1942), "Editorial"; and Yao Qingzeng, *Kangzhan geyan ji* (Chongqing: Zhongshan wenhua jiaoyuguan, 1938).

28. See discussion in David Parkin, "Political Language," *Annual Review of Anthropology* 18 (1984): 353.

29. See, for example, Wen Zaidao et al., *Biangu ji*, pp. 265–267. Zhou Li'an, *Huafa ji*, pp. 110, 127.

30. See Ge Yihong, *Zhanshi yanju zhengce*, p. 31.

31. Liang Shiqiu, "Bianzhe de hua," *Zhongyang ribao*, 1 December 1938, p. 4.

32. For the furor created by this incident, see *Zhongguo kang-Ri zhanzheng shiqi dahoufang wenxue shuxi* 2:131–171. Liang's statement was repeatedly and unfairly criticized by Communist writers. Recently, the writer Ke Ling finally came to his defense, arguing that Liang's proposal was a reasonable one. Ke Ling attacked the notion of "total submission to the War of Resistance" as "a narrow and mechanical approach." See Ke Ling, *Wenyuan manyoulu* (Hong Kong: Sanlian shudian, 1988), pp. 124–125, 309.

33. Shen Congwen, "Yiban huo teshu," in *Zhongguo kang-Ri zhanzheng shiqi dahoufang wenxue shuxi* 2:142–146.

34. Wang Liaoyi, *Long chong bing diao zhai suoyu* (Shanghai: Guancha she, 1949), pp. 4–5.

35. See Hong Shen, *Kangzhan shinian lai*, p. 169.

36. See above, chapter 5, note 114 with associated quote.

37. *Wenxue chuangzuo* 1.3 (15 November 1942), "Editorial."

38. Quoted in Hong Shen, *Kangzhan shinian lai*, p. 87.

39. See my discussion in *Going to the People*, pp. 12–15.

40. See, for example, Xu Zhengrong, "Dao neidi qu," *JWRB*, 14 October 1937, p. 4; "Dao nongcun qu" (To the village), *Dongfang zazhi* 34.14 (16 July 1937): n.p.

41. Quoted in Leo Ou-fan Lee, "Literary Trends: The Road to Revolution, 1927–1949," in *Cambridge History of China*, vol. 13, pt. 2, pp. 453–454.

42. See Wang Yao, *Zhongguo xinwenxue shigao* 2:441–452. Interview with Wu Zuxiang, 4 November 1989, Beijing.

43. Tian Qin, *Zhongguo xiju yundong*, p. 91.

44. Ge Yihong, *Zhanshi yanju zhengce*, pp. 23–24. Interview with Ge Yihong, 28 September, 20 October, and 4 November 1989, Beijing.

45. Hong Shen, *Kangzhan shinian lai*, pp. 83–88 (paraphrased).

46. *XJSD* 1.1 (16 May 1937): 30; see also pp. 8, 19, 20–21, 22, 29.

47. See Zhang Jinglu, ed., *Zhongguo xiandai chuban shiliao* 3:32–33.

48. Ibid., pp. 33–34.

49. Gan Yunheng, "Kangzhan shiqi de shige zhongxin huodong," in *Kangzhan yu yishu*, p. 33.

50. For the Chinese Communists' anti-urban legacy, see Maurice Meisner, *Marxism, Maoism, and Utopianism* (Madison: University of Wisconsin Press, 1982), esp. chaps. 2 and 3.

51. See Keith M. Baker, "Introduction," in Baker, ed., *The French Revolution and the Creation of Modern Political Culture*, p. xii.

52. For the repeated use of these terms, see Zhang Geng, ed., *Yanggeju xuan*, pp. 21 (*xin shehui*), 289 (*jiu shehui*), 296 (*shoukuren* and *dangjiaren*), 16 and 45 (*laodong*), 11 and 50 (*shengchan*), 8 and 127 (the Eighth Route Army), 62 and 225 (the Chinese Communist Party). Communist songs also abound with these terms. See, for example, *Kang-Ri zhanzheng gequ xuanji*, 4 vols. (Beijing: Zhongguo qingnian chubanshe, 1957).

53. See Zhang Geng, ed., *Yanggeju xuan*; and *Kang-Ri zhanzheng gequ xuanji*.

54. On social reforms in the border regions, see Mark Selden, *The Yenan Way in Revolutionary China* (Cambridge, Mass.: Harvard University Press, 1971); on the Party's organizational strength, see Tetsuya Kataoka, *Resistance and Revolution in China: The Communists and the Second United Front* (Berkeley and Los Angeles: University of California Press, 1974), esp. pp. 300–301.

Glossary

Names and titles are not included in the glossary if they appear in the bibliography.

Ai Wu 艾蕪
An E 安娥
Babai haohan sishou Zhabei 八百好漢死守閘北
Bai Chongxi 白崇禧
Bai Yunpeng 白雲鵬
Baijia xing 百家姓
Baimaonü 白毛女
Banjiao manhua 半角漫畫
baodao hua 報道畫
Baofengyu zhong de qige nüxing 暴風雨中的七個女性
Baowei Lugouqiao 保衛蘆溝橋
Batou luozi banbao 八頭騾子辦報
Bayi jutuan 八一劇團
Beijing xinwen xuehui 北京新聞學會
Beiping xinwen zhuanke xuexiao 北平新聞專科學校
Bianqu minzhong jutuan 邊區民衆劇團
bianqu wenhua 邊區文化
biao de shi 表的是
bibao 壁報

Bo Gu (Qin Bangxian) 博古（秦邦憲）
bu dang, bu mai, bu si, bu mang 不黨, 不賣, 不私, 不盲
caizi 才子
Cao Yu 曹禺
chaguanju 茶館劇
Chahua nü 茶花女
Chang'an minzhong jutuan 長安民衆劇團
"Changcheng yao" 長城謠
chaoran huajia 超然畫家
Chen bao 晨報
Chen Cheng 陳誠
Chen Liting 陳鯉庭
Chen Yi 陳毅
Chen Yuanyuan 陳圓圓
Chen Yunshang 陳雲裳
Cheng Yanqiu 程硯秋
Chuju 楚劇
chunlian 春聯
Chunliu she 春柳社
ci 詞
cong Kaerdeng dao jietou 從卡爾登到街頭

359

Cui Wei 崔嵬
"Da hui laojia qu" 打回老家去
dacheng yipian 打成一片
Dadao jushe 大道劇社
dadao Riben diguozhuyi 打倒日本帝國主義
dagu 大鼓
dang bagu 黨八股
dangjiaren 當家人
dao jietou qu 到街頭去
dao neidi qu 到內地去
dao nongcun qu 到農村去
Dawan bao 大晚報
Dawei Luo 大衞羅
daxi 大戲
Dayu shajia 打漁殺家
dazhong 大衆
Dazhong shenghuo 大衆生活
Dazhong wenyi 大衆文藝
Dazhong zhexue 大衆哲學
dazhonghua 大衆化
Deng Tuo 鄧拓
difang baozhi 地方報紙
Ding Li 丁里
Ding Song 丁悚
Diren datui le 敵人打退了
Dong Xiaowan 董小宛
douzheng yangge 鬥爭秧歌
duige 對歌
erliuzi 二流子
"Erqi kangzhan" 二期抗戰
Ershi nian mudu zhi guai xian-zhuang 二十年目睹之怪現狀
Fan wuguan 反五關
fan'an xi 翻案戲
fanshen 翻身
"Fanshen ge" 翻身歌
Fanshen jutuan 翻身劇團
Fei Xiaotong 費孝通
fengci hua 諷刺畫
"Fengyang huagu" 鳳陽花鼓
Fuguihua (Fu Shu'ai) 富貴花(富淑媛)
fukan 副刊

Fuqi shizi 夫妻識字
fushere 輻射熱
Gao Minfu 高敏夫
Gao Yongchang 高永常
Ge Nenniang 葛嫩娘
Gong nong sanzi jing 工農三字經
Guan Dexing (Xin Liangjiu) 關德興(新靚就)
Guan Shanyue 關山月
Guangdong xiju yanjiusuo 廣東戲劇研究所
guanggao hua 廣告畫
Guangrong deng 光榮燈
Guangxi ribao 廣西日報
Guangxi shengli yishuguan 廣西省立藝術館
Gudao 孤島
gujun zuozhan 孤軍作戰
Guodu 過渡
Guofu yisheng 國父一生
guojia xingwang, pifu youze 國家興亡,匹夫有責
guojia zhishang, minzu zhishang 國家至上,民族至上
Guojia zongdongyuan huabao 國家總動員畫報
Gushi bian 古史辨
Hai pai 海派
Haiguo yingxiong 海國英雄
Hangzhou jizhe gonghui 杭州記者公會
hanjian 漢奸
Hanju 漢劇
hao 耗
Hao yi ji bianzi 好一計鞭子
Heinu yutian lu 黑奴籲天錄
Hokusai 北齋
Hong Jun 洪鈞
Honglou meng 紅樓夢
houfang 後方
Hu Shi 胡適
hua zheng wei ling 化整為零
huaju 話劇

Huang Shaogu 黃少谷
Huang Wennong 黃文農
Huang Xuchu 黃旭初
Huang Zhenxia 黃震遐
Huangjin daxiyuan 黃金大戲院
huo de baozhi 活的報紙
huobaoju 活報劇
Huoshao Hongliansi 火燒紅
蓮寺
Huozhuo Bai Jianwu 活捉白
堅武
Ichigō 一号
Itagaki Seishirō 板垣征四郎
Jiangcun xiaojing 江村小景
Jiang Feng (Nanhai Shisanlang)
江楓(南海十三郎)
Jiang Han yuge 江漢漁歌
Jiang Qi 蔣旂
*Jiang weiyuanzhang kangzhan
liangzhounian gao junmin*
蔣委員長抗戰兩週年告軍民
jianzhi 剪紙
Ji'exian shang 饑餓線上
jiefang 解放
jiehua 解畫
jietou 街頭
jietou wenhua yundong 街頭文
化運動
jietouju 街頭劇
jietoushi 街頭詩
jilu hua 記錄畫
Jin Ping Mei 金瓶梅
Jin Shan 金山
Ji'nan jushe 暨南劇社
Jin-Cha-Ji 晉察冀
Jin-Cha-Ji ribao 晉察冀日報
Jin-Ji-Lu-Yu 晉冀魯豫
Jin-Sui 晉綏
Jin-Sui dazhong bao 晉綏大眾報
Jin-Sui ribao 晉綏日報
Jing bao 京報
Jing bao 晶報
Jing pai 京派
Jingan zuan 金鋼鑽

jingbian zhuyi 精編主義
Jinghua yuan 鏡花緣
jingshen bujixian 精神補給線
Jingyun dagu 京韵大鼓
jiu shehui 舊社會
jiuping zhuang xinjiu 舊瓶裝
新酒
jiuwang 救亡
Jiuwang manhua xuanchuandui
救亡漫畫宣傳隊
"Jiuyiba xiaodiao" 九一八小調
Jizhe jie 記者節
Jizhe zhi jia 記者之家
Kaerdeng xiyuan 卡爾登戲院
kang dao di 抗到底
Kangdi huabao 抗敵畫報
Kangdi yanjudui 抗敵演劇隊
Kangjian tongsu wenku 抗建通
俗文庫
Kang-Ri gao yu yiqie 抗日高於
一切
"Kang-Ri shan'ge" 抗日山歌
Kang-Ri zhanzheng 抗日戰爭
kangzhan bagu 抗戰八股
Kangzhan huakan 抗戰畫刊
Kangzhan manhua 抗戰漫畫
Kangzhan ribao 抗戰日報
katun 卡吞
Ke Zhongping 柯仲平
keguan 客觀
Kong Shangren 孔尚任
Kong Xiangxi 孔祥熙
Kongjun dazhan 空軍大戰
koutou xuanchuan 口頭宣傳
kuaiban 快板
kuileiju 傀儡劇
Kuriyagawa Hakuson 厨川白村
la yangpian 拉洋片
langman 浪漫
Lao Can youji 老殘遊記
Lao Zhang de zhexue 老張的
哲學
laobaixing 老百姓
Laobaixing bao 老百姓報

laodong 勞動
laodong yingxiong 勞動英雄
Laoniangpo zhu xunlian 老娘婆住訓練
Leiyu 雷雨
Leting dagu 樂亭大鼓
Li bao 立報
Li Jiefu 李劫夫
Li Liewen 黎烈文
Li Shaoyan 李少言
Li Shutong (Hongyi) 李叔同（弘一）
Li Xiangjun 李香君
Li Xiucheng zhi si 李秀成之死
Li Zongren 李宗仁
Liang Qichao 梁啟超
liangmianpai 兩面派
Liangyou huabao 良友畫報
lianhuantu 連環圖
lie wei 列位
Lihua dagu 梨花大鼓
Lin Shu 林紓
lishiju 歷史劇
litihua 立體化
Liu Baoquan 劉寶全
Liu Fu 劉復
Liu Han geju yanyuan zhanshi jiangxiban 留漢歌劇演員戰時講習班
Liu Zhiren 劉志仁
Lu Xun yishu xueyuan (Luyi) 魯迅藝術學院（魯藝）
Lu Zhixiang 陸志庠
Luyi gongzuotuan 魯藝工作團
Ma Ke 馬可
man 漫
manbi 漫筆
manhua 漫畫
Manhua hui 漫畫會
Manhua Riben qin Hua shi 漫畫日本侵華史
Manhua yanjiuhui 漫畫研究會
Manhua yu muke 漫畫與木刻
manhua zhan 漫畫戰

"Maoguo chunqiu" 貓國春秋
Mei Lanfang 梅蘭芳
Mei niang 眉娘
Meihu 郿鄠
"Meng Xiangying fanshen" 孟祥英翻身
Mianzi wenti 面子問題
Mingmo yihen 明末遺恨
mingshi 名士
mingxi 名戲
Minjian ji 民間集
minjian wenyi 民間文藝
Minsheng bao 民生報
Minzhong xijushe 民眾戲劇社
minzu manhua 民族漫畫
minzu xingshi 民族形式
MK muke yanjiuhui MK 木刻研究會
modeng nüxing 摩登女性
Modeng she 摩登社
muke 木刻
muke manhua 木刻漫畫
Mulan shi 木蘭詩
Nahan 吶喊
Nan gui 南歸
Nan she 南社
Nanguo banyuekan 南國半月刊
Nanguo dianying jushe 南國電影劇社
Nanguo she 南國社
Nanguo yishu xueyuan 南國藝術學院
Nankai 南開
neihangren 內行人
ni zu shen xian 泥足深陷
nianhua 年畫
Nie Rongzhen 聶榮臻
Niehai hua 孽海花
Niu Wen 牛文
Niu Yonggui guacai 牛永貴掛彩
nongcun 農村
nongmin 農民
nongmin jutuan 農民劇團

Nongmin kangzhan congshu 農民抗戰叢書

nüxia 女俠

Pan Gongzhan 潘公展

"Peidu zan" 陪都讚

Penggong an 彭公案

Ping'an shu 平安書

pingjia bao 平價報

Pingju xuanchuandui 平劇宣傳隊

Pingju yanjiuhui 平劇研究會

pinglun 評論

Pu Xixiu 浦熙修

qianghua 牆畫

Qianzi wen 千字文

Qin Luozheng 秦洛正

Qin Shouou 秦瘦鷗

Qiu Haitang 秋海棠

Qiu Jin zhuan 秋瑾傳

qiuba shi 丘八詩

Qu Yuan 屈原

quan dang ban bao 全黨辦報

quanmin dongyuan 全民動員

qunzhong 群衆

Riben gui 日本鬼

Rongyu junren zhiye xunliansuo 榮譽軍人職業訓練所

Rou Shi 柔石

ruo wen 若問

Sa Kongliao 薩空了

"San Mao" 三毛

Sange panni de nüxing 三個叛逆的女性

Sanhu tushu yinshuashe 三戶圖書印刷社

Sanren fengci manhua zhan 三人諷刺漫畫展

Sanjianghao 三江好

santou 傘頭

sanxian 三弦

Sanzi jing 三字經

Saodang bao 掃蕩報

saoqing dizhu 騷情地主

seqing manhua 色情漫畫

Sha Ding 沙汀

Shaan-Gan-Ning 陝甘寧

Shang qianxian 上前線

Shanghai manhuajie jiuwang xiehui 上海漫畫界救亡協會

Shanghai meishu zhuanke xuexiao 上海美術專科學校

Shanghai poke 上海潑克

Shanghai xiao tongbao 上海小同胞

Shanghai xijujie jiuwang xiehui 上海戲劇界救亡協會

Shanghai xinwen jizhe lianhuanhui 上海新聞記者聯歡會

Shanxi xisheng jiuguo tongmenghui 山西犧牲救國同盟會

Shanyaodan (Fu Shaofang) 山藥旦 (富少舫)

Shao Lizi 邵力子

Shao Piaoping 邵飄萍

"She yu furen" 蛇與婦人

Shen Yiqian 沈逸千

sheng yu youhuan, si yu anle 生於憂患, 死於安樂

shengchan 生產

Shenghuo ribao 生活日報

Shenghuo shudian 生活書店

Shenghuo zhoukan 生活週刊

shenghuoju 生活劇

"Shi ba mo" 十八摸

Shi bao 時報

Shi'erba liandao 十二把鐮刀

Shigong an 施公案

Shijie ribao 世界日報

Shijie wanbao 世界晚報

Shishi xinbao 時事新報

shou yapo 受壓迫

shoukuren 受苦人

Shu Yan 舒湮

shuanghuang 雙簧

Shucai jiuguo 輸財救國

Shuihu zhuan 水滸傳

shulaibao 數來寶

shuntianyou 順天遊

Shuoshu zu 說書組
Sifan xiashan 思凡下山
Silang tan mu 四郎探母
"*Song dage*" 送大哥
"*Songhuajiang shang*" 松花江上
Suanming xiansheng 算命先生
Sun Fuyuan 孫伏園
Suzhou yehua 蘇州夜話
tai Ou hua 太歐化
Taihangshan jutuan 太行山劇團
tanci 彈詞
Tang Enbo 湯恩伯
Tang Huaiqiu 唐槐秋
taoshan 逃山
Tianjin manhua 天津漫畫
Tongsu duwu biankanshe 通俗
  讀物編刊社
tongsu wenyi 通俗文藝
Tuhu 屠戶
tuzhi 土紙
Wang Jingwei 汪精衛
Wang Ming (Chen Shaoyu)
  王明(陳紹禹)
Wang Tao 王韜
"*Wang xiansheng*" 王先生
Wang Youyou 汪優遊
Weina jushe 葳娜劇社
Wen Xiangshuan 溫象拴
wenhua bingzhan 文化兵站
wenhua huoxianwang 文化火
  線網
Wenhua jie 文化街
wenmingxi 文明戲
wenren hua 文人畫
wenren lunzheng 文人論政
Wenxue yuebao 文學月報
wenyi che 文藝車
Wenyi tuji 文藝突擊
*wenzhang xiaxiang, wenzhang
  ruwu* 文章下鄉，文章入伍
Wu Dingchang 吳鼎昌
Wu Woyao 吳沃堯
Wu Youru 吳友如
Wu Zuxiang 吳組湘

*Wubai dadaodui zhansi Xifeng-
  kou* 五百大刀隊戰死喜峯口
wumian huangdi 無冕皇帝
Wushen quannian huabao 戊申
  全年畫報
wusheng 武生
Wutaishan heshang kangzhan
  五台山和尚抗戰
Xiandai 現代
Xiang Jie 香姐
xiangcun wenyi 鄉村文藝
Xiangju xuanchuandui 湘劇宣
  傳隊
xiangsheng 相聲
xiangtu yu 鄉土語
xianshiju 現實劇
xiao bao 小報
"*Xiao Chen liu Jing waishi*"
  小陳留京外史
xiao jiaoniang 小嬌娘
xiao shimin 小市民
Xiao Tongzi 蕭同茲
"*Xiao yanzi*" 小燕子
xiaopinwen 小品文
xiaoxing bao 小型報
Xibei wenyi 西北文藝
Xibei zhandi fuwutuan 西北戰
  地服務團
"*Xiezhan Juyongguan*"
  血戰居庸關
xigezao 洗個澡
xiju xiaxiang 戲劇下鄉
xin meishu yundong 新美術
  運動
xin shehui 新社會
Xindi jushe 新地劇社
xingeju 新歌劇
xinju 新劇
xintianyou 信天游
xinwen 新聞
xinwen bagu 新聞八股
Xinwen bao 新聞報
xinwen gongzuo de youjizhan
  新聞工作的游擊戰

xinwen jizhe 新聞記者
Xinwen xuekan 新聞學刊
Xinwenxue yanjiuhui 新聞學研究會
Xiongmei kaihuang 兄妹開荒
"*Xiu hebao*" 繡荷包
Xu Ying 徐盈
xuanchuan 宣傳
Xuezhan Lugouqiao 血戰蘆溝橋
Yan Haiwen 閻海文
Yan Yangchu 晏陽初
Yan-Fu dazhong 鹽阜大衆
yang bagu 洋八股
Yang Chaochen 楊朝臣
Yang Gang 楊剛
yang jiaotiao 洋教條
Yang Shengfu 楊生福
Yang Wencong 楊文聰
yangge 秧歌
Yangmen nüjiang 楊門女將
Yao Ziqing 姚子青
Ye Yinquan 葉因泉
Yefu (Zheng Yefu) 野夫（鄭野夫）
Yiba yishe 一八藝社
Yiduo honghua 一朵紅花
Yijiang chunshui xiang dong liu 一江春水向東流
Yishi bao 益世報
yishiju 儀式劇
yishu de bailei 藝術的敗類
Yishu jushe 藝術劇社
"*Yiyongjun jinxingqu*" 義勇軍進行曲
youxingju 遊行劇
yu jiaoyu yu yule 寓教育於娛樂
Yue Fei (Yue Wumu) 岳飛（岳武穆）
Yue zhuan 岳傳
yue'er 悅耳
Yueju jiuwang fuwutuan 粵劇救亡服務團
yumin zhengce 愚民政策
yuyi hua 寓意畫

"Zai yiyuan zhong" 在醫院中
Zeng Pu 曾樸
Zeng Xiaogu 曾孝谷
Zhandi baozhi gongyingdui 戰地報紙供應隊
zhandi jizhe 戰地記者
Zhang Chuyuan 張初元
Zhang Shanzi 張善孖
Zhao Dan 趙丹
Zhao Zhankui 趙占魁
Zhao Ziyue 趙子曰
Zhengfeng 整風
Zhengqi ge 正氣歌
zhengyan de xiazi 睜眼的瞎子
zhiyehua 職業化
Zhong Wancai qijia 鍾萬財起家
zhong zhi cheng cheng 衆志成城
Zhongguo huabao 中國畫報
Zhongguo lüxing jutuan 中國旅行劇團
Zhongguo qingnian xinwen jizhe xuehui 中國青年新聞記者學會
Zhongguohua 中國化
Zhongguohua de manhua 中國化的漫畫
Zhonghua pingmin jiaoyu cujinhui 中華平民教育促進會
Zhonghua quanguo manhua zuojia xiehui 中華全國漫畫作家協會
Zhonghua quanguo wenyijie kangdi xiehui 中華全國文藝界抗敵協會
Zhonghua xijujie kangdi xiehui bianqu fenhui 中華戲劇界抗敵協會邊區分會
Zhongshen dashi 終身大事
Zhongyang tongxunshe 中央通訊社
Zhongyang tushu zazhi shencha weiyuanhui 中央圖書雜誌審查委員會

Zhou Enlai 周恩來
Zhou Shoujuan 周瘦鵑
Zhou Xinfang 周信芳
Zhou Zuoren 周作人
Zhu De 朱德
zhuangyuan 狀元
zhuanmenhua 專門化

zhuizi 墜子
Ziye 子夜
Ziyou hun 自由魂
"Ziyou tan" 自由談
Zuihou yi ji 最後一計
Zuoyi jutuan lianmeng 左翼劇
  團聯盟

Bibliography

NEWSPAPERS AND PERIODICALS

Baoxue jikan 報學季刊 (Journalism quarterly). Shanghai, October 1934–August 1935.

Beifang wenhua 北方文化 (Northern culture). Zhangjiakou, March–August 1946.

Bianqu qunzhong bao 邊區羣眾報 (Border region people's press). Yan'an, 1940–1948.

The Chinese Social and Political Science Review. Beijing, 1916–1938.

Dagong bao (DGB) 大公報 (Impartial daily; original title *L'Impartial*). Tianjin, Hankou, Chongqing, Hong Kong, 1931–1945.

Duli manhua 獨立漫畫 (Independent cartoons). Shanghai, September 1935–February 1936.

Fenghuo 烽火 (Beacon-fire). Shanghai, Guangzhou, September 1937–August 1938.

Guangming (GM) 光明 (The light). Shanghai, June 1936–October 1937.

Huashang bao 華商報 (Chinese commercial press). Hong Kong, April 1941–December 1941.

Jiefang ribao (JFRB) 解放日報 (Liberation daily). Yan'an, 1941–1947.

Jin-Cha-Ji huabao 晉察冀畫報 (Shanxi-Chahar-Hebei pictorial). N.p., July 1942–December 1945.

Jiuwang manhua (JWMH) 救亡漫畫 (National salvation cartoons). Shanghai, September–November 1937.

Jiuwang ribao (JWRB) 救亡日報 (National salvation daily). Shanghai, Guangzhou, Guilin, 1937–1941.

Kang dao di (KDD) 抗到底 (Resisting till the end). Hankou, Chongqing, January 1938–November 1939.

Kangzhan sanrikan 抗戰三日刊 (War of Resistance three-day press; also known as *Dikang sanrikan* 抵抗三日刊 [Resistance three-day press]). Shanghai, August–November 1937.

Kangzhan wenyi (KZWY) 抗戰文藝 (Resistance literature and art). Hankou, Chongqing, May 1938–May 1946.

Kangzhan wenyi yanjiu (KZWYYJ) 抗戰文藝研究 (Studies on resistance literature and art). Chengdu, 1982–.

Kangzhan xiju 抗戰戲劇 (Resistance drama). Hankou, November 1937–July 1938.

Lunyu (LY) 論語 (The analects). Shanghai, September 1932–August 1937.

Quanmin kangzhan 全民抗戰 (United resistance). Hankou, Chongqing, 1937–1941.

Quanmin zhoukan 全民週刊 (United weekly). Hankou, January–June 1938.

Renjian shi 人間世 (This human world). Shanghai, April 1934–December 1935.

Shen bao 申報 (Shanghai news). Shanghai, 1931–1949.

Shidai manhua (SDMH) 時代漫畫 (Modern cartoons). Shanghai, January 1934–June 1937.

Taibai 太白 (Venus). Shanghai, September 1934–September 1935.

T'ien Hsia Monthly. Shanghai, 1935–1941.

Wanxiang 萬象 (Phenomena). Shanghai, July 1941–June 1945.

Wenhua xianfeng 文化先鋒 (Cultural pioneers). Chongqing, Nanjing, 1942–1948.

Wenxian 文獻 (Documents). Shanghai, October 1938–May 1939.

Wenyi yuekan 文藝月刊 (Literary monthly). Nanjing, Hankou, Chongqing, August 1930–November 1941.

Wenyi zhendi 文藝陣地 (Literary battleground). Shanghai, Chongqing, April 1938–November 1942.

Xiju chunqiu (XJCQ) 戲劇春秋 (Drama annals). Guilin, November 1940–October 1942.

Xiju shidai (XJSD) 戲劇時代 (Drama times). Shanghai, May 1937–August 1937.

Xinhua ribao 新華日報 (New China daily). Hankou, Chongqing, 1938–1947.

Xinwen jizhe (XWJZ) 新聞記者 (The reporter). Hankou, April 1938–March 1941.

Xinwenxue shiliao (XWXSL) 新文學史料 (Historical materials on the new literature). Beijing, 1978–.

Xinwen yanjiu ziliao (XWYJZL) 新聞研究資料 (Research materials on journalism). Beijing, 1979–.

Xinwen zazhi 新聞雜誌 (News magazine). Hangzhou, May 1936–February 1937.

Yan'an wenyi yanjiu 延安文藝研究 (Research on Yan'an literature and art). Xi'an, 1984–.

Yenching Journal of Social Studies. Beijing, June 1938–July 1950.

Yuzhou feng (YZF) 宇宙風 (Universal wind). Shanghai, Guangzhou, Guilin, Chongqing, September 1935–August 1947.

Yuzhou feng yikan 宇宙風乙刊 (Universal wind, II). Shanghai, March 1939–December 1941.

Zazhi 雜誌 (The magazine). Shanghai, 1937–1945.

Zhandi 戰地 (Battleground). Hankou, March–June 1938.

Zhongyang ribao 中央日報 (Central daily). Nanjing, Chongqing, 1929–1945.

BOOKS AND ARTICLES

A Ying 阿英 (Qian Xingcun 錢杏邨). *Bixue hua* 碧血花 (Jade blood flower). Beijing: Zhongguo xiju chubanshe, 1957.

——— (Wei Ruhui 魏如晦). "*Bixue hua* renwu bukao" 「碧血花」人物補考 (Additional analysis of *Jade Blood Flower*). *Wanxiang* 1.1 (1 July 1941): 41–43.

———. "Shanghai ge huaju jituan chunji lianhe gongyan wenxian jiyao" 上海各話劇集團春季聯合公演文獻輯要 (A collection on the joint spring performances of Shanghai drama organizations). *XJSD* 1.1 (16 May 1937): 243–254.

———. "Shanghai shibian yu dazhong gequ" 上海事變與大衆歌曲 (The Shanghai Incident and popular songs). In *Xiandai Zhongguo wenxue lun* 現代中國文學論 (Essays on modern Chinese literature), edited by Qian Xingcun. Shanghai: Hezhong shudian, 1933.

———. *Yang E zhuan* 楊娥傳 (The story of Yang E). Shanghai: Chenguang chuban gongsi, 1950.

———. *Zhongguo nianhua fazhan shilüe* 中國年畫發展史略 (A brief history of the development of Chinese New Year pictures). Beijing: Zhaohua meishu chubanshe, 1954.

———, ed. *Kangzhan dumuju xuan* 抗戰獨幕劇選 (Selected one-act plays during the War of Resistance). N.p.: Kangzhan duwu chubanshe, 1937.

Agulhon, Maurice. *Marianne into the Battle: Republican Imagery and Symbolism in France, 1789–1880*. Cambridge: Cambridge University Press, 1980.

Ai Qing 艾青. "Di yi ri" 第一日 (The first day). *JFRB*, 18 August 1941.

———. "Jiefangqu de yishu jiaoyu" 解放區的藝術教育 (Art education in the liberated areas). In *Zhonghua quanguo wenxue yishu gongzuozhe daibiao dahui jinian wenji*. N.p.: Xiuhua shudian, 1950.

———. "Wu Manyou" 吳滿有 (Wu Manyou). *JFRB*, 9 March 1943.

————. "Zhankai jietoushi yundong" 展開街頭詩運動 (Launch a street poetry movement). *JFRB*, 27 September 1942.

Ai Qing and Jiang Feng, eds. *Xibei jianzhi ji* 西北剪紙集 (A collection of papercuts from the Northwest). Shanghai: Chenguang chubanshe, 1949.

Ai Siqi 艾思奇 et al. *Yangge lunwen xuanji* 秧歌論文選集 (Selected essays on *yangge*). N.p.: Xinhua shudian, 1944.

Akiyoshi Kukio 秋吉久紀夫. *Kahoku konkyochi no bungaku undō* 華北根拠地の文学運動 (The literary movement in the northern China border regions). Tokyo: Hyōronsha, 1976.

————. *Kōsei Soku bungaku undō shiryō shū* 江西蘇区文学運動資料集 (Collected materials on the literary movement in the Jiangxi Soviet). Tokyo: Tōkyō daigaku Tōyō bunka kenkyūjo, 1976.

Asada Kyōji 浅田喬二. *Nihon teikokushugika no Chūgoku* 日本帝国主義下の中国 (China under Japanese imperialism). Tokyo: Rakuyū shobō, 1981.

Auden, W. H., and Christopher Isherwood. *Journey to a War*. New York: Random House, 1939.

Baker, Keith M., ed. *The French Revolution and the Creation of Modern Political Culture*. Vol. 1. Oxford: Pergamon Press, 1987.

Bakhtin, Mikhail. *The Dialogic Imagination: Four Essays*. Edited by Michael Holquist, translated by Caryl Emerson and Michael Holquist. Austin: University of Texas Press, 1981.

Bao Tianxiao 包天笑. "Ba yue shisan" 八月十三 (13 August [1937]). *JWRB*, 15 October 1937.

————. "Wenhuajie de xijidui—xiao cezi" 文化界的襲擊隊—小冊子 (The culture shock troops—pamphlets). *JWRB*, 17 October 1937.

Baoluo 保羅. "Zhankai xiju de youjizhan" 展開戲劇的游擊戰 (Launching drama guerrilla warfare). *Kangzhan xiju* 1.1 (16 November 1937): 6–9.

Baqian li lu yun he yue—Yanju jiudui huiyilu 八千里路雲和月—演劇九隊回憶錄 (Eight thousand *li* of clouds and moon—the memoirs of the Ninth Drama Troupe). Edited by Yanju jiudui duishi bianji weiyuanhui 演劇九隊隊史編輯委員會 (The Editorial Board of the History of the Ninth Drama Troupe). Shanghai: n.p., n.d. (epilogue dated 1988).

Bedeski, Robert E. "China's Wartime State." In *China's Bitter Victory*, edited by James C. Hsiung and Steven I. Levine. Armonk, N.Y.: M. E. Sharpe, 1992.

Bi Keguan 畢克官. "Jindai baokan manhua" 近代報刊漫畫 (Cartoons in modern journalism). *XWYJZL* 8 (November 1981): 68–87.

Bi Keguan and Huang Yuanlin 黃遠林. *Zhongguo manhua shi* 中國漫畫史 (A history of Chinese cartoons). Beijing: Wenhua yishu chubanshe, 1986.

Bi shang Liangshan 逼上梁山 (Driven up Mt. Liang). Edited by Pingju yanjiuhui. N.p.: Xinhua shudian, 1945.

Bi Yao 碧遙. "Qin Liangyu" 秦艮玉 (Qin Liangyu). In *Guofang xiju xuan* 國防戲劇選 (Selected national defense plays). N.p.: n.p., n.d.

Bigsy, C.W.E., ed. *Approaches to Popular Culture.* Bowling Green, Ohio: Bowling Green University Popular Press, 1976.

Bo Han 伯韓. "Shangbing daoqing" 傷兵道情 (The tale of a wounded soldier). *Quanmin zhoukan* 1.11 (19 February 1938): 174.

Boorman, Howard L., ed. *Biographical Dictionary of Republican China.* 4 vols. New York: Columbia University Press, 1967–1971.

Boyle, John H. *China and Japan at War, 1937–1945: The Politics of Collaboration.* Stanford: Stanford University Press, 1972.

Brandon, James R. *Theatre in Southeast Asia.* Cambridge, Mass.: Harvard University Press, 1967.

Broder, David S. *Behind the Front Page.* New York: Simon & Schuster, 1987.

Brooks, Jeffrey. *When Russia Learned to Read: Literacy and Popular Literature, 1861–1917.* Princeton: Princeton University Press, 1985.

Bu Shaofu 卜少夫. *Zhandi jizhe jianghua* 戰地記者講話 (Lectures for the war correspondent). Guiyang: Wentong shuju, 1942.

Burke, Peter. *Popular Culture in Early Modern Europe.* London: Temple Smith, 1978.

Cai Ruohong 蔡若虹. *Ku cong he lai* 苦從何來 (Where does hardship come from?). Shanghai: Chenguang chuban gongsi, 1948.

Cambridge History of China. Vol. 13: *Republican China, 1912–1949.* Pt. 2. Edited by John K. Fairbank and Albert Feuerwerker. Cambridge: Cambridge University Press, 1986.

Cao Bohan 曹伯韓. *Jietou bibao* 街頭壁報 (Street wall newspapers). Shanghai: Shenghuo shudian, 1937.

———. *Xuanchuan jishu duben* 宣傳技術讀本 (Propaganda techniques reader). N.p.: Shenghuo shudian, 1938.

Cao Juren 曹聚仁. *Caifang waiji* 採訪外記 (Unofficial interviewing). Hong Kong: Chuangken chubanshe, 1955.

———. "Ping Zhao Wangyun *Nongcun xiesheng ji* ji qi tishi" 評趙望雲「農村寫生集」及其題詩 (A review of Zhao Wangyun's *Rural Sketches* and his poetic inscriptions). *Shen bao,* 30 January 1934.

———. "Xiandai Mulan Tang Guilin de ceying" 現代木蘭唐桂林的側影 (A profile of Tang Guilin: a modern-day Hua Mulan), *Zazhi* 5.1 (16 June 1939): 56.

———. "Zhandi guilai" 戰地歸來 (Returning from the battlefield). In Tian Han et al., *Zhandi guilai.* Shanghai: Zhandi chubanshe, 1937.

Censer, Jack R., and Jeremy D. Popkin, eds. *Press and Politics in Pre-*

Revolutionary France. Berkeley and Los Angeles: University of California Press, 1987.

Chadourne, Marc. *China*. Illustrated by Miguel Covarrubias. New York: Covici Friede, 1932.

Chang Zhiqing 常芝青. "Zai *Jin-Sui ribao* de niandai li" 在晉綏日報的年代裏 (Reminiscences of my experience at *Shanxi-Suiyuan Daily*), in Zhang Jinglu, ed., *Zhongguo xiandai chuban shiliao*. Vol. 4.

Changjiang 長江 (Fan Changjiang 范長江). "Dao Jiluan xiansheng" 悼季鸞先生 (In memory of Mr. Zhang Jiluan). *Huashang bao*, 8 September 1941.

———. "Diao Datong" 弔大同 (Mourning Datong). In Changjiang et al., *Xixian xuezhan ji*. N.p.: Zhanshi chubanshe, n.d.

———. "Jianli xinwen jizhe de zhengque zuofeng" 建立新聞記者的正確作風 (Establishing the correct attitude for reporters). *XWJZ* 1.2 (1 May 1938): 5.

———. "Liangnian lai de xinwen shiye" 兩年來的新聞事業 (Journalism in the past two years). *XWJZ* 2.2 (1 August 1939): 1–6.

———. "Lugouqiao pan" 蘆溝橋畔 (Beside the Marco Polo Bridge). *DGB* (Tianjin), 23–25 July 1937.

———. *Saishang xing* 塞上行 (Journeys on the frontier). Tianjin: Dagong bao, 1937.

———. *Tongxun yu lunwen* 通訊與論文 (Correspondence and essays). Chongqing: Xinhua chubanshe, 1981.

———. "Tuibu yu jinbu" 退步與進步 (Retrogression and progress). *XWJZ* 2.10 (16 March 1941): 1–3.

———. "Yi ye zhanchang" 憶夜戰場 (Recalling the battlefield at night). In Tian Han et al., *Zhandi guilai*. Shanghai: Zhandi chubanshe, 1937.

———. "Yige xinwen jizhe de renshi" 一個新聞記者的認識 (A journalist's understanding). In *Kangzhan de jingyan yu jiaoxun*, edited by Qian Jiaju, Hu Yuzhi, and Zhang Tiesheng. N.p.: Shenghuo shudian, 1939.

———. "Zenyang fa zhanshi dianxun yu xie zhandi tongxun" 怎樣發戰事電訊與寫戰地通訊 (How to file and write war dispatches). *XWJZ* 1.4 (1 July 1938): 5–6.

———. "Zenyang tuijin Guangxi difang xinwen gongzuo" 怎樣推進廣西地方新聞工作 (How to advance local journalism in Guangxi). *Jianshe yanjiu* 1.2 (15 April 1939): 33–34.

———. "Zhanshi xinwen gongzuo de zhenyi" 戰時新聞工作的真義 (The true meaning of wartime journalistic work). *XWJZ* 1.6–7 (10 October 1938): 18.

———. *Zhongguo de xibei jiao* 中國的西北角 (The northwest corner of China). Tianjin: Dagong bao, 1937.

————, ed. *Cong Lugouqiao dao Zhanghe* 從蘆溝橋到漳河 (From the Marco Polo Bridge to the Zhang River). Hankou: Shenghuo shudian, 1938.

————, ed. *Huaihe dazhan zhi qianhou* 淮河大戰之前後 (Before and after the Battle of the Huai River). N.p.: Jiangsheng shushe, 1938.

————, ed. *Lunwang de Ping-Jin* 淪亡的平津 (The fall of Beiping and Tianjin). Hankou: Shenghuo shudian, 1938.

————, ed. *Xixian fengyun* 西線風雲 (Battles on the western front). Shanghai: Dagong bao, 1937.

Changjiang et al. *Xixian xuezhan ji* 西線血戰記 (Bloody battles on the western front). N.p.: Zhanshi chubanshe, n.d.

Chen Baichen 陳白塵. *Shaonian xing* 少年行 (A youthful journey). Beijing: Sanlian shudian, 1988.

Chen Bosheng 陳博生. "Zuo xinwen jizhe de jige yuanze" 做新聞記者的幾個原則 (Several basic principles for the journalist). *XWJZ* 1.1 (1 April 1938): 6–9.

Chen Chin-yun. "Art Chronicle." *T'ien Hsia Monthly* 11.3 (December–January 1940–1941): 270–273.

Chen Fukang 陳福康. *Zheng Zhenduo nianpu* 鄭振鐸年譜 (Chronological biography of Zheng Zhenduo). Beijing: Shumu wenxian chubanshe, 1988.

Chen Jiying 陳紀瀅. *Baoren Zhang Jiluan* 報人張季鸞 (Journalist Zhang Jiluan). Taibei: Wenyou chubanshe, 1957.

————. *Hu Zhengzhi yu Dagong bao* 胡政之與大公報. (Hu Zhengzhi and *Dagong bao*). Hong Kong: Zhanggu yuekanshe, 1974.

Chen, Karl Chia. "The Undeclared War and China's New Drama." *Theatre Arts* 23.12 (December 1939): 895–900.

Chen Lifu 陳立夫. *Zhanshi jiaoyu fangzhen* 戰時教育方針 (Educational policies during the war). N.p.: Zhongyang xunliantuan junshizhengzhibu jiaoguan yanjiuban, 1939.

———— (Chen Li-fu). *Four Years of Chinese Education (1937–1941)*. Chungking: China Information Committee, 1944.

Chen Qiancun 陳前村. "Bianjiang neidi yu dushi de xinwen xiezuo" 邊疆內地與都市的新聞協作 (News cooperation between the border areas, the interior, and the cities). *Baoxue jikan* 1.1 (10 October 1934): 77–80.

Chen Wangdao 陳望道, ed. *Xiaopinwen he manhua* 小品文和漫畫 (Personal essays and cartoons). Shanghai: Shenghuo shudian, 1935.

Chen Yanqiao 陳烟橋. "Lu Xun xiansheng yu banhua" 魯迅先生與版畫 (Mr. Lu Xun and wood carvings). *GM* 1.12 (25 November 1936): 780–783.

Chen Yifan 陳依範 (Jack Chen). "Folk Art and Drama in North-West China To-day." *Our Time*, May 1946, pp. 213–214.

Chen Yiyuan 陳逸園. "Kang-Ri shan'ge" 抗日山歌 (Anti-Japanese

mountain songs). *Quanmin zhoukan* 1.13 (5 March 1938): 196–197.

———. "Wenzhang xiaxiang" 文章下鄉 (Literature must go to the countryside). *Quanmin kangzhan* 64 (10 April 1939): 909.

Chen Yongliang 陳永倞. "Xiezuo jietouju zhi guanjian" 寫作街頭劇之管見 (My views on street play writing). *Zhongyang ribao*, 23 September 1938.

———. "Yanchu jietouju ersan shi" 演出街頭劇二三事 (Several issues in staging street plays). *Zhongyang ribao*, 7 October 1938.

Ch'en, Yung-fa. *Making Revolution: The Communist Movement in Eastern and Central China, 1937–1945*. Berkeley and Los Angeles: University of California Press, 1986.

Chen Ziai 陳子艾. "Woguo min'ge de tishi yu gelü" 我國民歌的體式與歌律 (The form and musical rule of Chinese folk songs). *Kanshou zhidao* 38 (1988): 33–36.

Cheng Cangbo 程滄波. "Zhongguo ziyoushi shang yiwei duli de jizhe —Cheng Shewo xiansheng" 中國自由史上一位獨立的記者—成舍我先生 (Mr. Cheng Shewo—an independent journalist in the free history of China). *Baoxue* 2.1 (June 1957): 6–8.

Cheng Jihua 程季華, Li Shaobai 李少白, and Xing Zuwen 邢祖文, eds. *Zhongguo dianying fazhanshi* 中國電影發展史 (History of the development of Chinese film). 2 vols. Beijing: Zhongguo dianying chubanshe, 1963.

Cheng Qiheng 程其恆. *Zhanshi Zhongguo baoye* 戰時中國報業 (China's wartime newspapers). Guilin: Mingzhen chubanshe, 1944.

Cheng Shewo 成舍我. *Baoxue zazhu* 報學雜著 (Essays on journalism). Taibei: Zhongyang wenwu gongyingshe, 1956.

———. "Wo suo lixiang de xinwen jiaoyu" 我所理想的新聞教育 (My ideal journalism education). *Baoxue jikan* 1.3 (29 March 1935): 105–114.

———. "Women xuyao 'pingjia bao'" 我們需要「平價報」 (We need "inexpensive newspapers"). *Dongfang zazhi* 39.9 (15 July 1943): 24–27.

———. "'Zhidan' yi ke jiandi" 「紙彈」亦可殲敵 ("Paper bullets" can also annihilate the enemy). *DGB* (Hankou), 13–15 May 1938.

———. "Zhongguo baozhi zhi jianglai" 中國報紙之將來 (The future of Chinese newspapers). *Wenhua yuekan* 2 (March 1934): 75–78.

Ch'i, Hsi-sheng. *Nationalist China at War: Military Defeats and Political Collapse, 1937–45*. Ann Arbor: University of Michigan Press, 1982.

China Handbook, 1937–1943. Compiled by the Chinese Ministry of Information. New York: Macmillan, 1943.

China Handbook, 1937–1945. Compiled by the Chinese Ministry of Information. New York: Macmillan, 1947.

China Handbook, 1950. Compiled by the China Handbook Editorial Board. New York: Rockport Press, 1950.

China Year Book, 1936. Edited by H.G.W. Woodhead. Shanghai: North China Daily News, 1936.

Chow, Tse-tsung. *The May Fourth Movement.* Cambridge, Mass.: Harvard University Press, 1960.

Clausewitz, Carl von. *On War.* Edited and translated by Michael Howard and Peter Paret. Princeton: Princeton University Press, 1976.

Coble, Park M. *Facing Japan: Chinese Politics and Japanese Imperialism, 1931–1937.* Cambridge, Mass.: Council on East Asian Studies, Harvard University, 1991.

Cohen, Paul A. *Between Tradition and Modernity: Wang T'ao and Reform in Late Ch'ing China.* Cambridge, Mass.: Harvard University Press, 1974.

Collins, Irene. *The Government and the Newspaper Press in France, 1814–1881.* London: Oxford University Press, 1959.

Coupe, W. A. "Observations on a Theory of Political Caricature." *Comparative Studies in Society and History* 11.1 (January 1969): 79–95.

Cox, Beverly J., and Denna Jones Anderson. *Miguel Covarrubias Caricatures.* Washington, D.C.: Smithsonian Institution Press, 1985.

Crowley, James B. *Japan's Quest for Autonomy: National Security and Foreign Policy, 1930–1938.* Princeton: Princeton University Press, 1966.

Croizier, Ralph. *Art and Revolution in Modern China: The Lingnan (Cantonese) School of Painting, 1906–1951.* Berkeley and Los Angeles: University of California Press, 1988.

Da xiao Riben 打小日本 (Smashing little Japan). N.p.: Rongyu junren zhiye xunliansuo, n.d.

Darnton, Robert. "The Symbolic Element in History." *Journal of Modern History* 58.1 (March 1986): 218–234.

Davis, Natalie Z. "The Historian and Popular Culture." In *The Wolf and the Lamb: Popular Culture in France*, edited by Jacques Beauroy, Marc Bertrand, and Edward T. Gargan. Saratoga, Calif.: Anma Libri, 1977.

———. *Society and Culture in Early Modern France.* Stanford: Stanford University Press, 1975.

Dianshizhai huabao 點石齋畫報 (Dianshizhai Studio pictorial). 10 vols. Preface dated 1884.

Ding Cong 丁聰. *Zuotian de shiqing* 昨天的事情 (Yesterday's events). Beijing: Sanlian shudian, 1984.

Ding Dong 丁東. "Bianqu ji jiefangqu de xiaoxingbao" 邊區及解放區的小型報 (Tabloids in the border regions and the liberated areas). *JFRB*, 17 May 1945.

Ding Ling 丁玲. "Lüetan gailiang Pingju" 略談改良平劇 (A brief discussion on reforming Beijing opera). *Wenyi zhendi* 2.4 (1 December 1938): 495–497.

Ding Ling and Xi Ru 奚如, eds. *Xibei zhandi fuwutuan xiju ji* 西北戰地服務團戲劇集 (Collection of plays of the Northwest Front Service Corps). Hankou: Shanghai zazhi gongsi, 1938.

Ding Yanzhao 丁言昭. "*Fangxia nide bianzi* dansheng, liuchuan he yanbian" 「放下你的鞭子」誕生、流傳和演變 (The birth, circulation and evolution of *Lay Down Your Whip*). *Shanghai xiju* 101 (28 April 1986): 30–31.

Dolby, William. *A History of Chinese Drama*. London: Paul Elek, 1976.

Dong Sheng 東生. "Fengjian shili zai baozhi shang" 封建勢力在報紙上 (Feudalistic influence in the [Chinese] press). In Zheng Zhenduo, *Haiyan* 海燕 (The petrel). Shanghai: Xin Zhongguo shudian, 1932.

Dower, John W. *War Without Mercy: Race and Power in the Pacific War*. New York: Pantheon Books, 1986.

Duara, Prasenjit. *Culture, Power, and the State: Rural North China, 1900–1942*. Stanford: Stanford University Press, 1988.

Duus, Peter, Ramon H. Myers, and Mark R. Peattie, eds. *The Japanese Informal Empire in China, 1895–1937*. Princeton: Princeton University Press, 1989.

Eastman, Lloyd E. *The Abortive Revolution: China Under Nationalist Rule, 1927–1937*. Cambridge, Mass.: Harvard University Press, 1974.

———. "Nationalist China During the Sino-Japanese War, 1937–1945." In *Cambridge History of China*, vol. 13: *Republican China, 1912–1949*, pt. 2, edited by John K. Fairbank and Albert Feuerwerker. Cambridge: Cambridge University Press, 1986.

———. *Seeds of Destruction: Nationalist China in War and Revolution, 1937–1949*. Stanford: Stanford University Press, 1984.

Eberhard, Wolfram. *A Dictionary of Chinese Symbols: Hidden Symbols in Chinese Life and Thought*. London: Routledge & Kegan Paul, 1986.

Eksteins, Modris. *Rites of Spring: The Great War and the Birth of the Modern Age*. Boston: Houghton Mifflin, 1989.

Elshtain, Jean B. "Women as Mirror and Other: Toward a Theory of Women, War, and Feminism." *Humanities in History* 5.2 (Winter–Spring 1982): 29–44.

Elvin, Mark, and G. William Skinner, eds. *The Chinese City Between Two Worlds*. Stanford: Stanford University Press, 1974.

Epstein, Israel. *The Unfinished Revolution in China.* Boston: Little, Brown, 1947.

Fan Changjiang. *See* Changjiang.

Fan Dazeng. *See* Xiao Fang.

Fan Tong 凡同 (pseud.). "Nongcun tongxun de pinruo" 農村通訊的貧弱 (The paucity of rural communication). *XWJZ* 2.10 (16 March 1941): 28–29.

Fang Bai 方白. "Tongsu wenyi jiqiao tan" 通俗文藝技巧談 (On the techniques of popular literature). *KZWY* 4.2 (25 April 1939): 48–52, 64.

Fang Meng 方蒙. *Fan Changjiang zhuan* 范長江傳 (Biography of Fan Changjiang). Beijing: Zhongguo xinwen chubanshe, 1989.

Fang Xiang 方向. *Fang Xiang muke xuanji* 方向木刻選集 (Selected woodcuts of Fang Xiang). 2 vols. Taibei: Gongtong yinshuachang, 1956.

———. "Kangzhan, muke yu wo" 抗戰、木刻與我 (The War of Resistance, woodcuts, and me). In *Kangzhan wenxue gaishuo*, edited by Li Ruiteng. Taibei: Wenxun yuekan zazhishe, 1987.

Fang Zhizhong 方之中. "Minzu ziwei yu manhua" 民族自衛與漫畫 (National defense and cartoons). *Manhua he shenghuo* 1.3 (10 January 1936): 11.

Fanjian ji 反間計 (Counterespionage). N.p.: Junshi weiyuanhui houfang qinwubu zhengzhibu, 1939.

Feng Yi 馮毅. "Manhua Zhongguo jin bainian xuelei shi" 漫畫中國近百年血淚史 (China's struggle in the past hundred years in cartoons). *Zazhi* 6.2 (20 January 1940): 36–40.

Feng Yingzi 馮英子. "Fuzhi difang xinwenzhi" 扶植地方新聞紙 (Promoting local newspapers). *XWJZ* 1.4 (1 July 1938): 23–24.

———. "Huiyi Changjiang" 回憶長江 (Reminiscences of Fan Changjiang), *XWYJZL* 28 (December 1984): 145–159.

———. "Jianli difang baozhi he dihou baozhi" 建立地方報紙和敵後報紙 (Establishing local newspapers and newspapers behind enemy lines). *Minzu gonglun* 1.6 (20 February 1939): 118–123.

Feng Yiyin 豐一吟 et al. *Feng Zikai zhuan* 豐子愷傳 (Biography of Feng Zikai). Hangzhou: Zhejiang renmin chubanshe, 1983.

Feng Yuxiang 馮玉祥. *Feng Yuxiang kangzhan shige xuan* 馮玉祥抗戰詩歌選 (Selected poems on the War of Resistance by Feng Yuxiang). Shanghai: Nuhou chubanshe, 1938.

———. *Kang-Ri de weida minzhong* 抗日的偉大民眾 (The great masses in the War of Resistance). Guilin: Sanhu tushu yinshuashe, 1938.

Feng Zikai 豐子愷. *Chexiang shehui* 車箱社會 (Compartment society). Shanghai: Liangyou tushu yinshua gongsi, 1935.

————. *Ertong xiang* 兒童相 (Sketches of children). N.p.: Kaiming shudian, 1945.

————. *Feng Zikai sanwen xuanji* 豐子愷散文選集 (Selected essays of Feng Zikai). Shanghai: Shanghai wenyi chubanshe, 1981.

————. *Gushi xinhua* 古詩新畫 (Old poems in new paintings). N.p.: Kaiming shudian, 1945.

————. *Husheng huaji* 護生畫集 (Paintings on the preservation of life). 6 vols. Reprinted Taibei: Chunwenxue chubanshe, 1981.

————. *Jiaoshi riji* 教師日記 (A teacher's diary). Chongqing: Wanguang shuju, 1947.

————. *Jieyu manhua* 劫餘漫畫 (Cartoons after a narrow escape). Shanghai: Wanye shudian, 1947.

————. *Kechuang manhua* 客窗漫畫 (Traveler's cartoons). Guilin: Jinri wenyishe, 1943.

————. *Manhua de miaofa* 漫畫的描法 (Cartooning methods). Shanghai: Kaiming shudian, 1948.

————. "Shengji" 生機 (The instinct for life). In Feng, *Yuanyuantang zaibi* 緣緣堂再筆 (Essays from the Yuanyuan Studio, supplement). N.p.: Kaiming shudian, 1948.

————. "Tan kangzhan gequ" 談抗戰歌曲 (On resistance music). *Zhandi* 4 (5 May 1938): 98–100.

————. "Yishu bineng jianguo" 藝術必能建國 (Art must be able to establish a nation). *Yuzhou feng yikan* 2 (16 March 1939): 52–53.

————. *Yishu quwei* 藝術趣味 (A taste for art). N.p.: Kaiming shudian, 1946.

————. *Yuanyuantang jiwai yiwen* 緣緣堂集外遺文 (Supplement to essays from the Yuanyuan Studio). Edited by Ming Chuan 明川. Hong Kong: Wenxue chubanshe, 1979.

————. *Yuanyuantang suibi* 緣緣堂隨筆 (Essays from the Yuanyuan Studio). Shanghai: Kaiming shudian, 1948.

————. *Zikai manhua* 子愷漫畫 (Zikai's cartoons). Shanghai: Kaiming shudian, 1931.

————. *Zhandi manhua* 戰地漫畫 (Battlefield cartoons). Hong Kong: Yingshang buliedian tushu gongsi, 1939.

————. *Zhanshi xiang* 戰時相 (Wartime cartoons). N.p.: Kaiming shudian, 1945.

————. "Zhongguo jiu xiang ke dashu" 中國就像棵大樹 (China is like a big tree). *Yuzhou feng yikan* 1 (1 March 1939): 5–6.

Fitzpatrick, Daniel. *As I Saw It*. New York: Simon & Schuster, 1953.

Forman, Harrison. *Report from Red China*. New York: Henry Holt, 1945.

Freedberg, David. *The Power of Images: Studies in the History and Theory of Response*. Chicago: University of Chicago Press, 1989.

Fu, Po-shek. "Passivity, Resistance, and Collaboration: Intellectual

Choices in Occupied Shanghai, 1937–1945." Ph.D. diss., Stanford University, 1989.

Furet, François. *Interpreting the French Revolution*. Translated by Elborg Forster. Cambridge: Cambridge University Press, 1981.

Furuya Tetsuo 古屋哲夫, ed. *Nitchū sensōshi kenkyū* 日中戰爭史研究 (Studies on the Sino-Japanese War). Tokyo: Yoshikawa kōbunkan, 1984.

Gan Yunheng 甘運衡. "Kangzhan shiqi de shige zhongxin huodong" 抗戰時期底詩歌中心活動 (The song-centered movement during the War of Resistance). In *Kangzhan yu yishu*. Chongqing: Duli chubanshe, n.d.

Gans, Herbert. *Popular Culture and High Culture: An Analysis and Evaluation of Taste*. New York: Basic Books, 1974.

Gao Lihen 高黎痕. "Tan jiefang qian Shanghai de huaju" 談解放前上海的話劇 (On preliberation Shanghai drama). In *Shanghai difangshi ziliao* 上海地方史資料 (Materials on Shanghai local history), vol. 5. Shanghai: Shanghai shehui kexueyuan chubanshe, 1986.

Gao Tian 高天. "Pubian jianli 'wenhua bingzhan'" 普遍建立「文化兵站」 (Widely establish "cultural war stations"). *XWJZ* 1.9–10 (10 December 1938): 12–13.

———. "Zhandi tongxun de xin dongxiang" 戰地通訊的新動向 (New trends in frontline dispatches). *XWJZ* 1.6–7 (10 October 1938): 16.

Ge Gongzhen 戈公振. *Zhongguo baoxue shi* 中國報學史 (A history of the press in China). Reprinted Taibei: Xuesheng shuju, 1964.

Ge Yihong 葛一虹. *Zhanshi yanju zhengce* 戰時演劇政策 (Wartime drama policies). Shanghai: Shanghai zazhi gongsi, 1939.

———, ed. *Zhongguo huaju tongshi* 中國話劇通史 (A history of Chinese spoken drama). Beijing: Wenhua yishu chubanshe, 1990.

Geertz, Clifford. *The Interpretation of Cultures*. New York: Basic Books, 1973.

Geipel, John. *The Cartoon: A Short History of Graphic Comedy and Satire*. Newton Abbot, Eng.: David & Charles, 1972.

Gendaishi shiryō: Nitchū sensō 現代史資料：日中戰爭 (Documents on contemporary history: the Sino-Japanese War). 5 vols. Tokyo: Misuzu shobō, 1964–1966.

Gerstlacher, Anna, et al., eds. *Woman and Literature in China*. Bochum, W. Ger.: Brockmeyer, 1985.

Gewurtz, Margo S. "Tsou T'ao-fen: The *Sheng-huo* Years, 1925–1933." Ph.D. diss., Cornell University, 1972.

Goldman, Merle. *Literary Dissent in Communist China*. Cambridge, Mass.: Harvard University Press, 1967.

Gu Jiegang 顧頡剛. "Women zenyang xiezuo tongsu duwu" 我們怎樣寫作通俗讀物 (How we write popular materials). *KZWY*

2.8 (29 October 1938): 114–117.

———. "Xisheng" 犧牲 (Sacrifice). *Dazhong zhishi* 1.3 (20 November 1936): 14–15.

Gu Yuan 古元. "Chuangzuo suibi" 創作隨筆 (Jottings on my art). *Banhua yishu* 1 (June 1980): 7–8.

———. "Minjian jianzhi" 民間剪紙 (Folk papercuts). *Beifang wenhua* 2.1 (1 June 1946): 44–45.

Gu Zhongyi 顧仲彝. *Liang Hongyu* 梁紅玉. Shanghai: Kaiming shudian, 1941.

Guangweiran 光未然 (Zhang Guangnian 張光年). "Jietouju de yanchu fangfa" 街頭劇的演出方法 (Methods of staging the street play). *DGB* (Hankou), 17 December 1937.

———. "Lun jietouju" 論街頭劇 (On street plays). *Xin xueshi* 2.2 (25 October 1937): 86–87.

Gunn, Edward M. *Unwelcome Muse: Chinese Literature in Shanghai and Peking, 1937–1945*. New York: Columbia University Press, 1980.

Guo Moruo 郭沫若. *Hongbo qu* 洪波曲 (Great wave melody). Hong Kong: Yixin shudian, n.d.

———. "Kangzhan song" 抗戰頌 (Ode to the War of Resistance). *Kangzhan sanrikan* 1 (19 August 1937): 3.

———. "Lixing yu shouxing zhi zhan" 理性與獸性之戰 (The battle between reason and bestiality). *Wenhua zhanxian* 1 (1 September 1937): 7.

———. *Zhanshi xuanchuan gongzuo* 戰時宣傳工作 (Wartime propaganda). N.p.: Zhongyang lujun junguan xuexiao, 1938.

Ha Hua 哈華. *Yangge zatan* 秧歌雜談 (Miscellaneous essays on *yangge*). Shanghai: Huadong renmin chubanshe, 1951.

Han Qixiang 韓起祥. *Han Qixiang yu Shaanbei shuoshu* 韓起祥與陝北說書 (Han Qixiang and the northern Shaanxi storytelling). Edited by Shaanxi sheng quyi shouji zhengli bangongshi, Shaanxi sheng qunzhong yishuguan. N.p.: n.p., 1985.

———. *Liu Qiao tuanyuan* 劉巧團圓 (The reunion of Liu Qiao). N.p.: Shenghuo, Dushu, Xinzhi, 1949.

———. *Zhang Yulan canjia xuanjuhui* 張玉蘭參加選舉會 (Zhang Yulan participates in the election). N.p.: Xinhua shudian, 1946.

Han Qixiang and Wang Zongyuan 王宗元. *Shishi zhuan* 時事傳 (A current affair). N.p.: Xinhua shudian, 1946.

Hanson, Haldore. *Fifty Years Around the Third World*. Burlington, Vt.: Fraser, 1986.

Harbsmeier, Christoph. *The Cartoonist Feng Zikai: Social Realism with a Buddhist Face*. Oslo: Universitetsforlaget, 1984.

Hata Ikuhiko 秦郁彦. *Nankin jiken* 南京事件 (The Nanjing Incident). Tokyo: Chūō kōronsha, 1990.

————. *Nitchū sensōshi* 日中戰争史 (History of the Sino-Japanese War). Rev. ed. Tokyo: Kawade shobō shinsha, 1961.

Hatano Yoshihiro 波多野善大. *Kok-Kyō gassaku* 国共合作 (The Guomindang-Communist alliance). Tokyo: Chūō kōronsha, 1973.

Hayford, Charles W. *To the People: James Yen and Village China*. New York: Columbia University Press, 1990.

He Fangyuan 何方淵. "Lishiju lunzhan" 歷史劇論戰 (Debates on historical plays). *Zazhi* 13.2 (10 May 1944): 153–156.

He Jingzhi 賀敬之. "Wei renmin yishujia lizhuan" 為人民藝術家立傳 (To write a biography for a folk artist). *Quyi* 207 (15 October 1989): 5–6.

He Qifang 何其芳. "Cong souji dao xieding" 從搜集到寫定 (From gathering to recording). In *He Qifang wenji* 何其芳文集 (Collected essays of He Qifang), vol. 4. Beijing: Renmin wenxue chubanshe, 1983.

He Rong 何容. "Tongsu yunwen qianshuo" 通俗韻文淺說 (A short introduction to popular rhymes). In Lao She et al., *Tongsu wenyi wujiang*. Chongqing: Zhonghua wenyijie kangdi xiehui, 1939.

————. "Zenyang shi wenzhang xiaxiang" 怎樣使文章下鄉 (How to make literature go to the countryside). *KDD* 10 (16 May 1938): 17–19.

Higonnet, Margaret R., et al., eds. *Behind the Lines: Gender and the Two World Wars*. New Haven: Yale University Press, 1987.

Hinton, William. *Fanshen*. New York: Vintage Books, 1968.

Holm, David. *Art and Ideology in Revolutionary China*. Oxford: Clarendon Press, 1991.

Hong Shen 洪深. *Kangzhan shinian lai Zhongguo de xiju yundong yu jiaoyu* 抗戰十年來中國的戲劇運動與教育 (The Chinese drama movement and education in the decade since the War of Resistance). Shanghai: Zhonghua shuju, 1948.

————. "Kangzhan shiqi zhong de xiju yundong" 抗戰時期中的戲劇運動 (The drama movement in the War of Resistance). *Xiju kangzhan* 1.1 (16 November 1937): 2–4.

————. "Xinwen dianying yu baozhi" 新聞電影與報紙 (News films and newspapers). *Baoxue jikan* 1.2 (1 January 1935): 23–25.

————, ed. *Zhongguo xinwenxue daxi* 中國新文學大系 (A compendium of the new literature in China). Vol. 9. Shanghai: Liangyou tushu yinshua gongsi, 1935.

Hong Shen and Xu Xuan 徐萱. *Sili qiusheng* 死裏求生 (From the jaws of death). N.p.: Shenghuo shudian, 1938.

Honig, Emily. *Sisters and Strangers: Women in the Shanghai Cotton Mills, 1919–1949*. Stanford: Stanford University Press, 1986.

Hora Tomio 洞富雄. *Nankin daigyakusatsu* 南京大虐殺 (The Nanjing massacre). Tokyo: Gendaishi shuppankai, 1984.

———, ed. *Nitchū sensō Nankin daizangyaku jiken shiryō shū* 日中戦争南京大残虐事件資料集 (Materials on the Nanjing massacre during the Sino-Japanese War). 2 vols. Tokyo: Aoki shoten, 1985.

Hou Weidong 侯唯動. "Ke Zhongping lingdao Bianqu minzhong jutuan" 柯仲平領導邊區民衆劇團 (The Border Region Popular Drama Troupe headed by Ke Zhongping). *XWXSL* 18 (22 February 1983): 146–151.

Hrdličková, V. "The Chinese Storytellers and Singers of Ballads." *Transactions of the Asiatic Society of Japan*, 3d ser., 10 (August 1968): 97–115.

Hsiao Ch'ien. *See* Xiao Qian.

Hsiung, James C., and Steven I. Levine, eds. *China's Bitter Victory: The War with Japan, 1937–1945*. Armonk, N.Y.: M. E. Sharpe, 1992.

Hsu, Tao-Ching. *The Chinese Conception of the Theatre*. Seattle: University of Washington Press, 1985.

Hu Daojing 胡道靜. *Xinwenshi shang de xin shidai* 新聞史上的新時代 (The new era in the history of journalism). Shanghai: Shijie shuju, 1946.

Hu Feng 胡風. *Jian, wenyi, renmin* 劍、文藝、人民 (Sword, art and literature, and the people). Shanghai: Nitu she, 1950.

Hu Jiwei 胡績偉. "Ban yizhang renmin qunzhong xiwen-lejian de baozhi—huiyi Yan'an *Bianqu qunzhong bao*" 辦一張人民群衆喜聞樂見的報紙—回憶延安「邊區羣衆報」 (Running a newspaper loved by the people—reminiscences of Yan'an *Border Region People's Press*). *XWYJZL* 30 (April 1985): 1–27.

Hu Jinquan 胡金銓. *Lao She he tade zuopin* 老舍和他的作品 (Lao She and his works). Hong Kong: Wenhua shenghuo chubanshe, 1977.

Hu Kao 胡考. "Baodao hua" 報道畫 (Reportage picture). *Huashang bao*, 3 December 1941.

———. "Jianli kangzhan manhua de lilun" 建立抗戰漫畫的理論 (Formulate theories for the national resistance cartoon). *Zhandi* 2 (5 April 1938): 34–35.

———. "Xiwang yu manhuajie" 希望於漫畫界 (Hopes for the cartoon circle). *Qianqiu* 15 (1 January 1934): 7–8.

———. "Zhanshi de manhuajie" 戰時的漫畫界 (Cartoonists during the war). In *Kangzhan yu yishu*. Chongqing: Duli chubanshe, n.d.

Hu Lanqi 胡蘭畦. *Hu Lanqi huiyilu* 胡蘭畦回憶錄 (Memoirs of Hu Lanqi). 2 vols. (vol. 1, 1901–1936; vol. 2, 1936–1949). Chengdu: Sichuan renmin chubanshe, 1985–1987.

———. *Zhandi ernian* 戰地二年 (The second year at the battlefield). N.p.: Laodong funü zhandi fuwutuan, 1939.

Hu Man 胡蠻. "Kangzhan banian lai jiefangqu de meishu yundong" 抗戰八年來解放區的美術運動 (Artistic activities in the liberated areas during the eight-year War of Resistance). *JFRB*, 19 June 1946.

Hu Mengxiang 胡孟祥. *Han Qixiang pingzhuan* 韓起祥評傳 (A critical biography of Han Qixiang). Beijing: Zhongguo minjian wenyi chubanshe, 1989.

Hu Sha 胡沙. "Shaanbei yangge" 陝北秧歌 (*Yangge* in northern Shaanxi). *Beifang wenhua* 1.6 (16 May 1946): 28–31.

Hu Yichuan 胡一川. "Huiyi Luyi muke gongzuotuan zai dihou" 回憶魯藝木刻工作團在敵後 (Reminiscences of the activities of the Luyi Woodcut Work Team behind enemy lines). *Meishu* 5 (October 1961): 45–48.

Hu Zhengzhi 胡政之. "Xinwen jizhe zui xuyao you zerenxin" 新聞記者最需要有責任心 (Journalists most need a sense of responsibility). In *Baoren zhi lu*, edited by Wang Wenbin. Shanghai: Sanjiang shudian, 1938.

Hua Junwu 華君武. "Xiangcha buduo" 相差不多 (Close resemblance). *JFRB*, 2 August 1943.

Huang Fengzhou 黃鳳洲. "Huiyi 'Nong jian suo'" 回憶"農講所" (Reminiscences of the Peasant Movement Training Institute). *Meishu* 5 (25 September 1977): 10–11.

Huang Mao 黃茅 (Huang Mengtian 黃蒙田). *Du hua suibi* 讀畫隨筆 (Essays on painting). Hong Kong: Renjian shuwu, 1949.

———. *Huajia yu hua* 畫家與畫 (Artists and art). Hong Kong: Shanghai shuju youxian gongsi, 1981.

———. "Huihua Zhongguohua tanxie" 繪畫中國化談屑 (Remarks on the sinification of art). *JWRB*, 12 May 1940.

———. "Liao Bingxiong jiushi" 廖冰兄舊事 (Reminiscences of Liao Bingxiong). *Dagong bao* (Hong Kong), 17 September 1983.

———. "Manhua de xuanchuan fangshi" 漫畫的宣傳方式 (Propaganda methods in cartoons). *Kangjian tongsu huakan* 2.2 (1 July 1942): 16–20.

———. *Manhua yishu jianghua* 漫畫藝術講話 (Lectures on cartoon art). Shanghai: Shangwu yinshuguan, 1947.

Huang Mengtian. *See* Huang Mao.

Huang Miaozi 黃苗子. "Kangzhan yilai de Zhongguo manhua" 抗戰以來的中國漫畫 (Chinese cartoons since the beginning of the War of Resistance). Preface to *Quanguo manhua zuojia kangzhan jiezuo xuanji*, edited by Huang Miaozi. N.p.: Zhanwang shuwu, 1938.

———. "Tan manhua" 談漫畫 (Speaking of cartoons). *Manhuajie* 7 (5 November 1936): n.p.

———. "Wo de manhua lilun" 我的漫畫理論 (My cartoon theory). In *Xiaopinwen he manhua*, edited by Chen Wangdao. Shanghai: Shenghuo shudian, 1935.

———, ed. *Quanguo manhua zuojia kangzhen jiezuo xuanji* (*QGXJ*) 全國漫畫作家抗戰傑作選集 (Selected works of Chinese cartoonists on the War of Resistance). N.p.: Zhanwang shuwu, 1938.

Huang Shiying 黃士英. "Manhua gailun" 漫畫概論 (An introduction to cartoons). In *Xiaopinwen he manhua*, edited by Chen Wangdao. Shanghai: Shenghuo shudian, 1935.

Huang Tianpeng 黃天鵬. *Zhongguo xinwen shiye* 中國新聞事業 (The journalism enterprise in China). Shanghai: Xiandai shudian, 1932.

———, ed. *Baoxue congkan* 報學叢刊 (Collected works on journalism). Vol. 1, no. 2. Shanghai: Guanghua shuju, 1930.

———, ed. *Xinwenxue lunwenji* 新聞學論文集 (Selected essays on journalism). Shanghai: Guanghua shuju, 1930.

———, ed. *Xinwenxue minlunji* 新聞學名論集 (Renowned lectures on journalism). Shanghai: Shanghai lianhe shudian, 1930.

Huang Yanpei 黃炎培. *Yan'an guilai* 延安歸來 (Returning from Yan'an). In *Bashinian lai* 八十年來 (In the past eighty years). Beijing: Wenshi ziliao chubanshe, 1982.

Huang Yuanlin 黃遠林. "Kangzhan shiqi jiefangqu de manhua" 抗戰時期解放區的漫畫 (Cartoons in the liberated areas during the War of Resistance). *KZWYYJ* 13 (15 May 1984): 65–69.

Huang Yuansheng 黃遠生. *Yuansheng yizhu* 遠生遺著 (The writings of Huang Yuansheng). 4 vols. Shanghai: Shangwu yinshuguan, 1924.

Huang Zhigang 黃芝崗. "Zenyang liyong difangxi zuo kangdi xuanchuan" 怎樣利用地方戲作抗敵宣傳 (How to utilize regional dramas for resistance propaganda). *Kangzhan yishu* 1 (1 September 1939): 1–7.

Hung, Chang-tai. "Female Symbols of Resistance in Chinese Wartime Spoken Drama." *Modern China* 15.2 (April 1989): 149–177.

———. "The Fuming Image: Cartoons and Public Opinion in Late Republican China, 1945 to 1949." *Comparative Studies in Society and History*, forthcoming.

———. *Going to the People: Chinese Intellectuals and Folk Literature, 1918–1937*. Cambridge, Mass.: Council on East Asian Studies, Harvard University, 1985.

———. "New Wine in Old Bottles—The Use of Folk Literature in the War of Resistance Against Japan." *Hanxue yanjiu* (Chinese Studies) 8.1 (June 1990): 401–423.

———. "Paper Bullets: Fan Changjiang and New Journalism in Wartime China." *Modern China* 17.4 (October 1991): 427–468.

———. "Reeducating a Blind Storyteller: Han Qixiang and the

Chinese Communist Storytelling Campaign." *Modern China* 19.4 (October 1993): 395–426.

———. "War and Peace in Feng Zikai's Wartime Cartoons." *Modern China* 16.1 (January 1990): 39–83.

Hung, Shuen-shuen. "Feng Tzu-k'ai: His Art and Thought." M.A. thesis, Michigan State University, 1986.

Hunt, Lynn. *Politics, Culture, and Class in the French Revolution*. Berkeley and Los Angeles: University of California Press, 1984.

Huo Gong 豁公 (pseud.). "Kangdi *zhuzhici*" 抗敵竹枝詞 (Anti-Japanese *zhuzhici* songs). *Kangdi zhoubao* 1 (18 September 1937): 5.

Ienaga Saburō 家永三郎. *Taheiyō sensō* 太平洋戦争 (The Pacific war). 2d ed. Tokyo: Iwanami shoten, 1990.

Imahori Seiji 今堀誠二. *Chūgoku no minshū to kenryoku* 中国の民衆と権力 (Chinese people and power). Tokyo: Keisō shobō, 1973.

Inkeles, Alex. *Public Opinion in Soviet Russia: A Study in Mass Persuasion*. Cambridge, Mass.: Harvard University Press, 1950.

Ishijima Noriyuki 石島紀之. "Kōnichi sensōshi kenkyū no kadai to hōhō" 抗日戦争史研究の課題と方法 (Problems and methods for the study of the Anti-Japanese War). *Chikaki ni arite* 3 (March 1983): 30–36.

Israel, John. "Chungking and Kunming: Hsinan Lienta's Response to Government Educational Policy and Party Control." In *Kangzhan jianguoshi yantaohui lunwenji* 抗戰建國史研討會論文集 (Proceedings of the conference on China during the period of the Sino-Japanese War, 1937–1945). Taibei: Institute of Modern History, Academia Sinica, 1985.

Ji Zhi 季植. "Guanyu 'muke manhua'" 關於「木刻漫畫」(On "woodcut cartoons"). *Xinhua ribao*, 19 March 1942.

Jia Zhi 賈芝. "Lao Suqu de min'ge" 老蘇區的民歌 (Folk songs in the old Jiangxi Soviet area). *Minjian wenyi jikan* 1 (1950): 46–57.

Jiang Feng 江豐. "Guanyu 'fengci huazhan'" 關於「諷刺畫展」(On the "Satirical Cartoon Show"). *JFRB*, 15 February 1942.

Jiang Shuchen 蔣曙晨. "Li Furen" 李敷仁. *Xinwenjie renwu* 新聞界人物 (Journalism personnel) 8 (April 1987): 1–164.

Jiangxi Suqu wenxueshi 江西蘇區文學史 (A history of literature in the Jiangxi Soviet period). Edited by Jiangxi shifan daxue zhongwenxi, Suqu wenxue yanjiushi. Nanchang: Jiangxi renmin chubanshe, 1984.

Jianxun 建勳. "Xin meishu yundong zhankai zhong—wo de jidian yijian" 新美術運動展開中—我的幾點意見 (My personal views of the New Art Movement). *Huashang bao*, 6 August 1941.

"Jieshao Tongsu duwu biankanshe jianshi ji gongzuo" 介紹通俗讀物編刊社簡史及工作 (A brief history of the Popular Reading Publishing House and its work). *KZWY* 1.4 (14 May 1938): 32.

Jin-Sui jiefangqu muke xuan 晉綏解放區木刻選 (Selected woodcuts from the Shanxi-Suiyuan Liberated Region). Chengdu: Sichuan renmin chubanshe, 1982.

Johnson, David, Andrew J. Nathan, and Evelyn S. Rawski, eds. *Popular Culture in Late Imperial China*. Berkeley and Los Angeles: University of California Press, 1985.

Johnson, Kay Ann. *Women, the Family, and Peasant Revolution in China*. Chicago: University of Chicago Press, 1983.

Judd, Ellen R. "Cultural Articulation in the Chinese Countryside, 1937–1947." *Modern China* 16.3 (July 1990): 269–308.

Kang-Ri zhanzheng gequ xuanji 抗日戰爭歌曲選集 (Selected works of songs in the War of Resistance). 4 vols. Beijing: Zhongguo qingnian chubanshe, 1957.

Kang-Ri zhanzheng shiqi de Zhongguo xinwenjie 抗日戰爭時期的中國新聞界 (Chinese journalism during the War of Resistance). Edited by Zhongguo shekeyuan xinwen yanjiusuo 中國社科院新聞研究所 (Institute of Journalism Research, Academy of Social Sciences). Chongqing: Chongqing chubanshe, 1987.

Kang-Ri zhanzheng shiqi Yan'an ji ge kang-Ri minzhu genjudi wenxue yundong ziliao (KRZZY) 抗日戰爭時期延安及各抗日民主根據地文學運動資料 (Materials on the literary movement in Yan'an and other anti-Japanese democratic base areas during the War of Resistance). 3 vols. Edited by Liu Zengjie 劉增傑 et al. Taiyuan: Shanxi renmin chubanshe, 1983.

Kangzhan banian muke xuan 抗戰八年木刻選 (Woodcuts of wartime China). Edited by Zhonghua quanguo muke xiehui 中華全國木刻協會 (China Woodcut Association). Shanghai: Kaiming shudian, 1946.

Kangzhan yu yishu 抗戰與藝術 (The War of Resistance and art). Chongqing: Duli chubanshe, n.d.

Kataoka, Tetsuya. *Resistance and Revolution in China: The Communists and the Second United Front*. Berkeley and Los Angeles: University of California Press, 1974.

Ke Ling 柯靈. "Kangzhan zhong de Feng Zikai xiansheng" 抗戰中的豐子愷先生 (Mr. Feng Zikai in the war). In Wen Zaidao et al., *Biangu ji*. Shanghai: Yingshang wenhui youxian gongsi, 1938.

———. *Wenyuan manyoulu* 文苑漫游錄 (Wandering in the literary garden). Hong Kong: Sanlian shudian, 1988.

Kedward, H. R. *Resistance in Vichy France: A Study of Ideas and Motivation in the Southern Zone, 1940–1942*. Oxford: Oxford University Press, 1978.

Kedward, H. R., and Roger Austin, eds. *Vichy France and the Resistance: Culture and Ideology*. London: Croom Helm, 1985.

Keen, Sam. *Faces of the Enemy: Reflections of the Hostile Imagination*. San Francisco: Harper & Row, 1986.

Klein, Mina C., and H. Arthur Klein. *Käthe Kollwitz: Life in Art*. New York: Schocken Books, 1975.

Kong Xiaoning 孔曉寧. "Fan Changjiang xinwen tongxun de tese" 范長江新聞通訊的特色 (The journalistic style of Fan Changjiang). *XWYJZL* 23 (January 1984): 1–23.

Lai Guanglin 賴光臨. *Liang Qichao yu jindai baoye* 梁啟超與近代報業 (Liang Qichao and modern journalism). Taibei: Shangwu yinshuguan, 1968.

Lai Shaoqi 賴少其. "Manhua yu muke" 漫畫與木刻 (Cartoons and woodcuts). In *Kangzhan de jingyan yu jiaoxun*, edited by Qian Jiaju, Hu Yuzhi, and Zhang Tiesheng. N.p.: Shenghuo shudian, 1939.

Lai Xinxia 來新夏, ed. *Tianjin jindai shi* 天津近代史 (Modern history of Tianjin). Tianjin: Nankai daxue chubanshe, 1987.

Lan Hai 藍海. *Zhongguo kangzhan wenyi shi* 中國抗戰文藝史 (History of the literature and art of the Chinese War of Resistance). Ji'nan: Shandong wenyi chubanshe, 1984.

Langer, Susanne K. *Feeling and Form*. New York: Charles Scribner's Sons, 1953.

——. *Mind: An Essay on Human Feeling*. Vol. 1. Baltimore: Johns Hopkins Press, 1967.

Lao She 老舍 (Shu Qingchun 舒慶春). "Da ke wen—wenyi zuojia yu kangzhan" 答客問—文藝作家與抗戰 (Questions and answers—writers and the War of Resistance). *Yuzhou feng yikan* 2 (16 March 1939): 54–56.

——. "Duo xi duo xie" 多習多寫 (Learn more and write more). *Wenhua xianfeng* 1.14 (1 December 1942): 9.

——. "Guanyu Wenxie" 關於文協 (On the All-China Resistance Association of Writers and Artists). *YZF* 73 (16 August 1938): 38–40.

——. *Gushu yiren* 鼓書藝人 (The drum singers). Beijing: Renmin wenxue chubanshe, 1980.

——. *Lao She quyi wenxuan* 老舍曲藝文選 (Lao She's selected writings on folk performing arts). Beijing: Zhongguo quyi chubanshe, 1982.

——. *Lao She wenji* 老舍文集 (Collected essays of Lao She). 14 vols. Beijing: Renmin chubanshe, 1980–1989.

——. "Nü'er jing" 女兒經 (Classic for women). In *Lao She wenji*, vol. 13. Beijing: Renmin chubanshe, 1988.

——. *San si yi* 三四一 (Three, four, one). N.p.: Duli chubanshe, 1939.

——. "Tongsu wenyi de jiqiao" 通俗文藝的技巧 (The techniques of popular literature). *KDD* 25 (1 August 1939): 2–8.

————. "Wang Xiao gan lü" 王小趕驢 (Wang Xiao drives a donkey). *Wenyi zhendi* 1.3 (16 May 1938): 77–78.

————. "Wo zenyang xie tongsu wenyi" 我怎樣寫通俗文藝 (How I write popular literature). In *Lao She quyi wenxuan.* Beijing: Zhongguo quyi chubanshe, 1982.

————. "Xianhua wode qige huaju" 閒話我的七個話劇 (About my seven plays). *Kangzhan wenyi xuankan* 抗戰文藝選刊 (Selected writings from *Resistance Literature and Art*) 1 (April 1946): 26–29.

————. "Zhizuo tongsu wenyi de kutong" 製作通俗文藝的苦痛 (The difficulty of writing popular literature). *KZWY* 2.6 (15 October 1938): 89–92.

Lao She and Song Zhidi. *Guojia zhishang* 國家至上 (The nation above all). Shanghai: Xinfeng chuban gongsi, 1945.

Lao She et al. *Tongsu wenyi wujiang* 通俗文藝五講 (Five lectures on popular literature). Chongqing: Zhonghua wenyijie kangdi xiehui, 1939.

Lao Xiang 老向 (Wang Xiangchen 王向辰). "Guanyu *Kang-Ri sanzi jing*" 關於抗日三字經 (On the *Anti-Japanese Three-Character Classic*). *KZWY* 1.7 (5 June 1938): 19.

————. *Huangtu ni* 黃土泥 (Yellow mud). Shanghai: Renjian shuwu, 1936.

————. "Kang-Ri qianzi wen" 抗日千字文 (Anti-Japanese thousand-character classic). *KDD* 20 (16 January 1939): 7–9.

————. *Kang-Ri qianzi wen, sizi jing* 抗日千字文、四字經 (Anti-Japanese thousand-character classic and four-character classic). N.p.: Zhengzhong shuju, 1938.

————. "Kang-Ri sanzi jing" 抗日三字經 (Anti-Japanese three-character classic). *KDD* 5 (1 March 1938): 2–4.

————. "Kangzhan geyao" 抗戰歌謠 (Songs of resistance). *YZF* 78 (16 May 1939): 265, 268, 271.

————. "Kangzhan sinian lai de minzhong duwu" 抗戰四年來的民眾讀物 (Popular readings published in the four years of the War of Resistance). *Wenyi yuekan* 11.7 (7 July 1941): 33–38.

————. "Lunan dasheng" 魯南大勝 (The resounding victory in southern Shandong). *YZF* 68 (16 May 1938): 114–115.

————. "Mu hanyi" 募寒衣 (Collecting winter clothing). *YZF* 109 (16 November 1940): 416–418.

————. "Tongsu wenyi de liliang" 通俗文藝的力量 (The power of popular literature). *Wenhua xianfeng* 1.14 (1 December 1942): 12, 11.

————. "Tongsu wenyi gailun" 通俗文藝概論 (An introduction to popular literature). In Lao She et al., *Tongsu wenyi wujiang.* Shanghai: Zhonghua wenyijie kangdi xiehui, 1939.

————. "Xiandai jiaoyu babi" 現代教育八弊 (Eight drawbacks in

modern education). *LY* 62 (1 April 1935): 677–684.

Lee, Leo Ou-fan. "Literary Trends: The Road to Revolution, 1927–1949." In *Cambridge History of China*, vol. 13: *Republican China, 1912–1949*, pt. 2, edited by John K. Fairbank and Albert Feuerwerker. Cambridge: Cambridge University Press, 1986.

———. *The Romantic Generation of Modern Chinese Writers*. Cambridge, Mass.: Harvard University Press, 1973.

Lee, Leo Ou-fan, and Andrew J. Nathan. "The Beginning of Mass Culture: Journalism and Fiction in the Late Ch'ing and Beyond." In *Popular Culture in Late Imperial China*, edited by David Johnson, Andrew J. Nathan, and Evelyn S. Rawski.

Levine, Lawrence W. *Highbrow/Lowbrow: The Emerqence of Cultural Hierarchy in America*. Cambridge, Mass: Harvard University Press, 1988.

Leyda, Jay. *Dianying: An Account of Films and the Film Audience in China*. Cambridge, Mass.: MIT Press, 1972.

Li Bozhao 李伯釗. "Dihou wenyi yundong gaikuang" 敵後文藝運動概況 (A survey of the literary movement behind enemy lines). In *KRZZY*, vol. 2.

Li Furen 李敷仁, ed. *Laobaixing shelunji* 老百姓社論集 (Selected editorials of *The Common Folk*). Xi'an: Laobaixing biankanshe, 1940.

Li Gongpu 李公樸. "Yige zhanxin de gejudui" 一個嶄新的歌劇隊 (An innovative opera troupe). *Quanmin kangzhan* 69 (5 May 1939): 988–989.

Li Hua 李樺. "Kangzhan qijian de muke yundong" 抗戰期間的木刻運動 (The woodcut movement during the War of Resistance). *Xin Zhonghua* 4.8 (16 September 1946): 36–40.

———. "Lu Xun xiansheng yu muke" 魯迅先生與木刻 (Mr. Lu Xun and woodcuts). *Minzhu shijie* 3.8 (1 November 1946): 23.

Li Ji 李季. *Wang Gui yu Li Xiangxiang* 王貴與李香香 (Wang Gui and Li Xiangxiang). N.p.: Shenghuo, Dushu, Xinzhi, 1949.

———. "Wo shi zenyang xuexi min'ge de" 我是怎樣學習民歌的 (How I studied folksongs). In *Li Ji yanjiu zhuanji* 李季研究專集 (Collected essays on the study of Li Ji). Fuzhou: Haixia wenyi chubanshe, 1985.

———, ed. *Shuntianyou er qian shou* 順天遊二千首 (Two thousand follow-heaven-roaming songs). Shanghai: Shanghai zazhi gongsi, 1950.

Li Jiarui 李家瑞. *Beiping suqu lüe* 北平俗曲略 (A brief account of popular songs in Beiping). Beiping: Lishi yuyan yanjiusuo, Academia Sinica, 1933.

———. "Tan dagushu de qiyuan" 談大鼓書的起源 (On the origin of drum singing). *Renjian shi* 31 (5 July 1935): 24.

Li Jinghan 李景漢 and Zhang Shiwen 張世文, eds. *Dingxian yangge*

xuan 定縣秧歌選 (Dingxian plantation songs). N.p.: Zhonghua pingmin jiaoyu cujinhui, 1933.

Li Ke 李克. *Hao Mengling kangdi xunguo* 郝夢齡抗敵殉國 (Commander Hao Mengling dies a hero's death). Wuchang: Tongsu duwu biankanshe, 1938.

Li Liangrong 李良榮. *Zhongguo baozhi wenti fazhan gaiyao* 中國報紙文體發展概要 (An outline of development of journalistic style in Chinese newspapers). Fuzhou: Fujian renmin chubanshe, 1985.

Li Lun 李倫, Wei Chenxu 魏晨旭, Ren Guilin 任桂林, et al. *San da Zhujiazhuang* 三打祝家莊 (Three attacks at Zhu Mansion). Beijing: Zhongguo xiju chubanshe, 1957.

Li Mo 李默 et al. "Guomindang fandongpai chajin baokan mulu" 國民黨反動派查禁報刊目錄 (A list of banned newspapers and journals by the Guomindang reactionaries). In *Zhongguo xiandai chuban shiliao*, edited by Zhang Jinglu, vol. 4. Beijing: Zhonghua shuju, 1959.

Li Puyuan 李樸園. "Guanyu xiju de yige shiyan" 關於戲劇的一個試驗 (On an experiment in drama). *Minyi zhoukan* 9 (9 February 1938): 12.

Li Qun 力羣. "Xizhanchang shang de muke yundong" 西戰場上的木刻運動 (The woodcut movement on the western front). *Wenyi zhendi* 4.5 (1 January 1940): 1377–1378, 1383.

———. "Xuanchuanhua zai nongcun" 宣傳畫在農村 (Propaganda pictures in villages). *Dikang sanrikan* 17 (13 October 1937): 8.

Li Ruiteng 李瑞騰, ed. *Kangzhan wenxue gaishuo* 抗戰文學概說 (An account of wartime literature). Taibei: Wenxun yuekan zazhishe, 1987.

Liang Bing 梁冰. "Kaifeng jiuwang juyun de yipie" 開封救亡劇運的一瞥 (A glimpse of the national salvation drama movement in Kaifeng). *JWRB*, 27 April 1938.

Liang Guozhang 梁國璋. "'Yanju qingqidui' chuanguo le zhandi" 「演劇輕騎隊」穿過了戰地 ("The Drama Light Cavalry" galloping across the battleground). *XJCQ* 2.1 (25 May 1942): 62–64.

Liang Shiqiu 梁實秋. "Bianzhe de hua" 編者的話 (Editor's note). *Zhongyang ribao*, 1 December 1938.

———. "Huiyi kangzhan shiqi" 回憶抗戰時期 (Remembering the War of Resistance). In Su Xuelin et al., *Kangzhan shiqi wenxue huiyilu*. Taibei: Wenxun yuekan zazhishe, 1987.

Liao Bingxiong 廖冰兄. *Bingxiong manhua* 冰兄漫畫 (Liao Bingxiong's cartoons). Guangzhou: Lingnan meishu chubanshe, 1984.

———. "Guanyu manmu hezuo" 關於漫木合作 (On the cooperation between cartoonists and woodcut artists). *JWRB*, 22 February 1940.

Liao Jingdan 廖井丹. "*Kangzhan ribao* de zhandou suiyue" 抗戰

日報的戰鬥歲月 (Years of arduous struggle at *Resistance War Daily*). *XWYJZL* 29 (February 1985): 56–78.

Liao Mosha 廖沫沙 et al. *Yi Deng Tuo* 憶鄧拓 (Remembering Ding Tuo). Fuzhou: Fujian renmin chubanshe, 1980.

Liao Quanjing 廖全京. *Dahoufang xiju lungao* 大後方戲劇論稿 (A draft history of drama in the hinterland). Chengdu: Sichuan jiaoyu chubanshe, 1988.

Libo. *See* Zhou Libo.

Lin Fei 林蜚. "Yanju yu guanzhong" 演劇與觀眾 (Staging plays and the audience). *JWRB*, 28 April 1938.

Lin Jianqi 林建七. "Zhongguo de manhua yu muke" 中國的漫畫與木刻 (Cartoons and woodcuts in China). *Yue bao* 1.2 (15 February 1937): 452–453.

Lin Jing 林婧. "Zai xiangcun zhong yanju de liangzhong zaoyu" 在鄉村中演劇的兩種遭遇 (Two encounters when staging plays in the rural area). In *Kangzhan de jingyan yu jiaoxun*, edited by Qian Jiaju, Hu Yuzhi, and Zhang Tiesheng. N.p.: Shenghuo shudian, 1939.

Lin Shan 林山. "Gaizao shuoshu" 改造說書 (Reforming storytelling). *JFRB*, 5 August 1945.

Lin Yutang 林語堂. *A History of the Press and Public Opinion in China*. Chicago: University of Chicago Press, 1936.

———. "*Shen bao* de yiyao fukan" 申報的醫藥附刊 (*Shen bao*'s medical supplement). *YZF* 18 (1 June 1936): 270–271.

———. "Suo wang yu *Shen bao*" 所望於申報 (My hopes for *Shen bao*). *YZF* 3 (16 October 1935): 115–116.

Ling He 凌鶴. Preface to *Manhua he shenghuo* 漫畫和生活 (Cartoons and life) 1.3 (20 January 1936): 3.

Link, Perry. *Mandarin Ducks and Butterflies: Popular Fiction in Early Twentieth-Century Chinese Cities*. Berkeley and Los Angeles: University of California Press, 1981.

Link, Perry, Richard Madsen, and Paul G. Pickowicz, eds. *Unofficial China: Popular Culture and Thought in the People's Republic*. Boulder, Colo.: Westview Press, 1989.

Lippmann, Walter. *Public Opinion*. New York: Harcourt, Brace, 1922.

Liu Cunren 柳存仁. "Jin shinian lai woguo huaju yundong de niaokan" 近十年來我國話劇運動的鳥瞰 (General survey of the Chinese spoken drama movement in the past ten years). *Dafeng* 92 (20 June 1941): 3074–3077.

Liu Jian 劉澗. "Ruhe shi huaju shenru dao nongcun qu" 如何使話劇深入到農村去 (How to make spoken dramas penetrate the rural areas). *Kangzhan xiju* 2.2–3 (May 1938): 80–81.

Liu Nianqu 劉念渠. "Wo xiang liudong yanjudui jianyi" 我向流動演

劇隊建議 (A few suggestions for the drama traveling troupe), *Kangzhan xiju* 1.2 (1 December 1937): 39–40.

Liu Qun 劉群. *Zhanshi de xuanchuan gongzuo* 戰時的宣傳工作 (Propaganda work during the war). Shanghai: Shenghuo shudian, 1937.

Liu Ruming 劉汝明. *Liu Ruming huiyilu* 劉汝明回憶錄 (Memoirs of Liu Ruming). Taibei: Zhuanji wenxue chubanshe, 1966.

Liu Shi 柳湜. "Dazhong wenhua yundong yu minzu jiefang" 大衆文化運動與民族解放 (The popular culture movement and national salvation). *Dushu shenghuo* 3.9 (10 March 1936): 391–393.

———. "Difang ribao qikan bianji yaodian shangque" 地方日報期刊編輯要點商榷 (A few important questions on editing local newspapers and magazines). *XWJZ* 1.2 (1 May 1938): 7–9.

———. *Jietou jianghua* 街頭講話 (Street talks). N.p.: Shenghuo shudian, 1936.

Liu Wenqu 劉問渠. "Chuangzao xinwen xiezuo de xinxing" 創造新聞寫作的新型 (Creating new news-writing styles). *Xinwen zhanxian* 2.2–3 (16 May 1942): 24–25.

Liu Xinhuang 劉心皇. *Xiandai Zhongguo wenxue shihua* 現代中國文學史話 (A history of modern Chinese literature). Taibei: Zhengzhong shuju, 1971.

Liu Yazi 柳亞子 (Yazi). "Zatan A Ying xiansheng de Nan Ming shiju" 雜談阿英先生的南明史劇 (On Mr. A Ying's Southern Ming historical plays). *Wenxue chuangzuo* 1.2 (15 October 1942): 52–57.

———. "Zatan lishiju" 雜談歷史劇 (On historical plays). *XJCQ* 2.4 (30 October 1942): 49.

Liu Yun 柳雲. "Hongjun de geyao" 紅軍的歌謠 (Folk songs of the Red Army). *Dafeng* 4 (5 April 1938): 106–109.

Liu Yunlai 劉雲萊. "Huabei dihou geming baokan de chuangjian" 華北敵後革命報刊的創建 (The founding of revolutionary newspapers behind enemy lines in Northern China). *XWYJZL* 29 (February 1985): 95–98.

Liu Zhenqing 劉枕青. *Manhua gailun* 漫畫概論 (An introduction to cartoons). Changsha: Shangwu yinshuguan, 1939.

Liu Zhuzhou 劉竹舟. "Zenyang zuo zhandi jizhe" 怎樣做戰地記者 (How to be a war correspondent). *Xinwen zhanxian* 2.2–3 (16 May 1942): 16–20.

Liu Zucheng 劉祖澄. "Guanyu xinwen jizhe zhiye diwei queli wenti" 關於新聞記者職業地位確立問題 (Questions about establishing the status of the journalism profession). *Baoxue jikan* 1.1 (10 October 1934): 57–59.

Liu Zunqi 劉尊棋. "Zhandi jizhe de yixie yinxing" 戰地記者的一些印象 (A few impressions of a war correspondent). In *Kangzhan de jingyan yu jiaoxun*, edited by Qian Jiaju, Hu Yuzhi, and Zhang

Tiesheng. N.p.: Shenghuo shudian, 1939.

Low, David. *Autobiography*. New York: Simon & Schuster, 1957.

———. *A Cartoon History of Our Times*. New York: Simon & Schuster, 1939.

———. *Years of Wrath: A Cartoon History, 1931–1945*. New York: Simon & Schuster, 1946.

Lowenthal, Leo. *Literature, Popular Culture, and Society*. Palo Alto, Calif.: Pacific Books, 1961.

Löwenthal, Rudolf. "Printing Paper: Its Supply and Demand in China." *Yenching Journal of Social Studies* 1.1 (June 1938): 107–121.

———. "Public Communications in China Before July, 1937." *Chinese Social and Political Science Review* 22.1 (April–June 1938): 42–58.

———. "The Tientsin Press: A Technical Survey." *Chinese Social and Political Science Review* 19.4 (January 1936): 543–558.

Lu Di 陸地. "Muke zai baozhi shang de zhendi" 木刻在報紙上的陣地 (The woodcut front in the newspapers). *XWYJZL* 10 (December 1981): 182–191.

———, ed. *Zhongguo xiandai banhua shi* 中國現代版畫史 (A history of Chinese engraving). Beijing: Renmin meishu chubanshe, 1987.

Lu Dingyi 陸定一. "Tan Yan'an *Jiefang ribao* gaiban" 談延安解放日報改版 (On the reform of Yan'an's *Liberation Daily*). *XWYJZL* 8 (November 1981): 1–8.

———. "Wenhua xiaxiang—Du 'Xiang Wu Manyou kanqi' yougan" 文化下鄉—讀「向吳滿有看齊」有感 (Sending culture down to the village—Thoughts after looking at "Emulating Wu Manyou"). *JFRB*, 10 February 1943.

Lu Shaofei 魯少飛. "Kangzhan yu manhua" 抗戰與漫畫 (The War of Resistance and cartoons). *Dikang sanrikan* 15 (6 October 1937): 8–9.

Lu Xun 魯迅. "Kaisui Kelehuizhi banhua" 凱綏·珂勒惠支版畫 (Käthe Kollwitz's prints). *Zuojia* 1.5 (15 August 1936): 1224–1227.

———. "Kaisui Kelehuizhi muke 'Xisheng' shuoming" 凱綏·珂勒惠支木刻「犧牲」說明 (On Käthe Kollwitz's "Sacrifice"). In *Lu Xun quanji* (Complete work of Lu Xun), vol. 8. Beijing: Renmin wenxue chubanshe, 1981.

——— (Qiejie 且介). "Manhua er you manhua" 漫畫而又漫畫 (Cartoons, again cartoons). In *Xiaopinwen he manhua*, edited by Chen Wangdao. Shanghai: Shenghuo shudian, 1935.

———. "Mantan 'manhua'" 漫談「漫畫」 (On cartoons). In *Xiaopinwen he manhua*, edited by Chen Wangdao. Shanghai: Shenghuo shudian, 1935.

———. "Tan muke yishu" 談木刻藝術 (On woodcuts). *Wenlian* 1.1

(5 January 1946): 5–6.

Lu Yi 陸詒. "Ji Zhongguo qingnian jizhe xuehui de chengli dahui" 記中國青年記者學會的成立大會 (On the inauguration of the Chinese Young Journalists Society). *XWJZ* 1.2 (1 May 1938): 17–18.

———. "Tan dangqian de zhandi xinwen gongzuo" 談當前的戰地新聞工作 (On current journalistic work at the front). *XWJZ* 1.6–7 (10 October 1938): 17.

———. *Zhandi pingzong* 戰地萍踪 (Battlefront experience). Beijing: Renmin ribao chubanshe, 1985.

Lu Zipei 盧子培. "Huazhong jiefangqu baozhi zazhi yilan" 華中解放區報紙雜誌一覽 (A survey of newspapers and magazines published in the liberated areas in Central China). In *Zhongguo xiandai chuban shiliao*, edited by Zhang Jinglu, vol. 3. Beijing: Zhonghua shuju, 1956.

Lü Fu 呂復. "Kangdi yanjudui wushi zhounian zuotanhui qianyan" 抗敵演劇隊五十周年座談會前言 (An introduction to the symposium commemorating the fiftieth anniversary of the founding of the Anti-Japanese Traveling Drama Troupes). Unpublished paper, 5 October 1988, Wuhan.

Lucie-Smith, Edward. *The Art of Caricature*. Ithaca: Cornell University Press, 1981.

Ma Yanxiang 馬彥祥. "Duiyu jiuju de zai renshi" 對於舊劇的再認識 (A new understanding of traditional dramas). *Beida banyuekan* 6 (1 June 1948): 13–14, 17.

———. "Jiuju kangzhan" 舊劇抗戰 (Traditional dramas for resistance), *KZWY* 1.10 (25 June 1938): 127.

———. "Ruhe renshi difangju" 如何認識地方劇 (How to correctly understand regional dramas). *Renmin wenyi* 1.3 (15 March 1946): 60–63.

———, ed. *Zuijia kangzhan juxuan* 最佳抗戰劇選 (The best resistance war plays). Hankou: Shanghai zazhi gongsi, 1938.

McDougall, Bonnie S., ed. *Popular Chinese Literature and Performing Arts in the People's Republic of China, 1949–1970*. Berkeley and Los Angeles: University of California Press, 1984.

Mackerras, Colin. "Theater and the Masses." In *Chinese Theater: From Its Origins to the Present Day*, edited by Colin Mackerras. Honolulu: University of Hawaii Press, 1983.

MacKinnon, Stephen R., and Oris Friesen. *China Reporting: An Oral History of American Journalism in the 1930s and 1940s*. Berkeley and Los Angeles: University of California Press, 1987.

Mai Dong 買冬 (pseud.). "Taiyuan de jiuwang shuci yundong" 太原的救亡書詞運動 (The national salvation storytelling movement in Taiyuan). *Shen bao zhoukan* 2.25 (27 June 1937): 564.

Mao Dun 茅盾. "Dazhonghua yu liyong jiu xingshi" 大衆化與利用舊形式 (Popularization and the use of old forms). *Wenyi zhendi* 1.4 (1 June 1938): 121.

Mao Zedong (Mao Tse-tung) 毛澤東. *Mao Zedong xinwen gongzuo wenxuan* 毛澤東新聞工作文選 (Selected journalism writings of Mao Zedong). Beijing: Xinhua chubanshe, 1983.

———. *Selected Works of Mao Tse-tung.* 4 vols. Peking: Foreign Language Press, 1967.

———. "Zai *Jiefang ribao* gaiban zuotanhui shang de jianghua" 在「解放日報」改版座談會上的講話 (Talks at the forum on the reform of *Liberation Daily*). In *Mao Zedong xinwen gongzuo wenxuan.* Beijing: Xinhua chubanshe, 1983.

———. "Zengqiang baokan xuanchuan de dangxing" 增强報刊宣傳的黨性 (Strengthen newspapers and magazines in propagating the Party's policy). In *Mao Zedong xinwen gongzuo wenxuan.* Beijing: Xinhua chubanshe, 1983.

———. "Zenyang ban difang baozhi" 怎樣辦地方報紙 (How to run a local newspaper). In *Mao Zedong xinwen gongzuo wenxuan.* Beijing: Xinhua chubanshe, 1983.

Mauldin, Bill. *Up Front.* Cleveland: World, 1945.

Meisner, Maurice. *Marxism, Maoism, and Utopianism.* Madison: University of Wisconsin Press, 1982.

Meng Qiujiang. *See* Qiujiang.

Miao Peishi 苗培時, ed. *Geyao congji* 歌謠叢集 (Collected folk songs). N.p.: Taofen shudian, 1947.

Mo Ye 莫耶. "Liping de fannao" 麗萍的煩惱 (Liping's distress). In *Shenghuo de bolan.* Xi'an: Shaanxi renmin chubanshe, 1984.

———. *Shenghuo de bolan* 生活的波瀾 (Waves of life). Xi'an: Shaanxi renmin chubanshe, 1984.

Monas, Sidney. "St. Petersburg and Moscow as Cultural Symbols." In *Art and Culture in Nineteenth-Century Russia*, edited by Theofanis G. Stavrou. Bloomington: Indiana University Press, 1983.

Morley, James William, ed. *The China Quagmire: Japan's Expansion on the Asian Continent, 1933–1941.* New York: Columbia University Press, 1983.

Mosse, George L. "Two World Wars and the Myths of the War Experience." *Journal of Contemporary History* 21.4 (October 1986): 491–513.

Mowrer, Edgar A. *The Dragon Wakes: A Report from China.* New York: William Morrow, 1939.

Mu Mutian 穆木天. *Kangzhan daguci* 抗戰大鼓詞 (War of Resistance drum songs). Hankou: Xinzhi shudian, 1938.

———. "Wenyi dazhonghua yu tongsu wenyi" 文藝大衆化與通俗文藝 (The popularization of literature and popular literature).

Wenyi zhendi 2.8 (1 February 1939): 638–643.

———. "Yong zhanzheng huida zhanzheng" 用戰爭回答戰爭 (Use war to answer war). In *Kangzhan song*, edited by Tang Qiong. Shanghai: Wuzhou shubaoshe, 1937.

Mukerji, Chandra, and Michael Schudson, eds. *Rethinking Popular Culture: Contemporary Perspectives in Cultural Studies*. Berkeley and Los Angeles: University of California Press, 1991.

Murphey, Rhoads. *Shanghai: Key to Modern China*. Cambridge, Mass.: Harvard University Press, 1953.

———. "The Treaty Ports and China's Modernization." In *The Chinese City Between Two Worlds*, edited by Mark Elvin and G. William Skinner. Stanford: Stanford University Press, 1974.

Nash, Vernon, and Rudolf Löwenthal. "Responsible Factors in Chinese Journalism." *Chinese Social and Political Science Review* 20.3 (October 1936): 420–426.

Ning 寧 (pseud.). "Xin meishu yundong" 新美術運動 (New art movement). *Huashang bao*, 19 June 1941.

Ono Kazuko. *Chinese Women in a Century of Revolution, 1850–1950*. Edited by Joshua A. Fogel. Stanford: Stanford University Press, 1989.

Ou Mei manhua jingxuan 歐美漫畫精選 (Selected cartoons from Europe and America). Edited by Qian Gechuan 錢歌川. N.p.: Zhonghua shuju, 1943.

Ouyang Yuqian (Ouyang Yu-chien) 歐陽予倩. *Dianying banlu chujia ji* 電影半路出家記 (My film career). Beijing: Zhongguo dianying chubanshe, 1962.

———. "Gaige Guixi de buzhou" 改革桂戲的步驟 (Steps toward reforming Guangxi opera). In *Ouyang Yuqian yu Guiju gaige*, edited by Guangxi yishu yanjiuyuan, Guangxi shehui kexueyuan. Nanning: Guangxi renmin chubanshe, 1986.

———. *Huaju, xingeju yu Zhongguo xiju yishu chuantong* 話劇、新歌劇與中國戲劇藝術傳統 (Spoken drama, new opera, and the Chinese dramatic tradition). Shanghai: Shanghai wenyi chubanshe, 1959.

———. "Huiyi Chunliu" 回憶春柳 (Spring Willow Society recollected). In *ZGHJYD*, vol. 1.

———. *Liang Hongyu* 梁紅玉. Hankou: Shanghai zazhi gongsi, 1938.

———. "Mingri de xingeju" 明日的新歌劇 (Tomorrow's new operas). *XJSD* 1.1 (16 May 1937): 69–74.

———. "The Modern Chinese Theatre and the Dramatic Tradition." *Chinese Literature* 11 (November 1959): 102–123.

———. "Mulan congjun" 木蘭從軍 (Mulan joins the army). *Wenxian* 6 (10 March 1939): F1–F31.

———. *Ouyang Yuqian wenji* 歐陽予倩文集 (Collected works of Ouyang Yuqian). 2 vols. Beijing: Zhongguo xiju chubanshe, 1980.

———. *Pan Jinlian* 潘金蓮. Shanghai: Xindongfang shudian, 1928.

———. "Shan'ge" 山歌 (Mountain song). *JWRB*, 10 October 1937.

———. "Tan wenmingxi" 談文明戲 (On civilized drama). In *ZGHJYD*, vol. 1.

———. *Taohua shan* 桃花扇 (*The Peach Blossom Fan*). Beijing: Zhongguo xiju chubanshe, 1957.

———. "Zaitan jiuxi de gaige" 再談舊戲的改革 (Another discussion of the reform of old dramas). *Shen bao zhoukan*, 2.7 (21 February 1937): 139–142; 2.8 (28 February 1937): 166–167; 2.12 (28 March 1937): 257–258.

Ouyang Yuqian yu Guiju gaige 歐陽予倩與桂劇改革 (Ouyang Yuqian and reform of Guangxi opera). Edited by Guangxi yishu yanjiuyuan and Guangxi shehui kexueyuan. Nanning: Guangxi renmin chubanshe, 1986.

Ozouf, Mona. *Festivals and the French Revolution*. Translated by Alan Sheridan. Cambridge, Mass.: Harvard University Press, 1988.

Paine, Robert. "When Saying Is Doing." In *Politically Speaking: Cross-cultural Studies of Rhetoric*, edited by Robert Paine. Philadelphia: Institute for the Study of Human Issues, 1981.

Parkin, David. "Political Language." *Annual Review of Anthropology* 18 (1984): 345–365.

Passin, Herbert. "Writer and Journalist in the Transitional Society." In *Communications and Political Development*, edited by Lucian W. Pye. Princeton: Princeton University Press, 1963.

Pepper, Suzanne. *Civil War in China: The Political Struggle, 1945–1949*. Berkeley and Los Angeles: University of California Press, 1978.

Phelps, Dryden L. "Letters and Arts in the War Years." In *China*, edited by Harley F. MacNair. Berkeley and Los Angeles: University of California Press, 1946.

Pickowicz, Paul G. *Marxist Literary Thought in China: The Influence of Ch'ü Ch'iu-pai*. Berkeley and Los Angeles: University of California Press, 1981.

Pocock, J.G.A. *Politics, Language, and Time: Essays on Political Thought and History*. New York: Atheneum, 1973.

Press, Charles. *The Political Cartoon*. East Brunswick, N.J.: Associated University Presses, 1981.

Průšek, Jaroslav. "Urban Centers: The Cradle of Popular Fiction." In *Studies in Chinese Literary Genres*, edited by Cyril Birch. Berkeley and Los Angeles: University of California Press, 1974.

Qian Jiaju 千家駒, Hu Yuzhi 胡愈之, and Zhang Tiesheng 張鐵生,

eds. *Kangzhan de jingyan yu jiaoxun* 抗戰的經驗與教訓 (Experience and lessons during the War of Resistance). N.p.: Shenghuo shudian, 1939.

Qian Junrui 錢俊瑞. "'Zhun hanjian' lun" 「準漢奸」論 (On would-be traitors). *Xin xueshi* 2.3 (10 November 1937): 110–111.

Qian Xingcun. *See* A Ying.

Qianli 千里. "Zhongguo xiju yundong fazhan de niaokan" 中國戲劇運動發展底鳥瞰 (A general survey of the development of the Chinese drama movement). *Beidou* 2.2 (20 January 1932): 51–57.

Qianyu. *See* Ye Qianyu.

Qiejie. *See* Lu Xun.

Qin Xianci 秦賢次, ed. *Kangzhan shiqi wenxue shiliao* 抗戰時期文學史料 (Historical materials on wartime literature). Taibei: Wenxun yuekan zazhishe, 1987.

"Qingzhu 'Jiuyi' jizhe jie" 慶祝「九一」記者節 (Celebrating September 1st, Journalists' Day). *Xinwen zazhi* 1.8–9 (5 September 1936): 1, 23.

Qiujiang 秋江 (Meng Qiujiang 孟秋江). "Dazhan Pingxingguan" 大戰平型關 (The great battle at the Pingxing Pass). *DGB* (Hankou), 5–14 October 1937.

———. "Ketong de Zhangjiakou" 可痛的張家口 (Lament for Zhangjiakou). In *Xixian fengyun*, edited by Changjiang. Shanghai: Dagong bao, 1937.

———. "Nankou yuhui xian shang" 南口迂迴線上 (Outflanking the enemy at the Nankou Pass). *DGB* (Hankou), 3–4 October 1937.

———. "Tuishou Yanmenguan" 退守雁門關 (Withdrawing to guard the Yanmen Pass). *DGB* (Hankou), 30 September–2 October 1937.

———. "Zenyang zuo zhandi xinwen jizhe" 怎樣做戰地新聞記者 (How to be a war correspondent). *XWJZ* 1.6–7 (10 October 1938): 20.

Qu Junong 瞿菊農. "Miaoxie nongcun shenghuo de wenzhang" 描寫農村生活的文章 (Articles depicting village life). *YZF* 40 (1 May 1937): 168.

Qu Qiubai 瞿秋白. *Jietou ji* 街頭集 (Street essays). Shanghai: Xia she, 1940.

———. *Qu Qiubai wenji* 瞿秋白文集 (Collected works of Qu Qiubai). 4 vols. Beijing: Renmin wenxue chubanshe, 1953–1954.

Rawski, Evelyn S. *Education and Popular Literacy in Ch'ing China*. Ann Arbor: University of Michigan Press, 1979.

———. "Elementary Education in the Mission Enterprise." In *Christianity in China: Early Protestant Missionary Writings*, edited by Suzanne Wilson Barnett and John King Fairbank. Cambridge, Mass.: Committee on American–East Asian Relations of the Department of History in collaboration with the Council on East Asian Studies, Harvard University, 1985.

Rawski, Thomas G. *Economic Growth in Prewar China*. Berkeley and Los Angeles: University of California Press, 1989.

Rhodes, Anthony. *Propaganda*. New York: Chelsea House, 1976.

Rivers, William L. *The Opinionmakers*. Boston: Beacon Press, 1965.

Rowe, William T. *Hankow: Conflict and Community in a Chinese City, 1796–1895*. Stanford: Stanford University Press, 1989.

Rupp, Leila. *Mobilizing Women for War: German and American Propaganda, 1939–1945*. Princeton: Princeton University Press, 1978.

San Tzu Ching: Elementary Chinese. Translated and annotated by Herbert A. Giles. Reprinted Taibei: Literature House, 1964.

Schechner, Richard. *The End of Humanism: Writings on Performance*. New York: Performing Arts Journal Publications, 1982.

Schram, Stuart R. *Mao Tse-tung*. Harmondsworth, Eng.: Penguin Books, 1967.

———. *The Political Thought of Mao Tse-tung*. Rev. ed. New York: Praeger, 1969.

Schramm, Wilbur. *Mass Media and National Development: The Role of Information in the Developing Countries*. Stanford: Stanford University Press, 1964.

Schudson, Michael. *Discovering the News: A Social History of American Newspapers*. New York: Basic Books, 1978.

Schwarcz, Vera. *The Chinese Enlightenment: Intellectuals and the Legacy of the May Fourth Movement of 1919*. Berkeley and Los Angeles: University of California Press, 1986.

Scott, A. C. *Literature and the Arts in Twentieth-Century China*. New York: Anchor Books, 1963.

Scott, Joan W. "Rewriting History." In *Behind the Lines: Gender and the Two World Wars*, edited by Margaret R. Higonnet et al. New Haven: Yale University Press, 1987.

Scribner, R. W. *For the Sake of Simple Folk: Popular Propaganda for the German Reformation*. Cambridge: Cambridge University Press, 1981.

Selden, Mark. *The Yenan Way in Revolutionary China*. Cambridge, Mass.: Harvard University Press, 1971.

Sha Kefu 沙可夫. "Huabei nongcun xiju yundong he minjian yishu gaizao gongzuo" 華北農村戲劇運動和民間藝術改造工作 (The village drama movement and the reform of folk art in North China). In *Zhonghua quanguo wenxue yishu gongzuozhe daibiao dahui jinian wenji*. N.p.: Xinhua shudian, 1950.

———. "Huigu yijiusiyi nian zhanwang yijiusier nian bianqu wenyi" 回顧一九四一年展望一九四二年邊區文藝 (Base area culture and art: 1941 in retrospect and 1942 in prospect). In *KRZZY*, vol. 2.

Sha Yan 沙雁. "Ping *Kang-Ri sanzi jing*" 評抗日三字經 (A critique of *Anti-Japanese Three-Character Classic*). *KDD* 11 (1 June 1938): 19–20.

Shaanbei min'ge xuan 陝北民歌選 (Selected folk songs of northern Shaanxi). Edited by Lu Xun wenyi xueyuan. N.p.: Xinhua shudian, 1949.

Shanghai fengqing 上海風情 (Amorous Shanghai). N.p.: Lantian shubao zazhishe, n.d.

Shanghai manhua 上海漫畫 (Shanghai cartoons). Shanghai, 1928–1930.

Shanghai shenmi zhinan 上海神秘指南 (Mysterious guide to Shanghai). Shanghai: Datong tushushe, n.d.

Shanxi wenyi shiliao 山西文藝史料 (Historical materials on literature and art in Shanxi). Vol. 2. Taiyuan: Shanxi renmin chubanshe, 1959.

Shen Congwen 沈從文. "Yiban huo teshu" 一般或特殊 (Generality and specificity). In *Zhongguo kang-Ri zhanzheng shiqi dahoufang wenxue shuxi*, vol. 2. Chongqing: Chongqing chubanshe, 1989.

Shen Qiyu 沈起予. "Zhongguo manhuajia cong Sulian dailai de liwu" 中國漫畫家從蘇聯帶來的禮物 (Gifts brought back from the Soviet Union by a Chinese cartoonist). *GM* 1.9 (10 October 1936): 570–572.

Shen Xiling 沈西苓 et al. *Jietou yanju* 街頭演劇 (Street plays). N.p.: Guofang xiju yanjiuhui, 1938.

Shen Zhenhuang 沈振黄. "Duiyu manhua xuanchuan gongzuo de yijian" 對於漫畫宣傳工作的意見 (My views about cartoon propaganda work). In *Kangzhan de jingyan yu jiaoxun*, edited by Qian Jiaju, Hu Yuzhi, and Zhang Tiesheng. N.p.: Shenghuo shudian, 1939.

Sheridan, James. *Chinese Warlord: The Career of Feng Yu-hsiang.* Stanford: Stanford University Press, 1974.

Shi Yan 石燕. "Litihua de zhandi caifang" 立體化的戰地採訪 (The three-dimensional frontline interview). *XWJZ* 1.6–7 (10 October 1938): 14–15.

———. "Xinwen gongzuo de zhuanxingqi" 新聞工作的轉型期 (A transition period for journalism). *XWJZ* 1.9–10 (10 December 1938): 6.

"Shisan yue" 十三月 (Thirteen months). In *Kang-Ri Shibeicha* 抗日十杯茶 (War of Resistance "Ten cups of tea"). Wuchang: Tongsu duwu biankanshe, 1938).

Shou Ming 受銘, ed. *Kangzhan gequji* 抗戰歌曲集 (Selected songs of the War of Resistance). Vol. 2. Hankou: Shenghuo shudian, 1938.

Shu Qingchun. *See* Lao She.

Sih, Paul K. T. *Nationalist China during the Sino-Japanese War, 1937–1945*. Hicksville, N.Y.: Exposition Press, 1977.

Skinner, G. William, ed. *The City in Late Imperial China*. Stanford: Stanford University Press, 1977.

Smedley, Agnes. *Battle Hymn of China*. New York: Alfred A. Knopf, 1943.

Snow, Edgar. *Red Star over China*. New York: Random House, 1938.

Song Zhidi 宋之的. "Xiezuo *Wu Zetian* de zibai" 寫作武則天的自白 (A personal statement about writing *Empress Wu*). *GM* 3.1 (10 June 1937): 43–45.

Spufford, Margaret. *Small Books and Pleasant Histories: Popular Fiction and Its Readership in Seventeenth-Century England*. Cambridge: Cambridge University Press, 1981.

Stein, Gunther. *The Challenge of Red China*. New York: Whittlesey House, 1945.

Stevens, Catherine. "Peking Drumsinging." Ph.D. diss., Harvard University, 1973.

Styan, J. L. *Modern Drama in Theory and Practice*. 3 vols. Cambridge: Cambridge University Press, 1981.

Su Guangwen 蘇光文. *Kangzhan wenxue gaiguan* 抗戰文學概觀 (An introduction to wartime literature). Chongqing: Xinan shifan daxue, 1985.

Su Xingzhi 蘇醒之. "Kangzhan zhong de woguo baozhi" 抗戰中的我國報紙 (Newspapers in the War of Resistance). *Dafeng* 91 (5 June 1941): 3038–3041.

Su Xuelin 蘇雪林 et al. *Kangzhan shiqi wenxue huiyilu* 抗戰時期文學回憶錄 (Reminiscences of wartime literature). Taibei: Wenxun yuekan zazhishe, 1987.

Sun, Shirley Hsiao-ling. "Lu Hsun and the Chinese Woodcut Movement, 1929–1936." Ph.D diss., Stanford University, 1974.

———. *Modern Chinese Woodcuts*. San Francisco: Chinese Culture Foundation, 1979.

Szyk, Arthur. *The New Order*. New York: G. P. Putnam's Sons, 1941.

Takehisa Yumeji 竹久夢二. *Kodomo no sekai* 子供の世界 (The children's world). Tokyo: Ryuseikaku, 1970.

Tang Qiong 唐瓊, ed. *Kangzhan song* 抗戰頌 (Ode to the War of Resistance). Shanghai: Wuzhou shubaoshe, 1937.

Tang Ren'an 唐忍安. "Difang baozhi" 地方報紙 (Local newspapers). *Baoxue jikan* 1.1 (10 October 1934): 17–36.

Tang Tao 唐弢. *Duan chang shu* 短長書 (Short and long book). Shanghai: Nanguo chubanshe, 1947.

———. *Touying ji* 投影集 (Projections). Shanghai: Wenhua shenghuo chubanshe, 1940.

Tang Yifan 唐一帆. "Kangzhan yu huihua" 抗戰與繪畫 (The War of

Resistance and painting). *Dongfang zazhi* 37.10 (16 May 1940): 26–28.

Tang Zhenchang 唐振常, ed. *Shanghai shi* 上海史 (A history of Shanghai). Shanghai: Shanghai renmin chubanshe, 1989.

Taylor, George E. *Japanese-sponsored Regime in North China.* New York: Garland, 1980.

Te Wei 特偉. "Faxisi he yishujia" 法西斯和藝術家 (Fascism and artists). *Huashang bao*, 16 July 1941.

———. "Lian ren dai yi" 連人帶椅 (Throw them out together with the chairs). *Huashang bao*, 13 November 1941.

Teradaira Tadasuke 寺平忠輔. *Rokōkyō jiken* 蘆溝橋事件 (The Marco Polo Bridge Incident). Tokyo: Yomiuri shimbunsha, 1970.

Tian Han 田漢. "Nanguo she shilüe" 南國社史略 (A brief history of the South China Society). In *ZGHJYD*, vol. 1.

———. *Tian Han zhuanji* 田漢專集 (Collected works of Tian Han). N.p.: Jiangsu renmin chubanshe, 1984.

———. "Women de ziji pipan" 我們的自己批判 (Our self criticism). In *Tian Han zhuanji*. N.p.: Jiangsu renmin chubanshe, 1984.

———. *Yingshi zhuiyilu* 影事追憶錄 (Film memoirs). Beijing: Zhongguo dianying chubanshe, 1981.

———. "Zhongguo huaju yishu fazhan de jinglu he zhanwang" 中國話劇藝術發展的徑路和展望 (The path and the future of the development of Chinese spoken dramatic art). In *ZGHJYD*, vol. 1.

Tian Han, Zhong Baihua 宗白華, and Guo Moruo 郭沫若. *San ye ji* 三葉集 (Clover). Shanghai: Yadong tushuguan, 1923.

——— et al. *Zhandi guilai* 戰地歸來 (Returning from the battlefield). Shanghai: Zhandi chubanshe, 1937.

——— et al., eds. *Zhongguo huaju yundong wushinian shiliao ji (ZGHJYD)* 中國話劇運動五十年史料集 (Historical materials on the Chinese drama movement of the last fifty years). 3 vols. Beijing: Xiju chubanshe, 1985.

Tian Jian 田間. *Shici* 誓辭 (Oaths) . Shanghai: Xinwenyi chubanshe, 1953.

———. "Tian Jian zishu" 田間自述 (Autobiography). *XWXSL* 25 (22 November 1984): 104–111; 29 (22 November 1985): 105–121.

Tian Jin 田進. "Kangzhan banian lai de xiju chuangzuo" 抗戰八年來的戲劇創作 (Drama productions in the eight years of the War of Resistance). *Wenlian* 1.3 (5 February 1946): 25–27.

Tian Qin 田禽. *Zhongguo xiju yundong* 中國戲劇運動 (Chinese drama movement). Shanghai: Shangwu yinshuguan, 1946.

———. "Zhongguo zhanshi xiju chuangzuo zhi yanbian" 中國戰時戲劇創作之演變 (The development of Chinese wartime drama production). *Dongfang zazhi* 40.4 (29 February 1944): 53–57.

Ting, Lee-hsia Hsu. *Government Control of the Press in Modern*

China, 1900–1949. Cambridge, Mass.: East Asian Research Center, Harvard University, 1974.

Tong, Hollington K. *China and the World Press*. N.p.: n.p., n.d. (preface dated February 1948).

Tozer, Warren W. "The Foreign Correspondents' Visit to Yenan in 1944: A Reassessment." *Pacific Historical Review* 41.2 (May 1972): 207–224.

Tung, Constantine. "Lonely Search into the Unknown: T'ian Han's Early Plays, 1920–1930." *Comparative Drama* 2.1 (Spring 1968): 44–54.

Turner, Victor. *Dramas, Fields, and Metaphors: Symbolic Action in Human Society*. Ithaca: Cornell University Press, 1974.

Usui Katsumi 臼井勝美. *Manshū jihen* 満州事変 (The Manchurian Incident). Tokyo: Chūō kōronsha, 1974.

Van Slyke, Lyman. "The Chinese Communist Movement During the Sino-Japanese War, 1937–1945." In *Cambridge History of China*, vol. 13: *Republican China, 1912–1949*, pt. 2, edited by John K. Fairbank and Albert Feuerwerker. Cambridge: Cambridge University Press, 1986.

Vohra, Ranbir. *Lao She and the Chinese Revolution*. Cambridge, Mass.: East Asian Research Center, Harvard University, 1974.

Wagner, Rudolf G. *The Contemporary Chinese Historical Drama*. Berkeley and Los Angeles: University of California Press, 1990.

Wang Dunqing 王敦慶. "Manhua de xuanchuan xing" 漫畫的宣傳性 (The propaganda nature of cartoons). *SDMH* 17 (20 May 1935): n.p.

———. "Manhua zhan" 漫畫戰 (Cartoon warfare). *JWMH* 1 (20 September 1937): 1.

———. "Seqing manhua de zanyang" 色情漫畫的讚仰 (In praise of erotic cartoons). *SDMH* 26 (20 February 1936): n.p.

Wang Liaoyi 王了一 (Wang Li 王力). *Long chong bing diao zhai suoyu* 龍蟲並雕齋瑣語 (Talks at the Dragon-and-Insect Carving Studio). Shanghai: Guancha she, 1949.

Wang Lin 王琳. "Ji Han Qixiang shuoshu" 記韓起祥說書 (On Han Qixiang storytelling). *Beifang wenhua* 2.6 (16 August 1946): 52–53, 47.

Wang Ping 王坪. "Tian Han zai 'feixu shang'" 田漢在「廢墟」上 (Tian Han in the ruined city of Changsha). *Juchang yishu* 9 (20 July 1939): 14–15.

Wang Pingling 王平陵. "Tongsu wenxue zai shangdui" 通俗文學再商兌 (A further discussion of popular literature). *Wenhua xianfeng* 1.14 (1 December 1942): 2–5, 8.

Wang Qi 王琦. *Xin meishu lunji* 新美術論集 (Collected essays on new art). Shanghai: Xin wenyi chubanshe, 1951.

Wang Weimin 王衛民, ed. *Zhongguo zaoqi huaju xuan* 中國早期話劇選 (Selected early Chinese spoken dramas). Beijing: Zhongguo xiju chubanshe, 1989.

Wang Wenbin 王文彬, ed. *Baoren zhi lu* 報人之路 (The journalist's road). Shanghai: Sanjiang shudian, 1938.

Wang Xiangchen. *See* Lao Xiang.

Wang Xianzhong. "Beijing Folk Customs in the Works of Lao She." *Chinese Literature*, Summer 1985, pp. 197–209.

Wang Xunzhao 王訓昭 et al., eds. *Guo Moruo yanjiu ziliao* 郭沫若研究資料 (Research materials on Guo Moruo). 3 vols. Beijing: Zhongguo shehui kexue chubanshe, 1986.

Wang Yao 王瑤. *Zhongguo xin wenxue shigao* 中國新文學史稿 (A draft history of modern Chinese literature). 2 vols. Shanghai: Shanghai wenyi chubanshe, 1982.

Wang Ying 王瑩. "Wang Ying xie gei Yingzi de xin" 王瑩寫給英子的信 (Wang Ying's letters to Yingzi). *XWXSL* 30 (22 February 1986): 20–40.

Wasserstrom, Jeffrey N. *Student Protests in Twentieth-Century China: The View from Shanghai.* Stanford: Stanford University Press, 1991.

Wei Ruhui. *See* A Ying.

Weitz, Margaret. "As I Was Then: Women in the French Resistance." *Contemporary French Civilization* 10.1 (1986): 1–19.

Welch, David. "Introduction." In *Nazi Propaganda: The Power and the Limitations*, edited by David Welch. London: Croom Helm, 1983.

Wen Tianxing 文天行. *Guotongqu kangzhan wenxue yundong shigao* 國統區抗戰文學運動史稿 (A history of the wartime literature movement in the Guomindang-controlled territories). Chengdu: Sichuan jiaoyu chubanshe, 1988.

Wen Yiduo 聞一多. "Shidai de gushou—du Tian Jian de shi" 時代的鼓手—讀田間的詩 (The drummer of our age—on reading Tian Jian's poems). In *Wen Yiduo quanji* 聞一多全集 (Complete works of Wen Yiduo), edited by Zhu Ziqing 朱自清 et al., vol. 3. Hong Kong: Nam Tung Stationery, n.d.

Wen Zaidao 文載道 et al. *Biangu ji* 邊鼓集 (Border drums). Shanghai: Yingshang wenhui youxian gongsi, 1938.

Wen Zhenting 文振庭, ed. *Wenyi dazhonghua wenti taolun ziliao* 文藝大眾化問題討論資料 (Source materials on the discussion of how to popularize literature and art). Shanghai: Shanghai wenyi chubanshe, 1987.

Wen Zongshan 文宗山. "Tongsu wenyi yu tongsu xiju" 通俗文藝與通俗戲劇 (Popular literature and popular drama). *Wanxiang* 2.5 (1 November 1942): 134–137.

White, Stephen. *The Bolshevik Poster*. New Haven: Yale University Press, 1988.

White, Theodore H., and Annalee Jacoby. *Thunder Out of China*. New York: William Sloane, 1961.

Wilkinson, James D. *The Intellectual Resistance in Europe*. Cambridge, Mass.: Harvard University Press, 1981.

Wilson, Dick. *When Tigers Fight: The Story of the Sino-Japanese War, 1937–1945*. Harmondsworth, Eng.: Penguin Books, 1983.

Wohl, Robert. *The Generation of 1914*. Cambridge, Mass.: Harvard University Press, 1979.

Wolf, Margery, and Roxane Witke, eds. *Women in Chinese Society*. Stanford: Stanford University Press, 1975.

Wu Guanyin 吳貫因. "Xinwen zhiyehua yu kexuehua" 新聞職業化與科學化 (Journalism made professional and scientific). In *Xinwenxue minlunji*, edited by Huang Tianpeng. Shanghai: Shanghai lianhe shudian, 1930.

Wu Zuguang 吳祖光. *Wu Zuguang lunju* 吳祖光論劇 (Wu Zuguang on drama). Beijing: Zhongguo xiju chubanshe, 1981.

Xi Zhengyong 席徵庸. *Ban Chao ding Xiyu* 班超定西域 (Ban Chao pacifies the Western Region). Changsha: Zhonghua pingmin jiaoyu cujinhui, 1938.

Xia Yan 夏衍. *Baitou jizhe hua dangnian* 白頭記者話當年 (Memoirs of an old reporter). Chongqing: Chongqing chubanshe, 1986.

———. *Lan xun jiu meng lu* 懶尋舊夢錄 (Autobiography). Beijing: Sanlian shudian, 1985.

———. "Sai Jinhua" 賽金花. *Wenxue* 6.4 (1 April 1936): 553–590.

———. "*Shanghai wuyan xia* houji" 「上海屋簷下」後記 (Postscript to *Under Shanghai Eaves*). In Hui Lin 會林 et al., *Xia Yan yanjiu ziliao* 夏衍研究資料 (Research materials on Xia Yan). Beijing: Zhongguo xiju chubanshe, 1983.

Xiang Linbing 向林冰. "Kangzhan yilai tongsu wenyi yundong de fazhan yu quexian" 抗戰以來通俗文藝運動的發展與缺陷 (The development and problems of the popular literature movement since the war). *Dushu yuebao* 1.1 (1 February 1939): 6–8.

———. "Xian jieduan tongsu wenyi de quexian ji qi kefu" 現階段通俗文藝的缺陷及其克服 (The problems of the current popular literature and their solutions). *KZWY* 4.4–5 (10 October 1939): 127–129.

Xiang Peiliang 向培良. "Lun jiuju zhi buneng gailiang" 論舊劇之不能改良 (On the idea that traditional drama cannot be reformed). *Shen bao*, 6 September 1935.

Xiang Shiyuan 項士元. "Ruhe shi xinwen shiye zhenzheng minzhonghua" 如何使新聞事業真正民眾化 (How to truly popularize journalism), *Baoxue jikan* 1.3 (29 March 1935): 93–97.

Xiang Zhongyi 尚仲衣. "Yujiu Zhongguo bixu kaifa minzhong yun-dong" 欲救中國必須開發民衆運動 (To save China we must develop the mass movement). *Xin zhanxian* 3 (1 January 1938): 75–76.

Xiao Fang 小方 (Fang Dazeng 方大曾). "Baoding yi nan" 保定以南 (South of Baoding). In *Cong Lugouqiao dao Zhanghe*, edited by Changjiang. Hankou: Shenghuo shudian, 1938.

———. "Cong Niangziguan dao Yanmenguan" 從娘子關到雁門關 (From the Niangzi Pass to the Yanmen Pass). In Changjiang et al., *Xixian xuezhan ji.* N.p.: Zhanshi chubanshe, n.d.

Xiao Jianqing 蕭劍青. *Manhua Shanghai* 漫畫上海 (Shanghai in cartoons). Shanghai: Jingwei shuju, n.d.

Xiao Qian (Hsiao Ch'ien) 蕭乾. *The Dragon Beards Versus the Blue-prints: Meditations on Post-War Culture.* London: Pilot Press, 1944.

———. *Wei dai ditu de lüren—Xiao Qian huiyilu* 未帶地圖的旅人—蕭乾回憶錄 (Traveler without a map—the memoirs of Xiao Qian). Hong Kong: Xiangjiang chuban gongsi, 1988.

Xie Bingying 謝冰瑩. *Junzhong suibi* 軍中隨筆 (Miscellaneous essays in the army). Shanghai: Kangzhan chubanbu, 1937.

———. *Nübing zizhuan* 女兵自傳 (Autobiography of a woman sol-dier). Chengdu: Sichuan wenyi chubanshe, 1985.

Xie Liuyi 謝六逸. *Bai longmenzhen* 擺龍門陣 (Chat). Shanghai: Bowen shudian, 1947.

———. "Dazhongyu he baozhi" 大衆語和報紙 (Popular language and newspapers). *Shehui yuebao* 1.5 (15 October 1934): 14–16.

———. "Zhanshi de xinwen jizai" 戰時的新聞記載 (Wartime news). *Kangzhan* 5 (3 September 1937): 10.

Xin minzhu zhuyi geming shiqi gongnongbing sanzi jing xuan 新民主主義革命時期工農兵三字經選 (Selected *Worker-Peasant-Soldier Three-Character Classics* during the New Democratic Rev-olutionary Period). Edited by Zhongguo geming bowuguan bian-xiezu. Beijing: Wenwu chubanshe, 1975.

Xinbo 新波. "Wusheng de zhadan" 無聲的炸彈 (Silent bombs). *Huashang bao*, 7 May 1941.

———. "Xiang Sulian ji shijie jinbu de huajia xuexi" 向蘇聯及世界進步的畫家學習 (Learn from Russian and other progres-sive artists of the world). *Huashang bao*, 30 July 1941.

"Xinwen jiaoyu jiguan gaikuang" 新聞教育機關概況 (A brief survey of journalism education institutions). *Baoxue jikan* 1.2 (1 January 1935): 115–127; 1.3 (29 March 1935): 147–150.

Xiong Foxi 熊佛西. *Foxi lunju* 佛西論劇 (Xiong Foxi on drama). Shanghai: Xinyue shudian, 1931.

———. *Guodu ji qi yanchu* 過渡及其演出 (Staging *Crossing*). N.p.: Zhengzhong shudian, 1947.

———. "Wo de wenyi xizuo shenghuo" 我的文藝習作生活 (My

artistic life). *Wenyi chunqiu* 4.1 (15 January 1947): 142–146; 4.2 (15 February 1947): 132–137.

———. "Wo duiyu chuangzao xingeju de yidian yijian" 我對於創造新歌劇的一點意見 (My personal views on reforming new opera). *Yicong* 1.2 (July 1943): 6–7.

———. *Xiju dazhonghua zhi shiyan* 戲劇大衆化之實驗 (Experiment in the popularization of drama). N.p.: Zhengzhong shudian, 1947.

———. "Zenyang zuoxi yu zenyang kanxi" 怎樣做戲與怎樣看戲 (How to act and how to enjoy a play). *Yue bao* 1.4 (15 April 1937): 894–900.

———. "Zhengzhi, jiaoyu, xiju, sanwei yiti" 政治、教育、戲劇、三位一體 (The trinity: politics, education, and drama). *Xiju gangwei* 1.1 (15 April 1939): 3–5.

Xu Baishi 須白石. "Tan muke" 談木刻 (On woodcuts). *Shen bao*, 2 December 1933.

Xu Banmei 徐半梅. *Huaju chuangshiqi huiyilu* 話劇創始期回憶錄 (Reminiscences of the initial stage of spoken drama). Beijing: Xiju chubanshe, 1957.

Xu Baohuang 徐寶璜. "Xinwenxue dayi" 新聞學大意 (General principles of journalism). In Xu Baohuang and Hu Yuzhi 胡愈之, *Xinwen shiye* 新聞事業 (Journalism enterprise). Shanghai: Shangwu yinshuguan, 1924.

———. "Xinwenzhi yu shehui zhi xuyao" 新聞紙與社會之需要 (Newspapers and the needs of society). In *Baoxue congkan*, edited by Huang Tianpeng, vol. 1, no. 2. Shanghai: Guanghua shuju, 1930.

Xu Beihong 徐悲鴻. "Quanguo muke zhan" 全國木刻展 (All-China woodcut exhibition). Reprinted *JFRB*, 16 March 1943.

Xu Maoyong 徐懋庸. *Jietou wentan* 街頭文談 (Street essays). 1936; Shanghai: Guangming shuju, 1946.

Xu Zhengrong 許崢嶸. "Dao neidi qu" 到內地去 (To the hinterland). *JWRB*, 14 October 1937.

Xu Zhucheng 徐鑄成. *Jiuwen zayi* 舊聞雜憶 (Reminiscences). Hong Kong: Sanlian shudian, 1982.

———. *Zhadan yu shuiguo* 炸彈與水果 (Bombs and fruit). Hong Kong: Sanlian shudian, 1983.

Xu Zhuoyun (Hsu Cho-yun) 許倬雲 and Qiu Hongda (Chiu Hung-dah) 丘宏達, eds. *Kangzhan shengli de daijia* 抗戰勝利的代價 (The costs of China's victory in the War of Resistance). Taibei: Lianjing chuban shiye gongsi, 1986.

Xuan Wenjie 宣文傑. "Kang-Ri zhanzheng shiqi de manhua xuanchuandui" 抗日戰爭時期的漫畫宣傳隊 (The Cartoon Propaganda Corps during the War of Resistance). *Meishu* 6 (25 July 1979): 37–39.

Xubai. *See* Zeng Xubai.

Yang Cunbin 楊村彬. *Qin Liangyu* 秦良玉. N.p.: Sichuan shengli xiju jiaoyu shiyan xuexiao bianzuan weiyuanhui, 1940.

———. *Zhan'ge* 戰歌 (War songs). Changsha: Zhonghua pingmin jiaoyu cujinhui, 1937.

Yang Fangzhi 楊放之. "*Jiefang ribao* gaiban yu Yan'an zhengfeng" 解放日報改版與延安整風 (The reform of *Liberation Daily* and Yan'an's Rectification Campaign). *XWYJZL* 18 (March 1983): 1–5.

Yang Han 楊涵, ed. *Xinsijun meishu gongzuo huiyilu* 新四軍美術工作回憶錄 (Reminiscences of art work in the New Fourth Army). Shanghai: Shanghai renmin chubanshe, 1982.

Yang Hansheng 陽翰笙. *Fengyu wushinian* 風雨五十年 (My fifty turbulent years). Beijing: Renmin wenxue chubanshe, 1986.

———. "Zhongguo xiju zhong de xinjiu nüxing" 中國戲劇中的新舊女性 (The new and old female characters in Chinese dramas). *Wencui* 1.6 (13 November 1945): 18–21.

Yao Jiguang 姚吉光 and Yu Yifen 俞逸芬. "Shanghai de xiaobao" 上海的小報 (Mosquito newspapers in Shanghai). *XWYJZL* 8 (November 1981): 223–244.

Yao Qingzeng 姚慶曾. *Kangzhan geyan ji* 抗戰格言集 (Collected maxims on the War of Resistance). Chongqing: Zhongshan wenhua jiaoyuguan, 1938.

Yazi. *See* Liu Yazi.

Ye Qianyu 葉淺予. *Hua yu lun hua* 畫餘論畫 (On paintings). Tianjin: Renmin meishu chubanshe, 1985.

———. "Lüetan Zhongguo de manhua yishu" 略談中國的漫畫藝術 (A brief discussion of Chinese cartoon art). *Renwen yikan*, 12 December 1948, p. 30.

——— (Qianyu). "Manhua de minzu xingshi" 漫畫的民族形式 (The national form of cartoons). *Huashang bao*, 1 October 1941.

———. *Ye Qianyu manhua xuan—sanshi niandai dao sishi niandai* 葉淺予漫畫選—三十年代到四十年代 (Selected cartoons of Ye Qianyu from the 1930s to the 1940s). Shanghai: Renmin meishu chubanshe, 1985.

Yeh, Wen-hsin. *The Alienated Academy: Culture and Politics in Republican China, 1919–1937*. Cambridge, Mass.: Council on East Asian Studies, Harvard University, 1990.

"Yidong yanju yundong teji" 移動演劇運動特輯 (Special issue on traveling drama troupes). *GM* 3.3 (10 July 1937): 188–195.

Ying Sun 鷹隼 (pseud.). "Guanyu *Mulan congjun*" 關於「木蘭從軍」 (On *Mulan Joins the Army*). *Wenxian* 6 (10 March 1939): F32–F35.

Yiqun 以群. "Yijiusier nian Yu Gui ge zhanqu juyun pingshu" 一九四二年渝桂各戰區劇運評述 (Review of the drama movement in Chongqing, Guilin, and other war zones in 1942). *Wenxue chuangzuo* 1.6 (1 April 1943): 119–125.

You Jing. *See* Yu Ling.

Yu Da 余大. "Cong qiantou hua dao tu dianying" 從牆頭畫到土電影 (From wall paintings to local films). *Meishu* 11 (15 November 1958): 39–40.

Yu Feng 郁風. "Yong yanshe poxiang Faxisi" 用顏色潑向法西斯 (Let's wage an art war against Fascism). *Huashang bao*, 16 July 1941.

Yu Ling 于伶 (You Jing 尤兢). *Dazhong juxuan* 大眾劇選 (Selected popular plays). Hankou: Shanghai zazhi gongsi, 1938.

Yu Zhigong 于志恭. "Feng Yuxiang xiansheng yu wenyijie" 馮玉祥先生與文藝界 (Mr. Feng Yuxiang and literary and art circles). *XWXSL* 19 (22 May 1983): 244–249, 161.

Yuan Changchao 袁昶超. *Zhongguo baoye xiaoshi* 中國報業小史 (A short history of the press in China). Hong Kong: Xinwen tiandishe, 1957.

Yuanxin. *See* Zheng Zhenduo.

Zai Mu 宰木. *Lun kangzhan qizhong de wenhua yundong* 論抗戰期中的文化運動 (On the cultural movement during the War of Resistance). Shanghai: Shenghuo shudian, 1937.

Zang Kejia 臧克家. "Chule kangzhan shenme dou mei yiyi" 除了抗戰什麼都沒意義 (Everything is insignificant except resistance). In *Kangzhan song*, edited by Tang Qiong. Shanghai: Wuzhou shubaoshe, 1937.

Zeng Xubai 曾虛白 (Xubai). "Wenxue zuopin yu xinwen zuopin" 文學作品與新聞作品 (Literary works and news reports). *XWJZ* 1.1 (1 April 1938): 9–10.

———. *Zeng Xubai zizhuan* 曾虛白自傳 (Autobiography of Zeng Xubai). Vol. 1. Taibei: Lianjing chuban shiye gongsi, 1988.

———, ed. *Zhongguo xinwen shi* 中國新聞史 (A history of the press in China). 2 vols. Taibei: Guoli Zhengzhi daxue xinwen yanjiusuo, 1966.

"Zenyang bianzhi shibing tongsu duwu" 怎樣編製士兵通俗讀物 (How to compile popular reading materials for soldiers). *KZWY* 1.5 (21 May 1938): 34–36.

Zhang Cuifeng 章翠鳳. *Dagu shengya de huiyi* 大鼓生涯的回憶 (Reminiscences of my life as a drum singer). Taibei: Zhuanji wenxue chubanshe, 1967). English translation by Rulan Chao Pian, in *CHINOPERL Papers* 13 (1984–1985): 12–99.

Zhang Ding 張仃. "Manhua yu zawen" 漫畫與雜文 (Cartoons and miscellaneous essays). *JFRB* 23, 25 May 1942.

———. *Zhang Ding manhua* 張仃漫畫 (The cartoons of Zhang Ding). Shenyang: Liaoning meishu chubanshe, 1985.

Zhang E 張諤. "Wo hua manhua de jingguo" 我畫漫畫的經過 (My experience in cartooning). In *Xiaopinwen he manhua*, edited by Chen Wangdao. Shanghai: Shenghuo shudian, 1935.

Zhang Geng 張庚. "Huiyi Yan'an Luyi de xiju huodong" 回憶延安魯藝的戲劇活動 (Reminiscences of the drama activities at the Lu Xun Academy of Art in Yan'an). In *KRZZY*, vol. 1.

———. "Lun bianqu juyun he xiju de jishu jiaoyu" 論邊區劇運和戲劇的技術教育 (On the drama movement and education in dramatic technique in the border region). *JFRB*, 11–12 September 1942.

———. "Luyi gongzuotuan duiyu yangge de yixie jingyan" 魯藝工作團對於秧歌的一些經驗 (Some experience of performing *yangge* of Luyi's Work Team). *Xiju yu yinyue* 1 (1 March 1946): 1; 2 (1 April 1946): 3–5.

———. "Muqian juyun de jige dangmian wenti" 目前劇運的幾個當面問題 (Problems facing the current drama movement). *GM* 2.12 (25 May 1937): 1492–1495.

———, ed. *Yanggeju xuan* 秧歌劇選 (Selected *yangge* plays). Beijing: Renmin wenxue chubanshe, 1977.

Zhang Guangnian. *See* Guangweiran.

Zhang Guangyu 張光宇. "Guonei meishujie de qingzhuang" 國內美術界的情狀 (The current art scene in China). *Huashang bao*, 25 June 1941.

———. *Xiyou manji* 西遊漫記 (Journey to the West). Beijing: Renmin meishu chubanshe, 1983.

Zhang Jiluan 張季鸞. *Jiluan wencun* 季鸞文存 (Selected writings of Zhang Jiluan). 2 vols. Tianjin: Dagong bao, 1947.

———. "Xinwen jizhe genben de genben" 新聞記者根本的根本 (The essential of the journalist's essentials). In *Baoren zhi lu*, edited by Wang Wenbin. Shanghai: Sanjiang shudian, 1938.

Zhang Jinglu 張靜廬. *Zai chubanjie ershinian* 在出版界二十年 (Twenty years in the publishing world). Hankou: Shanghai zazhi gongsi, 1938.

———. *Zhongguo de xinwen jizhe yu xinwenzhi* 中國的新聞記者與新聞紙 (Chinese reporters and newspapers). Shanghai: Xiandai shuju, 1932.

———, ed. *Zhongguo xiandai chuban shiliao* 中國現代出版史料 (Historical materials on publishing in contemporary China). Vols. 3 and 4. Beijing: Zhonghua shuju, 1956–1959.

Zhang Junxin 張俊鑫. "Zai xiangxia yanju" 在鄉下演劇 (Performing in the rural areas). In *Kangzhan de jingyan yu jiaoxun*, edited by Qian Jiaju, Hu Yuzhi, and Zhang Tiesheng. N.p.: Shenghuo shudian, 1939.

Zhang Leping 張樂平. *San Mao liulangji quanji* 三毛流浪記全集 (The complete "Wanderings of San Mao"). Beijing: Renmin meishu chubanshe, 1984.

Zhang Wenyuan 張文元. "Zhongguo manhua yundong de huigu yu qianzhan" 中國漫畫運動的回顧與前瞻 (The past and future of the Chinese cartoon movement). *Wenchao yuekan* 2.3 (1 January 1947): 604–608.

Zhang Youluan 張友鸞. *Zhanshi xinwenzhi* 戰時新聞紙 (The wartime press). Chongqing: Zhongshan wenhua jiaoyuguan, 1938.

Zhanshi xinwen gongzuo rumen 戰時新聞工作入門 (A primer for wartime journalism). N.p.: Shenghuo shudian, 1940.

Zhao Chaogou 趙超構. *Yan'an yiyue* 延安一月 (One month in Yan'an). Nanjing: Xinmin bao she, 1946.

Zhao Huishen 趙慧深. "Zai Zhongguo lüxing jutuan" 在中國旅行劇團 (In the China Traveling Drama Troupe). *Juchang yishu* 6 (20 April 1939): 20–25.

Zhao Jingshen 趙景深. "Feng Zikai he tade xiaopinwen" 豐子愷和他的小品文 (Feng Zikai and his personal essays). *Renjian shi* 30 (20 June 1935): 14–16.

———. "Juyongguan" 居庸關 (The pass at Juyong). *JWRB*, 12 October 1937.

———. "Pingxingguan" 平型關 (The pass at Pingxing). *JWRB*, 14 October 1937.

———. "Shuo dagu" 說大鼓 (On drum singing). *Renjian shi* 21 (5 February 1935): 19–22; 22 (20 February 1935): 20–25.

———. *Zhanshi daguci* 戰時大鼓詞 (Wartime drum songs). N.p.: Zhanshi chubanshe, 1938.

Zhao Junhao 趙君豪. *Shanghai baoren de fendou* 上海報人的奮鬥 (The struggle of Shanghai's journalists). N.p.: Erya shudian, 1944.

———. *Zhongguo jindai zhi baoye* 中國近代之報業 (A history of the modern press in China). N.p.: Shangwu yinshuguan, 1940.

Zhao Kunliang 趙坤良. "Xinwen jiujing shi shenme?" 新聞究竟是什麼 (What is news?). *Baoxue jikan* 1.4 (15 August 1935): 47–51.

Zhao Mingyi 趙銘彝. "Wei zuoyi juyun kaipi dadao—ji 'Daodao jushe'" 為左翼劇運開闢大道—記「大道劇社」 (Breaking the ground for the left-wing drama movement: on the Great Way Drama Club). *Wenyi yanjiu* 2 (25 April 1980): 69–71.

Zhao Qingge 趙清閣. *Kangzhan xiju gailun* 抗戰戲劇概論 (An outline of wartime drama). Chongqing: Zhongshan wenhua jiaoyuguan, 1939.

Zhao Shuli 趙樹理. *Zhao Shuli wenji* 趙樹理文集 (Collected works of Zhao Shuli). Vol. 1. Beijing: Gongren chubanshe, 1980.

Zhao Wangyun 趙望雲. *Zhao Wangyun nongcun xiesheng ji* 趙望雲農村寫生集 (Zhao Wangyun's rural sketches). Tianjin: Dagong bao she, 1934.

Zheng Boqi 鄭伯奇. "Shenme shi xin de tongsu wenxue" 什麼是新的通俗文學 (What is new popular literature?). *Xin Zhonghua zazhi* 5.7 (10 April 1937): 89–91.

———. "Xin tongsu wenxue lun" 新通俗文學論 (On new popular literature). *GM* 2.8 (25 March 1937): 1267–1272.

Zheng Junli 鄭君里. *Lun kangzhan xiju yundong* 論抗戰戲劇運動 (On the anti-Japanese drama movement). N.p.: Shenghuo shudian, 1939.

Zheng Zhenduo 鄭振鐸 (Yuanxin 源新). "Baowei minzu wenhua yundong" 保衛民族文化運動 (The movement for protecting national culture). *Wenyi zhendi* 5.1 (16 July 1940): 1–5.

———. "Chatu zhi hua" 插圖之話 (On illustrations). *Xiaoshuo yuebao* 18.1 (10 January 1927): 1–20.

———. *Jie zhong de shu ji* 劫中得書記 (Books obtained in the midst of calamity). Shanghai: Gudian wenxue chubanshe, 1956.

———. "Shao shu ji" 燒書記 (Book burning). In *Zheju sanji* 蟄居散記 (Memoirs of life as a recluse). Shanghai: Shanghai chuban gongsi, 1951.

———. "Shi shu ji" 失書記 (Losing books). *Fenghuo* 9 (31 October 1937): 1–2.

———. *Zhongguo banhuashi tulu* 中國版畫史圖錄 (History of Chinese prints). 20 vols. Shanghai: Zhongguo banhuashi she, 1940–1947.

Zhongguo kang-Ri zhanzheng shiqi dahoufang wenxue shuxi 中國抗日戰爭時期大後方文學書系 (A comprehensive compendium of literature in the hinterland during the anti-Japanese war). 20 vols. Chongqing: Chongqing chubanshe, 1989.

Zhonghua quanguo wenxue yishu gongzuozhe daibiao dahui jinian wenji 中華全國文學藝術工作者代表大會紀念文集 (A commemorative volume of the All-China Writers and Artists Congress). N.p.: Xinhua shudian, 1950.

Zhou Erfu 周而復 et al. *Yanggeju chuji* 秧歌劇初集 (First collection of *yangge* plays). Chongqing: Xinhua ribao, 1944.

Zhou Fei 周飛. "Zhongguo de xibei jiao" 中國的西北角 (On *The Northwest Corner of China*). *Guowen zhoubao* 13.39 (5 October 1936): 41–43.

Zhou Gangming 周鋼鳴. "Lun xian jieduan de yanju yishu" 論現階段底演劇藝術 (On current dramatic art). *Wenyi zhendi* 5.1 (16 July 1940): 64–76.

Zhou Jianchen 周劍塵. *Liang Hongyu* 梁紅玉. N.p.: Xinyi shudian, 1940.

Zhou Li'an 周黎庵. *Huafa ji* 華髮集 (White-haired). Shanghai: Yuzhou feng she, 1940.

Zhou Libo 周立波 (Libo). "Houhui yu qianzhan" 後悔與前瞻 (Regrets and prospects). *JFRB*, 3 April 1943.

Zhou Wen 周文. "Gaibian min'ge de yidian yijian" 改編民歌的一點意見 (Ideas for revising folk songs). *KZWY* 3.8 (4 February 1939): 126.

Zhou Yang 周揚. "Yishu jiaoyu de gaizao wenti" 藝術教育的改造問題 (The reform of art education). In *KRZZY*, vol. 1.

Zhou Yang, Xiao San 蕭三, and Ai Qing et al. *Minjian yishu he yiren* 民間藝術和藝人 (Folk arts and folk artists). Zhangjiakou: Xinhua shudian, 1946.

Zhou Yibai 周貽白. *Hua Mulan* 花木蘭. Shanghai: Kaiming shudian, 1941.

Zhu Xingyi 朱幸薏. "Wo suo xiji yu manhuajie de" 我所希冀於漫畫界的 (My hopes for cartoon circles). *Duli manhua* 4 (10 November 1935): 3.

Zigang 子岡 (Peng Zigang 彭子岡). "Yanhuo zhong de Hanyang" 烟火中的漢陽 (The city of Hanyang in flames). *DGB* (Hankou), 12 August 1938.

Zou Taofen 鄒韜奮. "Benkan yu minzhong" 本刊與民衆 (This magazine and the people). In *Taofen wenji* 韜奮文集 (Selected writings of Zou Taofen), vol. 1. Shanghai: Sanlian shudian, 1956.

———. *Huannan yushengji* 患難餘生記 (Records of a troubled life). Beijing: Sanlian shudian, 1980.

———. "*Shenghuo ribao* de chuangban jingguo he fazhan jihua" 生活日報的創辦經過和發展計劃 (The founding and the development plan of *Life Daily*). In *Renmin de houshe* 人民的喉舌 (Mouthpiece of the people). Fuzhou: Fujian renmin chubanshe, 1980.

Zuo Lai 左萊 and Liang Huaqun 梁化群. *Suqu "Hongse xiju" shihua* 蘇區「紅色戲劇」史話 (A history of "red theaters" in the Jiangxi Soviet). Beijing: Wenhua yishu chubanshe, 1987.

Index

Page references to illustrations are in italics.